DAUGHTERS
OF THE
DIASPORA

DAUGHTERS
OF THE
DIASPORA

AFRA-HISPANIC WRITERS

Editor
Miriam DeCosta-Willis

Ian Randle Publishers
Kingston • Miami

First published in Jamaica 2003 by
Ian Randle Publishers
11 Cunningham Avenue, Box 686
Kingston 6

ISBN 976-637-077-X paperback
ISBN 976-637-133-4 hardback

A catalogue copy of this book is available from the
National Library of Jamaica

and in the United States by
Ian Randle Publishers, Inc

ISBN 0-9729358-0-0 paperback
ISBN 0-9729358-1-9 hardback

www.ianrandlepublishers.com

Book and cover design by Errol Stennett
Printed and bound in the United States of America

For my daughters,

Elena, Erika, Monique

descendants of Sally, a tall, slender, dark-skinned girl who was brought up in the hold of a slave ship from Dahomey, West Africa around 1760 and sold on the shores of Virginia. The daughters of that diaspora carry on the creative and intellectual tradition of our foremother – a healer, conjurer and wise woman.

Contents

CONTENTS

CONTENTS

Preface

In the lull between papers at the 1991 International Symposium on Afro-Hispanic Literature, I began listing Afra-Hispanic* writers and critics of that literature who might collaborate on this anthology. Although only one woman – Yvonne-América Truque – was among the five writers attending the conference and only two women writers – Shirley Campbell and Aida Cartagena Portalatín – were the subjects of papers, I realised that we were witnessing, in the early 1990s, the emergence of a tradition of Black women writing in the Spanish Americas. That same feeling – that we were on the cusp of a significant cultural phenomenon – prevailed at Howard University in the early 1970s, when students and professors were reading and writing about Nicolás Guillén, Manuel Zapata Olivella, Nelson Estupiñán Bass, and other male hispanophone writers of African descent. That cultural movement led to the publication, in 1977, of *Blacks in Hispanic Literature*, a collaborative work intended to chart the early history and evolution of Afro-Hispanic literature.

The 1970s also marked the advent of another cultural movement: a literary tradition forged by African American women writers and scholars. The publication of *The Bluest Eye, Revolutionary Petunias*, and *The Black Woman* in 1970 was later reinforced by the publication of two studies – *Sturdy Black Bridges: Visions of Black Women in Literature*, one of the first anthologies to include African and Caribbean women, and *All the Women Are White, All the Blacks Are Men, But Some of Us Are Brave*, an early product of Black feminist scholarship – which solidified the field of Black Women's Studies as a discipline with both a creative and scholarly foundation. Literary critics cannot underestimate the importance of North American writers such as Alice Walker, Toni Morrison, and Audre Lorde in inspiring other women of colour throughout the world to add their voices to the literary discourse of their countries. As the editors of *Breaking Boundaries: Latina Writings and Critical Readings* point out, Black women writers 'provided a female context. To this day, Latina writers may express a debt to Black women writers'. I also owe a debt to Black women writers and scholars who have had a significant impact on my own personal and intellectual development, particularly during the 1980s when I was teaching and writing at a small, historically Black college in the South. In 1983, a grant from the United Negro College Fund enabled me to spend a year at libraries throughout the country doing research on early African American women writers. That experience gave me an insight into the writers' lives and literature: their self-representation and social construction; their language and style, omissions and silences. That experience was also invaluable to me in the 1990s, when I began teaching and writing about Black hispanophone women writers in the Americas.

The past decade has marked the emergence of women writers as a new and powerful voice in Afro-Hispanic literature, so much so that it is possible to speak of the *mujerización* (womanisation) of that literature. The gender shift is evident in two phenomena: the proliferation of publications by women and an increase in scholarship on women writers. In the past ten years, for example, Luz Argentina Chiriboga has published eight books: Nancy Morejón, four *poemarios*; Soleida Ríos, three collections of verse and an edited volume; Marta Rojas, an edited text and two novels, with a third in press; Excilia Saldaña, two works of poetry; and Mayra Santos-Febres, a novel, short story collection and three volumes of poetry. The decade also witnessed the production of important scholarship on these writers, as literary critics produced translations, wrote essays, published books and organised conferences. Since 1990, four major works have been translated into English – Argentina Chiriboga's *Drums Under My Skin*, Aida Cartagena Portalatín's *Yania Tierra* and Mayra Santos-Febres' *Urban Oracles* – while a collection of Excilia Saldaña's poetry, in translation, was recently published and a bilingual edition of Nancy Morejón's complete works is in production. The essays and bibliography in this volume indicate the scope and depth of recent scholarship on Afra-Hispanic writing. Literary critics such as Caroll Mills Young, Gabriel Abudu, Elba Birmingham-Pokorny, Claudette M. Williams, Aida Heredia, and Flora M. González have made women's writing the primary focus of their research, while Ian I. Smart, Dellita Martin-Ogunsola, M'Baré N'Gom, and Donald K. Gordon have examined the texts of women writers within other critical or geographic contexts. The first conference dedicated to the work of a single Afra-Hispanic writer, Nancy Morejón, was held at the University of Missouri, Columbia in 1995, and the papers from that conference appeared in a special issue of the *Afro-Hispanic Review*. In 1999, the Howard University Press published *Singular Like a Bird: The Art of Nancy Morejón*, the first book devoted to the writing of a single author.

Daughters of the Diaspora will continue the archaeological project of excavating, preserving and disseminating the writing of African-descended women by examining their work within a critical context. The collection contains the creative writing (poetry, fiction, essays and personal narratives) of 20 Spanish-speaking women, as well as interviews and interpretive essays by fifteen scholars from Africa, Canada, the Caribbean, and the United States. Its objectives are to give voice to writers from the Spanish Americas, to provide English translations of representative texts, to give information on the lives and works of writers, to trace the historical evolution of a literary tradition and to offer critical contexts for understanding and interpreting the literature. This volume will contribute to the literary history of women throughout the Americas by recovering the texts of forgotten or neglected writers such as Virginia Brindis de Salas and Carmen Colón Pellot, by focusing attention on emerging writers like Cristina Cabral and Mayra Santos-Febres, and by placing established writers such as Julia de Burgos and Aida Cartagena Portalatín within a wider discursive tradition. Reflecting upon issues of ethnicity, sexuality, social class, and self-representation, these writers shape a revolutionary discourse that questions and subverts historical assumptions and literary conventions. Unfortunately, many accomplished writers such as Cuban Cristina Ayala, Latina Sandra María Esteves, and Puerto Rican Angela María Dávila had to be excluded because of time and space restraints, but information on these writers appears in the introduction.

It is hoped that this survey of Afra-Hispanic literature will stimulate more extensive and sustained research on these writers and others who have been omitted – except for the token one – from anthologies, biographies and critical studies of Afro-Hispanic literature (where 'all the Blacks Are Men') and of Latin American women's literature (where 'all the Women Are White').

Daughters of the Diaspora is intended for anglophone readers who enjoy the literature of other countries, for students who want to expand their cultural horizons, for teachers intent on enriching the experiences of their students and for scholars who are open to new and challenging research opportunities.

---

* The term 'Afra-Hispanic', an adjective that characterises hispanophone women of African descent, is adapted from the term coined by Joanne M. Braxton and Andrée Nicola McLaughlin in their anthology *Wild Women in the Whirlwind: Afra-American Culture and the Contemporary Literary Renaissance*. This form is particularly appropriate in a gendered language such as Spanish, in which the vowel endings of nouns and adjectives often denote gender.

Acknowledgements

Many thanks to the writers, literary critics, and translators – friends and colleagues all – whose patience and encouragement sustained me through the long period of this anthology's gestation. Donald Gordon was the first to answer the call, and with such grace and generosity of spirit. Cuban poet Nancy Morejón has lent her support throughout, introducing me to Excilia Saldaña and Marta Rojas, providing information on Cristina Ayala, and sending a book of Rafaela Chacón Nardi's poetry. I could not have completed this collection without Marta Rojas' detailed letters and frequent e-mails or without the blessings of Soleida Ríos who communicates with Ochún and Yemayá. Aché! My circle of friends fully embraced this project: Janet Hampton read manuscripts and solved computer glitches, Marvin Lewis answered every urgent cry for help, Dellita Martin-Ogunsola was a sister scholar in every way, Edward Mullen sent copies of Juana Pastor's poetry, James Davis shared his research on Afra-Dominican writers, and Caroll Young provided information on Afra-Uruguayan writers and introduced me to Cristina Cabral and Beatriz Santos. I am so grateful to Cathy Jenkins for her computer expertise and to J. Rolando García for handling communication with María Nsue Angüe.

Other generous *amigos y compañeros* – Elba Birmingham-Pokorny, Gabriel Abudu and, especially, Antonio Olliz Boyd – never refused a request to translate into English just one more poem or essay. Elba introduced me to the work of Mayra Santos-Febres, while Gabriel put me in touch with Soleida Ríos and sent copies of Cristina Ayala's poetry from Havana's Biblioteca Nacional. William Luis and Rosemary Geisdorfer Feal, who have supported my work in many ways, read submissions, wrote evaluations, and even edited a manuscript or two. I am also indebted to Mariela Gutiérrez for her early contribution, to Khara Cannon for translating an essay on Angela María Dávila, to María Zielina Limonta for her article on María Nsue Angüe, and to Dolores 'Lola' Aponte-Ramos whose research on Puerto Rican writers was invaluable. Other scholars helped along the way: Herbert Rogers of Baltimore's Pratt Library kept me abreast of new web sites and recent publications; Clementina Adams gave me a copy of *Common Threads*, her study of Black women writers; Franklin Gutiérrez sent me *Evas terrenales*, his bibliography of Dominican women writers; and Patricia Bell-Scott kept me focused on my research and centered in my writing. My thanks also to Ballard Gilmore who braved the chill of a Washington spring, to photograph a very reluctant subject. I am grateful to the president and dean of the University of Maryland, Baltimore County, who approved a fall 1999 sabbatical leave that enabled me to complete some of the initial groundwork for this anthology. I am especially indebted to my friend and colleague Acklyn Lynch, former Chair of the Department of Africana Studies, who has always supported my scholarship and who suggested that I contact Ian Randle about publishing this collection. I am most appreciative of the efficiency, professionalism and seriousness of purpose with which he and his staff, particularly Lisa Morgan and Dahlia Fraser, have treated this project. When I received a note card from classmate Patricia Theiss, I realised that Bermuda artist Shan Kelly-Cecilio's depiction of African-descended women as proud and confident agents of their own destiny captures the vision that inspired *Daughters of the Diaspora*.

Finally, I am so blessed to have a family – mother, son, three daughters, and seven grandchildren – who forgive my failings and understand my commitment to research on the rich heritage and inspiring history of our people.

Introduction

'This Voyage Toward Words': Mapping the Routes of the Writers

Miriam DeCosta-Willis

Words are the medium through which I understand the worlds I inhabit, visit or dream about. Therefore, when I write I take notes, draw maps of departures and destinations, find my routes into the page.

Mayra Santos-Febres

Women Writers and Literary Production

In her short story 'La escritora' ('The Woman Writer'), Puerto Rican poet and novelist Mayra Santos-Febres examines the possibilities – the routes – open to the female artist who must navigate the tenuous straits between survival, on the one hand, and creativity, on the other. In her reflections on the creative process, Santos-Febres constructs a metafiction, a story within a story, that examines and interrogates itself through the words and actions of three characters, all women writers: the writers/characters in the two stories and the writer/narrator (Santos-Febres' alter ego) who comments on the text. Through this fictional guise, Santos-Febres examines the social, economic, and physical conditions under which women produce literature. The protagonist of the internal story (whose narrative is in italics) is a pregnant college student who quits her lover, plans an abortion, and puts her writing on hold. The other writer (whose text is in roman letters) is a divorced graduate student and office worker who has to 'cook, iron, mop, and take care of the kids' while trying to complete her short story. She lists the reasons for her writer's block – children, work, bills, and divorce – but then concludes that *she* is responsible for her failure. Through such fictional characters, Santos-Febres illustrates the material obstacles to writing such as overwork, family responsibilities sexual needs, personal relationships, and isolation ('long nights in a monastic habit'). However, in her narrative asides (enclosed in parentheses), she explores the psychological and technical demands of the 'voyage toward words': self-revelation, anxiety of influence, limited narrative control, and duplicity (assuming characters' voices, using literary tricks of the trade, and playing games with allusions and metaphors). The narrator, in her view, is a conjuror or trickster, a liar who creates a 'portrait of a life so different from my own. I, who have never been divorced, who doesn't know what it's like to be pregnant' (*Urban Oracles*).

The challenges facing the woman artist, which Santos-Febres examines in 'La escritora' are all too evident in the 'life portrait' of another Puerto Rican writer whose personal experiences are paradigmatic of the struggle between creativity and survival. The figure of Julia de Burgos haunts the pages of contemporary writers such as Angela María Dávila, Sandra María Esteves, and Sherezada 'Chiqui' Vicioso, who pay homage, in their essays and poems, to their literary foremother. 'She [Julia] fashioned herself into an untamed bird,' writes Dominican poet Vicioso, 'oblivious to any type of restriction in its search for life and love' (*Julia*). But for these writers, the life of Burgos – that daughter of a 'sensitive *mulata* woman', that *jíbara* who studied French and Greek and Latin and Portuguese, that uppity coloured woman who defied conventional views on race and class in lines such as 'Ay, ay, ay, I am black, pure black, / kinky hair and Kaffir lips / and flat Mozambican nose' is something of a cautionary tale: How to survive in a world that refuses to recognise its brilliant, gifted daughters. Burgos' writing could not sustain her or save her mother's life. In 1938, the twenty-four-year-old writer travelled throughout Puerto Rico in *carros públicos,* trying to sell a collection of self-published poems to pay for the medical treatment of her mother, who was dying of cancer. But the books did not sell and her mother died anyway. Today acknowledged as one of Puerto Rico's greatest poets, Burgos could barely make a living teaching in rural schools, distributing free breakfasts to children, and working in New York garment factories and newspaper offices before dying – at age thirty-nine – of pain and poverty and pneumonia on a street in Harlem.

Burgos made the mistake of trying to live from her writing. Contemporary women are not so naive; they know that coloured folk will not get paid to sit and write. University-educated by and large, the twenty writers in this volume are also teachers, editors, professors, journalists, administrators, social workers, radio/television commentators, performers, media specialists and independent consultants. Some have even worked in blue-collar jobs – two as domestics and two others as factory workers. Only a few are 'married with children', while the others – divorced, widowed, or single by choice – lead active, non-traditional lives, totally committed to

Como difundir
el mensaje

their work, honing their craft and plying their trade in the literary marketplace. This is not to say that they are not 'human' or 'womanly'. They are incredibly adventurous women, always on the move – from Costa Rica to Zimbabwe and Bogotá to Barcelona – reciting poetry to music, attending conferences and organising for peace and justice. Even so, life for them 'ain't been no crystal stair'. Several have migrated or been exiled; one was born in prison and another was taken from her mother at birth; one has survived cancer and radiation; some have lost children or lovers; and others, like Julia and Lourdes and Excilia, died young of asthma, pneumonia, and liver failure. But . . . they wrote, always. Four months before her death, Burgos penned a wistful letter to her sister Consuelo from the hospital on Welfare Island where she had been committed: 'I want to look at my river again', she wrote wistfully, 'with the same peaceful, longing eyes that I did when I was its sweetheart'.

detalles
de la
de la
vida

These details of their lives suggest that the Afra-Hispanic writer needs more than a 'room of her own' (with lock and key) and money to support herself; to write, she also needs support from the literary establishment, including editors, publishers, distributors, and reviewers. Literary production is difficult in countries where there is a small publishing industry or where the works of women and Blacks are not priorities in the literary marketplace. Laurence Prescott notes:

> Generally published at the author's expense in limited print runs and by modest presses, [the works of Afro-Colombian women] do not receive commercial publicity nor newspaper reviews by the literary establishment which could evaluate, edit and stimulate the writers. (191)

Many early writers such as Juana Pastor and Cristina Ayala of Cuba and Virginia Brindis de Salas of Uruguay, like their nineteenth-century African American counterparts, published their poems in the periodical press. Important in this regard is the emergence of Black periodicals such as *Rumbos, Nuestra Raza, Revista Uruguaya, La Conservación*, and *Mundo Afro* in Uruguay; *Letras Nacionales* in Colombia; and *Africa 2000* and *El Patio* in Equatorial Guinea. These journals were founded and edited by Black male writers such as Pilar Barrios, Manuel Zapata Olivella, and Donato Ndongo-Bidyyogo who encouraged women to submit their work for publication. In the past twenty years, African American journals such as the *Afro-Hispanic Review, Black Scholar, Callaloo,* and *PALARA* (Publication of the Afro-Latin American Research Association) have published literature by and about Afra-Hispanic writers such as Nancy Morejón, Julia de Burgos,

Argentina Chiriboga, Excilia Saldaña, and others. A few Black women writers have also been involved in the publishing business. Aida Cartagena Portalatín founded the Dominican journal *La Poesía Sorprendida* and the publishing house La Isla Necesaria, while Yvonne-América Truque co-founded, with her French-Canadian former husband, CEDAH (Centre d'Études et de Diffusion des Amériques Hispanophones). Given the effort, time, and expense of operating such institutions, however, most of these journals and presses were short-lived.

Afro-Hispanic writers, in general, and Black women writers, in particular, have faced daunting problems in the publication and dissemination of their works. Julia de Burgos self-published her *Poema en veinte surcos*, but her *Poemas exactas a mí misma*, for which she was unable to find a publisher, has been lost. Brindis de Salas' *Pregón de Marimorena* and *Cien cárceles de amor* have been out of print for many years, and the manuscript of her *Cantos de lejanía* has disappeared. Although more publishing opportunities exist in cities such as Havana, Santo Domingo, San Juan, Quito, and Bogotá, economic conditions and political considerations often determine which texts are published or reprinted. In the past decade, works by or about Afra-Hispanic writers, some in English translation, have been published in the United States by small (often minority-run) presses such as the Afro-Hispanic Institute, Azul, Arte Público, Black Scholar, Howard University, and Lumen. For some writers, however, publication in that country is problematic for personal and political reasons. Sherezada Vicioso explains: 'I never thought of publishing in the United States because as a Latina, I felt unable to deal with the publishing establishment in that country'. Cuba, where literary production has been a priority of the revolutionary government, provides an illuminating example of the ways in which economic and political vicissitudes have affected writing and publishing. In spite of institutional support for its publishing industry and the strength of such publishers as Ediciones Unión and Editorial Letras Cubanas, the early works of Nancy Morejón, Soleida Ríos, Georgina Herrera, and Excilia Saldaña are out of print. A major obstacle to publication in Cuba has been the shortage of paper in the past decade. Marta Rojas recently wrote that, although her third novel *El haren de Oviedo* has been accepted for publication, its production this year or next depends upon the availability of paper. During the 'special period' following the collapse of the Soviet Union, Cuban publishers produced a limited number of *plaquettes* or hand-made chapbooks, such as Morejón's *Balada de un sueño* and *El río de Martín Pérez y otros poemas*, which are noted for their originality and artistic beauty. Another problem in Cuba and other small countries is the

¿Cómo defines tu π?

distribution of books and access to the media. For example, only one of Soleida Ríos's eight books has been reviewed in a literary or cultural journal in spite of the fact that she was singled out as a 'new voice' in poetry of the post-Revolution.

Escriben prosa que π

Genres and Themes

Although they also write prose, thirteen of the twenty writers included in this volume are poets, partly for cultural reasons, because in Latin America poetry is a popular art form, rooted in a rich, oral, Afro-Indo-Hispanic tradition. Nuyorican poet Sandra María Esteves underscores the appeal that this urban 'poetry for the people' has had in her Latino community, particularly during the 1960s.

> We mingled and read poems to each other, in our houses, on university tours, at the Nuyorican Poets Cafe and the New Rican Village, at a political rally in Chicago, in the Central Park Delacourt Theater, at the gates of the White House, in schools, community centers, and other multi-purpose locations, indoors, outdoor, on buses and trains… ('Letter' 119)

Poetry can be performance art at its best: Eulalia Bernard in African robes giving a spirited interpretation of 'My Black King'; singer Marta Valdés and Nancy Morejón performing the poet's 'Polished Stone' in Mexico; and Yvonne-América Truque accompanied on the drums by Diego Marulanda at Toronto's Mixed Art Festival. Poetry can touch the mind and the spirit. In Cartagena Portalatín's 'A Woman is Alone', it raises philosophical questions about the human condition, and in Edelma Zapata Pérez's 'Ancestral Fears', it invokes the power and presence of the gods. Because poetry has such different functions, contemporary women writers use varied forms: free verse with its multiple rhythms and tempos but also traditional, primarily Hispanic, verse forms, such as *baladas, romances, sonetos, sones, tangos, cantos, elegías,* and *elogios.*

Except for Dominican Cartagena's poetic *Escalera para Electra* (1980) and Ecuato-Guinean María Nsue Angüe's *Ekomo* (1985), most first novels by Afra-Hispanic writers have been published in the past decade. These include *Bajo la piel de los tambores* (1991) by Argentina Chiriboga, *El columpio de Rey Spencer* (1993) by Marta Rojas, and *Sirena Selena vestida de pena* (2000) by Mayra Santos-Febres. The most innovative of these in its form, language, and characterisations is *Sirena,* a remarkable tour de force by one of Puerto Rico's most gifted prose stylists. The narrative, about a young singer and an aging transvestite, captures the textures and rhythms of dimly-lit gay bars, where men and women deal with their ambiguous sexuality in a vibrant and tactile language that bips and bops across the page. Santos-Febres' short story collection, *Pez de vidrio* (*Urban Oracles* in the English translation) is also a ground-breaking work, similar in its inventiveness to Cartagena's *Tablero*, a volume of stories published in the Dominican Republic in 1978. Mayra Santos-Febres and especially Excilia Saldaña of Cuba draw on Afro-Latin American oral prose forms such as proverbs, tales, myths, antiphonal patterns, and *patakínes* (Yoruba legends) to create folk tales that express the beliefs and customs of their communities. But the essay is the prose genre to which many of the Daughters are attracted; two of the most important collections of essays are Chiqui Vicioso's *Algo que decir* (1991), which contains critical studies of women's literature, and Nancy Morejón's *Fundación de la imagen* (1988), essays on literary and cultural criticism. The most significant nonfiction writer, however, is Marta Rojas, a prolific Cuban journalist whose articles, essays, and novels are exceptional for their language, fictive devices, and stylistic innovations.

It is curious that first-person narratives (diaries, memoirs, testimonials, and autobiographies), which are so important in Afra-American literature, are seldom the genre of choice of Black Hispanic women. In fact, Sherezada Vicioso's 'An Oral History', Sandra María Esteves' 'Open Letter to Eliana', and Edelma Zapata Pérez's 'Coming to Consciousness' were requested by editors, while the narratives of Shirley Campbell, Soleida Ríos, and Marta Rojas were written for this anthology. Other genres that have received little attention by writers and even less attention by literary critics are radio/ television scripts, including those written by Georgina Herrera of Cuba and Uruguayan Beatriz Santos – both of whom work in that media – and dramatic works such as Vicioso's *Wish-ky Sour* and Morejón's short, poetic *Pierrot y la luna*. Although Chiriboga, Herrera, and Saldaña have written award-winning books for children, Saldaña points out in 'Reflections on My Poetic Work' that the writers of children's literature have to deal with publishing delays, lack of promotion, and the absence of critical studies. Her essay reveals that many creative writers are also exceptional literary critics who demonstrate in their self-reflective essays a broad knowledge of literature, an awareness of intertexuality in their writing, and a clear sense of the thematic, stylistic, and ideological direction of their work. Examples of critical reflections include 'Las poéticas de Nancy Morejón', as well as two interviews in this volume: Georgina Herrera's 'The Lion's Version of the Jungle', and Mayra Santos-Febres' 'The Page on Which Life Writes Itself'.

Evident in both the critical and creative work of Afra-Hispanic writers is their commitment to social and political change in their countries.

Sometimes overtly but more often subtly, their poetry and fiction focus on issues about which they are deeply concerned: Sherezada Vicioso on discrimination against Dominican immigrants, Lourdes Casal on tensions between Cubans and Cuban-Americans, Eulalia Bernard on racial prejudice in Costa Rica, Argentina Chiriboga on the erasure of Black women from Ecuadorian history, and Cristina Cabral on sexism in Uruguay. One of the most powerful political pieces – similar to David Walker's *Appeal* in its passion and stylistic innovations – is Aida Cartagena Portalatín's *Yania Tierra*, a long, epic poem that lays bare the bloody pages of Dominican history. Her cryptic rewriting of history is heightened by fictive devices – intercalation of songs and poems, contrapuntal alternation of lyrical and dramatic passages – that make *Yania* a beautiful work of art rather than a didactic treatise. Committed writers such as Cartagena would probably agree with Santos-Febres, who explains:

> My work reflects all of that [abhorrence of racism, violence, and homophobia]. But a literary text will always be more than politics. It has to be. Because literature is about imagination and freedom of expression; it can serve political purposes, but it is fueled by struggles of the soul.

In spite of this caveat, her political views are evident in the dedication of a short story to *'all the Puerto Rican political prisoners jailed in federal prisons by the US government since 1960'*.

One of the most important social and political questions that Caribbean and Latin American writers of African descent raise is that of race: What does it mean to be a *negra* or *mestiza* or *mulata* in a country that defends and validates European colonisation and acculturation? Race is a major component of identity for many writers, particularly those from Cuba, Costa Rica, Uruguay, and other countries where pride in the African cultural heritage is valued in the *casa* and the *barrio*. Cuban writers Cristina Ayala, Marta Rojas, Georgina Herrera, Excilia Saldaña, and Nancy Morejón underscore the significance of African culture in the formation of national identity. Supported by the pro-Africa discourse of the Revolution, the Afro-Cuban cultural tradition is evident in every facet of Cuban life, particularly in its art, music, and literature. Georgina Herrera wrote 'First Time in Front of a Mirror' after seeing her face reflected in an African mask, and the female persona of her 'Sedi Ibu', a poem full of African allusions, proudly maintains, 'I never forget / who I am, from whence I came, to whom I'm indebted'. In 'The Lion's Version of the Jungle' Herrera says, 'I always liked being Black, having this tranquility. I was proud of our large mouths and our wide noses'. Uruguayan Virginia Brindis de Salas

colonización mental

expressed the same pride and self confidence in the 1940s – before the Black-is-beautiful vogue – when she wrote: 'I'm a Black woman, / because I have black skin'. In her poems, interviews, and narratives, Costa Rican Shirley Campbell expresses the significance of race in her self-image. She writes:

> I accept myself
> unequivocally free
> unequivocally black
> unequivocally beautiful

Race, however, is not unproblematic. Some writers question the black-white dichotomisation of race in the United States. They deal, instead, with the nuances and subtleties of *mestizaje* (racial and cultural mixing) or hybridisation in the Spanish Americas, where the mixing of Natives, Africans, and Europeans has produced a lexicon of ethnicities: *pardos, mestizos, zambos, mulatos, morenos,* et cetera. In spite of real differences in racial definitions in the Americas, what is undeniable is the denial of race by some individuals and countries that have internalised the racist ideology of the dominant culture. Mental colonisation is the subject of Frantz Fanon's *Black Skin, White Masks,* a seminal study of the psychological effects of European colonisation. In her essay 'Oh Lord, I Want to be White' and her book-length study *Charcoal and Cinnamon*, literary critic Claudette Williams examines Carmen Colón Pellot's rejection of blackness and internalisation of racist values. In her collection of poetry, *Ambar mulato* (1938), the Puerto Rican poet depicts a mulatto woman 'in the throes of a crisis of racial identity' (100). Williams demonstrates that mulatto identity depends upon a denial of blackness and that mulattoes are often complicit in their racial erasure. The denial of race and creation of 'raceless' poetry were more prevalent among early writers, who held precarious positions in plantation society. The legacy of that reductive mentality is evident in countries where the myth of European origin still prevails, where people of colour are called *indios* (Indians) or *trigüeños* (light-skinned people), and where dark-skinned people are considered Haitians in disguise. In 'The Journey Inward', for example, scholar Aida Heredia explains: 'The Dominican Republic suffers from a politics of social and cultural identity informed by a concept of a nationalism that is rooted in the supposed ideal of a Spanish origin'. Dominican poet and essayist Sherezada Vicioso elaborates:

> In Santo Domingo, the popular classes have a pretty clear grasp of racial divisions, but the middle and upper-middle classes are very

deluded on this point. People straighten their hair and marry 'in order to improve the race', etc., etc., and don't realise the racist connotations of their language or their attitude. In the United States, there is no space for fine distinctions of race, and one goes from being 'trigüeño' or 'indio' to being 'mulatto' or 'Black' or 'Hispanic'. ('An Oral History')

(Yet, when one examines the photographs in Franklin Gutiérrez's *Bibliography of 150 Dominican Women Writers,* it is evident from their skin colour, hair texture, or facial features that many writers are of African descent.)

Coming to terms with one's racial identity and accepting one's difference can be a difficult process, according to Colombian poet Edelma Zapata Pérez. In 'The Consciousness-Raising of an Afro-Indo-Mulatto Woman Writer', she writes: 'My life in the capital marked the discovery of my blackness – a slow, painful, and anguished road toward my origins'. It is ironic that the experience of living in the United States, where the Civil Rights and Black Power Movements radicalised so many Blacks, forced some Afra-Hispanic writers to confront, for the first time, their own identity as women of African descent. Sherezada Vicioso explains in 'An Oral History' how her experience of racism in the United States forced her to confront and to adopt the 'Black identity as a gesture of solidarity'. Before her 'enlightenment', Cuban-American poet and college professor Lourdes Casal called herself a *mulata*. '[A] Cuban of mixed ancestry (white, black and Chinese)', she reflects, 'I considered myself to be like Cuba – a mulatress in an essentially mulatto country'. But her participation in the US freedom struggle made Casal aware of her blackness, of the significance of her colour and hair texture.

In the view of many Black women writers such as Shirley Campbell, identity is anchored in gender as well as race. In a recent poem, 'Persona', Nancy Morejón writes : 'Who is that woman / who is present in all of us fleeing from us, / fleeing from her enigma and her distant origin?' That woman wants to distance herself from other women, from her problematic and enigmatic self, and from her (African? slave? illegitimate?) roots. She chooses the easy way out – flight – because the search for the female self is too hard, too painful, and too complicated. That woman represents all of us who are caught in the struggle between flight and the difficult journey within to self-knowledge. In their poems and short stories, their essays and novels, the Daughters explore gender – sexual identity and its associated social and cultural characteristics – as it has been constructed by the society in which they live. Although their writing sometimes represented women in traditional roles as wives and mothers, early writers often wrote 'genderless' poetry on neutral subjects such as nature and God in an effort to erase their female identity and gain acceptance by the male literary establishment. But not Burgos, who rejected the feminine (passive, submissive, frivolous) self in her powerful 'To Julia de Burgos'.

> You are only the ponderous lady very lady;
> not me; I am life, strength, woman.
> You belong to your husband, your master; not me;
> I belong to nobody, or all, because to all, to all
> I give myself in my clean feeling and in my thought.

That poem is probably the first feminist manifesto written in Spanish by a woman of African descent.

Many of these writers, however, do not call themselves feminists, because they do not want their work pigeonholed by labels ('feminist', 'black', or 'communist') and because they consider feminism a Euro-American ideology that is exogenous to their culture. Nancy Morejón voices this attitude in an often-quoted interview. She says, 'I think that the task of a womanist (let's talk with Alice Walker's term which I love very much) in our region should be something related to our society and to our history' ('Womanist' 266). In spite of such disclaimers, there is a decided feminist consciousness in the works of many contemporary Afra-Hispanic writers, who create strong and independent female characters; rewrite national history through their portraits of revolutionary women; describe grandmothers, othermothers, and literary foremothers who have shaped their work; support a female culture of artists and workers; examine women's inner worlds (their psychology and spirituality); underscore in their lives and works the importance of female deities such as Yemayá, Ochún, and Oya; write an 'autobiography of the body' that explores sexual desire and the female body; question femininity and women's traditional roles in patriarchal societies; examine the effect that silence, isolation, and invisibility have on female agency and creativity; and expose both private and public acts of violence and discrimination against women.

In the novel *Jonatás y Manuela*, for example, Ecuadoran Argentina Chiriboga creates a fictional character with historical roots, who is the prototype of the New Black Woman: she is creative, political, courageous, aware, intelligent, militant, and self-directed. A homely, cross-dressing woman, she is also the antithesis of the beautiful, half-white, hip-shaking rumba dancer who peopled the pages of *negrista* poets for decades. We see reflections of the Jonatás prototype in other Black female protagonists: Rojas' Lucila Mendes, Morejón's Mujer Negra, Cabral's Warrior Woman, Cartagena's Yania, and Truque's Mujer Batalla. Such characters originate in a revisionist ideology in which women are the subjects – rather than objects – of national history. The fictional personae are often based on figures who have been erased from Latin American history, such as Jonatás, an enslaved Ecuadoran who liberated slaves and fought for independence from Spain, as well as María de la Luz Sánchez and María Rita Armand, nineteenth-century leaders of Cuba's antislavery movement. Many fictional characters, such as Lunda Uyanga in *Bajo la piel de los tambores* and Ba-Lunda in *Jonatás y Manuela*, are also based on ancestral figures, particularly grandmothers, life-giving and -affirming culture bearers who pass on creative gifts – African songs, tales, myths, beliefs, and deities – to a long line of coloured daughters and granddaughters. Cuban novelist Marta Rojas, for example, is indebted to her grandmother, Cecilia Martínez, whose stories about slavery have enriched her novels. In countless poems, Excilia Saldaña pays tribute to her grandmother, Excilia Saldaña Bregante, who nurtured her body and creative spirit. She writes: 'I discovered in my blood / with suddenness a grandmother / a female / and an extended line / of mothers singing'.

It is likely that neither their grandmothers nor their mothers would have approved of the openness with which contemporary writers deal with sexual desire and the female body. As usual, Julia de Burgos was the first to break the silence, writing lyrical, sensual and passionate poetry to her lover, the Man River of Loiza. 'Coil yourself', she urges, 'upon my lips and let me drink you, / to feel you mine for a brief moment'. The erotic poetry of contemporary Afra-Hispanics is more explicit, and they describe female pleasure in various forms. Uruguayan Beatriz Santos writes: 'Your semen's burning lava / begets butterflies / in my dark womb'. Cuban novelist Marta Rojas uses irony and erotically-charged language to evoke the protagonist's womanliness and to satirise the slaveowner's lechery in *Santa lujuria o papeles de blanco* (Holy Lust or White Papers). The most daring and radical writer, in terms of her fictive depiction of eroticism and sexuality, is thirty-something Mayra Santos-Febres, whose novel and short stories deal, on occasion, with fellatio, masturbation, pedophilia, transvestism, voyeurism, necrophilia, and homoeroticism (in fact, she is the only Afra-Hispanic writer to portray gays and lesbians in her work) – not to titillate but to explore, artistically and empathetically, the depth and diversity of human beings. Her fictional characters, even the adolescents, prisoners, and sex workers who are preyed upon by dirty old men, prison guards, and johns, maintain control over their bodies, which become sites of power and resistance. Santos-Febres describes, for example, Dulce M, who was imprisoned for her support of Puerto Rican independence. 'She put her finger in where occasionally the guards searched her, and she said, "This is mine and it doesn't matter if in a few minutes they come to take it away from me, for now it's still mine, mine."' She then takes possession of her own body in a deliberate act of defiance.

Evolution Of A Literary Tradition
The Spanish Caribbean: 'Five Centuries of Rains and Moons'

The earliest Afra-Hispanic writers emerged in the Spanish Caribbean, where their poetry and prose describe their lived experiences, their literary models, the periods in which they lived, and particularly, the social and historical contexts of their work. The Spanish conquest and colonisation of Cuba, Puerto Rico, and Santo Domingo led to the slaughter of natives, importation of enslaved Africans, and creation of a plantation society. It is estimated that between 1502 and 1870, approximately two million Africans were brought to the Spanish colonies (Palmer 66), and, although they contributed substantially to the culture and economy of the region in the seventeenth and eighteenth centuries, they were far from willing participants in the colonisation of the New World. The Africans' resistance to slavery through rebellions and insurrections, through flight and marronage, was intensified after the Haitian Revolution of 1790–1804, when slave rebellions – in which Black women often played prominent roles – erupted throughout the Caribbean. The nineteenth century was marked by the struggle for emancipation, which lasted from 1824 to 1886, and by wars of independence in which the colonies struggled for freedom from European domination. The postcolonial period has also been marked by turbulence: civil wars, revolutions, dictatorships, economic recessions, and military occupation by the United States.

It is against this historical background of displacements and disjunctures that the literature of African-descended women in the Spanish Caribbean must be examined. Their literature is fragmentary and discontinuous; it is characterised by silences and lagunas – what Cocco de Filippis calls 'Feminine Parentheses' (26) – in its evolution. Three early poets – Juana Pastor, Salomé Ureña de Henríquez, and Cristina Ayala – are paradigmatic in the archaeological reconstruction of this literary tradition because they reveal, in different ways, how women artists and intellectuals dealt with their creative gifts. The life of the first known Afra-Hispanic writer is shrouded in mystery, but we hear her voice, however faint, echoed in rare books and the pages of a few scholarly papers. Juana Pastor, described as a free *parda* or brown-skinned woman, was born in the 1700s in Havana's Jesús María barrio. Like her contemporary, African American poet Phillis Wheatley, she may have been taught to read and write, study geometry and grammar, compose poetry, and recite Latin (in all of which she excelled) by a former slaveowner; or she may have attended one of the small schools for free coloured and white children that sprang up in colonial Havana; or she might have been an autodidact, like the nineteenth-century Afro-Cuban poet Plácido. At any rate, she stood out in that community of wealthy Creoles, European immigrants, and upwardly-mobile mulattoes. She became 'a teacher of the most distinguished ladies of her time' (López Prieto liv), and she wrote flawless prose and poems full of Christian piety and patriotic zeal. But we can only wonder what her life must have been like in that colony of planter elites, where Cubans of African descent, including slaves and free Blacks, made up 44 per cent of the population by 1775 (García Agüero 358).

Later called the 'Black Avellaneda' (an allusion to the nineteenth-century Cuban novelist Gertrudis Gómez de Avellaneda), Pastor inhabited the tenuous terrain of the mulatto in a race-conscious society that was becoming increasingly Black in spite of attempts to hide its nappy roots. Did she recite her poetry at *tertulias* or literary salons? Was her work published in broadsides and newspapers? Was she proud of her dark skin? Did she embrace her identity as a woman of African descent? Like other colonial writers, Juana Pastor took themes from classical or biblical texts, composing formal, derivative verses – the same 'stiff, struggling ambivalent lines' that, according to Alice Walker, characterised Wheatley's poetry (200). Although she did not publish a book and most of her poetry is not extant, a few of her *décimas* (poems of ten-line stanzas) have survived in the introduction to an 1881 anthology. According to Antonio López Prieto, Pastor improvised the following poem on November 27, 1815:

> I pity the godless,
> Lament the inept,
> Flatter the favorite,
> And laugh at the haughty.
> Wise, I also spurn
> The coarse knave
> Who dares violate my honor,

But I always know, by
Faith, that I am his rib,
And that I must love him. (liv-lv)

Pastor imitated European models because her readers undoubtedly came
from the small circle of Cuba's intellectual elite, which included few
women and even fewer Blacks. She would have disdained the rich folk
tradition of the *barrio* and the slave plantation, where, according to
Esteban Montejo, Afro-Cubans danced the *zapateo* and *tumbandera*, ate
masango and *ochinchín*, worshipped the *orishas,* played *güiros* and
timbales, and sang 'Toma y toma y toma caringa / pa' lo viejo palo y
cachimba' (Barnet 71).

Like Juana Pastor, the Dominican poet Salomé Ureña de Henríquez
(1850–1897), 'whose features clearly showed her grandmother's African
descent' (Grossman 12), ignored her country's vernacular tradition (as
did most nineteenth-century writers) in favour of neoclassical verses
about nature, nationalism, and nurturing. Although the two poets used
similar themes and styles, Ureña, who has been called the 'founding
poet' of the Dominican Republic, achieved the fame that eluded Pastor.
Ureña may have been the better poet (too little of Pastor's work remains
to judge), but she also enjoyed privileges – a superior education,
professional opportunities, and publication of a book – as the daughter
and wife of educated, upper-class men. She was taught by her mother
and grew up surrounded by books in a house frequented by literary
figures. (Apparently, her racial origin was not problematic in a country
that denies its African roots. Although it is estimated that one-quarter
of the population is Black and two-thirds is mulatto, Dominicans with
money and/or education are classified as 'White'.) In 1880, Ureña
published *Poesías*, a collection of thirty-three poems that includes
'Anacaona', which is based on legends about the Taino queen who
was killed by the Spanish conquistadors. It is significant that this educator
and poet sought the ethnic origins of her country in its indigenous
population, whose culture was virtually eradicated, while she ignored the
Afro-Dominican culture that was quite visible. Ureña, described as a militant
advocate of national independence and women's rights, also founded the
Instituto de Señoritas, the first secondary school for women in the
Dominican Republic. Although she is hailed 'for her dedication to the
struggle for a better society in which women would be a vital and integral
part' (Cocco de Filippis 19), the 'better society' that she envisioned did
not include Afro-Dominicans.

The first Afra-Hispanic writer to break the silence about race was Cristina Ayala, who was born in 1856, six years after the birth of Salomé Ureña de Henríquez, in the small town of Güines, Cuba. Perhaps because of her humble origins (for her mother was a slave), or because she lived in the country, where *campesinas* tended to be more race-conscious, or because she matured during the struggle for emancipation and independence, Ayala wrote openly about race in carefully crafted, didactic poems full of pain and moral indignation. She wrote 'A mi raza' (To My Race), for example, in response to a pamphlet entitled 'Cuba y su gente' (Cuba and Its People) in which Blacks, especially women, were denigrated. Written in 1888, two years after the abolition of slavery in Cuba, her poem is both a defence and an apologia.

> It is not the black race, no;
> although some people say so,
> who is responsible
> for 'that time now passed'.

'That time' probably alludes to slavery because one of the ironies of post-emancipation racism was blaming the victim (the slave) for his own bondage. The poet continues by exhorting Afro-Cubans to strive for education and moral perfection in order to erase the stigma that society has placed on them. To women, she writes:

> And, we women
> carrying out our mission
> have the obligation
> to understand our duties.

Little is known about Cristina Ayala, the subject of a study by Carlos Alberto Cervantes and a short tribute by Nancy Morejón, who considers Ayala her literary foremother. Like Esteban Montejo, Ayala was taken from her slave mother to be raised by a *madrina* or godmother until she was five years old, at which time she was reunited with her mother. As a child, she attended a poor neighbourhood school where she learned little, but she loved literature and became an avid reader. She began writing poetry when she was only seven years old and published her first poem 'Al Valle de Güines' (To the Güines Valley) in 1885. She wrote extensively between 1885 and 1920, and gave poetry readings, including one at the Sociedad Gran Maceo de Santa Clara in 1911. Her ballads, sonnets, and poetic tributes to Plácido and José Martí appeared in more than twenty local newspapers and journals, including *El Pueblo Libre* (Free People) and *El Sufragista* (The Suffragist). The titles of these periodicals suggest that she participated in the social and political movements of the period. As Morejón notes, 'Cristina wrote and struggled against slavery, against social inequality based on race or gender, as well as in support of national independence for Cubans of all types, origins, and colors' (7). In 1926, perhaps as a tribute to the poet on the occasion of her death (date unknown), a volume of her collected poetry, *Ofrendas mayabequinas*, was published in Güines with a prologue by Valentín Cuesta Jiménez. This volume, however, is extremely rare: there is a copy in Cuba's National Library and another in the Fondo Antiguo de la Sociedad Económica de Amigos del País in Güines. Morejón points out: 'The country's literary history does not record, in any of its major sources, the important work of this Black, rural, feminist and woman poet and journalist'. Gabriel Abudu noted in a letter to this editor that '[a]nother important Afro-Cuban writer of the early 20th Century was María Dámasa Jova, who published a fine collection of poetry in 1927'.

In the two decades that followed publication of Cristina Ayala's and Dámasa Jova's poetry, two major writers emerged in the Spanish Caribbean – Julia de Burgos in Puerto Rico and Aida Cartagena Portalatín in the Dominican Republic – to open up new routes to the page. (Although Carmen Colón Pellot published her *Ambar mulato* with its self-rejecting 'Oh Lord I Want to be White' at the same time, her work harkened back to an earlier period when women produced timid, tentative verses that reinforced their precarious status in racist, patriarchal societies.) Burgos and Cartagena – through both their innovative works and their unconventional lives – struck out for the high seas. Following in their wake came a long line of talented island women: Dominican Sherezada Vicioso; Puerto Ricans Angela María Dávila and Mayra Santos-Febres; Cubans Marta Rojas, Rafaela Chacón Nardi, Georgina Herrera, Nancy Morejón, Excilia Saldaña, and Soleida Ríos. Although Chacón Nardi and Angela María Dávila are not included in this volume, they have gained recognition for their writing. Chacón was born in Havana in 1926 to a Martinican mother and a Cuban father. A prize-winning poet and an educator with a doctorate in pedagogy, she has published twenty books, including the following poetry collections: *Viaje al sueño* (Voyage to the Dream) in 1948, *Del silencio y las voces* (Of Silence and Voices) in 1979, and *Una mujer desde su isla canta* (A Woman From Her Island Sings) in 1994. Gifted with a lilting, lyrical voice, she writes about her island's beauty, music's birth, and a soldier's song. Angela María Dávila (1944) has published only two collections of poetry: *Homenaje al ombligo* (Tribute to the Belly Button) in 1967, written with José María Lima as a kind of erotic dialogue, and *Animal fiero y tierno* (Animal Fierce and Tender) in 1977. She has been acclaimed as one of Puerto Rico's most inventive poets for her linguistic innovations and use of vernacular language.

A new generation of Afra-Hispanic writers has emerged in the Dominican Republic, but they seldom write about race; instead, they examine issues relating to class and gender in a patriarchal society. Her experiences in the US made Sherezada Vicioso aware of problems in her own country: 'Like racism, for example. Class differences. Santo Domingo is a very societally structured city. The situation of women is atrocious'. Vicioso and others of her generation are college-educated academics and writers who belong to workshops and groups such as the Círculo de Mujeres Poetas (Circle of Women Poets). University professor Jeanette Miller (b.1944), for example, has gained critical acclaim for her poetry, plays, movie scripts, and nonfiction. In poems such as 'The Woman Whom I Know' from *Fichas de identidad* (Identity Papers), she examines the weaknesses and pretensions of Dominican women: 'The woman whom I know / wields invisible fingers / diffused voice / and straightened hair'. An educator, labour lawyer, and poet, Ida Hernández Caamaño (b.1949) reveals how domesticity thwarts the woman artist when she asks, in a poem from *Viajera del polvo* (Dust Travelling Woman): 'How is poetry possible from hands busy with detergent, spices and heroics?'

Also born in 1949, Josefina de la Cruz Martínez is the only novelist of this group. Besides *Una casa en el espacio* (A House in Space), she has published four collections of poetry and a book of literary criticism based on her doctoral dissertation. Dulce Ureña (1960) has represented her country at literary events in the Caribbean and Latin America, and poetry from her *Preámbulo* and *Babonucos* has been anthologised in *Common Threads* and *Sin otro profeta que su canto*. Between 1985 and 1999, Angela Hernández Nuñez (b.1954) has published four books of poetry and five collections of short stories. A chemical engineer, educator, and political activist, she has, according to Franklin Gutiérrez, made a major contribution to feminism in the Dominican Republic through her activism and scholarship (92). A member of the Generation of 1980, Carmen Sánchez Aponte (b. 1960) published two poetry collections before winning the National Poetry Prize in 1996 for *Demando otro tiempo* (I Demand Another Time) in 1996. Another young writer, Aurora Arias Almánzor (b.1962), has degrees in art education and clinical psychology and has edited several magazines and newspapers, including one for the Center of Investigation for Women's Action. Her publications include two collections of poetry and two of short stories. One of the most prolific and accomplished writers is Ylonka Nacidit-Perdomo, who has published six books of poetry and four works of literary criticism in the past decade. Although a lawyer by training, she has worked as a journalist and librarian to promote Dominican culture and literature.

Central America: 'Memorizing the Map of Your Scars'

Although the European conquest and colonisation of Central America follows the same pattern as does that of the Caribbean, there are significant differences in its ethnic history, in its 'map of scars'. The indigenous population was reduced but not eradicated by wars and massacres; free and enslaved Africans were 'disappeared' through assimilation into the majority Indo-Mestizo-European population; a second diaspora of Blacks from the British West Indies occurred in the late nineteenth and early twentieth centuries; Afro-Anglo-Hispanics are fewer in proportion to the majority Mestizo population; and most of these descendants of West Indians live along the Caribbean coast. Many North Americans find it difficult to believe that there was or is a visible Black presence south of the Río Grande, but it is estimated that approximately 0.2 million enslaved Africans were imported into Middle America (Palmer 70). Gonzalo Aguirre Beltrán reports that in Mexico, for example, there were 20,569 Blacks by 1570 and 35,089 by 1646, but he concludes, 'What is the significance of 15, 20 or 35 thousand Blacks diluted by 50 million Mexicans?' (198). Luz María Martínez Montiel, a Mexican anthropologist of African descent, has also documented the African presence in Central America in a series of articles and books (Adams 210–16). Descendants of enslaved Africans – visible in the dark skins, wide noses, and coarse hair of Afro-Hispanics in rural towns and coastal cities – are called 'Colonial Blacks' to distinguish them from West Indians who later migrated to Central America to work on railroads, banana plantations, and the Panama Canal. According to Lourdes Martínez-Echazábal, 'Colonial Blacks assimilated the language, religion and customs of the Spanish colonizer . . . [and] they identify with an (Afro)Hispanic, rather than with an (Afro)British cultural tradition' (126).

In his *Central American Writers of West Indian Origin: A New Hispanic Literature*, Ian Smart was one of the first scholars to document the emergence of an hispanophone literature by writers of Anglo-Antillean descent. Included among the writers is Eulalia Bernard, one of Central America's first Black women writers, who published her first collection of poetry, *Ritmohéroe*, in 1982. Since then, other women writers, such as Shirley Campbell (Costa Rica), Juanita Mitil (Panama), June Beer and Mariana

Yonüsg (Nicaragua), and Mirma Martínez (El Salvador) have added their voices to the literary discourse. Both Bernard and Campbell have now published several books and, through reviews, translations, and scholarly critiques of their work, are gaining an international reputation. The other writers are little known outside of their countries, although some of their poems have been anthologised and/or translated into English. The poetry of Juanita Mitil, for example, has appeared in the *Afro-Hispanic Review* and *Erotique Noire / Black Erotica*. A poet and journalist, she is active in the women's movement and serves on the board of the Acción Reivindicadora del Negro Panameño (ARENEP).

The anthology *Ixok Amer-Go: Central American Women's Poetry for Peace* includes the works of other African-descended writers from Central America. Poet and painter June Beer (1935–1986) lived on Nicaragua's Caribbean coast, where she supported Sandinismo, promoted cultural activities, and served as contributing editor to the bilingual newspaper *Sunrise*. In poems such as 'La parcela' (Land Plot) and 'Vacacionej en Cornailan' (Vacations on Corn Island), she recounts, in the dialect of Anglo-Caribbean immigrants, the social and economic difficulties of coastal dwellers. At the end of 'La parcela' she writes, 'Peruese gerente de sonrisa guabinosa / mi dio sólo rialej paembarcarme y despuej qitarme la parcela' (But that banker with the fishy smile / gave me just enough money to get in debt / and then took my land). Mariana Yonüsg was born in Venezuela but, since 1978, has lived in Nicaragua, where she participated in the freedom struggle. In 1985, she won the Gregorio Aguilar Barea Prize for Poetry, and her work has been published in *Nuevo Amanecer* and *La Chachalaca*, the magazine of Nicaragua's Ministry of Culture. A medical specialist in cervical cancer and oral rehydration, she writes lyrical and militant poetry dealing with the complexities of love and the horrors of war, hunger, and poverty. In 'Remembering Guillén: Affirmations to Explain the Death of a Child', she writes:

[This child] died from crossing, barefoot and alone,
the long sadness,
died from having centuries of hunger and cold,
died from not having crayon-painted dreams,
died not knowing a smile
nor the brevity of Sundays
nor what is hidden beneath the circus tent. (Anglesey 420)

Mirma Martínez was born in 1966 in El Salvador, where she coordinates the cultural publication of the Salvadoran Art and Cultural Workers Association.

She has completed a collection of her work, *Paralelo a su ausencia* (Parallel to Your Absence), and her poetry has been published in such literary magazines as *El Pregón*, *Códices*, and the cultural supplement of *El Mundo*.

South America: 'Placentas Buried in This Land of Musicians and Poets'

Like the descendants of enslaved Africans in Central America, the Black populations of many South American countries have disappeared or been absorbed by the *mestizo* population. In a compelling article, 'Racism: "Original Sin" of Argentine National Identity', an Afro-Argentine reports that in 1778, 40 per cent or 80,000 of the 210,000 inhabitants of the Río de la Plata region were 'negros, mulatos y zambos' (Molina 50–51), but that the official policy of *blanqueamiento* or whitening, introduced in the mid-nineteenth century, resulted in the 'disappearance' of Blacks. It is estimated that from the sixteenth to the nineteenth century, half a million slaves were brought to Spanish South America to work in the mines and on sugar and coffee plantations (Palmer 70). They were sold at slave auctions in colonial cities such as Cartagena, Maracaibo, Buenos Aires, and Montevideo, where they served as domestics and artisans. The majority, however, were sent to the grasslands and coastal plains of New Granada, where they established majority-Black enclaves in such places as Chocó, Colombia and Esmeraldas, Ecuador. It was in these enclaves and in the coastal cities that Afro-Latin American culture began to flourish. The first writers emerged in the late nineteenth and early twentieth centuries, and they founded newspapers to publish their writing. None of these pioneering writers, however, was female.

The founding mother of Afra-Uruguayan literature and one of the first Black women writers in Latin America is Virginia Brindis de Salas, who published two slender volumes of poetry in the 1940s and then disappeared from letters and life, leaving few traces of her existence. The newest star on that country's literary horizon is poet and essayist Cristina Cabral, who wrote a great deal but published little before coming to the United States to pursue doctoral studies in Latin American and Afro-Hispanic literature. Another emerging writer is performing artist Beatriz Santos, whose essays and books on Afro-Uruguayan society, particularly the role of women, have helped to preserve her country's African legacy. In his anthology of Black Uruguayan poets, Alberto Britos Serrat provides poems by and biographical sketches of three Black women writers, including Cabral. Britos also cites the work of poet and painter Clelia Nuñez Altamiranda, who was born in Montevideo in 1906. Beginning in 1960, she published poems in local newspapers and gave readings from her unpublished collection *Esencia y voz del pensamiento* (Essence and Voice of Thought). Two of her most interesting poems include 'A Nicolás Guillén', an ode to the Cuban poet on his visit to Uruguay, and 'Canto negro' (Black Song), which highlights the cultural and historical contributions of Africans in the Americas. Myriam Tammara La Cruz Gómez, born in Montevideo in 1951, pursued graduate studies in physics and medicine after completing her bachelor's degree. Her sentimental poems, such as 'Black Woman', 'Your Eyes', and 'Homeland', treat love, motherhood, and nationalism in traditional styles and forms. In a conference paper, literary critic Caroll M. Young examined the writing of Sara Prieto and María Julia Bicca, two emerging writers; and in 'The New Voices of Afro-Uruguay', Young cites other Afra-Uruguayan writers, including Marta Gularte, América Ribero, and Beatriz Ramírez. Of particular significance, according to the critic, is Maruja Pereira, a contemporary of Virginia Brindis de Salas and founder of the first Black women's political party, the Comité de Mujeres Negras Por la Paz y Contra el Fascismo. Little, however, is known about Pereira's life and work.

The best known Afra-Colombian writer is poet and essayist Yvonne-América Truque, whose bilingual Spanish-French *Proyección de los silencios* was published in 1986. She migrated to Canada in the 1980s and is critical of political corruption and exploitation of the poor, themes that figure prominently in her work. Both of her sisters – Sonia and Colombia – are writers, following in the footsteps of their father, Carlos Arturo Truque (1927–1970), the distinguished Afro-Colombian poet and short story writer. Born in Buenaventura, Colombia, Sonia Nadhezda Truque edits an international, bilingual (Spanish-French) poetry journal, and she writes articles and book reviews. Her publications include an anthology of children's poetry, a book of verse, and several collections of short stories. Colombia Truque has also published poetry as well as a book of short stories, *Otro nombre para María y otros cuentos* (Another Name for María and Other Stories). Edelma Zapata Pérez, daughter of Colombian poet and novelist Manuel Zapata Olivella, is also a writer, who recently published her first collection of poetry, *Ritual con mi sombra*.

In *Common Threads* (27–34), Clementina Adams describes the work of Eyda María Caicedo Osorio, an emerging writer, who was born in Chocó, a coastal province of Colombia with a substantial Black population. Caicedo has published a novella, *La hija del aguijón-I* (The Sting's Daughter-I), which deals with discrimination against poor Blacks by religious leaders, corrupt politicians, and wealthy professionals. Laurence Prescott describes four other Afra-Colombian women writers, including poet María Teresa Ramírez, Luz Colombia de González, whose first book was cited in *El Tiempo*, Maura Valentine González, whose *Poemas de la vida* (Poems About Life) was published under the pseudonym 'Ebony Pearl', and Teresa Martínez de Varela Restrepo (b. 1914). According to Adams, Martínez de Varela is a poet, novelist, essayist, and biographer, who was born in Quibdó, Chocó but who lives in Bogota, where she has worked as a teacher and administrator. Sometimes writing under the pseudonym Lisa de Andráfueda, she has published the biography of an Afro-Colombian hero, an historical novel *Guerra y amor* (War and Love), and sentimental poems such as 'My First Love' and 'Trilogy of a Kiss'.

Although two Afra-Hispanic writers – Martínez de Varela and Brindis de Salas – published collections of poetry in the 1940s, Black women did not produce a body of literature until the 1980s and 1990s. One of the most prolific of these writers is Argentina Chiriboga of Ecuador, who has in the past decade published a children's book, an anthology, two collections of poetry, and three critically acclaimed novels.

North America: 'No Promised Land, Nor Paradise'

Many Afra-Hispanic writers who were born in or have migrated to North America in search of education and employment have ambivalent feelings about that region. Some like the security and stability that they experience in the North; others feel disoriented and displaced in a land that is alien to them in language and culture; and still others superimpose the history of northern exploitation on their memories of home. Colombian-Canadian Yvonne-América Truque writes:

There is no promised land, nor paradise
No homeland to cling to
After the long voyage
And a seedless return.

Lourdes Casal (1938–1981), who migrated to the United States from Cuba because she could not accept its revolutionary ideology, represents in her life and work the paradigmatic experience of the Latina. In 'For Ana Veldford' she voices contradictory feelings about her adopted country, proclaiming, 'And still New York is my home. / I am ferociously loyal to this acquired *patria chica*' but also lamenting, 'I will always remain on the margin, / a stranger among the stones'. Lourdes wrote in both English and Spanish; she wrote nonfiction in English because her scholarly writing was intended for US academics, but her poetry and prose were written in Spanish, her native tongue. Cuban-born Beatriz Rivera (b.1957) also lives in New York, where she is completing a doctorate in Spanish after receiving a master's in philosophy from the Sorbonne. Her two novels, *Midnight Sandwiches* and *Playing with Light*, and her collection of short stories, *African Passions*, are written in English with occasional Spanish words and phrases. This writer alludes at times to Cuban cultural myths, and she deals with personal rather than political issues. Perhaps Rivera and Casal reflect their generational differences: Lourdes was radicalised by the Civil Rights Movement of the 1960s, while Rivera was shaped by the pop culture of the 1980s.

Similar differences are apparent in the themes and preoccupations of two Dominican-Yorks. Loida Maritza Pérez (1963) recently published her first novel, *Geographies of Home*, which deals with a young New York woman who feels trapped in the stifling immigrant culture of her conservative and religious Dominican parents. The protagonist is more concerned, almost narcissistically so, with personal questions about identity and place rather than with the deeper social and political problems that Caribbean immigrants encounter in a hegemonic, White, Anglo society such as the United States. Like Lourdes Casal, Sherezada Vicioso lived in New York during the 1960s and '70s and participated in the freedom movement. Her poems and essays, therefore, reflect her pain and outrage at the plight of poor immigrants in that country. 'If you stay in New York too long', she writes, 'you begin to get worn down by it. Anyone who is in the least sensitive can't help but feel bruised by the destruction of our people'. Eventually, she became ill and retreated into silence. Finally, she returned home.

Social and political issues also inform the writing of Puerto Rican-Dominican-Latina writer Sandra María Esteves. The titles of poems such as 'For Lolita Lebrón', 'Anonymous Apartheid', and 'For Fidel Castro' underscore her commitment to racial equality, Puerto Rican independence, and revolutionary politics. One of the best known and most acclaimed Latina writers, Esteves is an award-winning poet, essayist, performer, graphic artist, and producer, who became director of the African Caribbean Poetry Theater, an arts organisation that presents poetry readings and theatre productions. She recounts the emotional experience of attending a reading at the National Black Theater in Harlem, where she heard 'nontraditional, nonclassical, free-form poetry that addressed itself to the immediate issues of our collective existence'. Her publications include three volumes of poetry: *Yerbabuena* (1980), which is said to have established an urban Latina aesthetic and thematic; *Tropical Rains: A Bilingual Downpour* (1984); and *Bluestown Mockingbird Mambo* (1990). The dynamic and revolutionary spirit that infuses her work is apparent in this definition: 'A poem', she writes, 'is a simple truth that blows up like a bomb in your head'.

Africa: The Motherland

The Republic of Equatorial Guinea, which gained its independence from Spain in 1968, after more than 150 years of colonial domination, is the only Spanish-speaking country in sub-Saharan Africa. Its colonial legacy is apparent in the social, political, and economic problems that have beset the country since independence. During the brutal dictatorship (1968–1979) of Francisco Macias Nguema, for example, one-third of the population, including most intellectuals and professionals, went into exile in Gabon, Cameroon, or Spain. Although two autochthonous writers, both males, published their novels during the final years of Spanish hegemony, a national literature did not emerge until the end of the Macias regime, when Ecuato-Guineans published their writing, founded journals, and organized cultural centers in Malabo, the capital. These organisations supported the writing of women such as Raquel Ilombe (1939–1992), pseudonym of Raquel Del Pozo Epita, who produced a book of poems, *Ceiba,* in 1978. Called 'poet of the rain, poet of the sun' by another writer, she was born on the island of Corisco to a Spanish father and Bantu mother but was raised in Spain. She also published *Leyendas guineanas* (1981), traditional stories for children, completed an unpublished book of poetry, *Nerea, Ausencia, Amor, Olvido*, and was writing *20 años de ir y venir a Guinea* a year before her death. María Nsue Angüe, the best known woman writer of Equatorial Guinea, has lived most of her life in Spain, where she published *Ekomo*, based on the cultural traditions of the Fang, the largest ethnic group in her homeland. Emerging authors also include Ana Sohora, Caridad Riloba, Mercedes Jora, and Trinidad Morgades Besari, who began writing while attending the Universidad Nacional de Guinea Ecuatorial. Morgades Besari has published essays and short stories in the country's two literary magazines *El Patio* and *Africa 2000*, but she is best known for the play *Antigona*, which uses African cultural elements (dance rhythms and drum beats) to reinterpret Greek drama.

The 'long journey' of writers María Nsue Angüe and Raquel Ilombo from their African Homeland to an Otherland – that is, perhaps, strange and distant – is emblematic of the many diasporas about which Afra-Hispanic Daughters write. The most traumatic, of course, was the African

Diaspora, when entire nations, after enduring captivity and enslavement, were subjected to a perilous journey across the Atlantic to the Americas, where they were sold at auction and forced to labour on sugar, cotton, and coffee plantations. The experience of that first 'scattering of people far from their ancestral homelands' is embedded in the cultural memory of the Daughters, whose poetry and prose remind readers of a shared myth of origin and of a shared history and culture. Curiously, some writers have retraced their ancestors' steps and made the journey back to their roots. That journey has often been unsettling but also transformative. There have been other diasporas, other dislocations and disjunctures, that have shaped racial, cultural and national identity: the Afro-Antillean diaspora of English-speaking West Indians to the coasts of Central and South America in the late nineteenth and early twentieth centuries, the self-exile and dis-exile (return home) of Cubans after the Revolution, the migration of Dominicans to the United States, the movement of Puerto Ricans from the island to the US mainland, and the flight of Ecuato-Guineans to Spain. Diasporas have profoundly affected the writing of Black Hispanic women because these movements mark imaginary spaces of dislocation and discontinuity. Yvonne-América Truque writes of the 'long voyage' away from home and of the 'seedless return' to a country that no longer feeds the spirit. Writers who have crossed borders between countries, cultures, and languages into strange and alien Otherlands reveal feelings of displacement, isolation, and despair, but, ironically, this estrangement, this defamiliarisation, makes them look at themselves with new eyes. Afra-Hispanic literature has thus been enriched by the migratory and exilic experiences of writers who have had to re-examine identities, revision their *patria*, and chart radically different routes to the page.

Works Cited

Adams, Clementina R. *Common Threads: Afro-Hispanic Women's Literature.* Miami: Ediciones Universal, 1998.

Aguirre Beltrán, Gonzalo. *La población negra de México: Estudio etnohistórico,* 3rd edition. Mexico: Universidad Veracruzana, 1989.

Anglesey, Zoë, ed. *Ixok Amer-Go: Central American Women's Poetry for Peace.* Penobscott, Maine: Granite Press, 1987.

Barnet, Miguel. *Biografía de un cimarrón.* Mexico: Siglo Veintiuno Editores, 1968.

Braxton, Joanne M. and Andrée Nicola McLaughlin, eds. *Wild Women in the Whirlwind: Afra-American Culture and the Contemporary Literary Renaissance*. New Brunswick, N. J.: Rutgers University Press, 1990.

Britos Serrat, Alberto, ed. *Antología de poetas negros uruguayos*. Montevideo: Ediciones Mundo Afro, 1990.

Cervantes, C[arlos] A[lberto]. 'Juana Pastor'. In *Sobre la poesía negrista*. Edited by Oscar Fernández de la Vega, 11-16. New York: n.p., 1985.

___. *Plácido y Cristina Ayala: Disertación histórico-crítica, leída en la noche del 28 de juno de 1927 en el salón de actos de Unión Fraternal*. Havana: Imprenta Estrella, 1927.

Cocco de Filippis, Daisy. *Sin otro profeta que su canto: Antología de poesía escrita por Dominicanas*. Santo Domingo: Taller, 1988.

DeCosta-Willis, Miriam, ed. *Singular Like a Bird: The Art of Nancy Morejón*. Washington: Howard University Press, 2000.

DeCosta-Willis, Miriam, Reginald Martin, and Roseann P. Bell, eds. *Erotique Noire / Black Erotica*. New York: Doubleday, 1992.

Esteves, Sandra María. 'Open Letter to Eliana (Testimonio)'. In *Breaking Boundaries: Latina Writing and Critical Readings*. Eds, Asunción Horno-Delgado et al., 117-121. Amherst: The University of Massachussetts Press, 1989.

García Agüero, Salvador. 'Lorenzo Menéndez (o Meléndez) – El negro en la educatión cubana'. *Revista Bimestre Cubana* 39 (1937): 347-65.

Grossman, Judith. 'La musa de la patria'. *Women's Review of Books* 17 (September 2000): 12.

Gutiérrez, Franklin. *Evas terrenales: Biobibliografías de 150 autoras dominicanas*. Santo Domingo: Comisión Permanente de la Feria del Libro, 2000.

López Prieto, Antonio, ed. *Parnaso cubano: Colección de poesías selectas de autores cubanos desde Zequeira a nuestros días*. Havana: Miguel de Villa, 1881.

Martínez-Echazábal, Lourdes. 'Hybridity and Diasporization in the "Back Atlantic": The Case of *Chombo*'. *PALARA* 1 (Fall 1997): 117-29.

Molina, Lucía Dominga. 'El racismo: Pecado original de la identidad nacional Argentina'. *PALARA* 4 (Fall 2000): 50-3.

Morejón, Nancy. 'Sobre Cristina Ayala'. *Revista del Vigia* 1 (1996): 7.

___. 'A Womanist Vision of the Caribbean: An Interview'. In *Out of the Kumbla: Caribbean Women and Literature*. Edited by Carole Boyce Davies and Elaine Savory Fido. Trenton, N. J.: Africa World Press, 1990.

Palmer, Colin. 'African Slave Trade: The Cruelest Commerce'. *National Geographic* 182 (September 1992): 63-91.

Pastor, Juana. 'Décimas (November 27, 1815)'. In *Parnaso cubano: Colección de poesías colectas de autores cubanos desde Zequeira a nuestros días*. Edited by Antonio López Prieto. Havana: Miguel de Villa, 1881.

Prescott, Laurence E. 'Negras, morenas, zambas y mulatas: Presencia de la mujer afroamericana en la poesía colombiana'. In *Colombia: Literatura y cultura del siglo XX*. Edited by Isabel Rodríguez Vergara. Washington: Organization of American States, 1995.

Smart, Ian. *Central American Writers of West Indian Origin: A New Hispanic Literature*. Washington: Three Continents Press, 1984.

Walker, Alice. 'In Search of Our Mothers' Gardens'. *Double Stitch: Black Women Write About Mothers & Daughters.* Edited by Patricia Bell-Scott et al., 196-205. Boston: Beacon Press, 1991.

Williams, Claudette M. *Charcoal and Cinnamon: The Politics of Color in Spanish Caribbean Literature.* Gainesville: University Press of Florida, 2000.

Young, Caroll M. 'The New Voices of Afro-Uruguay'. *Afro-Hispanic Review* 14 (Spring 1995): 58-64.

Virginia Brindis de Salas

Virginia Brindis de Salas

URUGUAY

(1908–1958)

The life of this pioneering Afro-Uruguayan poet is shrouded in mystery and, most recently, in controversy. Highly acclaimed by the Afro-Uruguayan community as a writer and intellectual, Brindis de Salas was the first Black woman writer in South America to publish two books, and, according to poet Gabriela Mistral, she was the first Afro-Uruguayan literary figure to gain international attention. Although she was said to have been born in Montevideo, the daughter of José Brindis de Salas, she published her first poem 'Mi corazón' (My Heart) in the journal Acción *under the name Iris Virginia Salas. By 1946, when her first collection of poetry was published, she had appropriated the name Virginia Brindis de Salas as well as a relationship to a noted Black family. Indeed, the editors of* Acción, *who took credit for introducing 'Iris's' poetry to the literary world, wrote that she was the 'descendant of a family of great renown in intellectual circles'. In 'Mis dos tíos ilustres' (My Two Illustrious Uncles), a speech delivered in Buenos Aires and published in her second volume, she claims a familial relationship to Claudio Brindis de Salas, the great Cuban violinist, and Gabino Ezeiza, the famous Argentine* payador *or guitarist-singer from the River Plate region.*

Described by her contemporaries as a shy, quiet woman, Virginia Brindis de Salas is depicted in a photograph as a pensive intellectual with a penchant for books. She belonged to the Circle of Black Intellectuals, Artists, Journalists, and Writers (CIAPEN), which included such important literary figures as Pilar Barrios, Juan Julio Arrascaeta, and Carlos Cardoso Ferreira, and she was a founder and contributor to Nuestra raza *(Our Race), a Black journal published in Montevideo from 1917 to 1950. Her first collection of poetry,* Pregón de Marimorena *(Brown Mary's Street Call), is considered the first major publication by a Black Uruguayan writer. In*

2

militant poems such as 'Race?', 'Black Lament', 'The Colored Maid', and
'Song for a South American Black Boy', Brindis de Salas became the voice
of Uruguay's poor, Black underclass of domestics, street vendors, and
sugarcane workers. In 1949, she published Cién cárceles de amor (One
Hundred Love Laments), but a third volume, Cantos de lejanía (Faraway
Songs), remained unpublished and is probably now extant. A race woman
in every sense, she traces in her poetry the African roots of Uruguayan
culture and describes Black popular culture – the songs, ritual dances
(tango and conga), ancestral drums, and ceremonies such as Candombe,
as well as Black archetypes and culture-bearers such as the gramillero or
male ancestral figure; and she protests political, economic, and social
conditions such as Yankee imperialism, racial oppression, and poverty in
Montevideo's slums.

In spite of the poet's accomplishments, there has been a one-man
'campaign to write Virginia Brindis de Salas out of Uruguayan literary
history', according to Marvin A. Lewis. Alberto Britos Serrat, who
enthusiastically reviewed Pregón in 1946, suggests in his Antología de
poetas negros uruguayos (1990) that Brindis de Salas did not actually
write the poetry attributed to her. Such accusations abound in the history
of Black women's literature, but literary historians Lewis and Caroll Mills
Young, who have done extensive research in Uruguay, convincingly dispute
Britos' claim. Although her books are now out of print, Virginia Brindis
de Salas' poetry has been widely anthologised in such collections as Antología
de la poesía negra americana (1953), Schwarzer Orpheus (1954), The
Image of Black Women in 20th-Century South American Poetry (1987),
Voices of Negritude (1988), and Daughters of Africa (1992).

Hallelujah!

Redeeming chorus shouting
from the Antilles
to the Plate River
and in the sea-like river
exclaims:
Hallelujah!

People of America,
I am yours.
I was born in you;
because of you I exist
and so I say:
Hallelujah!

So many people
are there in the street
and there is no one
who maintains
silence:
Hallelujah!

Many are those
who are going to work
and there are also many
who hardly eat
but yet would wish to sing:
Hallelujah!

I have legs
with which to walk;
they will not falter.
I go everywhere
without hesitation.
Hallelujah!

Translated by Ann Venture Young

Pregón Number One

Take my verses
Marimorena.
I know that you have to drink them
like a shot of rum,
but as a fair exchange
I want your anguish,
Marimorena.

I want your anguish,
I want your suffering,
all of your suffering
and the tilt of your mouth
when you laugh
like a crazy woman,
Marimorena,
drunk
not so much on wine
as on misery.

Your voice,
never singing lullabies
to your children
or grandchildren,
a pariah's voice
gently proffers
the daily newspaper.

There is no one to quiet you
for four cents a paper;
no one can refuse to buy one
so as to lighten your burden.

Cont'd

Let me see your face Marimorena,
for its expression captivates,
causing sorrow and pity.

They owe you so much,
Marimorena,
the ones who write
and whom you pay
with your pennies,
with your sales pitch,
in the morning
and in the afternoon
thousands of times;
on the other hand you
pay dearly for
their journalism,
their political propaganda
all their defects, their selfishness,
their false and dull careers.

Marimorena
sells newspapers every day;
Marimorena
suffers every day
her burden.

Translated by Ann Venture Young

The Conga

Drummer, beat,
beat the drum, drum.

Let it run,
the river which springs on your forehead.

On with it, negra,
On with the ancestral conga.

Drummer, beat,
beat the drum, drum.

Look what a pretty figure
the dancing girl makes:
her tinted hair like
foam on the sea.

From the whirl
of her dizzyness,
a seafarer
in a storm.

My goodness, how amazing!
Wide skirt,
petticoat,
moving in the breeze
the whirl of her dancing.

A blond girl
pale and slender
as a candle
from the cathedral.
How the flame
flickers in vain,

Goodness!
her hands
try to plunge
through the breeze
in search of a fire
which will burn
her feet, blood and veins;
and her head,
confused now,
turns and turns again
dazed by
the syncopation
of her dancing.

Look at her face
Negra *Manuela!*

Look what a face
the girl makes,
charmed by the "conga"
and the "conga" players;
the drummers
design in her
convulsions
and their expressions
which force
that "poor little girl"
to dance, spinning
like a noria
in a sea breeze.

Negra *Manuela,*
look at your little friend;
as she yields
to the tumult
of saxophones.
She is drunk
as if on palm wine

and she's spiced
with cinnamon,
ginger,
aroma of the jungle in bloom.

Even her hair
which at first was
blond, silky
in croquignole curls
now turns the color
of smoke rings
when she moves
her whole body;
her conspicuous protrusions
from chest to belly
move freely:
lying in wait for
the sharp tooth
of desire.

Negra *Manuela,*
look at the drum
when your little
friend dances!

In disarray
her whole flesh
undulating
from side to side…

Look at the girl!

You will believe if you
listen to the drums
beat for her
far from the floor
of the jungle.

Listen to the drums beat for her.

Bah! if she only knew
in her ambiguous form
that she wants
to be clothed in black,
to smell of earth
and ardent nights;
completely desirous
completely fervent
close to the drum
and the drummers;
near the drum-head
and the drummers;
entirely oblivious
entirely contented.
Even her face
has changed!

Stridently
the trumpet
lends rhythm and cadence.

Your little friend dances,
Negra *Manuela.*

Now the night lights
grow dim.

Ay, and they carry her,
Negra *Manuela,*
to her house
on a stretcher.

Translated by Ann Venture Young

The Unmasking of Virginia Brindis de Salas:
Minority Discourse of Afro-Uruguay

Caroll Mills Young

Virginia Brindis de Salas is the leading black woman poet of Uruguay and is considered to be the most militant among Afro-Uruguayan writers. According to Richard Jackson, her poetry comes closer to 'shaking the famous black fist' (108) than does that of her contemporaries, Pilar Barrios, Juan Julio Arrascaeta, and Carlos Cardoso Ferreira. Unfortunately, little about her life is known: her date of birth, for example, has been recorded as both 1908 and 1920. Janheinz Jahn writes that Brindis de Salas was born in Montevideo in 1920, to José Brindis de Salas, but the author does not provide her mother's name. At present, the only available date of death is 1958.

Brindis de Salas published two volumes of poetry: *Pregón de Marimorena* (The Call of Mary Morena) in 1946, and *Cien cárceles de amor* (One Hundred Prisons of Love) in 1949. In *Cien cárceles,* the editor notes that a third volume of poetry, *Cantos de lejanía* (Songs from Faraway), is forthcoming, but that collection was never published. Other than Pilar Barrios, Virginia Brindis de Salas is only the second black Uruguayan writer whose work appears in book form.

Pregón de Marimorena and *Cien cárceles de amor* represent both the intellectual fervour of Brindis de Salas and the cultural reality of Afro-Uruguay. In the prologue to *Pregón,* Julio Guadalupe, a Uruguayan poet and contemporary of Brindis de Salas, lists her among the best women poets of the River Plate area: 'Virginia Brindis de Salas, the first and only black Uruguayan woman poet, quiet and shy, unlike the majority of American women poets who lavish in popularity, has remained virtually anonymous, until the publication of this, her first book' (8-9). Brindis de Salas's tough-minded interpretation of Afro-Uruguay, love for her people, originality, sincerity, irony, refusal to conform to traditional poetics, and cynicism are several of the distinctive characteristics that rank her among the best poets in the Southern Cone.

Although both volumes of poetry are important cultural documents, *Pregón* represents the poet's most innovative attempt to reflect the social

11

reality of Afro-Uruguay. The collection is divided into four parts: *baladas* (ballads), *pregones* (street calls or shouts), *tangos,* and *cantos* (songs). Each section of poetry presents a different aspect of Afro-Uruguayan culture. The themes of *Pregón* focus primarily on racial discrimination, hegemony of the dominant culture, black pride, Africa, and the poverty and oppression of Afro-Uruguayans. Her poetic style reflects the folkloric traditions and oral culture of Afro-Uruguayans. It is a poetry without elaborate metaphors and images, and the tone of her work ranges from anger to joy. As a poet, she frees herself from the bonds of the dominant discourse by taking 'the shout' of the street vendor Marimorena – her struggle, song, and joy – and moulds them into free verse. Moreover, Brindis de Salas chooses for her stage the slums of Afro-Uruguay and poetically magnifies its deplorable conditions. Her leading characters are the poor and the oppressed, and, in their defence, she attacks those who ignore and reject them. In contrast, she praises those, like Marimorena, who manage to overcome misery, poverty, hunger, and prejudice. The song 'Aleluya' (Hallelujah) best describes her mission as a defender of and a speaker for the poor:

Aleluya!
Son muchos
los que van a trabajar
Y muchos son también
los que apenas comen
y quisieran cantar.   (58)

(Hallelujah!
Many are those
who are going to work
and there are also many who
hardly eat
but yet would wish to sing.)*

In these lines, Virginia Brindis de Salas describes her own personal battle against oppression and her struggle to improve the living conditions of poor Afro-Uruguayans. In the ballad, 'Es verdad, sí señor' (It's True, Sir, It's True), she defends her struggle for equal rights:

Hay quien vive para comer
y quien come para vivir;
quien ve para creer

y quien lucha para sufrir. (20)
(There is he who loves to eat
and he who eats to live
he who sees to believe
and he who fights to suffer.)

The closing lines of the poem reveal her alliance with other black writers in the Southern Cone, the Caribbean, and the United States, who have chosen to fight oppression. Similarly, 'La hora de la tierra en que tú duermes' (The Hour on Earth in Which You Sleep) is a call for everyone, black or white, to take off his/her blindfolds and join the struggle against racial injustice.

In the poet's struggle to disclose the social ills of Afro-Uruguay, the poems of *Pregón* became weapons in the struggle; each poem conveys a powerful message to the ruling majority. In her *baladas*, Brindis de Salas begins her battle by depicting the poverty and misery of children living in the slums of the black community. The ballad 'Prez para los niños sin canto' (Prayer for Children Without a Song) illustrates these conditions.

Allí están mis niños,
ellos son los más pobres
En ese patio inmundo
todo, destartalado
no hay hamacas, ni muñecas . . . (25)
(There are my children
the poorest ones
living in that filthy
dilapidated patio,
no hammocks, no dolls . . .)

Both 'Prez' and 'El cerro' realistically describe the slums of the black community, where children have barely enough to eat; the poems serve as strong messages to a society that victimises innocent children by allowing them to live in such deplorable conditions.

In her rebellion against the dominant group, Brindis de Salas writes the ballad 'El pan legendario' (Legendary Bread) as a reminder of the hard labour of the poor. She emphasises that without the sweat of their brow there would be no bread to eat. Another concern of Brindis de Salas is the image of a white God. She challenges that image in 'Cristo negro" (Black Christ):

Cristo negro manoseado
por la audacia y por la fuerza,
dejarás tu mansedumbre
de cordero y tu vergüenza. (27)
(Black Christ,
Abused by audacity and power
You will bequeath your
meekness and your shame.)

The black Christ is a symbol of the bloodshed and suffering of Afro-
Uruguayans.

In the poet's attempt to change the social ills of Uruguay and to draw
more attention to the day-to-day struggles of the poor, she captures the
pregón or cry of the black street vendor in a poetic form. The *pregón* is
one of the oldest oral art forms in Uruguay, because it originated during
slavery. During the colonial period, black men and women performed
unpleasant and burdensome domestic tasks. After completing the tasks,
slaves had to go through the streets and sell their masters' wares. It was
common to see black women, skilled in making candy, *empanadas* (meat
pies), or cakes selling their goods in the street. From sunup to sundown,
the cries of the black street vendors filled the air with rhythmic and
melodious sounds (*Pregones* 31). According to Rubén Carámbula, the
towncriers who sold their wares in the streets of colonial Montevideo
were recognised by their songs – a kind of short melody with an initial
syllable in the middle or at the end of the *pregón* (*Negro* 199).

In the second section of *Pregón,* there are three poems about
Marimorena, the central protagonist, who sold newspapers. Here, Brindis
de Salas connects the past to the present by emphasising that the *pregón*
is an art form symbolic of the enslavement of poor blacks in Uruguay.
Although free, Marimorena is still enslaved by society because she struggles
to exist. The first *pregón* suggests the pain and sacrifice involved in
Marimorena's daily labor.

Tu voz,
que nunca arrulló
a tus hijos
ni a tus nietos
y es voz de paria
arrulla mimosamente
toda la prensa diaria. (34)

(Your voice
never singing lullabies
to your children
or grandchildren,
a pariah's voice
gently proffers
the daily newspaper.)

Marimorena earns only a few pennies from peddling papers all day,
yet her long hours of work are unappreciated by those whose papers
she sells:

¿Cuánto te deben
Marimorena
esos que escriben
y que tú pagas
con tus vintenes (35)

(They owe you so much,
Marimorena,
The ones who write,
and whom you pay
with your pennies)

Unaware of the political propaganda, the buyers' egotism, and their
ideologies, Marimorena, who is illiterate and unaware, works to feed her
family. In the second *pregón*, Brindis de Salas underscores Marimorena's
working conditions:

No hay sol que te arredre nunca,
ni lluvia que te aglutine.
Y si se empapa tu nuca
o chapotean tus botines,
vas adelante y pregonando
como heraldo en los mitines (37)

(There's no sun that frightens you,
nor rain that weakens you
If your clothes are soaked
or your boots are wet,

you keep peddling papers,
like a herald angel)

In the last lines, Brindis de Salas attacks those who become wealthy from the painful labor of Marimorena, who barely earns enough to buy bread. The third *pregón* calls attention to those who, like Marimorena, earn a living selling papers on the streets of Uruguay. It serves as a tribute to those who support the Uruguayan economy and whose cries are daily reminders of the struggle to survive.

Like many black Uruguayan writers, Virginia Brindis de Salas gained an identity from her African roots, as is evident in her use of the tango as a poetic form. The poem rhythmically evokes the dance that was created by African slaves. According to Nestor Ortíz Oderigo, the word *tango* is an Africanism – a corruption of 'Shango', god of thunder and storms in Yoruba mythology (Lewis 21). Traditionally, ritualistic dances and songs accompanied the evocation of such gods. When transferred to the New World, these dances and songs took the same name as the secret society. Thus, the present-day *tango* and *candombé* are derived from the ritualistic dances of slaves who were transported to Brazil and the River Plate area (Carámbula 177). To illustrate this Afro-Uruguayan tradition, Brindis de Salas includes three tangos, which capture the fast-moving, rhythmic pace of the dancers and singers.

Danza
que bailaron los esclavos,
parche y ritmo
en su elemental rueda de gallo.
Yimbamba – yimbamba
Yimbamba – yambambé;
son tus caderas
y tus pies. (46)

(The Dance,
that the slaves danced,
drum and drumbeat,
the dance of the peacock.
Yimbamba – yimbamba
Yimbamba – yambambé;
Your hips sway,
and your feet move.)

The drum language, 'yimbamba – yambambé', mixed with Spanish words, adds to the intensity of the dance. Likewise, the onomatopoetic reproduction of the song and the sounds of the piano evoke the ceremonial invocation to the gods:

Aheeé
canta el chico
Ahooó
canta el "piano" (46)

(Aheeé
the young man sings
Ahooó
the piano plays)

Brindis de Salas' poetic reproduction of the tango is another example of minority discourse that evolved from the slave experience of black Uruguayans.

In the last section of *Pregón de Marimorena*, Brindis de Salas includes four songs that capture the spirituality of black Uruguayans. 'Canto para un muchacho negro americano del sur' (Song for a South American Black Boy) encourages black elders to pass their pride and wisdom on to the youth:

Muchacho con orgullo de bantú
que cantas:
Ya ho . . .,
ge . . ., ge . . .,
ge . . ., ge . . .,
tangó!
Abuelito,
gramillero
siempre lo recuerdas tú
dile a este muchacho americano
qué era el bantú. (50)

(Boy with the pride of the Bantu
who sings
Ya ho . . .,
ge . . ., ge . . .,
ge. . ., ge. . .,
tangó
Grandfather,

Griot,
You, who remember it,
Tell this South American boy
who the Bantu were.)

The poet underscores the importance of Afro-Uruguayan culture by contrasting the innocence of the young boy with the wisdom of the grandfather, who is the Afro-Uruguayan culture-bearer. Most importantly, Brindis de Salas enhances the grandfather's role as the *gramillero,* one of the most respected men in the black community. Traditionally, a healer and lead figure in the tango and *candombé,* the *gramillero* is one of the most popular and well-known figures of Afro-Uruguayan culture (Carámbula 61). The *gramillero* is a repository of knowledge and the narrator of Afro-Uruguayan history, especially the legacy of the Bantu-speaking slaves who were brought to Montevideo. It is his task, therefore, to inform the youth of their African heritage and to instruct them in the traditions and customs of their people.

In the prologue to *Cien cárceles de amor,* Isaura Bajac de Borjes describes the poems as laments, because they are emotionally intense and full of pain and suffering. Brindis de Salas criticises the oppressor with a sarcastic and bitter voice. Her use of free verse exemplifies her rebelliousness in refusing to follow traditional poetic patterns. In a letter to Brindis de Salas, Humberto Zarrilli describes the collection as 'el más completo de poesía negra que se publica en el Uruguay' (the most representative black poetry that has been published in Uruguay) (*Cien* 7). Chilean poet Gabriela Mistral proclaimed *Cien cárceles* an artistic success and described Brindis de Salas as the first black literary figure to cross continental lines. In a letter, Mistral wrote:

> Sing beloved Virginia, you are the only one of your race who represents Uruguay. Your poetry is known in Los Angeles and in the West. I have learned of your recent work through diplomatic friends, and, may God grant that this book be the key that opens coffers of luck to the only brave black Uruguayan woman that I know. (8-10)

Thus, Brindis de Salas was well received as an artist, and her poetry was recognised for its aesthetic merit and for its depiction of the black Uruguayan experience.

Cien cárceles de amor is a collection of twenty-three poems, including five dedicated to poets such as Marta De Mezquita, Elvira Comas Vieytes, Montiel Ballesteros, and José C. Santos. The poet's sarcastic title, 'One

Hundred Prisons of Love', is indicative of the tone and themes of the collection. She uses a direct approach to protest the terrible abuses inflicted on Afro-Uruguayans. The sometimes bitter and angry poems treat pain, forgiveness, despair, hope, and freedom. While the compositions vary thematically, Brindis de Salas deals primarily with oppression, identity, and self-affirmation. Although not all of the poems in *Cien cárceles* treat the black experience in Uruguay, this analysis will focus on those that do. Poems such as 'Abuelito Mon' (My Beloved Grandfather), 'La criada de color' (The Colored Servant Girl), 'Navidad Palermitana' (A Palermo Christmas), 'Cantos' (Songs), 'Negros' (Blacks), and 'Lamento negro' (A Black Man's Lament) move away from the ballads, songs, and folk customs of *Pregón;* the poems in *Cien cárceles* present a more personal interpretation of the black experience.

'Abuelito mon' is written in memory of the poet's ancestors, who worked in the sugarcane fields. In the poem, rum is symbolic of the pain and toil of blacks who produced the beverage for the pleasure of whites. This drink, which the persona will not allow to touch her lips, evokes a painful memory of an unjust society.

> Me cabe el cañaveral
> en cuatro dedos de ron.
> Poco paga el yanqui ya
> por este millón de cañas
> que el negro sembró y cortó.
>
> (I can fit the canefield
> in a swig of rum.
> The Yankee can't pay
> enough for the millions of canereeds
> that the Black man has sown and cut.)

The poet criticises the Yankee who earns millions of dollars but pays little to blacks. For Brindis de Salas, the Yankee is a twentieth-century slaveowner. Therefore, the poet wants to rid Uruguay of its oppressor, and poetry becomes her weapon in this battle. She writes: 'Y mataré con mi boca / lo que con balas no mato' (21). (I will kill with my verses / what bullets cannot). The poem ends on a bitter, angry note, as Brindis de Salas contrasts the sleeping, contented *yanqui* with the sad, desperate black man. The poet urges Afro-Uruguayans not to drink rum because it makes the Yankee wealthy and powerful:

Pero como el negro suelta
agua, triste como yo.
Mientras el yanqui en el bar
duerme su siesta de ron. (22)

(The Black man's sweat runs like
water, sorrowful like me.
While the Yankee in the bar
sleeps off his rum.)

'La criada de color' describes the psychological and physical pain that a black woman endures as a domestic servant. The opening lines evoke the beauty of Africa, which symbolises the lost freedom of Afro-Uruguayans. Brindis de Salas depicts the young woman as a humble servant who wears an artificial smile of happiness. This smile is the mask that Afro-Uruguayans wear to protect themselves from a harsh society:

La risa agudizada sobre sus dientes blancos,
Guarda en lo más profundo castigos de otra raza;
Como pasión ferviente de querer libertarse,
Del ímpetu despótico con que se le rebaja. (25)

(A striking smile upon her white teeth
guards the deepest punishments of another race;
like the burning desire of wanting to be free,
from the tyrannical violence that demeans her.)

The final lines describe the feeling of inferiority and the emotional torture that Afro-Uruguayans are forced to endure: 'It is a smile of anger / . . . that brings forth drowned rebellions and / reverent bows of servitude' (26) The poem ends on a critical note, as Brindis de Salas attacks the dominant culture for its treatment of the black servant girl.

Brindis de Salas addresses the question of her own identity in the poem, 'Cantos':

Yo negra soy
Porque tengo la piel negra
¡Esclava no!...
Yo nací de vientre libre, (32)

(I'm a Black woman,
because I have black skin.
I am not a slave!
I was born free,)

The poet feels that her skin color should not bind her to the vestiges of slavery. Therefore, she calls upon the Afro-Uruguayan gods – Legbá, Dembolá, Uedó, and Avidá – for strength. The evocation of their names brings forth the power and strength to rid the country of its racial and social inequities. As a proud black woman, Brindis de Salas affirms her racial heritage by refusing to call upon Christian gods and insists that one's beliefs and skin color should not determine one's place in society.

On a lighter note is the poem, 'Navidad palermitana' (A Palermo Christmas). Here, the poet offers a beautiful description of the barrio Palermo, an Afro-Montevidean community, on Christmas night. The poem vividly depicts shining stars, a round white moon, colorful decorations, and people dancing the *candombé*. The Christmas celebration evokes memories of the poet's ancestors and their African-derived customs. In the next lines, she mentions the ancestral drum, a symbol of strength and survival, which has survived the rigors of slavery:

Reminiscencia africana
Que reviven los morenos
En nuestra fiesta cristiana.
Recinto de los esclavos
Del viejo Montevideo,
En donde por vez primera
Repico mi tamboril. (24)

(Memories of Africa
that my people relive
on this day of Christian celebration
In the slave quarters
of Old Montevideo
where for the first time
I played my tamboril.)

Although Brindis de Salas is critical of society – and her anger and bitterness are unequivocal – she is also optimistic. In 'Lamento negro' (Black Lament), she describes the anguish, pain, and misery Afro-Uruguayans have endured without losing their desire for freedom and a better future. She begins with the rhetorical question: 'Sabe, compañero, ¿Que cosa me hicieron?' (37) (Brother, do you know what they did to me?). 'Lamento negro' is a sensitive poem that holds Afro-Uruguayans blameless for the oppression and racism of the society.

In *Cien cárceles de amor* and *Pregón de Marimorena*, Brindis de Salas poetically evokes the social and cultural reality of Afro-Uruguay. Both volumes of poetry are testimonies to the oppression of her people. Although the compositions differ widely in style, they connect thematically and reflect the collective experiences of Afro-Uruguayans. Each poem communicates a message and becomes a vehicle to foster social change. The poet uses a personal tone to involve everyone in the struggle for racial and social equality. For Afro-Uruguayans, the poems in *Cien cárceles* and *Pregón* represent their daily struggles to exist, the racism, the social inequities in society, the customs, the music and dance of the black Uruguayan community. The life-like depiction of Marimorena and the vivid descriptions that emerge from each composition are designed to inspire Afro-Uruguayans to change and to reform their society. In contrast, for the oppressor, the poet's goal is to produce feelings of guilt and shame, as she reports the cruel reality of Black Uruguayans. Both *Cien cárceles de amor* and *Pregón de marimorena* reproduce the voices of Afro-Uruguayans, a silent minority that is not responsible for the socio-economic conditions in which they live. The volumes are intended to promote social change in Uruguay; they exemplify the poet's crusade for solidarity, equality, and dignity.

Virginia Brindis de Salas is not a traditional female writer who limits herself to themes of physical love and the relationships between men and women; nor does she write of maternal love or the problems of being female in a patriarchal society. As a poet, she writes from the perspective of a black in a racist society. As an individual and a poet, she suffered the consequences of her militancy and her candor. Her boldness in describing the negative conditions of Afro-Uruguayans often alienated her from other black writers who wanted to impress others with the intellectual genius of the black Uruguayan community. Nonetheless, her work is a defiant discourse that develops themes of racial pride and the struggle for the political, social and economic freedom of blacks everywhere. Today, the life of Brindis de Salas still remains a mystery. How could a writer who was acclaimed as the voice of Afro-Uruguayans be ignored for so many years after her death? There are several possible answers to this riddle. Between 1948 (just before the publication of *Cien cárceles de amor*) and 1960, Uruguay experienced a severe economic crisis, which resulted in increased political and social tensions, economic stagnation, inflation, and currency devaluation (Weinstein 33-36). It would be safe to conjecture that Brindis de Salas and her supporters were unable to secure the funds to publish *Cantos de lejanía*. In addition, her racial militancy and the lack of solidarity among black intellectuals following the death of Pilar Barrios (1889-1974) may have led to the devaluation of her work. Although Mistral read Brindis de Salas's poetry in Los Angeles, only one other document indicates that her work was available outside of Uruguay. In 1954, a German translation of 'Tango Número Tres' was published in Jahnheinz Jahn's anthology *Schwarzer Orpheus* (Black Orpheus).

Most recently, her poems have appeared in Margaret Busby's anthology of black women writers, *Daughters of Africa* (1992), and in Julio Finn's *Voices of Negritude* (1988). Over the last ten years, critics such as Richard L. Jackson, Marvin A. Lewis, Ann Venture Young, and Lemuel A. Johnson have given critical attention to the work of Brindis de Salas. These critics have suggested that her poetry is significant because it contributes to the interpretation of the black experience in Uruguay and South America. The life and work of this pioneering writer indicate that black writers in Latin America are often invisible and critically neglected, for as Lemuel Johnson notes, 'it is doubly regrettable that both volumes of poetry [by Brindis de Salas] are now out of print' (28). Hopefully, studies such as this one will lead to more comparative studies of black women writers throughout the world.

*Editor's Note: Unless otherwise indicated, all translations are those of Caroll Mills Young.

Works Cited

Brindis de Salas, Virginia. *Cien cárceles de amor.* Montevideo, n.p., 1949.

___. *Pregón de Marimorena.* Montevideo: Sociedad Cultural Editora Indoamericana, 1946.

Busby, Margaret. *Daughters of Africa.* New York: Pantheon Books, 1992.

Carámbula, Rubén. *Negro y tambor: Poemas, pregones, danzas y leyendas sobre motivos del folklore afro-rioplatense.* Buenos Aires: Editorial Folklórica Americana, 1952.

___. *Pregones del Montevideo colonial: Candombe, compars de los negros lúbolos*. Montevideo: Editores Mosca, 1987.

Finn, Julio. *Voices of Negritude*. London: Quartet, 1988.

Jackson, Richard L. *Black Writers in Latin America*. Albuquerque: University of New Mexico Press, 1979.

Jahn, Janheinz. *Schwarzer Orpheus*. Muchen: Hanser Verlag Munchen, 1954.

Johnson, Lemuel. "'Amo y espero": The Love Lyric of Virginia Brindis de Salas and the African American Experience in the New World'. *Afro-Hispanic Review* 3.3 (1984): 19-29.

Lewis, Marvin A. *Afro-Hispanic Poetry, 1940-1980: From Slavery to 'Negritud' in South American Verse*. Columbia: University of Missouri Press, 1983.

Pereda Valdés, Ildelfonso. *El Negro en el Uruguay: Pasado y presente*. Montevideo: Revista del Instituto Histórica y Geográfico del Uruguay, 1965.

Weinstein, Martin. *Uruguay: Democracy at the Crossroads*. Boulder: Westview Press, 1988.

Young, Ann Venture. *The Image of Black Women in 20ᵗʰ Century South American Poetry*. Washington: Three Continents Press, 1987.

Carmen Colón Pellot

$\mathcal{C}$ARMEN $\mathcal{C}$OLÓN $\mathcal{P}$ELLOT

PUERTO RICO

(b. 1911)

This early poet is an elusive literary figure because very little is known about her life, and she published only one collection of poems, Ambar mulato *(1938), when she was in her twenties. Born in Arecibo, Puerto Rico in 1911, she became a teacher and journalist, associated at one time with the newspaper* El Imparcial. *According to literary critic Efraín Barradas, 'Her poetry. . . is a direct and personal expression of her negritude. (Of her mulattoism, the poet would point out).' She is preoccupied with Puerto Rico's colour hierarchy, as she reveals in a poem dedicated to her teacher, the poet Carmen Gómez Tejera: 'Teacher / because I was born dark / of slave's blood / I might not understand / the full whiteness of your brilliant mind'. Written in the first person and autobiographical in its tone and feeling, her poetry reveals that she was an educated woman of African descent who identifies herself, ethnically, culturally, and phenotypically, as a mulatto. Colón began writing at a time when* negrista *poetry was at its height in the Spanish Caribbean and when Puerto Rican poet Luis Pales Matos was the preeminent practitioner of that reductive and primitivist poetics, but she brings a different perspective – that of a coloured woman – to the genre.*

Oh Lord, I Want to be White!
(Mulatto Prayer)

On the steep, shy
virgin slopes of the mountains
the orange tree bears blossoms
with goodness perfumed.

Untainted in their beauty
and pure their whiteness;
my fingers do not break them
nor my voice stain them.

Oh, my Jesus!
Oh Lord, I want to be white!

The pond of water revels
in its green birth,
for the stars converse
in its clear brightness.

It shows no sign of the poppy
that is in my scarlet dream;
my songs do not taint it
and my mind does not disturb it.

Oh, my Jesus!
Oh Lord, I want to be white!

The waves unfurl
their foamy crests on the beach;
in innocent playfulness,
rising, falling.
The sea has its mantilla
and I have my guitar;

the sea is decked as a bride,
I am dressed in scarlet.

Oh, my Jesus!
Oh Lord, I want to be
blond and white;
like the foam,
like the pond,
like the blossoms
of the orange trees
on my mountain.

Translated by Claudette Williams

Roots of Mulata Envy

I envy you,
white cloud;
you fall in love in the arms
of the wind.
you alone can frolic
among the virile trees
of the high mountains;
they pay tribute to you
for your chastity and beauty

No one praises me in song;
norms, Christian laws
enslave me.

The sky smiles on you;
space pampers and regales you
you give all to the sun, as you fancy
voluptuous and vague
amid the shining kisses
and the caresses of the rainbowed light.

No one seeks my brown smiles;
no one worships me,
though I have sap
in my warm, bubbling goblets.

Your color is snowy;
my inheritance is tanned.

While I splash in mud
you are rocked in white;
atop the world,
scorning the lowly swamps.

In the quiet night;
the handsome stars
wink at you.
You float, flirtingly
and you rendezvous
with the most handsome
one who seeks your love.

And so, seeing you so free;
seeing myself, so enslaved,
a cold sadness comes over me
and I feel such deep envy
of you, white cloud.

Translated by Claudette Williams

The Land is a Mulatto Woman

The land is a mulatto woman,
a mulatto woman is the land;
with her strong, lustful smell
and her cinnamon colour.

The hills are her warm breasts,
breasts of a restless woman;
breasts filled with green desire
caressed and kissed by the sun.

The fiery lashes
leave her subdued and still;
then the ploughing man
sates his zestful appetite.

The land is a mulatto woman,
a mulatto woman is the land;
with her springs of life waters
and her furrows in waiting.

Translated by Claudette Williams

'Oh Lord I Want to be White':
The Ambivalence of *Mulatez* in Carmen Colón Pellot's *Ambar mulato*

Claudette Williams

Ambar mulato (*Ritmos*)[1] is a collection of 23 poems with a prologue that is integral to their understanding. It was published by Carmen Colón Pellot in Puerto Rico in 1938, after the heady years of the *negrista* movement of which another Puerto Rican poet, Luis Palés Matos, was a leading figure in the late 1920s and the 1930s. The author implicitly denies participation in that movement when she informs us in her prologue that the work was written ' in the simple peace of the mountains, free from the direct influence of schools or complex environments'. *Ambar mulato* is, nonetheless, not totally unaffected by the literary ethos and ideological tendencies of the period. There are ways in which the poems in this volume both coincide with and deviate from *negrista* practice.

Colón Pellot attempts to color our reading of the work by setting out its ideological bases and socio-cultural context in the prologue. She establishes nationalism and race consciousness as the mainstays of her poetry, describing it as 'mulatto and Puerto Rican like my race itself'. This characterization lays tacit claim to the racial, and inferentially, cultural hybridity of Puerto Rican society. Race is the recurring motif that unites the different poems in the collection. Eight have titles with racial references and almost all make allusions to race. Affirmation of a mulatto identity, which the poet equates with the identity of the nation is the collection's dominant motif: 'I shall strum in the air / my brown guitar, humming the rhythms / of its mulatto strings' ('When All is Done', 54). 'Soft and sweet was my voice; / brown my skin / and my body / an urn of unpoured wine'. ('Exodus', 11). These expressions are part of the broader Caribbean anti-colonial effort to reclaim the power of self-definition. Nevertheless, some poems bear witness to a contradiction that has beset the decolonization process: the effort to establish a Caribbean identity has not always been attended by a radical break with alienating colonial modes of thought. For example, the poem 'White Love Motifs' is punctuated with racial stereotypes and reinforces the hierarchy of racial preferences characteristic of Caribbean societies. Its evocation of white, mulatto and black women is accompanied by the conventional associations. Flower imagery is reserved for the white woman, the decorative appendage: 'fragile gardenias', 'lilac caresses' (52). The mulatto woman, on the contrary, is invested with sensuous signs:

> Happy and smiling is my rhythm
> My life and my skin of music are made
> On wild scales
> of golden-brown notes (52)

The black woman is linked atavistically with African savagery:

> The moment is a hymn of triumph;
> The moment of my jungle.
> The red senses resound
> a distant echo of drumbeats.
> The sounds of the fragrant jungle!
> The wild kingdom
> of the new race,
> its song aflame
> in the burning bonfire
> that accompanies my savage dance (52)

In the prologue, Colón Pellot is careful to acknowledge and celebrate the strong influence of African-ancestored people in Puerto Rican national life: 'the coloured race has had a significant influence on the life of our island'. Yet, she betrays a certain racial anxiety in her equally careful discrimination between mulattoes and the (presumably inferior) full-blooded blacks she refers to in stereotypical terms: 'the perfect Negro does not exist here, that is, the superstitious *ñáñigo* type. Our present population is *jíbaro* sprinkled with mulatto'.[2] In this context the use of 'perfect Negro' to distinguish full-blooded blacks from mulattoes produces a curiously ironic effect in that, while seeming to validate the African ancestry of the Puerto Rican people the poet is, in fact, repudiating it. These full-blooded blacks, with their continuing links to an African past, she implies, exist (elsewhere) but not in Puerto Rico. Colón Pellot's 'perfect Negro' is, we suspect, akin to the *negrista* stereotype of the black savage. Her representation of the Negro is also reminiscent of a similar denial of blackness that has long prevailed in the Dominican Republic, which considers its own black population less African and therefore superior to blacks from Haiti and other areas of the Caribbean. Colón Pellot's definition of the mulatto as 'not black' evokes an earlier characterization of the mulatto woman as 'not white':

> You are not white, *mulata,*
> your hair is not pure gold
> your neck is not like silver,
> your eyes do not mirror
> the sky's heavenly blue. (qtd in Morales 197)

This construction of the *mulata*'s identity by Francisco Muñoz del Monte (a white Dominican poet writing in Cuba in the nineteenth century) reflected the whites' desire to keep the mulatto class in its place and thereby preserve white racial purity and supremacy. Colón Pellot's statement stems from an analogous fear of blackness which she perceives as a threat to *mulatez*. It is this self-contradiction that engaged Raymond T. Smith in his study of the multiracial notion of the Caribbean. 'Before ethnic identity can be transcended.' Smith claimed, 'it must be asserted, ... in order to ensure the stature, participation and self-respect of everyone in the local community.' (Smith, 54).

Colón Pellot's discrimination between mulatto and black is also encoded in the language she assigns to the speakers in different poems. Standard Spanish is the language of the collection's dominant mulatto voice; it is the language of the 'mulatto / Puerto Rican poetry' referred to in the prologue. The aberrant Afro-Spanish speech of the poems 'Ugly Mixture' and 'The Bride's Veil', however, presume Negroid speakers.

> Lord, that mixture so ugly
> Black and *jíbaro* all mix' up!
> Hear me, my chile, Negress Panchita
> You gots to be careful (47)

The origins of this racial bias can be traced back to slave society. With the emergence of the mulatto class, slave society created a color spectrum as the basis for assigning positions in the Caribbean's racial hierarchy. In the pigmentocracy, brown-skinned mulattoes occupied a position above black-skinned Negroes, but below whites. Eric Williams has referred to the historical contempt mulattoes felt for blacks. He notes that the mulatto caste in slave society despised the black side of its ancestry: 'With the prestige of white blood in their veins, they refused to do laboring work. They despised the "no-good niggers'" (58). Their relative superiority to blacks was partial compensation for the mulattoes' status as inferior to whites, to whom they were in turn more acceptable.

Despite this development, however, the white racial bias of slave society has remained substantially unchanged. Puerto Rican writers of varying racial backgrounds have in general submerged this discomfiting truth beneath their fixation with the nationalistic significance of the mulatto's racial hybridity. In *Ambar mulato* poems such as 'Song to the Mulatto Race' belong to this tradition of nationalist rhetoric. The poem takes a diachronic look at the mulatto's history going back to the Moorish occupation of Spain, the Spanish conquest of America, the transatlantic slave trade and black-white liaisons that produced the mulatto:

the *conquistadores*
with hands of iron;
slave boats sent
to cross the seas.
And in the warm shade
of the palm trees;
on the ridges, valleys and hills,
the *conquistadores*
of Spanish race,
and the black slaves
engendered my mulatto race;
they fused their genes
and in a nuance and graceful bundle
They created my people!
  To the ambitious mulatto race
I sing my song!
Great race that studies
meditates;
strong race that imposes its beliefs;
and draws among the white race
its golden stream of desires
Mulatto and proud is the race
  To whom I raise my song! (22)

Such an idealization of *mulatez* is a constant of Puerto Rican *negrista* poetry and is a response to the nation-building imperative of the 1920's and 1930's. It effaces, however, the problematic aspects of the mulatto's past. Apart from the cursory admission of the inhumanity of the slave trade, the author glosses over and perhaps even obscures the brutality that often accompanied race mixing, promoting instead the rhetorical view of *mulatez* as felicitous union and synthesis. In a 1942 poem that he entitled 'The Mulatto Woman' and dedicated to Colón Pellot, Puerto Rican mulatto poet Fortunato Vizcarrondo construes the mulatto woman's duality as perfect racial equilibrium, ascribing superiority to neither her African nor her European heritage, but to the new and discrete type they have produced:

> I am with this mixed blood,
> A new breed of woman: the Mulatto woman,
> Fifty percent black,
> Fifty percent white
> Blessed, black woman, blessed
> Was your love for the white man,
> For out of the union
> Came a mixture that is stronger
> Than your race and the Caucasian (qtd in Morales 1976, 58)

Colón Pellot is likewise concerned more with symbolism and less with reality. In the prologue, she amplifies this nationalist myth by attributing special creative endowments to the mulatto's race: 'My mulatto poems ... rise to delicate emotional heights, because the mulatto possesses a keen psychic sense'.

'Brown Girl' gives a more fairy-tale account of the process of miscegenation and reproduces the sensual *mulata* cliché:

> A flash of light
> struck my black pupil,
> and my pearly skin
> Turned to brown
> My hair curled
> into a thousand black seashells
> and wherever I go
> my musical rhythms
> inspire sweet words ...
> 'Your eyes like a dagger
> are killing me, Brown Girl!' (26)

Although in the prologue she unconsciously deprecates real blacks and their Africa-derived culture, in 'Princess' Colón Pellot consciously upholds the romantic myth of a paradisiacal Africa:

an enchanted kingdom of colors
a legendary country, a Garden of Eden
Over valleys of light and chimeras
amid sleeping beaches
siestas under palm trees (33)

It would appear then, that the only Africa that the rhetoric of *mulatez* will accommodate and claim as heritage is an Africa with royal associations. The European component of *mulatez* is celebrated in 'Arecibeñas', in which the poet pays tribute to her hometown Arecibo, using comparably romantic vocabulary:

fair enchanted princess
dressed in a bundle of gold ...
pretty white princess ...
    Evening in my village
granddaughter of Isabel the Great
    Evening in Arecibo
vision of a noble race (12-13)

Male poets in the Hispanic Caribbean (who historically have controlled the field of literary production) have shown extreme fascination with mulatto women as erotic bodies, while they have de-emphasized sexuality in their portrayals of mulatto men. For female poets, on the other hand, sexuality (male or female) is less likely to be an obsession. Colón Pellot's disclaimer in the prologue – 'my mulatto verse is not inspired primarily by the sexual theme' – indicates her intention to shun the reductive ahistorical stereotype. Yet, in 'The Land is a Mulatto Woman' she comes close to the *negrista* practice:

The land is a mulatto woman,
a mulatto woman is the land
with her strong, lustful smell
and her cinnamon color. (49)

While the poet reproduces the *negrista* view of the *mulata*'s sexuality as wanton lust in this poem, she is mainly appropriating that long-standing

Western patriarchal discourse that has identified woman with the land (nature) in its creative and nurturing functions. Colón Pellot confirms the stereotype of female sexual passivity and its antithesis, male sexual dominance. She has sought, however, to adapt the inherited convention to suit the local reality by her specific racial identification of the woman as mulatto. This representation also affirms the creative possibilities of the *mulata*'s sexuality, thereby dismantling the *negrista* projection of a non-reproductive eroticism onto the mulatto woman.

Although it is the woman of African descent who has come to embody non-white sexuality, the discourse of sexuality in Spanish Caribbean literature is predicated upon race rather than gender. In 'Mullato!' Colón Pellot also affords us a rare perspective of a sexualized mulatto man, using the conventions of the discourse:

> Mulatto, your eyes
> are like a black inferno of love,
> a liquid fire rages in your gaze
> melting my heart,
> and boiling in my soul
> happy like the magic of alcohol.(24)

Here, the poet has recourse to imagery used in a nineteenth-century depiction of the mulatto woman by Cuban poet Bartolomé Crespo Borbón:

> pepper that pleases the eye
> but sets the mouth on fire;
> liqueur with soothing smell
> and intoxicating effect
> Spanish fly that sometimes vivifies
> and sometimes kills. (qtd. in Morales 310)

Representations of the mulatto woman as aesthetic, sexual or ideological object have effaced many aspects of her problematic past and painful present. Two poems in *Ambar mulato* problematize the *mulata* image by abandoning the nationalistic rhetoric of the period and using a more personal and authentic voice to explore the psychic dilemma of a notionally 'real' mulatto woman. 'Oh Lord, I want to be White!' and 'Motifs of Mulatto Envy' challenge the preceding notions that the mulatto woman is the unequivocal beneficiary of her proximity to the white female model. The *mulata* persona does not rest confidently on her superiority over blacks. 'Oh Lord, I Want to be White' is the cry of a *mulata* in the throes of a crisis of racial identity:

> Oh, my Jesus!
> Oh, Lord I want to be
> blond and white:
> like the foam,
> like the pond
> like the blossoms
> of the orange trees
> on my mountain. (46)

The poet's choice of a first-person discourse allows her to personalize the *mulata*'s plight and to lay bare the discrepancy between literary stereotype and lived reality. This *mulata* exhibits the other side of the Negrophobia seen in the prologue: the yearning to be white. Although the concept of whiteness is embodied euphemistically in images from the natural environment (orange blossoms, foam, pond), what the *mulata* hankers after is the white woman's beauty; she wants to be white and blond. Her inferiority complex is mirrored even in the arrangement of ideas in the poem, much of which gives priority to the elaboration of images of whiteness, thereby indicating its status as the aesthetic ideal.

This poem is a tragic illustration of one psychic consequence of the dominance of white aesthetic standards. Self-alienation results from the *mulata*'s obsession with an inaccessible whiteness. Not only does the use of a private voice making supplication to God heighten the intensity of her desire, but the obvious futility of her quest seals her tragedy. In defining herself, the *mulata* persona also makes use of the language of Christian morality, which attaches spiritual values to color. She desires whiteness not only as a physical ideal, but also for its association with virtue and chastity. Hence, she characterizes white beauty as 'unpolluted' and 'immaculate' and attributes qualities such as virginity and sanctity to whiteness. Obliquely, the *mulata* portrays herself as the negation of purity, as that which tarnishes and defiles. Her self-image depends totally on her perception of her white counterpart. She has internalized that perception of race that has led to the aesthetic, sexual and moral devaluation of the colored woman. So the desire to be white is also accompanied by the desire to escape the stigma of sinful sex traditionally associated with her black taint (represented in the allusion to the prostitute, the proverbial 'scarlet woman').

'Motifs of Mulatto Envy' with its equally explicit title, highlights the link between the *mulata*'s race and her social status:

And so, seeing you so free
seeing myself so enslaved
an old sadness comes over me
and I feel such deep envy
of you white cloud. (4)

Contrapun!

Again the contrapuntal characterization of the *mulata* and her white counterpart forms the poem's structural frame. As in the first poem, the speaker uses the euphemistic image of the cloud to represent the dominance of whiteness. The location of the cloud, like that of the blossoms of the orange tree growing on the mountain in the preceding poem, is a spatial representation of the socio-racial distance between the two women. While the cloud is identified with superior space and its elements – the wind, the sun, the sky and the stars – the *mulata* identifies with the lowly earth. The earth image does not bear the usual connotations of creativity and fertility but is associated with the pollution and unwholesomeness of mud and swamps.

Colón Pellot's poem highlights the social origins of the *mulata*'s psychological dilemma. The contrast between the acceptance accorded the white woman and the exclusion experienced by the *mulata* foregrounds the correlation between skin color and social status. It is the system of power relations that confers freedom, virtue and beauty on the white woman and that guarantees her a place, while placing restrictions on the *mulata* because of her black taint. Her representation of her condition as a form of enslavement links this black taint back to the institution of slavery and its supporting ideology, and suggests a continuation of that bondage through the surviving caste system. But although the speaker's recognition of the injustice of the race-class division implies some measure of protest, she acquiesces to the notion of her own inherent inferiority. Her questioning of the existing racial value system that discriminates against her stems from a desire, not to change the system, but to rise to the dominant position in the racial hierarchy. Both poems illustrate well the process of cultural conditioning whereby her internalization of white supremacist ideology determines the *mulata*'s self-perception. Her desire to be white is self-denying and results in unhappiness. It is one manifestation of a psychological attitude which, in the words of Erna Brodber, 'diverts time and mental energy from more creative activities and, most detrimental of all, crystallizes an inferiority complex' (36). These confessions of self-alienation displace the glorified image of the *mulata* as sexual or aesthetic object and demythify the nationalist rhetoric that has consecrated her as an inert symbol of racial integration and harmony. Shown as a feeling subject, she does not conform to their rhetorical image.

Ambar mulato is testimony to the centrality of race in Caribbean discourse. In treating this subject, Colón Pellot speaks with not one but many poetic voices and assumes shifting and sometimes irreconcilable positions. She sums up this fact succinctly in 'My Poetry':

> My poetry is paradoxical
> My poetry is all in one
> in the confused amalgam of my chaos ...
> So am I: like my poetry (6-7)

In the collection the textual affirmation of her racial identity coexists with a subtext of racial disparagement; the rhetorical treatment of *mulatez* as metaphor is undermined by the depiction of *mulatez* as lived reality. The color amber in the collection's title is, consequently, not only a fitting generic metaphor for the mulatto's racial in-betweenness but aptly expresses the instability of the author's specific ideological posture.

Notes

1. Carmen Colón Pellot. *Ambar mulato (Ritmos)*. (Puerto Rico: Arecibo, 1938). All quotations, included in parenthesis in the text, are from this edition. The translations are mine.
2. A *ñáñigo* is a member of an Afro-Cuban secret society of ancestor worshipers (*ñañiguismo*). The *jíbaros* are white Puerto Rican small farmers.

Works Cited

Brodber, Erna. *Perceptions of Caribbean Women: Toward a Documentation of Stereotypes*. University of the West Indies, Cave Hill, Barbados: Institute of Social and Economic Research, 1982.

Colón Pellot, Carmen. *Ambar mulato (Ritmos)*. Puerto Rico: Arecibo, 1938.

Morales, Jorge Luis, ed. *Poesía afroantillana y negrista (Puerto Rico, República Dominicana, Cuba)*. Río Piedras, Puerto Rico: Editorial Universitaria, 1976.

Smith, R. T. 'People and Change'. *New World*, 2 (1966): 49-54.

Williams, Eric. *The Negro in the Caribbean*. New York: Negro Universities Press, 1942.

Julia de Burgos

JULIA DE BURGOS

(1914 –1953)

*Called an 'icon of Puerto Rican feminism and pro-independence passion',
Julia de Burgos is acknowledged as one of her country's most important
poets because of the power of her voice. She was born in a rural area of
Puerto Rico to impoverished* jíbaros *(peasants), Francisco Burgos Hans
and Paula García de Burgos, the latter described as a 'sensitive mulatta
woman'. The oldest of thirteen children, six of whom died of malnutrition
and poverty, Julia moved with her family to a slum in Río Piedras, where
she obtained a scholarship to attend high school. Burgos, a brilliant student
who spoke fluent English and studied Latin, Greek, French, and Portuguese
over the course of her life, received a degree from the University of Puerto
Rico's normal school and taught in a rural school. A daring and
unconventional woman, she married twice – first, journalist Rubén
Rodríguez Beauchamp in 1934 and then musician Armando Marín in
1943 – but the love of her life was Dr Juan Isidro Jiménez Grullón, a
prominent Dominican whose wealthy parents disapproved of his
relationship with a* mulata *and 'drinking divorcée'. She was, indeed, a
free spirit and a self-defined woman. For two years, she lived with Jiménez
Grullón in Cuba, met other Cuban and Latin American poets, and wrote
some of her finest lyrical poetry. In 1942, Burgos returned to New York,
where she wrote weekly articles for* Pueblos Hispanos, *while struggling to
make a living in a series of demeaning, low-paying jobs – as a saleswoman,
laboratory assistant, garment worker – and suffering from increased
isolation, alcoholism, and depression. She died of pneumonia on the
streets of Harlem in 1953, and, because she had no identification, was
buried with other indigents in Potter's Field.*

*Julia de Burgos began writing and reciting poetry to considerable
acclaim, although her first collection,* Poemas exactos a mí misma *(Poems*

Exactly Like Me), completed in 1937, was never published and is presumed lost. The body of her work, written primarily between 1933 and 1943, is quite small: she self-published and distributed two small collections – Poema en veinte surcos *(Poems in Twenty Furrows) and* Canción de la verdad sencilla *(Song of the Simple Truth), in 1938 and 1939 respectively, while a third collection,* El mar y tú *(The Sea and You), which she could not get published, appeared posthumously in 1954. Other poems, essays, and journalistic pieces were published in Cuban, Puerto Rican, and North American journals, magazines, and newspapers.*

Her lyrical poetry, which deals with themes of love, death, and solitude, voices the thoughts and feelings of a vigorous and independent woman who questions and challenges the place of the female, the Black, and the jíbaro *in Puerto Rico's neo-colonial society. In her signature poem 'A Julia de Burgos' (To Julia de Burgos), the poet creates a female persona whose song of the self is strong, passionate, and powerful. While 'A Julia' articulates a strong feminist consciousness, 'Ay ay ay de la grifa negra' (Cry of the Kinky Haired Girl) affirms the African identity and racial awareness of a Black female persona. At a time when other Puerto Rican poets such as Palés Matos depicted the Black woman as an inferior sexual object, Burgos subverted* negrista *poetics into an affirmation of racial pride. Burgos's most sensual and erotic poetry appears in* Canción, *a collection of verse that celebrates the female body and physical union through images of nature: rivers, trees, and birds. Perhaps her most celebrated poem is 'Río Grande Loiza' (Man River Loiza), an erotic evocation of a woman's longing for sexual freedom and fulfilment.*

Julia de Burgos was also an accomplished prose writer, as is apparent in her essays, articles, and speeches in favor of Puerto Rican independence. A member of the Nationalist Party and secretary general of the Women's United Front for a Constitutional Convention, she often lectured on political issues. When she was only twenty-two, for example, she delivered a speech 'La mujer ante el dolor de la patria' (The Woman Faces the Country's Pain) at a rally to gain the support of her sisters. In 1945, she won the Journalism Prize of the Instituto de Literatura Puertorriqueña for her essay 'Ser o no ser es la divisa' (The Emblem is Whether or Not to Be). Julia de Burgos was a rebellious woman and a militant writer, whose iconoclastic and transgressive texts revolutionised Puerto Rican literature.

Cry of the Kinky Haired Girl

Ay, ay, ay, I am black, pure black;
kinky hair and Kaffir lips;
and a flat Mozambican nose.
A jet black woman, I cry and I laugh
at the thrill of being a black statue;
of being a piece of the night, where
my white teeth flash like lightning;
and being a black whip
that is twisted on blackness
to shape the black nest
where the crow lies.
Black piece of blackness where I carve myself
ay, ay, ay, for my statue is all black.
My grandfather was the slave they say
the master bought for thirty pieces of silver.
Ay, ay, ay, my grandfather was the slave
that's my pain, that's my pain.
Had he been the slave master,
that would have been my shame;
for among men and among nations,
if the slave has no rights,
the master has no conscience.
Ay, ay, ay, the sins of the white king,
let the black queen wash them in forgiveness.
Ay, ay, ay, my black race is slipping away
with a buzz toward the white race it flies
to sink in its clear waters;
or perhaps the white race will grow dark in the black.
Ay, ay, ay, my black race is slipping away
running with the white race to become brown;
to become the race of the future,
fraternity of America!

Translated by Claudette Williams

Río Grande de Loíza

Río Grande de Loíza!...Elongate yourself in my spirit
and let my soul lose itself in your rivulets,
finding the fountain that robbed you as a child
and in a crazed impulse returned you to the path.

Coil yourself upon my lips and let me drink you,
to feel you mine for a brief moment,
to hide you from the world and hide you in yourself,
to hear astonished voices in the mouth of the wind.

Dismount for a moment from the loin of the earth,
and search for the intimate secret in my desires;
confuse yourself in the flight of my bird fantasy,
and leave a rose of water in my dreams.

Río Grande de Loíza!...My wellspring, my river
since the maternal petal lifted me to the world;
my pale desires came down in you from the craggy hills
to find new furrows;
and my childhood was all a poem in the river,
and a river in the poem of my first dreams.

Adolescence arrived. Life surprised me
pinned to the widest part of your eternal voyage;
and I was yours a thousand times, and in a beautiful romance
you awoke my soul and kissed my body.

Where did you take the waters that bathed
my body in a sun blossom recently opened?

Who knows on what remote Mediterranean shore
some faun shall be possessing me!

Who knows in what rainfall of what far land
I shall be spilling to open new furrows;
or perhaps, tired of biting hearts
I shall be freezing in icicles!

Río Grande de Loíza!...Blue. Brown. Red.
Blue mirror, fallen piece of blue sky;
naked white flesh that turns black
each time the night enters your bed;
red stripe of blood, when the rain falls
in torrents and the hills vomit their mud.

Man river, but man with the purity of river,
because you give your blue soul when you give your blue kiss.

Most sovereign river mine. Man river. The only man
who has kissed my soul upon kissing my body.

Río Grande de Loíza!...Great river. Great flood of tears.
The greatest of all our island's tears
save those greater that come from the eyes
of my soul for my enslaved people.

Translated by Jack Agüero

To Julia de Burgos

Already the people murmur that I am your enemy
because they say that in verse I give the world your me.

They lie, Julia de Burgos. They lie, Julia de Burgos.
Who rises in my verses is not your voice. It is my voice
because you are the dressing and the essence is me;
and the most profound abyss is spread between us.

You are the cold doll of social lies,
and me, the virile starburst of the human truth.

You, honey of courtesan hypocrisies; not me;
in all my poems I undress my heart.

You are like your world, selfish; not me
who gambles everything betting on what I am.

You are only the ponderous lady very lady;
not me; I am life, strength, woman.

You belong to your husband, your master; not me;
I belong to nobody, or all, because to all, to all
I give myself in my clean feeling and in my thought.

You curl your hair and paint yourself; not me;
the wind curls my hair, the sun paints me.

You are a housewife, resigned, submissive,
tied to the prejudices of men; not me;
unbridled, I am a runaway Rocinante
snorting horizons of God's justice.

You in yourself have no say; everyone governs you;
your husband, your parents, your family,

the priest, the dressmaker, the theatre, the dance hall,
the auto, the fine furnishings, the feast, champagne,
heaven and hell, and the social, "what will they say."

Not in me, in me only my heart governs,
only my thought; who governs in me is me.
You, flower of aristocracy; and me, flower of the people.
You in you have everything and you owe it to everyone,
while me, my nothing I owe to nobody.

You nailed to the static ancestral dividend,
and me, a one in the numerical social divider,
we are the duel to death who fatally approaches.

When the multitudes run rioting
leaving behind ashes of burned injustices,
and with the torch of the seven virtues,
the multitudes run after the seven sins,
against you and against everything unjust and inhuman,
I will be in their midst with the torch in my hand.

Translated by Jack Agüero

Pentachrome

Today, day of the dead, parade of shadows...
Today, shadow among shadows, I delight in the desire
to be Don Quijote, or Don Juan, or a bandit
or an anarchist worker, or a great soldier.

Today I want to be a man. My longings burn me
to be a bold and combative Captain
fighting in the febrile Spain of Valencia,
bound to the ranks of the loyal faction.

Today I want to be a man. I would be Quijote.
I would be the true Alonso Quijano,
one of the people today converting into heroes of life
the shadow heroes of the immortal madman.

Today I want to be a man. The boldest bandit
of the Seven of the City of Ecija. The wildest
of those who flew on seven horses,
challenging everything with blunderbuss and dagger.

Today I want to be a man. I would be a worker,
cutting cane, sweating my shift,
with my arms up, my fists on high,
snatching from the world my piece of bread.

Today I want to be a man. Climb the adobe walls,
mock the convents, be all a Don Juan;
abduct Sor Carmen and Sor Josefina,
conquer them, and rape Julia de Burgos.

Translated by Jack Agüero

Letters to Her Sister Consuelo

In 1939, Julia de Burgos published Canción de la verdad sencilla *(Song of the Unadorned Truth) and met Juan Isidro Jiménez Grullón, who inspired some of her best love poetry. After a brief visit in 1940 to New York, where her poetry was well received, she journeyed to Cuba. As this letter reveals, she was delighted to be reunited with her lover, but Burgos became increasingly unhappy because of her isolation in Cuba and Grullón's refusal to acknowledge their relationship publicly.*

Havana, Cuba
Thursday, June 27, 1940

My dearest Consuelo,

Although you won't believe it, I'm in Cuba, the beautiful land of Martí. Who would have believed three years ago that I would travel across the lands of America! I owe everything to Juan, my eternal beloved. I knew that in following him, I myself was going to achieve all my innermost desires, and now you see that it's happening. The New York experience, the prologue to our pilgrimage, could not have been more grotesque. But it served to make us drink in, with more intensity and vehemence, all the sweet and mellow charm of other things even sweeter, more beautiful, and more ours. Such as Cuba. When this blessed land, framed by palm trees on a carpet of green light, rose before me yesterday morning, my eyes watered and my heart warmed.

Consuelín, for the first time I walked on the free land of Indo-Hispanic America! It is a wonderful thing. I invoked Martí while remembering all the Puerto Rican blood spilled in Cuba for the Independence Movement. Where are those men today? The Cuban flag, stretched across the horizon, gave me a terrible feeling of sadness. It is so similar to its sister: ours. However, ours waves only in the pure hearts of those who have known how to protect it from the violent wind that has uprooted the shame of most of our people. Consuelín, never forget that to have true social justice in our country – whether it's called communism or whatever – the one-starred flag that defines us as Hispanoamericans in America first has to wave freely and alone over every building, every palm tree, and every crossed heart.

I will go on. My last days in New York were awful. I was overcome by a terrible attack of nerves, which reached a climax on the bus taking me from New York to Miami, a trip that lasted 42 hours altogether. In the seat, I slept only two hours. I felt very strange things. I heard all of you speaking to me, as clearly as if I had you next to me. It was terrible. When I caught the boat in Miami, I calmed down a little and slept. A two-hour trip, and then Havana. From the deck I saw Juan waiting for me. What deep emotions I felt! Imagine, there had been almost a month and a half of absence. I had to pay duty to Customs for the books. I went down into the arms of my beloved, who filled my life with love and tenderness, helping me to calm down a little.

He took me to visit some sites. How beautiful Havana is! The life that one leads here is Parisian, elegant and peaceful. Yesterday we rode on a bus and a streetcar, getting to know some of the city, which is huge. They call it Little Paris. And there are no Germans . . . (yet). Last night we went out to walk. We sat down at an open-air café, located on very wide sidewalks. Here, there are many Paris-style cafés like that one. There are bands with women musicians, especially *mulatas*. We spent a pleasant bit of time watching people pass by. Then we continued walking and he showed me the monument to Martí, and the monument to Máximo Gómez. We strolled along the Martí Promenade, which extends for several blocks, with trees and benches on both sides. The promenade faces the sea and close by is the monument to Gómez, the Dominican Hero of Cuban independence. Imagine, Consuelito, how much emotion I experienced, feeling what I had never felt; drawing close to lofty monuments that symbolise men and represent native lands. Drunk with patriotic exuberance, we continued toward the cathedral. It is something marvellous, built by Spain in the 18th century. Imagine, Consuelo, what a contrast in emotions I felt and what a paradox. From the heroes of the Revolution we went on to admire and to take in another of the country's monuments, which inspired those heroes of independence. Cuba and Spain were united in our eyes and our emotions. And both made us feel tall, impressed, silent. Because if Cuba, not America, freed itself from the arm or yoke of Spain, it could never free itself from its soul. And in art it is also the soul of Spain. If the institutions responsible for protest no longer exist, why not admire the spiritual and artistic channel that the Motherland left us, running in our land forever? Well then, we went toward the cathedral, which lies tangled up in a swarm of narrow, zig-zagging alleys. They were lighted with lanterns, and from each alley surged little, old, indistinct houses with balconies. In the middle of them is the cathedral, very old and secure in its unshakeable centuries. In front is the

Cathedral Plaza with three buildings on the other sides. On one of them there is a restaurant, and Juan tells me that it is a gathering place for several poets and writers such as Guillén. Fascinated, we stayed there a long time looking at all that. Juan's eyes swam into the night's river, over the buildings, and went ashore in mine, leaving behind this epoch. We were in Spain.

Today we will continue wandering through the city. And he will introduce me to several writers. I feel so happy in his arms. On Saturday we will leave for Santa Clara, six hours from here, where he will give a lecture. I still don't know definitely where I'll be living. So, write me a letter adddressed to Juan at 111 Aguadulce, but don't put my name. Write: Dr. J.I. Jiménez Grullón, c/o J. Bosh, 111 Aguadulce, Havana, Cuba.

Hug everyone there. I will write you all. Now things are becoming clear. You know I love you so much.

Julita

When her relationship with Jiménez Grullón ended, Burgos returned to New York, where she worked in a variety of low-paying jobs and then married Armando Marín. Plagued by alcoholism, overweight, and bouts of depression, the poet spent extended periods at Goldwater Memorial Hospital, where she was diagnosed with cirrhosis of the liver. Still struggling bravely to overcome physical and emotional problems, Burgos wrote this letter to her sister just four months before her death.

Goldwater Memorial Hospital
Ward D-12 Welfare Island
NYC – April 7, 1953

My adored Consuelito:

Your last letter ended by comforting me in this struggle between my thirst to live and my desire to be once again in my country near all that I most love in the world, in the boundless sense of this expression. I know, and your words strengthen me in it, that my keyword is hope. Since I have been able to endure until now, sometimes impatient, other times rebellious, but most often with the stoic and aggressive resignation of the fighter who will not surrender, I can take a little more of this medicine, which after all, looking at it realistically, can be beneficial not only to me, but to thousands of people who will gain in the future from my experimental treatment. At this point, in spite of my moral and mental decline, my physical health is improving and will help repair the relative harm done to my spirit and to my mental equilibrium.

I feel strong, my mental health depends on you more than on anyone, so be patient and plan your trip more calmly, for the time when all the flowers of Puerto Rico open to await my arrival and when the beaches are adorned in their prettiest blue to receive my life whole and healthy as before. I want to spend several days sunbathing by the sea, as in the days of our childhood, and I want to look at my river again with the same peaceful, longing eyes that I did when I was its sweetheart.

On Tuesday several patients and I went in Red Cross buses, with nurses and everything, to see a movie at the Rivoli Theater on Broadway. I spend all my sad hours participating in many of the hospital's activities. This is a human spectacle worthy of the best literary work, a work of elevation and respect for the one who has fallen through an act of nature. I will tell you more.

For now, hug the whole family for me. Send me a peso to buy a bit of cloth for some pajamas or a robe. I am size 42.

I adore you,

Julita

Editor's translation

I Am The Life, The Strength, The Woman
Feminism in Julia de Burgos' Autobiographical Poetry

Consuelo López Springfield

During the depression of the 1930s, when labor unrest sparked nationalist literary movements throughout the entire Caribbean, Puerto Rico's Julia de Burgos published her first book of lyrical poems. Only two others would follow.[1] She died in 1953, at the age of thirty-nine, poor, sick, and lonely in the immigrant port city of New York. Critics tell us that her radical politics, non-traditional lifestyle, and destructive romantic liaisons contributed to alcoholism and to eventual self-estrangement.[2] Facing death in her final poem, she maintained an ardent faith, nonetheless, that even "here…in depths of tears and sorrows over this vast empire of solitude and darkness" she would find "the voice of freedom" (Solá 158).[3] Nearly forty years after her tragic death on the streets of New York, she is the most celebrated of Puerto Rican poets. Her popularity has much to do with her ideological consciousness, her struggle to free herself from social and literary confinement, to redefine herself, her art, and her society.

In her introduction to Julia de Burgos' *I Was My Own Route [Yo misma fuí mi ruta]*, María M. Solá opposes autobiographical interpretations of Burgos' self-exploratory poems. Her "artistic goal," she writes, "was to communicate emotions, not anecdotes from her private life." To equate Burgos' poetry with autobiography, Solá argues, "would validate the myth she had fought against: of a martyr to love, the beautiful and talented young woman who gave herself up to alcoholism because her one true love abandoned her" (10). Although Solá recalls Burgos' thematic fusion of feminism and nationalism, she minimizes her desire for artistic legitimacy. Burgos' poems not only explore life's profound meanings, but they also articulate a life's vocation. It is not in the recollection of daily events where Burgos signifies self-invention; at the heart of her autobiographical poetry lies a rhetorical quest to justify a female poetics. Burgos' poems are allegorical constructs that impart, in the most intense and profound way, her efforts to achieve "wholeness" by rewriting the plots of patriarchal culture. To understand her autobiography, one must consider the ramifications of writing within the two competing patriarchal discourses of colonialism and nationalism.

Although women have been involved in shaping political events and have held major political positions in Puerto Rico, they have been underrepresented among playwrights, novelists, essayists, and poets. Diana Vélez reminds us that until the 1960s, "there had been little overtly feminist writing, with some important exceptions such as Luisa Capetillo's work" (35). As in all Caribbean societies where writers cannot support themselves and their families through writing and where they depend on the critical response of foreign literary critics (with the current exception of Cuba), the challenge to Puerto Rican women has been even more taxing. The dearth of prominent women writers reflects not only the economic condition of women but also, and equally important, their marginalization in social and literary circles. Nowhere is this more evident than in the poetry of Julia de Burgos.

Burgos began writing in the wake of the Romantic movement which had dominated Puerto Rican literature in the nineteenth and early twentieth centuries.[4] Antonio García de Toro points out that not only were women protagonists rare in romantic dramas but that frustrated love was also a recurring theme. Female characters were forced into submission by their fathers, seduced by men, and driven to suicide (29). During the era in which Burgos published (1937–1946), literary traditions compelled women who aspired to literary careers to accommodate to male constructions of gender.[5] To establish her reputation as a poet, Burgos negotiated her own space between female aesthetics and male-constructed literary conventions. Her foremost "text" was the romance; but within its margins, she demanded female empowerment.

Because it resembles the traditional *novelas* so popular among women readers throughout Latin America, her life-story almost insists on being treated as a romance narrative. The eldest of thirteen children, six of whom died of malnutrition, Julia Constanza Burgos García was born into rural poverty three years before the Jones Act imposed U.S. citizenship on Puerto Ricans. She helped her mother, a "sensitive mulatta" (Zavala-Martínez 6), with parenting and household chores, and together they would visit the Loiza River, which would later figure as Burgos' spiritual abode. In the countryside, she often rode horseback at her father's side, and he would tell her stories of the great men of history and of romance fiction. She read widely among historical romances, showed an early penchant for poetry, and studied at high schools in Río Grande and Río Piedras, finishing in three years. Her parents' willingness to sacrifice their farm to provide for her education enabled her to join members of Puerto Rico's small middle class who attended the University of Puerto Rico. It was there where she first became involved in Nationalist Party agitation and the demand for national sovereignty and human justice entered her verse, eventually permeating it.[6]

Burgos earned a teaching certificate in 1933, worked in a food program with P.R.E.R.A. (Puerto Rico's Economic Rehabilitation Agency), married in 1934, taught school briefly in the countryside, divorced in 1937, and attempted to support her family through writing. Although Puerto Rico suffered severely during the economic depression and few could purchase books, she traveled throughout the island by public transport [carros públicos], trying to sell her first book of poems, Poem in Twenty Furrows [Poema en veinte surcos] to help defray the cost of her mother's medical treatments for cancer. Less than three months after her mother's death in 1939, Juan Jiménez Grullón, a Dominican intellectual, took her to New York and afterwards to Cuba, where for two years she lived alone in a boardinghouse as his mistress. She met several Latin American writers of renown, composed many of her finest lyrical poems, and enrolled briefly at the University of Havana. Her lover ended their relationship by giving her a plane ticket to Miami. She left for New York, where she worked at odd jobs and quickly remarried. Before moving temporarily to Washington, D.C., she wrote briefly for an Hispanic weekly. Her marriage on the wane, her life increasingly isolated in New York City, Burgos turned to drink, to poetry, and to self destruction.

Biographical critics, privileging male authority, highlight her father's role in initiating Burgos into a world of the imagination. The destructive effects of his alcoholism are brought to light hastily and only in reference to her own alcohol addiction. Her solitary journeys, often at night through the countryside to fetch her inebriated father home, are not treated in terms of its humiliating effects on a young girl; they are interpreted as fanciful adventures adding to her resourcefulness and lust for independence. This critical stance perpetuates romantic myth-making (which Solá astutely reproaches). It also fails to address Burgos' aesthetic response to male authority – both paternal and literary. Not only did she resist collective pressure to adhere to female roles, but she also struggled within and against a cultural ambience that left no ample space for feminist writers.

While Burgos assigns her mother a nurturing role in nostalgic recollections of childhood in her autobiographical poetry, allusions to her father are notably absent. Freudian critics might contend that she transferred love of father to her lover who fulfills a paternal role. To a Lacanian, Burgos' act of writing assumes a phallic semblance. If one were to assign a cultural reading within the context of Latin America's literary history, it could also be argued that as the *word* signifies the power of the conquering *sword* over the voiceless oppressed, Burgos' appropriation of the word challenges the subordination of the silent female to male authority. In fact, her poetic vitality springs from dual impulses or what Rachel Blau De Plessis refers to as a split between her sensual needs, "the one congruent with feminine scripts of abasement and submission, the other a criticism of that structure of desire and that psychic career" (27). The social "script" can be construed as offering to social analysis what "ideology" offers to cultural analysis:

> "a generic term for the processes by which meaning is produced, challenged, reproduced, transformed."…So too literature as a human institution is, baldly, organized by many ideological scripts. Any literary convention – plots, narrative sequences, characters in bit parts – as an instrument that claims to depict experience, also interprets it. No convention is neutral, purely mimetic, or purely aesthetic. (2)

The romance, emphasizing male valor and female suffering, plays a pivotal role in Burgos' narrative choices. Tania Modleski explains that romancers assimilate the view that "it is possible really to be taken care of and to achieve that state of self-transcendence and self-forgetfulness promised by the ideology to love" (37). In Burgos' "romance plot" where love is reciprocal and passivity is renounced, the absence of love, nonetheless, signals psychic death. The poet-protagonist's feelings fluctuate between ecstasy and depression, depending on her intimate circumstances. In "A Night of Love in Three Cantos" ["Noche de amor en tres cantos"], a poem about sexual ecstasy, the self is likened to a flower opening to the mystical voice of a lover on a star-filled night. While birds soar from her hands toward "eternal heavens," the two lovers share the laughter "which subdues all tears." The lyrical poem describes the power of a lover to inspire the poetic "voice" (Burgos, *Canción* 22-24).[7] Conversely, feelings of despondency inform "Call Out My Number" ["Dadme mi número"], published posthumously in 1954:

> Hardly can I stand up to the world,
> lashing itself whole against my consciousness...
> Call out my number! I don't want to wait
> until even love has broken off...
> (Inseparable dream that follows me
> as footprints follow my steps.) (Marzán 61-63)

Burgos' "romance plot" conveys the love of a deeply spiritual and sensual woman for a male lover who moves increasingly in and out of her life. The self is at once defiant, a supporter of nationalist and proletarian struggle, and a tormented victim of love. Most importantly, she is a committed artist who, while searching for a social niche from which to express her views, examines restrictions placed on female roles. In "To Julia de Burgos," she ridicules conventional women:

> The voice that rises in my poems is not your voice; it is mine;
> you are the covering and I the essence;
> and between us lies the deepest abyss.
> You are the cold doll of social lies,
> and I the virile glimmer of human truth.

She goes on to denounce the "housewife, resigned submissive / bound to the prejudices of men." Her "true" self is "Rocinante untamed / smelling out the just horizons of God" (Burgos, *Antología* 23).[8]

Marginalized in patriarchal society and uninvolved in women's labor struggles, Burgos sees no room for internal changes within contemporary female culture. Because she allows for no alternative community, she rejects the repressed "other" who is but a victim of male hegemony. Socially powerless, she seeks through the act of writing an escape from male constructions of gender. In the "male" plots of European fiction, she discovers, paradoxically, empowering metaphors of self.

Burgos' identification with male heroes can be traced to her early exposure to literature. Yvette Jiménez de Báez reveals that – besides listening to her father's recitations of *Don Quijote*, tales of *Robinson Crusoe*, Marco Polo, Bolívar, and Napoleon – she read avidly from imported adventure books. In high school, she savored the thrilling exploits of Alexander Dumas' *The Three Musketeers* (1893); E. Phillips Oppenheimer's *The Vanished Messenger* (1914); Mary Johnston's best-selling romance set in colonial Virginia, *To Have and To Hold* (1900); Anthony Hope Hawkins' *The Prisoner of Zenda* (1894); and Rafael Sabatini's *Scaramouche*. Burgos preferred, Báez adds, "the novels and adventures of her favorite writer, Henry [sic], an English author of historical romances" (19). The "English author," however, was none other than George Alfred Henty (1832–1902), creator of such popular Victorian "boys" books as *A Final Reckoning* and *With Moore at Corunna* (1898), which involves a death-defying rescue of a noblewoman from a convent and from Jacobean mobs.

Writing within the perimeters of male discourse, Burgos weaves heroic quests into a self-centered autobiographical project. Because "the mythologies of gender conflate human and male figures of selfhood, aligning male self-hood with culturally valued stories" (Smith 50), Burgos rejects the silent, self-effacing stories of women for the public, self-promoting myths of male autobiography. In "Pentachromatic" ["Pentacromia"], her most disturbing poem, excluded from Báez's biographical text, she claims cultural authority by identifying with masculine self-metaphors. The poem is an indictment of society's repression of female sexuality, the confinement of female culture (represented by a convent), and the marginality of women's literary voices,

> Today I want to be a man. Climb over the walls,
> mock the nunnery, be a perfect Don Juan;
> rape Sister Carmen and Sister Josephine, make them yield,
> and then take Julia de Burgos by force.[9]

Her longing to emerge rebellious in fraternal throngs is played out in several poems of social protest. In "Pentachromatic" her identification with masculinity can be seen as a feminist strategy to refute gender-specific roles. While Burgos represents two opposing sides of her inner self in this autobiographical poem, self-violation signifies a victory over female passivity. Unrestrained by social conventions, the rebellious self purges "Julia de Burgos" of pretension and false piety. Her identification with sexual oppression also reflects female "masochism," evidence of "the pervasiveness of masculine ideology in patriarchal culture" (Modleski 38). If we were to interpret Burgos' metaphorical "rape" within the romance genre, we would find, as Modleski indicates, that "her desire to be taken by force (manifest content) conceals anxiety about rape and longings for power and revenge (latent content)" (48). A third interpretation, also overlooked by critics, is that the poem was intended as a mock-epic.

Its "theme" is a longing for power: sexual and artistic power. Burgos rebels not only against conventional sexual restrictions that are central to white, Spanish-Catholic patriarchal societies, but also against female archetypes and traditional narratives of domestic virtue. She tells us that although she wants to create tales of lust and adventure, male convention allows her the only option of producing counter-plots. Her "female script" thus attempts to transcend the divided self "by both protesting and endorsing the feminine condition"(Modleski 37). Eliana Rivero describes her strategy of dual representation in terms of a dialectical process that expresses "an individual and intimate perspective and the attitude of an observer" (40). Within this dichotomy, "'there are various levels of discourse," she writes; there is the "I," an ontological object, and the "I," who reflects on individual and social histories. To this, she adds a third "I," the "collective self" who represents "the speaker's racial and sociocultural conscience" (35). Burgos, herself, explains in "Oh, the slowness of the Sea" ["Oh, lentitud del mar"] that she felt forced "to give, to multiply myself / divide myself into complex paths" (Burgos, *El mar* 58). In "Pentachromatic," she appropriates male metaphors to emphasize the subordination of women writers to male conventions.

Burgos' preeminent quest was, after all, a poetic one. We know that to support herself and her impoverished family through writing, she traveled extensively for two years reciting and selling her first book. In a letter to her sister, she describes her trajectory. "I'm getting my next book ready which I'll call *The Sea and You* [*El mar y tú*]" she writes. "I have to publish a book a year" (de Báez 45). Later, hearing that the Biblioteca de Autores Puertorriqueños were thinking of publishing *The Sea and You*, she expresses delight that "while the government of this country repudiates me for fighting for the welfare of humanity, its own people, my Puerto Rican people, honor and protect me spiritually and materially... [It] is my strength to go on!" (de Báez 64). Regrettably, the poem was not published until 1954, after her death.

Although she presents her self as split into multiple speaking voices, Burgos consistently asserts her identity as a woman seeking immortality through verse. She ponders "what will they call me when I am only a memory, / a rock on a deserted island? / a carnation placed between wind and shadow." To this, she answers assuredly, "they'll call me poet."[10] Again, in "Bitter Song" ["Canción amarga"], she writes: "Nothing upsets me, but I'm sad." She concludes, "it must be the caress of futility, / the unending sorrow of being a poet."[11] In the whimsical "I've Lost a Verse" ["Se me ha perdido un verso"], she denounces masculine literary conventions. The male tradition is likened to "the rigid valor of four erect angles" and to "murky water belonging to centuries of inertia" which leaves her feeling "silenced," and "dressed in flesh devoid of words." The poem leads up to a cry of individual poetic triumph:

You are the world's today; the affirmation, the strength.
Revolution which shatters the curtains of time!

It is in the act of writing where she finds the essential meaning of life. "I find myself," she explains, "in finding my verse."[12]

Burgos' aesthetics embraces the rhythms of female life, the emotions, and physical changes that occur in the on-going process of maturity that leads, inevitably, to death. She turns inwardly to observe herself in relation to the landscape she inhabits. In "Río Grande de Loiza," her most acclaimed poem, the poet-narrator journeys into a metaphysical past where "all my childhood was like a poem in the river / And a river was the poem of my first dreams." As Burgos looks backward and forward into a time conditioned by a history of conflict, she reflects on the emergence of her poetic voice. Her female "script" traces her poetic evolution through life-cycles beginning with evocations of maternal inspiration at the river's edge, proceeding to celebrate secret longings in adolescence and sexual joy in maturity, all the while questioning her artistic future:

> Who knows in what rainstorms of what far lands
> I will be pouring to pen new furrows;
> Or if, perhaps, tired of biting hearts
> I will be frozen in crystals of ice!

The poem functions on different levels which correspond to life-cycles. Her poetic source, the maternal flow of life, becomes a lover and, finally a "tear" of compassion for her colonized people:

> Río Grande de Loiza!...Great river. Great tear.
> The greatest of all our island tears
> But for the tears that flow out of me
> Through the eyes of my enslaved people. (Marzán 53-55)[13]

The central image of the "great river" is paradoxical. Although the river embodies traditional "feminine" properties – spirituality, affinity to nature, and sensual longing – it also bears "masculine" attributes. The "Man River" is, at once, the source of her creative longing and a symbol of sexual fulfillment. One is reminded of Burgos' use of "verile" in describing her inner truth in "To Julia de Burgos" and her rejection of conventional gender roles in "Pentachromatic." In the latter poem, the narrator identifies with the masculine while rejecting the feminine, socialized self. In "Río Grande de Loíza," Burgos' autobiographical persona, personified in nature, demands sexual independence. The last two lines, linking themes of love, artistic vocation, and social justice can be compared to plot "twists" in women's novels. Nancy K. Miller calls them "a form of insistence about the relation of women to writing" (39). Burgos justifies her womanhood, her talent, and her trust in the power of the pen to revise social contracts. While confronting gender and colonial oppression in her quest for artistic mastery and love, she turns conventional allegories into subversive texts.

In addition to a "male-authored canon" and a masculine system of representation, Burgos faced "the yet unstable limits of budding national literatures" (Molloy 81). In "Ay ay ay, the Black's Kinky Hair" ["Ay ay ay de la grifa negra"], a collective "I" is transparent. Burgos invents an allegory where self and national identities merge. Puerto Rico's legacy of colonial and racial oppression becomes the terrain for an exploration into self identity as well as a quest for racial reconciliation.[14] In a society where Western cultural hegemony is deeply valued and where whiteness stands as a paragon of beauty, Burgos turns to her African-Caribbean heritage, to the mulatta's beauty, strength, and power to heal as a unifying archetype. Although the poem appears in several anthologies of Puerto Rican poetry, it is largely ignored by critics who see the representation of the self as an inauthentic attempt to capture the popular "negrista" style of her friend, Luis Palés Matos. Ostensibly, the poem exemplifies Burgos' sympathy for the oppressed, but a closer examination reveals equivocation in her attitudes toward male authority. Burgos objectifies the black woman, transforming her into an object, a sculpture, a thing to be observed and owned:

Ay, ay, ay, I am kinky-haired and pure black;
kinky is my hair, mine are *cafrería* lips
and my flat nose is from Mozambique.
Completely black, tear and river black
I am a black statue;

The "I" becomes a "black vine" and, finally, "black race and white merge / I become a triguña," the "woman of the future alliance of America." The perspective shifts from woman as object to woman as a vitalizing force. Internal time alternates as well from a past history of slavery to a future time of unity and solidarity. Burgos' oscillation between objectification and vitalization reflects the cultural ambiguity one often finds in *negrista* poetry. Burdened, in addition, by awkward poetic tonalities and rhythms, the poem nonetheless underlines the positive role of *mestizaje*, or "hybridization" in the history of the Americas. The romantic motif prevails in the use of objectification and exotic imagery; but a feminist ideology can be found at the poem's core.[15] The "sins of the white king" are, after all, "washed in forgiveness" by a black woman who is not a slave but a "queen," an equal.

This historical perspective stands at odds with a national cultural history that affirms the centrality of Spanish male, not African female heritage.

At the time when Burgos wrote "Ay, ay, ay, the Black's Kinky Hair," not only were women refused a place in history but black history was denied. Writer Ana Lydia Vega recalls that up until the late 1960s, black culture was seen as inferior in Puerto Rico: "We were brought up ignorant of all of it, ignorant of history, because in school, history ended in 1898 [when the U.S. took control of the island]." She added that one learned "absolutely nothing about our African heritage because it was 'taboo.' It was completely concealed by the elite class" (4). Critics overlook that Burgos was the first published Puerto Rican female poet to adopt a "mulatta" identity. In "Ay ay ay, The Black's Kinky Hair," she argues that popular approbation of that identity can lead to a process of collective redemption:

Ay ay ay my black and white race merge
making me trigueña;
the woman of the future
alliance of America! [16]

Gordon K. Lewis points out that in Antonio S. Pedreira's "canonical text," *Insularismo*, for instance, the mulatto is rendered as "a racially lost person who collaborates but does not create, follows but does not lead, and is incapable of independent social initiative" (183). Puerto Rican writers, with such exceptions as Palés Matos, depicted the "Puerto Rican Man" as *el jíbaro*, a light-skinned peasant (a *mestizo* of Indian and Spanish descent) from the interior of the island who provided for his dependent family. While writers personified the homeland as female, the incarnation of patriotic ideals, its civilizing elements were masculine. In the foreground, one finds images of cane-cutters and coffee pickers, *hacendados* [landowners], and local patriots. As Juan Gelpí explains, Puerto Rico's cultural nationalism is expressed in a patriarchal discourse that is, at once, hierarchical and populist. This "paternalistic rhetoric" upholds "metaphors" of a national "family" held together by a "father" who claims elite, male privilege over his "children" (298).

In Burgos' nationalist rhetoric, the influence of male cultural authority cannot be dismissed; her oppressed proletariat are *jíbaros*, cane-cutters, a collective mass, not the female tobacco strippers and needleworkers who organized throughout Puerto Rico for improved working conditions. [17] Women might have been integral disciples of the Nationalist Party, but its leadership was dominated by patriarchs who espoused the sanctity of

Spanish culture, language, Catholicism, and the traditional family unit. Its leader, the brilliant orator, Pedro Albizu Campos, who emulated Irish nationalism, envisioned Puerto Rico as a culturally homogeneous race fighting against North American Protestantism, imperialism, and racism.[18] To redefine herself, to infuse the national allegory with an emerging consciousness of womanhood and racial admixture, Burgos faced a dual colonialism that was, and still remains, pervasive in Puerto Rican culture. Her struggle to evolve as a poet in the midst of cultural oppression finds its greatest expression in "I Was My Own Path" ["*Yo misma fui mi ruta*"]:

> I wanted to be like men wanted me to be;
> an attempt at life, a hide and seek game with myself.
> But I was made of todays,
> And my feet planted over the promised land
> could not stand to walk backwards,
> And went forward, forward... (Acosta-Belén 12)[19]

In her "female script", she foresaw a transformation where boundaries separating men and women would be surmounted and power relations revised. As an individual genius, fighting for artistic recognition from a state of self-imposed exile, she recognized that her quest would only achieve collective endorsement in a future born out of the womb of discord. Her belief in the "alliance of the Americas," with women in the forefront, invites artistic challenge. As Françoise Lionnet reminds us, "the female subject must learn to create new images" that are "vivid enough to superimpose themselves on the old myths they mean to transform and sublate" (215).

Notes

1. *Poema en viente surcos* was published in 1938 (San Juan: Imprenta Venezuela), *Cancion de la verdad sencilla* in 1939 (San Juan: Imprenta Baldrich). *El mar y tú*, completed in 1940, was published posthumously in 1954.
2. For an excellent interpretation of Burgos' place within the feminist movement, see Edna Acosta-Belén's "Puerto Rican Women in Culture, History and Society" (12).
3. "Farewell in Welfare Island" was written in English.

4. Rosalina Perales explains that "modern theatre" did not emerge in Puerto Rico until the 1940s when Emilio S. Belaval and Leopoldo Santiago Lavadero formed the Areyto group. See "Theater of Friction: New Currents in Puerto Rican Theatre," *Sargasso* 7 (1990): 27.

5. Critics tend to examine the sociological fabric of Puerto Rican literature within the political context of colonialism. Only recently has the negative portrayal of women received critical attention. Rosario Ferré provides an engaging and vigorous analysis of contemporary Latin America's male canon in *El coloquio de las perras* (Río Piedras: Editorial Cultural, 1990).

6. In 1936-1937, Burgos wrote children's radio plays for the Department of Instruction's "La Escuela del Aire." She was fired for her views on independence.

7. Translations are mine.

8. Translations are mine.

9. I have chosen Julio Marzán's translation of "Pentacromía," in *Inventing a Word*. However, I find his translation of the line "raptar a Sor Carmen y a Sor Josefina, rendirlas," as "carry off Sister Josephine and Sister Carmen, seduce them" to be too mild. I have thus offered my own translation which communicates the defilement implicit in her images of sexual self-violation.

10. "Poem for my Death" ["Poema para mi muerte"], in *El mar y tú* (92).

11. "Cancion amarga," in in *El mar y tú* (35).

12. The poem defies my translation talents.

13. Translated by Grace Schulman

14. Spanish and U.S. domination stimulated racism in Puerto Rico. It is more often expressed in covert rather than in overt ways. The popular expression, "who is your grandmother," illustrates both a tendency to depreciate one's African heritage and an awareness that most "family trees" have African "roots." In today's consumer society, economic success facilitates upward social mobility; however, in Burgos' time, few could advance if they were black and/ or poor.

15. I agree with Sandra Lee Bartky that "as long as [women's] situation is apprehended as natural, inevitable, and inescapable, women's consciousness of themselves… is not yet feminist consciousness." This only emerges "when there exists a genuine possibility for the partial or total liberation of women" (14).

16. English translation by the author.

17. See Yamila Azize's *La mujer en la lucha* (Río Piedras: Editorial Cultural, 1985).

18. Pedro Albizu Campos (1891-1965), a dark-skinned Harvard graduate and leader of the Puerto Rican Nationalist Party, travelled extensively throughout Latin America to stimulate support for an alliance of Hispanic nations. He defended organized labor, armed struggle against U.S. imperialism, and social justice for the poor. Unjustly sentenced for inciting a rebellion against U.S. rule in 1952, he was not released until 1965, four months before his death. See Federico Rives Tovar, *Albizu Campos: El Revolucionario* (New York: Plus Ultra, 1971).

19. Translation by Edna Acosta-Belén.

Works Cited

Acosta-Belén, Edna. "Puerto Rican Women in Culture, History, and Society." *The Puerto Rican Woman*. Ed. Edna Acosta-Belén. New York: Westport, 1986.

Bartky, Sandra Lee. *Femininity and Domination*. New York: Routledge, 1990.

De Plessis, Rachel Blau. *Writing Beyond the Ending*. Bloomington: Indiana University Press, 1985.

de Báez, Yvette Jiménez. *Julia de Burgos: Vida y poesía*. Río Piedras: Editorial Coquí, 1966.

de Burgos, Julia. *Antología Poética*. Río Piedras: Editorial Coquí, 1979.

— *Canción de la verdad sencilla*. Río Piedras: Ediciones Huracán, 1982.

— *El mar y tú*. Río Piedras: Ediciones Huracán, 1981.

— *Yo misma fui mi ruta*. Ed. María M. Solá. Río Piedras: Ediciones Huracán, 1986.

de Toro, Antonio García. *Mujer y patria en la dramaturgia puertorriqueña*. Madrid: Editorial Playor, 1987.

Gelpí, Juan. "*Las tribulaciones de Jonás* ante el paternalismo literario." *La Torre* 19 (julio 1991).

Lewis, Gordon K. *Notes on the Puerto Rican Revolution*. New York: Monthly Review Press, 1974.

Lionnet, Françoise. *Autobiographical Voices*. Ithaca: Cornell University Press, 1989.

Marzán, Julio, trans. and ed. *Inventing a Word*. New York: Columbia University Press, 1980.

Miller, Nancy K. *Subject to Change: Reading Feminist Writing*. New York: Columbia University Press, 1988.

Modleski, Tania. *Loving with a Vengeance*. New York: Methuen, 1984.

Molloy, Sylvia. *At Face Value: Autobiographical Writing in Spanish America*. New York: Cambridge University Press, 1991.

Rivero, Eliana. "Dialéctica de la *persona* poética en la obra de Julia de Burgos." *Revista de Crítica Literaria Latinoamericana* (Lima) II.4 (1978).

Smith, Sidonie. *A Poetics of Women's Autobiography*. Bloomington: Indiana University Press, 1987.

Vega, Ana Lydia. "Women and Writing in Puerto Rico: An Interview with Ana Lydia Vega." With Consuelo López Springfield and Elizabeth Hernández. *Callaloo* 17 (Summer 1994): 816-25.

Vélez, Diana. "Cultural Constructions of Women By Contemporary Puerto Rican Women Authors." *The Psychosocial Development of Puerto Rican Women*. Ed. Cynthia García Coll and María de Lourdes Mattei. New York: Praeger, 1989.

Zavala-Martínez, Iris. "A Critical Inquiry into the Life and Work of Julia de Burgos." *The Psychosocial Development of Puerto Rican Women*. Ed. Cynthia García Coll and María de Lourdes Mattei. New York: Praeger, 1989.

Aida Cartagena Portalatín

ᴀ̸ida ᴄartagena ᴘortalatín

DOMINICAN REPUBLIC

(1918–1994)

One of the Dominican Republic's most outstanding writers and intellectuals, Cartagena Portalatín published fourteen books, including two novels, nine collections of poetry, and several works of nonfiction. She was born in Moca, where she founded the cultural society 'Lumen' and began publishing poetry at age fifteen, under the pseudonym Lirio del Valle. After obtaining her doctorate from the Universidad Autónoma de Santo Domingo, she studied music and art theory at the School of Plastic Arts in Paris. As an artist and cultural activist, she helped modernise and universalise Dominican literature through her activities as an editor, anthologist, and publisher. During a career that spanned five decades, Portalatín served as a university professor and director of the Museo de Antropología in Santo Domingo. She co-founded La Poesía Sorprendida (Poetry Surprised), an organisation of surrealist-inspired poets, who advocated artistic and intellectual freedom. The group established a publishing house, which produced three of her early books, and it also published a literary journal, edited by Portalatín, which was closed down by the Trujillo regime. An independent woman who rejected the traditional roles of wife and mother, she travelled throughout Europe and the Americas, where she met some of the foremost writers of the period.

On her return to the Dominican Republic, she co-founded La Isla Necesaria (Necessary Island), which published two of her poetry collections: Mi mundo el mar *(My World the Sea) and* La mujer está sola *(Woman is Alone), a feminist text which deals with such themes as silence, blood, and women's rituals. A provocative thinker and powerful writer, Cartagena Portalatín's feminist consciousness and racial awareness are manifest in her poetry and prose, which expose the oppression of Blacks, women, and Haitian migrant workers. The long narrative poem* Yania Tierra, *for example,* documents the pernicious effects of European colonialism, American imperialism, and Dominican dictatorships. In her collection of short stories, Tablero *(Checkerboard)*, she examines the problems of race, class, and gender which confront Dominican women, and she explores the constraints of women's traditional roles in Dominican society. The sociopolitical subtext of her prose is underscored by her use of language, particularly dialogue, rhetorical questions, and colloquial speech. Unlike many Dominicans who deny their African origins, Portalatín reveals her African roots in poems such as 'Mi mamá fue una de las grandes mamás del mundo' (My Mama Was One of the Great Mamas of the World) and in her anthology Culturas AFRICANAS: Rebeldes con causa *(AFRICAN Cultures: Rebels with a Cause)*.

She has also written nonfiction and literary criticism, and has edited the volume Narradores dominicanos *(Dominican Narrators)*. Her experimental novels include Escalera para Electra *(Staircase for Electra)*, which won the prestigious Biblioteca Breve Prize in Spain, and La tarde en que murió Estefanía *(The Afternoon Estefanía Died)*, a novel written in verse, which attacks patriarchal dominance and corrupt politicians. Literary critic Daisy Cocco de Filippis calls Portalatín the most important woman writer in twentieth-century Dominican literature, because she pioneered the demystification of women by writing about those who were no longer submissive housewives.

Black Autumn
elegy

'Echoing drums, echoing on…'

I know it was already autumn,
without leaves and a lark's song
I, who cry for the trees, for fish and doves,
reject the white men of the South,
those whites with their hatred aimed at black men.
I'd never question their motives
because they would answer
that in Alabama both races can blossom.
After the summer of Medgar W. Evers,
came the fall of four black girls.

The funeral procession of so many caskets.
That procession clouding happiness
the beaten drums, echoing on
Until when? Those four black bodies.
The light of their dark skin brightening the earth.
The time for joy has gone.
Afflicted, even the earth cries…
Even Death weeps for these four black girls.
Who can fill the empty place they leave? Brutally murdered.
Death owns death and no one else should dare to use it.
Their tender bones will lift up their race.
Their curly hair will knit flags.
Four were the girls murdered in the church,
four immortal torches sown in the South.
How can one spell F R E E D O M in Alabama? – I ask.
I who cry for the trees, fish and doves.

Translated by Daisy Coco de Filippis

A Woman is Alone

A woman is alone. Alone with herself.
With open eyes and open arms.
With a heart opened by a wide silence.
She awaits in the desperate and despairing night
without losing hope.
She believes herself to be in the leading vessel
lit by creation's saddest light.
She has sailed away, fleeing from love,
the North wind guiding her flight.

A woman is alone. Binding her dreams with dreams,
the remaining dreams and the open Antillean skies.
Thoughtful and quiet, she faces a stony, aimless world,
lost in the meaning of its own word,
its own useless word.

A woman is alone. She believes everything to be nothing.
And no one speaks to her of the joy and sorrow to be found
in the blood that leaps, that flows,
in the blood which nourishes or dies of death.
No one comes forward to offer her clothing to dress
her naked, self-defining, weeping voice.

A woman is alone. She feels and her truth drowns
in thoughts which speak of the beauty of a rose,
of a star, of love, of man and of God.

Translated by Daisy Coco de Filippis

Wasted Effort

Ayayay, Auntie! Prebis arrived with the Dominicans who'd left the country. A plane from Nuevayork brought her to spend Christmas, if you'd seen her, dressed like Barajita the woman from the capital or like Comaisita from La Vega, with necklaces on top of necklaces, watches and more watches, plus a blonde wig. And you couldn't even count what they took out of the car this morning: ten suitcases, four boxes, artificial flowers and two dolls. And so, didn't she ask you about me? That American name 'Prebis' is nonsense concocted by my godmother Prebisteria Sánchez and as you say she puts on so many airs, it looks like she's trying to fool everyone in Guaco. I'm not interested in Fran-Francisco, but tell me: What else did you see? Auntie-Godmother, I didn't talk to her, after a while an engineer or architect arrived with a big envelope full of Dominican money to exchange for American money. Ayayay, Auntie, so many bills.

News about Fran-Francisco spread all over town. And they all came to see her: neighbours, brothers and sisters, godparents, friends, etc. etc. Madame Prebis was the talk of the town that Christmas. Prebisteria no longer washed clothes for pay, Prebisteria no longer ironed for pay, Prebisteria no longer screwed around for pay, now Prebisteria thought the folk from Guaco were trash.

However, lucky for her, three days later Andrejulio showed up at her house to see her and to bring back memories. He got a hold of Prebisteria and of a transistor radio that she bought for her daughter. The radio brought them closer together, they listened to Dominican stations, preferably those from the capital and, over the longwave, one from Aruba or Bucaramanga, and, while lying on the cot, request programmes. Madame Prebis said she was a fan of Montiel. And Sergeant Valenzuela made them dedicate 'Bésame mucho', sung by Sarita Montiel, to her, and if there was no interference, Andrejulio wanted to hear Fidel's speeches from Havana. Four days later, she ordered a box-spring like the one she had in Nuevayork, and of course, of course, ayayay, Auntie, what luxury! They threw away the folding cot and of course, of course, she slept better listening to the radio and prolonging her conversations, et cetera, but she still wasn't happy because for all that I work overtime and now that business about my daughter not living here is unforgivable, and all the things I brought my Calandria and her children, and the people here delight in telling me that she's dancing in a cabaret in the capital. I think I made a mistake in not having her baptised. Who knows if it's the devil's work. Everything happened so fast, the priest took the aspergill full of holy water in one hand and the civil registry in the other, I told you that it happened so fast, he threw the registry to my godfather and looking at us with old owl eyes, he yelled: That's not a decent name, and left her unbaptised. The priest was offended by her name. Calandria was a bird's name, not a person's, and it wasn't in the saint's calendar.

Calandria. It was for her that I made those sacrifices, working overtime to come here, to bring her everything. Somewhat moved, Andrejulio invited her to visit the capital. Ayayay, Auntie, what a mistake! The driver spun the steering wheel around six times after the highway patrolman searched the luggage, and he, like Andrés, explained that Madame Prebis didn't have a licence because she lived in Nuevayork. Andrés, Andrés, Andrejulio, how life treats me! Those early-risers, so as not to get in trouble, might crush or suffocate you in the subway, hanging by a strap on the way to the factory, and up to three dozen sheets daily for Cannon, and if they are pillowcases, up to six dozen, and when I finish I get up and turn off the machine and think that I'm going to collapse, but, Andrés, money, lots of money, and when I return here thinking about you and Calandria, that daughter who took after me, you remember me Andrejulio before I wore myself out like this and lost my exuberance, remember Andrés what happened to me with you in the ravine, sometimes I think I have memories like a registry in my head, where is it all going now? Ay, my sweet boy, the pains are killing me and wearing out my body and that Calandria is dancing in a cabaret, and you are so indifferent now, you spend only half a night on the box-spring for fear some other woman will bear your children or for fear of the guerilla that radio stations and newspapers threaten us with, and to think that in ten days I have to catch a plane, ay Andrés that plane over here, over there, up and down like crazy and me with an aching body and bones that I thought would snap apart.

Andrejulio kept his promise and they reached the capital, it was as difficult to get to Villa Duarte as it was in the days of the revolution. There was the cabaret where Calandria danced, there a friend took care of the children, there, there…. And they don't let that Andrés fellow go in, Andrés, I want to go in, Andrés, my daughter. But a policeman arrived and another policeman and another policeman, and the people were backing up. Madame Prebis motioned to the one with the most stripes, she gave him ten pesos as a 'gift' and the package with the address. Take everything to Calandria. The dresses are for her and the jerseys for the children. Tell them we'll see each other next year even if I have to get here by swimming.

When they returned to Guaco the transistor radio broke the news about the arrests and the shutting down of Villa Duarte. The announcer explained very clearly: 'This morning there were explosions near Seco Bridge, next to the cliff where a full regiment seized Amaury. Then, at ten o'clock, in upper Duarte, Tuerto, the alleged member of a gang of bandits, fell.' Ayayay, Auntie, what a trip so, so . . . !

Madame Prebis decided not to return home, the Americans had to restore order in her country, the Americans had to manage everything. Auntie, ayayay, what a crazy woman! But three years later, physically worn out by work in heat or not, in rain or not, in snow or not, washing, ironing, running, cooking, trouble, et cetera, victim of a nervous breakdown, they sent her back home. She who had wasted all her energy in American industry. Ayayay, Auntie, remember they sent you Prebisteria Sánchez.

*Translated by Linda S. Collins**

*Editor's Note: Professor Aida Heredia assisted with the translation of idiomatic Dominican words and phrases.

Aída Cartagena Portalatín: A Literary Life. Moca, Dominican Republic, 1918–94

Daisy Cocco de Filippis

Hombres no han llorado
Porque caen los hombres.
Cómo llorar la muerte de una rosa?
   (Aída Cartagena Portalatín)
(Man has not mourned
because men have fallen.
How can one mourn the death of a rose?)[1]

The most important woman writer in twentieth-century Dominican Republic, Aída Cartagena Portalatín was born and raised in the small coffee-plantation town of Moca. A folder of her early poems and an iron determination accompanied her to the capital city of Santo Domingo in the early 1940s. There she became part of a group of Dominican poets who were collaborating on *La Poesía Sorprendida,* the literary journal which was closed down in 1947 by the Trujillo regime. Her first collections of poems were published during this period: *Del sueño al mundo*[2] in 1944 and *Víspera del Sueño*[3] and *Llámale verde*[4] in 1945. In his essay on Portalatín, Baeza Flores, the Chilean poet who was co-founder and collaborator of the journal, points out:

> Desde este primer poema, que aparece en la revista, podemas sentirlo que será el aporte de Aida Cartagena a la poesia dominicana en el siglo XX: Es un enjambre de imágenes, metáforas, símbolos. Hasta entonces ninguna mujer, en la lírica dominicana, se había atrevido a una escritura poética tan rica en tropos, en contenidos metafóricos y significaciones.[5]
>
> (From this her first poem, which appears in the journal, we can sense what will be Aída Cartagena's contribution to Dominican literature in the twentieth century: It is an amalgam of images, metaphors, symbols. Until then no other woman, in Dominican lyric, had dared to write a poetry so rich in tropes, metaphorical content and significance.) (de Filippis. p. 1)

Her early poems, however, also present a poet who is lost in a world she cannot control, and desolation permeates her work, as seen in the poem 'Asolados' ('Sunburnt'):

Luna ceniza de mañana clara.
Parecerá que cubrirá la tierra
toda una nube blanca.
¿Quién tendrá un solo rayo?
Ha caído el cielo en una sombra.
Sol sin brazos, desdibujado
por un bregar de nubes.
(Moon of ashes in the morning light.
An immense white cloud seems
to cover the earth.
Who has even one ray of sunlight?
The sky has fallen into shadow.
Armless sun, obscured
By struggling clouds.) (de Filippis, pp. 51-2)

'Sunburnt' is an example of the poetry written at a time when Portalatín had to find a way to fit into a society in which she had no accepted function. Having refused to marry or to emulate Dominican role models of the time, she faced a period of great uncertainty in her life which manifested itself in her use of language. A careful reading of 'Sunburnt' leads to the conclusion that although the poem is syntactically correct, it is semantically hollow. The development of the poem is precisely a denial of its title. Since it denies all possibility of a mimetic representation, the poem can be perceived as the manifestation of another landscape: the inner world of the poet.

Emma Jane Robinett, one of her translators, commenting on Portalatín's early poetry, has pointed out that:

There is also a kind of energy and restlessness in these early poems that will not be satisfied to remain forever confined within those outmoded male definitions of what language and forms and subjects are proper for a woman who is also a poet. We can sometimes feel the poet's impatience with indirection and a great desire to confront herself and her world openly. (de Filippis, p. 19)

The closing down of *La Poesía Sorprendida* forced Portalatín into a decision: she had to travel in order to break down the barriers limiting her life. To a younger generation of Dominican women writers, Portalatín's travels have come to symbolize Dominican woman's flight from her imposed surroundings, her home, and her taking on a world until then closed off from women's experience. In fact, Portalatín's poems of this period indicate that they were written in such diverse places as Athens, New Delhi, London, Paris, New York, and Santo Domingo. In a recent interview with the writer of this article, Portalatín confirmed this interpretation of her work and explained how much her travels and associations with such influential writers as André Breton and Pablo Neruda had changed her poetry, giving it strength and audacity.

This newly found energy and self-assurance spilt over into every aspect of her life. On her return to Santo Domingo in the 1950s, Portalatín undertook the rigorous task of being co-founder and co-editor of a series of publications which appeared under the name of 'La Isla Necesaria'. This collection published the works of young as well as older poets who were writing without the benefit of *apoyo oficial*. This was Portalatin's way of taking a stand against a system she did not approve of but could not openly confront. In 'La Isla Necesaria' she also published her own books of poetry under the titles of *Una mujer está sola*[6] and *Mi mundo el mar,*[7] and her monograph on the works of the painter Vela Zanetti.

José Alcántara Almánzar, the Dominican sociologist and critic, explains this new stage in Portalatín's craft:

> Con *Mi mundo el mar,* la poetisa [sic] abrió una nueva etapa de su producción. Dejó el verso plurimétrico por una prosa poética de gran densidad, puso énfasis en el entorno antillano y asumió el papel de protagonista en las seis estancias que forman el libro. La poetisa [sic] devino, a un tiempo, sujeto y objeto de su poesia. Sujeto porque es ella quien vertebra cada una de las partes que componen la obra; objeto porque se visualiza a sí misma como una unidad integrada al habitat marino que aborda.[8]
>
> (With *Mi mi mudo el mar,* the poetess [sic] opened a new cycle in her production. She left behind a plurimetric verse for a poetic prose of great density, she placed emphasis on the Antillean context and took on the role of protagonist of the six sections which make up the book. The poetess [sic] became at the same time subject and object of her poetry. Subject because it is she who vertebrates each one of the parts which make up the work; object because she visualizes herself as a unit integrated to the marine habitat she delineates.)

Almánzar's comments serve to underline to what extent Portalatín's poetry had changed. Thus, on her return to the island, the poet was ready to make another journey: a literary one. Woman's journey in the literary is discussed in Elaine Showalter's article 'Walking in the Wilderness' where Showalter points out that:

> Women writing are not then inside and outside of male tradition: they are inside two traditions simultaneously... Indeed, the female territory might well be envisioned as one long border, and independence for women, not a separate country, but as open access to the sea.[9]

In a poem written during this period, Aída Cartagena Portalatín finds herself in that territory which is no territory, the border, the fringes, or at the door of a new beginning which follows the rejections of a woman's assigned place, and its consequent isolation:

UNA MUJER ESTÁ SOLA
Una mujer está sola. Sola con su estatura.
Con los ojos abiertos. Con los brazos abiertos.
Con el corazón abierto como un silencio ancho.
Espera en la deseperada y desesperante noche sin perder
la esperanza.
Piensa que está en el bajel almirante
Con la luz más triste de la creación.

(A WOMAN IS ALONE
A woman is alone. Alone with herself.
With open eyes and open arms.
With a heart opened by a wide silence.
She awaits in the desperate and despairing night without
       losing hope.
She believes herself to be in the leading vessel
lit by creation's saddest light.)
(de Filippis, p. 71-2)

Sherezada (Chiqui) Vicioso, a Dominican sociologist and one of the most outspoken Dominican poets of our day, calls *A Woman is Alone* the 'First Feminist Manifesto' written in the Dominican Republic. Vicioso points out that this is the first time that there is 'una voz que admite por primera vez las limitacionies de su condición de mujer y sus limitaciones politicas...' ('a voice that acknowledges for the first time the biological and political limitations imposed on women'). Furthermore, Vicioso affirms that:

Este período en la creación poética de Aída, en el cual está más cerca que nunca de crear su propia literatura verdaderamente femenina en la República Dominicana, cambia con la muerte de Trujillo en 1961 cuando Aída publica *La voz desatada y La tierra escrita*.[10]

(This period when she [Portalatín] comes closer to creating her own literature and establishing the basis for a truly feminist literature in the Dominican Republic, changes with Trujillo's death in 1961 when Portalatín publishes *La voz desatada* and *La tierra escrita*.)

Dominican literary criticism of Portalatín's work is controversial. To date, an in-depth study of her work, life, and times has not been written. There are many issues that need to be addressed; in particular, how Portalatín's development as a writer has been influenced by the historical and economic situation of the Dominican Republic and her own class, gender, and race. Unfortunately, the limited scope of this study, the introduction of the writer to English-speaking readers, precludes such an incursion. It is hoped, however, that these considerations will weigh heavily on future, more extensive studies of her work. In the existing criticism in the Dominican Republic, however, there is much difference of opinion. For critics such as José Alcántara Almánzar[11] or Ramón Francisco,[12] it is not until the poetry of the 1960s that Portalatín gains a true poet's voice. For others, like Vicioso, *A Woman is Alone* is Portalatín's finest hour. What a reading of her work makes clear, however, is that her poetry of the period, stripped of vague adjectives and yielding a strong language, sets the tone that will prevail in her later works. In *A Woman is Alone,* Portalatín shows her determination to strike down the lofty pedestals to which women seemed to have been so comfortably relegated by men in the past. With Cartagena Portalatín's works of this period begins the demythification of the role of women in the literature of the Dominican Republic. Significantly, it was in the 1950s that Portalatín discarded from Dominican poetic language such favored terms as *sumisa, virginal,* and *blanca,* as she began to redefine the boundaries of female experience.

In the 1960s Portalatín took on a more active role in educational, cultural, and literary institutions, an involvement which was to last the better part of three decades. She worked and taught at the Universidad Autónoma de Santo Domingo in various capacities, including Adjunct Professor of Art History, Colonial Art, and the History of Civilization. She also served as co-ordinator of programs in history and anthropology and as editor of the university's Annals and the journal of the humanities division. At that time she also edited a series of 'Cuadernos de las Brigadas Dominicanas' which gave a voice to a generation of writers who protested the Trujillo regime and its legacy: a North American invasion and a civil war. Her commitment to these activities, however, did not keep her from a continued dedication to her craft. During this decade Portalatín also wrote two collections of poems, *La voz desatada*[13] and *La tierra escrita*,[14] and she edited an anthology of Dominican short stories,[15] published in 1978 in Venezuela.

In the 1960s, having come to terms with her independence and her right to her own voice, Portalatín's concerns became those of humanity as a whole and, in particular, those of the peoples victimized by bigotry and racism:

Memorias negras
tono 1
vertical camino derribado
reducido a esencia original
fatalidad: el hombre
su problema inherente
simplemente la raza.

(Black Memories
tone I
Vertical road trampled
reduced to its original being
misfortune: said simply
race is the problem
man inherits.)
(de Filippis, pp. 111, 116)

In a courageous blow for Dominican racial identity, until recently linked to the European not to the African ancestor, Portalatín speaks of her own racially mixed background, and for the first time in Dominican poetry a poet faces her own racial identity without having to resort to euphemisms or justifications:[16]

Elegía Segunda
MI MADRE FUE UNA DE LAS GRANDES MAMAS del mundo.
De su vientre nacieron siete hijos que serán en Dallas,
Memphis o Birmingham un problema racial
(ni blancos ni negros)

(Second Elegy
MY MOTHER WAS ONE OF THE GREAT MOTHERS of the world.

From her womb were born seven children who would be in
Dallas, Memphis or Birmingham a racial question.
[Neither black nor white])
(Translated by Emma Jane Robinett; de Filippis, pp. 93-4)

The poems of *La voz desatada* and *La tierra escrita* present a poet who
has come to terms with her independence and right to her own voice. Since
then Portalatín's poetry reflects her concern for humanity as a whole and her
compassion for the victims of racial and social injustice. One of her finest and
most poignant poems of this period is 'Otoño negro' where she repudiates
the particularly brutal murder of four innocent victims of racial bigotry:

Sé que era otoño sin alondras ni hojas.
Yo que lloro al árbol, al pez y a la paloma
me resisto a los blancos del Sur
a esos blancos con su odio apuntando a los negros.
No les pregunto nunca, porque responderían
que en Alabama pueden florecer las dos razas.
Mas, después del Verano de Medgar W. Evers
hicieron un Otoño de cuatro niñas negras.

(I know it was already autumn,
Without leaves and a lark's song.
I, who cry for the trees, for fish and doves,
reject the white men of the South,
those whites with their hatred aimed at black men.
I'd never question their motives
because they would answer
that in Alabama both races can blossom.
After the Summer of Medgar W. Evers,
Came the Fall of four black girls...)
(de Filippis, pp. 95-6)

In this poem, the trees, fish, and doves, symbols of a graceful, innocent,
and generous nature, are the counterpoint to an act of gratuitous violence.
As can be seen in the fragment above, Portalatín has stripped her verse of
adjectives and has given it emotions as its only ornament. Yet her poetic
line, sustained by a strong and unyielding anger, maintains a lyricism and a
beauty which poignantly underscore the loss of possibilities: what might
be when both nature and men are in harmony.

Portalatín's inclusion of social concerns in her writings and her commitment to political causes, however, have met with criticism among some Dominican critics. Unlike Almánzar and Francisco, who pointed out the literary beauty and value of the works of this period, Manuel and Lupo Hernández Rueda, editors of *Antología panorámica de la poesía dominicana contemporánea 1912–1962*, characterize *La tierra escrita* as one of Portalatín's less fortunate publications:

> En su último libro de versos 'La Tierra Escrita' recurre a grafismos, diálogos, técnicas periodísticas e imágenes cinematográficas, usando como centro aglutinante una preocupación por el hombre y por sus libertades inculcadas. A pesar de la actualización que ella ha dado al mundo circundante, lo mejor de su poesía se nos ofrece en sus primeras publicaciones y en 'Una mujer está sola', sobre todo en esta última donde expresa con valentía su drama interior.[17]
>
> (Portalatín resorts to graphics, dialogues, the techniques of journalism, and the imagery of the cinema, using as a binding center her concern for mankind and his usurped freedoms. In spite of the sense of urgency she gives to the world, the best of her poetry is given to us in her earlier works and in a *Woman is Alone,* especially the latter where she valiantly portrays her inner drama.)

Manuel and Lupo Rueda, of course, betray their own allegiance to the *Poesía sorprendida,* a literary movement which advocated a poetry concerned mainly with form and style, a poetry written for its own sake and not at the service of a social cause. Critics outside the Dominican Republic, however, have praised Portalatín's experiments with form and her concern for social justice which are also at the core of her novel *Escalera para Electra,*[18] one of the finalists of the prestigious Seix-Barral award in 1969 where it was praised as

> ... especie de Electra tropical o, mejor aún, nudo vital en que se desarrollan los mitos de la Hélade y se aboceta la problemática de un mundo rural conmocionado por pasiones...Numerosas reflexiones sobre el oficio de novelar coexisten con los acontecimientos que se narran imbrican en ellos, determinan el relato y aclaran sus perfiles. [19]
>
> (... a sort of Electra of the Tropics, or better yet, the vital knot where myths of Hellas and the complexity of a rural world shaken by emotion are developed...There are numerous reflections about the craft of the novel which are narrated and intertwined to determine the narration and to sharpen profiles.)

Experiments with form and political and social engagement define her later works. *Tablero,*[20] a collection of short stories that portray the lives of women, is born out of these concerns. In 'They Called her Aurora. A Passion for Donna Summer,' the story that opens the book, Colita, the protagonist, is a symbol of a social group that has been denied a voice, name, and identity:

Mami me decía Colita. Colita García. Pero la señora Sarah me inscribió en la escuela pública con el nombre de Aurora. ¡Nada de Colita! gritó. Seguí sintiéndome interiormente Colita y oyéndome en la voz de los otros.

(Mami used to called me Colita. Colita García. But Mistress Sarah registered me in public school by the name of Aurora. Forget about Colita! She screamed. But I felt like a Colita that they all called Aurora.)

In *Tablero Checkerboard,* Portalatín created the space in which the lives of women, of the Colitas of Dominican culture, are played out by others with the same precision, deliberation, and cold-heartedness that it takes to win at this seemingly innocent game.

In *En la casa del tiempo* (1984),[21] her last work of fiction to be published to date, Portalatín's experimentation with form and content culminate in an angry verse characterized by the reduction of the poetic line which has gained strength and has become the visceral shriek of an anguished poet who needs to shake down the foundations of injustice:

Memorias negras
tono 5
ay, ay, ay, ay
asesinaron otra vez a Africa
otra vez en Sharpeville
ooooooh ooooooh
OoooooooooooooooH
nadie grita: castigo

(ah, ah, ah, ah
they've murdered Africa again
once again in Sharpeville
ooooooh ooooooH
OoooooooooooH
no one shouts: curses)
(de Filippis, p. 115)

Thus for Cartagena Portalatín, as she confirmed in a recent conversation, in her writings there is no return to a concern for the rose. A poet, short-story writer, novelist, essayist, editor, and college professor, Portalatín still has a very active role in Dominican literary circles. The author of 14 books her last four, published in the 1980s – *Yania tierra* (poetry),[22] *La tarde en que murió Estefanía* (novel),[23] *En la casa del tiempo* (poetry) and *Las culturas africanas: rebeldes con causa* (essays)[24] – bear witness to her continued support of the struggle against racism and social injustices and her experimentation with literary form.

Several tributes to her work include: 'De poetas a poetas, recital de poesia, tributo a Aída Cartagena Portalatín del Círculo de Mujeres Poetas' (in 1984, the newly-formed Circle of Dominican Women Poets dedicated a recital of their poetry to Portalatín, in acknowledgement of the role she played in paving the way for women's issues in Dominican literature); Sosa's anthology *La mujer en la literatura* (a 1966 collection of essays about women writers, including many studies of Portalatín's work); Daisy Cocco de Filippis's *Bilingual Anthology of the Poetry of Aída Cartagena Portalatín* (1988, the first ever bilingual edition devoted to the poetry of a single Dominican writer). These activities serve to underscore the fact that she is an author who must be considered, studied, and understood, if one is to write about Dominican literature in the twentieth century. Although in her seventies and retired from her university duties, Portalatín continued to write (she had a novel in progress) and remained involved in her craft and in her country. Until her passing in June, 1994, Portalatín remained clear-headed and committed to the cause of justice, still searching for new means of creative expression and determined to influence the course of Dominican letters in years to come.

Notes

This essay was first published in York College, CUNY, Proceedings of Women of Hispaniola Conference, Executive Report, Vol. 1, no. 2, 1993.

1 . Daisy Cocco de Filippis (ed.), *Sin otro profeta que su canto, antología de poesía escrita por dominicanas / From Desolation to Compromise: A Bilingual Anthology of the Poetry of Aída Cartagena Portalatín* (Santo Domingo: Taller, Colección Montesinos 10, 1988), pp. 47-8. Subsequent references to this volume are cited in the text as de Filippis.

2. Aída Cartagena Portalatín, *Del sueño al mundo,* Ciudad Trujillo: *La Poesía Sorprendida,* Colección 'El Desvelado Solitario,' 1944.

3. Aída Cartagena Portalatín, *Víspera del Sueño,* Ciudad Trujillo: *La Poesía Sorprendida,* Coleccion 'El Desvelado Solitario,' 1945.

4. Aída Cartagena Portalatín, *Llámale verde,* Ciudad Trujillo: *La Poesía Sorprendida,* Coleccion 'El Desvelado Solitario,' 1945.

5. Alberto Baeza Flores, *La Poesía dominicana en el siglo xx, generaciones y tendencias, poetas independientes. La poesía, sorprendida, suprarealismo, dominicinidad y universalidad (1943–1947) II* (Santiago: Universidad Católica Madre y Maestra, Colección Estudios 22, 1977), p. 621.

6. Aída Cartagena Portalatín, *Una mujer está sola,* Ciudad Trujillo: Colección 'La Isla Necesaria,' 1955.

7. Aída Cartagena Portalatín, *Mi mundo el mar,* Ciudad Trujillo: Colección 'La Isla Necesaria,' 1953.

8. José Alcántara Almánzar, *Estudios de poesía dominicana* (Santo Domingo: Alfay Omega, 1979), p. 274.

9. Elaine Showalter, 'Walking in the Wilderness, ' *New Feminist Criticism* (New York: Pantheon, 1985), p. 264.

10. Sherezada (Chiqui) Vicioso, in *La mujer en la literatura, Homenaje a Aída Cartagena Portalatín,* ed. José Rafael Sosa. (Santo Domingo: Editora Universitaria, 1986), p. 82.

11. Almánzar, *Estudios de poesía dominicana.*

12. Ramón Francisco, *Literatura Dominicana 60* (Santiago: Universidad Católica Madre y Maestra, Colección Contemporáneos 7, 1969).

13. Aída Cartagena Portalatín, *La voz desatada,* (Santo Domingo: Brigadas Dominicanas, 1962).

14. Aída Cartagena Portalatín, *La tierra escrita,* (Santo Domingo, Brigadas Dominicanas, 1967).

15. Aída Cartagena Portalatín (ed.), *Narradores dominicanos* (Caracas: Monte Avila, 1978).

16. For a study of women and racial identity in Dominican poetry, see the introduction to de Filippis.

17. Manuel and Lupo Hernández Rueda (eds.), *Antología panorámica de la poesía dominicana contemporánea 1912–1962* (Santiago: Universidad Católica Madre y Maestra, Colección Contemporáneos 12, 1972).

18. Aída Cartagena Portalatín, *Escalera para Electra,* 2nd edn (Santo Domingo: Colección Montesinos, 1980).

19. Quoted in Sosa (ed.), *La mujer en la literatura,* p. 9

20. Aída Cartagena Portalatín, *Tablero,* (Santo Domingo: Taller, 1978).

21. Aída Cartagena Portalatín, *En la casa del tiempo* (Santo Domingo: Colección Montesinos, 1984).

22. Aída Cartagena Portalatín, *Yania tierra* (Santo Domingo: Colección Montesinos 5, 1984).

23. Aída Cartagena Portalatín, *La tarde en que murió Estefanía* (Santo Domingo: Colección Montesinos, 1984).

24. Aída Cartagena Portalatín, *Las culturas africanas: rebeldes con causa* (Santo Domingo: Colección Montesinos 5, 1986).

Marta Rojas

M ARTA R OJAS

CUBA

(b. 1931)

An award-winning Cuban journalist who gained fame through her coverage of the Moncada Trial in 1953, Marta Rojas won the prestigious José Martí National Prize for Journalism in 1997. In a career that has spanned more than four decades, the 'Woman Journalist of Moncada' has served on the staffs of Revolución *and* Granma; *has travelled throughout Asia, Europe, and the Americas; was a war correspondent in Vietnam and Cambodia; and served as a special correspondent in Nicaragua. Those experiences led to the publication of books of historical testimony, including* El juicio del Moncada *(The Moncada Trial), and* Escenas de Viet Nam *(Scenes from Vietnam). Her interest in history began when she was hired, while a student at Havana's School of Journalism, to transcribe documents for a noted scholar. Her knowledge of history has had a decisive effect on her writing style: on the clarity and precision of her language, on her ability to distance herself from her subject, and on her attention to significant details. Those skills are also evident in* El que debe vivir *(He Who Must Live), an historical account of two revolutionary heroes which won the Casa de las Américas award, and* La cueva del muerto *(Dead Man's Cave), a testimonial narrative that was translated into English and made into a documentary film.*

The daughter of a tailor and seamstress, Rojas was born in Santiago de Cuba, where she grew up reading books, going to the movies, and listening to stories about her family's African and Spanish ancestors. She wrote her first work of fiction, the unpublished El dulce enigma, *while still in secondary school. Her novel* El columpio de Rey Spencer *(Rey Spencer's Swing), the first in a trilogy on Cuban history, racial origins, and national identity, was published in 1993. A postmodern historical romance composed of documents (letters, diaries, interviews, and data) that appear on a computer screen, it deals with Cubans of Caribbean descent, whose Haitian and Jamaican forebears migrated to Cuba to work in the canefields. The product of extensive historical research, Rojas' second published novel* Santa lujuria o papeles de blanco *(Holy Lust or White Papers) underscores the fluidity of racial boundaries, the commodification of skin colour, and the institutionalisation of whitening in Cuban colonial society.*

Marta Rojas is a consummate artist, whose fiction and nonfiction reveal a sensitivity to language and skilful craftmanship. Her dramatic writing style – evident in her realistic delineation of characters, poetic descriptions of place, and complex structuring of plot – has been shaped by her journalistic skills, knowledge of history, and familiarity with films and cinematic montage. The noted Cuban novelist Alejo Carpentier said of Rojas, 'A lively talented writer with . . . great insight, a direct, precise style, and the gift of showing many things with few words'.

The Sweet Enigma of a Writer's Life: A Personal Narrative

I was born several hundred miles from Havana in Santiago de Cuba, which is the most important city after Havana. At the beginning of the conquest and during the Colonial Period, it was the capital of the island and it was simply called 'Cuba'. I was born in the city with the help of a midwife (that is to say, my birth did not take place in a hospital). The date was May 17, 1932, although, when my birth was recorded, my father wrote down another date – but it is very clear that I was born under the sign of Taurus. The oldest of my two siblings was male and the youngest is female; I am eight years older than my sister, and my brother, who died rather young, was four years older than I.

My maternal grandmother was Black. She was born free, but she was the daughter of slaves in the city of Matanzas, near Havana. My maternal grandfather was Spanish. The two of them lived together and had nine children, the youngest of whom was my mother. She was born in Matanzas on January 25, 1900, at the turn of the century. My father was a typical mulatto from Santiago, a man of French, African, and Spanish ancestry. His last names are Rojas Fereaud, and my mother's are Rodríguez Martínez. My father met her when she was twenty-one or twenty-three years old, and they soon married. My father went to Matanzas to find work. The couple then moved to Santiago, where my two siblings and I were born and raised, but every year, we would go and see our grandmother.

My father was a tailor of *haute couture*, and my mother was also a high-fashion dressmaker. She did needlework with my aunts and older cousins (on my father's side), who sewed in their own homes, and I learned to cut and sew perfectly while watching them. My father worked for a while in a tailor shop, when there were important orders to fill; later, he worked with my mother at home, but he also used to own a small candy factory. We always lived in very large houses with patios and backyards, and each one of us had her/his own bedroom. The houses were antique in style: simple and austere but very clean, airy, and pleasant. That meant that, fortunately, I was never crowded and was able to develop my own individuality. In a period of economic crisis, when I was around seven years old, we moved to the country because no one was having elegant clothes made. We lived in the country, fairly close to Santiago, for a year and a half.

I was an exceptionally happy child, because my maternal grandfather pleased me in everything; that is, in accordance with his means, he satisfied each child's whim – chocolates, roller skates, and rides in his convertible. He was Spanish, and he had a small business that was adequate for that city. (My mother was his only daughter so when she got married, he went to live in Santiago. My grandmother and the other children stayed in Matanzas.) He took a trip to Spain that lasted several years, because he and his sisters became ill; that trip coincided with the economic and political crisis. I saw then how hard extreme poverty can be, but my mother never tried to conceal problems from us. The situation improved, but not much.

I wanted to study music – piano – but I didn't have the money to pay a music teacher and, much less, to buy a piano. Instead, I satisfied that artistic need through a craving for the cinema, and, since it was very inexpensive, I went to the movies every afternoon. In my childhood, adolescence, and young adulthood, I saw thousands of films. I used to pay for my movie tickets, because my mother, aunts, and cousins would give me little sewing jobs and ten or fifteen cents as gifts, so I always had a little money. I always spent at least two hours working. It was something I had to do, according to my parents, 'so that you will be still for a while'. Thus, I learned to handle the sewing needle and to buy threads and laces in the linen stores. Maybe that is why I tend to dress up my characters.

I learned to read and write from a retired teacher who used to give classes to the neighbourhood children, and when I was nine, I entered public school at the third grade level. It was an incomparable school, an annex to the Normal School or School for Teachers. My older brother went to a different school – also public – and then Mirtha, the youngest child, was born after I told my mother that I wanted to have a sister. I spent little time with her, however, because her godparents, who didn't have any children, took her with them when my mother was working, and then later I moved to Havana. Eventually, she won a prize – a trip to New York – in a hair styling contest that I had encouraged her to enter. She returned to New York to stay in 1960, and got married. That is another story, but we love each other very, very much.

I was a good student in elementary school but not outstanding, just normal. I talked in class, took mountain climbing trips, and played a lot, especially the typical games of little girls. I learned easily at school and entered the Instituto de Segunda Enseñanza in Santiago de Cuba before the customary age. I wanted to study medicine and become a doctor; my cousin was a doctor, so I learned medical formulas and read books on surgery. I understood, however, how difficult it would be for me to study that field; the books cost a lot of money and my parents worked night and day to support and educate us. In those days, there wasn't a medical school in Santiago, but there was one in Havana. The most expensive things at the university were the books and tuition. My brother, who was studying business in Santiago while working at the school, gave me ten pesos a month when I went to Havana.

I think it was my mother who discovered my literary vocation because whenever I returned from the movie theatre, I liked to retell the plot the way that I wanted it to be. The endings were seldom the same, and when my parents went to see these movies, they realised that I had added or eliminated things. One day, my mother said to me, 'Well, little Jules Verne, how did the movie *Cumbres Borrascosas* end?' When I recounted the ending that I liked, she called me an 'inventor', but she didn't scold me for that, adding, 'At least you don't lie about other things'. I did well on my composition assignments and examinations, and I even helped my classmates with their writing.

When I was in my third year at the lyceum, I discovered through the radio – for the radio was on almost all day in my house while my mother sewed – that Françoise Sagan, a French teenager, had written a romance novel. I told my classmates that if that French girl had written a novel, I could do it too. On returning from the Institute, I would lock myself in the bedroom and start writing. (The walls of my bedroom were covered with photos of American movie stars; I used to write to them in Hollywood, and their secretaries sent me the stars' photos). The next day during recess, I would read chapters to my female friends and to the males too. I called the novel *El dulce enigma*, and I wrote in the prologue that it dealt with the conflicts of adolescents. The novel took place in a Cuban historical context. I have not dared to read it again because it was awful, but it had all of the intrigues that captured the attention of my listeners. I added things that they found 'most beautiful' and, based on my listeners' reactions, I intensified or reduced the emotional tone. It was a sensational game, which lasted about four months. That year I passed my courses 'by the skin of my teeth', as they say.

One afternoon at dinner, I heard on the radio news that registration was open at Havana's School of Journalism and that the tuition was only four pesos. Right away, I told my parents that it would be better for me to go to Havana to study journalism instead of medicine, because I enjoyed writing. So, I travelled alone to Havana when I was only sixteen years old, passed the entrance examination, and began studying journalism. I was not the top student, but I was one of the best in my class. I have always enjoyed living life to the fullest, so I could not see spending hours and hours studying when, with what I knew, I could easily pass my courses. So I never aspired to win medals or scholarships. I never failed a course and even received some 'outstandings' and 'notables', but I was not the valedictorian of my graduating class. I preferred to go to a concert or party on Sunday, or to visit and talk with people. I also used to visit the Medical School, because some of my classmates from the Institute were studying there.

I found the professors at the School of Journalism to be very warm and helpful, although I was from a distant province and didn't have a journalist or intellectual among my relatives. During the fifties, I acquired my first job editing newscasts in the new field of television. I took a course in television broadcasting with the expectation of working in that area after graduation, which was possible because at that time many companies wanted to have a beautiful Black or mulatto on their payroll to hide evidence of racial discrimination.

So that my parents would only have to pay for my rent and other necessities, I took a difficult but interesting job at the National Library. I had to transcribe eighteenth- and nineteenth-century documents for a writer, Manuel Moreno Fraginal, who was doing research for *The Sugar Mill*, a book about the sugar industry that became a classic. The salary was low because it was a temporary job, but the complicated exercise of deciphering texts became very important for my literary work.

When I was a child, I used to read all kinds of magazines and newspapers that my parents bought, and I used to listen to the BBC. I began reading early, because my father had a barber friend who read the books that his clients left in the barbershop. The first books that I read were the complete works of Honoré de Balzac. I also read Jules Verne and a collection called *The Treasure of Youth*, and later I read *Madame Bovary*, *Hell* by Henry Barbasse, *The Plague* by Curzio Malaparte, Margaret Mitchell's *Gone With the Wind*, and *Don Quixote* as well as the biographies of Fouché, Napoleon, Catherine the Great, Abraham Lincoln, Simón Bolívar, José Martí, and Eva Perón.

I cannot be certain that reading the books of my father's friend, the barber, influenced my future writing – with the exception, perhaps, of Balzac and *Don Quixote* – but they did instill in me the habit of reading. As an adult, I preferred more concrete things and, among the Hispanic writers, the ones who impressed me the most were Cirilo Villaverde (the nineteenth-century novelist who wrote *Cecilia Valdés*), Rómulo Gallegos, Alejo Carpentier, and Jorge Luis Borges. As you can see, they are very dissimilar; they have absolutely nothing to do with one another in theme, concept, or form. To this, I must add something of great importance to me: my fondness for history and socio-political essays, some of which are very difficult but which I read as an intellectual exercise. There is a book among books that few writers master; it is the Bible. I have almost completely underlined it; I am not a religious militant, but neither am I an agnostic. I believe that faith is comforting at special moments, and I am fascinated by the synthesis of the Bible's writing.

Besides literature, influences in my work include, first, the plastic arts and then music. But anything can become a tool for a writer, from a television commercial to a theatrical programme; the most important thing is the critical observation of life in the present and in the past.

I believed in social justice even before I knew its definition and also in unlimited solidarity without expectation of recompense. I have not studied Marxism (or any philosophy, for that matter) in great depth, but I have studied the theme because I would be ignorant if it were totally unknown to me. In my house, people talked a lot about national and international politics, my country's Wars of Independence, the political frustrations of the First Republic, and World War II, about which I was interested, though I was very young. I believe that my father was affiliated with the Authentic Revolutionary Party, but he was not a politician. In my house, I learned the work ethic and humanism. Later, when I was a student in Havana, I sympathised with the Orthodox Party, which supported administrative reform, anti-corruption, and national sovereignty. That was not unusual because most of the young people, especially students, used to march in support of that party. Fidel Castro was associated with that party, but I knew him only by name, from reading in the newspapers about his battles against corruption as a student.

I gained political awareness during the Moncada Trial of 1953, and, more specifically, when I heard Fidel's famous pronouncement, *History Will Absolve Me*. I was in the courtroom as a newly-graduated journalist, and I was very bold to be there. I was deeply moved by what Fidel said about the reasons for the Revolution and about the socio-political programme of his group. The essence of the programme involved structural changes to achieve social justice and human rights. When I heard him, although I was willing to follow the ideas he enunciated, I thought that in Cuba these ideas would be an unattainable chimera. I was wrong. The incipient Revolution triumphed, and I became a part of it.

Translated by Elba Birmingham-Pokorny

from Holy Lust or White Papers

Set in colonial Cuba, Rojas' novel narrates the story of Lucila Méndes, a mulatto, who has a son by Don Antonio, a wealthy White Creole. Antonio buys 'white papers' from the Spanish crown to transform his son from coloured to white, while Lucila, forced to rename herself Isabel de Flandes, serves as the boy's governess. Although Lucila later marries Captain Albor, who buys white papers for her, she and her brother are important members of the Afro-Cuban community. This chapter includes a narrative by Lucila's son Filomeno – now a wealthy, educated adult – in which he describes an Afro-Cuban ceremony and the arrival of fugitive slaves from Georgia.

Finally, Lucila Méndes would become queen of the confederation of *cofradías* at the big house on San Carlos Street, whose grounds covered an entire city block. It was a world comparable to a *cabildo* sui generis of Congo royalty, even though it wasn't the only one like it in Spanish America. It was a world where people of colour invited Whites to their ball. Lucila, a real, honest-to-goodness, bona fide White woman, authenticated by royal decree, would preside over the ceremony that followed the Creole dinner, which would be topped off with rum and Madeira wines.

Captain Albor's comments cast a pall over the dinner guests seated around the table: he spoke about the Black leader from the Venezuelan provinces who had taken up arms against the Spanish that same year: 1795. According to Albor, the man's name was José Leonardo Chirino, and he was 'Frenchified' like Nicolás Morales of Bayamo.

'And listen to this, my friends', he added. 'In Santo Domingo, a group of slaves belonging to the Marquis of Iranda rose up against Governor García. Almost all the Blacks and mulattoes there are ranch hands, who ride horses and carry poles and skinning knives. Since Spain has given up the island, leaving it to the French, I have seen wealthy Dominicans rushing to Cuba, while others head for Puerto Rico and the less fortunate set out for Venezuela'.

The reply to his comments was dead silence, for the guests refused to touch the sacrilegious topic of Haiti. The fiesta finally ended, and Filomeno described it somewhat bitterly in his *Report* this way:

'With a stick in one hand and a *güiro* in the other, José entered, erect, dressed in red and white, and speaking the ancestors' tongue, as he walked between two rows of his peers. "Siguaraya prepare a way / Nsiguaraya buy back Mamá Ungúnda / prepare a way for my sister ..." Tun, tun . . . went the pitchfork. After joining the people and jostling with them, the scoundrel had the nerve to sit down at the table.

'The magic dance and the evocatory music of different *cofradías* was about to begin, when my governess felt a kinship with her people. There were songs for the government and, later, songs for liberty as well as for war, work, death and a lot of other things.

'The Cuban-born Blacks from Havana and, even more, the African-born Cubans who witnessed all of this for the first time, found it somewhat strange that Lucila began the sacred ritual by pouring water and gazing into a crystal cup that was overflowing with liquid, while she prayed that my grandfather Filho Mendes might "protect and enlighten me".

'The dead White man, as she called him, was her patron saint – the bearded Portuguese to whom she offered water because he was very thirsty. Then she began to sing her monorhythmic song and to move her feet. The drumming began and the music became irresistible to those of the *cofradía* who followed her lead without missing a beat. The others repeated José's words – first, the chorus and then the refrain – with a whisper that became a sort of humming. José moved in and out, like Changó, because his colours (the red and white of the *orisha*) revealed who he was.

'The supple, undulating bodies, and the sonorous song, with unimagined timbres. The hips and feet, including those of Don Antonio and Albor, continued dancing, because the beat, though a bit ordinary, was good. I hid behind a curtain and watched how they began to move their whole bodies to the beat of the drum. The bodies of the real dancers moved in unison.

'A man – José – moved toward the centre, and Governess, who was in front, approached him dancing; slowly, they drew closer together without missing a beat, until they boldly thrust their stomachs together, after which they stepped back and another couple took their place. Caridad danced to the rhythm while continuing to fan herself, and Salvador, in a cord-fringed skirt instead of the palm-leaf *mariwó* that others wore, raised his hands and shook his pelvis as he danced.

'On observing these mimetic dances, I went to Father Piño, who didn't know what to do, and told him: "There you see them, talking to each other through the dance and the drum."

'Once more, Queen Lucila, my governess, moved to the forefront with an erotic, insinuating and shameless dance of the imagination. Shaking her skirts and moving with complete abandon, she shimmied up to the musicians, provocatively and seductively, each move more suggestive than the last, while the music – above all, the music of the three sacred *batá* drums – kept up with her. The other woman, the mulatto Caridad, danced in the style of her class, while holding little Gracián, my brother. At an opportune time, Governess – my governess who was now their queen – took the child away from her. The oldest ones in the group danced with more decorum, without abandoning the rituals.

'It was still daylight and nothing escaped me. The large, old, plain drums made of almond tree trunks were played with bold frenzy and bare hands (I avoid saying "with a closed fist", which is a vulgar expression) by musicians who sat on top of their instruments to produce a louder sound. This sound blended with that of the brass instruments, the maracas, and the bracelets of the Blacks. And when the sheepskins on the drums reverberated excessively, mixing their sound with that of the dancing (which I've already described), masked clowns and little devils with mysteriously garbled speech, controlled by the spirits, began to appear calling out to Sambiá, just as we prudent Catholics might invoke our God, Our Lord.

'In order to understand how the spirit of that ceremony changed in such a strange way, you have to read the following segment taken from my "Narrative of the Epiphany", where I reveal a surprising fact:

'At the height of the Afro-Cuban society's concert, Griego strolled into the drawing-room of my governess, Queen Lucila, and whispered something to her; she assented with a gesture, since the two of them always understood each other. With the approval of my governess, Griego took the Marquis by the arm and led him outside. Griego was more flushed than usual and had bloodshot eyes; I don't know if this resulted from strong drinks that he had consumed or if something had happened.

'I followed them, of course . . . . They went through the garden toward the gate that leads to the narrow lane, where the Pilot (now Captain) Cortés de Navia lived. There, there was a group of blacks, surrounded by soldiers under the command of the lieutenant from the San Marcos Barracks. Right away, the lieutenant told the Marquis my father that his commanding officer was away on another mission and was not at his post. That was why he had come to see the Marquis, knowing that he held a high position in the kingdom. The blacks who were there in front of him were fugitive slaves from neighbouring plantations belonging to North Americans. In spite of the currents and strong winds, they had landed at St Augustine, Florida, in two fairly large but decrepit boats.

'Half-naked, the Blacks were shivering from the cold. They had delusions of gaining freedom on the island of Haiti, to which North American Blacks frequently fled, or, preferably, of joining the Seminole Indians. But a sudden shift in the stormy winds had turned them around and brought them straight to these shores. The wind had changed course quite quickly. One of them knew something of the sea, because he had been a slave of the Portuguese, who were acquainted with such things.

'The Blacks agreed with the officer's version. Two of the group, who had come from the little island of Fernandina, were somewhat skilled (though not much) in the Spanish language, but Griego almost always had to translate their English.

'There were not more than twelve of them, males and females, more males than females, and three boys and one little girl, whom I am not including in the group of twelve or so. To the surprise of this writer, my father the Marquis immediately gave them refuge and made them comfortable. I mean by this, that he gave them shelter, food, and clothes, because their own were tattered and soaking wet. He also promised to return their boats as soon as these were repaired; after the boats were mended, the people could use them to fish for food to eat or sell. As for the men, they were all free, but would remain under Griego's protection; my father would protect the women because they were quite young; the same went for the boys and girls.

'Griego, who knew how to handle such matters, told the Canary Islander from La Muralla de Aguas Claras to get the necessary supplies: food, shelter, and clothing for the newly-arrived fugitives. Again, I marvelled at how the Marquis my father had remedied that terrible injustice.

'But the thing that most amazed me happened later. I will tell you in this *Report* what happened when Don Antonio invited the runaways to see how happily our Blacks spent the Day of Epiphany, a day of Christian devotion, in union and fellowship with their masters.

'The newly-arrived fugitives' entrance in the drawing room, where they had been invited, was a surprise to those already present. But even greater was the cry of amazement from the fugitives themselves on seeing there such an array of different-shaped drums, including the three sacred *batá* drums, which were unknown to them because drums had been completely forbidden to slaves by their English masters. Because of their English heritage or because of customs that were passed down to them, the North Americans also prohibited, under threat of severe punishment, the playing of drums even though the so-called colonies were now independent. For this reason, their Blacks took such delight in our domain.

'During the celebration, the Georgians, more than the others, sang with high-pitched, falsetto voices, much like high sopranos. But they didn't know how to dance, because they were unfamiliar with the drums; they hadn't even seen such drums until that moment. These people who had landed in St Augustine looking for freedom did not come from Africa, although it is said that there are also stringed instruments in Africa. Who knows whether they were born in Georgia or Mississippi. As I later observed, they were familiar with violins similar to the ones played by the light-skinned musicians whom my father Don Antonio brought to Florida when he came from Cuba some months before aboard the *Saeta de Albor*.

'One of the North Americans, apparently from Georgia or Virginia as I had overheard, had brought something that resembled a violin, although it was closer to a guitar. It was kind of round; it had four strings, I believe; and it was called a banjo. He had made it himself.

'The recent arrivals, including the children, placed their rough hands, which were blistered by the oars during the storm, on the cured skins of the drums, and, when one of the Cuban blacks or mulattoes beat out a musical tune or a sacred piece on the well-tuned drum skins, the people from Georgia or thereabouts snapped their fingers, keeping time with the beat. They did it in such a way and with such precision and rhythm that those same fingers were transformed into musical instruments, impossible to imitate in that so-called orchestra or whatever you call it.

'Then the recent arrivals, as I again refer to them, piqued the interest of our drummers, who, given the amazement of our musical maestro De la Hoz, didn't have the skill to reproduce that sound with either their fingers or the palms of their hands. It seems as if the people whom we had just rescued, in addition to their musical clapping, sang out with great force and with a special timbre in their voices, as I have already written; their voices were different and worthy of opera singers. Although I haven't seen any operas, they have been described to me.

'They sounded to me like something unknown. When I asked Captain Albor, who was knowledgeable about a lot of things, if he had ever heard, either in Brazil or the Venezuelan provinces, music made by snapping fingers or clapping hands, or if he had heard anything like those sad songs that seemed to come from beyond the grave, he replied that he hadn't. He had heard something almost like it, not a lot like it, but similar, less vibrant, among Blacks in the smaller, English islands of the Caribbean.

'With the keen perception of plain, ordinary people, as my father always says, some and then others rapidly learned the rhythms and melodies that enabled them to join in uninhibitedly with the other group. Voices, clapping, and finger snapping mixed with drum beating, the jubilant sounds of *güiro* scrapping and metallic instruments. The sounds of flutes and other wind instruments mixed with the hum of violins and a harp plucked by a black woman. Vibrations came from the bamboo sticks that the Mexican cook from the Saeta had taken from his marimba and from the harp and guitar played by Melchor de Puella, and even from the complex sounds of the four-stringed banjo.

'Suddenly, it became quiet. We heard a solo voice with an other-world sound, and then the voices of the runaways formed a chorus. José María, the Florida Vitier, suddenly accompanied them, drawing silvery sounds from a make-shift piano: an Erard table.

'With that aptitude for creativity that true musicians have, the ball reached a climax in such a way that Spanish words fail me in describing it. All I can say is that just as dawn unfolds into full daylight, as the prophets say, so it was with that musical gathering, I repeat and affirm. Dazzling songs and dances were performed through the generosity of my father, in imitation of what the king himself would have done.

'Something else happened that deserves to be recorded in this narrative; it is somewhat difficult to describe, but here it is:

'Although I knew how similar ceremonies took place in the *igbodú* room or the pantheon (I was always snooping about in there), primarily on Christian religious days, it shocked me to see Governess twirling about in her own circle, without stopping until she fell to the floor with voluptuous shudders, as if dead from the spirited, diabolic dancing that accompanied the sacred litanies, so difficult to perform and so embarrassing to me.

'The music stopped, but I could still hear some of those solemn voices, like tortured sounds or desperate wails coming from swollen throats and lips that barely opened, but when they did I could see down their throats to the uvula.

'For a little while longer, I could still hear the sad, melodious songs of the Georgia fugitives, who left the main drawing room with the rest of the group carrying the drums, ceremonial objects, and more sophisticated instruments that the light-skinned, coloured musicians from Santiago de Cuba had brought aboard the Saeta for the concert. The Marquis planned the concert to shower my old governess with kindness. That is the conclusion that I reached'.

Translated by Antonio Olliz Boyd

Glossary

Cofradía: a brotherhood or organisation of Afro-Cubans who belong to the same ethnic group.

Cabildo: an Afro-Cuban socio-religious organisation.

Güiro: Cuban musical instrument.

Orisha: Gods or saints of the *santería* religion, which originated in West Africa, particularly among the Yoruba.

Mariwó: According to the author, 'it is a tunic or short skirt made out of fibre or straw; it is used in ceremonies or dances of African origin'. It is probably similar to the raffia skirts worn in African dance ceremonies.

Marta Rojas' *Santa Lujuria* and the Transformation of Cuban History Into Mythic Fiction

Miriam DeCosta-Willis

The novel *Santa lujuria o papeles de blanco* (Holy Lust or White Papers) by award-winning Cuban journalist Marta Rojas is significant for several reasons. First, it is unique in the corpus of Afro-Hispanic literature because it is one of only two novels by a Cuban woman of African descent (Rojas in both cases) and because this literary work, like Nancy Morejón's epic poem 'Mujer negra', Cristina Cabral's powerful lyric 'Memoria y resistencia', and Argentina Chiriboga's historical novel *Jonatás y Manuela*, focuses on the role of the African-descended woman in the transformation of Spanish American history. The novel is also important because it participates in the contemporary scholarly and literary discourse on slavery that was initiated in the 1970s and '80s by Black writers throughout the Americas.[1] *Santa lujuria* is a subversive and iconoclastic text, which serves as a counterdiscourse to the 'official' story, written by the founding fathers whose master texts created and preserved the disinformation that undergirded Cuban colonial history: to wit, the benevolence of slavery in the colonies, the mitigating influence of the Roman Catholic Church, the licentiousness of Africans, and the pure blood (*pureza de sangre*) of the Creole elite. Rojas inverts that history, demonstrating through a fictional text based on meticulous archival research, the violence of slavery, the complicity of the Church, the sexual depravity of the slaveowners, and the nappy roots of the Creoles.

Rojas has explained in numerous letters, interviews, and a memoir the significance of history in her personal, intellectual, and professional development as a writer. Her knowledge of history comes from various sources, including academic courses, research in libraries and archives, journalistic training, and – equally important – the oral testimony of family members, including her maternal grandmother Cecilia Martínez (1886–1958), the granddaughter of enslaved Africans.[2] While Rojas was a student at Havana's School of Journalism taking courses in Cuban and Latin American history, she had a formative experience that shaped the direction of her writing: she conducted research at the Biblioteca Nacional, where she transcribed eighteenth- and nineteenth-century documents for Manuel Moreno Fraginals, who was writing *El ingenio: complejo económico social cubano del azúcar,* a major work on Cuba's sugar industry. Ten years ago, she began research at the Archivo de Indias on eighteenth-century institutions and laws, particularly the law that gave male colonists the right to land and *women.* This research formed the basis for *Santa lujuria,* a study of slavery's legacy in the politics of property and identity. While in Madrid in 1999, Rojas conducted additional excavatory research at the Tribunal Supremo on Estéban Santa Cruz de Oviedo, the protagonist of her third novel, *El harén de Oviedo.*

The writer's love of history, however, began at home, where her parents and grandparents discussed slavery, Cuban history, and their forebears' participation in the wars of independence. 'Mi abuelo', Rojas explains, 'hablaba siempre de que por aquellas calles [las de Santiago de Cuba donde nació ella] había caminado Maceo' (My grandfather always said that Maceo had walked in those streets) (Elizalde 1997, 3). One of her first published articles, at age fourteen, was entitled 'Antonio Maceo, héroe epónimo' (Suardiaz 1997, 3). The question of the validity of oral testimony – particularly that by and about African people – as a source of historical truth is raised by one of the characters in *Santa lujuria,* who maintains that 'La Historia tiene que ser *escrita* ... sin *omisiones sospechosas,* ni tratándose de *infelices esclavos*' (History must be *written* ... without *suspicious omissions,* and should not deal with *wretched slaves*) (39, emphasis added). This statement suggests that conservative historiography has traditionally rejected nonscribal testimony, especially that of Blacks, as history.[3]

Drawing upon oral and written history, including maps, photographs, chronicles, and legal documents, Marta Rojas has created a work of fiction that examines the archetypes, historical events, and institutions that have shaped colonial Cuba. *Santa lujuria,* with its genesis in scholarly research, is an historical novel that reinterprets the past, demonstrating the effect of history on characters, examining the place of archetypes in history, and presenting the author's concept of history. The novel exhibits many of the characteristics of the historical romance, a genre that Jane Campbell calls a radical literary mode 'in which heroes and heroines depict values that run counter to those of an oppressive culture' (x–xi). In the romance novel, historical events such as slave rebellions and wars of independence acquire a symbolic or mythic significance; characters, such as Lucila Mendes and her brother José, are archetypal figures designed to counter negative stereotypes; the inflated language of the text, with its stylised diction and complex figures of speech, depicts an idealised reality; and the narrative is complicated by numerous sub-plots, intercalations, polyvocality, and constantly shifting scenes. Because of its theme – the legacy of slavery in Cuban history – *Santa lujuria* also belongs to the genre of the contemporary neo-slave narrative, a genre that, according to recent studies by Elizabeth Ann Beaulieu and Ashraf H. A. Rushdy, has been a major development in African American fiction of the past three decades. Rushdy writes: 'Having fictional slave characters as narrators, subjects, or ancestral presences, the neo-slave narratives' major unifying feature is that they represent slavery as a historical phenomenon that has lasting cultural meaning and enduring social consequences' (Rushdy 1997, 533). In this essay, I shall analyse Marta Rojas' text as an historical novel that, like the neo-slave narrative, depicts the effects of chattel slavery on the social, cultural, and demographic development of Cuba; and that, like the generic romance, deconstructs and transforms Cuban history through the creation of originative myths that convey a transcendent vision of historical truths.

Santa lujuria o papeles de blanco, the second in a trilogy that examines the racial construction of Cuban society, is set in Cuba and Florida between the 1770s and 1820s, when the Spanish colony was undergoing a rapid social and economic transformation to a plantation society dependent upon slave labour. The cast of characters, including slaves, free Blacks, Creoles, Spanish noblemen, and European immigrants, reflects the racial and ethnic diversity of a colour-conscious population beset by racial tensions. The action of the novel focuses on the quest of the female protagonist, a woman of African descent, for greater social and economic mobility – both for herself and her biracial son – in an oppressive society that validates White skin colour and European family lineage. The protagonist's quest for self-realisation is set against a traumatic social and historical background: the burgeoning of Cuba's Black population, gender imbalance in the colony, sexual violence against Black women, revolution in Saint Domingue, fear of a Haitian-style revolution, slave rebellions in Cuba, and retaliatory violence against rebel leaders. Among the political and philosophical issues interrogated by Rojas in her fictional treatment of slavery are the social construction of race, class divisions, gender relations, European colonialism, and a market economy built on human exploitation.

In the same way that the neo-slave narratives of African American writers such as Ishmael Reed, Sherley Anne Williams, and Charles Johnson are shaped by their participation in the Black Power and Black Arts movements of the 1960s, so Marta Rojas' vision of history is forged by her personal and professional involvement in the Cuban Revolution of 1960, which challenged scholars and creative writers to deconstruct pre-revolutionary historiography – a cultural production that seldom acknowledged the contributions of Afro-Cubans to the forging of national identity and to the creation of a revolutionary ideology and praxis through their struggle for liberation and independence. If *Santa lujuria* has its genesis in historical texts, it is also indebted to nineteenth- and early twentieth-century Cuban literary works, including such narratives as Cirilo Villaverde's *Cecilia Valdés* (1879), Martín Morúa Delgado's *Sofía* (1891), Alejo Carpentier's *El reino de este mundo* (1933), and Reinaldo Arenas' *La loma del ángel* (1987) because Rojas' novel enters into intertextual dialogue with these earlier works, interrogating, challenging and transforming them through her own unique vision, style, and perspective.

One of the strengths of Rojas' novel is the delineation of character, which is central to the development of the theme of Cuban identity, an identity that is symbolised by the protagonist Lucila Mendes, who effects, through her roles as mother, religious leader, and culture bearer, the feminisation of Cuban history. Her role in articulating the social and political significance of *cubanidad* is apparent in her response to her son and his half-brother, who suggest that Cuba should be aligned, culturally and politically, with Europe or North America. Lucila protests, '[Y]o creo que como ustedes nacieron en Cuba y sus padres también, aquella es su tierra' (I think that, since you and your parents were born in Cuba, that is your country) (278). Intelligent, courageous, and resourceful, this biracial woman rises above her circumstances – her race, gender, and class – to take control of her life, to become the agent of her own destiny, and to reinvent herself as Doña Isabel de Flándes, a powerful, wealthy, and respected woman. Ironically, an act of dis-possession – of her name and identity – facilitates her social mobility. After seducing and impregnating the sixteen-year-old Lucila, Don Antonio, a Creole slaveowner, changes her name from Lucila to Isabel and her identity from mother to nursemaid. As I explained in the essay 'Name It and Claim It', nomination or the act of naming permits the name-giver to claim and to possess the territory of others, including the bodies of the enslaved. Don Antonio is fully aware of the relationship between nomination and possession. When his slave concubine objects to being called by the name of his former mistress, saying 'Yo no soy Isabel de Flandes, yo soy Caridad' (I am not Isabel de Flandes, I am Caridad), he responds, arrogantly and contemptuously, 'Eres lo que yo desee' (You are whatever I desire) (18). Although Lucila *permitted* herself to be renamed ('Se dejó nombrar por el marqués Isabel de Flandes' [31]), hers is not a passive act of submission, because she literally *becomes* Doña Isabel: the poor, illiterate, mulatto mistress becomes the wealthy, literate, white wife, partly through the efforts of men: her son taught her to read and write, and her husband bought the *papeles de blanco* that whitened her. A sign of her vertical mobility – from *parda* to *blanca,* from mistress to wife – is her horizontal movement from one geographic area to another. Born in Santiago de Cuba, she lives in Havana but moves to St Augustine, Florida, where she becomes a successful jewellery designer and merchant. This fictional representation of Lucila as an independent and financially secure woman is historically valid, as Jane Landers points out in *Black Society in Spanish Florida*: 'Once free, women of African descent in Florida . . . managed plantations, operated small businesses, litigated in the courts, and bought and sold property, including slaves' (144). Using her spiritual gifts and the knowledge obtained from her mother, Lucila also becomes a powerful leader in the Afro-Cuban community.

Lucila / Isabel is an idealised figure whose characterisation emanates from the Genteel Tradition, which depicts women as gentle, feminine, and lady-like; she has the regal bearing and courtly manners of a queen, as noted by one of the male characters: '[N]o era igual a las demás mujeres, a ninguna. "¡Es una reina! esa bendita dueña"' (She was not like other women, not a one. 'She is a queen! that blessed lady') (238). She is a messianic figure of considerable secular and spiritual power, as revealed in two significant episodes: first, as queen of the *cofradía* or Afro-Cuban socio-religious society, she leads the community in its celebration of the Fiesta del Día de los Reyes; second, she conducts the *santería* ceremonies (ritual baths, sacred meals, and rites of purification) that will elevate her son to the ranks of the Spanish nobility. Like her historic prototypes, María de la Luz Sánchez and Graciana Grajales, Lucila is committed to social and political reform; she manumits slaves, teaches them to read and write, and harbours rebel leaders. Although she passes from one racial category to another, thus gaining social respectability, Lucila's birth relegates her to an ambiguous status in colonial society: 'era y no era una señora según el canon social' (she was and she was not a lady according to the social canon) (278). She cannot attain the status and power of her son, now a Spanish grandee, but Lucila is the figurative Founding Mother of Cuba's upper class, for it is from her body that future generations of national leaders – the writers, municipal judges, and government officials – emerge. Through her characterisation of Lucila / Isabel, Marta Rojas demythologises Cuban history and creates a countermythology of Cuba's origin, for the myth of the Black Founding Mother offers a different version of reality, one that subverts 'official' history, according to which Cuba was founded by White, male Europeans whose social, economic, and political values shaped the new country.

While Lucila Mendes is, perhaps, the most complex and dynamic character in *Santa lujuria*, she, like most characters in historical romances, is a static figure who does not evolve psychologically. Indeed, many of the characters are archetypes who represent various aspects of Cuban identity: Lucila's slave mother, 'la negra Aborboleta', for example, is an ancestral figure who represents the personal and familial legacy of slavery, while Aborboleta's son José is a cultural hero (like Mackandal, Nat Turner, and Cinque), who proposes a revolutionary overthrow of the existing social and political order. The villain Don Antonio epitomises the worst traits of the Cuban Creole slaveocracy, their greed, arrogance, and lust. Both he and his son are fictional representations of historical figures, whom Marta Rojas discovered in books on Cuban genealogy; she even found the registration document that consigned Francisco Filomeno, the son of a free Black woman and Antonio Ponce de León, to an orphanage (Castañeda 11). The fictional Filomeno, however, does not end up in an orphanage; instead, he inherits his father's fortune and titles. Don Antonio's acts of sexual license and perversion – rape, adultery, pseudo-necrophilia, and semi-incest (sex with his wife's *hermana de leche*) – underscore the meaning of the novel's title. Indeed, the theme of unbridled male sexuality serves to unify this episodic novel: the theme is explicit in graphic descriptions of bacchanalia and in the use of religious language as sexual metaphors (thus, the adjective *Holy* Lust); it is also apparent in the book's title and cover – a painting 'Vasallo a caballo' (Vassal on Horseback) by Santiago Armada, which depicts, according to the novelist, a phallus-man who represents the erotic conquest of the West Indies.[4] In her feminist revision of history, Rojas demonstrates that the territorial conquest of the Americas was effected, in part, upon the bodies of African women who birthed the Bastard Son, women such as Aborboleta, Lucila, Caridad, María Luz, and the two *valetsas* impregnated by Filomeno. Like the biblical Prodigal Son or Joseph Campbell's mythic Hero, the Bastard Son – of African and European descent – is a figure who embodies the values, institutions, and history of his society. Francisco Filomeno, Lucila and Don Antonio's biracial son, known as the 'marquesito de color quebrado' (broken-coloured little marquis) represents that figure. A brilliant judge, linguist, and writer whose memoir serves as a contrapuntal narrative within the fictional text, Filomeno seeks whiteness for self-validation. He is, according to Cuban critic Daniel García Santos, the Michael Jackson of the nineteenth century (6). After the deaths of his White wife and son, Don Antonio, now without an heir, decides to whiten and legitimise his natural son through the purchase of papers that will change the boy's racial classification from *pardo* to *blanco*, allow him to inherit wealth and titles, and facilitate his ascension in colonial society.

The antithesis of Filomeno and Antonio and the most compelling male character is Lucila's slave brother José. Also an idealised and messianic figure, he is a revolutionary hero, an *ogboni* or religious leader, and a trickster who feigns madness to avoid execution. He is modelled after the historical José Antonio Aponte, member of a *lucumí* secret society and an Oni-Shangó with secular and spiritual powers, who led a Haitian-inspired conspiracy to abolish slavery and the slave trade in Cuba. The language of both José and Lucila reveals their conceptualisation as idealized archetypes. They are bilingual: in their daily lives, they speak an elegant and graceful 'castellano muy castizo' (very pure Castillian), but in the rituals of the *regla* (*santería* religion), they chant a pure and ancient *lucumí,* derived from the Yoruba people of West Africa. Their knowledge of *lucumí* language and customs – an example of what Robert Stepto calls 'tribal literacy' – demonstrates the significance of African culture in the formation of Cuban identity. As fictional characters, Lucila and José bear witness to the profound relationship between religion and language, a relationship that William W. Megenney skilfully analyses in the chapter 'El Lenguaje Bozal y su Papel en las Religiones Afrocubanas y Afrocaribeñas' from his book on Cuba and Brazil (37–46). In the novel, *el lenguaje bozal* functions as a sacred and hermetic linguistic code, facilitating communication between the initiated. Even Filomeno, the grandson of a Black slave, understands his ancestors' *lenguaje bozal,* but he disparages knowledge of a code that he despises: 'La traducción le hice yo, pues el trato obligado con ellos me permitió entender *ese lenguaje salvaje de tan mal gusto*' (I did the translation, because my obligatory dealings with them allowed me to understand that savage and tasteless language) (89, emphasis added). José reveals his dexterity in both languages in a long, first-person narrative in which he recounts the story of his capture and trial:

> '*Emo ya okua-ana kaaroso* (castigo sin compasión, mato al que se atreva a faltarme)', con voz de chirrido y falsete. Y más estridente aún, y a todo lo que daban sus pulmones: '*¡Egua mi laki! ¡Egua mi laki!* (háblame, háblame)' (249)

> ('*Emo ya okua-ana kaaroso* (I'll punish without compassion, I'll kill whoever dares offend me)', in a cracking, high-pitched voice.

And even more strident, and with the full force of his lungs, he shouted: '*Egua mi laki! Egua mi laki*! (speak to me, speak to me).')

Although an unlettered slave, his facility in Spanish is evident in his vocabulary (words such as 'chirrido' and 'estridente') and in his flawless use of the subjunctive and imperative modes ('se atreva' and 'háblame'). Significantly, none of the Afro-Cuban characters speaks the demotic language of the folk – the dialect of Nicolás Guillén's Vito Manué or of Alejo Carpentier's Menegildo. The only example of the vernacular language is the anonymous ditty sung by a slave: 'Centella que bá bené / yo sube arriba palo' (Lightnin' gonna come / I go run up the pole) (91). Thus, unlike the characters often depicted by the *negrista* and *afro-criollo* writers of the 1930s and '40s, there is nothing quaint, folksy, or picturesque about the free or enslaved Blacks in Rojas's novel. Their stylised diction and inflated language suggest that these humanised and civilised characters, like those in other historical romances, depict abstract concepts and ideal states of consciousness.

Although Creoles and Europeans are prominent in the cast of characters, Rojas' novel clearly focuses on Cubans of colour, who are described by language (*bozales* and *ladinos*), by degree of blackness and/or whiteness (*negros, pardos, morenos, mulatos, mulatos achinados, mestizos,* and *mestizos de negro e india*) and, finally, by status (*esclavos, cimarrones, coartados,* and *libertos*). Rojas' fictional depiction of Black Cuban society is corroborated by historical studies. As Franklin W. Knight points out in *Slave Society in Cuba*, Blacks were subjected to a strict caste system that privileged free people of colour over slaves, and urban over plantation slaves; slaves were further divided into *bozales* or 'negros de naciones', who spoke only their native African languages; *ladinos,* including *peninsulares* who spoke some Castillian; and *criollos,* who were born and raised in Cuba. Among the latter, Knight adds, status depended on colour, position, and wealth, but status could be enhanced through marriage or the purchase of prestigeous social or military positions. The multipicity of racial categories attests to the widespread bastardisation of Cuban society, a society in which *el derecho de bragueta* (law of the fly) was sanctioned by royal decree and was widely practised by the planter elite. Because there were fewer White women than men in the colonies,[5] as Rojas' novel indicates (for Antonio's dead wife Mercedes Criloche is the sole example), Creole aristocrats took – by law or force – Black women as slave concubines or mistresses of colour. When Antonio's slave Caridad refuses to have sex with him in his dead wife's bed, he notes that it is an 'acto de insumisión y franca rebeldía contra *el derecho de bragueta*' (act of insubmission and flagrant rebellion against the law of the fly) (15), and he threatens to take her child – *his property*, he stresses – away from her. In *Santa lujuria*, such unions produce many biracial offspring, including Lucila, Filomeno, Paloma, Graciano, and Juana, all of whom are examples of what scholars call the bastardization of Cuban colonial society.

From an historical point of view, one of the most interesting features of the novel is its portrait of the Afro-Cuban community, particularly those free, urban Blacks who worked as teachers, carpenters, musicians, tailors, masons, and blacksmiths in Havana, Santiago de Cuba, and St Augustine, Florida. Rojas' depiction of this group, their customs and lifestyles, is realistic and historically valid, but individuals become mythic representations of the values and aspirations of their community. Such fictional characters include Lucila's lover Miguel Villavicencio, the organist of Santiago's Cathedral; the mulatto teacher and poet Nicolás; painter Vicente Escobar; and Salvador Hierro, a *negro criollo*, whose *papeles de blanco* accord him a position in the Batallón de las Milicias Disciplinadas de Pardos y Morenos de La Habana, a position that gives him the right to wear a military uniform, to carry arms, and to be buried in church. These fictional characters have historical prototypes, whose lives have been documented by scholars. In his article on Blacks in Cuban education, for example, Salvador García Agüero discusses the contributions of seventeenth-century, Afro-Cuban teachers such as Lorenzo Menéndez and poet Juana Pastor, the earliest Black female voice in Cuban literary history. The population of free people of colour increased substantially as a result of miscegenation. According to Knight, there were about 36,000 free people of colour in Cuba in 1774, but that number more than tripled to 153,000 by 1841 (22). During that period, the number and percentage of Blacks (both slave and free) in the Cuban population increased rapidly; they made up 44 per cent of the Cuban population in 1775, but that percentage increased to 60 per cent by 1844, according to García Agüero (358).

Another phenomenon – the slave trade – contributed to what Knight calls the Africanisation of Cuba during the colonial period. The historian estimates that between 1790 and 1820 – roughly, the period of Rojas' novel – more than 385,000 enslaved Africans were brought to Cuba. In chapter five, Rojas captures the violence of that trade in human flesh by recounting the story of fifteen-year-old Jackín, an enslaved African princess, who was raped, impregnated, shared with another man, sold naked in Havana's slave market, and, finally, ripped apart by dogs when she tried to escape. Ironically, her story is told, through flashbacks, in the voice and from the point of view of her rapist, the pilot Francisco Cortés de Navia, ironically called 'Good

Angel'. This is one of the most graphic, dramatic, and skilfully crafted episodes in the novel, because it narrates the horrors of the Middle Passage, as these are experienced by an individual African woman.

The story of Jackín reveals the ways in which Marta Rojas contextualises history in *Santa lujuria* by creating complex, representative characters or archetypes, such as *la esclava* and *el negrero*, who enact their personal dramas against an historical background. The author creates the background or context through precise and detailed settings; descriptions of laws and customs of the period; and allusions to historical figures, dates, and events. Several scenes underscore the skill with which the novelist conveys a sense of time and place, while creating very different tones: the joy of the fiesta with its music, dances, and chants; the plaintive lament of the Georgia fugitives, whose slave songs convey their pain; and the humour of Isabel's first sexual encounter with her younger lover. In such scenes, Rojas uses wit, irony, word play, hyperbole, double entendres, and figures of speech for dramatic effect. One of the most humorous chapters in the book deals with Juana, a young, beautiful, and sexually inexperienced mulatto nun who nurses Filomeno back to health and, in the process, discovers the use of the male organ. Tongue in cheek, Rojas writes that both the nurse and her patient found that she had a talent: 'esa bendita disposición para el alivio del hombre' (that blessed aptitude for man's relief) (97). Like Reinaldo Arenas, she juxtaposes a twentieth-century, sensual and irreverent attitude toward sex against prudish, conservative, nineteenth-century sensibilities, to great humorous effect.

Rojas' witty and wicked bedroom scenes, like Shakespeare's comic interludes, leaven the more serious episodes that deal with war, independence, slavery, conspiracies, and executions. Throughout the novel, there are constant allusions to historical events of the period, including a slave rebellion in Oriente Province, a military uprising in Chile, and France's annexation of Catalonia. These events are buttressed by references to historical figures such as José Antonio Aponte and Simón Bolívar, José Bonaparte and Jean Lafitte, Queen María Luisa and Carlos IV of Spain. There is even a long passage dealing with the epistolary debate between Benjamin Banneker and Thomas Jefferson over the intelligence of Blacks. The specific dates of battles, invasions, and royal decrees also give authenticity and verisimilitude to this historical romance; according to the text, Blacks defended Havana against the English in 1763; there was a slave rebellion in Venezuela in 1795; and the king issued a decree on February 20, 1773, protecting fugitive slaves in Trinidad. From the point of view of its historicity, one of the most significant parts of the novel deals with Spanish colonial life in St Augustine, Florida, where Cuban colonists established contact with Seminole Indians and fugitive slaves from Georgia. Rojas explained that this section is based on vague memories of a half-day visit to St Augustine in the 1950s, Minnie Moore-Wilson's *The Seminoles of Florida* (1909), and material (pamphlets, maps, and census reports) sent to her by friends in the United States. A meticulous researcher and an avid reader of biographies and histories, Rojas is gifted with a prodigious memory for details, which enables her to capture the sights, sounds, and rhythms of a previous era.

Through its evocation of time and place and its creation of idealised and heroic characters, *Santa lujuria o papeles de blanco* transforms Cuban history into mythic fiction embodying cultural values – spirituality, independence, and desire for freedom – that are rooted in the Afro-Cuban experience. Dramatic events in the novel, such as the death of Jackín, escape of María Luz, and beheading of Salvador – events recorded in historical documents or related through oral narratives – acquire a symbolic or ideological significance, because they demonstrate the sexual and racial violence of a feudalistic society bent on the exploitation of human beings.

Notes

1. The contemporary literary discourse on slavery has produced such neo-slave narratives as Maryse Condé's *Moi, Tituba, Sorcière . . . Noire de Salem*, Caryl Phillips' *Cambridge*, Toni Morrison's *Beloved*, Manuel Zapata Olivella's *Changó el gran putas*, Sherley Anne Williams' *Dessa Rose*, Cubena's *Los nietos de Felicidad Dolores*, and Charles Johnson's *Middle Passage*.
2. In a note to the author dated 12 June 2000, Rojas explained: 'En cuanto a mi abuela, ella nació libre en el vientre. Aquí los españoles dictaron una Ley de Vientres Libres a finales de siglo y los hijos de esclavos nacían libres. Sus padres eran esclavos criollos, y los abuelos de mi abuela [eran] africanos'. (With respect to my grandmother, she was born free in the womb. The Spanish passed a Law of Free Wombs at the end of the century, and the children of slaves were born free. Her parents were Creole slaves, and the grandparents of my grandmother [were] Africans.)
3. For example, most North American historians viewed as outrageous the claim by the Hemings family – passed down, orally, from one generation to another – that they are the descendants of president Thomas Jefferson . . . that is, until scientific evidence substantiated their claim.
4. Marta Rojas wrote to the author on 9 June 2000: 'El nombre del pintor es Santiago Armada y firmaba Chago; era historietista (comic) diseñador, dibujante y pintor. Ese cuadro que se toma para la portada de mi libro se

llama "Vasallo a caballo" y a mi juicio no es un hombre sobre un falo sino un falo-hombre y la idea que él representaba fue el hecho de la conquista erótica de las Indias. El leía pedazos de mi novela cuando yo la pasaba en limpio en el periódico y un día me dijo que para él se simbolizaba plásticamente así. El murió poco después, a los 52 años de asma, y cuando le entregué el texto a la editora le enseñé el cuadro. Ya tenía idea de usar uno clásico "El Eros y Psiquis", cuya reproducción compré en un Museo de España, pero ella votó por "Vasallo a caballo' (The painter's name is Santiago Armada, known as Chago; he was a cartoonist, designer, sketcher, and painter. The canvas that is used on the cover of my book is called 'Vassal on Horeseback' and, in my opinion, it is not a man mounted on a phallus, but a phallus-man, and the idea that he represents is that of the erotic conquest of the Indies. Chago read parts of my novel when I was revising it at the newspaper office, and one day he told me what it symbolised visually for him. He died of asthma shortly afterwards, at age 52, and when I gave the book to my editor, I showed her the canvas. Previously, I thought of using a classical painting of 'Eros and Psyche', a reproduction of which I had bought in the Spanish Museum, but she voted for 'Vassal on Horseback'.)

5. Table 8 in Knight's *Slave Society in Cuba* indicates that in 1841, there were 227,144 White males but only 191, 147 White women in Cuba (86). The Black male population was almost twice that of females: 281,250 males to 155,245 females. In his *Biografía de un cimarrón*, Esteban Montejo reported that the result of the gender disparity was the appropriation of Black females by White males, who left Black men without sexual partners.

Works Cited

Beaulieu, Elizabeth Ann. *Black Women Writers and the American Neo-Slave Narrative: Femininity Unfettered*. Westport, Conn.: Greenwood Press, 1999.

Campbell, Jane. *Mythic Black Fiction: The Transformation of History*. Knoxville: The University of Tennessee Press, 1986.

Castañeda, Mireya. 'Lust for Identity'. *Granma Internacional* (April 1999): 11.

DeCosta-Willis, Miriam. 'Name It and Claim It: Ethnic Literature, Literary Criticism, and the Politics of Alterity'. Keynote Address. Afro-Hispanic Literature and Culture Conference. Magnolia, Arkansas, Fall 1993.

Elizalde, Rosa Miriam. 'Marta Rojas, Premio Nacional José Martí, "El periodismo es algo estrictamente personal"'. *Granma Internacional* (April 30, 1997): 3.

Moreno Fraginals, Manuel. *El ingenio: complejo económico social cubano del azúcar*. Havana: Editorial de Ciencias Sociales, 1978.

García Agüero, Salvador. 'Lorenzo Menéndez (o Meléndez) – El negro en la educación cubana'. *Revista Bimestre Cubana* (1937): 347-65.

García Santos, Daniel. "*Santa lujuria*, novela de Marta Rojas." *Juventud rebelde* (14 July 1999): 6.

Knight, Franklin W. *Slave Society in Cuba During the Nineteenth Century*. Madison: The University of Wisconsin Press, 1970.

Landers, Jane. *Black Society in Spanish Florida*. Urbana: University of Illinois Press, 1999.

Megenney, William W. *Cuba y Brazil: Etnohistoria del empleo religioso del lenguaje afroamericano*. Miami: Ediciones Universal, 1999.

Rojas, Marta. Letters to the author. Undated (ca. 1998), November 5, 1999, June 12, 2000.

___. *Santa lujuria o papeles de blanco*. Havana: Editorial Letras Cubanas, 1998.

Rushdy, Ashraf H. A. 'Neo-Slave Narrative'. In *The Oxford Companion to African American Literature*. Edited by William L. Andrews et al. New York: Oxford University Press, 1997.

___. *Neo-Slave Narratives: Studies in the Social Logic of a Literary Form*. New York: Oxford University Press, 1999.

Suardíaz, Luís, 'Marta Rojas, el trabajo es mi mejor premio'. *Granma* (February 22, 1997): 3.

Eulalia Bernard

E ULALIA B ERNARD

COSTA RICA

(b. 1935)

The daughter of Jamaicans who migrated to Costa Rica's Caribbean coast at the beginning of the 20th century, poet and essayist Eulalia Bernard Little writes in three languages: Spanish, English, and Mecatelio (mek-a-tel-yu), the Creole of Limón, the coastal province where most Blacks settled. When her first book, Ritmohéroe, *appeared in 1982, Bernard became the first Costa Rican woman of African descent to publish a collection of poetry. In his prologue to the book, novelist Quince Duncan writes that 'RhythmHero represents a milestone in the national literature' of their country. Her work also includes* Negritud *(1976), a recording of 27 poems which later appeared in print, and two other poetry collections:* My Black King *(1991) and the forthcoming* Ciénaga (Quagmire). *In her poetry, written in traditional forms, she uses humour, irony, and dramatic tension to treat themes such as the African cultural heritage, relationships between men and women, and the sociopolitical problems of poor Blacks. Noted as a performance artist who gives spirited readings of her verse, Bernard conveys the sounds and textures of the vernacular language, and she captures the rhythms of* afrocostarricense *music and dance. Bernard, a political activist and human rights advocate concerned about the status of Blacks and women, has expressed her militant views in lectures, essays, and conference papers such as 'Negritude, Women and Culture', 'Meditation for Reflection: Experiences of a Griot', 'New Essay on Existence and Political Freedom', and 'The Universality of Women's Culture: A Contribution of Caribbean Women Writers to the Demystification of Gender Roles'.*

Eulalia Bernard grew up in Puerto Limón (the capital of the province), the youngest of seven children born to Carolica Little Crosby, a teacher, and Cristopher Bernard Jackson, a tailor. After the untimely death of her father in the 1940s, she was sent to San José, where she obtained her primary education at the Colegio de Nuestra Señora de Sión, before returning to Limón to attend the Colegio Diurno. In 1972, Bernard obtained a bachelor's degree in English from the University of Costa Rica, and she has also studied at the University of Wales in England and at the Cêntre de Récherche Pédagogique at Bordeaux, France. An educator, diplomat, and television producer by profession, she has held a number of challenging posts, including cultural attaché to Jamaica, director of educational television programmes for the Ministry of Public Education, special delegate to the United Nations, and professor of English at the University of Costa Rica, where she introduced the first course in Black culture of the Americas.

As critics of her work have indicated, Bernard is an engagée *writer, who is committed to Black solidarity, race and gender equality, the deconstruction of racial stereotypes, and the revision of Costa Rican history to reflect the contributions of its indigenous and African-descended people. In poems such as 'Hymn to Jamaica', 'Antillean Essence', and 'Requiem for My Jamaican Cousin', she pays homage to the Black immigrants 'whose sweat germinated / a little piece of this land' through their labour in Limón's cocoa and banana plantations; and in the dedication to her first book, she writes:*

To my ancesters and their
descendants who have
contributed in forging
our homeland through love.

Now That I Am Yours Limón

Now yes for I am yours Limón
Now yes I dare to look at you
Now yes I dance in your teasing circle
Now yes I memorise the map of your scars
I carry in my hands vestiges of your history
I carry in my womb Jacobin revolutions
Now yes for I am yours Limón
Now that they venerate your old buildings
Now that your brothels are houses of culture:
afroindigenoushispanicjewishchinese;
Now that your men are no longer "roll-on-roll-off"
Now that your women are no longer flesh for ignorant sailors
I carry on my feet the long walks of bygone days
I carry in my eyes the torrent of your waters
Now yes for I am yours Limón
Like you I run to the sea and am renewed

Editor's translation

We

We the ones who long for other seas
We the ones who dream of other forests
We the ones who sense other gods
We are others here
We are others there
We are others.

We who see other seas
We who worship other gods
We who live in other forests
We are alone here
We are alone there
We are loneliness.

We who breathe other airs
We who intone other songs
We who invoke other gods
We live dead here
We die alive there
We are dead.

Loneliness!
You are ambushed in death.
Life!
You are ambushed in loneliness.
Death!
You are ambushed in life
We are ambushed.

Let's cut down those forests
Let's look for new seas
Let's invent our gods
Let's intone new songs
We are.

Editor's translation

What Fi Do?*

What a molote!
Look like a viaje to the moon,
This paseo to Portete.

Mary you ready ya?
The rice and beans ya está?
No forget the crocus bag . . . you hear?
Fi pick up the basura,
You understand? . . . after
The pachanga done.

Hie - jie! . . . What a basilón!
Me can't wait fi the time to come.
I hope the camión no broke down
And lef' we pan the ground.

That would be a big tirada.
No sa! . . . What fi do?! . . .
We going have a real basilón
Camión or no camión . . . and done!

* In Limón, Costa Rica, the people are bilingual and the language is a mixture of English and Spanish.

molote: *hubbub*
viaje: *trip*
paseo: *picnic*
Portete: *beach in Limón*
rice and beans: *typical dish*
ya está?: *Is it ready yet?*
crocus bag: *burlap sack*
basura: *garbage*
pachanga: *'live it up' time*
basilón: *hell of a good time*
camión: *bus*
tirada: *nuisance*

'Our Weapon Is Strong Language'
A Conversation With Eulalia Bernard

Shirley Jackson

A gifted writer, Eulalia Bernard is the first female griot of African descent in Latin America to be recognised by academics and government officials. I was first introduced to her work several years ago through a small volume of poetry entitled *Ritmohéroe,* which has since become a textbook in the Costa Rican school system. Little did I know then that I would subsequently have many opportunities to talk with the poet both in the United States and in Costa Rica. The conversation that appears below is derived from formal interviews and informal discussions that we had in person and over the telephone during a three-year period, which began in October 1995 and ended in March 1998. Many of our discussions took place while Bernard was writing an essay, 'Meditation for Reflection: Experiences of a Griot', which she presented at an international conference in Washington, DC in 1997 and which she published in her most recent book, *Griot* (1998).

SJ: In the poem 'Stupified Casualness' you wrote that your name is 'something Bernard'. Why did you write 'something' instead of Eulalia?

EB: I want to stress that Black names are not legitimate, historically speaking; they are anonymous, plantation names. 'Bernard' has French roots and is western. We can reject our names or we can accept and build on them.[1]

SJ: Being declared the 'Griot of the Americas' is very important to you. Why?

EB: All my life I have been fighting and writing about the importance of our African heritage. I am one of the first female poets in Latin America to do this.

SJ: In 'Meditation for Reflection: Experiences of a Griot',[2] you wrote: 'The griots are our guides on the journey. If we lose them, we experience great loss and suffering, becoming non-dialectical and non-dialectic. Let us follow the teachings of our griots and put diadems on their foreheads'. Tell me something more about these concepts.

EB: Griots are important people. We griots are preachers, who express the power of words. We have a verbal history. 'Nuestra arma es la palabra fuerte' [Our weapon is strong language].

SJ: Have you written any articles based on your research?

EB: My research is contained in my work.

SJ: The idea that human beings are made of stellar material is something that most astronomers now agree with. The beauty of your work lies in the fact that you remain true to your ancestors. Your poems image primal forces in unique ways that make the invisible concrete. Some of the ideas in 'Griot No. 2' remind me of this concept.[3] Explain the idea of woman as deity in the following poem:

I know that the gods
are revealing me;
They tell me to stretch my beauty.
They tell me that erection is perfection.
Love seeds the soil,
and brings forth yams of all colours. (8)

EB: The earth is the mythological Black Madonna, who brings yams to coloured people. *Yam* is the verb 'to eat' in Akan and African Costa Rican culture. Are you familiar with the Odirwa Festival?[4]

SJ: In the essay 'Meditation' you wrote: 'We use our water to clean and transport us to our gods'. What does 'water' mean, and what does it have to do with the ancestors?[5]

EB: Water is life, and life is wisdom. The griot, who cannot come without water, is also wisdom. I am here because of water. I pray over water. Semen is water.

SJ: Some cultures consider the night sky with its embedded stars as a symbol of fertility; the black sky represents the female's womb and the stars represent the male's semen. Do you have this concept in Afro-Costa Rican culture? Are there any folkloric stories related to these ideas?[6]

EB: The Anansi stories are not very clearly compiled, because the collectors have left out the meaning.

SJ: In 'Meditation', you also wrote: 'We have the knowledge of the four elements of nature. We catch the balls and fix them in the air as we wish, when we wish'. What do you mean by this?

EB: 'Balls' refers to basketball, negritude balls, and my ball. I am working to reclaim the balls: the male testicles of knowledge. We are called *raro* [strange or weird] by Whites. In the article about me in *La República*, the Whites portray us as not having anything. They say,

'The thing is that they – Black Costa Ricans – are different'. I am considered a strange person because I write in English and Spanish. But I am not strange; I am talented. They like to say that Black men are weird and don't have balls. But we have to look at the inner movement, the spirit that cannot be captured and put into missiles.

SJ: What did you mean in 'Meditation' when you wrote: 'We do not immigrate; we rotate'.

EB: We are moving, rotating like the planets. We are global because our genes are everywhere, and we can recognise our people by their physical features. Blacks were the first people spoken about in ancient history. We explored the world – America and other places. Slavery also globalised our people.

SJ: Can you elaborate more on the relationship between music and globilisation.

EB: The whole idea of globalisation is ironic, politically. Technology is static, but art is dynamic. Today, rap music is more technology than art. When it first started, rap was art: the lyrics were direct, rhythmical, and aggressive. The rapper's language is powerful and focused. But rap, like reggae, was diminished by the vulgarity and the rappers' conduct. Rap in church. Don't throw it away; use it as a political platform. The form of rap is very African; Anansi stories and proverbs, for example, are rap art forms.

SJ: You have said that you are very political.

EB: I am very political.

SJ: Did your parents fuel your activism in any way?

EB: My mother and father were Maroons. My father and my godfather marooned to Cuba. I am a Maroon. Remember Nzinga?[7] My history goes way back to Africa. I am an Akan.[8]

SJ: What would you like people to know about your political activism?

EB: Open spaces!

SJ: What do you mean by 'open spaces'? Does this have anything to do with the fact that your father was a tailor?

EB: [Smiles.] I can do a lot of patchwork: mental patchwork with a purpose. In the campaign, I had to run hard.

SJ: What were you campaigning for?

EB: I ran for vice president of the Partido Liberal Nacional – something that had never before happened in Limón.[9] I made the Whites understand that we Blacks are not invisible or hidden, that we want a piece of the pie that we paid for four hundred years ago.[10] I want people to see me as a national political figure; I don't want them to ghettoise me as a leader of Blacks from a particular district. People need leaders, not just Black leaders from Limón or some other distsrict. I tell the young people of Limón that if they can't find what they need here, then leave!

SJ: What can you add about your political life?

EB: I always have a goal and a plan for my people. I want to be valued, to help break down racial stereotypes based on the way we speak or move. Rhythm, for example, is valued by Blacks, just as sports are valued by White people. Rhythm is not something to caricaturise. I dance my poetry. I am rhythmical.

SJ: Tell me more about rhythm.

EB: Rhythm – not the colour of the skin – is the essence of Africanness. You can be white as hell but, if you have the genes, that rhythm is going to come out even if you dance Russian ballet. We are the only race that has rhythm. See the way we walk. It is not that we walk slowly. We are not lazy. Whites call our rhythm lazy. They call us *indulgente* and *perezoso* [lazy], but we are not lazy.

SJ: What are your thoughts on language?

EB: We have not lost our intonation, which is very African. African Americans, for example, speak an African language with English sounds and structure. The Creole language, which is the oldest and newest thing we have, is rich, rhythmical, and fascinating. In Haiti, Limón, and Jamaica, we speak with such freedom. Creole poems, which are not dry, are rooted in the way our people see the world. Whites, on the other hand, lost their Creole language, which became homogeneous without any distinguishing features.

SJ: Costa Rica is really beautiful; it is considered to be an ecological paradise in Central America. There is clear air. There is sun. How does the climate affect your work?

EB: I'm a very urban person. When I say 'urban' I don't mean that exclusively because there is a lot of nostalgia for the ecosystem in my poetry. I did the first television programme on ecology, showing that Limón was a province where people had preserved nature in its purest form. No one had to tell Black Limonese to do this, because they love nature. In Limón every house has trees. My mother planted a tree for each child who was born. Mine is a *salsa* tree, and that tree appears in my poems.

SJ: You are very creative in your dress, and you have a keen sense of design. Is that because of your father, who was a tailor?

EB: I like to be seen, not hidden.

SJ: You also wear your hair in the traditional African style.[11] When I was in Johannesburg, South Africa, I saw African women with traditional hair styles like yours, working in the Holiday Inn. I also saw Luo women and children living on the remote island of Mboko in the Winan Gulf area of Lake Nyanza (Lake Victoria) at the source of the Nile River, wearing their hair like yours. Is your short hair style something recent?

EB: I was the first Black woman in Costa Rica to wear my hair like this.

SJ: When did you start wearing your hair in this style?

EB: In the early 1970s, when people said, 'She won't comb her hair'. Whites now wear this style too, but of course their hair is different. My hair is easy to comb in the morning, and I don't use hair spray. I'm getting ready to travel soon, and I have an easy hair style that looks nice. My mother wore her hair natural; she parted it in the middle and braided it to the back. This modern style is more eye-catching and flattering to the face.

SJ: I remember your saying that you dress for Black men. Why?

EB: It is important for us to remember our origins, our mothers, and, particularly, Black men.

SJ: You have said that you are a mother, but what does 'mother' mean to you?

EB: I use 'mother' in the tribal sense. You have children, so you are a mother. I am a mother to all children.

SJ: Tell me more about your mother.

EB: My mother was an extraordinary woman!

Notes

1. For a fuller explanation of the importance of names in traditional African societies, see chapters one and three in Hehi Metu Ra Enkamit's *African Names*.

2. This essay was written for the International Cultural Conference on Africa and the Diaspora, sponsored by the Foreign Language Research Council on Africa and the Diaspora, during the gala celebration at the Hyatt Regency Hotel in Washington, DC on Saturday, May 3, 1997. The Research Council has since expanded its mission to include interdisciplinary topics and currently carries the name 'Research Council of Languages and Cultures in Africa and the Diaspora: Origin, Influence & Legacy'.

3. The poem, 'Griot No. 2', was written for the International Cultural Conference: Africa & the Diaspora, and it was completed on April 8, 1997.

4. For more information on traditional festivals in Africa, see R. S. Rattrag's *African Cultures in Religion and Art in Ashanti.*
5. In his *Introduction to African Religions,* John S. Mbiti explains the meaning of water in traditional African cultures.
6. Information on African Costa Rican culture can be obtained from Carlos Meléndez and Quince Duncan's *El negro en Costa Rica.* See also *Light from Ancient Africa* by Na'im Akbar, *Foundations of African Thought* by Chukwunyere Kamalu, and *African Philosophy* by Albert Mosely.
7. For many years, the African queen Nzingha and her troops resisted efforts of the Portuguese to bring Angola under colonial rule. For a more detailed description of Queen Nzingha, see 'African Warrior Queens' by John Henrik Clarke.
8. Eulalia Bernard traces her ancestry back to the Akan people of Ghana, West Africa. Tradition has it that Nyame, the first Queen Mother of the Akan, is a spiritual force who came to earth after being separated from a spiritual portion of the moon in our solar system. See Eva L. R. Meyerowitz's *The Akan of Ghana* and Muata Abhaya Ashby's *The Hidden Properties of Matter.*
9. Bernard is referring to the National Liberation Party elections held in Costa Rica from November 1997 to January 1998.
10. In July 1996, the newspaper *La Republica* ran a series of articles on the political discord between residents of Limón province and the Costa Rican government. Bryce-LaPorte and Trevor Purcell also present an historical overview of the current situation of Blacks in Costa Rican society in 'A Lesser-Known Chapter of the African Diaspora: West Indians in Costa Rica, Central America'.
11. For a photograph of Eulalia Bernard wearing the traditional African hairstyle, see the back cover of the first edition of *Ritmohéroe.*

Works Cited

Akbar, Na'im. *Light from Ancient Africa.* Tallahassee: Mind Productions, 1994.
Ashby, Muata Abhaya. *The Hidden Properties of Matter.* Miami: Cruzan Mystic Books, 1996.
Bernard, Eulalia. *Griot.* San José, Costa Rica: Adventist Foundation, 1998.
___. *My Black King.* Eugene, Oregon: World Peace University, 1991.
___. *Ritmohéroe.* San José, Costa Rica: Editorial Costa Rica, 1982.
Bryce-LaPorte and Trevor Purcell. 'A Lesser-Known Chapter of the African Diaspora: West Indians in Costa Rica, Central America'. In *Global Dimensions of the African Diaspora.* Edited by Joseph E. Harris, 137-157. Washington, DC: Howard University Press, 1993.
Clarke, John Henrik. 'African Warrior Queens'. In *Black Women in Antiquity.* Edited by Ivan Van Sertima. New Brunswick: Transaction Publishers, 1992.
Enkamit, Hehi Metu Ra. *African Names.* Washington, D. C.: Ser Ap-Uat Press, 1993.
Kamalu, Chukwunyere. *Foundations of African Thought.* London: Karnak House, 1990.

Mbiti, John S. *Introduction to African Religions*. Oxford: Heinemann, 1991.

Meléndez, Carlos and Quince Duncan. *El negro en Costa Rica*. San José: Editorial Costa Rica, 1993.

Meyerowitz, Eva L. R. *The Akan of Ghana: Their Ancient Beliefs*. London: Faber & Faber, 1958.

Mosely, Albert G. *African Philosophy: Selected Readings*. Englewood Cliffs, N.J.: Prentice Hall, 1995.

Rattrag, R. S. *African Cultures in Religion and Art in Ashanti*. New York: Oxford University Press, 1969.

Eulalia Bernard: A Caribbean Woman Writer and the Dynamics of Liberation

Ian I. Smart

The burgeoning West Indian Central American literature accords a special respect and recognition to women's special role as leaders, consistent not only with all other West Indian literature, but with the essential tenor of African cultures and civilizations. There appears, however, a gap between theory and practice as the proclaimers of woman's greatness are primarily men.[1] The question that must be posed is whether this gap springs from an internal contradiction – hypocrisy – or from an internal one, i.e., historical forces entirely beyond the control of West Indian Central Americans, a nondominant ethnolinguistic minority group (black West Indians, a majority group in their respective territories and Islands, have only recently begun to take control of their societies). This paper examines the theme of liberation in the work of Eulalia Bernard for an answer to this question.

In his introduction to Bernard's first book, *Ritmohéroe*,[2] Quince Duncan asserts: "El papel de la mujer se agiganta en todas las culturas en que la tierra es la base de la economia" (18). Cheikh Anta Diop, the renowned Senegalese scientist, historian, Egyptologist, and thinker, suggests that the especially important role women have enjoyed in African societies is the result of their discovering and harnessing of agriculture. In support of his claim, Diop cites the predominance of matriarchal systems as "characterized by the collaboration and harmonious flowering of both sexes, and by a certain preeminence of women in society, due originally to economic conditions, but accepted and even defended by man."[3] Further supporting evidence lies in the fact that whereas there has been an "absence of queens in Greek, Roman, or Persian history… In contrast during those epochs, queens were frequent in Black Africa." Along with the example of Queen Candace of Meroitic Sudan, who resisted the colonizing armies of Augustus Caesar,[4] there are those of the Ashanti Queen Yaa Asantewa and Queen Nzinga of Ndongo-Matamba, symbols of resistance to the British and Portuguese respectively (Diop 143).

Strong, black women enjoy a preeminent role in the fictive universe created by novelists as a mirror of Caribbean society. Literary historians consider Jamaican H.B. DeLisser's *Jane's Career* (1913), the first important Caribbean novel. It is the first regional novel to portray a native black (and in this case, a woman), as the central protagonist. Claude McKay's *Banana Bottom* (1933) is perhaps the second most important of the pioneer Caribbean novels. Again in this novel, the chief protagonist is a black woman of rural origin.

West Indian literature continues this trend which is, in part if not in whole, attributable to its culture's historical roots deeply planted in African culture and civilization. One need only think of Mrs. Rouse in the pivotal *Minty Alley* (1936) by the Trinidadian C.L.R. James; the mother figure in Barbadian George Lamming's *In the Castle of My Skin* (1953); the corresponding grandmother figures: M'man Tine of the Martinican Joseph Zobel's *La Rue cases-negres* (1950); or Miss 'Mando of *The Harder They Come* (1980) by the Jamaican Michael Thelwell. In Cubena's universe the dominant figure is Nenen, a principal source of inspiration to Cubena as artist and as human being. These powerful women are not isolated cases in either fiction of the real world of West Indian life. It is difficult to think of any fictional female characters who do not correspond to these patterns of preeminence.

Central American West Indian literature creates a fictional universe populated by tenacious black women in effective leadership roles. In Duncan's two most important novels, the female protagonists are of equal, if not greater, importance vis-a-vis their male partners. In *La paz del pueblo*, it is Sitaira who has the last word: a laugh of profound satisfaction that wells up from her watery, final resting place. Although Lorena of *Los cuatro espejos* dies early in the course of the novel, it is her death that triggers all of the action. Thus she becomes the central character. There are many other examples of strong female protagonists in Caribbean literature. Among them we could also cite the names of La señora Mariot of *La paz del pueblo*, or Mama Bull of both this novel and the short story, "La rebelión pocomía," or Tidam Frenchi from Cubena's powerful first novel, *Chombo*.

Eulalia Bernard's artistic activity, like that of the other Central American West Indian writers, makes a statement about the fundamental existential enterprise of the "tribe" or ethnolinguistic minority group, namely, the process of adjustment to the host environment. This adjustment is basically a process of liberation from the constraints attending any dominated minority group.

Bernard's book begins and ends with poetic pieces, "Seamos libres" and "Nosotros" respectively, that define her vision of liberation. The first of these poems starts with a bald negation, a "¡No!" that indicates the poet's conscious rejection and hence free choice. What the poet opts for is absolute self-generosity in a heterosexual relationship. Such generosity unhesitatingly and unstintingly practiced on her part, seems to elicit a free flow of mutual self-giving that she likens to the rush of waters flowing from the opened gates of a canal lock (certainly the Panama Canal contributed to the creation of this image). The poem is characteristically brief, and reads:

> ¡No!, no me hables así
> desvela tu cuerpo
> ¡No!, no busques excusas
> por tu ausencia, tus defectos;
> abracémonos como las esclusas y
> dejemos el agua expelida
> correr libremente
> por el canal de la vida
> ¡Seamos amigos
> seamos libremente amigos! (23)

Leaving aside any bitter recriminations, the persona proclaims that generous, sensual self-giving is the sure path to liberation in male-female relationships.

The term "nosotros" that constitutes the title of Bernard's closing poem has the narrowly private and eminently romantic acceptance of "you and me." However, in this poem it is given the sense of "all of us," both men and women, and not "nosotras" a distinctly feminist code word. The sense of the poem is then quite clear and complements "Seamos libres." Bernard's social concerns are not gender-based, but group- and race-based. "Pressed to the wall" by all of the pressures attendant on any dominated culture, the group must not "lay down and die," but triumph by "fighting back" with its cultural resources. This is the vigorous summons issued in the final three lines of the poem: "Forjemos nuestros dioses / Entonemos frescos cantares / Nosotros somos" (92). There are resounding echoes of Cubena's vigorous self-assertion in *Chombo*[5] or Gerardo Maloney's summons at the end of his "Elaborando nuestros nombres," "...has heredado un nombre / despierta y fórjalo en hombre." [6] The "tribe" will only survive by pulling together, liberation is "black" or "West Indian," not "woman's."

The poem "Equilibrio" focuses squarely on the physical aspects of love between man and woman. The persona's sentiments are consistent with those expressed in "Seamos libres," the poem in its entirety reads:

Entró en mi
de repente;
el equilibro buscado
en mi cuerpo
con tu cuerpo,
en mi mente
con tu mente.

Yo me icé,
tú descendiste
y, nos equilibramos
en perfecto amor. (53)

Perfect love, as a real possibility, is seen as a harmonious balance that evolves from the complete giving of body and mind through lovemaking. In "Cariño," the persona's sentiments appear to carry the self-giving to extreme self-abasement – the role stereotypically ascribed to women. It begins with the invitation: "Entra; acomódate; / quítate los zapatos;" (58). This self-sacrificing maternalism could be seen as a manifestation of vulnerable tenderness; vulnerability is human. Note, moreover, that the persona expects her partner to accept his own vulnerability unashamedly. The poem ends not on a note of feminine vulnerability, but rather of superiority: "yo te cuidaré; / toda la tarde, toda la noche; / todo el tiempo…" (58). Superhuman strength flows from this generous, unhesitating giving; giving the poet establishes as a precondition for liberation.

The poet makes it clear that liberation is not license, for the precondition is always some form of ascesis. This is the message of "¡Soy del gremio!" the opening stanza expresses an awareness of, and a strong attraction to, nature.

¡La atmósfera!, sí
Era algo quizá como
un despertar rodeado de dioses.
que cantaban, sin encerrar
egoísmo en sus voces (25)

The persona's response is an automatic: "y, yo, ¡sí! yo, sentí la gana / de ¡saltar de la cama / a la fiesta de la mañana!" This sense of freedom is specious, however. To its alluring call she answers firmly in the final couplet:

"Pero, no pude. /Soy del gremio!" (26). Reason prevails, liberation comes through a committed course of action in solidarity with the group.

The facets of the theme of liberation that surface in Bernard's poetry are the same as those in the work of other Caribbean poets. [7] Her identity is militantly West Indian, as she proclaims in "Esencia antillana." Each of the three stanzas of this work begins with a "¡No!" that resoundingly declares the poet's conscious and deliberate rejection of the logic of colonization, her intelligent acceptance of, and commitment to, the group's cultural heritage. The fnal verse proclaims:

¡No! Antillano,
Necio eres si enterrar
tu etnia prefieres,
que tus ojos, tu pelo, tú,
en esencia, eres
Antillano. (50)

The vision of the West Indian group, exiled in a foreign land and caught up once more in a new plantation existence, is given expression in "Requiem a mi primo jamaiquino":

Su sudor germinó
un pedacito de esta tierra
inhóspita y fertil del trópico
que no será nunca tierra patria
pues cedularse jamás pudo
mi primo jamaiquino. (35-6)

In poems like "Carbúnculo" and "Infancia alegre," Bernard's nostalgia for childhood compares with Duncan's in his collection, *Una canción en la madrugada*. And in "Revoltijo," the poetic possiblities of the daily realities of West Indian life are sensitively woven into the fabric of art. In this sense Bernard's work closely resembles that of Cubena, Maloney, and Duncan. The following verse, for example, celebrates some of these "little things" of daily existence:

¡Oló! que no falten los patacones,
un poco de macarrones, con salsa
china y como postre
un "pan bun" no caería mal. (72)

A somewhat similar listing of cherished childhood memories presented in "Infancia alegre" includes: "Gustaba escoger arroz, / dejar lo sucio afuera" (47). The "escoger" seems a literal translation of the West Indian English expression "to pick rice," meaning to clean it. This linguistic peculiarity, a feature of West Indian culture and literature, is responsible for puns such as this one from "Himno a Jamaica": "Jamaica / 'akee', 'akee', / aquí pa'mí' 'pattie', 'pattie,' / allá pa'ti" (88). Ackee and patty are two particularly important food items in Jamaican culture.

Religion also plays an important part in the Caribbean struggle for liberation[8] which explains the importance of the religious theme in Duncan's work.[9] In her "Y el negro rezó," for example, Bernard's poem begins with: "Y el negro rezó / pero Jesus no lo oyó" (81). Midway through the poem the *negro* radically changes his approach: "el negro no más rezó / el negro el fusil tomó" (81). The dramatic result given in the lines following is: "el negro habló y habló / Jesús lo oyó" (82). The poem recalls Nicolás Guillén's "Sabas" in its call to vigorous action to redress the wrongs of oppression. Bernard, however, cleverly manages to castigate the official church and coopt it into the struggle.

Eulalia Bernard's poetic stance on the question of liberation appears to betray no gender-based conflict. Both as a woman and as an artist she is harmoniously integrated into her group. She thereby further indicts the group's oppressors, exonerates its artists, and further advances the cause of its liberation.

Notes

1. The principal figures of the new Central American West Indian literature are: Quince Duncan from Costa Rica and the Panamanians Carlos G. Wilson (Cubena) and Gerardo Maloney. I shall make reference to the following works by Duncan: *Una canción en la madrugada* (San José: Ed. Costa Rica, 1970); his first collection of short stories: *La rebelión pocomía y otros relatos* (San José: Ed. Costa Rica, 1976); his latest collection of short stories; and two of his novels, *Los cuatro espejos* (San José: Ed. Costa Rica, 1973); and *La paz del pueblo* (San José: Ed. Costa Rica, 1978). Specific reference is also made to the following novel by Cubena, *Chombo* (Miami: Ed. Universal, 1981).

2. Eulalia Bernard, *Ritmohéroe* (San José: Ed. Costa Rica, 1982). Prior to the release of this work, Bernard's poetry was available in the US principally on an LP recording.

3. Cheikh Anta Diop, *The African Origin of Civili:ation*, ed. Mercer Cook (New York: Hill, 1974) 145.

4. See John G, Jackson, *Introduction to African Civilizations* (Secaucus, New Jersey: Citadel, 1970) 32 and Chancellor Williams, *The Destruction of Black Civilization* (Chicago: Third World P, 1976).

5. See Ian Smart, *Central American Writers of West Indian Origin: A New Hispanic Literature* (Washington, D,C: Three Continents P, 1984) 69-79.

6   This poem, along with three others, was published in a special issue of the Panamanian journal *Revista Nacional de Cultura 5* (1976), 102.

7. See Smart, 87-108.

8. Consider the Sam Sharpe and Paul Bogle rebellions in Jamaica, Voodoo's role in the Haitian revolution, and the current Rastafarian movement in Jamaica and the entire Caribbean region.

9. See Smart, 51-64.

Georgina Herrera

GEORGINA HERRERA

CUBA

(b. 1936)

Although she grew up in the provincial town of Jovellanos, where the* *literary talents of poor Black girls were seldom recognised or nurtured,* *Georgina Herrera began writing while quite young and published her* *first poems in Havana periodicals, including* El País *and* Diario de la* *Tarde, when she was only sixteen. Many of her later poems capture the* *pain and loneliness of her growing-up years: the poverty ('Our family* *was so poor. / So poor / that there was never enough for a photograph'),* *the despair of a loveless home, her absent father, her mother's death* *when Georgina was fourteen. In 1956 – three years before the Cuban* *Revolution – Herrera moved to Havana, where she worked as a domestic;* *in the home of her wealthy employees she met writers who encouraged* *her to publish and take courses. Although she took a course or two,* *including one in typing that enabled her to get a job with a radio station,* *Herrera had little formal education and, as a writer, was primarily self-* *taught. In 1962, through the support of writers associated with* El Puente* *publishing house, she produced her first collection of poems* G. H., *which* *took its title from her initials. During that period, she married novelist* *Manolo Granados (whom she would later divorce) and had two children:* *Ignacio Teodoro, who became a poet, and Anaísa, who was killed in a* *car accident in 1992. After the birth of her children, motherhood* *became a central theme in Herrera's work, particularly the poems in* *Gentes y cosas (People and Things), published in 1974, and* Granos* *de sol y luna (Grains of Sun and Moon), a 1978 publication. The* *poems that deal with her own mother, however, poems such as 'Mami'* *and 'Family Fear', explore the complexities and difficulties of a* *relationship fraught with fear, anxiety, and regret – regret for words* *unspoken and feelings unexpressed.*

Characterised as a poet of the post-revolution, Herrera's work is remarkably free of the ideological rhetoric that marks so much of her generation's poetry. With her 'shy poetic voice', as Eliseo Diego describes it, she strives for clarity and precision in language, concision in thought and image, and a fluid, lyrical style that is deceptively simple. Although her Golpeando la memoria *(Striking Memory), which includes autobiographical pieces about the life of a poor village girl, was never published, poems from the collection appeared in other works, such as* Grande es el tiempo *(Great is Time), 1989, and* Gustadas sensaciones *(Delicious Feelings), 1997. Some of her most powerful poems are those in which she affirms her identity— and, by extension, that of all Black Cuban women – as a woman of African descent. In 'First Time in Front of a Mirror', she sees her own face in the terracotta mask of an African woman, and in 'Ibu Sedi', a poem about Yemayá's daughter, she writes, 'I never forget / who I am, from whence I came, to whom I'm indebted'. Presently, she is working on* Siete mujeres, *a collection of poems about seven women of African origin, as well as an anthology of poetry about women. She is also completing a book of children's stories entitled* ¿Quién quiere vender los gallos del Señor Gallero? *(Who Wants to Sell the Farmer's Roosters?). Her poetry has been translated into several languages and anthologised in Margaret Randall's* Breaking the Silences *and Margaret Busby's* Daughters of Africa. *A member of the National Council of UNEAC and president of the Radio Section of the Cuban Association of Film, Radio and Television, Herrera has written novels, short stories, and plays for radio. At one time, she was affiliated with the editorial office of* La Unidad, *and she presently works as a scriptwriter for the Cuban Institute for Radio and Television.*

---

* Poet Nancy Morejón wrote to the editor: 'Jovellanos is a town near Matanzas whose population was predominantly Black because of slaves who settled there even before the formal abolition of slavery. So its nickname was Bemba'.

Street of the Women of the World

On the other side of that line, up the hill,
we couldn't walk.
The decent ones, or those
who passed for such till one learned otherwise,
switched direction, expression,
everything, at the mere mention of that street.
The fact that it bore the name
of a general in an old war
didn't mitigate the shame.
To pronounce 'Calixto García'
in any house in my village
was like calling on the devil.
Risking a bit
I'd say
it was like mentioning the noose
in the hangman's house.
And Calixto García couldn't even
really be called a street. It was a rutted road
where you ran into piles of old wood
pretending to be walls,
roofs, floors.
But as I was saying, Calixto García,
street or road, from where it began
down by the tracks
to where the village was no longer village
was the street of the 'women of the world'.
Ladies like no others, those women
sat or leaned against a wall,
simple women, waiting to trade
one moment of the habitual rigidity
of those who came
looking for something more
than the passive formality

always on hand at home,
nothing to do with love
in those village customs.
By memory's light, because my eyes
have lost them, let me introduce
those women: formal, refined, serious,
women who gave more than they got
in that daily buying and selling
as one could.
Out of my memory they appear on this paper,
speaking of that difficult time, long as an era
May they all be blessedly remembered
always.

Translated by Margaret Randall

First Time in Front of a Mirror
(On observing an excavated head, *Olokum walode ife*, made of clay)

Someone says that
this is not the face I see,
that it is not I in front of the mirror,
clearer, recognising myself?

Or . . . making this head again?
What I see
I am, a thousand years back, or more:
claiming my right.
My hand passes from that face to mine
that is only one, and two.
It ascends, gropes
the holy chin,
the spacious mouth. Yes,
with ample space, so that a single kiss
suffices
to ask a blessing from the wind,
the earth, the fire, the mist.
Now my hand touches the nose.
From one side to the other of this face,
the two.
That nose . . . my God; in the meadow
for me only, what they call the Universe,
where I do as I please
trapping fragrances.
Scent of fire, storm,
earth and water joined,
scent of love, unending life
enters through it;
total nourishment for my blood.
My hand, at last, reaches the extreme point
of both faces:
the cheeks, the forehead. I caress

just a little lower until I find the eyes.
I look as they stare at me.
Incredible eyes
where sadness extinguishes and revives the flames.
I am. Mirror or born again.
I am.

Translated by Linda S. Howe

Ibu Sedi

In my ancestors' language
I say everything
that my Only Mother wishes.
From Abeckuta, *where*
that deceivingly flaccid woman was born,
as Olosí,
I was chosen to speak.
Among many of my relatives' heads
she searched out mine, put her hand on it and said:
'You are lucumisa'.
From her mouth all
the stars in the sky spoke in the name
of Abolá. *She, the one*
who wears a silver chain on her ankles.
Omi Sande *calls me.*
I am her daughter, legitimate.
Her voice here, her noises,
her movement like irumí,
her acho ayiri.
I make my way slowly toward
the gourd of water that no one sees or cares about.
She puts it on my head for my own sake, and it suffices.
I'm indebted to her.
I name her seven times
with her seven names;
after which I say:
'Ororó irawá, *morning dew', and always*
she envelops me, as if she were
oyá bá soró,
and she makes iré aye *on my cheeks*
so that I never forget
who I am, from whence I came, to whom I'm indebted.
I call her again and she comes

from the depths of the oceans.
She comes, takes what I offer her.
She gently blesses me, slowly,
with branches from the ifefe *and* okableba; *I have*
iresi *until my dying day.*

Translated by Linda S. Howe

Glossary

Abeckuta: land of Yemayá, goddess of the sea; a hill in Africa; the name of a *lucumí* king.
Abolá: female saint; one who rules.
acho ayiri: blue clothes.
ifefé: rush.
iré aya: a tattoo the *lucumí* wear on their cheeks.
iresí: great luck; a big star.
irumi: movement of water.
lucumisa: feminine for *lucumí*, a Yoruba in Cuba.
okableba: corn.
Olosí: principal woman.
Omi Sande: daughter of Yemayá.
oyá bá soró: falling rain.

'The Lion's Version of the Jungle'
A Conversation with Georgina Herrera

Linda S. Howe

LH: Do you remember when you published your first poems?

GH: The first poems appeared in 1952 and 1953.

LG: Approximately how many poems did you publish?

GH: Well, I published only a few, because I lived inland. I lived in Jovellanos, a tiny village in Matanzas. In those days, it wasn't easy to send poems to Havana. I sent poems four times before coming to live in Havana, and every time I sent something they published it.

LH: What kind of poetry did you publish?

GH: Oh, the first poem that I published was a very sad, deep poem called 'Green Branch'. It was very reflective. It goes like this:

> An enravished mother rocks her beloved son in his little cradle. The afternoon breeze gently sways the branch on high to the drowsy lullaby of the green leaves. In their mute and sad language, they bend in search of something that vanishes into the earth. Do those green branches by chance bend their leaves to the ground seeking comprehension or tenderness, love, comfort for those who don't understand or love each other? There is so little tenderness in this world . . .

I was about sixteen. We had no reading habits in my house. We were poor people. I don't like to speak about my poverty, because nowadays everyone is so proud that they were poor, even those who were not. Now, everyone wants to be poor. I prefer not to talk about it, but we were very poor. In my house, no one knew what books were, nothing of the sort. Nevertheless, at school, my teacher, the school principal, took my hand one day and said, 'Child, come here. Whose work are you plagiarising?' She couldn't understand how I could use such unusual words at my age. Later, all the teachers became my good friends and great admirers of my poetry. I had a poetry notebook, which was a common thing to have. The other girls wanted my notebook because everyone copied from it, but I wrote my own poems.

LH: Were you recognised as a poet before moving to Havana? As a local poet at least?

GH: No. Well, one day when we were pledging allegiance to the flag, the principal said, 'Here is a future poet with great potential'. Just imagine, that's the way I started. I didn't really take it seriously, because I had no reason to be a poet. There was no literary ambience around me; there was no literary movement or anything of the sort in my village. I was aware of the fact that I was different. I already had the devil in me. When I was twenty years old, I came to Havana. Then I remembered the newspapers where I had been sending things. I went to the editorial offices, and they were very kind to me. Then I published some more. I got to know some writers, and I studied at night.

LH: Which writers?

GH: Onelio Jorge Cardoso, Félix Pita Rodríguez, Joaquín Santana . . . not many. Really, there wasn't an intellectual movement yet, at least not a centralised one. At night I studied hard, and I attended a course for secretaries. When the Revolution occurred, I was introduced to the *El Puente* group. I also met the staff at Página Dos of Prensa Libre, who had their own group of literati. I was involved with both groups.

LH: How did you meet José Mario, editor of *El Puente*?

GH: I met him through his Argentine friend, who was a theatre instructor.

LH: Did José Mario ask you to show him some of your poetry?

GH: Yes, and so did Ana María Simo. When they read my poetry, they became very interested and said, 'Look, you have to change a couple of things'. They began to collaborate with me, making me edit things, because they were so enthusiastic about my work. So, I changed a few things in the poems. When I finished, I remember that they said, 'What title are you going to give your book? It's ready!' I said, 'Well, I don't know'. They said, 'Start thinking of a title' but I didn't give it much thought. Everybody was excited about the idea of publishing a book, but I wasn't. I'm embarrassed to tell you that I'm the kind of person you always have to be after to do things. But one day they said, 'Hey, the book is ready. Now you only need the book cover'. But I couldn't face the fact that I had a book of my own. Ana María and José Mario decided to call it *G.H.* which are my initials. 'We're going to call it *G.H.* so that it sounds hip'.

LH: I found only one article that claimed to be about *G.H.*, although it was not actually about *G.H.* It concerned poetry written before *G.H.*, which seemed to be intensely intimate poetry, full of feelings and anguish. In an article published in *Lunes de Revolución*, Luis Suardíaz said something to that effect. I found criticism on *Gentes y cosas*, but hardly any on *G.H.*

GH: No, there are only two critical articles on *G.H.* My poems from the fifties were published in *El País* and *Excelsior* and *Diario de la Tarde*. At the onset of the 1959 Revolution, there was a newspaper called *Diario del Tarde* that published revolutionary poetry, and I wrote three sonnets dedicated to Fidel. They published them as if they were something great.

LH: Nevertheless, in *Gentes y cosas*, I didn't find much poetry that praised the Revolution. After reading most of your poetry, one could say that it is intimate, that you do not use a specifically revolutionary aesthetic. Well, I hardly find any revolutionary elements in your poetry.

GH: No. I was constantly criticised for that. I used to be a real revolutionary, completely convinced in those days, but I didn't take to praising it all the time. Sometimes you saw how they granted literary prizes to some serious botch-work, and you wondered what was going on.

LH: But you did write some things about the Revolution at certain moments.

GH: A few, when I felt motivated. Otherwise, not.

LH: So, just when you felt like doing it.

GH: I can't write poetry on request. What happened was that the notorious 'upwardly mobile' were assigning jobs to people, and they did it to convince themselves that they were doing the right thing. They looked for people who shared their ideas, who could write poetry of adulation [for the Revolution]. Sometimes a critical poem, if it's good criticism, is more valuable than a panegyric poem. Of course, if you simply wrote, even if you didn't say anything against the Revolution, you were ostracised. It was worse, because they would say, 'What is this person doing?' One day, in the excitement of those times, Eliseo [Diego] came to me. He had been my teacher when I was young. He taught a very interesting course on children's literature at the National Library. He came to me and asked me to show him some of my poetry. He adored *G.H.* When we met again at UNEAC, he asked me to show him some more things. One day, he came to me and said, 'Georgina, I'm calling you to thank you'. He was very ceremonious. 'But why, Eliseo?' I asked. 'Because you gave me real poetry to read. These days when one has to live reading, surrounded by so much bad work, we have to be thankful when someone writes poetry'. I had more things published than other people did. They always published what I wrote.

LH: Was there a time when you didn't publish anything?

GH: When other things happened. For example, when I had my son, I devoted myself to my son. I think that being a mother is the only interesting thing, but I go on writing poetry. There is a series of poems dedicated to my children, the poems to Ignacio and Anaísa. Twice in the OPAAL (Organisation for Solidarity with the People of Asia, Africa, and Latin America), they made mural poems, and they asked me for poems for that book. After that, I wrote a book of poetry for children, so I went on writing quite a lot. One day, they called me from the publishing house and said that a book that I was supposed to publish had been ruined. They returned the ruined copy and paid me for the whole thing. They said that time had passed and that my topics were not relevant any more, so they told me to write new poems.

LH: They didn't publish the poems?

GH: They didn't publish the poems. Then I wrote another book, *Golpeando la memoria* (Striking Memory). Why did I write this book? Because they gave me such a hard time at the publishing house, saying that was enough sad poetry and all that. I knew that I had a very painful past – my childhood – so I told myself: Let's see if I can write a book about this experience. I wrote poems about the school parade, the Day of the Kings, everything that was part of a poor girl's life in a village. That book received special mention in a UNEAC contest. The book wasn't published, but it won honourable mention.

LH: Do you have *Striking Memory* at home?

GH: Yes, but later I published the poems in other books. Others are out of print, because they were about the streets, about the improvement of village life, and they were a bit exaggerated. That was the only time that I spoke with my heart on my sleeve. Some poems will never be published. I'm not going to publish those poems now. I have already overcome that phase. So then I published *Golpeando la memoria*, and after that *Granos de sol y luna* (Grains of Sun and Moon), after which I didn't publish anything until *Grande es el tiempo* (Great is Time). I worked for a long time on a book of children's stories that I haven't finished yet, a book called *¿Quién quiere vender los gallos del señor gallero?* (Who Wants to Sell the Farmer's Roosters?). It's a very nice book. I will finish it someday. And since then I haven't written anything. Writing poetry is like that, sporadic. I don't write poetry with a topic in mind, as other people do. I only write when I feel that I really need to. I have some poems that – we'll see. Loose poems, lots of loose poems scattered about that I'm writing now, many about women, a lot of reflections, reflections about Black women.

LH: Were you involved in the Black cultural movement in Cuba? Some groups listened to the music, talked about Black affairs, read Malcolm X, and had discussions.

GH: I was not involved in that, but they were my people. I too am Black. They were the people I talked to, with whom I had all kinds of relationships. And so, well, we did speak about that, but not in an active way, not even in secret. At that time, creating a group meant dividing the country. The great fear existed that groups with those ideas could develop, because we were a republic that raised questions. But, in fact, the idea is attractive, because we, as Blacks, always feel that we are left out. I was never very involved. We discussed it [Black culture], I heard about it, and I had my opinion about it, but Manolo [Granados, Georgina's husband in the sixties], for example, was much more active.

LH: He was very active, and Tomás González was too.

GH: But many people, in spite of the fact that they were not active (and I don't know why), were considered part of the Black Power problem. They had plenty of problems. I'll tell you something. That was a period that marked many people. A lot of people are still afraid; they've become more conservative to avoid any problems.

LH: Do you think that the problems that several Black intellectuals and artists had here in Cuba seriously affected Black writing, especially the aesthetics, the themes, and maybe the avoidance of Black issues?

GH: Well, I don't think so, because at the end of the day, if the Black Cuban intellectual actually felt like writing literature, he would have done it, as a few did. Somebody would have published it, and people would have read it clandestinely, or maybe not, but they would have written it.

LH: Well, it's written somewhere but not published. I have searched and I can't find many things published.

GH: No, there's no such thing. I don't know of it either. And I can tell you now calmly and with peace of mind that I am not worried about those things. Now I am writing more about the Black problem. I'm more reflective now. There are two poems in this packet that I'm giving you that are essential to me. One is called 'Ibu Sedi', and it's about Omi Sande, Yemayá's daughter in Yoruba. The other one is called 'Primera vez ante un espejo' (First time in Front of a Mirror). Once, I was with Rogelio [Martínez Furé] looking at a book. We started laughing at the very old images that looked like us. And then he said, 'Look at those Black people – what serenity! But they are the same people who were beaten; that's why their looks have changed. It's the way they have been treated'. We saw a terracotta mask that was about two thousand years old, and I said, 'Rogelio, look how it resembles me!' I was looking at it, and I was so astonished at that moment, because I was fully aware that I accepted myself as I was. I always liked being Black, having this tranquillity. I was proud of our large mouths and our wide noses. All of that is in the poem.

LH: I don't know. I may be mistaken, but are you obsessed with the idea of death?

GH: Very much so. I was a potential suicide when I was very young. However, I was afraid that I might not die in the act. I couldn't face that possibility. But then things changed. After I gave birth to my son, I became extremely fond of life. I was virtually afraid of death for that reason. I became so fond of life after that. I learned to appreciate it, to look at it from different points of view that I had never considered before. Every morning when I wake up, I'm so grateful; it's as if I were being born again. I love life very much. But then, death . . . I know that death is the victor in all of our battles, because after that . . . even if the spiritualists say that there is another life, all I know is this one, where I have spun my web, my life, in my own way. Death has dealt me many blows. My mother died when I was only fourteen, so I couldn't have a real relationship with her when I grew older. I always thought that they didn't love me at home. I am sure that if my mother had lived, if we had communicated, if there had been more time for us both . . . I have written a lot about this. But, well, it's over. Then I had a problem when I got married, divorced, and loved another man. We had a beautiful relationship, really beautiful, but he died too. And then there was my daughter's death. But even before my daughter's death, which is the worst thing that ever happened to me, I already had the impression that death was always predetermined.

LH: When did your daughter die?

GH: In 1992, at the beginning of 1992.

LH: You had already written a lot of poetry about death.

GH: A lot. A lot.

LH: And about anguish and suffering, because even though children and love were positive things, they were also things that made you suffer.

GH: Very much. I felt that I was very affected by suffering. I was emotionally crippled by my love for this man and the children, in apparently uncomplicated circumstances. But they weren't uncomplicated. I was alone with two kids. I really had a hard time, because they were very difficult children. I would still have them if I had to do it over again, but it's an experience that didn't turn out as I had expected. In a poem about my mother I say, 'Seguro que hubo amor, pero escaseó el tiempo para darnos a conocer cuando yo fuese mayor y ella más vieja' (Surely there was love, but there wasn't enough time for us to get to know each other, when I was grown and she was much older). I still remember my mother's last morning in the house. 'La habitación de la que es dueña / la instalan como si fuese una extranjera / allá como nunca se está ahora . . .' (In the house she ruled / they placed her as if she were a stranger / now more than ever she is present …).

LH: You also speak about people who live on your block: crazy women, spinsters.

GH: Spinsters, mistresses. They are very specific women who were always around and still support the Revolution.

LH: Why do you call them spinsters?

GH: Why? Because of the way they live. A spinster is someone I can't comprehend. She is a woman who never let a man lay hands on her. I can't understand that. And the thing with the mistresses is that they have been misunderstood.

LH: Why misunderstood?

GH: Because I think that one must be incredibly strong to be a man's lover in the days when being a wife was what everybody strove for, no matter what humiliation one might suffer. At least here this was very common. Being a man's mistress meant being ostracised by society. This woman had no access to anything, thanks to this man. From time to time, whenever men wanted or could, they would abuse their mistresses. Well, I think that the word 'mistress' itself means a lot of things. The mistress was the one whom the man loved, but sometimes being a mistress was merely a label for the other experience outside the house – the affair.

LH: There is an interesting poem, 'Enemy', in *People and Things* that I want to ask you about.

GH: I made it concise because of Eliseo. The poem 'Enemigo' is a very long poem, and Eliseo told me one day, 'Georgina, everything you say, say it using as few words as you can. Everything you write in poetry, the fewer words the better'. Talking about this poem, he said, 'What you say in the last lines is a whole poem in itself'. When I wrote, 'Entre los dos sentados un pequeño rey ríe siniestramente, es para siempre' (Between the two sitting, the little king laughs in a sinister manner, as always), that's the end of the poem. I learned my lesson. I remember that I published it like that. But from then on, I reduced all the poems that were verbose. For example, my poem about the mistresses was very long, but I reduced it and left it like this. 'Islas son a veces por oscuras palomas habitadas, otras van cayendo, lavando heridas en ciudades viejas. Entonces son diablos'. (At times, islands are inhabited by dark pigeons, others are falling, cleaning wounds in old cities. Then they're devils).

LH: Somebody was talking to me about your poetry, and they mentioned pain and hope, the problems of a poor Cuban family before the Revolution. Do you think that you explicitly express all that?

GH: I don't know. People think that when you suffer, you suffer because you were poor. People assume that your father was violent and your mother rude, but they don't understand me correctly, because I know a lot of people who were very poor, but they were happy anyway. In one line, I say that I was a restless child, always looking for fruit and opening bottles – situations in my life that were like those of any other child. So I don't think it was as they said. I don't think you can come to that conclusion reading my poetry.

LH: I think that it was an ideological or political issue, because I read an article that stated that Georgina is a poet in this country thanks to the Revolution.

GH: I read that. I think that it is on the flap of *G.H.* No, I didn't appear with the Revolution. It simply opened many doors for me. I took various courses on many things. I kept up with the times and caught up with matters that I hadn't known before.

LH: In a sense, you can't criticise that kind of praise, but, on the other hand, it implies that the merit isn't so much yours. That's what struck me. Eliseo Diego wrote a very interesting article, published in *Cuba*. He concentrates on your poetry, rather than crediting the Revolution with your talent.

GH: That was when I worked at the editorial office of *La Unidad*. When the first book came out, he took the first copy off the press and said, 'Georgina, there is an article about you that is going to come out in *Cuba*'. He was extremely enthusiastic about my poetry.

LH: It was the most interesting of all the articles, because it dealt with your poetry. He didn't feel an obligation to make your poetry accord with revolutionary aesthetics. He spoke specifically about your poetry. He says that you have a very shy poetic voice, but that you express yourself more openly in the second book. He comments that in your book *No se vuelva al exterior* (Don't Reveal Yourself), 'Georgina speaks about the people and the things that she internalised in her youth, that are a part of her because they are in her memory. Also, the poetry expresses the anguish of her past, of her former loneliness . . .' Well, he emphasises that the notable change is a more expressive, audacious voice.

GH: Well, I don't know whether it's true. My first book of poems was that of a mere child. I knew what I was doing when I became aware of the fact that I was a woman writing poetry. From that moment, I maximised my experiences. Being a woman is something different. It's about the mastery of language and certain experiences that motivate me to write poetry.

LH: Do you think that the critics misinterpret your intimate poetry, seeing it more as a poetry of pure sentiments?

GH: I am shy. I am a very shy woman. Many people don't like me; they think that I don't say 'Hello' in the street because I am very conceited. But I am the absolute opposite of conceited. They don't realise that I am shy. I don't want to force anyone. I don't want to impose myself on anyone, so it's a question of timidity. But I am the shy one. What is often overlooked is how the critic handles things. There is another question about my poetry, and it's that I try to write poetry without complicated metaphors. I think that you can't make things too complicated for people, because even if you know what you mean, people might not understand. That's why every time that one of my poems turns out to be too complicated – and sometimes that happens – I have to work on it, search for words that might make it more accessible to others, because people make mistakes. They don't possess the absolute truth.

LH: Well, critics are also free to interpret.

GH: Yes, they are. But critics must be a bit better, too. I think that a critic must become a critic just like someone else becomes something. Not everybody has natural ability. That is an art, too. People say, 'Your poetry is nice; it's bad, it's good; it resembles that of so-and-so; it shows the influence of . . .' Critics go beyond all that, but I let them do it.

LH: They also write a bit about the feelings that you express in your poetry. Do you really think that human beings are so fragile? The poetic voice in your poems is quite fragile; it is that of a person who suffers intensely or who has a lot of . . .

GH: Some people are not fragile. It's just that they are more vulnerable, more sensitive than others.

LH: Would you say vulnerable rather than fragile?

GH: Yes, good things affect me more. I am sure that I enjoy more those things that normally don't excite other people. Those things affect me. So, it's very relative whether I am fragile or strong, in the sense of good and evil, because sensitivity is the same for both things. The things that most human beings remember and insist on are things that make us suffer. But there are many pretty and virtuous things. With regard to searching for sensations – I enjoy the dusk, the afternoon when it rains. The sound of rain is something incredible. The rainbow, the reflection of something, a tree, a ripple on the water. Those things are divine to me. That's important! In that sense I do think that I have suffered a lot and devoted much time to my suffering. But I was never very communicative. Now I am; I like to speak about things that I didn't express before. Now, I am much more open. I'll tell you, the death of somebody very dear to me helped me become this way. When my mother died, I wrote poems that said that we should have communicated more. When the man whom I loved so much died, I realised that there were so many things that were left unsaid, that I should have told him. When my daughter died, it was the same thing. But what a coincidence that everybody whom I loved was dying, and it was I who still had something to say! I'm very hermetic. I want people to know that I have my good moments, that I love people, that I'm thankful, and that I receive love from people. If not, I'll ask for what I need. Otherwise, one becomes extremely unbalanced.

LH: What did your daughter think of your poetry?

GH: She was not interested. She was interested in dancing; the only thing that she liked to do was dance. She was an extroverted child, very crazy. One of the things that I couldn't understand was why she was the way she was. I didn't want her to be different. But that was the way she was. She hardly had anything to do with me, almost nothing. One day, a long time after her death, I told my son that I thought she hadn't loved me. And he said, 'But, Mama, how can you say that?' I never got anything from her, and I am very affectionate. I loved my children very much. I never received any love from her. He told me, 'But, Mama, she loved you so much! You can't say that!' That was traumatic for me. Something happened. No, there was no communication. But the proof that I did love her is there; it's there in the poems. People are very understanding, because from the moment that one loses a child, people know that the loss is awfully sad. Nonetheless, I have written about it. So there's proof that I loved her dearly, but something never clicked; we didn't communicate. Well, it's my burden, and there's no way to resolve it now. So now I make an attempt, every time I am around people. I love them and I want them to know that I love them. I want them to know that I am satisfied with our loving. We'll see what happens!

LH: You have written so much poetry about your children as a form of communication?

GH: Yes. My daughter read the poems.

LH: She read the poems? But she didn't really pay attention to them?

GH: No, she didn't pay too much attention to them. It wasn't her way of expressing herself.

LH: So, tell me. You spoke before about what you are doing now. Explain that.

GH: I'm working on a project, a collection of poems about seven women, African women, women who are still alive. It seems that the project is growing now. It's going to comprise more than the seven women. It may include more Black women who are still living. People ignore what these women have done and what they can do. So I am going to focus on that at the moment. We must tell the lives of women. We must recognise the people who have done something. I have a poem called 'Termínalo por mí' (Finish it for Me), which is in one of my books. That woman existed in my house. I used to listen to my grandmother's sisters. They told me that they had been slaves and what they had done. A short time ago, there was a lecture on a slave rebellion that occurred in the Alcancía Sugarmill. It was a great event, well organised. But when all was said and done, I asked why the two Black women who had participated in the rebellion hadn't been mentioned. I think I have my work cut out for me. There is an African proverb that I read not long ago that says, 'While the hunter writes his stories about the jungle, the hunter also has to give the lion the right to tell his version of the jungle'. That is a great truth. Everyone has to write his own stories, because each has his own perspective.

LH: I don't know if you have read things by Alice Walker or . . . ?

GH: Oh, a lot. Incredible!

LH: Or by Toni Morrison, who is also a novelist?

GH: We don't have so much from her.

LH: Yes, that is the problem, that literature doesn't always arrive here.

GH: And once it arrives, we have to cram against each other and sign up on a list, taking our turn to read the books. But I do realise that literature by Black women in the States is strong, very beautiful, and maybe because it's newer, because they've written about the things that happen to their people, written about themselves. It's a style, a certain form of expression.

LH: That's why I appreciate Nancy Morejón's poetry. She speaks about intelligent Black women.

GH: And she points out the importance of her roots, her identity.

LH: And she uses an active poetic voice that presents a subject who fought in wars, who was a Maroon, who fought during the Cuban Revolution – the idea being that there is an active Black woman who takes part in Cuba's history. She doesn't merely dance and move her hips.

GH: The general image of the [Black] Cuban woman is of the dancer. One year, I was in Czechoslovakia meeting with people from many countries, and I was the only Black. When it came time to dance, everyone wanted to dance with me, because they thought . . . . There was a huge German who was giving me a hard time because he could dance and I couldn't. He asked, 'How is it that you don't know how to dance?' It's only a myth that Black people can dance. I am Black, and I can't dance. I can't dance.

LH: But that is the cliché, the image developed in literature, with the Harlem Renaissance, Josephine Baker, the fascination with primitivism.

GH: But as I tell you, those things [racism and prejudice] don't disappear. It took me a long time to come to terms with that. Well, you understand that if something affects you, and you know that it's unfair . . . although we overcame . . . but I realised that I was not going to solve anything with my rage. I write. I create. There is a reality that you recreate, but you also have to transform it. You have to do what you can with a goal in mind if you want that reality to change. In my writing, I will never describe Black people as the bad guys. On the contrary, I want to give priority to Black women, who are capable of loving, who are affectionate women, who are trying to surpass their circumstances.

Toward a Definition of the Self in the Poetry of Georgina Herrera

Gabriel A. Abudu

Before the 1959 Revolution the voice of the Black woman was not prominent in Cuban literature; there were few Black women writers then, and those who appeared in literature were often presented as objects of literary discourse. After the Revolution, with massive literacy campaigns, the formation of cultural organisations, and the establishment of publishing houses, doors were opened to women, who became the producers as well as the readers of literature. Just as writers such as Nicolás Guillén and Marcelino Arozarena had opened up the Latin American literary canon in the thirties by introducing Black themes, motifs, subjects, and language, Black women would in turn open up the Afro-Hispanic canon by incorporating their own voices, visions, feelings, and language. It was important, as Mary Helen Washington argued in the case of Black women writers in the United States, that 'for purposes of liberation, black women writers will first insist on their own name, their own space' (xvii). For Afro-Hispanic women writers, making themselves heard was also crucial in their search for true identity and self-fulfilment, for the voice in the Afro-Hispanic canon hitherto had been a male one that could not adequately represent the Black woman's point of view. Yet, the importance of having one's own voice heard in the canon is underlined by Jackson when he states: 'By seizing the tools of power, which is what language and literature represent, [Black authors] are opening up the canon a little wider' (6). Blas Jiménez echoes this sentiment on the empowering role of language as medium of literary creation when he states: 'El acto de crear es en sí un acto de fuerza. Cuando creamos imponemos nuestra voluntad sobre aquellos que serán tocados, de una u otra forma, por nuestro producto creativo .... En este proceso vivimos los impulsos que nos llegan de la necesidad de autodefinirnos .... ' (The act of creating is in itself an act of force. When we create we impose our will on those who will be touched, in one way or another, by our creative product. In this process we experience the impulses that arise from the necessity of self-definition)(5). On the other hand, a gender-specific literary discourse is advocated by the Afro-Ecuadorian author Luz Argentina Chiriboga when she explains: 'La concepción de los hombres es diferente, pues poetizan a la mujer como un objeto sensual y sexual, en cambio mi poesía es una toma de conciencia femenina, una nueva retórica para expresar mi cosmovisión' (The concept of men is different, because they poeticise the woman as a sensual and sexual object; on the other hand, my poetry is a feminine consciousness-raising, a new rhetoric for expressing my cosmic vision) (Feal 13). The necessity for a gender-specific literary discourse is evident in an even more direct appeal by the Cuban writer Nancy Morejón, who states: 'Women also have a special vision that is born of pain, and pain smartens one up a great deal' (Béhar and Suárez 133). Literary creation and the transforming power of language are thus viewed as instruments for self-affirmation, social transformation, and historical rectification. Afro-Hispanic women writers seek to be active participants in the formulation of a new literary discourse that has a wider embrace.

The Cuban government in the early sixties rightly saw art as a medium of empowerment, and sought to cultivate artistic talent in areas of creative endeavour among a population whose level of literacy before the Revolution had been very low. Georgina Herrera was one of those women whose artistic talents were brought to the fore thanks in large measure to the fervent cultural atmosphere that was nurtured by the Revolution. Women writers such as Herrera, Nancy Morejón, and Excilia Saldaña have helped to establish a core of Black women's writing in Cuba, thus opening up the Afro-Hispanic literary canon. These writers define their identities by creating their own poetic spaces within which they construct their artistic worlds. In so doing they regain control of their destinies. As Catherine Davies states, they have inscribed themselves into Afro-Cuban literary discourse, and have thereby established 'a tradition of black women's writing' ('Women Writers' 145). Each writer has posited her own 'I' as subject of literary discourse and has thus helped to 'wrest the individual black subject out of anonymity, inferiority and brutal disdain' (Willis 213).

Herrera published her first major work, *G.H.*, in 1962. However, it is with the appearance of her three later books, *Gentes y cosas* (People and Things) in 1974, *Granos de sol y luna* (Grains of Sun and Moon) in 1979, and *Grande es el tiempo* (Time is Great) in 1989, that she makes a solid mark on the Cuban literary landscape and on Afro-Hispanic literary discourse. In her poetry, motherhood and womanhood become the centre of poetic expression, and they are examined from the woman's perspective. Her poetry encompasses a broad range of themes, particularly love, death, nature, and history. All these thematic components of her poetic world are viewed from the perspective of a central self which employs the transforming power of language to create a new poetic vision. She was born in 1936, and grew up in the village of Jovellanos, in the Matanzas province of Cuba. Chronologically, she is an elder member of the first generation of Cuban writers whose main works began to appear shortly after the 1959 Revolution. Poetry provided Herrera with an avenue to channel her creative abilities and to communicate her vision of the world. Her poetry emanates from her life's experiences. As such, it contains biographical details that explain the poet's philosophy of life and help us to understand the impact of these experiences on her poetic expression. These experiences include her personal struggles with motherhood, death, and abandonment. In the short poem 'La melancolía' (Melancholy), for example, Herrera paints a portrait of the world within which she has to function:

A un lado están los hijos, el trabajo
con sueldo regular,
algunos libros
que los demás no tienen,
los elogios, los sueños,
el entrañable amor hacia la vida
y tus semejantes. (*Granos* 40)

(On the one hand are the children, the work
with regular pay,
some books
that others don't have,
the praises, the dreams,
the deep-set love for life
and for others like yourself).*

Her children, her work as a writer, her modest means, the few privileges that she enjoys, her successes and her failures, her dreams, her love of life and of others in spite of difficulties and scarcities – these are the thematic units that make up Herrera's poetic world. What is most remarkable in her poetry is the deep love of life, which results in an outward movement toward others, toward nature and history, with the self acting as the anchor that binds all the different spaces within which the poet functions. Herrera's philosophy of life is further explored in

'Vivir' (Living) where, in the midst of insurmountable difficulties, her poetic sensibilities discover a strong *raison d'être* in protecting the delicate flower from the intrusive and destructive breeze:

> Entonces el viento
> surge entre tú y la flor; intenta en ella
> no sé qué asunto contra la ternura.
> Tú, con tus manos, la proteges, luchas
> contra el intruso. Hallas
> así el motivo de la vida. (*Granos* 54)

> (Then the wind
> arises between you and the flower; it attempts
> on it some design against tenderness.
> You, with your hands, you protect it, you fight
> against the intruder. You find
> thus the reason for life.)

She discovers a natural human inclination toward destruction; against this weakness she juxtaposes the delicate beauty of the flower. The flower is a metaphor for the precarious beauty that Herrera discovers in human beings, and it is a symbol that recurs consistently in her poetry. Protecting this delicate human beauty in her multiple role as mother, wife, neighbour, and friend, is the goal which the poet has established for herself. Herrera's temperament is also clearly expressed in 'Es fácil olvidar la dicha' (It is Easy to Forget Joy), where the feeling of joy is presented as a fickle experience, while pain seems to endure forever:

> Ser feliz es como vivir al día;
> suena la dicha
> dentro del corazón
> igual que música.
> Pero se gasta . . .
> Es fácil olvidarla.
> Sin embargo, la pena . . .
> Es otra cosa.
> Asible y fuerte.
> ¿Alguien puede zafarse de su abrazo?
> Resulta ser como la tumba;
> se entra

en su interior y no se sale. (*Gentes* 59)
(Being happy is like living day by day;
happiness sounds
inside your heart
like music.
But it wears off . . .
It is easy to forget it.
However, pain . . .
That is something else.
It grips you strongly.
Can anyone escape from its embrace?
It turns out that it is a tomb;
one goes inside
and never comes out.)

While happiness is equated with the aesthetic pleasure of music, pain is equated with the ontological experience of death. Since happiness is a temporary experience and pain is a permanent one, there is a rather disquieting sense of existential despair and emptiness that permeates the entire poem. Indeed, in Herrera's poetry, happiness is always tempered by the sempiternal presence of death.

The simple, modest provincial life that Herrera experienced in her hometown of Jovellanos is conveyed to us in several of her poems. In 'El patio de mi casa' (The Backyard of My House) the poet remembers the childhood silence around her house: 'Patio sin otro ruido / que el silencioso andarlo' (Backyard with no other noise / but the silent walk around it), the poverty she suffered: 'mis pies descalzos' (my bare feet), and the emotional solitude she endured: 'Sitio para mí sola, donde la ternura / y su modo simple de crecer . . . / me fue vedado' (A place for me alone, / where tenderness / and its simple way of growing up . . . / was denied me). The empty, lonely backyard left a deep void in Herrera's life:

Patio perdido y ya recuperado
pues regresa
desde el fondo de un sueño
como un hueco en la infancia. (*Grande* 55)

(Backyard lost and now recovered
for it returns

from the deeps of a dream
like an emptiness in childhood)

These childhood memories, recuperated by an adult Herrera, shaped by the poetic word, and enlarged by an expansive vision of the world, sometimes return with the force of a furious thunderstorm. Another poem which describes Herrera's modest childhood world is 'La pobreza ancestral' (Ancestral Poverty), where the poet again recalls the poverty that her family endured during her childhood:

Pobrecitos que éramos en casa.
Tanto
que nunca hubo para los retratos;
los rostros y sucesos familiares
se perpetuaron en conversaciones. (*Grande* 21)

(How poor were we at home.
So poor
that there was never enough for portraits;
family faces and events
were preserved in conversations.)

In this short poem, the importance of the oral tradition in the transmission of history and ideas is underscored. The oral tradition (songs, fables, rituals, legends, myths) was a crucial medium through which much of Afro-Cuban culture survived. In the absence of pens, paintbrushes, and photographs, historical events and personalities are transmitted from generation to generation through the oral medium. Thus, the myths and legends that assured the survival of a people and the continuity of a culture are transformed into an immediate and personal experience for the poet.

The most tender moments in Herrera's poetry occur when she examines the theme of motherhood. In fact, much of her poetry centres on her role as mother, and her children often serve as inspiration for artistic creation. As she explains to Linda Howe, motherhood is a most interesting experience for her. As Catherine Davies also notes, Herrera takes her role as a mother very seriously ('Writing the African Subject' 39). It is no wonder then, that much of her poetry deals with the theme of motherhood, which is no more a limiting frame of reference that was often used as an instrument of oppression to confine the Caribbean woman and suppress her aspirations. Here it is celebrated and cherished, and it is a constant source of poetic inspiration. It is presented as a source of pride and joy for the Black woman. In Herrera's poetry, the woman re-appropriates the theme of motherhood for herself, and transforms it into an instrument of positive self-affirmation. For Herrera, the pains of motherhood are sometimes sharp, but the liberating joys of this condition are obvious in the poetic persona that we encounter in her poetry. A mother's infinite pride and joy are presented in 'La que antepone a todo la ternura' (The Woman Who Puts Tenderness Before All Else), from *Gentes y cosas*, where a mother walks along with her daughter on her shoulders, exhibiting a love that transcends space and time. The gods of Western mythology are not capable of capturing the depth of this woman's joyful mood. Repudiation of Western mythology as incapable of understanding the transcendent dimensions of this woman's true feelings is, in effect, a rejection of foreign standards of evaluation, judgment, and measurement. As is frequent in Herrera's poetry, the child becomes an integral part of the woman's existential experiences, not just a biological extension of her being. Even where biological reproduction is examined, the poet prefers the joys of childbirth to an aristocratic life, as she states in 'El parto' (Childbirth). Certainly, Herrera is aware of the anguish and anticipation of watching a child grow up, mature, and become independent, as we observe in 'Ultimo elogio como niña' (Last Praise as a Child) and 'De pronto crece' (She Grows Quickly), both from *Grande es el tiempo*. Still, motherhood is not viewed as a condition that should be rejected. It undergoes a rebirth in Herrera's poetry, where it is re-evaluated and celebrated through a Black Caribbean woman's poetic vision.

The passion with which motherhood and children are presented in Herrera's poetry is apparent in several other poems of *Gentes y cosas* and *Granos de sol y luna*. In *Gentes y cosas*, for example, Herrera wrote an entire section dedicated to her two children, where she explores the everyday challenges of being a mother and raising her children by herself. In the first poem of *Gentes y cosas*, 'Los hijos' (Children), nature is employed in strong metaphorical language to illustrate various aspects of life:

Un día
la inmensa tierra blanda (el corazón)
rota amanece.
Ese árbol que son los hijos
casi que se compara al cielo en su tamaño.
Pues, entonces,

agua de riego oculta
va en los ojos.
Sangre abono queda relegada.
(One day
the immense soft earth (the heart)
awakes broken through.
That tree which is the children
is almost like the sky in size.
Well, then,
irrigating water is hidden
in the eyes.
Blood now becomes fertiliser.)

The nature-inspired comparisons in this poem create parallels and points of convergence between mother earth and the woman, both presented as sources of life. This parallelism allows the poet to integrate herself into nature: the heart/womb breaks open like the earth breaking loose; the children sprout out of the womb like seedlings sprouting out of the earth, and they grow up like trees growing out of the earth; as water nourishes the plant's growth, tears of joy also accompany the children's growth, and life-giving blood is the fertiliser for the children to grow on.

The joys and challenges of motherhood are examined in 'Anaísa', a poem dedicated to Herrera's daughter Anaísa. As she watches Anaísa on her second birthday she remembers the joy she felt on the day that the baby was born. Anaísa is presented as someone who provides the poet with the right equilibrium in her life, one who helps her to correctly manage happiness and sorrow. This centre of equilibrium that Herrera finds in motherhood will be profoundly shaken when her daughter dies tragically in Havana in 1992. In a second poem also titled 'Anaísa', the daughter is described as a little flower that brightens Herrera's night of sadness with her movements, her voice, and her eyes; she is the joy that puts an end to the poet's perpetual melancholy: 'Eres exactamente / la mitad del canto indispensable / para quebrar esto de ser triste / casi por vocación' (You are precisely / one half of the indispensable song / to break this sadness that I bear / almost by vocation). In 'Canción de cuna' (Lullaby), Anaísa is presented as the poet's inspiration, and as a queen she receives her mother's adoring attention. In 'Las dos mitades de mi sueño' (The Two Halves of My Dream), the poet indicates that her identity, her dreams, and aspirations as a woman, would be incomplete without her children:

Ambos me han hecho
una mujer hermosa.
Una mujer que tiene
la más inmensa historia
por contar.
Todo el dolor que venga
será pequeño, comparado
a tanto amor creciendo en sus tamaños. (*Gentes* 17)

(Both of them have made me
a beautiful woman.
A woman who has
the biggest story
to tell.
All the pain that may come
will be small, compared
to so much love growing within them.)

For Herrera, the children's love has made her a more complete person and it will compensate for any pain she may have to suffer in life.

Anaísa reappears in 'Preguntas que sólo ella puede responder' (Questions That Only She Can Answer) from *Granos de sol y luna*, as Herrera examines the mysteries of love and motherhood. In a series of questions she reflects on the problems of being a mother, and on the special relationship between herself and her daughter. Although the questions are directed toward Anaísa, the focus of the reader's attention is Herrera, who seeks to comprehend why she loves her daughter so dearly, and why the two are so inseparable. From the tone of this poem it is obvious that there is a strong bond between mother and daughter, that they both understand the mysteries of motherhood, and that only they as women are capable of deciphering the magic of womanhood. We also witness Herrera execute her role as a protective mother in '¿De noche? Con los hijos' (Night Time? With the Children), where she covers her children to protect them from the effects of inclement weather. In 'Con la mejilla sucia y no lo sabe' (She's Unaware That Her Cheek Is Dirty), the stain left by a child's kiss is perceived as the mark of a mother's happiness. In 'Ella durmiendo' (She's Asleep), the poet contemplates her daughter, trying to protect her, but fully aware that as she grows up she will experience the same pains of life that afflicted her mother:

A esta niña le llegará su hora,
la doblará el dolor más ambicioso
cuando una espina con flor la ronde,
pero si es sabia
tendrá ventura.
Por ahora, duerme apacible. Sea
lo más posiblemente largo
el sueño suyo. (*Granos* 32)

(This girl's time will come,
the most ambitious pain will make her bend over
when a thorn with flower pursues her,
but if she is wise
she will be happy.
For now, she is sleeping peacefully.
May her dream be
as long as possible.)

In Herrera's poetry love is a multifaceted experience. Besides the
love for her children, there is the love between men and women. In the
section 'Otras gentes' in *Gentes y cosas*, Herrera deals extensively with this
aspect of love. In 'Enemigos' (Enemies), she relives the anguish of loving
and leaving, an experience which she views as a painful and cruel reality
of life: 'Pues la vida es así. / Aceptemos sus leyes' (Well this is life. / Let's
accept its laws). A sense of fatalistic resignation thus sets in. In 'Ruptura'
(Break Up) the moon, which had been a witness to their blissful love, has
now become a distant luminous disc devoid of symbolism and indifferent
to the human drama unfolding below. Time has also intervened and dissolved
the original passion. In 'Dedicatoria' (Dedication) Herrera explores the
sensual aspects of love, as the persona becomes totally consumed by her
love for a man. The effects of the man's presence on her are equivalent to
the effects of a wind blowing through a village. The man sweeps her away,
plucking her off like the wind plucks a fragile leaf from a humble tree.
What she experiences at that moment is a very intense feeling of love.
'Sentencia' (Sentence) on the other hand, depicts the end of an affair. The
force of poetic expression is achieved through the repetition of the negative
'nunca' at the beginning of the three sentences that make up the poem.
This force is capped by a strong double negative toward the end of the
poem, as the legendary love of the woman and the man is now relegated
to a distant background: 'Y nunca / ya más será ese río / múltiple de mi

boca / lugar donde tu sed desaparezca' (And never / ever more will that / multiple river of my mouth / be the place where your thirst disappears) (*Gentes* 43).

As time passes the pains associated with romantic love become more and more intense. 'Esa manera de morir' (That Manner of Dying), for example, captures a moment of emotional barrenness as the poetic subject confronts infertile, destructive love. For her this kind of love is like a rock on which nothing thrives, a hard, barren, hostile atmosphere that provides no nourishment for the roots of human sentiment to thrive:

Amor le llaman
los que a su sombra grande se tendieron.
Yo le diría:
piedra marina, donde
mi corazón de peces fue golpeado,
tierra
tremendamente dura
que le negó humedad a mis raíces.
Cielo que despidió mi estrella
y la hizo errante. (*Granos* 41)

(Those who laid themselves down in its big shade
call it love.
I would call it:
ocean rock, where
my heart was hit with fishes,
tremendously hard
earth
that denied my roots moisture.
Sky that expelled my star
and made it wander about.)

A sense of abandonment emerges in this poem, leading to a rather cynical view of love and human relationships. Nature images become strong points of reference for the woman/mother/lover to project her feelings of betrayal and disappointment. In a sarcastic tone, she describes love as the ocean rock that did not protect her vulnerable heart from ravenous fish, a dark sky which had no place for her bright star to shine.

In *Grande es el tiempo* there is also some discussion of the theme of love. In this book, Herrera establishes a delicate world full of sensual images and sometimes suggestive eroticism. In 'Agradecida al hombre que me ama' (Grateful to the Man Who Loves Me), self-sacrificing love is portrayed as a field of suspense in which a man lives. The only balance which he finds is in the pendulum that swings him back and forth between the two insecure poles of luck and fatalism that define the boundaries of this precarious relationship. The sensuality and tenderness of love is often presented through the image of a flower – rose, begonia, lily, flamboyant – because love, like flowers, is perceived as a beautiful but delicate relationship that is easily destroyed. When love becomes distant or vanishes, the flowers in Herrera's poetry lose their colours and the persona's life is filled symbolically with dead flowers, as in 'Desamor' (Lack of Affection). The breakup in the relationship with the man occurs in 'Lo irremediable' (Incurable), when the two lovers gradually fade away from each other:

Aunque es bonito
se irán haciendo más distantes tus visitas
hasta que al fin nos convenzamos.
Tú, de que no existo.
Yo, de que te he inventado. (*Grande* 81)

(Although it is beautiful
your visits will get more and more scarce
until we are finally convinced.
You, that I do not exist.
I, that I have invented you.)

From the preceding discussions, it is obvious that life, children, motherhood, and love are themes that give structure and meaning to Herrera's poetry. She also confronts the question of death. Her personal experience with death provides the background for her interest in this theme: her mother died when she was very young, her second husband also died, and more recently, her daughter perished in an accident. These experiences seem to make death an immediate and ever present reality for the poet. In *Granos de sol y luna*, death as a final and inevitable journey is explored in the poem 'Despedida a los que quiero y mueren' (Farewell to Those Loved Ones Who Die). In *Grande es el tiempo*, Herrera discusses the impact of her mother's death on her own life in the poem 'Mañana última' (Last Morning): that event destroyed part of her childhood and marked the beginning of her life-long obsession with death. As she states in the poem, death deprived her of any chances of ever expressing her love for her mother:

Y así empezó mi asunto con la muerte.
Seguro que hubo amor,
pero escaseaba el tiempo de mostrarlo
y hacer que lo entendiera.
Y a partir de ese día
todo fue ya inútil. Se hizo tarde
para sentarnos a hablar y conocernos
cuando yo fuese mayor y ella más vieja. (*Grande* 53)

(My problem with death started this way.
Sure there was love,
but there was no time to show it
and let her understand.
And from that day onward
everything became useless. It was too late
for us to sit down and talk and get to know each other
when I grew up and she got older.)

In the section titled 'Vecinos' in *Gentes y cosas*, Herrera deals with the deaths of her neighbours. Through these neighbours she explores this transcendent reality of human existence. At the same time, the poet immortalises those socially marginalised persons who led unconventional or anonymous existences, and who precisely because of their unconventional lifestyles may be viewed as social rebels. She rescues such persons as the spinster, the mistress, and the guerrilla fighter's wife from the certain oblivion that they would all have faced. The poet begins this section of the book with a short untitled poem which establishes an abstract, philosophical approach to the theme of death and provides an appropriate prelude:

Con esos ojos de mirar la vida
se puede mirar la muerte
como una estrella más . . . (*Gentes* 21)

(With such eyes from watching life
one can look at death
as one more star)

Death is juxtaposed to life, making the human being's most profound existential experiences tangential and complementary opposites. In spite of the horror that it evokes, death is presented as a reality of human existence that must be accepted. We are reminded about death's cruel twists in 'Una niña: su muerte' (A Little Girl's Death), where the darkness and vastness of the night stand in remarkable contrast to the little girl's diminutive body. The terrible finality of the event cannot be avoided, and the impossibility of any return from that journey can only be couched in a painful sigh of resignation.

Herrera also participates in the redefinition of history as it pertains to her identity as a Black Cuban, Caribbean, and Latin American woman. There is an interest in narrating the untold truth of Latin American history from the perspective of those whose voices have been ignored: Indians, Blacks, and women. In 'Los conquistadores' (The Conquerors), she recalls the Spanish conquerors, who ushered in the period of colonisation and slavery, phases of history marked by violence, degradation and dehumanisation of Blacks and Indians. For the poet, the violence that the European conquerors committed against the land and the people has guaranteed them a dark place in the history of the Americas:

Y buscaron mujer, porque del cuerpo
la vida, interminable, les brotaba.
Tuvieron tierras y mujer. Y odio,
desesperada pasión,
y un sitio oscuro entre la historia. (*Gentes* 35)

(And they looked for a woman, for from their bodies
life, endless life, was sprouting.
They had land and women. And hate,
desperate passion,
and a dark place in history)

This violence, hatred, and prejudice of the white Europeans provoke some indignation and lead to a discussion of Latin American and Caribbean destiny. In 'Historia americana, nuestra' (American History, Ours), Herrera questions the myth of the White conqueror when she makes an Indian warrior announce to his superior: 'No son dioses' (They Are Not Gods). The conqueror, who had been perceived as a god by the Aztec ancestors of this warrior, has now been humanised and his head has been symbolically cut off to emphasise his mortality.

Herrera is not only concerned with rewriting Cuban and American history; she also shows a keen interest in re-connecting with African history. Her poem 'Africa' is a moving tribute to the African continent.

The extent of personal involvement is exemplified by the use of the second person subject pronoun 'tú' for the continent, thereby personifying it, humanising it, and establishing a relationship based not only on intellectual awareness and historical reality, but on emotional bonding with the African continent as a mother figure. Herrera expresses a strong consciousness of her African ancestry and notes that her identity as a human being – her physical beauty, her dreams, and her sensibilities – is intricately linked to her African heritage. She identifies not only with the physical entity, but also with the legendary and mythical Africa, whose gods are identical to the Afro-Cuban deities. Africa provides a paradigm (Davies, 'Writing the African Subject' 41; Kubayanda 181); it is presented 'as consciousness, as metaphor, as a utopian subject, as mother, as a source of authority' (Kubayanda 184). There is a sense of exaltation, admiration, respect, and profound love from a daughter who identifies with a protective and idealistic mother Africa that inspires her in every aspect of her life:

> Amo esos dioses
> con historias así, como las mías:
> yendo y viviendo
> de la guerra al amor o lo contrario.
> Puedes
> cerrar tranquila en el descanso
> los ojos, tenderte
> un rato en paz.
> Te cuido. (*Grande* 14-15)

> (I love those gods
> with stories like this, just like mine:
> coming and going
> from war to love or vice versa.
> You can close your eyes
> in quiet rest, give yourself
> a moment of peace.
> I care for you.)

Africa is also evoked in the poem 'Respetos, presidente Agostinho' (Respects, President Agostinho), which is also a tribute to the grandfather who awakened Herrera's interest in Africa by telling her stories of the slave trade, legends, and myths of the continent. The idealistic and utopian Africa

is again presented at the beginning of the poem, but this paradigm of
excellence is broken by the violent intrusion of foreign forces:

> Según abuelo, Africa
> era un país bonito y grande como el cielo, desde
> el que a diario, hacia
> el infierno occidental, venían
> reyes encadenados, santos
> oscuros, dioses tristes. (*Granos* 48)

> (According to grandfather, Africa
> was a country as big and beautiful as the sky, from
> where every day, toward
> the infernal west, came
> kings in chains, Black saints, sad gods.)

Herrera then pays homage to Angolan president Agostinho Neto, whose
sense of humanity, and whose love for freedom and justice, make us identify
and sympathise strongly with him as a victim of Portuguese colonialism.
Neto is reunited with the poet's grandfather at the latter's grave, where he
engages in a dialogue with the grandfather, thus achieving mythical and
legendary status.

Like many Black women writers of her generation in Cuba and the
Caribbean, Georgina Herrera is also interested in the way certain women
have confronted the historical challenges of their times. She focuses on
several strong women figures who led exemplary lives. She draws energy
and inspiration from strong Black women who rebelled and helped to
shape the course of history. One such figure is Doña Ana de Souza of
Angola, who fought against the Portuguese colonisation of her land. In
order to underscore the cruelty of the Portuguese invaders and colonisers,
Herrera employs the image of the delicate and beautiful flower to contrast
with and bring out the barbarous nature of the invaders. She feels immense
respect and admiration for Doña Ana de Souza, and views her as a model
of pride, defiance, and inspiration: 'Yinga, / señora, agua limpia donde
quiero / verme reflejada'. (Yinga, / my lady, clear water where I want / to
see a reflection of myself) (*Granos* 12). Another strong historical figure to
whom Herrera pays tribute is Fermina Lucumí, a black slave who fought
for freedom during the Cuban slave revolts in the early part of the nineteenth
century. Herrera also pays tribute to the heroines who helped to change
history in one way or the other, but who have been deliberately silenced

by mainline historical discourses. By resurrecting them in her poetry, Herrera accords them the immortality that they rightly deserve. She sees their unnoticed rebellion and heroism as worthy of emulation and preservation. Accordingly, she pays homage to such heroines as the young girls who in 1942 helped to prevent the destruction of the Kiev railway, and to Carmen Castillo, wife of a fallen Chilean guerrilla leader. These female characters, who acted courageously during periods of immense racial and/or gender bias, are presented as 'subjects of history' (Davies, 'Writing the African Subject' 41), and in a sense, as precursors of the modern Afro-Hispanic woman's struggles against invisibility. Herrera resurrects these forgotten figures in an effort to rewrite history so as to include the voices that are ignored in historical canons.

Herrera's poetry is a deeply personal and intimate one as she relives in her writings the experiences that have been boldly engraved into her memories. Although her rhetoric is not a militant or propagandistic one, there is certainly an underlying current of dissatisfaction with traditional historical and literary discourses. One therefore detects a tone of quiet resentment, defiance, and rebellion. She refuses to let the traditional role of women be a limiting framework of reference within which someone else shapes her identity. The strong focus on her role as a mother is meant to reevaluate women and motherhood and to view the world on her own terms. Since motherhood is a central factor in the definition of her as a woman, she re-appropriates this condition and places it not at the peripheries, but at the centre of her poetic discourse. There seems to be a rejection of the streak of Western feminist thought that devalues motherhood as a means of attaining equality and self-fulfilment. It is for this reason that we find so many poems focusing on the joys of motherhood. It is also for this reason that her children figure so prominently in her poetry. I believe that this act of placing motherhood and children at the centre of her poetic discourse is, in itself, an act of rebellion.

As we have seen from the discussion in this essay, Herrera is also concerned with redefining history. She challenges traditional historical discourse by resuscitating heroines who rebelled against oppression, and according them their rightful place in history. Such heroines become models of defiance and inspiration for the modern Black Caribbean woman in her struggle for equality. Even the women who led unconventional lives and were perceived as social outcasts are rebelling against traditional social values through their unconventional lifestyles. Questioning traditional historical and literary discourse is part of the larger task of redefining class, race, and gender. This framework provides a centre of stability for Herrera's poetic persona. It is within this framework and from this stabilising centre that Herrera, like other Afro-Hispanic women writers, has been able to engage in a discourse of validation as she asserts her own identity. By questioning historical and literary canons, by questioning traditional gender relations, by questioning societal values, by questioning foreign value systems, she successfully 'proclaims voice, subject, and the right to history and place' (Willis 213). This is the right that she seeks as she explores the diverse thematic units that make up her existential universe, and it is a right that she wishes to bestow even posthumously, on the Black heroines of the past.

* All translations of poems from Spanish into English are mine.

Works Cited.

Anim-Addo, Joan, ed. *Framing the Word. Gender and Genre in Caribbean Women's Writing*. London: Whiting and Birch, 1996.

Béhar, Ruth, ed. *Bridges to Cuba / Puentes a Cuba*. Ann Arbor: University of Michigan Press, 1995.

Béhar, Ruth and Lucía Suárez. 'Two Conversations with Nancy Morejón'. In *Bridges to Cuba*. Edited by Ruth Béhar, 129-139. Ann Arbor: University of Michigan Press, 1995.

Davies, Catherine. 'Women Writers in Twentieth Century Cuba: An Eight-Point Survey'. In *Framing the Word. Gender and Genre in Caribbean Women's Writing*. Edited by Joan Anim-Addo, 138-168. Whiting and Birch, 1996.

___. 'Writing the African Subject: The Work of Two Cuban Women Poets'. *Cultural Review* 4.1 (1993): 32-48.

Feal, Rosemary Geisdorfer. 'Entrevista con Luz Argentina Chiriboga'. *Afro-Hispanic Review* 12.2 (1993): 12-6.

Greene, Gayle and Coppélia Kahn, eds. *Making a Difference: Feminist Literary Criticism*. London and New York: Methuen, 1985.

Herrera, Georgina. *G.H.* Havana: Ediciones El Puente, 1962.

___. *Gentes y cosas*. Havana: Ediciones Unión, 1974.

___. *Grande es el tiempo*. Havana: Ediciones Unión, 1979.

___. *Granos de sol y luna*. Havana: Ediciones Unión, 1978.

Howe, Linda. ' "The Lion's Version of the Jungle": A Conversation with Georgina Herrera' in this volume.

Jackson, Richard L. 'The Emergence of Afro-Hispanic Literature'. *Afro-Hispanic Review* 10.3 (1991): 4-10.

Jiménez, Blas. 'El escritor afro-hispano y el proceso creativo'. *Afro-Hispanic Review* 14.1 (1995): 3-9.

Kubayanda, Josaphat Bekunuru. 'The Phenomenon of Recognition: The African Ideal in the Caribbean Text'. *Journal of Caribbean Studies* 8.3 (Winter 1991): 175-185.

Washington, Mary Helen. *Midnight Birds*. Garden City, N.Y: Anchor/ Doubleday, 1980.

Willis, Susan. 'Black Women Writers: Taking a Critical Perspective'. In *Making a Difference: Feminist Literary Criticism*. Edited by Gayle Greene and Coppélia Kahn, 211-37. London and New York: Methuen, 1985.

Lourdes Casal

LOURDES CASAL

CUBA / UNITED STATES

(1938–1981)

Although she was born into the Cuban middle class and moved to the United States because of political differences with the revolutionary government, Lourdes Casal eventually became a fervent supporter of the Revolution and laboured, through her writing and her activism, to effect a reconciliation between Cubans inside and outside of the island. A poet, essayist, and short story writer, she is best known for the poem 'For Ana Veldford', included in the collection Palabras juntan revolución *(Words Foment Revolution), published shortly after her death. In her poetry, she deals with the feelings of loss, isolation, and alienation that beset the exile who is separated from her native country, but she also recognises that the experience of exile can be an opportunity for social and political transformation. Her other writings include* Los fundadores: Alfonso *(The Founders: Alfonso), a collection of short stories;* El caso Padilla *(The Padilla Case), a work of nonfiction;* Itinerario ideológico *(Ideological Itinerary), an anthology published posthumously; and several monographs. With three other writers, she also edited and wrote the introduction to a collection of essays,* Contra viento y marea *(Against the Wind and Tide).*

The daughter of a doctor and a teacher, Casal grew up in Havana, where she attended private schools and graduated from the Universidad de Villanueva. After migrating to the United States in 1961, she obtained master's and doctoral degrees in social psychology from the New School for Social Research in New York and became active in the liberation struggles of the 1960s. She taught at such institutions as Dominican College of Blauvelt, Brooklyn College, and Rutgers University, where much of her scholarship focused on the social and political problems of her native country. Her essay 'Africa ante el problema cubano' (Africa in Relation to the Cuban Problem), written after a trip to that continent, her monograph 'Race Relations in Contemporary Cuba', and her doctoral dissertation 'Images of Cuban Society Among Pre- and Post-Revolutionary Novelists' suggest the depth of her research on Cuba.

After her first trip back to Cuba in 1973, Casal became increasingly involved in efforts to reunite the Cuban community, although she realised that, as a 'political tourist' who had spent most of her adult life in exile, she had a daunting challenge. Throughout her life, she struggled to understand the significance of the Cuban national identity, and of her own identity as a woman of African, European, and Chinese descent. That struggle is reflected in many of her poems and short stories, which deal with childhood memories, family legends and myths, and Afro-Cuban religious figures. She brings to her work a profound knowledge of history, a strong sense of place, and an artist's eye for illuminating detail.

For Ana Veldford

Never a summertime in Provincetown
and even on this limpid afternoon
(so out of the ordinary for New York)
it is from the window of a bus that I contemplate
the serenity of the grass up and down Riverside Park
and the easy freedom of vacationers resting on
    rumpled blankets,
fooling around on bicycles along the paths.
I remain as foreign behind this protective glass
as I was that winter
– that unexpected weekend –
when I first confronted Vermont's snow.
And still New York is my home.
I am ferociously loyal to this acquired patria chica.
Because of New York I am a foreigner anywhere else,
fierce pride in the scents that assault us along any
    West Side street,
marijuana and the smell of beer
and the odour of dog urine
and the savage vitality of Santana
descending upon us
from a speaker that thunders, improbably balanced on
    a fire escape,
the raucous glory of New York in summer,
Central Park and us,
the poor,
who have inherited the lake of the north side,
and Harlem sails through the slackness of this sluggish
    afternoon.
The bus slips lazily,
down, along Fifth Avenue;
and facing me, the young bearded man
carrying a heap of books from the Public Library,

and it seems as if you could touch summer in the
  sweaty brow of the cyclist
who rides holding onto my window.
But New York wasn't the city of my childhood,
it was not here that I acquired my first convictions,
not here the spot where I took my first fall,
nor the piercing whistle that marked the night.
This is why I will always remain on the margins,
a stranger among the stones,
even beneath the friendly sun of this summer's day,
just as I will remain forever a foreigner,
even when I return to the city of my childhood
I carry this marginality, immune to all turning back,
too habanera *to be* newyorkina,
too newyorkina *to be*
– even to become again –
anything else.

Translated by David Frye

Patria chica: home town or province
Habanera, newyorkina: from Havana, New Yorker.

Profile of My City

I
My city's profile yellows
and wears thin, always moving
in my memory,
yet
always becoming a mass of images pressed by years.

City I loved as I love no other
city, person or conceivable thing;
city of my childhood,
where everything was mine without question,
where I was real as the walls,
unquestionable landscape.
Ten years
without singing it or speaking to it but in distance;
my city's crater always shining
in absence;
pit that defines me and traces
the irregular map of my nostalgia.

II
If I've lost it,
I've lost it twice,
lost it in the eyes of my face
and in my memory's tenacious eye.

I don't want to forget it and it goes
in spite of sudden waves
of names and vague
images:
Soledad, Virtudes, Campanario,
Peña Pobre *one summer afternoon*
and that tiny park,

thick with birds,
when they gather to usher sundown in,
flocks calling in dreams
beyond O'Reilly's *hours*
of books and beards.

III
Bits of city
fragments out of context, the links lost.

How do you get to, where did it come from, where did
    that bus go?
What's happened to that city of mine?

Prepositions,
unarticulated
questions.
I've been gone too long now.
You forget me.
May you bloom.
Forever.

Translated by Margaret Randall

I Live in Cuba

I live in Cuba.
I've always lived in Cuba
even when I thought I existed
far from the painful crocodile
I've always lived in Cuba.
Not on the easy island
of violent
blues
and superb palms
but on the other,
the one that raised its head
on Hatuey's indomitable breath,
that grew in palenques and conspiracies,
that staggers and moves forward
in the building of socialism,
the Cuba whose heroic people lived through the sixties
and didn't falter,
who's been darkly, silently
making history
and remaking herself.

Translated by Margaret Randall

The Founders: Alfonso

Wei wu wei
Do without doing

Great-granddaughter 1

My grandmother used to tell me that when her father was seventy years old and blind " this was fifty years after his arrival in Cuba " he would fly into a seething rage if he found so much as one piece of furniture out of place. He would roam the house like some infallible guardian of order in the world, setting chairs straight and checking that tables were in their proper position. Very erect, with his grey moustache cascading down over his hairless chin, he used his gnarled hands to see the world and to reconstruct it. Wearing his inevitable blue espadrilles, he walked with confident step, his impeccably ironed guayabera loose over his white drill trousers.

Five decades on from the hellish journey and, at last, the dream of respectability, somewhat modified, it's true, but made real, no doubt, in the geometric precision of the formal living room: the mahogany and wickerwork furniture, the piano, the six-foot-tall mirror, the vast tapestries and the chandelier filtering its unnecessary light through the hundreds – thousands? – of pieces of carved crystal.

Three excited taps of his walking stick would presage the coming storm " a chair left at a careless angle or, worse, an unfamiliar object blocking a path previously left open – followed by fulminations against the murderous intentions of the other inhabitants of the house.

Once order was restored, Alfonso López would flop into the armchair in the dining room.

Alfonso 1

You would flop into the armchair and when you felt the familiar pressure of the wickerwork on your bony spine, you knew that everything was in its place. Then, you would close your eyes (or leave them open, it made no difference) and look back, which is all you can do with your eyes closed and/or when you're blind and with seventy years behind you. You didn't smoke – ten years tending the leaves in the fields made you lose your taste for tobacco early on – although you had always lived off those who did smoke and it seemed to you that all the memories you had of your life came to you wreathed in smoke. As if every memorable event in your life had taken place in some small, smoke-filled room.

History 1

The importation of coolies to Cuba began in July 1847 (Zulueta & Co. of London, a Spanish ship, the *Oquendo*, 206 Chinese) and progressed slowly at first, then with great vigour from 1853 onwards, continuing busily and, of course, profitably – there is no need to say for whom – until 1874, the year of the visit to Havana of the imperial envoy, the mandarin Chin-Lan-Pin, investigator-into-the-fate-of-the-sons-of-the-great-empire-contracted-to-work-in-the-empire-of-New-Spain. Alerted by Eça de Queiroz, he decided to leave the deceptive capital and travel into the hinterland. As a result of his report, the trade contract was terminated.

The contract: four dollars a month for eight years. In southern China, during the death agony of the Manchu dynasty, that seemed like a fabulous sum. Besides, Manila wasn't so very far away and Tai-Lay-Sun was, of course, Manila. When the journey went on longer than expected – the voyage to Cuba took one hundred and fifty days – the dreams grew bitter. How many committed suicide? Others resorted to rebellion, only to die having gained control of ships they had no idea how to sail. There are legends, tales, about ghost ships, phantasmal clippers, spotted adrift on the high seas and boarded sometimes by sailors who were met by horrific scenes, the spectral spectacle of between three and five hundred corpses. Freedom and its price.

Alfonso 2

Your father – Wu Liau – had been a follower of Hung-Hsui-Chuan. You had heard him talk about the Kingdom of the Great Peace and about the Way and about Christ and the Revolution, probably in as confused a fashion as you remember it now. When your father was captured along with other rebels, a mandarin from Fukien sold him to Tanco, the Colombian who traded in coolies. Your father committed suicide, hanging himself the night before they were due to set sail. You vaguely remember the hard times that followed. Having six children and being the widow of a rebel was not much help in a country where poverty required so little encouragement, in an empire that was clearly in an advanced state of decomposition. So a few years later, you decided to take the place on the ship rejected by your father. Perhaps Taiping, the Kingdom of the Great Peace, could flower across the seas, in the lands of New Spain. Perhaps you could return one day and be a man and not the plaything of mandarins and other petty tyrants.

Even forty years later, the Spanish expression 'They made a Chinese fool out of you' still rankled. You heard your son Alejandro use it once quite innocently. You were already almost completely blind, but you still had the use of your hands and you clouted him so hard that he fell backwards into one of the flowerbeds in the courtyard. Manila, the Manila that became Havana without you realising it: months and months of blueness – the Pacific is an inhuman, transhuman ocean-days and evenings and nights of sun and cold and salt seeping into your very bones; days and nights and evenings of pressing your face into the wooden deck to try and escape the stench of five hundred piled-up, half-naked bodies, and always that blueness and then land – which was not, however, *the* land – and the journey by train and then another ship and more blueness and, at last, New Spain.

How many people did you see die by your side? Some were carried off by strange fevers, others by terrible diarrhoea, others simply, silently, slipped overboard. The dream of the Great Peace and the dream of death.

Now, however, that you could flop into the armchair and feel the wickerwork against your bony spine, now that you could prescribe exactly where the table with the vase on it should go, now that your dog came and lay across your blue espadrilles as soon as you sat down, now you finally felt at peace. And if this peace – the peace of espadrilles and of the formal living room, of the courtyard with the flower border and the begonias and the creeper and the penetrating smell of ylang-ylang on light summer nights – if this peace was not the Great Peace, it was at least yours … and it was enough.

Guilt? You have earned that peace, now that it makes no difference whether you have your eyes open or closed, for you have seen far too much in your time – too many wars and deaths in the years when your eyes still had light.

Wu Liau – you remember how they brought him and deposited him like a bruised bundle in the middle of the room before your own horrified eyes and your mother's screams. Thus ends the revolution – with a rope around your neck, a filthy shirt and two imperial guards dumping you unceremoniously on the ground without a word, with a hysterical widow and six orphans and you – the eldest son – crazy enough, one day, eight years later, commending yourself neither to God, the Devil nor to your ancestors, to go off in search of Tanco when you heard that he was back in Canton looking for workers.

You arrived in Cuba only to find yourself in the middle of another war. Your owner – sorry, your contractor – could not send you to the canefields (the fields in Oriente had been burned) and so he set you to work with tobacco in Alquízar, near Havana, where it was almost as if there was no war. Now you bore your owner's surname, López; they gave you the same Christian name too, Alfonso. A brand-new name, new and Spanish, for New Spain.

Later, they told you that according to Máiximo Gómez: 'There's no such thing as a Chinese deserter or a Chinese traitor'. But then you had only just disembarked and you were terrified by all the sounds and stories of war, and the Kingdom of the Great Peace seemed farther off than ever. Rumours about what was going on in the countryside reached even your field – it wasn't your field, of course, but López's, but let's not quibble over details – even relatively peaceful Havana. Many, many Chinese men fought in Las Guásimas (you didn't know it then, of course, but they began fighting the very day you disembarked, March 15, 1874). Pablo Chang used to tell you that – he was the one who wanted to rebel and take you with him. There are even Chinese commanders, Chang would say seductively, and suddenly you could imagine yourself as a mandarin, riding across the fields of Cuba at the head of hundreds and hundreds of horsemen, you in your embroidered clothes and wearing a cap adorned with glass buttons and a peacock feather. The bruised bundle of Wu Liau weighed too heavily in your memory, though, and by the time you had reached a decision, the war had ended. Later, you learned that Commander Sian used to travel barefoot and was the only one among his troops to own a poncho, threadbare and faded from countless washings. When he died, there was no one to place a coin in his mouth, nor even a coin to place there. And now, no one remembers them ... People do not even know that any Chinese fought in the war.

So, after a small war and another big war and after mini-wars and after lean years and fat years ... you have learned a lot. The husband of one of your daughters reached the rank of colonel in the 1895 war and what did he get for it? They shot that handsome negro, Colonel Isidro, in the back ... No, it certainly would not have been worth your while becoming a commander.

The Chinese men who threw themselves into the revolution obviously still had that Taiping madness going round and round in their heads ...'

History 2

The Empire was 'shaken to its foundations' by the Taiping rebellion (1850–64) or, rather, the Taipings emerged out of the rotten foundations of the

Empire. Hung Hsiu Chuan: visionary, prophet, military leader. An obscure peasants' revolt became a real revolution. No to the imperial aristocracy, no to Confucian ethics, no to ancestor-worship, no to the Manchu dynasty, no to private property. Yes to agrarian reform, to equality for women and language reform. No to landowners and mandarins. Yes to a revolutionary millenarianism tinged with a rather odd form of Christianity. The Taipings believed that their mission was to create heaven on earth " the Kingdom of the Great Peace that they solemnly proclaimed in Nanking when they took it in 1853.

The corrupting effects of power diluted the utopian puritanism of those early, difficult years, however; but what finally finished off the Taiping rebellion was the profits from the opium trade, which placed France and England firmly on the side of the Manchu dynasty, the Ever Victorious Army (made up of mercenaries led by an Englishman who called himself Charles George Gordon), and the landowners of Hunan who equipped the army of Tseng-kuo-fan, plus, perhaps, the fact that the rebellion was eighty years before its time. When Tseng-kuo-fan retook Nanking for the Empire, in 1864, it was clear that the extermination of the Taipings was only a matter of time.

Alfonso 3

Stripping the leaves was women's work. That was what Amalia did. Amalia was certainly different; she was a mulatta, none too bright, it's true, but fierce as they come, the daughter of a black female slave freed by her white master-father. Amalia, a worker in what was then Cuba's biggest factory (a corner shop by today's standards) in Güira de Melena, spelled it out to you when you tried to lure her up into the hills: 'Bit of paper, then talk,' she said, mocking you, imitating your pidgin Spanish. And she explained to you how her mother had taught her that you have to be firm with men, which was why she wasn't going to open her legs just yet. 'Not until we're married.' You turned on your heel and marched off without saying a word. Who did that little mulatta think she was! You had two daughters already and no one had ever made you sign a bit of paper before. You thought: 'She can have her treasure; however tightly shut she keeps her legs, it'll just be food for the worms one day anyway', and you spat through the gap where your left eyetooth used to be. You kicked the lemon tree so hard it nearly toppled over. Who the hell did that mulatta think she was! But you couldn't stop thinking about those prominent eyes, that small mouth and the jet-black hair caught up and held in place by a comb, and that mocking laugh and those hands and that intense cinnamon-coloured skin that burned your eyes and even now burned inside your pants. You gave the lemon tree another kick. You turned around. You threw a stone up at her window. She looked out. 'All right, we'll get married.' She smiled at you. 'When?' she asked. 'Whenever you want,' you said, smiling back.

'Any chance of an advance?' you asked, half-joking, half-serious. The window had already closed again when you heard her laughter. You shouted: 'See you tomorrow,' and leaped on your horse. That night you rode back and forth four times between her house and yours, unable to stop, your cock irremissibly erect, fighting to get out of your trousers. And you rode and rode; you felt as if you were drunk – and doubtless you were – drunk on Amalia and on the wind and on the doves and you rode until your exhausted horse's legs buckled under him, outside the door to the dairy – the dairy belonged to López, just as you once had – and you got off your horse and lay down on the ground next to him, and the following morning, they found the two of you still lying there, wet with dew, mouths open.

History 3

Between 1847 and 1874, some one hundred and twenty-five thousand 'Asians' arrived in Cuba. It is estimated that about ten thousand managed to return to China. In 1899, when the American administrators completed the census and stopped immigration, there were some fourteen thousand Chinese, most of them 'Californians' – that is, not coolies but Chinese immigrants who had arrived via the United States. In 1862, of the 346 suicides that took place in Cuba, exactly half – 173 of them – were Asians. So, over a period of about fifty years there were one hundred thousand deaths (due to suicides, beatings, wars, fevers and, of course, old age, but how do you catalogue the deaths from sadness?).

Esteban Montejo mentions the Chinese: 'A lot of us were slaves. Blacks, Chinese, Indians and various mixtures. The Chinese were always looking and thinking. The Blacks were always moving around, doing something. If the Chinese ever had a moment to sit, they would sit down and think … on Sundays or feast days, we would dance and the Chinese would sit and watch us, as if they were trying to work something out in their heads…'

Alfonso 4

They said in the village that the rebels meant business. At their head was Colonel Isidro, a huge negro, who could strangle a horse with his bare hands, the scourge of both Spaniards and Creoles. All his men were Black, they said, and when they struck at night, they would attack stark naked and machete in hand, in order to blend in with the darkness of the forest.

By then, the war had reached Occidente. You remembered the Taipings and gave them tobacco and, sometimes, pigs, but you also remembered Wu Liau's corpse and decided to stay with your family. Amalia had given you a daughter, Carmen – your first child in wedlock – as well as the longed-for son, Sebastián you called him (the name you would have liked, but which they did not give you). Your eldest daughter, Eugenia, had come to live with you too (her mother died in a smallpox epidemic). So you had your family to look after – the peace, the Great Peace begins at home. You had had quite enough problems with your second daughter – Leonor – the one you had with that woman from the Canary Islands who lived in Colón. Leonor turned out to be a rebellious tomboy, very much like Wu Liau and a little bit like you. She disappeared one night on horseback and nearly rode the poor animal into the ground trying to reach Oriente. She didn't make it; instead she joined up with Pancho Peréz's troops near Esperanza, and you had heard nothing since. One extremely uppity daughter and Carmen, who, by some miracle, survived smallpox and now this Colonel Isidro striding about the countryside naked … The Great Peace remained as far off as ever, despite the new house which your neighbours helped you build in the twinkling of an eye, despite the small farm – by then yours – where you planted vegetables and fruit trees and raised pigs and experimented with growing rice as they used to in Fukien, despite your cigarette stall which was flourishing, what with the village and the war, which, it seems, encouraged people to smoke more not less.

And now it was the rainy season and, one day, you got home late and found Amalia sitting on the doorstep with Sebastián in her arms, waiting for you, and when you saw her anxious, frowning face, you knew at once that something was wrong. 'That daughter of yours' – she weighed each word, emphasising the 'yours' – 'you've got to talk to her.' You sat down in silence and waited for her to speak. You took off your hat and hung it on one of the posts on the veranda. 'That daughter of yours takes no notice of anyone and she's as crazy as Leonor.' You shuddered. Leonor was a name that always made you feel as if you had been punched in the stomach and left gasping for air. Things must be really bad for Amalia to mention Leonor. You took off your left boot. 'That daughter of yours, Alfonso, she's only a kid of eighteen and she's already mixed up with men.' You took off your right boot, smiled and said gently: 'Amalia, you were only sixteen when we got married.' Amalia brought her hand down hard on the sill, making the door frame shudder and shaking the stool you were sitting on. 'Your daughter Eugenia is having an affair with Colonel Isidro.' 'Eugenia!' you thundered. She came to the door. She was wearing a red flower in her hair, a marpacífico. Years later you would often remember this scene and that flower was always the first thing to come to mind. 'Sit down!' She pulled over another stool and set it down opposite yours. She looked you straight in the eye and you saw yourself reflected in eyes identical to yours. 'What exactly is going on?' She held your gaze, as proud as yours. 'I'm engaged, Papa. My fiancé wanted to come and talk to you and I told Amalia so that she could ask your permission, but she just flew into a rage.' You were drumming your bare feet on the floor that your boots had left covered in mud. 'Is it Colonel Isidro?' you asked and Eugenia nodded. You took off your belt and dropped it on the floor, machete and all. 'I don't want you to be a widow before you're even married.' You had rolled your sodden shirt up into a ball and were gripping it in your left hand and punching it with your right. 'No one's going to kill Isidro. The man hasn't been born who could do that. We'll get married when the war is over, and that will be any day now. I just wanted you to know and to give us your blessing. No one else outside this house must know anything about it.'

You tipped the stool back so that it was leaning against the wall. The front legs were in the air and your bare, muddy feet rested on the front bar. Your daughter was still holding your gaze. 'You're a fool, Eugenia.' She said nothing, but kept her eyes fixed on yours. You jumped to your feet and stood a few inches away from her. She looked up, still with her eyes trained on yours. Amalia thought you were going to hit her. Eugenia said later that she knew you wouldn't. You took her face in your wet hands and kissed her on the mouth. 'Tell him to come and see me as soon as he can.' Then you picked up your straw hat and strode into the house.

History 4

The end of the war did, in fact, come swiftly – the end came with the arrival of the Americans. And vice versa. That signalled another beginning too. Many of the remaining Chinese had settled in Havana, in what later became Chinatown. It began in 1858 when Chang Ling settled in Calle de Zanja and opened a cheap restaurant there and Laig Sui-Yi opened a fruit stall.

The 'Californians' had started arriving in 1860 and they came with a few savings. They were the Chinese entrepreneurs, not just small businessmen but also illegal bookies and racketeers. By 1873 there was already a five-star restaurant in Dragones and a Chinese theatre. In 1878 the first newspaper was started.

Chinatown became fully established in 1913 when the doors for immigration, closed by the administrators, were reopened. Between 1913 and 1929, thirty thousand Chinese arrived, this time as ordinary immigrants. The dream of New Spain and of a new Cuba was clearly a powerful one.

Alfonso 5

It was Carmen's wedding day, the only time in your life when you got drunk. 'You really pushed the boat out,' the neighbours said. She was your last daughter to get married and you felt proud of a job well done. Five children (three daughters) and all of them decent folk. Not like your old friend, Salvador Monleón, the most respected patriarch in all Alquízar, who had so many children he didn't even know their names. He was a good stud was Salvador. He stayed on in the village when you all moved to Havana. No one knows exactly how many children he had, but on his birthday, you counted forty-five at the party, of all colours and sizes, some younger than his own grandchildren. It was Salvador who helped you when your contract had just expired and you almost had to sign on again because no one would employ you. He said: 'I need an honest man who's not afraid of hard work,' and he smiled as if to say that he knew you fulfilled both conditions. That was the day you began to be free. One of Salvador's daughters, Bértila, taught you to read and write Spanish, and it was in Salvador's house that you met Amalia, your wife, his wife's half-sister.

And on Carmen's wedding day when you saw him crouch down to come in through the door – he was a very big man – and saw him surrounded by the mist that was by then your constant companion, you knew with painful certainty that very soon you would never see him again and so you decided to get drunk with him on pure rum, in the name of all the good times you had had and of those that would never come again.

Since they had never seen you drunk, your children made a huge fuss. Carmen laughed hysterically and had such a terrible fit of hiccups she nearly had to cancel her honeymoon. Eugenia was angry and jealous that you should get drunk at Carmen's wedding, whereas at hers you had never touched a drop. Leonor sat down in an armchair beside you and matched you drink for drink – a whole bottle of cheap rum. At that point, Colonel Isidro arrived and said to her: 'You certainly live up to your rank as general' (that's how they always addressed Leonor after the war, although, in fact, she only ever made lieutenant). He joined you and Leonor and you each took a swig of brandy, straight from the bottle. And when Leonor said: 'I could drink you both under the table', you and Isidro accepted the challenge and bet a whole roast suckling pig for the whole family, to be paid for by the first to pass out, and two gallons of rum, to be paid for by the second. When the hour of reckoning came, you and Isidro were both sprawled on the floor and Leonor said: 'You see, you don't need balls to drink,' but when she went to get up, she keeled right over and they left the three of you out in the courtyard because you all stank to high heaven of brandy.

Great-granddaughter 2

Alfonso refused to live in Chinatown when he moved to Havana. He rented a house nearby, though, and sometimes he would go in search of smoked pork and sweet bread and sugar candy and glazed fruits.

Alfonso 6

And now you can flop into the armchair and feel the wickerwork against your bony spine and you can look back and see, through the smoke, that you lived through a lot of bad times, but a lot of good times too. You know that it is 1924 and you never expected to get this far. You stroke the handle of your walking stick and take a deep breath; you can fall asleep without fear now. After all, you have had the rare privilege of surviving and being able to die sitting in your armchair, surrounded by five children, five grandchildren, two dogs and a turtle.

Great-granddaughter 3

Ah, the great bearded dragon with eyes of fire and gaping mouth! Let's dance the dragon through the streets hung with little coloured lights and paper flags. Let's dance the dragon through the fireworks and the rockets. And let's wait for them to award the prize and the greenbacks and, finally, there'll be the party with rice wine to drink. But the dragon, after the parade, after the dreams, the dragon, deflated now, the dragon ... always ends up biting his own tail.

Translated by Margaret Jull Costa

Identity and the Politics of (Dis)Location in Lourdes Casal's Narratives of Place

Miriam DeCosta-Willis

Cuban writer and filmmaker Jesús Díaz understood, as only another artist could, the significance of place in the life and work of Lourdes Casal, when he wrote:

> Lourdes retornó. Pero verdaderamente no a La Habana, sino a ella misma, a su barrio, a su origen, a los sitios, al sitio permanente y sitiado en que vivimos, la patria, este sitio que también es de ella. (Díaz 119)

> (Lourdes returned. But not really to Havana, but to herself, to her barrio, to her roots, to the sites, to the permanent and situated sites in which we live, the homeland, this site that is also hers.)

Díaz suggests that the geographic site – the homeland – is both sign and symbol of individual and cultural identity, and that the return of the Prodigal Daughter, of the exile, is not merely a homecoming but also an act of reconnection and reconciliation. Indeed, the life of Lourdes Casal is emblematic of the complexities and contradictions of Cuban and Cuban American identity in a revolutionary era. Of African, Spanish, and Chinese descent, she was born in 1938, into what has been described as Havana's 'precaria pequeña burguesía mulata' (Consejo 120). The daughter of a doctor and a school teacher, she attended private schools, where, as she writes, 'the children of the bourgeoisie . . . [had] little contact with the black masses and other oppressed sectors of the population' ('Race' 21). She graduated from an elitist, parochial university, but when the Revolution triumphed in 1959, her political views reflected the political ideology of the White middle class with which she identified. And so, at age twenty-three, Lourdes Casal joined other exiles in a flight to the United States. Her radicalisation began in New York, where she attended graduate school, became a university professor, and participated in the liberation struggles of the 1960s.

Her experiences in this country were crucial to her identity formation as a Black, Cuban-American revolutionary. According to Nancy Morejón, '[I]t was only in the United States that Lourdes noticed what color she was, what kind of hair she had, that she was a woman' (Behar 135). In 1973, Casal became one of the first Cuban exiles to return to the island, a move that clearly marked her social and political transformation. She noted in an interview:

> Yo he sido una de esas personas que individualmente ha evolucionado de posturas extremadamente agresivas contra la Revolución Cubana hacia posturas menos agresivas ('Dos semanas' 9).

> (I have been one of those persons who has evolved, as an individual, from an extremely aggressive position toward the Cuban Revolution to a less aggressive position.)

A year after her first trip to Cuba, she co-founded the journal *Areíto*, helped organise the Brígida Antonio Maceo, and led a group of *maceítos* to Havana to seek the reunification of the Cuban people. In 1979, after the assassination of two allies and several threats on her life, Lourdes Casal moved to Havana, where she became seriously ill and died two years later at age forty-two. In spite of a daunting programme of study, teaching, and activism, Casal published several books, including collections of poetry, essays, and short stories.

Her life provides a context for interpreting Casal's narratives of space, those literary texts that derive their meaning from the physical and psychological relationship between the subject and the space that s/he inhabits. The narratives that I shall examine in this essay include poems from her collection, a memoir, and a short story. *Palabras juntan revolución* is divided into four sections, which oscillate between two distinct landscapes: Havana, the location of childhood memory; and New York, the site of transformation. The first section, 'El barrio regresa en sus sonidos' (The neighbourhood returns through its sounds), recreates the beloved world of a young girl, identified as 'la niña de las trenzas' (the girl with braids) whose words evoke a remembered landscape, idealised and romanticised, of Havana in the 1940s and '50s. It is the imaginary homeland that the exile has left behind: it is a place where memory recreates familiar tastes (ice cream and tamales), sounds (vendors' cries and dogs' barking) and visions (fresh flowers and old portraits); it is a place where family rites and rituals (Sunday rides and birthday parties) give form and texture to an orderly life. Poems about Afro-Cuban religious figures suggest that the family also observes the rituals of *santería*, which give stability and significance to their lives. The girl with the braids feels safe and secure in that spiritual space, under the protection of her mother and the orishas. In 'Ebbó', for example, the personae of the mulatto mother and the Orisha Yemayá Olokún are conflated – in the lines

'Yemayá, la madre, Lilia, / mulata preciosa' (14) – into a maternal figure who nurtures the child: 'Mi madre . . . me limpia / me protege / me retorna la quebrantada salud' (15) (My mother . . . cleans me / protects me / restores my once-broken health). Afro-Cuban Orishas do not create, in Casal's work, a poetics of the exotic; rather, they are signifiers of the African roots of Cuban identity. As Stuart Hall explains, African gods often serve in literature as coded signs of an identity that is formed by what Senghor calls the Presence Africaine, a fundamental element in the Caribbean imaginary (228-30).

Although the poems in 'El barrio' refer to several Havana landmarks, they are centred primarily in the domestic space of 'home', in the large, rambling house on Maloja Street in Los Sitios, where the extended family of uncles and aunts and cousins gathers to celebrate the girl's birthday. This is a site of comfort and privilege, for encoded in the poetry are signifiers of class: the father's black Studebaker and saxophone, the girl's lace dresses and taffeta ribbons, and the house with its patio and balcony. In that comfortable and ordered world of Havana's 'pequeña burguesía mulata', it was important that 'todo estaba en su lugar' (everything be in its place), a phrase that appears in the first poem, as well as in the short story about the Chinese ancestor who raged when furniture was misplaced. Indeed, any 'eruption of funk' threatened to destabilise that tenuous, precarious world, constructed of memory and fantasy. The reader senses beneath the surface of the words the anxiety of the 'I' who writes, as well as the tension that separates the narrator – the exile of the 1970s – from the girl, who is the subject of the written text. The narrator searches in vain for the uncomplicated self that she was and for the Edenic world that she once knew. She asks:

> . . . dónde está la que yo era
> cuando era mío aquel vestido azul . . .
> dónde se ha ido aquel mundo que conozco
> en mis huellas . . . (12)

> (. . . where is the one whom I was
> when that blue dress was mine . . .
> where has that world gone that I know
> through my footprints . . .)

This stranger (and here I use the figure – 'una extraña entre las piedras' – with which the narrator of the poem 'Para Ana Veldford' is identified) does not recognise herself in the child's fixed, essentialised identity. This stranger can no longer inhabit the closed and claustrophobic world of the mulatto bourgeoisie, because the comfort and security of that world come at too high a price: silence and complicity.

In distancing herself, physically and psychologically, from Havana of the 1940s, the exiled woman can deconstruct pre-revolutionary 'home' and 'nation' as sites of privilege, omission, and silence. Casal dares to 'speak the unspeakable', to uncover Cuba's 'hidden history' by recounting 'horrifying stories [that] were not to be told' ('Race' 12). She relates these stories in a short memoir, inserted into a scholarly essay, which serves as a counter-discourse to the officially sanctioned history of race in Cuba. Here, the narrator is a New York scholar writing in the 1970s, but the speaking subject is 'a young black Cuban', who heard terrifying stories about violence in the racial war of 1912, 'stories about blacks being hunted day and night, and black men being hung by their genitals' ('Race' 12). Equally upsetting was the conspiracy of silence about these atrocities, which were omitted from history books; and the complicity of Blacks, including family members, in suppressing these horrible memories. She reflects:

> It seemed aberrant to me, that memories which were still alive in participants and witnesses, even in victims and relatives of victims, could have been so completely obliterated from the collective consciousness, so completely erased from everyday discourse and from history books. ('Race' 12)

In this essay, language signifies shifts in social and political consciousness. The narrator employs a linguistic code – English – that is not her own, not her native tongue, because in voicing the unspeakable, she must defamiliarise the emotionally-charged experience. Casal's facility in an alien language also marks her movement from exile to diaspora and from displacement to immersion in the codes of another culture. She writes that, as a young, black Cuban, she was puzzled about the 'codes which regulated communications on race relations' ('Race' 12). But her location in the United States in the 1960s and her subject position as a student activist exposed her to a new set of codes on race and to a new vocabulary that included such words as 'sit-ins', 'demonstrations', and power to the people'.

Location, as this narrative demonstrates, is a useful metaphor in the representation of identity, because it often signifies a change in consciousness; metaphors such as bell hooks' margin/centre and Gloria Anzaldúa's borderland/la frontera become sites for exploring the complexities of race, gender, class, and sexuality in a postmodern world. What does it mean, then, for a subject to become dis-located, dis-placed, uprooted, deracinated . . . exiled? Casal explores the political and psychological ramifications of this phenomenon in several texts. In the short story 'Los Fundadores: Alfonso' (The Founders: Alfonso), for example, she draws upon history and myth to create a narrative of dis-location, a narrative about Cuba's Asian roots that was lost or forgotten or suppressed in the construction of national identity. The story relates the diaspora experience of men like Casal's great-grandfather, the son of Wu Liau, who grew up in China but was forced into exile by war and poverty. In the nineteenth century, he and some 100,000 other Chinese endured a five-month voyage through hell to become eight-year contract labourers in Cuba's tobacco fields for 4 dollars a month. Those experiences transformed Wu Liau's son, but the categories 'immigrant', 'Cuban', and 'contract labourer' cannot possibly describe his complex identity, aspects of which – the Christian name Alfonso López, the alien tongue, the unfamiliar customs – were forced upon him. He held fast, however, to the markers of his originary self: his moustache, hairless chin, and, especially, his dream of respectability.

According to Stuart Hall, 'identities are the names we give to the different ways we are positioned by, and position ourselves within, the narratives of the past' (223). In 'Los fundadores', Casal demonstrates how the nomadic experience – the movement from China to Cuba and from the tobacco fields to Havana – both shapes and metaphorises Alfonso's identity. Narrated in three segments – 'La biznieta', 'Alfonso', and 'Historia' – and from different points of view, the story recovers the forgotten past. Again, the writer dares to 'speak the unspeakable': the assassination of Taipan rebels, the stench and disease of the middle passage, and the deaths of thousands of Chinese Cubans through suicide and sadness. But 'Los fundadores' is more than a fictionalised biography of a Chinese ancestor; it is also an attempt by Casal to understand a part of her Cuban self that had long been suppressed. She writes that she had:

> . . . a burning set of questions deeply related to my own identity. . .
>
> [A]s a Cuban of mixed ancestry (White, Black and Chinese), I considered myself to be like Cuba – a mulatress in an essentially mulatto country. ('Race' 12)

Questions about identity – of both the self and the nation – have profound political implications, especially when the construction of self is grounded in difference – difference of race, class, and ideology.

One of the most important political problems that Lourdes Casal confronted in her life and writing was the question of the relationship between islanders and exiles. In her life, she bore passionate witness to the importance of reconciliation; in her prose, she examined the social and political complexities of reconnection. But it was in her poetry that she dealt, deeply and intimately, with her feelings about exile. In the poem 'Definición', she wrote:

> Exilio
> es vivir donde no existe casa alguna
> en la que hayamos sido niños (31)
> (Exile
> is living where there is no house
> in which we have been children)

The second and longest section of *Palabras,* entitled 'Tanto más vulnerable que la piedra' (Much More Vulnerable than Stone), includes many poems, such as 'Exilio / Orden del día' (Exile / Order of the Day), 'Hudson, invierno' (Hudson, Winter), and 'Domingo' (Sunday), which depict the place of exile: New York City. One of the most important of these narratives of space is 'Para Ana Veldford', which is widely recognised as Casal's signature poem. In this short, plaintive lyric she articulates the terrible dilemma of the dis-located. The first two-thirds of the poem is a love song to the city, in which images of light and warmth create an idyllic landscape. The narrator feels a connection to that place – 'Nueva York es mi casa. / Soy ferozmente leal a esta adquirida patria chica' (60) (New York is my home / I am fiercely loyal to that acquired *patria chica*.) – but she is separated from others by the window of a bus. Alone and isolated, she explains, 'Permanezco tan extranjera detrás del cristal protector' (I remain so foreign behind the protective glass). Her New York is an urban landscape, where the smell of marijuana and the sound of Santana's music linger in the streets of Harlem, and where the narrator identifies with others: 'nosotros, los pobres' (we, the poor). In the last section of the poem, the persona confesses that this is not the city of her childhood (of her first convictions, of her first fall), so she will remain forever on the margins, forever a stranger, a foreigner:

> demasiado habanera para ser newyorkina,
> demasiado newyorkina para ser,
> – aún volver a ser –
> cualquier otra cosa. (61)

> (too *habanera* to be *newyorkina,*
> too *newyorkina* to be,

– even to become again –
anything else.)

The subject, who speaks/writes from a particular place and time, is dislocated, and that displacement is signified by two symbolic spaces: New York and Havana. She realises that identity is not fixed or coherent but always in the process of becoming something else, and it is the 'otra cosa' that permits growth and transformation.

Kaminsky maintains that 'exile identity . . . is a function of the self's being tied to a particular place where it belongs, however tenuously' (22). No matter how she feels about New York, her *patria chica*, for Casal, the geographic space and symbolic place of her identity is Cuba, *la patria*, to which she is anchored by birth, culture, and language. She expresses the significance of The Return in a poem that connects Cuba to its African past:

De nuevo,
Yemayá,
voy recorriendo tu reino.

(Again
Yemayá,
I go running across your kingdom.)

and she ends the poem in the same way with the lines:

Repito con Obbatalá el viejo patakín
'La tierra.
La cosa está en la tierra'.

(With Obbatalá I repeat the ancient *patakín*
'The land
The thing is in the land'.)

The land was deeply rooted in the consciousness of Lourdes Casal, who explored in her poetry and prose the psychological and political effects of deterritorialisation, the displacement of people, meaning, and identities that is endemic to the postmodern world. Her experiences as an artist and intellectual revealed to her the paradox of exile in a strange land: on the one hand, it was alienating and isolating but, on the other, it permitted a revolutionary transformation.

Works Cited

Anzaldúa, Gloria. *Borderlands / La Frontera: The New Mestiza*. San Francisco: Spinsters /Aunt Lute, 1987.

Behar, Ruth and Lucía Suárez. 'Two Conversations with Nancy Morejón'. In *Bridges to Cuba: Puentes a Cuba*. Edited by Ruth Behar. Ann Arbor: The University of Michigan Press, 1995.

Casal, Lourdes. 'The Founders: Alfonso'. Translated by Margaret Jull Costa. *The Voice of the Turtle: An Anthology of Cuban Stories*. Edited by Peter Bush. New York: Grove Press, 1997.

___. *Palabras juntan revolución: poesía*. Havana: Casa de las Américas, 1981.

___. 'Race Relations in Contemporary Cuba'. In *The Position of Blacks in Brazilian and Cuban   Society*. Anani Dzidizienyo and Lourdes Casal. London: Minority Rights Group, 1979.

Consejo de Dirección de *Areito*. 'El Instituto de Estudios Cubanos o los estrechos límites del pluralismo'. *Areito* 9 (1984): 120-22.

Díaz, Jesús. 'Homenaje'. *Areito* 9 (1984): 118-20.

'Dos semanas en Cuba: Entrevista a Lourdes Casal'. *Areito* 9 (1983): 9-11.

Hall, Stuart. 'Cultural Identity and Cinematic Representation'. In *EX-ILES: Essays on Caribbean Cinema*. Edited by Mbye Cham. Trenton: Africa World Press, 1992.

hooks, bell. *From Margin to Center*. Boston: South End Press, 1984.

Kaminsky, Amy K. *After Exile: Writing the Latin American Diaspora*. Minneapolis: University of Minnesota Press, 1999.

Argentina Chiriboga

ARGENTINA CHIRIBOGA

ECUADOR

(b. 1940)

*With the publication of three novels, two collections of poetry, and several
works of nonfiction, Luz Argentina Chiriboga emerged in the 1990s as
one of Ecuador's most prolific and esteemed writers. She was born in the
coastal town of Esmeraldas but has lived for most of her adult life in
Quito, where she attended the Universidad Central and presently lives
with her husband, the distinguished poet and novelist Nelson Estupiñán
Bass. Her first writings included articles and short stories (one of which
won a prize in the José de San Martín Contest in Buenos Aires), which
were published in periodicals such as* Cultura, Débora, *and* Letras del
Ecuador. *One of her first books* Manual de ecología *(Ecology Manual), a
beautifully illustrated collection of poetry for children, reflects her
academic training as a scientist. In 1991, Chiriboga published her first
novel,* Bajo la piel de los tambores, *which examines the physical and
psychological development of a young mulatto woman who confronts
issues of race, gender, class, and sexuality. Translated into English by
Mary Harris,* Beneath the Skin of the Drum *is one of the first novels by a
Latin American writer of African descent. It is notable for its mysterious
characters, poetic language, and romantic ambience, all of which
contribute to the eroticism of the text. Eroticism is also the theme of
Chiriboga's* La contraportada del deseo *(The Back Cover of Desire), a
collection of poems that explore female desire through sensual images
and evocative language.*

*Two of the major themes of Chiriboga's work are the status of women
and the position of African-descended people in Ecuadorian society. These
interests are reflected not only in her writing but also in her intellectual
and cultural activities: she has attended conferences on Afro-Latin
American culture in Colombia and Panama, as well as the centennial*

celebration for Chilean poet Gabriela Mistral; she served as president of the National Union of Ecuadorian Women; and she has lectured on Ecuadorian literature and culture throughout the United States. A recent publication, Diáspora: Por los caminos de Esmeraldas (Diaspora: Through the Roads of Esmeraldas), is a study, based on extensive research, of Ecuador's African heritage. In Palenque: Décimas, a group of original poems derived from the Afro-Ecuadorian oral tradition, Chiriboga uses a popular verse form, the décima (a narrative poem of ten lines), to treat themes related to slavery and popular culture.

In her fiction, Chiriboga gives voice to women who have been silenced or omitted from the official history of Ecuador. Her second novel, Jonatás y Manuela, is a fictional treatment of the life of an historical woman – a slave from Chota – who led her mistress in a series of escapades to liberate slaves and battles to gain Ecuador's independence. En la noche del viernes (On Friday Night), her third novel, deals with the plight of a contemporary mulata who struggles in her work and in her relationships to achieve agency, independence, and self-awareness. In such narratives, novelist Chiriboga explores the ramifications of being Black and female in Latin America.

from

The Backcover of Desire

Untitled

Changó and Yemayá go by,
brushing by the night's thighs,
announcing songs and drums.
I write discovery, surrender,
movement,
and your voice remains
suspended in my memory.
Ancestral spirits
tumble headlong,
giving shape to disoblivion,
and your breath takes shelter
in my fragile triangle.

Translated by Rosemary Geisdorfer Feal

Untitled

Let my braid loose
so it may dance
in the wet wind.
I want to feel
its intoxicating language.
This wild,
elusive tangle
lights the fire that
makes me delirious.
It cries out
a full-bodied surrender,
and it casts shadows
on my nocturnal rebellions.
It soars, dances
with frightened wings
and when it flies about
it reveals its African origin.
My kinky hair
brings a frenzy
a swell of waves
an ancestor
who comes from afar.
This sheen so black
carries forth ancient codes.
Beneath these curls
with their cracking voices
my grandparents emerge.

Translated by Rosemary Geisdorfer Feal

Untitled

For Nelson

On these avenues
the waves of your ocean
lick my sleep
Your seafoam
leads me by the hand
toward the country of my desires.

In me
there is no wasteland.
In me
your word
besieged by moons
has sown a swarm of verses.

Without respite
we have travelled
through rains and rainbows
that exchanged
their language of colour
with our jubilation.

Bring your ear
close to me
and you will hear the murmur
of my palisades.
On my skin, indelibly engraved,
are your four cardinal points.

Translated by Rosemary Geisdorfer Feal

from

Drums Under My Skin

Early one Friday morning, Milton demanded that we make love. It ended with a scene in which I cried hysterically when it seemed, for a moment, that he was going away forever, taking my virginity as his prize. When he saw me convulsing in a fit of madness, he agreed to give up his bachelor life. "We'll get married," he said unwillingly.

Using the argument that we needed a man to help us run the farm, I succeeded, in the end, in convincing my mother that my marriage to Milton was convenient. I added that, if papa were alive, he would accept my marriage. Adela was supporting mama who was walking lifelessly. Solís waited for us with his marimba on the pier, which was almost full of soldiers who looked as if they were after someone. The people crowded together to watch my now famous wedding. Nicasio and Adela declared before the official that they knew that we were both single and that there was no reason why we should not be joined in matrimony. I looked at the half-hidden hands of our housekeeper, who had joined her middle fingers to show that she was not committing perjury. Fortunately, no one noticed the subtle, comical smile on Milton's face throughout the ceremony. I took his hand and felt sweat coming down his arm, but he let go when he saw that a lot of people were watching him. I was glad that I had made myself up in such a way that no one could see me blush at such disdain. "My God!" I murmured, intimidated by a voice resounding inside me. "I'll pass through Sikán," Rebe. I recognized his tone of voice. It was he. I inhaled the smell of this ideal man and felt his body brushing against mine. I imagined him stroking my hand, and as I felt his presence, I stepped back in time to taste the candy we had shared on my first trip to Quito. I closed my eyes to surrender myself to the memory of Julio Martínez.

A crowd followed us in canoe and on rafts to the farm, livening up the trip with cheers and guitar music. We butchered ten pigs, three young bulls, twelve chickens, and five ducks. While Milton and Nicasio served sugarcane liquor, Solís's marimba group, accompanied by women singing and responding, played *torbellinos* and *agualargas*. The couples returned to the makeshift dance floor after they had gotten some sleep beneath the most leafy trees, and the women served the stewed duck which, according to ancient belief, was the best way to replenish the energies of those who were waking up. In observance of an African rite established in Oriki, Milton and I were forced to eat a stew made with the testicles of a cautious bull. Mama shut herself up in her corner of bitterness and did not come out to join the guests in their merrymaking. Milton was circulating among the guests, showing that he could hold his liquor. The celebration lasted three days, the length of time which, according to the guests, would assure us of eternal happiness. Only then, for the first time and because he was drunk, did I hear Milton talk about his father. He revealed that his father never had time for his children, but was completely devoted to his animals, and that his mother would send his father's dinner pail every day to the different huts where he stayed and slept when night caught him. I was convinced of this one thing: the memory of Julio Martínez would be a lifebuoy in my shipwreck. At dawn the fourth day, the canoes slid downstream and the guests shouted their last hurrahs.

Milton's entry into the house accentuated mama's old age. She abandoned her place at the table and went to eat with Adela in the kitchen or invited the little children to lunch to continue their reading lessons. From then on, Millton assumed control of the farm and the account in the bank in Oriki. I no longer went to the pasture, to the corrals or to see the pigs. I was resigned to servitude – something which I had never imagined – and would prepare his favorite meats. I knew a long time ago that I was prepared to make happy the man destiny put in my path. It was a kind of secret pact I had made with reality. As long as Milton took care of Sikán and didn't stop me from participating in the fishermen's co-op, I had to resign myself to his indifference. I lived only for my senses, thinking about nothing transcendental. That was what mama disliked most, because she was convinced that I had been endowed at birth with abilities which I was wasting.

Months passed, almost a year. One afternoon, Milton came back from Oriki and called me by the wrong name. He had stopped liking green and had replaced it with violet. He came home with the smell of old things on his breath and rancid perfume on his clothes. I began to replace him bit by bit. I changed his voice. The memories of my single days were a sanctuary where I venerated the man from Argentina whom I always saw exactly as I had engraved him in my memory. I began to daydream and continued to talk in my sleep. Out of fear of mama, I started to hide Milton's faults, but he insulted me when I complained. "And that Julio Martínez who was your lover?" I would get very quiet. "See, you're not saying anything. You still think about him. That day in the palm grove when you got my name mixed up with his, I felt like kicking you." He would use ballads such as this one to reproach me: "Everything has turned against you. / Instead of hitting, you missed. / The one with whom you deceived me loved you and left you."

In my insomnia I would hear Milton's horse galloping as it rode through the early morning. Sultán and Napoleón would wake mama with their barking. Manuelita's persistent "No" pursued me night and day. At dawn one day, I heard a stair creak, and I hid the books of the co-op. "You big whore, are you waiting for Julio?" Milton slapped me, and a whiff of alcohol crossed my face. "Even when you're asleep, you call his name, you slut." I trembled at the thought that he could tell from my eyes that I was waiting for the man from Argentina and I cried in anger because I had lost the card with his address. I kept crying until the dogs barked again. Milton lifted me in the air, took me to bed and undressed me. "This is how that Julio used to make love to you." I cleared my mind, and I realized that clearing it didn't leave it empty because I filled it with repugnance. "I don't like you whispering with those people from the co-op. All they do is gossip." I freed myself from his arms and went to get the douche. This time, I doubled the amount of lemon juice.

When I returned, I saw him looking at the ceiling, his mouth still open as though he were enjoying me, and his hands still holding the shape of my breasts. I tiptoed over with the ax in the air. "Child, what are you going to do?" It was papa's voice. I looked to see where he was but didn't see him. I hid the weapon.

I was afraid of returning to the same old boring life, to the nights with cold feet, to the lonely Sundays and to my silence. Milton was passing his hands up and down my thighs as I read aloud beneath the shade of an avocado tree. "I'm going to build a house in El Salto." It was then that I argued with him, trying to understand the situation, trying hard not to shout or cry, and controlling my hands so as not to throw the book at him. We spoke until we were hoarse without being able to reach an agreement. He wanted to return to his former life, to enjoy the freedom of being a night owl. Realizing how risky a pregnancy could be, I went to the captain of *The Pharaoh* as soon as Milton went to the mountain.

It seemed to me that lemon juice was not a sure enough method to avoid having a child and that there were more modern ways to do so. I asked the captain to bring me three dozen condoms. I felt my cheeks get red with embarrassment, and I looked in my purse for my handkerchief. I turned the pockets inside out but couldn't find it. Someone had stolen it from me on the trip.

We were alone again, mama, Adela and I, once more in control of our house and of Sikán, without the feeling of having a child who would have been a projection of his father. When the captain came to the farm to personally deliver the order to me, Milton had already left the house under the pretext that I had guaranteed a bank loan for *Seablue* without consulting him. I began to realize that I could build my happiness without him. Mama's weeping intensified in the early morning, and she seemed to drown in her tears and her asthma. She was losing her strength and didn't get out of bed during the day. When Milton left, my mother ordered the return of the cattle, and I agreed with her. The animals bellowed in the nearby pasture.

It was Tuesday. The trees were dripping with dew, and the birds were practicing their musical scores. The stair creaked under Milton's boots, and his "Damn nigger whore!" echoed even in the river. "I married you out of pity." I dodged his punch. Then mama, remembering that she was once young, stood up in the doorway with papa's shotgun and aimed at Cevallos, determined to shoot him. He stepped back, scared. Then we heard him running quickly down the stairs and his horse galloping off. His Panama hat was lying in the living room.

Translated by Mary A. Harris

The Poetics and Politics of Desire: Eroticism in Luz Argentina Chiriboga's *Bajo la piel de los tambores*

Miriam DeCosta-Willis

Sexuality is one of the most problematic areas in the literary representation of Black women because the image of the loose woman – exotic, uninhibited, and predatory – haunts the pages of African American, Caribbean, and Latin American literatures. To counter the negative stereotype, early African American women novelists, such as Frances Watkins Harper and Nella Larsen, shaped a discourse of reticence about Black female sexuality and they created a bourgeois model of respectability – the genteel, fair-skinned mulatto – whose sexuality was repressed or thwarted but seldom celebrated. This model of respectability, however, seldom appears in Afro-Hispanic literature, where the hot-blooded *mulata* is the predominant figure. As Ann Venture Young and Claudette RoseGreen-Williams have pointed out, the Afro-Hispanic woman has been defined and constructed, traditionally, in terms of a reductive sexuality; the primitive exotic is at once desirable (an object), useful (a commodity), and dangerous (a predator). Contemporary women writers, however, unlike their predecessors who were constrained by social mores and literary conventions, celebrate female sexuality, represent sexually desiring subjects, and explore themes such as incest, lesbianism, and autoeroticism which were once taboo. In the pages of their sometimes political and often polemic works, female sexuality often becomes a feminist metaphor for woman's independence and autonomy.

In her first novel, Afro-Ecuadorian writer Luz Argentina Chiriboga explores the complexity and ambiguity of the Black female experience, treating female sexuality as a metaphor of resistance to the ideology of domination. *Bajo la piel de los tambores,* a narrative which subverts the orthodox construction of race, gender, and class in Hispanic society, signals the emergence of Black women's prose fiction in Afro-Hispanic and Latin American literatures. Traditionally, Afro-Hispanic novels recount the adventures of male protagonists such as Ascensión Lastre and José Antonio

Pastrana, while female characters – depicted as mothers, wives or lovers, who are relevant primarily in terms of their relationships to men – are invisible or marginal. Many male-authored novels and short stories describe violence toward women; in works like "Martes de Carnaval" and *Toque de queda,* rape and "violation of the feminine body [form] part of a larger discourse of violence, such as that of a dictatorship, integrating it into the repressive mechanisms of *de facto* governments" (López Morales 128). In such polemical texts – where women serve as metaphors of the political body and of the body politic (Hunt) – woman's pleasure is either absent or misrepresented, as Juyungo's rape of María de los Angeles demonstrates:

> A caressing bite on the shoulder elicited from her a gesture, a mixture of pain and *acquiescence* at the same time. She *yielded* gradually, finally *letting him kiss her*. ... Having felt that white girl *tremble, enjoy, sigh,* palpitate beneath him gave him more aplomb... *(Juyungo, 49-50, emphasis added)*

Male desire (especially when accompanied by force) does not automatically result in female pleasure. The notion that María could feel, under such circumstances, a "certain primitive and feminine curiosity for this tall and strong Black," and that she could "acquiesce," "yield," and "enjoy" rape by this stranger is a male fantasy rather than an accurate representation of female desire. Curiously María's "pleasure" is filtered through the mind of Juyungo: "Having felt that white girl ... beneath him."

Argentina Chiriboga's novel, which examines the sexual desire of an Afro-Ecuadorian woman, is a subversive text because it challenges the construction of female sexuality in patriarchal societies, where women, historically, were/are denied a right to their bodies through repression of their sexuality, the threat of sexual violence, and the denial of reproductive rights. Although not a *roman à thèse,* the novel deals, tangentially, with controversial themes such as marital rape, male libidousness, miscegenation, and birth control; and it undermines prevailing codes of social and literary propriety by representing female desire as a form of social and aesthetic resistance to ideologies of the family, school, and church. These institutions have traditionally repressed female sexuality outside the context of marriage, insisting that single women preserve the "priceless gem of virginity." As Espín points out, the precepts of the Catholic Church and the Hispanic concept of honor mandate female chastity (151-53).

The thematic impulses and fictive devices of *Bajo la piel* elaborate a rhetoric of insubordination which challenges these doctrines, while the novel deconstructs religious and racial archetypes. A White priest and nun (Father Cayetano Santacruz and Sister María de la Concepción) are sensual and passionate in spite of conventional representations of the clergy as asexual; and Black women (Sister Inés, Adela, and Nidia), stereotypically depicted as lusty, are asexual. These ironies are not lost on Rebeca. As she passes from adolescence to adulthood, from innocence to experience, she laments her "involuntaria virginidad," questions the prohibitions against female sexuality – represented textually by the "Pórtate bien" of maternal authority figures – and challenges conventions of female decorum which require modesty, passivity, and chastity.

The iconoclasm of the novel is apparent to literary critics such as Alfredo Rodas Reyes, who writes that it is a "[n]ovela de carácter social, personal y sicológico, talvez un poco cruda," perhaps "crude," in his opinion, because it is the work of a woman. Invoking the discourse of the body, Argentina Chiriboga writes honestly and frankly about sex and rites of desire without using what feminist scholars like Suleiman call "male language" – the four-letter words and explicit vocabulary that characterize the writing of a Peri Rossi or of an Ntozake Shange. As the author points out, "En cuanto al vocabulario que utilizo, no incluye 'malas palabras,' aunque considero que ninguna palabra es mala" ("Primera"). Neither, however, is hers a "discourse of reticence," characterized by "ladylike" language: euphemisms, circumlocutions, and coded words. She describes, for example, several female biological rituals: using sanitary napkins during menstruation and douching with lemon water for birth control. According to López Morales, "menstruation … has generally been silenced by masculine discourse" because male writers ignore bodily functions that are different from theirs (128-29). Argentina Chiriboga uses words like *los senos, el aborto, los preservativos,* and *el irrigador* – what Molly Hite calls the conventionally repressed "language of corporeality" (132) – to underscore the biological facts of womanhood and to affirm Rebeca's identity as a female subject. In terms of its subject, language, and themes, then, this novel is very much a feminist text.

On another level, *Bajo la piel* can be read as a sentimental novel which employs the rhetorical patterns and narrative strategies of romance fiction: a clandestine affair, the element of danger, a sense of risk and helplessness, fear of possession, and attraction to someone of a different age, race or class. In the romance novel, however, sex is customarily legitimized within the bonds of marriage. Argentina Chiriboga has written a first-person linear narrative, divided into three parts, which traces the social, sexual, and racial coming-of-age of Rebeca González, a young Black woman who leaves her coastal village to attend a parochial boarding school in Quito, where she encounters racial prejudice, confronts class privilege, and experiences a sexual awakening. Eventually, she returns to Oriki, marries an alcoholic, womanizing White man, has a brief affair with a priest, and discovers the identity of a mysterious lover. Her interracial marriage is, in part, an act of rebellion against her mother and the ethics of sexual conduct and of domestic deportment that the mother represents: "Odié a mamá y la forma que me había educado..." (122). In spite of her rejection of the "maternal destiny" of other women – her mother, Nidia Araujo, a former teacher; Adela Okú, their housekeeper, who observes African cultural traditions; and Sister Inés de Rosario, a Black nun and activist, who organizes women laborers – Rebeca is mired in a conventional romantic script. She seeks fulfillment and completion in the arms of a man because she has internalized the feminine values of her society; she defines herself and tests received conventions through her erotic relationships with men. After begging Millton to marry her, Rebeca surrenders control of Sikán, the successful ranch that she has established, to her husband, confessing that she was once "dispuesta a hacer feliz al hombre que el destino me pusiera en el camino" (141).

Rebeca is a complex and ambivalent woman whose identity is fragmented and shifting; she is a woman divided and in constant battle with her conflicted selves. The granddaughter of an African, she denies her racial self; the daughter of a modest rancher, she hides her rural self from her class-mates, the daughters of doctors, bankers, and generals, while she tells her parents that "Estas relaciones cuestan, pero son importantes para mi posición futura" (92). She is an "emerging" woman, who tries to free herself from other women's social scripts. On one hand, she is a daring and unconventional heroine, who sets out on a journey of self-discovery – a literal journey from Oriki to Quito and a figurative journey from silence to voice – but, on the other hand, she is hesitant and self-doubting. The novel's narrative strategies undermine the voice of the heroine, at the same time that they reinforce her sense of alienation, isolation, and powerlessness. Her first-person narrative does not begin with a strong and assertive "yo" but with a series of collective, first-person plural verbs, such as "disfrutábamos," "éramos," and "gozábamos," which dissipate the individual self into an amorphous collective group. The self first appears as the direct object pronoun *me* rather than the subject pronoun *yo*, indicating that the process of self-objectification has begun. Paradoxically, Rebeca is both the subject and the object of her discourse; as subject, she narrates the story of her sexual rite of passage, but, as object, she is "acted upon" as she acquiesces to the textual and sexual desires of others. She does not present herself as "I" until the fourth page of her narrative, and then only within the context of her mother's desire for the daughter's domesticity:

> Yo, consciente de que en el internado tejía la urdimbre de mi destino, oía lejanos los consejos de mamá que sólo dejaría de suspirar cuando me viera casada. (12)

Narration and description predominate in this novel, while interchange between characters often takes the form of indirect discourse ("Amelia nos había dicho que en el amor todo era permitido."). Dialogue is enclosed in long, run-on sentences without the orthographic conventions – dashes and indented paragraphs – which differentiate speakers. In the following passage, this narrative strategy masks the speech of Julio Martínez, while it suppresses Rebeca's voice within a masculine discourse:

> A medida que nos alejábamos, Sikán humedeció mis ojos, Por qué lloras, escuché con acento extranjero al desconocido, persona como vos no debe estar triste. (14)

Dashes, however, frame the powerful voice of Amelia Roca, the student-prostitute, during her interrogation by the police. Amelia speaks with confidence and authority, while Rebeca whispers about silence, entrapment, fear, and invisibility. Words and phrases such as "callamos," "sin comunión," "encerrada," "asomada," "asustada," and "de no verme" underscore the Afro-Ecuadorian's insecurity and self-doubt.

The language of the text – its words, figures, and images – shapes a poetics of desire that reinforces, dialectically, the structure and meaning of the novel. The fictive universe of the narrative is evoked through sets of erotic images – masks, mirrors, and enclosures – which frame a dialectic of covering and uncovering, of masking and unmasking, and of closing and opening. "Sexuality," as Carole S. Vance explains, "is simultaneously a domain of restriction, repression and danger as well as a domain of exploration, pleasure, and agency" (1). Rebeca experiences, particularly in her relationship with Father Santacruz, the erotic tension between these two concomitant aspects of sexuality: when she is in the confessional with the priest, she describes a feeling "oscilante entre el placer y el daño" (55). It is the passionate Zaragozan priest, the man of the warm breath, seductive *ceceo,* and black velvet mask, who arouses the young woman and introduces her to sensual pleasures – the scent of delicate perfumes, the touch of pearl rosaries, and the texture of lace mantillas – even as he claims her body:

Sus manos por mi cintura, sus manos por mis glúteos, sus manos por mis senos, sus manos, sus inquietas manos, arrimados a la pared sentí multiplicados sus dedos. (65)

Caught between the.sexual orthodoxy which she has been taught (ironically, by the sisters of Nuestra Señora de Guadalupe) and the desire which she feels, Rebeca inhabits an eroticized world of dark passages, hidden gardens, and deserted mansions – a sexualized landscape where the boundaries between reality and fantasy are blurred. Reality is fragile and tenuous, while appearances are deceptive: a female student is a man, another is a prostitute, and Julio Martínez turns out to be an historical figure.

The shifting identities of characters like Julio Martínez, Adela Roca, Vicenta Páez, and Father Santacruz reinforce the enigmatic and ambiguous texture of Rebeca's erotic world. On her journey to Quito, in the penumbra of a dark bus, she meets a mysterious stranger, dressed in blue jeans, boots, and a beret, who is one of the most tenuous but important characters in her narrative. As they whisper in the dark, she falls passionately in love with the handsome man, who becomes the idealized subject of her erotic fantasies. Rebeca discovers, on the last page of the novel, that Martínez, from whom she has received only one postcard and the promise of a rendezvous, is really the Cuban revolutionary, Che Guevarra. That revelation evokes, in the reader, a visual image of Alberto Korda's famous photograph of Che, "Guerillero Heróico," which adorns books, posters, and even buildings: Che of the deep, penetrating eyes and sensual mouth, his hair, long and dark, blowing in the wind. The illusory Julio/Che, a figment, perhaps, of Rebeca's inventive imagination, illustrates the way in which characterization – like theme, language, and structure – reinforces the erotic context of the narrative.

Argentina Chiriboga creates an exotic *mise en scène,* which seduces the reader and pulls her into the text. As the author explained in a recent interview: "[La novela] tiene un erotismo que fluye del texto, de su estructura, de ese ambiente juvenil en que se desenvuelve la vida de la protagonista" ("Primera"). The first page, for example, describes, in sensual and lyrical language, the seductive weekend rituals of the students. Words and images, such as the following, evoke a poetic landscape:

los límites de lo prohibido
la proximidad de la seducción
el atractivo de los amores fugaces
la época de disfraces
como cuerda de guitarra

It is a landscape without boundaries, illusory and timeless, where lovers engage in a circular dance, like the rhythm of the sea, "como olas que venían y se iban." The novelist's considerable gifts as a poet are evident in the skill with which she crafts her introduction; she describes an intimate terrain, presents the passionate players, establishes a languorous rhythm, and creates a sensual tone through her use of erotic images and figurative language. Her novel reveals the same graceful language and circular rhythm that characterize the poetry of her *La contraportada del deseo:*

En la cama
me crece toda la risa
que afluye de mis vendimias
íntimas.
Desarreglo el silencio
y voy hundiéndome (88-9)

The structure of the novel – the linear narrative and circular poetic form – reinforces the sexual tension of the pleasure-pain continuum. The first sentence prefigures the dialectical structure – the "partida doble" – of the text: "Disfrutábamos la vida por partida doble: éramos estudiantes internas del colegio … y gozábamos las ilusiones que nos brindaba el antifaz" (9). On a literal level, the narrative recounts the subject's search for identity, while, on a figurative level, the imagery structures a poetics of desire. Images, according to Houston Baker "allow us not only to map a topography of intimate human space but also to follow moments of human consciousness to the very functions … of intimacy and protection" (51).

The primary image of *Bajo la piel* is the mask, which charts the intimate terrain of Rebeca's consciousness: the tension between her desire for sexual fulfillment and her longing for social acceptance. The mask represents her division into subject and object; it signifies the psychic split between her inside self – the vulnerable, interior, hidden self – and the outside self, the façade that she presents to the world. Before engaging in erotic adventures with men, Rebeca and her friends, under the tutelage of a libertine and procuress masquerading as a student, don red velvet masks whose color and texture symbolize passion. The *antifaz* is both a protective device that hides the vulnerable feminine self and an outward, visible sign of sexual desire, which Rebeca puts on whenever she is aroused:

Cuando el *deseo* ascendía con urgencias me daban ganas de ir por mi *antifaz*. (128)

> Apelé al *antifaz,* con el que sentía más fuertes mis caudales y tenía la sensación de ocultar mis *deseos.* (134, emphasis added)

Rebeca conceals her sexuality behind the "mask" of femininity. Femininity, according to Irigaray, is prescribed by man and does not correspond to woman's desire, "which may be recovered only in secret, in hiding, with anxiety and guilt" (30). Ironically, that secrecy, with its attendant guilt and anxiety, is also a stimulus to the erotic imagination. One of the most provocative scenes in the novel illustrates how the mask functions as both sign of desire and symbol of protection. When a donkey becomes sexually aroused by her scent, Rebeca trembles at the sight of its erect organ and dons her mask before surrendering to Milton Cevallos in her first sexual encounter.

> … lentos rodamos por la hierba, sentí el vapor de la tierra mezclado con la baba del burro, los dedos de Milton deslizaron mi antifaz en tanto la tarde apagaba los trinos. (135)

Such scenes evoke, obliquely, the sexual fantasies of women: sex with an animal (the donkey), a stranger (Julio Martínez), and another woman (Vicenta Páez), but Rebeca verbally rejects such fantasies. When, for example, Vicenta Páez, a man dressed as a woman, propositions her, she comments: "En Sikán los caballos montan a las yeguas, pero nunca las yeguas hacen el amor entre ellas" (17). Homoeroticism, in her mind, is not a viable option.

Masks and other forms of covering – disguises, sunglasses, scarfs, wigs, and clerical habits – are signs in a semiotic code of sexual transgression, while acts of masking become elaborate mating rituals. According to Rolfe and Shalleck, masks are signs of freedom, which liberate, empower, and mystify, freeing people from inhibitions and permitting respite from social and moral laws. The evening and weekend trysts of Rebeca and her friends have the seductive magic of masked balls and carnival celebrations, as couples engage in elaborately staged rituals of seduction, marked by scenery (river banks and patios), special effects (music, dancing, and liquor), costumes and make-up (short skirts, black bikini panties, and Chanel No. 5). Bakhtin explains the significance of these Bacchanalian rituals:

> During carnival time life is subject only to its own laws, that is, the laws of its own freedom. It has a universal spirit; it is a special condition of the entire world, of the world's revival and renewal, in which all take part. (7-8)

Her mask permits Rebeca to participate in forbidden acts of pleasure, while it allows the priest to take on a new persona – sensual and sexual – with greater presence and power. As Rebeca notes, "sin el pelquín y sin el antifaz [el padre Cayetano] era una persona distinta" (37).

Other forms of masking are evident in the novel. Single women cover their faces with their hands and mantillas; nuns "take the veil," as they assume the mask of devotion, or, in the case of the hot-blooded Sister María de la Concepción, mask their passions; and men hide behind dark glasses, which are emblems of their social status and symbols of their depredation. In literature, the mask functions in various ways: in feminist texts, like Lucía Guerra's *Más allá de las máscaras,* it encodes the social conventions which thwart female sexuality, while in racial discourse, such as Paul Laurence Dunbar's "We Wear the Mask" and Frantz Fanon's *Black Skin, White Masks,* it signifies the dissimulation of Blacks in their relationships with Whites. Rebeca also uses the mask to conceal her racial identity. Ashamed of her grandmother, Lunda Uyanga, and of the African culture of her village, where she grew up hearing invocations to Changó and stories of runaway slaves, Rebeca at first rejects her racial and cultural identity, but, finally, embraces her Africanity:

> … ya no me dolió aquella raíz que antes, equivocada, deseaba esconder. Me sentí parte de la abuela, su consecuencia, oyendo sus tambores sonar bajo mi piel. (104)

She discovers, slowly and painfully, the connection between sexual exploitation, racial discrimination, and class distinctions in the duplicity of men who desire her sexually but reject her socially. Disillusioned, Rebeca learns that she is merely a commodity: "yo era un supermercado donde podría [Fernando] adquirir todo lo que deseara" (91). At his mother's insistence, Fernando Ponce, a medical student, abandons Rebeca "por ser negra y por ser mona [costeña]," while Milton Cevallos calls his wife a "¡Maldita negra puta!" The words *negra* and *puta* link race to sexuality, blackness to immorality, as Milton evokes the negative stereotype of the loose woman, while "mona" or "montubia costeña" (coastal woman) alludes to race and class. The pejorative term "coastal" connotes the social distance between the urbanites of Quito, located in the mountains, and the rural peasants of the coast, many of whom are descended from escaped African slaves.

Devastated by Fernando's racism and crushed by Milton's emotional abuse and violence, Rebeca retreats into silence and invisibility:

> … retorné al silencio de antes, tan lleno de amarguras … Frente al espejo tenía la sensación de no verme, sino de ver una mujer distinta y lejana. (136)

Her silence discloses the fissures in her relationships with men, while her mirror reveals what the mask conceals: her feminine self. As Rebeca gazes at herself, she sees an imaginary other – distant and different – and feels the disassociation of her body from her consciousness. Like the heroine of Parente Cunha's *Woman Between Mirrors,* she is fragmented, split, and broken in two. The mirror, like the mask, permits the reader to trace the development of Rebeca's consciousness and to "map the topography of [her] intimate human space." Whenever Nidia Araujo looks in the mirror, she sees her daughter; this double image suggests that, no matter how much Rebeca rebels, she is destined for her mother's fate – marriage and domesticity. Narcissistic and self-absorbed, Rebeca undresses and gazes on her youthful body:

> Por las noches ante él [mi espejo de cristal] me desnudo, observo complacida mi cuerpo azucarado, pido a la vejez que haga excepción conmigo. (44)

Looking into the mirror, she sees herself *as* body – with her wide hips, firm behind, and narrow waist. In this text however, the woman is more than the sum of her sexual parts, more than the eroticized female body described in *la poesía nalguista;* she is a whole body, composed of arms and feet and hands. She pleases herself as well as those who desire her when she dresses in short skirts and revealing sweaters; she walks seductively with graceful, undulating movements (so unlike the rigid body language of the nuns) "para que los hombres exclamaran un acentuado ¡Ay! a [su] paso" (10).

Rebeca feels the intensity of the male gaze, but she, too, looks at men with desire: she has "los ojos puestos en los hombres." Boldly, she asserts her right to look at men and to participate, voyeuristically, in their private rituals, even the intimate act of urinating in the woods:

> Tras apearse Milton escuché un chorro, no debía descubrirme, yo ya había dejado de ser aquella muchacha, lo había visto en aquel acto íntimo. (18)

In another passage, full of erotic tension, Rebeca and Juan Lorenti, the father of a classmate, gaze at each other in the rearview mirror of his car. Aroused by the ocular *pas de deux,* she looks at him and then lowers her eyes, coquettishly, while imagining the pleasure of seduction.

> Juan arregló el retrovisor de tal manera que sentí pegados sus ojos a los míos [y] yo dirigía mis ojos al retrovisor, se unía su persistente mirada con la mía... Nos miramos... imaginé que iba desnudándome:

primero desabrochó mi blusa, escurrió mi falda, pasó sus dedos por mi espalda, sentí arder mi sangre, me quitó el brassiere… (99)

Rebeca wants to define the terms of her sexuality, but she is hampered by internalized prescriptions of conventional femininity. Patriarchal societies, according to Michel Foucault attempt to control female sexuality through social sanctions, oppressive institutions, and repressive laws. Ironically, women often enforce the mores of patriarchal societies: thus, Inés, Adela, and Nidia are society's arbiters in the control of the young woman's sexuality. Rebeca is constrained by the "Pórtate bien" of older women – authority figures – who mandate virginity before marriage. When she fantasizes about an affair with Julio Martínez, she laments, "El Pórtate bien de mamá frenó entonces mi deseo…" (36); later, Sister Inés warns the girl, "Pórtate como una pebeta culta." Rebeca does not want to pay the price – marriage and childbearing – exacted of women for sexual expression, but she also understands that sexual transgression costs a great deal. Her fear of pregnancy is a serious deterrent to sexual expression, because she recalls all too vividly her visit – under the aegis of Sister Inés – to Virginia Méndez, a former student who was incarcerated for killing her illegitimate baby.

As a virgin, Rebeca can only imagine herself as a desiring woman – "a representation which [challenges] sexist notions of female sexual passivity" (hooks, 1989 136). She discovers early, however, that she is a desirable woman, the object of the male "outsider who experiences the sexed woman as an object of desire" (Hite 21), because Páez exposes himself to her, Santacruz fondles her, Ponti wants her, and Lorenti tries to seduce her. Two things finally release her from her inhibitions: the first experience of sexual pleasure and the knowledge that she is not pregnant. When she realizes that her lemon water douches have been effective for birth control, she yields to desire, first, with Milton Cevallos and, later, with Cayetano Santacruz, whom she embraces with complete abandon: "Sin intentarlo deslicé mis labios hacia su máximo punto de atracción ese instanter lo sentí vibrar, gemir…" (145) – a subtle allusion to fellatio. But Rebeca is not completely free; in the final analysis, she is the product of her socialization.

Although Rebeca achieves a kind of sexual freedom, she does not attain that wider freedom of the mind and spirit that will allow her to realize her full potential as a confident, secure, and independent woman, who calls into question her socially constructed identity as a middle-class, African-ancestored, Ecuadorian woman, but who eventually surrenders to a bourgeois femininity because she has internalized the socially-sanctioned values of a patriarchal society. Trapped in the conflicts between sexual orthodoxy and erotic pleasure, between received conventions and individual aspirations, the protagonist embodies the paradoxes and contradictions of the text: the representation of woman as both subject and object; the dialectical structure of a narrative that is both linear and circular; a poetics of *dédoublement* with images – masks and mirrors – that both reveal and conceal; and a feminist politics that is subsumed by a feminine ideology. On one level, *Bajo la piel de los tambores* is a subversive work which attempts, through innovative rhetorical strategies and fictive devices, to undermine masculinist structures of representation, but, on another level, it presents female sexuality as essentially receptive and passive.

Works Cited

Argentina Chiriboga, Luz. *Bajo la piel de los tambores*. Quito: Casa de la Cultura Ecuatoriana, 1991.

— *La contraportada del deseo*. Quito: Talleres Gráficos, 1992.

Baker, Houston. *Workings of the Spirit: The Poetics of Afro-American Women's Writing*. Chicago: The University of Chicago Press, 1991.

Bakhtin, Mikhail. *Rabelais and His World*. Bloomington: University of Indiana Press, 1984.

Dunbar, Paul Laurence. "We Wear the Mask." *Black Writers of America: A Comprehensive Anthology*. New York: The Macmillan Company, 1972.

Espín, Olivia M. "Cultural and Historical Influences on Sexuality in Hispanic/ Latin Women: Implications for Psychotherapy." *Pleasure and Danger*. Ed. Carole S. Vance. Boston: Routledge & Kegan Paul, 1984.

Estupiñán Bass, Nelson. *Toque de queda*. Guayaquil: Casa de la Cultura Ecuatoriana, 1978.

Fanon, Frantz. *Black Skin, White Masks*. New York, 1967.

Foucault, Michel. *The History of Sexuality, I*. Trans. Robert Hurley. New York: Vintage Books, 1990.

Guerra, Lucía. *Más allá de las máscaras*. Puebla: Premia Editora, 1984.

Harper, Frances Ellen Watkins. *Iola Leroy*. 1892. (rpt. Boston: Beacon Press, 1987).

Hite, Molly. "Writing – and Reading – the Body: Female Sexuality and Recent Feminist Fiction." *Feminist Studies* 14.1 (1988): 121-142.

hooks, bell. "'Whose Pussy Is This?' A Feminist Comment." *Talking Back: Thinking Feminist, Thinking Black*. Boston: South End Press, 1989.

Hunt, Lynn. *Eroticism and the Body Politic*. Baltimore: The Johns Hopkins Press, 1991.

Irigaray, Luce. *This Sex Which Is Not One*. Trans. Catherine Porter. Ithaca: Cornell University Press, 1985.

Korda, Alberta. "Guerillero Heróico." *Cuba: la fotografía del años 60*. Ed. María
E. Haya. Havana: Fototeca de Cuba.

Larsen, Nella. *Quicksand* and *Passing*. Ed. Deborah E. McDowell. New Brunswick.
New Jersey: Rutgers University Press, 1986.

López Morales, Berta. "Language of the Body in Women's Texts." Trans. María
Teresa Marrero. *Splintering Darkness: Latin American Women Writers in
Search of Themselves*. Ed. Lucía Guerra Cunningham. Pittsburgh: Latin
American Literary Review Press, 1990.

Ortiz, Adalberto. *Juyungo*. Trans. Susan F. Hill and Jonathan Tittler. Washington:
Three Continents Press, 1982.

Parente Cunha, Helena. *Woman Between Mirrors*. Trans. Fred P. Ellison and
Naomi Lindstrom. Austin: University of Texas Press, 1989.

Rodas Reyes, Alfredo. "Primera novela de Luz Argentina Chiriboga de Estupiñán."
El comercio. B-2. 25 March 1991.

Rolfe, Bari. *Behind the Mask*. Oakland: Personabooks, 1977.

RoseGreen-Williams, Claudette. "The Myth of Black Female Sexuaiity in Spanish
Caribbean Poetry: A Deconstructive Critical View." *Afro-Hispanic Review*.
12.1 (Spring 1993): 16-24.

Shalleck, Jamie. *Masks*. New York: The Viking Press, 1973.

Suleiman, Susan Rubin, ed. *The Female Body in Western Culture: Contemporary
Perspectives*. Cambridge: Harvard University Press, 1986.

Vance, Carole S., ed. *Pleasure and Danger: Exploring Female Sexuality*. Boston:
Routledge & Kegan Paul, 1984.

Wilson, Carlos Guillermo. "Martes de Carnaval." *Cuentos del negro Cubena*.
Guatemala, Landivar, 1977.

Young, Ann Venture. "The Black Woman in Afro-Caribbean Poetry." *Blacks in
Hispanic Literature: Critical Essays*. Ed. Miriam DeCosta. Port Washington,
N.Y.: Kennikat Press, 1977.

—. "Black Women in Hispanic American Poetry: Glorification, Deification and
Humanization." *Afro-Hispanic Review* 1.1 (January 1982):23-28.

—. *The Image of Black Women in 20th Century South American Poetry. A Bilingual
Anthology*. Washington: Three Continents Press, 1987.

Nancy Morejón

N ANCY M OREJÓN

CUBA

(b. 1944)

One of the most gifted and critically acclaimed of contemporary Cuban poets and intellectuals, Morejón was awarded her country's highest prize in literature, the 2001 Premio Nacional de Literatura for the body of her work. A member of the prestigious Academia Cubana de la Lengua, she has produced an astonishing number of publications, including works of poetry, essays, oral history, and literary criticism. Born in Havana, she grew up in a modest neighbourhood near the old city, where her working-class parents supported and nurtured the artistic ambitions of their only child. She began writing when she was nine and published her first collection of poetry, Mutismos (Silences) *in 1962, when she was only eighteen years old. Two years later, her* Amor, ciudad atribuida, *a tribute to her beloved city, appeared. While a student at the University of Havana, from which she received bachelor's and master's degrees in French language and literature, she attended lectures or classes given by some of Cuba's most distinguished writers, including Mirta Aguirre and José Lezama Lima. The protégé and literary executrix of Nicolás Guillén, Morejón published a second volume,* Richard trajo su flauta *in 1967, which clearly marks her emergence as an important poet of the post-Revolution. This hauntingly evocative work, in which she pays homage to her family and celebrates her African heritage, contains some of her most familiar poems, including 'La cena', 'Madre', 'Un patio de La Habana', and the title poem.*

While she continued to write, publishing Lengua de pájaro, Recopilación de textos sobre Nicolás Guillén, *and* Parajes de una época *in the 1970s, she also worked as an editor, journalist, and translator, serving as an arts promoter for the Unión de Escritores y Artistas de Cuba (UNEAC) and as an editor for* La Gaceta de Cuba. *During that decade, called the period of her 'literary disappearance', Morejón's poetry became more political; poems such as 'Mitologías', 'En el país de Vietnam', and her signature poem 'Mujer negra', reveal her commitment to the ideals that inspired the Cuban Revolution. The decade of the 1980s ushered in one of the poet's most creative and prolific periods, when she published some of her most sensual and lyrical poetry, including* Elogio de la danza *and* Piedra pulida, *as well as a collection of essays,* Fundación de la imagen. *During that same period, her work became increasingly known outside of Cuba through her poetry readings in other countries, the inclusion of her poems in major journals and anthologies, and their translation into more than ten languages. She gained the attention of readers and critics in this country through the publication, in 1985, of the bilingual* Where the Island Sleeps Like a Wing. *Morejón has also lectured at universities thoughout the United States and was the subject of a conference at the University of Missouri-Columbia in 1995, the papers of which were published in a special issue of the* Afro-Hispanic Review. *A collection of critical essays on her work,* Singular Like a Bird: the Art of Nancy Morejón, *was published by the Howard University Press in 1999.*

Although Morejón is committed to the deconstruction and revision of Cuban history, there is a creative tension in her work between poetry that is socially and politically engagé *and poetry that is deeply and profoundly lyrical. Her more recent work, as one critic suggests, is more hermetic; the poet seems to abandon themes of social and political significance. Collections such as* Paisaje célebre *(1993) and* Elogio y paisaje *(1996) certainly underscore the strength and maturity of the poet's gifts – her control of language and mastery of technical elements – but they also point to other themes and different techniques. For example, her poetry of the 1990s is more woman-centred. Although she rejects feminist politics and ideology in favour of Alice Walker's concept of womanism, Morejón reveals a class and gender consciousness in poems such as 'Persona' and 'Ana Mendieta', which deal with female identity, artistic expression, and cultural production. As a poet and essayist, Nancy Morejón continues to explore new directions in her art.*

Ana Mendieta

Ana was fragile as lightning in the sky.
She was the most fragile girl in Manhattan,
lit up always by the autumn rains,
her story burnt to ash upon the saddest lattice shutters.
Up on a balcony, Ana opened the windows
to lean out and watch the multitudes pass.
Like silhouettes of sand and clay
they walked by, on foot. Like a silhouetted
army of silent ants they were,
scattered in the constant wind of Lent
or burrowed into glass.
Ana loved the extras on that set
because they brought her remembrances,
old, resonant, sweet remembrances
of some side street in the South, in El Vedado.
Ana, cast into space.
Ana, our lady of despair,
yourself sculpted in the hostile cement of Broadway.
A desert, like the desert
you found in the orphanages,
a desert, yellow and grey, reaches you
and holds you tight, through the air.

Under Ana's balcony the trains rush past,
as the water flowed in some other time
through the gutters of that strange small town
of green aspens and the burning lamp.
Above the balcony of Ana, of noble Havana calling,
fly tutelary butterflies,
fly simple swallows, which emigrate,
as always, as usual, as everyone knows,
to vast cities aflame with comfort and with fright.

*Ana, a swallow is fluttering above your black hair
and the simple purity of that flight presaged your death*

Ana

A swallow of sand and clay.

Ana

A swallow of water.

Ana

A swallow of fire.

Ana

A swallow and a jasmine.

*A swallow that made the slowest of summers.
A swallow that scores the sky of Manhattan
towards a fictitious North we cannot quite see
or imagine, even farther North than so many vain
    illusions.
Ana, fragile as those vivid little crosses
that nest in the domes of certain medieval churches.
Ana, cast upon the mercy of the elements of Iowa,
    once again.
A black drizzle falls on your silhouette.
Your sleeping silhouettes lull us
like supreme goddesses of inequality,
like supreme goddesses of the new pilgrims of the West.
Ana simple. Lively Ana.
Ana with her enchanted orphan's hand.
Sleeping Ana. Ana, goldsmith.
Ana, fragile as an eggshell
scattered over the huge roots of a Cuban ceiba,
darkleaved, thickly green.*

Ana, cast into space.

Ana, gliding like a kite
above the red roofs of the great houses of the old Cerro.
Ana, what radiant colors I see,
and how they resemble certain paintings of Chagall
that you loved to follow through all the galleries of the
    Earth.
Your silhouettes, sleepy, calm,
tip up the multicolored kite
which flees Iowa, skirting indigenous cypresses,
and comes to rest on the sure clouds
of the mountains of Jaruco, in whose humid land
you have been reborn again, wrapped in a celestial
    moss
that dominates the rock and eaves of that place,
yours now, more than ever.

Translated by David Frye

"Rupestrian sculpture" carvings in the eaves of Jaruco by Ana Mendieta.

Lady of the Unicorn

Next to the French tapestries
looked on and given shape by the dust
throughout the ages;
in the cold dome of the hall
(*very* belle époque *and very* art nouveau)
abandoned by counts and kingdoms,
vanished friars and corsairs,
there shines a torso with its frigid hand
and the limp stare of an old fashioned lady.
Fatal lady of the unicorn,
anachronic fruit of the unexpected
for whom no one composed madrigals,
not even a simple hai-ku.
What thoughts, imperial shipwrecks,
might have crossed her brow
in the instant when the painter
had her pose for a thousand maravedis
never suspecting this other instant
in which an island girl
(from the so-called West Indies)
was to laugh with perplexed eyes
and imagine how it was possible
to live without swallows
bleeding stubbornly through each viceroyal cell?
Asexual lady of the unicorn,
might she have seen the Alcazar's gardens
or the mosques of Seville? Might she have read
Apollonian sonnets, sounded
the flageolet of her ancestors
who planted dew drops for their garden birds?
Who might have imagined it?
Who might have foreseen
that she'd reach our time

in velveteen and damask and frustration
fastened to the aberrant frame
of this cameo?
Rings, feathers, keepsakes, enamel-work,
satyrs, porcelain, market-place dwarfs...
And you, girl, with the natural instinct
of one who loves life and justice,
you see her, you try to understand her
in her polemical beauty,
although you may not find the excuse,
the aptest word for such deterioration
for such insipid pomp, for such ridicule
of the eyes of your most loved ones,
builders of the pyramids
that joyfully bespatter their encephalic unicorn.

Translated by Margaret Randall

Persona

Which of these women am I?
Am I not the one speaking
from behind the iron bars of a window with no style
that overlooks the abundance of all these centuries?
Am I perhaps the tall black woman
who runs and almost flies
to set astronomic records,
with her dark celestial legs
in their lunar spiral?
In which muscle of hers does my face take form,
planted there like an eleven-syllable line imported
from a country of forbidden snow?

I am at the window
and Antonio's wife walks by;
'the cute little neighbour from the other side', from a
    street with no shape;
'the mother – black woman Paula Valdés –'.
Who is the young man who pays for
her clothes and her food
and the vetiver fragrances that she now leaves behind
    as she walks?
What endures in me from that woman?
What unites the two of us? what separates us?
Am I perhaps the 'early morning wanderer',
who rents taxis during the night from jaguars
like a heron lying on the pavement
after having been hunted
    and exhausted
    and resold
around the Quinta de los Molinos
and the docks at the harbour?

They: I wonder who they are? or is that myself?
Who are these women who resemble me so much
not because of the colours of their bodies
but those devastating fumes
cast forth by our skin of an animal branded
by a strange fire that never ceases?
Why am I? Why are they?

Who is that woman
who is present in all of us fleeing from us,
fleeing from her enigma and her distant origin
with her lips muttering an incredulous prayer
or a hymn that is sung
after an ever recurring battle?

Are all my bones mine?
Whose could all my bones be?
Could they have bought them from me
at that distant public square of Gorée Island?
Is all my skin mine at all
or have they rather returned to me
the skin and bones of another woman
whose belly has been branded by another horizon,
another being, other creatures, another god?

I am at the window.
I know there is someone.
I know that a woman is flaunting my flesh and bones;
that she has sought me in her weary bosom
and that she finds me lost and in constant movement.
The night is buried under our skins.
The wise night arranges its bones and mine.
A bird from the sky has turned its light into our eyes.

Peñalver, 31 March 1999
Translated by Gabriel A. Abudu

from
Myth and Reality in Cecilia Valdés'

Cecilia: The Weakest Link

Like all fictional characters, Cecilia Valdés is an abstract construct based on a real human being. Much has been and will be written about the circumstances in which Cirilo Villaverde (1812-1894) created his heroine. At present, the historical status of the 'Little Bronze Virgin' is a minor concern; there has been more than sufficient discussion of that matter. Whether or not she really existed in Havana at the beginning of the nineteenth century, one thing is certain: Cecilia Valdés, the literary character, fully represents a given society at a specific period of time. This is the novelist's greatest accomplishment.

If we pay attention, as we should, to the time-honoured device of identifying the woman with the country (and the nation), we will notice how effective this device continues to be, even today. For Aragón, Elsa is France, the France that resisted Hitler's armies with stoicism and dignity. Let us think for a moment of a simple example, the novel *Nedjma* by Algerian writer Kateb Yacine. In the maze of a colonial world, *Nedjma* is the only option, the only form in which to recreate and evoke the symbolic ideals of a country. If, in the middle of the twentieth century, different writers continue to employ such a device, how can we doubt the imperative that motivated Villaverde to create this female character?

There is no doubt that Cecilia Valdés embodies the tragic condition of an island submitted to the implacable rigours of slavery, while slavery was, at the same time, the foundation of the Spanish colonialism. It is a secret to no one that African slavery in America, as on other continents, was one of the arches – not necessarily the most important one – erected to support the bases of European capitalism. Spain's colonial empire became one of the most extensive. The trade in Black Africans made possible the establishment of a system that was diseased from the moment of its inception; this trade was the axis or cornerstone of the colonies, whether they were Spanish, French, British, or Dutch. On the other hand, the slave trade was one of the most constant in the Antilles. This colonial system, speaking just among ourselves, created a society whose structure corresponds perfectly to that of an Egyptian pyramid.

If we begin at the base and not at the peak, we encounter the great mass of Black slaves imported from the west coast of Africa. Numerically, people of African descent constituted the majority of the Cuban population in the first quarter of the nineteenth century, the period in which Villaverde set his novel. Emerging with these people was a kind of *hampa,* a community that began forming on the outskirts of the capital; it was a society that operated outside of colonial law. A little above this first group are the free Blacks and mulattoes who work as artisans and perform various other types of work. We see at the same level of the pyramid, in similar numbers, a rural population, descended primarily from Spaniards and engaged in small-scale agriculture. Above the artisans/craftsmen of colour and the small farmers, there is a somewhat tentative middle class of White Creoles whose ranks are filled by plantation and sugarmill owners, individuals for all practical purposes who are economically ruined and who devote themselves to the liberal professions, generally speaking, as doctors and lawyers. At the very top of the pyramid are two social groups on which the colonial destiny of the island depends: the producers and businessmen, all White. Primarily Creoles as well as some Spaniards – long-time inhabitants of the island – belonged to the first group. Spaniards born in Spain belonged to the second group, which was the most powerful and pervasive as well as a staunch representative of the Crown.

The population of Cuba was rigidly stratified and subordinated to the service of the Spanish colonial treasury. Of course the mobility[1] of the pyramid was, although comfortable, proverbial. It depended on the prosperity or decline of the slave traders. The most authentic roots of Cuban nationality grew out of the slave trade and its intrigues; furthermore, it established the model that exists on all the other Caribbean islands, be they large or small. From another perspective, one observes a phenomenon that was significant to the colony's development: the entire population was economically active, as Manuel Moreno Fraginals has pointed out.

It is possible to signify on this phrase and add that the entire population was active from the 'social' point of view, in spite of the rigid caste divisions. *Cecilia Valdés* exemplifies, as does no other novel of the period, the race-mixing that was shaping our colonial society in the nineteenth century.[2] The protagonist's status as a woman adds the final ingredient. Thus, Cecilia is the weakest link.

One might ask, Why the 'weakest link'? It is not only because of her inferior position in the romantic triangle, a device that Villaverde employs to propel the dramatic action, but also because Cecilia herself really demonstrates the anguish of transculturation.

Cecilia is the crucible of this irreversible phenomenon. Historically, transculturation is at the centre of all human civilisations. In modern times, its breath touched all the great geographic zones of our America. The Caribbean stands out in this regard. This phenomenon is an undeniable fact; as we stated earlier, it is an irreversible fact of our cultures, because it defines them. It is important here to point out that the term *transculturation* that we use in this analysis was formulated by the great writer Fernando Ortiz, who had appropriated and transformed it from a term that Malinkowski had used, one that was known by the middle of this century by the name *acculturation*.[3]

Cuban society is the product of transculturation. So is Cecilia. Our culture is a hybrid, made up of elements from Hispanic and African cultures. Of what does transculturation consist? Of having been transplanted to a new world. We are no longer – without even thinking about it – Africans or Spaniards. A third component emerges from these two, which were brought to the island at almost the same time – in spite of contradictions, in spite of society's laws – and were established on the island by different and often antagonistic means.[4]

Transculturation and racial mixing – in the ethnic and sociocultural sense – define the unique condition of the Cuban nation. However, it is also necessary to point out that transculturation and racial mixing depend, as we know, on the time and the turning points of each period of change. Cecilia, whose persona illustrates the aforementioned phenomena, represents a phase of those turning points. The passage of time, from her period to ours, influences the subtle alterations and transformations in her characterisation. Clearly and tenaciously, the socialist revolution in Cuba has established as a priority its commitment to identifying and reclaiming the most legitimate roots of our identity. It is not in vain that our most determined affirmation of national culture dates from that period; of course, our warm connection to the Caribbean spirit also satisfies us. 'Cuba is an example of a New People, a *Pueblo Nuevo*', that is African American or, as Fidel recently stated, Latin American.

At first glance, Cecilia belongs to one of the humblest elements of the population. If we again consider the organisation of the so-called pyramid that we have just described, we will agree that beneath the layer in which we find Cecilia, there exists another even more exploited, if not the most exploited, segment of society: Black slaves. Nonetheless, Cecilia does not belong to that class. She is free. How, then, can we say that Cecilia is the weakest link? Cecilia is the weakest link because the vision with which Villaverde constructs the image of nationality, according to the way in which it is stratified, is determined by the concept of nation with which the Creoles and Spaniards from Spain – the producers and business class – were grappling at that point in history. Despite the antagonisms of those two groups, they agreed on this point. The most lucid pages of the novelist – who, like all writers, was conditioned by his background – are permeated, in this sense, by the ideology of men like José Antonio Saco, spokesman for the local oligarchy, whose ideas about the Cuban nation – for whose liberty he fought tirelessly, even to the point of suffering exile – excluded, systematically, the population composed of enslaved Black Africans imported by the slave trade. It was as much a conviction of the slave traders as of those who opposed them. Black slaves were not important to Cuban nationality. Saco's phobia against Black people is based on his antipathy to the slave trade but not to slavery. His goal: the same end (slavery) by other means. Therefore, Spaniards and Creoles, in one way or another, became enmeshed in the same complicated web that enabled them to survive. This concept, basically an elitist one, was abolished in practice and during the two wars of independence. Nonetheless, that was the concept that most informed Cirilo Villaverde when he began to arrange the elements that would lead him to the tragic character of Cecilia and to the dire final consequences. So it can be explained. The idea that a mulatto man and, in this case, a mulatto woman would want to cross the colour line can thus be explained. The last place in the country, condemned like some filthy mule stall, was sweetly reserved for the slave.

The Black slave was, above all, a Black slave. Represented as inferior – physically savage and morally depraved – he was always depicted as a being incapable of possessing any attributes whatsoever of the human condition. The slave was a *thing*. Or rather, to be more exact, the slave was a piece of merchandise subject to the market's most nefarious whims. The slave, source of labour, was relegated to the condition of an animal by those who exploited him. How can one even imagine that such a society could sustain itself without him? It is absurd and impossible to even imagine it, but that was the most profound conflict of our nineteenth century. It was not coincidental that political contradictions in that period revolved around the tragic destiny that had been devised for him. Therefore, even the slave's own descendants insisted on and learned how to distance themselves – furtively or openly – from the Black slave. These descendants – educated and informed by principles different from their true circumstances – also developed a phobia toward the Black slave, a phobia that degenerated into a collective neurosis. That is the hidden substratum from which Cecilia Valdés' tragic condition emerges. Her struggle can be summed up in her desire to distance herself as much as possible from her African – slave – ancestry. In that pyramid everyone aspired to exceed the limits of his/her social condition, climbing – poor things – out of their slippery bases to fill the higher ranks, the superior ranks. In the process, they used elaborate deceptions, among which the demon Sex was especially efficacious. That is the drama of Cecilia. The novel is about a poor, helpless, mulatto woman who attempts to scramble out of the way of the dikes when they break, while she tries to avoid the obstacles in her determination to forge a future for herself that is forever immobilised in circumstances of imminent exploitation. Cecilia does not want to be Cecilia. Trapped in the nets of her own making, she is the weakest segment of the pyramid.

Translated by Carol Beane

Notes

1. *El ingenio, complejo económico social cubano del azúcar*. (Havana: Editorial de Ciencias Sociales, 1978) 1-3.
2. Cirilo Villaverde, *Cecilia Valdés*. Havana: Imprenta Literaria, 1839.
3. Fernando Ortiz, *Contrapunteo cubano del tabaco y del azúcar* (Havana: Consejo Nacional de Cultura, 1963).
4. Ortiz. 'Los factores humanos de la cubanidad'. In *Orbita de Fernando Ortiz* (Havana: Ediciones Unión, 1973).

An Aesthetic of Women's Art in Nancy Morejón's 'Ana Mendieta'

Miriam DeCosta-Willis

In 'Mujer negra', Nancy Morejón depicts an independent, rebellious, and self-actualised female subject whose heroic deeds, metaphorised in transgressive speech ('I rebelled' and 'I rose up'), posit a radical revision of Cuban history with a Black woman as the iconic hero. 'Black Woman', however, obscures other poems that centre a female subject and that focus on different aspects of Cuban womanhood. As a writer and intellectual, Morejón has dealt in her poetry and essays with the history of literature, the aesthetics of art, and the creative process of the artist. As a result, some of her most intellectually challenging poems deal with the creative power of women as artists/workers. In 'Mujer negra', for example, the female subject points to her historical role as creator and procreator: 'Bordé la casaca de Su Merced y un hijo macho le parí' (I embroidered His Worship's coat and bore him a male child). In 'En el pais de Vietnam' (In the Country of Vietnam), two women make art through singing, even as they build pagodas and bamboo houses. In 'Obrera del tabaco' (Tobacco Worker), a female worker, among the most oppressed in pre-revolutionary Cuba, has written a poem: 'Pero ni sus hermanos, ni sus vecinos, / adivinaron *la esencia de su vida*. Y nunca supieron / del poema' (But neither her brothers, nor her neighbours, / divined the truth about her life. And they never knew about the poem) (19, emphasis added). This idea that art is the essence of life is evident in poems such as 'Elogio de la danza' (In Praise of Dance), 'Elogio de Nieves Fresneda' (Eulogy to Nieves Fresneda) and 'Alicia Alonso', which affirm dance as a form of creativity, a medium of self-expression, and a means of communion with nature. This essay will examine the ways in which Nancy Morejón represents the life and work of another artist and will analyse similarities and differences in the feminist aesthetics of Ana Mendieta and the womanist poetics of Nancy Morejón.

'Ana Mendieta', published in 1993 in *Paisaje célebre,* depicts the life and work of a Cuban American artist. Born in Havana in 1948, Mendieta was the daughter of wealthy and aristocratic parents; her father was an attorney, her grandfather a physician, and her great-uncle was president of Cuba in the 1930s. The artist's life, however, was characterised by a series of uprootings and disjunctures. In 1961, when she was twelve years old, she and an older sister were sent to the United States under the auspices of Operation Peter Pan, an organisation founded to relocate Cuban refugee children. Meanwhile, her father, who had been an early supporter of Fidel Castro, was imprisoned for twelve years. The sisters, who stayed in orphanages and foster homes in Iowa, were not reunited with their mother until 1966 and did not see their father until thirteen years later. According to Gerardo Mosquero, Mendieta commented on a return to Cuba in 1980, 'Estoy entre dos culturas' (I am between two cultures), because, although a Cuban by birth, she had grown up alone in a strange country where she did not know the language. After completing graduate studies in art at the University of Iowa, Mendieta moved to Mexico and then to New York, where she developed an avant-garde, woman-centred art that explored the relationship between nature and the female form. In an application for a grant from the New York State Council on the Arts, dated March 17, 1982, Mendieta wrote: 'Art must have begun as nature itself, in a dialectical relationship between humans and the natural world from which we cannot be separated' (Clearwater).

Mendieta was influenced in her work, according to the editor of *Ana Mendieta: A Book of Works,* by the myths, rituals, and goddesses of the African and Tainan cultures in Cuba. As a child, she learned of *santería,* the Afro-Cuban religion, from household servants and, later, she read the studies of anthropologist Lydia Cabrera. According to Mary Jane Jacob, Mendieta's interest in *santería* culminated in a feminist and woman-centred art that explored gender issues such as female sexualtiy and the female body. For Mendieta, art became a spiritual act, an act of magic, with the artist serving as the conduit or priestess. In works such as 'Burial of the Náñigo' (1976), where her silhouette is outlined by candles, she used her own body to underscore the presence and power of women. In 'Bird Transformation', the artist practised the ritualistic use of blood (considered in *santería* as ashé, the source of divine power, the essence of life); in this ritual the artist rubbed cow's blood on her body and then rolled in chicken feathers. Other installations inspired by Afro-Cuban religious practices include 'Ceiba Fetish' (Miami, 1981), 'Arbol de la vida' (1977), and 'Incantación a Olokún-Yemayá' (Oaxaca, Mexico, 1977). Yemayá, who represents womanhood, maternity, the sea, and Our Lady of Regla, is an important *orisha* or female deity in Mendieta's work. Significant symbols or images in her art include hands, fire, gunpowder, shells, and water.

The other important source of Ana Mendieta's artistic inspiration is the prehistoric art and mythology of the Tainos, the autochthonous people who inhabited the island until the Spanish conquest and colonisation of Cuba resulted in their decimation. Her interest in female goddesses, inspired by the reading of José Juan Arróm's *Mitología y artes prehispánicas de las Antillas* and of *Leyendas cubanas* is evident in earth sculptures such as 'Guabancex' (Goddess of the Wind), 'Itiba Cabubaba' (Old Mother Blood), and 'Alboboa' (The Beautiful One). In August 1980, Mendieta carved rupestrian sculptures – called 'earth art' or 'ecological art' – on the cave walls and rugged cliffs of the Escalera de Jaruco in Jaruco State Park near Havana. She described these life-size figures of Tainan goddesses as 'an intimate act of communion with the earth', and as 'a loving return to the maternal breast' (Marquera 54). These figures, for which Mendieta was well known in Cuba, were described by Mosquera as opulent and maternal feminine forms in repose (54). They were intended to protest what Mendieta called the 'deculturation' or destruction of indigenous cultures in Cuba during the colonial period. But hers was a fragile medium: the only record of her earth art is the series of photographic etchings taken by the artist for exhibition in art galleries. Her work, like her life, was ephemeral.

On September 8, 1985, Ana Mendieta plunged thirty-four floors to her death. Ironically, she cast her final earth-body sculpture on a cement sidewalk in Manhattan. She died mysteriously with everything to live for: she was not quite 37 years old, her career was on the ascendancy, and she had recently married the artist Carl Andre. Her husband, who was alone with her at the time of her death, was arrested, but, after 29 months of inquiry, he was acquitted for lack of evidence. Robert Katz, whose exhaustive study resulted in the publication of *Naked by the Window: The Fatal Marriage of Carl Andre and Ana Mendieta*, pointed to what he calls the 'strategy of silence by the art community', which refused to implicate Andre. Katz comments tersely: 'I know if Ana had been an Anglo and if Carl had been black, the art world would have lynched him' (Katz 375-383).

The life and work of this remarkable artist inspired one of Nancy Morejón's most finely crafted works, a poem in which the visual art of the sculptor is indelibly inscribed in the language of the text. In a 1993 interview, Morejón commented that 'Ana Mendieta's life is a beautiful life, full of contradictions and bitterness', and then she went on to discuss significant events in the artist's life and characteristics of her work: her tragic and mysterious death, her desire to reclaim her Cuban cultural heritage, her talent and success as an artist, and her interest in nature as revealed in her landscapes ('Guest' 2). Morejón concludes: 'So Ana was a genius, I think.

She was very young and very gifted'. The words of her poem allude to major events in Mendieta's life: her childhood in the great houses of the old Cerro in Havana, her adolescence in various orphanages in a small Iowa town, and her fall from a balcony in Manhattan. There are also allusions to her work: the mountains of Jaruco; goddesses, like the 'Goddess of the Wind', whom she sculpted in rocks and caves; silhouettes of sand and clay, which refer specifically to Mendieta's 1973–1980 'Silueta' Series; and a Cuban ceiba, which recalls her 'Ceiba Fetish'.

Significantly, Morejón alludes to the artist's death in very oblique and tangential ways: the first stanza describes the setting – a balcony in Manhattan above the cement streets of Broadway – and relates a brief, circuitous narrative about a fragile girl named Ana who opened the windows of her balcony and leaned out to watch the people below. In the sixteenth line, she writes, 'Ana, lanzada al vacio' (Ana cast into space), a line that is repeated and stands alone at the beginning of the final stanza. A reader unfamiliar with the circumstances of Mendieta's death might miss the clues – the repetition of *balcón* and images of flight ('vuelan las mariposas' [fly butterflies] and 'vuelan las simples golondrinas' [fly simple swallows]) – which appear in the second stanza. A couplet follows: 'Ana, una golondrina esta revoloteando sobre tu pelo negro / y el candor de ese vuelo presagiaba tu muerte' (Ana, a swallow is fluttering above your black hair / and the simple purity of that flight presaged your death). Significantly, Morejón does not reduce Mendieta's work to the tragedy of her death; nor does she politicise her death, citing it as another example of violence against women. In fact, she does not mention Carl Andre, his womanising, the unhappy marriage, the final struggle in their bedroom which left scratches on her body, or the husband's incarceration. The poet has loftier aims: she shifts the focus from the material to the spiritual, and from human mortality to the immortality of art.

The language of spirituality, apparent in certain allusions and images – *Cuaresma, crucecitas, cupula, iglesias medievales, diosas, peregrinos,* and *celeste* (Lent, little crosses, dome, medieval churches, goddesses, pilgrims, and celestial) – , creates a sacred space where art (Mendieta's sculpture) and nature (sand, water, and jasmine) merge. In its language, the poem elucidates Mendieta's belief that art is a spiritual act and that the artist serves as the agent of that spirituality. This idea of the artist as spiritual agent is also evident in Morejón's poetics, specifically in the significance of inspiration to her creative process. She writes:

> El grueso de mi obra ha nacido de la inspiración, es decir de esa intuición en éxtasis … La inspiración llega y me dejo llevar por ella. Es un rapto.

Sin embargo, cuando vuelvo a mi consciencia natural dejo mis manuscritos reposando en la gaveta. ('Poética')

(Inspiration – or, intuition in ecstasy – has given birth to the bulk of my work …. Inspiration comes and I let myself be carried away by it. It is rapture. However, when I become fully conscious, I leave my manuscripts lying on the desk).

The word 'inspiration' means, literally, 'A divine influence or action on a person believed to qualify him [or her] to receive and communicate sacred revelation'. Morejón's work, like that of Mendieta, is spiritual without being religious. Before the Revolution, Morejón's family observed the outward forms of Catholicism (she was baptised and received communion), but she was brought up as an atheist, who later gained respect for *santería* as a cultural practice and as a form of resistance during slavery ('Two' 626-27). Her spirituality takes different forms: 'La cena' (1967) and 'Peñalver 52' (1993) create an 'espacio amado', a sacred space where the family breaks bread and solidifies kinship ties, while 'Elogio de la danza' and 'Alicia Alonso' celebrate the erotic spirituality of an art that is embodied in the female form. Morejón evinces, in poems such as 'La dama de los perros' (The Lady of the Hounds) and 'La dama del unicornio' (The Lady of the Unicorn), a literary spirituality, grounded in medieval texts, particularly in the mystic works of Santa Teresa de Jesús. In the poem 'Ana Mendieta', spirituality is expressed in images of flight – of butterflies, swallows, and kites; images that suggest ascendancy and transcendency. Here, allusions to pilgrims and medieval churches evoke an ancient landscape, both mystical and mythological; in Mendieta's sculpture, images of Tainan rituals and myths evoke a different landscape – a terrain of sand and caves – which is also mysterious and mythological.

Ana Mendieta's belief in the dialectical relationship between nature and human life is implict in the imagery and structure of Morejón's poem, particularly in the following section:

Ana
Una golondrina de arena y barro.
Ana
Una golondrina de agua
Ana
Una golondrina de fuego.
Ana
Una golondrina y un jazmin.

(Ana
A swallow of sand and clay.
Ana
A swallow of water.
Ana
A swallow of fire.
Ana
A swallow and a jasmine).

The juxtaposition of woman and nature has many connotations: it evokes an African praise song; it suggests a religious ritual (the antiphonal chanting of the psalms); it is patterned after the call and response (a structuring element of neoAfrican art); and it illustrates the synthesis of two dialectically opposed elements. The dialectical juxtaposition of opposites is also apparent in Morejón's mythopoetic landscapes: an urban topography of Havana streets is set against the bucolic *paisaje* of the Jaruco mountains; a small town in Iowa contrasts with the hostile cement of Manhattan. The landscape of the fictitious north is sad and strange and frightening; it is a place of autumn rains and black showers, of orphanages and vain illusions, of strange towns and vast cities. All of these oppositions (rural and urban landscapes, Cuba and North America, woman and nature) underscore the contradictions in Mendieta's life, her feelings of loss and exile, her sense of being a part of two cultures and yet not fully in either. As Adrienne Rich would say, the poet is split at the root. The language of Morejón's poetry captures this sense of Ana Mendieta's deracination and estrangement – feelings that the artist communicates in her sculpture.

Ana Mendieta was doubly exiled: she was separated from both her mother and her motherland. As feminist psychoanalysts have indicated, the relationship with the mother is important not only for the emotional and physical growth of the daughter, but also for her intellectual and artistic development. This phenomenon of stimulating the child intellectually is what Nancy Chodorov calls 'mothering the mind'. Morejón has written and spoken often about the role that her mother, Angélica Hernández, played in nurturing her creativity. She said in an interview: 'Virginia Woolf decía que detrás de toda escritora permanecía el fantasma de su madre. . . . Porque es la madre la que alimenta una vocación, alienta la necesidad de escribir' (Virginia Woolf said that behind every woman writer stood the ghost of her mother . . . Because the mother is the one who nurtures a vocation, stimulates the need for writing) (Bianchi Ross 31). Clearly, it is the ghost of her mother that Ana Mendieta searches for in the goddesses and maternal figures that she carved in the caves of Jaruco. When Mendieta returned to Cuba in the 1980s, she often visited the home of Angélica Hernández, who seems to have served as her 'othermother'. According to Patricia Hill Collins, 'othermothers' or women who assist biological mothers or who share mothering responsibilities, are traditional in African and African American communities (119). The friendship between Morejón and Mendieta was strengthened by the 'mothering' of Angélica Hernández, as the poet explains:

> . . . my mother was a friend of Ana Mendieta. She knew Ana well. Ana was my friend. When Ana would come to Havana – I live in a very modest house, a little neighbourhood house – Ana would always come over to eat. She was someone who became very close to me. And all the people who have been my friends, who have been important to me, have been connected with my mother . . . . ('Two' 630)

Given the friendship between the two artists, it is interesting to note the way in which Morejón characterises the persona. Ana, the woman, was 4' 10" tall and weighed only 93 pounds when she died at age 37; Ana, the persona, is introduced as a fragile girl. Her fragility is underscored by the repetition throughout the poem of the adjective *fragil;* by past participles (*esculpida* and *esparcida),* and by figures of speech such as 'Ana, fragil *como una cascara de huevo*' (Ana, fragile as an eggshell) (emphasis added). Her 'pelo negro' (black hair) – the only allusion to the girl's physical appearance – is significant because the artist often used her long, black hair as an element in her body sculptures. Although the title presents the artist's full name, she is addressed in the body of the poem solely by her first name, indicating that the narrator has a close, intimate relationship with the persona. This relationship is further underscored by the use of the familiar pronoun *tu* and by direct discourse, as the narrator addresses the girl. The point of view shifts several times from the formal third person subject pronoun *Usted* to the familiar second person pronoun *tú*. Most of the first stanza is written in the third person, because the narrator is relating events from an emotional, temporal, and spatial distance. In line seventeen, however, the narrator uses the first person plural possessive adjective – *nuestra,* 'Our Ana' – to suggest a broader national relationship between *cubanas* or *compañeras*. Only once does the narrator speak in the first person singular; at the beginning of the last stanza, she comments: 'Ana, que colores tan radiantes veo' (Ana, what radiant colours I see).

Nancy Morejón and Ana Mendieta are artists who work in different media; Morejón creates word magic, while Mendieta shaped spirit forms. As I have suggested above, there were many similarities in their works and in their aesthetics. Their art expresses an intense, deep, and perhaps unconscious spirituality, of the kind that Alice Walker describes in her seminal essay, 'In Search of Our Mothers' Gardens'. Like Walker, they feel themselves a part of a generational line of female Artists/Saints who have 'handed on the creative spark' and who have ordered 'the universe . . . in Beauty'. Mendieta's work is grounded in the art of African and Tainan female storytellers and mythmakers, while Morejón underscores the influence of other women writers such as Mirta Aguirre, Emily Dickinson, and Gabriela Mistral. Both artists, particularly Mendieta, decode the difficult and complex messages left by women of the past. In the works of the poet and the sculptor, Yoruba goddesses such as Yemayá express the female imagination or represent the woman artist, as is apparent in Mendieta's 'Incantación a Olokún-Yemayá' and Morejón's 'Elogio de Nieves Fresneda', which conjures up the dance of Yemayá. They invent a language of complex imagery – of sand and sea – to express an intense longing for the land, for the mythopoetic landscape of Cuba. Their images of the land often have deeply symbolic meanings: the cottonsilk tree is sacred in African and Afro-Cuban mythology, as is the forest or *el monte,* which also served as a refuge for runaway slaves. Neither artist recreates the feminine text of some women artists, a text of domesticity, senitimental love, child rearing, woman's place, the private sphere, and female awakening.

Although they both illuminate the power and presence of women, Mendieta's woman-centred art is more radical, for it is grounded in the politics of feminism and environmentalism that emerged in the United States in the late 1960s. Morejón, on the other hand, carefully disengages herself from feminist politics and ideology. The difference in approach is evident in their treatment of the female subject. Mendieta is a subversive and unconventional artist, who examines female sexuality, uses blood as a signifier of womanhood, enacts rituals of menstruation and childbirth, and depicts the nude female body, while Morejón is more interested in the artistic, intellectual, and ideological significance of the woman in Cuban history and culture.

Finally, both artists articulate a revolutionary aesthetics that underscores the power of art in the social, cultural, and spiritual transformation of human beings.

Works Cited

Ana Mendieta: A Retrospective. New York: New Museum of Contemporary Art, 1987.

Bianchi Ross, Ciro. 'Nancy Morejón. "Soy muchas poetas"'. *Cuba Internacional*.

Clearwater, Bonnie, ed. *Mendieta, Ana. A Book of Works*. Miami Beach: Greenwood Press, 1993.

Collins, Patricia Hill. *Black Feminist Thought: Knowledge, Consciousness, and the Politics of Empowerment*. Boston: Unwin Hyman, 1990.

Jacobs, Mary Jane. *Ana Mendieta: The 'Silueta' Series*. New York: Galerie Lelong, 1991.

Katz, Robert. *Naked by the Window: The Fatal Marriage of Carl Andre and Ana Mendieta*. New York: Atlantic Monthly Press, 1990.

Morejón, Nancy. 'Alicia Alonso', 'Elogio de la danza', and 'Elogio de Nieves Fresnada'. In *Elogio de la danza*. Mexico City: La Universidad Nacional Autónoma de Mexico, 1982.

___. 'Ana Mendieta'. In *Paisaje célebre*, 39-41. Caracas: Fundarte, Alcaldia de Caracas, 1993.

___. '"Be My Guest": An Interview With Nancy Morejón'. By Ramón G. (typed transcript) January 16, 1993.

___. 'Hilanderas'. Manuscript copy.

___. 'Obrera del tabaco'. In *Octubre imprescindible*, 18-9. Havana: Ediciones Unión, 1982.

___. 'Poética por Nancy Morejón'. *Afro-Hispanic Review* 15 (Spring 1996): 6-9.

___. 'Spinning Woman'. Translated by J. R. Pereira. In *Ours the Earth*, 26-7. Mona, Jamaica: Institute of Caribbean Studies, 1990.

___. 'Two Conversations with Nancy Morejón'. By Ruth Behar and Lucía Suárez. *Michigan Quarterly Review* 3 (Summer 1994): 625-37.

___. 'A Womanist Vision of the Caribbean. An Interview'. By Elaine Savory Fido. In *Out of the Kumbla: Caribbean Women and Literature*. Edited by Carole Boyce Davies and Elaine Savory Fido, 265-9. Trenton, N. J.: Africa World Press, 1990.

Mosquera, Gerardo. 'Esculturas rupestres de Ana Mendieta'. *Areito* 7 (1980): 54.

Excilia Saldaña

EXCILIA SALDAÑA

CUBA

(1946–1999)

An award-winning Cuban poet, short story writer, and author of children's books, Saldaña is noted for her experimentation with forms, particularly her use of rhymed prose that blurs the generic boundaries between poetry and narrative. Form, however, is always appropriate to the context. Kele Kele, *for example, is a poetic prose piece that is structured like a Greek drama but is rooted in the Afro-Cuban oral tradition. A proponent of cultural* mestizaje *(the blending of Cuba's African and European heritage), she often conveys the rhythms and sounds of African poetry through traditional Cuban and Spanish verse forms, such as the son (song-poem) and* romance *(eight-line ballad). Like poets Nicolás Guillén and Marcelino Arozarena, Saldaña uses Afro-Cuban myths and folklore in her work, but her knowledge of* lucumí *or Yoruba culture, particularly its vocabulary and legends (called* patakín), *is based on extensive research in ethnographic history.*

The influence of Nicolás Guillén, a literary ancestor, is apparent in the long narrative poem Mi nombre (Antielegía personal) *(My Name [A Personal Anti-Elegy]), a kind of 'call and response' to one of Guillén's elegies. Saldaña's respect for the ancestors, whom she calls 'spiritual generators', is also evident in her depiction of the grandmother in* La noche *(Night). A symbol of* la patria *and of the heroic woman in Cuban history, the grandmother is an archetypal figure in the writer's poetry and life. In an interview, she said, 'My grandmother, Ana Excilia Bregante, was and is the most important person in my life'.* La noche, *written in the form of a lyrical dialogue between a child and her grandmother, has been critically acclaimed as one of Saldaña's most daring and experimental works because it exemplifies a new aesthetic, a new vision of artistic creation. Acknowledging her indebtedness to such masters of the lyric as*

José Lezama Lima, Saldaña said in a recent interview that she is searching for the roots of poetry, the 'internal essence of poetry', and a poetry without boundaries. Characterised by its metric dexterity, dramatic intensity, stylistic purity, formal control, and moral integrity, Saldaña's poetry is grounded in an ethic that is fundamental to Cuban national identity.

Saldaña has written over twenty books, some of which have been translated into seven languages. Besides those mentioned above, her publications include Soñando y viajando *(Dreaming and Travelling),* El refranero de La Víbora *(Book of Proverbs for the Snake), and* Cantos para un mayito y una paloma *(Songs for a Mayito and a Dove), the last of which demonstrates what she calls the 'music of story-telling'. (Significantly, her son and only child Mario Ernesto is called 'Mayito'.) Until her death on July 20, 1999, Excilia Saldaña served as visiting professor at the Feliz Varela Teaching Institute in Santa Clara and as an editor at Gente Nueva, a children's press in Havana.*

Autobiography

II
If we have to begin I want to tell you everything
it's not worth keeping it secret anymore
I was born one August 7th in 1946
a year and a day after Hiroshima
(remember? our neighbour's great achievement)
I was born because all attempts at abortion failed
and because I was stubborn even in that
my father was a playboy
(that's what they called them in those days
when the son of the family was a no good bastard)
well, it wasn't his fault
like it wasn't his fault that he smoked marijuana
gambled and screwed around
imagine the context
my trembling mother
the proverbial cavity
The thing is – as I was saying –
my father was a bit of a playboy
and I was born
When they saw me everyone knew what I'd be
my mother, a doctor
my grandfather, a druggist (the family name)
my grandmother, a teacher
the dog barked
(maybe she wanted me to be a bitch . . .)
I grew chubby and cross-eyed
abominably silly
samaritan by vocation
sister of charity, guardian angel
to birds, cockroaches and beggars
and one fine day when my high yalla
future was all but set

the Revolution came to power
(yes, I know you know all about Agrarian Reform and
  Socialism)
I'm not going to talk about that
but about my small anonymous life
collecting bullets and buttons
listening to the arguments of the adults
I want you to know I didn't understand a thing
but Fidel's hoarse voice sent shivers down my spine
I want to tell you my father slapped my face
the day I shouted 'Homeland or Death!'
(can you understand what that means
when there's never been an embrace?)
I want to tell you the blue birds are moulting
there's unjustified mourning this tedious dawn
the gods are so angry
and there's so very much lost
and so much
and even more.

Translated by Margaret Randall

from

My Name (A Family Anti-Elegy)

I am not I.
            I have not been born:
Without love nothing is begotten.
And if I am not,
                        who clings
to the breast flaccid and dry from bitterness:
Who spies on the Azure Bird?
For whom is time being held in a box?
All amazement is in the gaze.
All the brilliance of the Sun.
And all worlds turn above his head.

There is no time to lose:
                        but I get lost.
I cannot find myself among the palm trees. I look for
      myself
in the back yard anthill,
before the tubs of oleander,
under the galán de noche,
in the fierce grip of the ivy.
I call myself by my name
                        to keep myself company
relishing the idea that someone may find me.

The final answer lies behind the glass eyes of the last
      doll.
It is not because of nobility that I do not poke at the
      mystery.
It is not because of piety.
It is not because of love.
                        But because of fear.
We are all afraid:
                        In the house

we act like figures in a grotesque ballet,
on tip toe
>> *and with fearful finger*
>> *strangling the kisses.*
In the house we are all afraid.
Although it is only I who defies the crime by mocking
>> *its boundaries:*
A fugitive slave of the parks,
>> *hiding out at school*
with laughter as my small machete
>> *and my new scrawl:*
without land in my own land:
fleeing each day from the facedown beating
>> *and caning.*
And to top it all, without the consolation
>> *of angels,*
>> *without the pity*
>> *of angels,*
Because in tropic air angels do not answer.

My house is the first stop in hell:
The circle of knives and radio soap operas.
Between the sighs of the condemned ones
>> *and the telephone*
waiting for a voice,
>> *the magical eye of the master*
orders the rounds of the grandmother and the mother
holding each other's hands
>> *for all eternity.*
My mother and my father's mother.
>> *And I at the centre.*
They circle and they wheel.
>> *And I at the centre.*
They howl and they endure.
>> *And I at the centre.*
Everyone peers out. Everyone watches.
>> *And I at the centre.*
Where do I look for a lock for this iron grate?

In what place do I rise up or sink down
                    with full lungs,
                    with open branchia,
                    with the full freedom
of being and not dying?
                    Not in this human body.

And the one I am not dreams herself
                    a star
                        or a plant
                            or a sensitive stone,
while,

                    asthma glistens through the chest,
                        swells the rib cage,
                        slows the foot's gate,
                        dilates the pupils,
                        stains the nails,
                        leaps in the belly.
                        Exorcises.
Enemy and twin
            she's also here
with my mother and my father's mother
and with all those who circle in the rounds
where I am always
            at the centre
drunk with screams and curses, asking for
what others have in excess:
                    a gulp of air, noble and quiet
to calm the howl that I hold inside.
They never
        stopped the circle. No, they
dressed me in white
            or
scrubbed my skin to transparency: Alabaster
in place of arteries. Water
in the course of blood. Doves
where there are veins.

Of everything I am guilty and I accept that.
The one that I am not – but who usurps me by habit
   and fear –bites
                 the sophistication of the bread
                 like a caress:
Grinds the serpent.
              Swallows the sword whole.
              Opens the forbidden iron grate.
God inside my 10 year-old body.
Oh, vanity of vanities, conceit of teophagy;
neither my mother nor my father's mother could devour
an entire god, round, white, insonorous.
It is not I – but how well I feign it under a tender smile –
who now sits,
          not on the right
          nor on the left.
          But in the centre.
          On the throne made with tinsel and tins of
            jam preserves
dictating the future of her race for ever and ever.
And she chooses to save you, Ana Excilia Bregante,
             caressive mulatta from Atarés,
             mistress of oranges,
             owner of coral and canistel,
             mistress of pumpkin custard,
             grandmother and martyr
while the country is torn
          by bomb shells and corpses.
I save you
          and I save my name from oblivion and hell,
today,
       the 8th of December of 1956.

Translated by Flora M. González
and Rosamond Rosenmeier

Note:

galán de noche: Night jessamine; suitor of the night.

The Zeal for Self-Denomination in the Poetic Works of Excilia Saldaña

Flora M. González

Although Excilia Saldaña (Havana, 1946) is not yet well known in the world of literary criticism in the United States, the Cuban writer already has a substantial number of works which include collections of poetry, children's short stories and essays on Cuban literature in general.[1] We make mention of her collections of children's short stories which have received prizes in Cuba: *Cuentos para un mayito y una paloma* (Short Stories for a Mayito and a Dove) (Ismaelillo Prize, 1979, and the Rosa Blanca Prize, 1984), *Campay Tito* (Edad de Oro Prize, 1984), and *Kele Kele* (Rosa Blanca Prize, 1987). She has also published *La noche* (The Night) (Ediciones Gente Nueva 1989), an autobiographical poem, 'Mi nombre (Antielegía personal)' (My Name [A Personal Anti-Elegy]) (Ediciones Unión, 1991) and *El refranero de La Víbora* (The Book of Proverbs for The Snake) (Ediciones Unión, 1989) which place her at the forefront of current Cuban poetic production. Her remaining poetic works are in press and are entitled *La naranja transparente* (The Transparent Orange), *Y ahora voy a desnudarte* (I Shall Now Undress You), *Jícara de miel* (Honeycup) (Gente Nueva). Saldaña is also a member of the editorial board of Gente Nueva, which is devoted to literature for children and young people.

From a reading of 'My Name (A Personal Anti-Elegy)' and of the short story 'Las tres suspirantes' (The Three Sighing Sisters) (*Kele Kele*), we suggest that Excilia Saldaña dialogues with Nicolás Guillén and transforms the genre of the children's short story into a poetic space where the Baroque voices of Luis de Góngora and Sor Juana Inés de la Cruz, and the more contemporary ones of Lydia Cabrera, Nicolás Guillén and José Lezama Lima resonate anew. Saldaña's poetic voice resorts to the metrics of the traditional *romancero* to turn prose into poetry; her reinvention of the Afro-Cuban *patakín* (Yoruba legend) attempts to redefine the face of the Black woman in Cuban literature.

There exists in the works of Excilia Saldaña a pressing need to name herself. We have proof of this in the poem 'My Name (A Family Anti-Elegy)' and in the short story 'Kele Kele', published in 1991 and 1987 respectively.[2] In 'Kele Kele', the rewriting of a Yoruba legend, the woman, in conversation with the man, defines herself in this way:

> Ochún Na Owo Pipo,
> Ochún Obailú Chemi Loyá:
> the one who carries the igbá
> the one who will be with you always
> your woman,
> the queen of the honey,
> the owner of the oñí
> That's what I am, that's what you call me. (115)

The poem 'My Name' defines the writer in a much more personal way and concludes:

> My name
> in the name of those who've recently decided their name and their memories.
> My name
> to precipitate like rain on the pitcher of my archipelago.[3] (32-33)

This insistence on naming herself reflects what the North American critics Sandra M. Gilbert and Susan Gubar have called 'the anxiety of authorship'.[4] In their study of the English women writers of the nineteenth century, Gilbert and Gubar offer us a fitting theory on female creativity in the face of an almost exclusively male tradition. The anxiety of authorship does not refer to an anxiety of influence, but rather to the effort put forth by the woman writer who defines her own voice as she reinterprets and rereads patriarchal works from a defamiliarised perspective. Gilbert and Gubar speak of a new, daring rereading. The new woman writer has to define herself fearlessly. Her survival within a male tradition depends on her ability to reinvent herself as she seeks precursors who have survived the weight of the former tradition.

We must make clear that the rereading proposed by the North American critics does not suggest a play on reference in the manner of Eliot or Borges, where it is claimed that the creative mind does nothing more than say the same thing with a different voice. The woman's anxiety of authorship produces a search that is more intuitive than rational, a search where precursors reappear in heterogeneous dialogue in the memory of the creative mind, where no one authority is placed above the other. Causal relationships disappear in the reinvention of literary sources.[5] If we speak of an intuitive search and of heterogeneous dialogues, we must refer to the work of José Lezama Lima, who says:

> Our method would be closer to that technique used in fiction, which was proposed by Curtius, rather than to Eliot's method of myth criticism. Everything will have to be reconstructed, reinvented, and when the old myths reappear, they will offer us their incantations and their enigmas with an unfamiliar face. The fiction of myths are [sic] new myths, with new fatigues and terrors.[6]

Lezama refutes the idea of exhaustive knowledge in favor of a theory of 'creative assimilation' based on the reinterpretation of the virtual unknown. In his excellent study of the essay 'Imagen y posibilidad' (Image and Possibility), Fina García Marruz clarifies Lezama Lima's creative method:

> Through it he would like to suggest, more than a thesis about some aspect of his work, the very way in which he approaches poetry; not the deciphering of a body of images and ideas, but rather their incessant rupture into 'rings and fragments', since he also approached the texts of others in this way. He was not interested in their internal circular coherence, but was looking for their tangential relationship with other poetic methods and other systems. His reading was not linear, but algebraic; he was looking for unexpected interrelationships, like someone rubbing sticks together to see the intermediary, immortal spark fly. (249)

I paused at Lezama's idea of creative assimilation because I would like to suggest that the poetics of Excilia Saldaña has been nurtured by readings of Lezama Lima which, though not explicit in her work, have been assimilated to define her personal literary tradition. There is in the texts of Saldaña what García Marruz describes in the texts of Lezama: 'una cadena de resonancias, una nueva irrupción de lo naciente, que hace engañosa la aparente enemistad de los condicionamientos causales' (255) (a chain of resonances, a bursting forth of the new, which makes any apparent enmity with causal analyses deceptive).

I suggest we begin with a reading of 'My Name (A Family Anti-Elegy)', a poem which recognizes and converses with the poetry of Nicolás Guillén, specifically 'El Apellido: Elegía familiar' (The Last Name: A Family Elegy). Saldaña dedicates the poem to Guillén and to her grandmother: 'A Nicolás Guillén / El apellido entero. / A mi abuela Ana Excilia. / suyo mi nombre' (To Nicolás Guillén / The whole last name. / To my grandmother Ana Excilia. / my name is hers). After the dedication, Saldaña cites a well-known verse from Guillén's elegy: 'Me dijeron mi nombre. Un santo y seña para hablar con las estrellas' (I was told my name. A password to speak with the stars). Starting with the title, and continuing with the dedication, Saldaña establishes a dialogue and a whole series of correspondence with the poem and the work of Guillén.

'My Name' begins with the birth of Saldaña, and establishes the existence of the new being out of abandonment: '¿Dónde? / ¿Dónde está el que soy? ¿Qué olvido me malcría y tutela?' (5) (Where? / Oh where is one that I am? What obliviousness indulges and protects me?). The child is born into a house where fear reigns. Her father is absent, and her mother and grandmother are her companions. From the beginning, the poem establishes the search for the self in a hostile environment: 'No hay tiempo que perder: / pero me pierdo. / No doy conmigo entre las arecas. Me busco / en el hormiguero del patio'[7] (6) (There's no time to lose: / but I get lost. / I can't find myself among the areca palms. I look for myself / in the anthill in the courtyard). This feeling of being an orphan, at least not having a father, had already been expressed in another poem entitled 'Autobiografía'[8] (Autobiography). If in 'My Name' the anguish of not being able to find herself rules the verse, here the anecdote prevails:

> I was born because the contraceptives failed
> and also because I was stubborn
> my father an eccentric boy
> (that's what they called it at that time when the son
> of the family turned out to be a cuckold)
> in short it wasn't his fault
> nor was the fact that he smoked marijuana
> gambled and fornicated
> just imagine the circumstances
> my mother trembling
> the void (200)

In these two poems the desire is to establish a void, starting with the absence of the father who leaves his name but not his presence. This absence underscores the arbitrariness of the last name Saldaña, just like Guillén does in his family elegy:

And then I was given
what you see written on my card,
what I put at the end of all my poems
the thirteen letters
that I carry on my back through the street,
that always go with me everywhere (97)

The name becomes a series of letters, with no context, no history. In this elegy, Guillén devalues the 'given' last name, the last name of the European father who, within the historical context of a descendent of slaves, represents the rape committed on his mother and his forgotten last name 'Yelofe', 'Bakongo', 'Banguila', 'Kumbá' or 'Kongué' (100). Vera Kutzinski does a detailed study of the myths to which Guillén alludes in his elegy and draws this conclusion: 'In "El Apellido", as in "Sensemayá", Guillén is concerned with effacing structures of authority (or better, authoritarianism of various kinds) in an effort to open up a space where ideas of self and culture can be entertained without being subjected to the institutional requirements of an avowed ideology' (164). In representing European culture with a marble statue, the poet creates a blank space where he inscribes the myths of the vanquished cultures. Guillén's elegy alludes to the historical context in order to retrieve both the myths of the taínos (the tree with 'ramas oscuras movidas por los sueños' 98) (dark branches swayed by dreams), and the iconography of the 'Mandinga, Bantu, Yoruba and Dahomey' cultures (102).[9] 'The Last Name' reveals the transcultural imagination of the Caribbean which Guillén himself called *mestizaje*.[10]

The difference between Guillén and Saldaña lies in the very personal element present in Saldaña's approach to her name. Guillén's poem underscores his impersonal relationship with his last name with the passive voice: 'Y luego me entregaron / esto que veis escrito en mi tarjeta' (And then I was given what you see written on my card). Saldaña speaks of 'el pequeño y extraño nombre de los papeles oficiales' (30) (the small, strange name of the official papers). The two poets begin and end with the desire to liberate their own name, but Guillén actualizes this desire with a historical, mythical search while Saldaña does so with a historical, mythical, personal search. If Guillén starts by devaluing the personal in order to root his poetic self in the syncretic myths of the Caribbean, Excilia Saldaña establishes a search for her name in personal terms, in creationist terms in the manner of Vicente Huidobro:[11]

God inside my 10-year-old body.
Ah, vanity of vanities, concept of teophagy;
neither my mother nor my father's mother could devour
an entire god, round, white, insonorous.
It is not I – but how well I feign it under a tender smile –
That's not me – but how well I hide it beneath my
who now sits
      not on the right
          nor on the left
      But in the center
      On the throne made with tinsel and tins of jam preserves
dictating the future of her race for ever and ever. (11)

Guillén dialogues with a culture rescued by his own poetry. Saldaña parodies herself by standing as a goddess who claims to pronounce the future of her race. If her predecessor rescued the past, the only thing left for the poetess to do is to reinvent the future, a feat equivalent to that of Huidobro, who reinvents the universe. In order to avoid the final fall, Saldaña places herself in the present, in the concreteness of being. 'My Name' begins:

Goodbye, mouth of the dream without a fitting trade
reality in its place justly gained.
I take up another language. I call forth another dimension.
I investigate
on behalf of this blood
of now, and here,
on behalf of this skin
at times
stained and rough,
at times
refined as a madrigal
or
as a young girl's sigh. (4)

The poem follows an autobiographical course with the child-poet discovering her environment, her body, her sensuality and finally the circumstances of the Revolution of '59. Initially, the self occupies space within the child's body, then inside the house, and towards the end, outside, in the streets of Havana immediately following the fall of Batista. Indoors, the child feels exiled because she and her grandmother are the only ones in the family in favor of socialist change: 'Soy la niña exiliada en el día de la espera' (23) (I am an exiled girl in the day of expectation). The child begs her grandmother for help; the two of them could go out and create the revolution in the streets of Havana. But the grandmother offers her another alternative:

> It was my turn to lose.
>   But
> save me for when in you I go
> or when to me you come.
>   I'll wait for you
> with the bed made
>   odorous of vetiver grass and mint,
> with steamed milk smoking,
> with my lullabies and my Punchinello.
> Excilia,
>   you,
>   always Excilia:
>   name of my name:
>   grandchild,
>   guardian:
>   comrade. (28)

These lines represent the historical, personal moment when the child gives herself wholly to the cause of the Cuban revolution, and consequently has to leave the house. It is also the moment when the name is handed down, when the grandmother names her granddaughter. At this moment in the family history when the grandmother hands down her name, she makes the distinction between herself, a woman whose lot it was to lose, because she was the 'hija de mulata y de isleño' (26) (daughter of mulatto and islander), and Excilia, the granddaughter, who opposes the entire family and rebels. Saldaña describes the situation at home within the context of slavery in Cuba: 'Cimarrona de los parques apalancada en el colegio' (7) (A fugitive slave of the parks, / hiding out at school). This decision to rebel exiles her from the family home and thrusts her into the outside world where the poetess assumes her name with all the connotations of the historical moment and brings about her own liberation when she begets her son:

> I am not the inheritor of bewilderment.
> They banished my name and they banished me.

They condemned me to bear it
>from door
>to
>door
being the one who left or the one who also was left.
Insomniac of my bed, keeper of the fast at my table.
>nobody watches over it;
in the vortex of the cyclone
only those with a vocation for wind are admitted;
I am free within
>of the first freedom
to encounter my origin
in the son who engenders me. (29)

Excilia Saldaña names herself in terms of her historical circumstances; she names herself when she takes on her role as a revolutionary; but she also does so as a woman, a woman who does not beget her son but has been engendered by him. In the final analysis, it is the relationship between grandmother and granddaughter, a relationship that begets nothing, except the act of naming, that defines the young poetess:

Her slow finger traces the circle of my eternity:
seven letters:
my name to say yes,
my name to fill the space,
my word-name,
my poem-name. (16)

Towards the end, Saldaña breaks the link that she had established with Guillén in the dedication: 'No hablo del nombre que me dijeron / para poder hablar con las estrellas' (31) (I'm not speaking of the name that was told to me / so that I could speak with the stars). The poem-name of Excilia Saldaña ends with a whole series of qualifiers that link the name with nature ('Mi nombre / de pie y de camino . . . / de yagua y cieno' etc.)[12] (My name / of foot and road . . . / of palm and mire, etc.) and ends with:

My name
>in the name of those who've recently decided their names
>>and
>>>their memories.

> My name
>> to precipitate rain on the pitcher of my archipelago. (32-33)

Her name-word-poem is the water that gives and creates life in Excilia Saldaña's Caribbean universe. It is a poem rooted in the earth, in the belly of the mother and in the history of the Cuban women who participated in *cimarronaje*. With 'My Name', Saldaña pays homage to Guillén but also confronts the master by recreating her own historical moment, based on personal, not mythical experience.

In dialoguing with the title of Guillén's poem, Saldaña manages to start a conversation among equals, creating the illusion that the poem of the child-poet precedes that of the master: 'Mi Nombre', 'El Apellido' (My Name, The Last Name). Note the possessive in Saldaña's poem and the impersonal in Guillén's. The subtitle 'Antielegía' (Anti-Elegy) places Saldaña's poem in opposition to Guillén's. The creationist tone of the poetess casts a shadow over the previous god, her predecessor. The power to confront the master comes from her relationship with her grandmother, the giver of the name, the woman who incites her granddaughter to beget the name-poem.

Excilia Saldaña, a disciple of Guillén, learns the lessons of the master very well, but she also transforms them, assimilating unexpected references like that of the *vanguardista* Huidobro. In the words of Lezama Lima: 'Todo tendrá que ser reconstruido, invencionado de nuevo, y los viejos mitos, al reaparecer de nuevo, nos ofrecerán sus conjuros y sus enigmas con un rostro desconocido' (see note 5) (Everything will have to be reconstructed, reinvented, and when the old myths reappear, they will offer us their incantations and their enigmas with an unfamiliar face). Saldaña reinvents Guillén by creating implicit relationships with lines from Huidobro. This interrelationship of the Caribbean with the Chilean revitalizes Saldaña's poetry and, to a certain degree, reflects the cultural syncretism that Guillén codified as *mestizaje*.[13] Like Lezama Lima, Saldaña has recourse to the concept of poetic assimilation in order to invent a defamiliarized name, a face unfamiliar to the reader, that of the young Cuban poetess. If in our analysis thus far we have established the paradigm of poetic assimilation as the modus operandi of the Cuban poet, let us see how this poetic system works in a reading of 'The Three Sighing Sisters', the final short story of the collection *Kele Kele*.

There is no doubt that on a formal level, the short story is rooted in the oral Afro-Cuban tradition. The *patakín* or Yoruba legend begins and ends with a narrative framework. It begins with: 'Ayer me contó mi abuela que

Olofi tenía tres hijas . . .' (19) (Yesterday my grandmother told me that Olofi had three daughters . . .), and it ends with: 'Así termina la historia que hoy te vine a contar; ayer me la dijo mi abuela, mañana tú la repitirás' (41) (This is the end of the story that I came to tell you; my grandmother told it to me yesterday, and you will repeat it tomorrow). With this framework we start from the origins of the narrative genre in which the grandmother tells the story to the granddaughter, who then retells it on condition that it be repeated.[14] To facilitate this repetition, the narrator resorts to a whole series of formulas that make it easy to remember: 'Ayer me contó mi abuela que Olofi tenía tres hijas a cual de las tres más bellas; que Olofi tenía tres hijas a cual de las tres más buenas; que Olofi tenía tres hijas criadas de igual manera' (19)[15] (Yesterday my grandmother told me that Olofi had three daughters, each one vying to be the most beautiful; that Olofi had three daughters, each one vying to be the best; that Olofi had three daughters raised in like manner).

Although the typography deceives us with a page in prose, we immediately hear the octosyllable with *rima asonante* in the even lines. And this romance which comes from the epic, lyric tradition, this *patakín* is composed of narrative sections, dramatic sections and sections which incorporate other metrics of *arte menor*. However, the predominant metric system is that of the *romance*. We also recognise the repetitive use of dramatic clauses which have no purpose other than to link sections of the anecdote. The following is an example that is repeated with multiple variations in this *patakín*:

> Nothing is easy under the sun, rope always gets tangled up,
> and the three were consumed with sighing and grieving.
> – Ay – said the youngest.
> – Ay – replied the first.
> – Ay – responded the other.
> – Ay, ay, ay, what are you complaining about? – asked
> the pebbles, the insects and the forest. (19)

Note the contamination of the formulaic with actual expressions such as 'la pita siempre se enreda' (rope always gets tangled up) and with the thread of the Afro-Cuban legend that favors dialogue with the flora and the fauna of the mountain.[16] Before we proceed with a formal analysis of the *patakín*, it is appropriate that we give a brief summary of the narrative. In 'The Three Sighing Sisters', the three daughters of Olofi complain constantly because all three love one man 'con pasión justa y sincera' (19) (truly and dearly). The three love Orula, the orisha of divination, and the symbol of wisdom. Father Olofi, the chief deity of the Yoruba pantheon, sends them to Orula to get the best remedy for their woes. Orula prescribes work for them: 'Cuando el cuerpo labora se olvidan los suspiritos' (22) (Work for the body means sighs cannot reign). The three devote themselves to women's work in their zeal to win Orula by following his own prescription:

> From town to town,
> I peddle my ware,
> Orula, the wise,
> I'll catch him,
> I'll catch him,
> I'll catch him,
> I myself
> will marry him. (24-25)

They each set out in search of Orula and come across Ikú, death, who also loves Orula. The first two sisters follow the advice that work will alleviate their suffering. They fall victim to the lies told by Ikú, who insists that Orula has died, and they die of love. The third sister, the youngest of the three, confronts Ikú and exposes her lies. The dialogue to the death that ensues between the two shows brilliant mastery of the word on the part of the young girl.

The third episode of the *patakín* is the most significant because, in this case, the behavior of the young girl breaks with all social expectations for a woman in a society defined by paternalism. From the beginning, what characterizes this girl is the absence of fear in the multiple faces of death. At the first meeting, Ikú disguises herself as a crocodile. But to the surprise of Ikú, who thought that she looked so fierce, the young girl replies: '— Gracias, Ta Cocodrilo, tendré sumo cuidado en no tocarle el hocico. . . . yo con usted no me meto, no se meta usted conmigo' (33) (Thanks. Easy does it, Crocodile. I'll be very careful not to touch your mouth. . . . I'm not messing with you, and don't you mess with me). Note the use of humorous, colloquial language by the girl in order to defeat Ikú. It is noteworthy that her power lies in the mastery of language at all levels. Later Ikú describes the girl's powers in this way: 'Esta niña no es humana, parece una golondrina' (33) (This girl is not human, she appears to be a swallow). Here, emphasis is placed on the musicality of the language which, with her rhythmic singing, turns into poetry. When the girl plays down the exaggerations of death, Ikú responds with this aside:

'Usa bien el vocabulario' (34) (She uses words well). With the word, the girl overcomes death and wins her lover Orula.

This episode echoes a similar one by Lezama Lima, where the poet's apprenticeship is also represented as a meeting between two characters, one from the world above (the petty thief) and the other from below (the cat). I am referring to the episode found in Chapter IV of *Oppiano Licario*.[17] I quote Margarita Fazzolari who analyses it in the following way:

> The cat is a symbol of the double and of the analogous wisdom, according to what Lezama Lima has said in 'The Imaginary Eras: the Egyptians'. On the other hand, the petty thief is a symbol of the poet, Prometeo, the alter ego of Cemi, who steals fire from the gods. The petty thief throws a stone at the cat, and it insults him by saying: 'Fuck your mother'. Unperturbed, the boy replies: 'Fuck yours back'. Ironically, when these characters from the world above and the world below insult each other in a grotesque way, they are returning to the origins, alluding to the moment of Creation. (127)

The moment of creation arises from a verbal battle between the opponents. But if in *Oppiano Licario* the success of the petty thief depends on the intervention of Licario who cuts off the cat's head and later takes the petty thief to a crazy doctor, in Saldaña's episode the girl takes control of Ikú by herself. The vulgar verbal exchange between the girl and Ikú takes us back to that of the cat and the petty thief. Saldaña appears to rewrite Lezama's episode, but she does so with a poet-protagonist who needs no advocates, at least not explicit advocates. If it now seems evident to us that this episode echoes the work of Lezama Lima, we must also trace other poetic presences which are much more explicit in the episode of 'Las tres suspirantes'.[18]

With *Kele Kele*, Excilia Saldaña attempts to rescue an oral poetic tradition that is on the verge of disappearing: 'Como dice el viejo adagio africano: "Cada viejo que se muere es una biblioteca que se quem". Transcribamos esa biblioteca al lenguaje de nuestros días' (13) (As the old African adage says: 'Every old man who dies is a library that goes up in flames'. Let us transcribe that library to the language of our day). It is fitting to ask what is the poetic language of 'nuestros días' (our day) in the context of Saldaña's poetry. Let us follow the trail that the narrator leaves us in 'The Three Sighing Sisters'. If Excilia Saldaña attempts to rescue the Afro-Cuban tradition with epic, lyric chords, she does so in the shadow of Nicolás Guillén. It is not difficult to follow his tracks in the *patakín* that we are analyzing. In her zeal to infuse poetic chords into popular language, Saldaña pays homage to Guillén by playing with the rhythms of popular Cuban speech. We will mention two such moments in the text which echo the voice of the Afro-Cuban poet.

The first occurs when Orula makes his prediction concerning the illness of Olofi's daughters: 'Dice Ifá, digo y repito, que si usted me lo permite, yo la enfermedad les quito. Dice Ifá, digo y repito, que si el cuerpo está cansado, viene por si mismo el apetito. Dice Ifá, digo y repito, que cuando el cuerpo labora se olvidan los suspiritos. Dice Ifá digo y repito' (22) (So says Ifá, so say I and say I again, with your permission, I'll cure your pain. So says Ifá, so say I and say I again, tire your body and your appetite you'll regain. So says Ifá, so say I and say I again, that work for the body means sighs cannot reign. So says Ifá, so say I and say I again). This rhythmic repetition defines the work of Guillén, especially his *poemas-son*.[19] The second example makes a more direct reference with the play on the personal pronouns: 'Yo no digo que sí, yo no digo que no. Yo digo, que si tú quieres, te cuento yo' (23) (I don't say yes, I don't say no. I say that I'll tell you if you want me to). Let us recall Guillén's poem 'No sé por qué piensas tú' (I Know Not Why You Think) in which he plays with the pronouns 'yo' (I) and 'tú' (you):

> I know not why you think,
> soldier, that I hate you,
> we are the same
> I,
> you,
> You are poor, so am I;
> I'm from the underclass, so are you;
> Where did you get that,
> soldier, that I hate you?[20]

If the *patakín* begins and ends with the grandmother who symbolizes the voice of the oral Afro-Cuban tradition, and if there exist obvious traces of Guillén in the references, where do we place the voice of the foremother?

There is no doubt that the all-powerful figure that the young lover has to defeat is the figure of Ikú; that is, the figure of death. In her final attempt to defeat the young poetess, Ikú promises: 'Te convertiré en polvo, en olvido, en nada . . .' (38) (I'll turn you to dust, to oblivion, to nothingness . . .). With this sentence, Saldaña evokes the voice of Sor Juana Inés de la Cruz in Sonnet 145: 'Procura desmentir los elogios que a un retrato de la poetisa inscribió la verdad, que llama pasión'[21] (The poetess seeks to refute the praises rightfully sung to a portrait of hers, deeming them excessive). Faced with her own image, the Mexican poetess struggles to the death against Sonnet CLXVI of Góngora, her predecessor. Excilia Saldaña recreates the poetic dialogue between Góngora and Sor Juana in which Góngora's line 'en tierra, en humo, en polvo, en sombra, en nada' (to clay, to smoke, to dust, to shadow, to nothingness) becomes 'es cadáver, es polvo, es sombra, es nada' (it's a corpse, it's dust, it's shadow, it's nothingness) in Sor Juana.[22] Curiously, Saldaña adopts the syntax of Góngora's line. Saldaña and Góngora construct parallelisms based on the preposition 'en', (to) while Sor Juana emphasizes the verb 'ser' (to be). In imitating Góngora, Saldaña seems to have forgotten Sor Juana. However, that oversight is corrected when she rescues the word 'cadáver' (corpse) used by Sor Juana with the detailed description of Ikú: 'Ikú se quita la máscara, muestra los huesos, lanza una carcajada' (38) (Ikú takes off her mask, shows the holes, her smooth, bald head, rattles all her bones, bursts out laughing).

In her revision of Góngora's sonnet, Sor Juana mentions what Góngora did not want to make explicit in his poem: the cadaverous nature of death. With the macabre image of Ikú, the Cuban poetess brings to a literal level the word 'cadáver' (corpse) which Sor Juana so boldly added to Góngora's baroque concept of death. Saldaña's revision adds the word 'olvido' (oblivion) as if to underline her apparent oblivion to the line from Sor Juana. Saldaña forgets the word 'cadáver', but revives it with the unmasked, or rather, the prosaic image of Ikú, death, who bursts out laughing. With this play on poetic allusions, Excilia Saldaña brings to mind the creative act of Sor Juana de La Cruz, a poetess who 'se retrata' (paints her portrait) by parodying the great Baroque poet. To demarcate her own portrait, Saldaña resorts to the ruse used so well by Sor Juana in her 'Respuesta a Sor Filotea' (Reply to Sor Filotea): expressing one's thoughts through the voice of another.[23] Saldaña's voice projects beneath the shadows of Nicolás Guillén and José Lezama Lima in the same way that Sor Juana's voice projects beneath the shadow of Góngora. In order to assimilate the influence of the great predecessors, the two poetesses repeat the past creating 'interrelaciones inesperadas' (unexpected interrelationships) (García Marruz), ever anxious to paint a lasting portrait. Saldaña's good fortune is that she has a female poetic tradition to which she can have recourse when she establishes her own voice. The success that results from such a hard task produces an outburst of laughter.

Saldaña constructs her poetic image in apparent oblivion of her patriarchal past. Only the lines of Sor Juana Inés de la Cruz are explicit, while the voices of Guillén and Lezama are engraved in the rhythm and the humor of the girl's speech. The rhythm of the traditional *romance* is reborn in its present manifestations when she duplicates the popular speech of the mulatto woman from Havana, whom Guillén had already presented.[24] The oral Yoruba tradition reappears within the parameters of a new society in which the voice of a precocious child-poet (Sor Juana-Saldaña) is able to depose the masters of poetry (Góngora and Guillén). In order to invent her own poetic tradition, Saldaña resorts to Lezama's method of illuminating fragments of earlier texts to create 'una nueva irrupción de lo naciente' (a bursting forth of the new) (García Marruz 255). As Gilbert and Gubar had anticipated, the new writer silences the voices of the more recent patriarchal tradition (Guillén and Lezama), so that she can start a more explicit dialogue with Sor Juana Inés de la Cruz, her predecessor who dared to start a dialogue to the death with Góngora. The prose poems in *Kele Kele* establish a new tradition born of the poetic assimilation of European and Cuban heritage, of mothers and fathers who resuscitate in all their splendor so that they can be reinterpreted in the context of Saldaña's works.

Translated by Mary A. Harris

Notes
1.   See Flora González, 'De la tradición épico-lírica a la yoruba en *Kele Kele* de Excilia Saldaña', until now the only critical essay on Saldaña. The research and writing of the present article was made possible thanks to the academic support of the Office of Graduate Studies of Emerson College.
2.   All references to these texts will be made with page numbers in parentheses. The 'Works Cited' includes an up-to-date bibliography on the author.
3.   'My Name (A Personal Elegy)' is translated by Flora M. González and Rosemond Rosenmeier and is from their book *In the Vortex of the Cyclone*, a collection of poetry by Saldaña.
4.   See especially pages 49-53. I am grateful to the Cuban critic Nara Araújo for the correspondence between Saldaña's naming of the self, and Gilbert and Gubar's anxiety of authorship.
5.   For this definition of reading and creative writing, see the fourth chapter of Gustavo Pellón's book on Lezama Lima, 45-69. Through correspondence with Lezama Lima, who rejects literary pessimism in the manner of Eliot and Borges, the work of Saldaña also implicitly rejects Harold Bloom's theory of anxiety of influence.
6.   This reference comes from the Center for Literary Research of Casa de las Américas. *Interrogando a Lezama Lima*. (Barcelona: Anagrama, 1971), cited in Pellón.

7. These lines echo Canto IV of Vicente Huidobro in *Altazor*:

    'No hay tiempo que perder / Todo esto es triste como el niño que está
    quedándose huérfano' (104) (There's no time to lose / All this is sad like
    a child becoming an orphan). Huidobro and Saldaña begin with questions
    that underline the loneliness of the speaker. '¿En dónde estás Altazor?'
    (Where are you, Altazor?) says the Chilean poet in his first canto (88).
    Later on in this analysis I will speak of more correspondences between
    Saldaña and Huidobro. What is important is that Saldaña has taken a
    line from Huidobro which is repeated like a leitmotif in one of the best
    known poems of Latin America: 'No hay tiempo que perder' (104) (There's
    no time to lose). The poet breaks all ties with the universe and not only
    invents himself but reinvents poetic language. Saldaña takes this daring
    gesture from Huidobro and repeats it in order to invent her own name,
    even when the Cuban poetess knows how easy it is to get lost: 'No hay
    tiempo que perder: / pero me pierdo' (There's no time to lose: / but I
    am lost). The act of getting lost actualises the act of inventing the self
    with a play on words.

8. In *Breaking the Silences: An Anthology of 20th-Century Poetry by Cuban
    Women*. Translated and introduced by Margaret Randall, 200, 202.

9. See the analysis by Kutzinski, 151-164.

10. See Kutzinski, 134.

11. We must remember Huidobro's 'Arte Poética' which ends like this: "Por
    qué cantáis la rosa, oh Poetas! / Hacedla florecer en el poema; / Sólo para
    nosotros / Viven todas las cosas bajo el Sol. / El poeta es un pequeño Dios'
    (*The Selected Poetry of Vicente Huidobro* 3) (Why sing ye to the rose, oh
    Poets! / Make it bloom in the poem; / Only for us / All things live under the
    Sun. / The poet is a small God). The complete freedom of versification in
    Saldaña's poem also recalls the cantos of *Altazor* (*The Selected Poetry of
    Vicente Huidobro* 83-159).

12. This repetitive section towards the end of the poem recalls Huidobro's
    Canto VI (148-157) where the rhythm and the abundance of nouns anticipate
    the dispersion of poetic language. In Saldaña's case, the poem ends with
    the celebration of the word-poem, name-poem.

13. In his study on Nicolás Guillén and the Baroque, 'Guillén as Baroque',
    Roberto González Echevarría focuses on the interdependence and
    desecration of the codes of the African and European cultures in *Sóngoro
    cosongo y otros poemas*. In conclusion, the Cuban critic says: 'The constant
    transfer from the African to the European code no doubt wears away the
    authority of the former, but at the expense of revealing, of making profane
    the latter. There is a double unveiling: the authority of the European code
    is shown to rely on convention or imposition, not to be invested with any
    inherent superiority; but, by relinquishing its secrecy, the African code
    gives up its sacredness, that which would presumably make its claim to
    superiority' (211). These words will help us to formulate a method of analysis
    for the second part of this paper, where Saldaña plays with Baroque and
    Afro-Cuban influences.

14. It is imperative that we note here again the importance of the grandmother in Saldaña. In this *patakín*, the creative work is defined by the grandmother; in her poem 'Mi Nombre (Antielegía Familiar)', Saldaña dedicates the poetic work to Nicolás Guillén and to her grandmother Ana Excilia, who gave her her name: 'A Nicolás Guillén / El apellido entero. / A mi abuela Ana Excilia, / suyo mi nombre' (To Nicolás Guillén / The whole last name. / To my grandmother Ana Excilia, / my name is hers).

15. For the radical study of the formula in the oral tradition see Albert B. Lord, 'The Formula', 30-67.

16. We cite the well-known beginning of Lydia Cabrera's monumental work: 'Persiste en el negro cubano, con tenacidad asombrosa, la creencia en la espiritualidad del monte. En los montes y las malezas de Cuba habitan, como en las selvas de Africa, las mismas divinidades ancestrales, los espíritus poderosos que todavía hoy, igual que en los días de la trata, más teme y venera, y de cuya hostilidad o benevolencia siguen dependiendo sus éxitos y fracasos' (13) Lydia Cabrera, *El Monte*. (There persists in the Black Cuban, with surprising tenacity, the belief in the spirituality of the mountain. In the mountains and thickets of Cuba, as in the jungles of Africa, live the same ancestral deities, the powerful spirits whom he fears most and whom he still worships today, just like in the days of the slave trade, and on whose hostility or benevolence his successes or failures continue to depend). There is no doubt that Saldaña was deeply influenced by the work of Cabrera, a work which she knows in its entirety and which she imitates in *Kele Kele*, when, like Lydia Cabrera, she provides the reader with a dictionary of terms from the Afro-Cuban languages at the end of the text.

17. For an analysis of this chapter (93-109 Mexico, Ediciones Ena, 1997), see the essay by Margarita Fazzolari's essay 'Las tres vías del misticismo en *Oppiano Licario*', 125-133.

18. It must also be noted that *Oppiano Licario* and 'Las tres suspirantes' are prose works that establish a method of poetic creation.

19. I quote from Kutzinski in her 'Translator's Introduction' to Nicolás Guillén, *The Daily Daily*: 'There is no doubt that Guillén's *poemas-son* were a daring literary experiment. They not only called attention to racial prejudice and economic injustices but also put aside conventional poetic forms in favor of the *son*, a bold gesture that in itself made a powerful symbolic statement about Cuban culture and literature' (xi).

20. Nicolás Guillén, 'No sé por qué piensas tú', *Sóngoro cosongo y otros poemas*, 72.

21. Sor Juana Inés de la Cruz, *Obras completas*, 134.

22. Luis de Góngora, *Antología*, 148.

23. See the analysis of the 'Respuesta' by Josefina Ludmer: 'Tretas del débil', 47-54.

24. Gustavo Pérez Firmat speaks of the use of conventional poetic forms on the part of Guillén in 'Mulatto Madrigals': 'Speaking of his use of the romance in *Motivos de son* he has said that his intention was "amulatar el romance español, esto es, cubanizarlo, volviéndolo a ser pristino' (94) (to make the Spanish *romance* mulatto, that is, to make it Cuban, returning it to its pristine form).

Works Cited

Bloom, Arnold. *The Anxiety of Influence: A Theory of Poetry*. New York: Oxford UP, 1978.

Cabrera, Lydia. *El Monte (Igbo-Finda, Ewe Orisha, Vititi Nfinda)*. Miami: Colección de Chichereкú, 1986.

De la Cruz, Sor Juana Inés. *Obras completas*. Mexico: Editorial Porrúa, 1989.

Fazzalari, Margarita.'Las tres vías del misticismo en *Oppiano Licario*'. In *Coloquio Internacional sobre la obra de José Lezama Lima. Vol. II: Prosa*. Poitier, France: Centre de Récherches Latino-Américaines; Madrid: Editorial Fundamentos, 1984. 125-133.

García Marruz, Fina. 'La poesía es un caracol nocturno (En torno a "Imagen y posibilidad")'. *Coloquio Internacional sobre la obra de José Lezama Lima. Vol 1: Poesía*. Poitier, France: Centre de Recherches Latino-Américaines; Madrid: Editorial Fundamentos, 1984. 243-275.

Gilbert, Sandra M. and Gubar, Susan. *The Madwoman in the Attic: The Woman Writer and the Nineteenth-Century Literary Imagination*. New Haven: Yale UP, 1979.

Góngora, Luis de. *Antología*. Madrid: Espasa Calpe, 1971.

González, Flora. 'De la tradición épico-lírica a la yoruba en el *Kele Kele* de Excilia Saldaña'. *Actas del Congreso Beresit* II. Tomo II, Toledo, Spain: Cofradía Internacional de Investigadores, 1992. 171-77.

González Echeverría, Roberto. 'Guillén as Baroque'. *Celestina's Brood: Continuities of the Baroque in Spanish and Latin American Literature*, Durham: Duke UP, 1993. 194-211.

Guillén, Nicolás. 'El apellido: elegía familiar (1951)'. *Las grandes elegías de Nicolás Guillén*. Havana: Ediciones Fundación Guillén, 1993, 95-102.

___. 'No sé por qué piensas tú'. *Sóngoro cosongo y otros poemas*. Madrid: Alianza Editorial, 1980.

Huidobro, Vicente. *The Selected Poetry of Vicente Huidobro*. Ed., David M. Guss. New York: New Directions, 1981.

Kutzinski, Vera. 'The Carnivalization of Poetry: Nicolás Guillén's Chronicles'. *Against the American Grain: Myth and History in Carlos Williams, Jay Wright and Nicolás Guillén*. Baltimore: The Johns Hopkins UP, 1987. 131-235

___. 'Translator's Introduction'. *The Daily Daily, Nicolás Guillén*, Berkeley: U of California P, 1989. v-xxxvi.

Lord, Albert B. 'The Formula'. *The Singer of Tales*, Cambridge: Harvard UP, 1971. 30-47.

Ludmer, Josefina. 'Tretas del débil'. *La sartén por el mango*. Eds., Patricia Elena González and Eliana Ortega. Río Piedras: Ediciones Huracán, 1985. 47-54.

Pellón, Gustavo. *José Lezama Lima's Joyful Vision: A Study of Paradise and Other Prose Works*. Austin: U of Texas P, 1989.

Pérez Firmat, Gustavo. 'Mulatto Madrigals'. *The Cuban Condition: Translation and Identity in Modern Cuban Literature*. 80-94. Cambridge: Cambridge UP, 1989.

Saldaña, Excilia. 'Autobiografía'. *Breaking the Silence: An Anthology of 20ᵗʰ-Century Poetry by Cuban Women*. Trans., Margaret Randall, Vancouver: Pulp Press, 1982. 200, 202.

___. *Bulgaria, el país de las rosas.* Havana: Editorial Gente Nueva, 1987.

___. *Cantos para un mayito y una paloma.* Havana: Editorial Unión, 1984.

___. *Campay Tito.* Havana: Editorial Gente Nueva, 1988.

___. *De la isla del tesoro a la isla de la juventud.* Havana:Editorial Gente Nueva, 1978.

___. 'Deus'. *Lovers and Comrades.* Ed., Amanda Hopkinson, 121. London: The Women's Press, 1989. 121.

___. *Flor para amor.* Havana: Editorial Gente Nueva, 1980.

___. *Kele Kele.* Havana: Editorial Letras Cubanas, 1987.

___. 'My Name (A Family Anti-Elegy)'. Eds., Ruth Behar and Juan León. *Michigan Quarterly Review* 33.3 (Summer 1994): 543-47.

___. *El misterioso caso de los maravillosos cascos de Doña Cuca Bregante.* Havana: Editorial Capitán San Luis, 1992.

___. *La noche.* Havana: Editorial Gente Nueva, 1989.

___. 'Ofumelli'. *AfroCuba.* Eds., Pedro Pérez Sarduy and Jean Stubbs, 163-68. Brooklyn: Ocean Press, 1993. 163-168.

___. *Poesía de amor y combate.* Havana: Editorial Gente Nueva, 1981.

___. *El refranero de La Víbora.* Havana: Editorial Letras Cubanas, 1989.

___. *Soñando y vagando.* Reprint. Havana: Editorial Gente Nueva, 1980, 1989.

___. *Un testigo de la historia.* Havana: Editorial Gente Nueva, 1978.

Beatriz Santos

B EATRIZ S ANTOS

URUGUAY

(b. 1947)

A writer, cultural worker, and human rights activist in Montevideo, Uruguay, Beatriz Santos Arrascaeta has worked assiduously to document, preserve, and disseminate the history and cultural traditions of Uruguay's Black community. After a career in theatre, radio, and television, she has turned increasingly to writing as a means of stimulating interest in the contributions of Afro-Uruguayans. She began writing scripts for radio and television, as well as editorials and articles for Mundo Afro, *a contemporary Black newspaper which, like earlier periodicals such as* La Conservación *and* Nuestra Raza, *has given voice to Afro-Uruguayan writers. In the past decade, Santos has published three books, including* Historias de vida: Negros en el Uruguay *(1994), co-authored with Teresa Porzecanski;* Africa en el Río de la Plata *(1995) with Nene Lorriaga of Argentina; and* La herencia cultural africana en las Américas *(1998). The niece of poet Juan Julio Arrascaeta, known as the Langston Hughes of Uruguayan poetry, Santos has played a leading role in the renaissance of Black letters in her country.*

She grew up in Barrio Buceo, a Montevideo neighbourhood, where, after completing high school, she worked as a domestic before exploring opportunities in communications and the performing arts. A talented singer and dancer, she became active in theatre: she sang in Romeo and Juliet; *performed* candombé *with the Odín theatre group; and recently starred in* El desalojo de la calle de los negros *(Eviction on the Blacks' Street) by Afro-Uruguayan playwright Jorge Emilio Cardoso. In the 1980s, she turned to radio and television, writing and producing shows on Black culture, such as 'Sangre, Sudor, Tambor' (Blood, Sweat, Drum), for Channel 5, Televisión Española, and Danmarks Radio. The first Black to be listed in Uruguay's Who's Who,* Uruguayos por su nombre: sepa quien

278

es quien, *Santos has gained an international reputation for her workshops, lectures, and conference presentations in Africa, Brazil, and the United States. A leader of many cultural and political organisations, she is president and co-founder of the Centro Cultural por la Paz y la Integración (Cultural Centre for Peace and Integration), which strives to eliminate racial discrimination in Uruguay.*

Historias de vida *is a collection of ten personal narratives by Afro-Uruguayans, who relate their life stories in their own voices; these oral histories document what it means to be Black in Uruguay. Santos' second book is also a work of non-fiction, written in an objective, journalistic style; it is an historical account of Black life in the Río de la Plata region, from slavery to the present.* La herencia cultural *is a collection of essays by writers who deal with such topics as art, music, religion, race, and the status of Black women. Besides these major works, Santos has written essays, such as 'La esclavitud en el Uruguay' (Slavery in Uruguay), poems, three of which were published in a recent issue of the* Afro-Hispanic Review, *and folkloric tales about the beliefs, customs, and religious practices of Black Uruguayans. The writing of this artist and lecturer is designed to create racial pride and to raise awareness of the contributions of Blacks to their country.*

* I am indebted to Professor Caroll Mills Young, the literary agent of Beatriz Santos in the United States and a specialist in Afro-Uruguayan literature and culture, for providing me with copies of Santos' writing and for sharing with me critical essays and material from the forthcoming book on Afro-Uruguayan writers that she and Beatriz Santos are co-editing.

Black Griot

Last night a griot
visited me, told me
beautiful legends.
Told me about black nymphs
enchanted forests
small villages.
The griot sang about
the splendor
of my black town
before the white oppressor
destroyed all that.
A blue bird
folded my ravaged soul
in its arms
so it could sleep forever
in Africa's beautiful land.

Editor's translation

Fire

Your passion's fire
slowly consumes
the nectar
that my breasts exude
Your semen's
burning lava
begets butterflies
in my dark womb.
While in the desecrated
night
your song soothes
my hours' pain.

Editor's translation

Chulin's Fantasy

Chulin is a youthful man with a lively look, a teasing smile, and white hair. Eight years ago, Chulin forgot what time it was. He doesn't live by hunting but by fishing, with which he supports his wife and eight children.

The majestic Cerro[1] looks impassively over Chulin's small milk farm, which has been ruined by the weather. When he's fishing for his eight children, Chulin's skin becomes tanned by the sun. A witty and lively man, he laughs at life and defies poverty, but he also good-naturedly teases those who merit his deep respect.

His circle of friends drink together at Chulin's farm – men and women who struggle against poverty – while one of the baby girls makes a furrow on the ground with urine. Carnival magic envelopes the city. Poor folk forget their misery, Blacks their complexes, the rich their money, the elderly their tired bones. The stage is set: the children's smiles and their anxious pleas of 'Paint me, Mister'[2] encroach upon the night.

Chulin, imitating the majesty of the Cerro, walks tall, arrogant . . . . forgetting his milk farm, the smell of urine, the fish, and his wife.

Chulin has been transformed into a king.

Editor's translation

Notes

1. Cerro is the highest point in the city of Montevideo, Uruguary. It is a barrio that is populated primarily by descendants of immigrants. Politically, it is important because the inhabitants of the neighbourhood have always fought for the rights of workers.
2. 'Paint me, Mister' (pínteme señor) – During Carnival, the participants use a special make-up on their faces and, when the children kiss them, some of the make-up comes off on their faces. This is a very old custom that persists today.

Tía Coca[1]

On the day before the Drum Calls,[2] the spirits were very expectant. Dressmakers were all tangled up in feathers, boas, and sequins; they still had to repair and iron one dress or another. In the places set aside for the practice session,[3] people were assuaging their thirst and taking up collections to pass out watered-down wine or home-brew with lemon. Not all the drums were in shape to be played the next day. From time to time, someone punctured a drum-head while trying to tighten it or slashed a leather strap, so the slightest damned sound could be heard across the street. Of course there were lots of bets over which *comparsa*[4] would win. There was happiness and a lot of nervousness in the barrio. While this was going on, Tía Coca was lingering between life and death, but there was no orisha[5] who could save her, because she had interfered in an 'Exchange of Life'.[6] The uncle of one of the owners of the Lubolo Concierto[7] was dying of cancer, and it was Tía Coca's turn to carry out the discharge. People say that this work does not always turn out well, because sometimes the one who performs the ceremony can die. Tía Coca always said, 'On the day I die, let them bury me with drums'. And so it was. They held a wake at her house, across from the Charrúa Slum[8] where she lived. The rooms were packed with people. The scent of flowers wafted through the air. Not even a knife could fit in. Friends, acquaintances, relatives, and journalists attended the burial. Of course the curious showed up. At three o'clock in the afternoon on a marvellous sunny day, four people carried the casket. Six drums accompanied Tía Coca on her last Drum Call. Nene Casal danced the candombé steps[9] behind her, while entoning: 'Don't stay here, Coca. Go forth, old woman'.

Editor's translation

Notes

1. Tía Coca: In Spanish, *tía* means 'aunt', but here it is the title of respect that is given to a revered elderly woman by the community of believers. Tía Coca was a well known 'Mamá Vieja', a wise and respected priestess of *candombé*, the African-derived religion of the Afro-Uruguayan people. (Caroll Mills Young)
2. Drum Calls (*Llamadas*): Before the grand procession that was the highlight of the carnival celebration, groups of drummers would meet regularly to

practice. They would stand on certain street corners and 'call' to each other. (C.M.Y.)

3. Practice session (*ensayo*): Each group of drummers was composed of a different community group with its own name and identity. The group would practise in a certain place for two or three years to get ready for carnival, a cultural event that had evolved from the religious practices of *candombé*. The practice session was really a party without carnival costumes. The drummers lit bonfires to tune up their drums. (C.M.Y.)

4. *comparsa:* a group of dancers and musicians who participated in the carnival procession and competed for first prize for performance, costumes, etc. (C.M.Y.)

5. orisha: a saint in African-derived religions.

6. Exchange of Life (*troca de vida*): *candombé* ceremony for the dying.

7. Lubolo Concierto: the name of a musical or drumming group. (C.M.Y.)

8. Slum (*Conventillo*): Many old dilapidated mansions in Montevideo were built in the Spanish style with an interior courtyard surrounded by four walls. Some of these mansions are now overcrowded with Blacks, who have turned the yards into public places or slums. (C.M.Y.)

9. danced the *candombé* steps (*hacer gramilla*): 'hacer gramilla' means to dance the steps of *candombé*, which, in this case, is done by the 'sweeper' or the *gramillero*. The *gramillero* is a typical figure in Uruguayan *candombé*. The dance is always performed by a male, who symbolises the witch doctor of ancient African nations, the one who possesses wisdom and profound knowledge about herbal properties. (Beatriz Santos)

María Nsue Angüe

ℳaría 𝒩sue 𝒜ngüe

EQUATORIAL GUINEA / SPAIN

(b. 1948)

María Nsue Angüe was born in Ebebeyin (Río Muni) in a prison, where her mother had been incarcerated for her political views. Her family, who were devout Protestants, had a decisive influence on her religious and intellectual development. Her father, for example, urged her not to write like a European because her country needed a woman writer who could describe their culture. While quite young, she moved to Madrid and, after completing her primary education, she studied journalism for two years at the Instituto Lope de Vega and then took a job in Addis Ababa, Ethiopia. At age twenty-one, she returned to Equatorial Guinea to work in radio and television, and she immersed herself in the language, history, and culture of the Fang people from which she was descended. Although she has lived longer in Spain than in her native country, she acknowledges that the people and traditions of Equatorial Guinea inform and inspire her writing. A journalist by profession, she published several poems under the title 'Delirios' in the magazine Africa 2000, *but she revealed in an interview that she does not consider herself a real poet. Nsue became the first Equatorial Guinean woman to publish a novel when the Universidad Nacional de Educación a Distancia (UNED) in Madrid published* Ekomo *in 1985. A French translation of the novel was published ten years later by L'Amattan.*

Scholars have noted that Nsue, like other Equatorial Guineans, writes in a literary and 'internationally prestigious' Spanish rather than the 'Guinean Spanish' spoken in the country. In the novel, Fang names (Mba, Nnegue, and Nfumbaha) and a few Guineanisms (abaha, clotte, bipkwele) evoke the poetic and mythical world of the Fang. Ekomo, *which means 'concord' in the Fang language, depicts the life and death of a man, narrated from the point of view of Nnanga, the woman who loves him. According to literary critic María Zielina Limonta, 'Ekomo is a transgressive novel, and like many other African novels, it is mimetic; its aim is to teach, to document . . . .' She contends that the transgressive elements are apparent in the description and development of the female narrator, who makes the male characters aware that women are an important creative force in their culture. Although Nsue does not support the objectives of feminism, which she calls a 'sickness of developed countries', she admires the work of women writers such as Toni Morrison, Rosalía de Castro, and Carmen Laforet. She points out in an interview, however, that these writers have nothing to do with her own style or method of writing. She believes that writers – male and female, African and European – have an important role to play in communicating across cultures, particularly in the struggle against racism, xenophobia, and violence.*

A widow and mother of three children, María Nsue Angüe presently lives in Madrid, where she writes for Spanish and Guinean newspapers and sometimes directs plays such as La conspiración del cuatro *(The Conspiracy of the Four). She is active in cultural events and often gives readings of her work in cafes and theatres, accompanying herself on occasion with a drum. She has written more than a hundred short stories and traditional tales, including 'Paper Mask', 'The Eye of the Mountain', 'The Solitary Swallow', and 'The War of the Lesser Gods'. Some of these stories will be published in Spain in a collection entitled* Los dioses perdidos *(The Lost Gods).*

from

Ekomo

Between a little sun here and a little bit of shade there, it seemed as if rain would come at any moment that morning.

It is the chilly season and, because the sun is so timid, the children search for excuses not to go to school. The *awawa*[1] passes by on its way to the city, filled to capacity with people, pigs and chickens, and between a little sun here and a little bit of shade there, Ikaa remains behind on the ground with his little sack of coffee and his hand raised high, while a cloud of dust surrounds him.

The goats are quietly chewing up the grass; the pigs are forcefully rubbing themselves against some beams. The sound of the bus gradually fades away into the mountains.

With a little sun here and a little bit of shade there, the colour grey envelops the atmosphere. Smoke from the ash-blue roof tiles rises upward in search of an ash-blue sky. An ash-coloured white fog covers the tops of ash-coloured green trees.

Grey cabins with grey walls; grey is the colour of the old nipa palm leaves that cover the roofs.

With a little sun here and a little bit of shade there, it seems as if rain will come at any moment this morning. It is the grey-coloured morning of my little town.

In the *abaha*[2], the men are having a discussion. Everyone is talking about Nchama, that flirtatious hussy who committed adultery yesterday in the woods. The men talk, the women keep quiet. The young people listen and the children play. What's going on?

Little Nnegue saw a man, and his mother explained to him that he was the bogey-man. Yesterday afternoon, the child believed it. And in the middle of a little sun here and a little bit of shade there, Nnegue again saw the man, chatting with his father in the village. With eyes as wide as saucers, with his mouth open, full of fear, curiosity and doubt, and like someone anxious to know what is going on, he asked his father whether the bogey-man who ate up his mama in the woods would eat him up, pointing at the man with his dirty little finger. Now it is all clear, because in the midst of a little sun here and a little bit of shade there, he identified the man who made love to his mother under the shade of the bamboo, by the banks of the river.

The men talk, the women keep quiet, the young people listen and the children play.

How many lashes will Nchama get on her buttocks? The men discuss it among themselves. What should be the punishment for adulterers?

In the midst of a little sun and a little bit of shade, the day progresses little by little. The adulterous act is denied. The husband becomes furious. The mother cries and everyone boos her all together; a little, bleary-eyed boy, his head covered with ringworm, a *clotte*[3] tied around his neck, and his little body white with dust, pushes through the crowd to boo her at close range. And in the midst of a little bit of sun and a little bit of shade, someone grabs him by the ear to remind him that he should take more kindly to a piece of soap and a scrubbing sponge.

But . . . because the sun is timid and the season is chilly, children make excuses in order to avoid water.

The ducks quack, the forest sings. Male dogs bark as they chase the females. It is just one more morning in the jungle, the same as all the others. The men talk, the women are silent and in the midst of a little sun and a little bit of shade, the old man's voice is heard among the people. The people quiet down, the duck grows silent. The forest, indifferent to man, continues its song. The fog over the trees settles down, and a rooster, like a macho, cocks his head to one side and looks haughtily at the old man standing in the middle of the people.

'And let this be the judgment!' shouts the old man. 'For the adulteress, fifty whacks with a stick on her buttocks.' And he goes on to say, while clearing his throat, 'For the adulterer, two goats, thirty thousand *bipkwele*[4] and a hundred and fifty whacks with a stick. Because a woman is just like a child. She does not know what fidelity means. And so, her guilt is less. You should all remember what was said in the old days: 'Don't chase after your brother's woman'. That meant that a man should not fool around with someone else's wife, since she is like the leaves on a tree: her love follows the direction of the blowing wind. But a man, in this case, knows when he is doing wrong.

A murmur follows the silence. Between a little sun and a little bit of shade, everyone is preparing to leave by the door of the *abaha*, when a deadly, swift, suffocating silence falls and all eyes are transfixed upward, up to the sky.

The sun dies in the midst of a little bit of shade. The men, huddled together, look with fear and silence toward the sky. The clouds roll on. Black clouds quickly cover white clouds. No one remembers any longer the one hundred and fifty blows for the adulterer; no one remembers any longer the fifty whacks for the adulteress.

Even the child with a head full of ringworms and the curiosity so typical of children, peeks out from behind the others. With eyes wide open, he looks up.

What is happening in the sky is a miracle. Over a greyish background, a black cloud, fringed with an orange colour, traces a strange figure, while the sky, little by little, draws closer to the earth. Everyone follows what is going on, until in the midst of a little shade and a dead sun, a mound of something is clearly outlined. Someone lets out a frightened cry:

'It's a stone tablet! Look at its shape!'

The men look. The women look. The children look. Everyone looks toward the sky. Dismay overtakes the earth. Fear invades all hearts. The flames of the hearths lose their warmth. Bodies become cold, and minds ponder the question:

'What does all of this mean?'

The voice of the chief answers the voices of the people. The chief's voice is so deep with emphasis that it sounds as if it is coming from beyond the grave.

'This is a great sign from our forebears. This is a sign from Ancient Africa, the stone tablet of the powerful ones. Every time you see this sign drawn in the sky, you must understand that a powerful person is going to die in Africa. His death will be violent; it will be unjust. His death is unavoidable and, in protest, the heavens are giving you this warning. He is a man of historical importance; a man whom you will remember down through the centuries. This sign that you see today in the sky appeared to the ancients, when Africa was Africa. And when only African gods were worshipped in Africa. It is strange, very strange, that this should appear to us today, because it's been centuries since African skies have seen the announcement of such a violent death.'

Then Nfumbaba, the one who only recently had returned from Europe, drawing close to the elder, asked him:

'Does this mean, father, that one of us is going to die?'

The question floats in the air. The question shines on the faces of those present. The question mark is on Osha's lips, which he wets uneasily. The question mark stands out prominently in the stares of those present. 'It means', replies the old man, 'that a powerful person from Africa will leave earth to join the ancestors. His departure will be violent and unjust. The sky reigns over all this land and, in this land, there are many who are powerful. But . . . I ask myself: Who are the powerful in this land? You must understand that, when I speak of the land, I am talking about Africa, and I am not saying this just to hear myself talk, but for a long time now Africans have abandoned Africa and Africa [has abandoned] Africans. In Africa there are no longer any powerful people.'

The chief looks down at the ground and searches in the dust for the blood of those who were his ancestors. The old man lowers his gaze and searches beneath the dust for the dried-up blood of Africa. When he gets up, he asks this question, as if of himself:

'Today, who will that powerful person be, today who will return nature's strength to these lands, these very lands that have caused her children, the Africans, to become rebellious so that even the sky displays the great sign? We heard that, in the Congo, a young man named Lumumba is rising up against the invader and fighting for the freedom of Africans, but . . . who can assure us that it's true?'

Then Nfumbaha, again moving closer to the elder, says to him:

'Father, I have heard talk of Lumumba. People speak well of him. I would be very sorry if it were he who is to die, since without a doubt he is fighting for Africa and African freedom! Africa has to be free again. The African should fight so that this can become a reality. Each and every day, one hears a lot about the Congo and her freedom fight. Africa, like all the other continents in the world, needs progress and we Africans must struggle to see that this is brought about.'

The women, quite shaken up, return to their homes. The children, somewhat puzzled, draw into little groups and make strange drawings in the dust. The men stare at the sky. Everyone contemplates the miracle that is unfolding on high. As for the mountain, it remains firm, challenging man's destiny and his life.

Silence invades the land, along with fear, suspicion and premonitions.

A breeze, light as a breath, begins to blow, while raising particles of dust. I am no more than an outline against the background that surrounds me, which is the forest. My presence, hardly noticed, is nothing but an absence/presence whose value has nothing to do with the normal unfolding of events. I live and breathe aware of my own impotence.

I call Ekomo from the depths of my soul, of my being, but I feel him far away. Fearful of I don't know what, I feel obliged to call him, because without him I am nothing, nor can I become anything. I call him with the lips of my soul, even though my mouth remains sealed rebelliously against the anguished cry that emerges from within me when, as in a nightmare, my mind shouts:

'Ekomo!' with my eyes pinned to a certain place, where his existence is revealed to me through his spirit. Then, just like the others, I look at the mysteries up in the sky.

My mind shouts:

'Ekomo!' Finally I hear his mind call to me:

'Wait!'

Wait, he says to me and I wait in the dark depths of my soul. Nonetheless, I see how the women, my companions, go forward, each one with her husband, feeling better protected. Wait, he says to me, and I wait from the dark depths of my uncertainty and my loneliness. Ekomo went with his brothers to the parties in the city, I remind myself.

The others returned after the parties ended, but he stayed behind, bewitched by a woman of loose morals. Since then, since the coming of three moons, I have seen the *awawa* pass every day, flying through the dust like a white sea-gull, without stopping to let him off or let a letter slip through the little window to tell us what became of his life.

The people are impressed by the sign that appeared in the sky this morning.

From a dark corner of the kitchen, mother intones her prayers, grasping the rosary between her fingers. She knows that someone is going to die, and she prays like an evil-omened bird on learning that misfortune is near.

'*Santamariaaa Niaaa Zamaaa, Volo biaaa awaaaiaaa miseeemmm mbembeee caasooaamern.*'

For some time now, she has been accustomed to praying out loud for everything. Mother is known in the town for her laments and her prayers. While her mournful sounds fill the room, the day advances, unnoticed, with a little sun here and a little bit of shade there.

Mother's voice continues its singsong litany, when grandfather calls out to everyone from the *abaha,* warning:

'Let no one leave town until told to do so.'

Minds think. Eyes show the effort, and then the facial mask assumes the shape of the worried soul.

Overcome by timidity, the sun covers itself with a haze of little yellow clouds. The sign in the sky disappears and, while clouds float from one side to another like multicoloured pieces of gauze, from some indeterminate place, we hear a hen's cackling – monotonous, persistent, and racked with pain, like the moan of a strange soul that, although present, knows things that are incomprehensible to man.

Under the stares of those present, the grandfather, an old, long-ago man, gets up, machete in hand, and walks toward the sacred ceiba tree.

The master of the town, a traditional man, walks hunched over to where he knows that the ancestors lie and protect the taboos. In the grey morning, between a little sun and a little shade, minds reflect.

They imagine things, misfortunes; they imagine that when the grandfather returns, he will bring something that will amaze them. The townspeople, in their uncertainty, silently ask themselves whether the grandfather knows anything at all about the great sign that appeared that morning. The townspeople wonder if the grandfather can intervene in the death of the powerful one that was announced in the sky that morning.

And when the grandfather returns, enveloped in the pale light of morning, he carries in his right hand two bundles of secret herbs and in his left hand the machete. After leaving one of the bundles on the roof of the *ababa*, he enters the room and sits down at a flameless hearth and, like someone unmindful of those around him, he picks up the remaining bundle and, after rubbing it over his hands, gives the impression that he is just warming himself at the hearth. From time to time, he looks to either side, as if to say something to someone who is not there. His arms, old and ashen, make a dry sound as he rubs them together, one against the other, in the smoke from the burning embers.

The children look, the grown-ups look. Astonished, they all follow the movement of the grandfather's old hands.

Shortly thereafter, he gets up, shakes his hands up and down, right and left, and commands those present:

'Everyone go home! And don't anyone leave until I give the order to do so.' And as if nature itself were dependent upon the old man's order, at that very instant, between a little sun and a little bit of shade, the sun hides behind the clouds and great areas of darkness begin to descend over the forest. The clouds descend quickly, like evil-omened birds; black cloud gusts cover the sky, like torn pieces of a cloak. Men hurry toward their homes. From her corner, Mother chants her mournful litany, like the cackling of a hen. No longer is there a little sun, because suddenly it has become dark. The clouds descend more densely until they cover the nipa palm roofs. Mother says that it is the end of the world.

Later, only later, instead of rain, it begins to hail furiously. In the fenced-in yard, only the grandfather, the old man now without his walking-stick, stands motionless and rigid, holding the bundles up high while nature continues its roar, knocking over trees and covering the ground with crystal balls.

Not a house, nor a roof, nor an animal, nor a plant sowed by man suffers any damage. In the town, there was no damage attributed to nature. In spite of this, Mother, from her corner continues praying:

'*Santa Mariaaa Nia zamaaaa. Vólo biaaa awaala miseeem 'mbembe cassooo amen.*'

Translated by Antonio Olliz Boyd

Notes*

1. *Awawa:* Bus.
2. *Ababa:* A rectangular hut with half walls, located in the middle of the village, where men and the entire village meet to discuss important matters. It is also a place where villagers spend time conversing.
3. *Clotte:* A piece of cloth used by women as a 'dress'. It is wrapped around the body from the chest down to the ankle or the calf; in some cases, it is worn by men from the waist down. The word is a 'Pichinglis' adaptation of the English 'cloth'.
4. *Bipkwele:* plural of *ekuele*, the national currency of Equatorial Guinea.

*The editor is grateful to Professor M'baré N'gom for providing the explanatory notes.

Writing from the Soul: A Conversation with María Nsue Angüe

M'bare N'gom

Mbare Ngom: Who is María Nsué Angüe? Tell us something about yourself.

María Nsué Angüe: I am a widow, mother of three children and a Protestant.

MN: What have your years outside of your country been like, on both the personal and literary levels?

MNA: That question would have to be answered by others because I am not aware of any difference. Perhaps this long absence from my homeland has enabled me to look at the African world through a multicultural lens. As for my way of seeing things and acting, I am fifty per cent pure African and the other fifty per cent is Spanish. Everyone around me can see that, regardless of his or her race. I am also aware of this fact. Now then, when I write, I try to be one hundred per cent my own person. By this I mean that I have my own way of looking at things, judging them and writing about them.

MN: Have you ever participated in a literary contest or competition? What are the advantages or disadvantages (if any) of literary competitions in a country like Equatorial Guinea? By this I mean, can you assess the role that the Hispano-Guinean Cultural Center of Malabo plays in this?

MNA: No! And I don't intend to do so. I haven't had an opportunity to participate either as a contestant or a judge. But I think that the Hispano-Guinean Cultural Centre is doing important work because it promotes the country's new writers.

MN: In 1985, you published *Ekomo*, your first novel. Why this title and what does this novel represent for you? Have you published anything else since then?

MNA: Ekomo means 'agreement' and since the book is not a nationalistic prototype, it neither attacks nor fails to attack colonialism. This novel, in itself, represents no more than what any literary work represents for its author. If you've read it, it's just a panorama of the country in every sense. At least, that's what it is for me.

MN: Which literary genre do you handle best and why?

MNA: I don't know. That depends on the reader's criteria. Nonetheless, I would like to add that I write poetry with the same facility with which I write fiction. It depends on what strikes me at the moment. In the anthology you will see some things, so when I can, I'll send you some others that were published in one of the journals here. Personally, I believe that every writer must know how to handle herself in any genre, since in any case, one always writes from the soul, and within the soul there is some of everything.

MN: How much time do you devote to writing – daily, weekly, monthly?

MNA: I have no pre-determined schedule. I write only when I have the urge to do so, and for as long as it takes.

MN: What projects does María Nsue have?

MNA: A lot. But for the time being, I prefer not to reveal them.

MN: What do you think of the feminist movement? I mean, what can you tell us about the situation for women and for female writers in Equatorial Guinea?

MNA: I hate labels. On the other hand, in Guinea there are only two women writers: Raquel Ilombé, who, as you know, has lived for a long time in Spain where she's married to a Spaniard, and María Nsue Angüe.

MN: Which authors – Spanish, African or from other regions – have influenced you and your literary work?

MNA: I admire Rosalía de Castro very much; she is my principal role model, but I don't overlook others such as Carmen Laforet, Ana María Matute, Saint Teresa de Jesús and the Brönte sisters. Finally, I am fascinated by Toni Morrison, an author about whom I had heard nothing until she won the Nobel Prize. She is fantastic, mystical, clear and deep. She is a true artist!

MN: What is happening with traditional literature in Equatorial Guinea and what is the future of this literature? To what degree does traditional African literature influence or interfere with your creativity?

MNA: I really can't say. Traditional literature is practically nonexistent in written form. Its future will depend on those who want to write it down and on the interest of those who want to preserve it. Like any writer, I am interested in everything that I consider important for my writing and, as a Bantu, I personally admire the great richness of this genre, but I prefer to be personal when I write, which does not mean that I don't identify with or want to identify with my people.

MN: Tell us briefly about the present situation of Equatorial Guinean literature written in Spanish.

MNA: It is still at an embryonic stage, although its pioneers have given a lot of themselves. At times, one might conclude that there is a lack of ambition or inspiration at the moment of creation, but this is understandable given the condition in which the country presently finds itself. There is no challenge in spite of the fact that there is a lot that one can and possibly could write about, keeping in mind that there are authors such as Donato Ndongo who have the necessary ambition, style and drive. Another reason why things are as they are is because of those invisible but unavoidable barriers that impede one's literary productivity in countries beyond Gibraltar. One cannot write freely when the future looms so uncertain.

MN: Some years ago, the Guinean writer Juan Balboa Boneke spoke about a 'lost generation' in which he included himself. Do you believe that one can talk about a 'lost generation' of Guinean writers, and why?

MNA: I have a lot of respect for Boneke and for his opinions, but I would have to talk with him personally to understand his point of view and his motives for calling an entire generation lost, because I don't understand it.

MN: Taking the year 1953 as a starting point, how many generations of Guinean writers would you say there are? Could you briefly describe the periods?

MNA: For me, there is only one generation of Guinean writers if one considers Guinean literature as that produced by autochthonous people. Before us, there is only one work: *Cuando los combes luchaban* [The Battle of the Combes] by Leoncio Evita Enoy. And one work does not create an entire generation of writers, because you have to have more than a single writer to make a generation. As I understand it, a whole generation of writers includes an ensemble of diverse minds, different points of view, various sociocultural and religious levels. Furthermore, I would say that, if it were not for this peculiar moment that our history is going through right now, even the writers of today could not be called a 'generation' in the true sense of the word, because we have all been affected by the bitterness of our own historical crisis.

MN: This also brings us to what the Guinean writer Donato Ndongo-Bidyogo has called 'the silent years'. How would you evaluate that period from the literary point of view?

MNA: Donato is a good friend and a great writer. As for literature, I would say that all Africa has been silent for many years, so I can't confirm that this silence was only in Guinea.

MN: Poetry prevails over fiction in Equatorial Guinean literature written in Spanish. How can one explain this phenomenon?

MNA: We are Bantus whose elders produced literature in oral form, in which poetry, images, and onomatopoeia abound. It is logical that when we write, we identify ourselves as Bantus.

MN: Do you believe in 'art for art's sake' or do you think that the African writer must make a commitment based on the very different circumstances of the continent?

MNA: It depends on what you call commitment. I strongly believe that all writers must make commitments regardless of where they are from.

MN: What problems confront the Guinean writer of today?

MNA: The same ones that confront any other writer of the world: publishing, publicity, sales.

MN: What is it like for you to write in a foreign language, or a 'borrowed tongue'? Do you consider yourself a 'language thief', as Jacques Rabemananjara (Madagascar) used to say when referring to African writers in 1959?

MNA: I think in Spanish, I dream in Spanish and I have spoken Spanish for most of my life. If you consider Spanish to be a foreign language for me because I was not born on Spanish soil, my question is: Were the 300 million Spanish speakers in the world today born on the Iberian Peninsula? How could you argue that I am stealing a language that has always been mine, if I was only eight years old when I arrived in Spain and didn't know how to say even three words in Fang?

MN: To which audience is your writing directed? Who is your 'real reader'?

MNA: I address myself primarily to my children.

MN: How would you describe the decade from 1980 to 1990 with respect to the cultural creativity of Equatorial Guinea?

MNA: I have spent very little time in Guinea, and so I have very little contact with what is going on. I don't believe that I can answer such a serious question. In order to answer that question I would have to keep abreast of the Hispano-Guinean Cultural Centre's plans, and I have not done so. Donato Ndongo has led the Centre for many years; he would certainly be able to give you a good answer.

MN: What can you tell us about the future of Equatorial Guinean literature written in Spanish?

MNA: It is the same as any other future; you look in the direction that you wish to look. However, I do understand that literature is a matter about which you cannot speculate. You can speculate about the political or economic future of a country, but not about its art or the idiosyncrasy of its art, because, come what may, it will always be there waiting for a hand or a miraculous voice to give it life. Literature has neither a past nor a future. It is a continuous present. It depends on nothing but its own reality. Therefore, a question about its future is incomprehensible to me. I am a writer and I have great respect for literature about which I consider myself to be just one more element.

Translated by Antonio Olliz Boyd

Narrative of a Woman's Life and Writing
María Nsue Angüe's *Ekomo*

M'baré N'gom

Black African Hispanic literature or African literature written in Spanish is a cultural product seldom commented on outside of Equatorial Guinea [. . .with the exception of. . .] small groups in Madrid. Equatorial Guinea is the only Spanish-speaking country in Sub-Saharan Africa, and this circumstance alone has given it a unique position within the body of Hispanic or African literatures. . .

This article looks at certain aspects of the African Hispanic literary production, [especially as it pertains to Equatorial Guinea, and tries to determine its place among the feminine literary art forms with an African context.]

The literature of Equatorial Guinea written in Spanish has its basis in an historical environment that dates back to the 15th century, when the Portuguese and Spanish kingdoms initiated exploratory expeditions along the West African coast in their ambitious search for a route leading to the discovery of spices. The first written literary expressions were perhaps born under the rubric of exploratory expeditions and progressive occupation of the west coast of Africa. Within this context one can point to the appearance of the first pieces of literature of a so-called literary Africanism, which in turn becomes the colonial literature of the 19th century.[1] During the two and a half century period that Bernard Mouralis (1984) calls 'the colonial reality', this cultural production was largely the private domain of white males. This was the image of the corpus of writings that conformed to the colonial model of literature along the length and breadth of the African continent. Such was the case that up to 1969, in what was called Spanish Guinea, we could only find one piece of writing published by a woman, *Efún* (1954), attributed to Liberata Masoliver. However, this author was Spanish.

Equatorial Guinea's independence in 1969 establishes the framework, as in other parts of Africa at that time, for the advent of what some have called 'national literature'. Up to that time, Equatorial Guinean literature included only two works: *When the Combes² Fought* (1953) by Leoncio Evita Enoy and *A Spear Pierced the Boabi³* (1962) by Daniel Jones Mathama. More than a decade went by before the first literary work by an Hispanic African woman appeared: *Ceiba* (1978) by Raquel Ilombé (adapted from her real name, Raquel Del Pozo Epita). *Ceiba* is a collection of poems written between 1966 and 1977, in Madrid and Bata (Equatorial Guinea). . . . [T]he appearance of Raquel Ilombé's writing coincided with the publication in Africa's editorial market of the first literary works by women. Actually, it was toward the mid-seventies that the first writings by women began to appear in the display cases and on the shelves of both public and university libraries in Africa and Europe. In this regard, Beverly Ormerod points out that '1975, declared the International Year of the Woman by the UN, is an important date in that it points to the beginning of a literary output that kept on increasing through the years' ([author's translation] 12). For his part, Kembe Milolo plainly states that works by African women were actually initiated in 1976 (34).

The delayed literary production of Hispanic African women, when compared with that of their male counterparts, is due, as in other parts of Sub-Saharan Africa, to socio-historical, political and economic factors. In traditional African society, social organisation followed the dictates of particular groups and geographical regions as to whether they would be patriarchal, matriarchal or a combination of the two. In spite of the fact that the man occupied the principal positions in that universe, the woman was the real axis around which the community's organization and survival rotated. The woman also articulated a central (and critical) role in the arena[s] of education and traditional oral literature. O[ladele] Taiwo also reached this conclusion (4-10). Oral in origin, traditional literature was a powerful, didactic instrument that women fully employed for education. The use of tales, songs, satire, praise songs, and other genres allowed women not only to educate but also to impart culture to children. In this way, women, besides being culture bearers of the first rank, contributed immensely to the enrichment of traditional literature, which later became a source of African literatures written in European languages.

The advent of colonialism changed the women's situation because they lost many of their prerogatives, including their political power. . . . The creation of what Professor Amadou Diop calls the 'colonial space', marked by mercantilism and the indiscriminate exploitation of human and material resources in the 'new' territories, not only disturbed the organization of traditional society but also redefined its political and socio-economic structures. By introducing profound changes into the traditional social structure, the colonial system marginalized women by not assigning them any relevant roles in that new social, political, economic and territorial organisation. New values, above all economic, replaced subsistence farming with crops for export or rent. The system went from value based on use to value based on monetary gain. And agriculture, a collective activity which utilized both men and women up to that point, became, with structural modernization, almost exclusively male-dominated. New spaces such as urban centers appeared, as well as new institutions such as colonial administration, civil service, monetary value, and mercantile transactions. Likewise, colonial development projects only allowed the participation of men trained to utilize the new technologies, specifically, mechanization of the means of production, while women continued to follow old/ancient systems of production. In other words, the woman had no place in the colonial project.

> Technical training with a view toward increasing production is limited to men who are a part of the monetary system because of the 'slave trade'. Men are introduced to the modern world and the world of progress while women remain mired in traditional society.[4]

Women were, therefore, systematically eliminated from the institutions of modernization (education, professional training and economics), leaving them powerless and, consequently, voiceless. Women had almost no role in the construction of the National Project in the various African countries until the time of independence.

This reality is also reflected in cultural production. Until recently, African literature in general was synonymous with a male-generated cultural product. It was a universal culture where, except in rare instances, women's creative input was excluded. As Lloyd Brown observes:

> Women writers in Africa are the other voices, the silent voices whose works are rarely discussed and whose works seldom receive space in often repeated anthologies .... Few magazines both literary and professional, in the West as well as in Africa, have dedicated space and time to African women who write (3).

[The situation] in Guinea was even more complicated because five months after the election of the country's first president, Francisco Macías Nguema, Equatorial Guinea began its second journey into the desert. . . . [B]etween 1969 and 1979, the year of his overthrow, Francisco Macías established one of the bloodiest dictatorships that the African continent has ever known. He unleashed a ferocious and indiscriminate campaign of repression, venting his savagery, above all, on intellectuals who were persecuted without mercy. In the ten years that the Nguema dictatorship lasted, the cultural space underwent a period of drought, except for the laudatory pamphlets written by his followers. As poet Ciriaco Bakesa so correctly points out, 'silence was the eloquence of the strong within the national territory. Only those who remained silent gained merit, creating out of their silent existence a catalyst of themes for their literary future' (97).

It is, then, within that universe structured by a vertical viewpoint of the world – the masculine one – and with assigned gender roles and well defined competition that the literary production of María Nsue Angüe emerges.

María Nsue Angüe was born in 1948 in Ebebeyín (Río Muni), Equatorial Guinea. She is the mother of three children and has spent most of her life in Spain. In 1984, she published *Ekomo,* her first novel, erroneously classified by Professor Vicente Granados as Equatorial Guinea's first novel. There is no doubt that *Ekomo* is the first novel in post-colonial Equatorial Guinean literature written by a woman, but from a chronological perspective Leoncio Evita's *When the Combes Fought* and Daniel Mathama Jones's *A Spear Pierced the Boabi* were written before hers. Consequently, *Ekomo* is the third novel.

Ekomo is the story of a male protagonist of the same name, whose life story is told by Nnanga, the narrator-eyewitness female protagonist, who met Ekomo as a little boy in the company of his father, a sorcerer who went through jungle towns offering his services. Years later, Nnanga marries Ekomo, and remains with him until his death [caused by] a gangrenous leg. Nnanga is the epitome of fidelity. At no time during her dramatic wandering through the country in search of a cure for Ekomo's leg, does it occur to Nnanga to abandon him, in spite of the irreversible nature of his illness. Giving up a promising career as a dancer, she follows him and takes care of him until the end of his days.

Unlike the African feminist novels written in European languages (French, English, and Portuguese), where the action takes place primarily in an urban setting and whose protagonists are often well educated and westernized, *Ekomo* unfolds exclusively in the traditional world of the forest. The city appears in the novel only in passing and is tied to a tragic circumstance, the death of Ekomo.

On the other hand, in keeping with the tradition of the African woman's novel in general, *Ekomo* uses the personal form as a narrative strategy, which gives it an autobiographical stamp. María Nsue uses a male protagonist whose vicissitudes are narrated to the reader in the first-person [voice] by means of a narrator-witness protagonist. This device allows the author to validate her text and to create a certain distance between herself and the character through whom she speaks. This is what Patricia Meyer defines as 'hiding selves'; that is to say, that tendency which the woman-as-writer has of avoiding and/or of negating her 'ego', her individuality, although in the African text one might have to nuance the latter. Mary G. Mason also reaches a similar conclusion: 'To defend their excursions into autobiographical writing women create works in which the self is validated in linking with another: either husband, community, friend or God' (235). The narrator of *Ekomo,* herself, acknowledges this phenomenon:

> I am nothing more than the outline of a profile against the environs that surround me, which is the forest. My presence, slightly noticed, is nothing but a presence-absence whose importance has nothing to do with the normal process of what is going on.

By hiding herself behind a masculine character to tell the story, the narrator attempts, on the one hand, to legitimize her text, because in this way she can re-write the history of the African woman from the place that she occupies in the novel and in African society, through self-discovery and revelation. On the other hand, she transmits the Black African woman's *modus* of perception in a patriarchal world and a patrilocal society such as the Bantu of Guinea. Thus, the validation of feminine discourse, obscured by patriarchal structure, far from being an obstacle becomes part of a strategy whose final objective is to create a breach in patriarchal culture. As Sidonie Smith observes:

> Since the ideology of gender makes a woman's life script a non-story, a silent space, a gap in patriarchal culture, the ideal woman is self-erasing rather than self-promoting and her 'natural' story shapes itself not around the public, heroic life, but around the fluid, circumstantial, contingent responsiveness to others that, according to patriarchal ideology, characterises the life of woman but not autobiography. From that point of view, woman has no 'autobiographical self' in the same sense that man does. From that point of view she has no 'public' story to tell. (34)

In this sense, the 'I' that runs throughout *Ekomo* accomplishes, then, a double function. On the one hand, it is a social 'I', that is to say, inclusive and communal, by writing and representing the group's experiences in the final analysis. It is collective and not fragmented as in the autobiographical projects of the West. Here, we quote from James Olney's comparative study of Western and African autobiographies:

> The whole logic of African autobiography and the nature of the *bios* around which African autobiography forms itself are there in the notion that 'a person is what he is because of and through other people' or in the notion that the Sonjo people (as reported by John Mbiti) hold: 'I am because we are, and since we are, therefore I am'. An autobiography that takes its orientation in this premise will not say, as Jung's book says, 'I am as I am' but will say instead, 'I am as we are. . . ' For the life-portrait that the African autobiographer executes is not the portrait of 'moi, moi seul', where the subject makes a claim of absolute uniqueness and imagines that his experience is unrepeated and unrepeatable; instead, the African autobiographer executes a portrait of 'nous, nous ensemble', and the life shared by the group now – by the phyle – is one lived countless times before, shaped by the ritual stages of birth and naming, initiation, marriage, parenthood, eldership, and death that have given form to the life of this people for as far back as the legendary, mythic memory of people extends. (218)

On the other hand, 'I' is feminine, for as Maryse Condé has so aptly put it, 'the African woman doesn't direct herself to the world, but to her frustrated and desperate sisters. When she talks, she does it in the name of those women who do not have a voice, who suffer in the fields and who are only left with the ambiguous vestments of maternity' (32). Or, as Irene Asseba d'Almeida has said, 'she lends her voice to all of her mute sisters' (43). Therefore, in addition to being the voice of a marginal collective (of the 'woman who is written about' at least up to that moment), that 'I', from the moment of its appearance, belongs to the 'woman who is writing', [it is] a voice that attempts to construct an 'intellectual feminine space', also in the words of Almeida. That is to say, it is an alternative platform in a universe where the woman manages to free herself not only from a subordinate condition, but where she can also express her own vision of the world. So, that 'I' frames itself within a process of revealing the feminine experience in Africa.

Nnanga, the narrator-witness protagonist, does not accept the customs of the traditional world. She is a rebel. Since early childhood, her playmates were, contrary to the norm, her brother and her friends, whose secrets she shared and for whom she was a challenge in a broad sense. Perhaps this background is what led her to adopt the pen name 'Fire Dove'. The name is loaded with symbolism, because the dove not only stands for peace but also for freedom. Upon the death of her friend Mba, the midget, Nnanga turns to the dance as a means of liberation and she dedicates a dance to Mba during a popular celebration:

> While I was dancing, I knew that one shouldn't ever dance for no one in particular, but for someone so I danced for someone. I danced for my beloved midget . . . From that moment on, I understood that my dance would always be for my midget and the people on applauding me were unconsciously paying homage to the little dead man. (74)

Nnanga not only discovers the liberating capacity of the dance, but she also finds another power: the dance opens up other worlds, other horizons, by offering her an opportunity to leave town and learn about other places and other people.

Nnanga fully exploits the only attributes. . . that might give her a certain strength, a certain power: she uses her beauty and her body to open up her own cultural space within that monolithic patriarchal universe. These two traits constitute, in a way, the platform from which she attempts to destabilize that universe of rigid rules. The body, the trivialized and objectified female body, is the only thing whose existence and reality are not denied to women by patriarachal society, but the body is always available to the man whenever he so desires. But there lies the paradox. In spite of the fact that the female body is the basic pillar upon which patriarchal society rests and its very survival depends upon the woman, she remains absent from the public space of descision-making. And up to a certain point, Nnanga is conscious of this fact. That is why she no longer uses the body, her body, as an expression of submission but as an instrument of subversion, that is to say, as a weapon. 'I, Fire Dove, knew perfectly well what power I had acquired, and I was conscious of my own beauty. I already knew that I was irresistible to boys. I named myself goddess and I put myself on a pedestal without anyone placing obstacles in my way' (74-75).

Nnanga's last act of rebellion occurs when she twice violates tradition. Here, once again, her body is the major protagonist of that rebellion. Not only does she oppose the entire town, but she also confronts tradition, that is to say, the very foundations of traditional society. On the death of Ekomo, the widow Nnanga decides to cut short the mourning period, which had to be observed sitting down. So she rebels against the 'incarceration' of her body and rises to resume her daily activities in spite of the town's almost total disapproval. Then, although she has cut her hair as a sign of grief, she forbids that it be gathered up, as custom demanded: 'They give the impression from one minute to the next that they are going to let out a victory cry, a woman's last cry on being born on this earth .... Who will cry for this rebellion?' (193)

It is curious that the only support that Nnanga receives comes from her father, a participant in the dominant discourse. Thus, the first breaches appear in the structure of patriarchal society. Clearly, Nnanga's assault on traditional institutions through her refusal to carry out certain rituals can be considered as a reappropriation of her body and of the female's body in general.

Ekomo also raises the question, with all of its harshness, of the conflict between tradition and modernity. This conflict, with its origin rooted in the contact between the traditional world and the colonial world, is latent throughout the entire novel. In the beginning, it appears between mindsets and generations. After having attending school, travelled to Europe, and discovered other worlds and customs, Nfumbaba, one of the protagonists, returns home with a different outlook and perception of reality. Armed with these modern tools, he questions many aspects of his traditional society and begins, among other things, to challenge some of its taboos.

> Nfumbaba, today's African man of tomorrow, after having spent two rainy seasons in Europe, left his tradition buried in the books; he left there his personality and his African beliefs, and this man without a continent returned to his village under a European disguise but without the European inside. Half white, half Black. (85)

In this instance, two visions of the future are in opposition to each other. On the one hand, there is tradition that represents the desire for continuity and attachment to the repetitious social structures dominated by the elders; and, on the other, there is so-called progress which defends democratization and rejects traditional society, among other things. But the forces of change represented by Nfumbaba are not enough to undermine the foundations of traditional society, and he dies struggling to do so.

The battle between the Catholic religion and traditional religion is another facet of this conflict. Here, María Nsue touches on a very delicate problem, profoundly rooted in African tradition: polygamy. When the old man Oyono embraces the Catholic faith, he has to give up two of his three wives. For this reason, Oyono's wives have taken him to the Council of Elders, because they think that he intends to break with the rules of tradition. Furthermore, 'none wants to be left behind and each one wants what is due' (92). This episode is one of the best examples of the conflict dealing with two forms of understanding the universe, while at the same time it provokes an identity crisis and a crisis in social structures. It is a conflict that fragments the basic nucleus of the community: the family.

> Deep inside of me I cursed all men, especially that man of God who was attempting without any remorse of conscience, to upset a peaceful and happy family .... I cursed that white man because he had disgraced a family and had ruined some children, subjecting them to motherlessness. (92)

Oyono wants to save his soul and go to heaven when he dies; to do this he embraces an imported religion: Catholicism. Even Ekomo faces the same dilemma, but from a more dramatic perspective. Now tired of wandering through the forest in search of a native doctor who can alleviate his pains, he decides to reject herbal medicines and, thus, tradition, in order to find help and a cure in western medicine. Already near death, Ekomo seeks salvation for his soul in the Catholic religion, but he is torn by a tremendous dilemma:

> I betrayed the ancestors by denying them. What will become of me? I need to be baptized as soon as possible to free myself of this doubt. Now, I am neither in the grace of Jesus Christ nor in the grace of my forefathers. I need to know who I am and where I am going when I die. (173, 176)

Father Ndoug Akele, the eldest and wisest person in the village, cannot understand what that imported religion has that cannot be found in his. The cultural and psychological conflict becomes a crisis of identity, because it affects all strata of Guinean and African society, upsetting and fragmenting communal structures and provoking profound changes in behavioral patterns and in the people's cosmovision.

In conclusion, we should point out that María Nsue is the first woman to invade the exclusively masculine territory of the novel in Equatorial Guinea. *Ekomo* not only tries to break down stereotypes about African women in patriarchal discourse, but it also presents, for the first time, with great objectivity and from [both] an individual and [a] collective perspective, the world of the Bantu and Black African woman, which is so poorly handled in patriarchal discourse. Narrative focus in *Ekomo* presents a world of rigid structures often in decline. Actually, María Nsue goes beyond mere description of the Bantu woman's condition, because she exposes certain aspects of traditional African society. Her text, therefore, is framed by a process of recuperating a socio-cultural space that has been invaded and alienated: the woman's.

Translated by Antonio Olliz Boyd

Notes

1. Chronicles, travelogues, testimonials, memoirs, and books on hunting belong to this early period. The division of the continent among various European powers of the period, as well as the subsequent administrative control of the different territories, gave rise to colonial literature.
2. There is no translation for *combe*; it is the name of an ethnic group that lives in the Río Muni (Continental Guinea). It is a sub-group of the larger Fang group. *Cuando los combes luchaban* by Leoncio Evita is based on the traditions of this group.
3. *Boabi* means Chief (more or less) among the *fernandinos*. Daniel Jones Mathama's *Una lanza por el Boabi* is the story of the most prominent *boabi* of the former island of Fernando Poo.
4. Peuda Mbow. *The Senegalese Woman and the Colonial Experience*. Conference held in July, 1991, at the Cheikh Anta Diop University, Dakar. (Author's translation).

Works Cited

Aaron, Jane et al. *Out of the Margins: Women's Studies in the Nineties*. London: The Falmer Press, 1991.

Assiba d'Almeida, Irène. 'L'écriture féminine en Afrique noire francophone. Le temps du miroir'. *Les Etudes Littéraires* 24 (Autumn 1991).

Brown, Lloyd. *Women Writers in Black Africa*. Westport, Conn.: Greenwood Press, 1981.

Condé, Maryse. 'Anglophones et francophones, les frontières littéraires existent-elles?' *Notre Librairie* 65 (July-Sept. 1982).

Diouf, Mamadou. *Le Kajoor au XIXe siècle. Pouvoir Ceddo et conquête coloniale*. Paris: Khartala, 1990.

Mason, Mary. *The Other Voice: Autobiographies of Women Writers, Autobiography; Essays Theoretical and Critical*. Ed., James Olney. Princeton: Princeton University Press, 1980.

Meyer Spacks, Patricia. Cited by Carole Boyce Davies in 'Private Selves and Public Spaces: Autobiography and the African Woman Writers'. *CLA Journal* 3 (March 1991).

Mouralis, Bernard. *Littérature et Développement*. Paris: Editions Silex/ACCT, 1984.

Nsue Angüe, María. *Ekomo*. Madrid: UNED, 1984.

Olney, James. *The Value of Autobiography for Comparative Studies: African vs Western Autobiography: African American Autobiography*. Ed., William L. Andrews. Englewood Cliffs: Prentice Hall, 1991.

Smith, Sidonie. *A Poetics of Women's Autobiography: Marginality and the Fiction of Self-Representation*. Bloomington: Indiana University Press, 1987.

Taiwo, Oladele. *Female Novelists of Modern Africa*. New York: St. Martin's Press, 1981.

Sherezada 'Chiqui' Vicioso

$\mathcal{S}$HEREZADA ' $\mathcal{C}$HIQUI' $\mathcal{V}$ICIOSO

DOMINICAN REPUBLIC

(b. 1948)

A poet, essayist, and dramatist, Sherezada Vicioso, called 'Chiqui' by friends and family, is the daughter of María Luisa Sánchez and Juan Antonio Vicioso Contín. In 1967, when she was nineteen years old, she moved from the Dominican Republic to New York, where she lived for eighteen years working in factories and acquiring an education. She received a bachelor's degree in Latin American history and sociology from Brooklyn College and a master's in education from Columbia University. It was in New York, where she participated in the student movements of the 1960s as a member of the Third World Alliance, that she confronted and adopted her identity as a Black, Caribbean feminist, dedicated to freedom and equal rights for all. Travel to Africa, Central and South America broadened her understanding of the liberation struggle. In 1978, during a trip to Africa to coordinate a meeting of educators from Portuguese-speaking countries, she wrote poems such as 'Bissau' and 'Bafatá', inspired by Amilcar Cabral, the revolutionary hero. For four years, she served as director of cultural projects for a foundation in Río de Janeiro, Brazil. Her experiences in Nicaragua, where she worked with the children of imprisoned women, led to the publication of Bolver a vivir: Imágenes de Nicaragua *(Living Again: Images of Nicaragua) in 1985. On returning to the Dominican Republic, she worked as a columnist for two newspapers:* Listín Diario *and* El Nuevo Diario.

Vicioso also became active in Dominican cultural and intellectual activities, particularly those related to women. She co-founded the Círculo de Mujeres Poetas (Circle of Women Poets), which organised the first National Poetry Contest for Rural Women as a tribute to three poets, including Julia de Burgos and Aida Cartagena Portalatín. Much of her nonfiction deals with the literary contributions of Caribbean and

Dominican women writers. In 1990, she published Julia de Burgos la nuestra, *about the life and work of the foremother of Puerto Rican poetry, and a year later her* Algo que decir: Ensayos sobre literatura feminina, 1981-1991 *(Something to Say: Essays on Women's Literature) appeared. In 1997, she produced* Salomé Ureña de Henríquez (1859-1897): A cien años de su magisterio *(Saolmé Ureña de Henriquez (1859-1897): On a Hundred Years of Teaching), a biography of one of the founding poets of Dominican literature. She has garnered several awards for her writing and for her work on behalf of women: she received the prestigious Anacaona de Oro en Literatura Award and the Medalla de Oro Award as the most outstanding woman of the year. In 1997, she received the National Theater Award for her play* Wish-Ky Sour.

Also a gifted and committed poet, Vicioso published her first collection, Viaje desde el agua *(Voyage From the Sea) in 1981. In the autobiographical poem on the book's back cover, she alludes to the ineffability of verse: 'I go in search / of what I cannot define / I attempt it in poetry / . . . sometimes'. In poems such as 'Nueva York', 'Perspectivas', and 'Haití', she describes the daily assaults against the poor, the coloured and the women in urban centres and postcolonial countries. She is particularly concerned about the plight of working-class Dominican-Yorks who do not understand the language or the culture of the North, and who fall between the cracks in this alien society. Sherezada Vicioso has published two other collections of verse –* Un extraño ulular traía el viento *(A Strange Wailing of the Wind) in 1985 and* Internnamiento *(Internment) in 1992 – and her work has been translated and widely anthologised in the Dominican Republic and the United States.*

An Oral History *
(Testimonio)

I started writing when I was very young and found out that the best way to pass Math was to write a poem to the teacher... I began to become aware of the marginalized people in my country when I was an adolescent and worked in the barrios as part of a Christian youth volunteer group. Basically I am a poet, but I also write criticism about women's literature. I began to write in 1978 and published my first book of poetry, *Viajes desde el agua,* in 1981.

Up until about 1977, I regarded literature as a hobby of the petite bourgeoisie, but when I went to Cuba and spoke there with writers whom I very much admired, they showed me that a writer is also a cultural worker. Whereas I took note of this fact on an intellectual level, I realized it on an emotional one only when I went to Africa in 1978. I started writing criticism from 1982 on and published my second book in 1985 (*Un extraño ulular traía el viento*).

Both my books were written for Dominicans and were published in Santo Domingo. I never thought of publishing in the United States because, as a Latina, I felt unable to deal with the publishing establishment in that country. My first book was presented at the Las Américas bookshop and other places for Latinos in New York. After all, New York is the second most important city for Dominicans. The island has six million inhabitants and half a million live in New York. Economically, it's the most important. I never felt far from Santo Domingo when I lived in New York.

I first came to the United States in April 1967. Initially, I had wanted to be a lay nun and work in the barrios. Marriage repelled me, especially when I looked at my aunts, practically all of whom were divorced. I couldn't stand the idiocy of the whole scene: the danger of getting mixed up with someone when you were thirteen or fourteen, worrying about not having a boyfriend when you were sixteen. To me, becoming a nun was my path to freedom. I also wanted to study medicine. The one year I planned to stay eventually became seventeen.

My mother, who had left a year earlier, said I should go to the States in order to improve my English and to get to know the world before embarking on becoming a nun. I was very angry with her at the time, but she was right.

I come from a very special family with an intellectual background. On my father's side, my grandfather was a journalist and a writer, and my father is a poet and a well-known composer. My mother is a better poet than I am, but has never dared to write. She is the daughter of a peasant woman who worked in a tobacco factory and a Dominican oligarch who owned the factory and literally bought her when she was sixteen. My mother is a hybrid of two very distinct classes. I felt this when I went to school in Santiago.

In spite of having studied English in school, I found out, on my arrival in New York, that I didn't know very much. Like most Dominicans who come to the United States, I went to work in a factory: first a hat, and then a button factory (the acetone in which we had to wash the buttons damaged my eyes so that I have had to wear glasses ever since). I went to night school for a while, and then was accepted into a city-sponsored intensive English program, where I was paid to study.

My next job was as a telephone operator, and I quickly acquired a reputation as being extremely courteous to the customers, as my English still wasn't all that good and I said 'Thank you' to everyone, even if they insulted me. Then Brooklyn College opened its doors to minority students. They responded to a policy, initiated under the Johnson administration, whereby colleges were paid federal funds to admit minorities. I was one of eight Dominican students admitted to Brooklyn College.

Since there were only eight of us, and it was very tough to survive in such a racist atmosphere, we joined up with other minority students, principally Puerto Ricans, Blacks, other people from the Caribbean – we formed a Third World Alliance.

This was a real threshold for me; I had never known the people from Barbados or Trinidad, etc. My concept of the Caribbean, up to that time, had been limited to the Spanish-speaking part, and I discovered my identity as a *caribeña* in New York.

I was also racially classified at Brooklyn College, which was an interesting experience for me. In Santo Domingo, the popular classes have a pretty clear grasp of racial divisions, but the middle and upper-middle classes are very deluded on this point. People straighten their hair and marry 'in order to improve the race', etc., etc., and don't realize the racist connotations of their language or their attitude. In the United States, there is no space for fine distinctions of race, and one goes from being 'trigüeño' or 'indio' to being 'mulatto' or 'Black' or 'Hispanic'. This was an excellent experience for me. From that point on, I discovered myself as a Caribbean *mulata* and adopted the Black identity as a gesture of solidarity. At that time, I deeply admired and identified with Angela Davis, and ever since then, I have kept on identifying myself as a Black woman.

This opened another door; I learned about Frantz Fanon and other Caribbean theoreticians, and that finished Europe for me. I learned about the triangular trade and how we had financed Europe's development. I realized that capitalism was an impossible model to follow in our development. For me, this was discovering a universe. I only became a feminist much later.

When I first became more radical I was very much put off by feminism and people like Gloria Steinem and Betty Friedan – to me they were representatives of the white U.S. middle class who were busy telling us how *we* were being screwed by machismo. In a first stage I rejected this and, up to a point, I also had a false sense of solidarity with our men, who were racially oppressed as well. I felt that if we women criticized our men, we were only providing the racists with ammunition. This created a conflict of loyalties for me.

Discovering myself as a woman came much later. First I had to discover that I was part of a certain geographical area, and then, that I was Latin American. The great majority of the Latin American exiles converged on New York at that time – the Argentinians, the Uruguayans, the Chileans (Allende fell during those years) – so that, for me, New York became a kind of great doorway to this Latin American world.

Being in New York was very essential to my development. I would not be the woman I am today had I not gone to New York. I would have been the classic *fracasada* (failure) in my country because I know that I would not have found happiness in marriage and having children. I would have been frustrated, unhappy in a marriage, or divorced several times over because I would not have understood that within me was a woman who needed to express her own truths, articulate her own words. That, in Santo Domingo, would have been impossible.

Nevertheless, for the first ten years that I lived in New York, I was engulfed by a great silence; I could write nothing at all. The only poem I salvaged from this era was one about two young Puerto Ricans, aged sixteen and seventeen, who were shot by a bartender they had robbed of $100. I saw an article about it in the paper and it made me terribly sad. The poem ends with the line, 'sadness has never come so cheaply.' New York was, for me, a crushing kind of silence.

Still, all these experiences were being stored up inside of me. It's that kind of a process; things go in stages.

It was going to Africa that restored my essence as a *caribeña* for me. I went for three and a half months to work on coordinating the first meeting of ministers of education of the Portuguese-speaking African nations, and discovered Amílcar Cabral, the outstanding African cultural and revolutionary theoretician. Up to that point, I had never understood the important role that culture plays in effecting change. This was a central experience for me.

When I returned to the States, I was a different person; I suffered from severe depressions, which I now realize marked the death of one Chiqui and the birth of another. I figured the only thing that could save me was to return to the university, so I decided, at that point, to get an M.A. in Education from Columbia. I tried to work one more year in New York, but it was no good, and I returned to Santo Domingo.

I was there for four years, until last year, when I returned to the States. Some very difficult things happened during that time. The man with whom I had planned to restructure my life died of cancer. I was working terribly hard in my job as an educational coordinator. Basically, I had a kind of breakdown. I returned to the States to recuperate, and then went back to Santo Domingo. I've been there three months now.

I have really wanted to be a literary critic, yet once again I am denying my condition as a writer. The African experience had awakened me to the terrible problem of illiteracy in my country; 40% of the population is totally illiterate, another 40%, functionally so. I've always moved in this atmosphere of crisis and tension [between the two drives in my life]. Even now, I am teaching not literature but a course on Dominican education at the university.

I had to go back to Santo Domingo because, after a few years, living in the United States gave me a kind of physical malaise… When you first get here from your country, full of strength and energy, you get involved in a first stage of learning, absorbing, discovering. Then comes a time when you have to go back in order to revitalize yourself. If you stay in New York too long, you begin to get worn down by it. Anyone who is in the least sensitive can't help but feel bruised by the destruction of our people. Really. I saw it all the time in the Dominican community. Even though I had already acquired all sorts of New York rituals – I took perfumed baths in a flowered bathtub, swallowed my B_{12} vitamins, was into meditation – none of it was doing me any good. I realized I had to leave.

The New York experience, which was so crucial to my discovery of my Caribbean and racial identity, has made me a very, very critical person with respect to my own society. Things I never noticed before, I now see. Like racism, for example. Class differences. Santo Domingo is a very societally structured city. The situation of women is atrocious. I get almost rude about this because I can't stand the kind of sexist behavior that exists in my country. And for that, you pay the price of ostracism. It's really hard. By dint of having lived in the United States, I am considered a 'liberated woman,' which means that the men feel they have a green light to harass me sexually while the women distrust me. That's the most painful part. You come back to your country with a sense of intimate relationship and find that, for the most part, the principal *machistas* are the women themselves. And that's terrible. You find yourself confronted by an immense hostility that is a product of their own frustration. At first you ask yourself, 'what have you done to this woman to have her treat you like this?' And then you realize that you symbolize all the things that she has never been able to do, and perhaps never will: leave the country, study what she wants to. She may find herself tied down by three or four children, a husband that bores her, physical confinement, etc.; and you come along as a woman who can come and go as she wishes, write, be creative and productive, freely elect the man she wants to be with, and you become, for her, an object of hatred. It's really dreadful. And with the men, you represent a challenge to try and get you because you're different, but the real challenge is to dominate you. For the women, you are all they cannot be and that must be destroyed for survival. And you have to understand that so that you don't self-destruct. You can laugh off the first two or three aggressions, but by the fourth time, it really hurts.

As a writer I haven't yet been able to talk about my experiences in the States. At some moment in the future I will. Remember that New York was an experience of great silence for me. I feel that a time will come when I will be able to surmount what happened to me in New York and will be able to write about it. Remember, too, that the things I'm telling you in such a light vein today were wrenching experiences for me, especially discrimination. I still can't talk about it, but because I now have a better understanding of the creative process, I have learned not to push the creative instincts so that they won't become artificial. I know I have to let things come to the surface. The time will come when I'll be able to do it. I've written some sociological essays and some journalistic pieces on New York for a Santo Domingo paper in order to let my people know what's happening there, but in terms of literature I haven't yet been able to draw out what I have inside.

Because so many of my potential readers live in New York, I am definitely moving more and more toward publishing in the United States. I think people on the island would be interested as well.... We cannot avoid the 'invasion' of the Dominicans from the U.S. The whole country is changing: English is spoken all over – you feel the influence of the Dominicans who come back everywhere. I also think there will be interest in my writing in the States, first of all, because there are so many of us there, and second, because I will approach things with the particular viewpoint of a woman. I have a lot to tell about what New York did to my family. I had to assume a kind of paterfamilias role with respect to my siblings. A lot of it was very traumatic.

However, for the moment I'm more interested in women's issues, and especially in testimonials by Dominican women. I'm working on a book that is a collection of women's testimonials from the four years when I was here earlier. I've collected testimonials from all classes of women: peasants, factory workers, etc. I would like to be the voice of those who have no voice. Later, I'll be able to speak about New York.

In Santo Domingo there is a need to create a market for women's literature. As women, we have not yet discovered our power as consumers of books, but some day, when we discover this, perhaps we'll manifest this power by supporting women who write.

* The above interview with Dominican poet Chiqui Vicioso was taped and subsequently translated by Nina M. Scott at the Segundo Congreso de Creación Femenina, University of Mayagüez, Puerto Rico, on Nov. 17, 1987. Sincere thanks go to the staff of the University of Mayagüez who aided in the making of the tape.

Julia de Burgos. Our Julia

from *Algo que decir* (Something to Say)

In 1977, I was on my way to a workshop on César Vallejo's poetry, accompanied by a Puerto Rican poet, and when we reached the corner of 104th Street and Fifth Avenue, the poet said to me, 'Julia de Burgos collapsed here'.

Then I asked him something that we Dominicans always ask when she is mentioned: 'Who is Julia de Burgos?', and he told me that she was Puerto Rico's greatest poet, that she had come from the rural area, and that her poetry was extraordinary. He also told me that after she collapsed and was picked up by the ambulance, Julia was taken to the Mayflower Hospital, which was right around here, between 105th and 106th Streets and Fifth Avenue, but that they would not admit her because she was Hispanic, so they sent her to a Harle.n hospital.

This story made me feel, immediately, a tremendous solidarity with that woman, who was this above all: a woman, and a Caribbean woman at that. My first poem to Julia arose out of that experience ….

> This corner
> that I had overlooked
> like an insignificant corner
> now arises undressing itself
> with a strange haughtiness
> with a light that unfolds it
> that increases it, that quickens it.
> This corner
> where a sun – intimidated by the profound nakedness
> vacillates
> where 105th Street and Fifth Avenue
> merge into a pioneering solitary whole,
> claimed its place in space
> when Julia de Burgos lay down upon it
> inhabiting it again,
> through poetry.

I did not yet know Julia the poet, and even less Julia de Burgos, the Dominican, who was shared by a few of our country's exiles: Bosch, Miolán, Mainardi, Mir, and the rival to her Río Grande of Loíza, Juan Isidro Jiménez Grullón.

Woman-Society

Even as a child Julia was aware of the contradictions in Puerto Rico's social structure. She lived these contradictions in her own flesh when she lost several of her siblings, victims of the family's poverty (it was the decade of the 1920s), and when, like any tomboy, she accompanied her father on his rambles through the countryside, making herself into a wild bird unfettered by any restrictions in its quest for life and love.

So Julia, breaking all the rules that governed the behaviour of a 'proper' woman of the period, met and fell in love with a Dominican named Juan Isidro, divorced her husband, and followed her lover into exile, where, true to herself, she rose above the prejudices of those who viewed her as a Bohemian or, even worse, a 'poet'. According to Juan Isidro:

> At that time, my parents were there and found out about the romance (I think I told them myself); they sought information about Julia and were told that yes, Julia was a great poetess, but that she was not a woman concerned with the traditional values of home and family, that she had a tendency toward alcoholism, and so naturally, because my parents were staunch bourgeois, they opposed our relationship.

Julia responded to the slander with her *Canción de la verdad sencilla*, giving back to love, to passion, its true nature and its character as an elemental and simple impulse without the complications inflicted upon it by the city, colonialism, racial difference, and superimposed class divisions.

I was the most silent
of all those who journeyed to your port

I was not welcomed with slippery social rituals
nor muffled bells of ancestral reflections
my route was the savage song of birds
that flung my kindness into the wind.

I was not borne by boats laden with riches
nor did Oriental rugs raise my body
over ships my face appeared
whistling in the winds' curved simplicity.

I did not weigh the harmony of trivial pursuits
that your sparkle-filled hands promised
I thought only of the soil of my light spirit
the tragic abandonment hidden behind your face.

One day along the yellow shores of hysteria
many faces shadowed by ambition followed you
through a surge of tears wrested from the cosmos
voices slipped through without crossing your mystery

Life-Death

From each of those contradictions – thinking/feeling, country/city, colonial
subject/metropolis, woman/society – Julia emerges ever more naked, but
each time more whole, sustained in her search by a great rebellion against
death, which she defied ….

We are here to live, not to die
one dies in death, not in life
and she who has conquered death, in a way
has no right to surrender.

Julia fought death so much that, even when it seems to have won, she
mocks it and decides to die in the language that symbolises Puerto Rico's
death – English – in order to live in Spanish, where our hope lies ….

It has to be from here
forgotten but unshaken
among comrades of silence
deep into welfare island
my farewell to the world.

In 1987, there are few Dominicans, at least in the literary world, who
ask 'Who is Julia de Burgos?'
It has not been easy to make her known, not because of the anticipated
resistance that her iconoclastic attitude toward life provokes in mediocre

people, but because of the reaction of those who do not understand our common destiny as Caribbean countries or the unbreakable ties that bind our two islands. It is enough to say that Pedro Mir and Juan Bosch are both sons of Puerto Rican women, and that Julia would have been the mother of Dominicans had she not been destined to be the mother of humanity. To pay homage to the country that she loved so much but could never visit – the Dominican Republic – and to make known her support of our own real independence struggle is not only a moral obligation but another way of loving her.

Editor's translation

A Strange Wailing of the Wind

1

Before identity used to be palm trees
sea, architecture
it used to recall the nostalgic other details
the little girl kept asking her teacher
and there was a strange wailing of the wind.

2

Before love used to be gatherings
books, trains, speeches
passion and art themes
and the self exile . . . 'the party line' . . .
Only the little girl, or when the little girl
would arrive like a whirlwind
tear papers, rummage through books
spill coffee on the table
ignore her husband and write
on the impeccable whiteness (of the paper and of the
     bull's eye)
love would return like an epileptic roar
in the dawn of consciousness
and light unfolded by palm trees and blinds
and there was a strange wailing in the wind.

3

The walls of the number four used to reign in the empire
but it arrived with the abruptness of drums
with the sensorial remoteness of that which is near
the unsleeping apparition of strangeness
the numbers were revealed and the number seven
– like pincers striking against number four –
like a blue axe opening paths
in the blue forest where they were waiting together
Ochún and Yemayá and the question
announced the seventh empire of the lizard

4

Then identity used to be palm trees
sea, architecture
drums Yemayá, Ochún
and the momentary peace of the waters.
A rainstorm (water . . . nothing more)
like a circular origin of nothingness
And there was a strange wailing of the wind.

5

Then love used to be meetings
trains, speeches, Amilcar
the clear darkness of instinct
the 'Is it this?' converted into 'Who are you?'
and the number five a serpent with apples
and the number five a great S
hissing the name of an island
. . . and another name
like a trampoline of adolescent hopes
It is this! said the heart
It is this! they repeated for the first time
in agreement the little girl and the teacher
clinging to the airplane
as one does a pencil.

6

It was the everchanging empire of the number 5
with its serpents and apples
identity and love already united
were palm trees, sea, architecture
drums: Amilcar, Yemayá, Ochún
the clear darkness of instinct
the promise. The pencil, happiness
but there was a strange wailing of the wind.

7

Surreptitious announced the number four the return
    of Saturn
by surprise the walls were raised

an immense net ensnared the island in schemes
the letter S converted to silence
the number five in melted tar
and therefore
identity and love were now palm trees
sea, architecture
drums, Amilcar
Yemayá, Ochún
the dark darkness of the instinct
the pencil, sadness
and the absurdity of Is it this?
paralysed in the middle of the street
like a little girl in fright.
Is it this? like an ant
in a transparent plastic cubicle
Is it this? like an imploring cadaver
at war number five against number four
the universe became number nine
and there was a strange wailing of voices in the wind.

8
Mirror the island projected to the cosmos its sphere
and the shadow, in reflection
like a giant drill
rounded the edges.
The island became a ball
in the hands of a great circle of female teachers
carpenters, peasants, longshoremen, poets,
doctors, drivers, street vendors, peanut vendors
blind men, cripples, mutes, beauty queens,
traffic cops, police officers, workers, prostitutes
a ball in the hands of a great circle of school children
This we are! This you are! a wheel
crushing – without violence – the Is it this?

Translated by Aida Heredia and John Scott

The Journey Inward: Sherezada Vicioso's 'Un extraño ulular de voces traía el viento'

Aida Heredia

The Dominican Republic suffers from a politics of social and cultural identity informed by a concept of a nationalism that is rooted in the supposed ideal of a Spanish origin. With this self-conception of the Dominican people as a repository of the ideal of the Spanish past, the classes which exercise economic, intellectual and political power on this Caribbean island have persuaded the Dominican majority that Dominicans do not have links, in any profound sense, with the peoples of Africa brought to the island as exploited or unpaid labour. Such a politics has serious implications when considered from the perspective of the poverty, illiteracy, and human rights abuses which the Dominican majority confronts in its daily living. Thus, we ask ourselves: What is gained by embracing the ideology of the elites with respect to whiteness as the norm and ideal of national identity and as the sociocultural paradigm for Dominicanness? What are the advantages, symbolic[1] as well as material, for those who are not part of the elites? What is the effect on the Dominican people of living under a social structure that privileges whiteness? For a growing number of Dominicans the simple posing of these questions implies a disenchantment with dominant ideology. It is clear that the answers to these questions are many and varied, both at the individual and collective levels.

One voice that has struggled with these interrogatives is that of the Dominican writer Sherezada (Chiqui) Vicioso. In 1967, Chiqui Vicioso travelled to New York City. There she worked in a factory while she finished her study of English in night school. Later, she entered Brooklyn College, where she and seven other Dominicans joined a group of Puerto Rican, African American, and other Caribbean students to form the Third World Alliance. It was in the interaction with these persons of colour that Chiqui Vicioso discovered that her Caribbean self was multi-faceted. The dynamic of this (self)knowledge deepened through her relationships with African Americans, in whose community she learned the history of the struggles for equality and justice.

Influenced by these experiences, Vicioso began to re-examine her own culture and came to understand the profound racism which underlies social and economic policies in Dominican society. There was yet another definitive experience that was later to become part of the world view of our author. In 1978, Vicioso travelled to Africa as the coordinator of the first meeting of ministers of education of Portuguese-speaking African nations. Her work in that capacity culminated in her becoming acquainted with the revolutionary humanism exemplified in the practices and theories of the political leader Amilcar Cabral. Such experiences led Vicioso to a new consciousness with which she began to tackle two central issues: What is the nature and location of the heritage of the Dominican people? How does identifying with that nature and location mitigate the choices we must make to survive and advance individually and collectively?[2]

The search for answers to these interrogatives becomes a journey inward that reveals the national spirit of a people who are deceived in their historic memory. We embrace a national identity as defined by the dominant class as their only resource. We fail to see that this national identity, embodied in the institutions of prestige and power, denies and disfigures the tradition of resistance and struggle for liberty and dignity that Africans and their descendants waged during the colonial period. Without the transforming vision that recognises that those African men and women participated centrally in the processes of national formation, and that their presence is not simply an 'element' at the margin, as traditional Dominican history makes us believe, we Dominicans grow up deprived of a consciousness grounded in our true history.

But the Dominican people do not completely surrender to dominant ideology. We emigrate as alternate practice that comes to be one of the modes for surviving the machinery of oppression, a mode for negotiating our right to a better life. Emigration, principally to the United States, acquires a high value in the context of the official ideology; it implies a reconfiguration of our memory, of our consciousness, of our identity.[3] This is the experience of the persona in 'Un extraño ulular traía el viento' (A Strange Wailing of the Wind),[4] a poem in which Chiqui Vicioso addresses the possibility of the Dominican majority developing a new consciousness that enables them to recognise their own voices in the midst of crippling discourses about national identity advanced and manipulated by the dominant classes.

The reading of the first lines of the poem places us in the dynamic of a geographic space that brings to plain view the Dominican habit of identifying our 'self' and our roots as fundamentally Hispanic in origin. The signs – palm trees, sea, architecture – evoke the discourse of appropriation by the first colonisers. Keeping in mind the arguments concerning symbolic power, the sign 'architecture' alludes to the glorification of the Colonial City in Santo Domingo with its monuments, residences, battlements, churches, and other artefacts that seek to anchor our national 'self' to the zenith of colonial rule. In general, Dominican history is understood to begin with the arrival of Europeans. In the first lines of the poem, one can make out the traces of a mentality that, in the construction of social relationships, adopts as its own the myth of the superiority of white culture. But for the majority, there is a reality that clashes with the supposed privileges that are proclaimed by the defenders of the myth. For it is at the time of seeking access to a quality education, decent housing, adequate health services, and economic opportunity that the Dominican majority finds itself dispossessed, excluded, exploited.

In the figure of the female teacher, Chiqui Vicioso denounces an educational system that is the source of stereotypes: Africa – land of slaves, backward peoples, and given to violence; Europe – the standard of all that is good, beautiful, and desired. With the criminal repetition of such stereotypes the integral presence of men and women of African origin – possessors of cultures with profound spiritual, moral, philosophical and aesthetic values – is deformed and silenced in the minds of many Dominicans. Most Dominicans see themselves as a people of essentially Hispanic origin. This is one of the habits against which the writing of 'Un extraño ulular traía el viento' speaks and which the teacher embodies. The political impotence and the cultural alienation suggested in the teacher's character are well understood in the context of what Kesho Scott calls the habit of surviving, a term that describes people's adjustments and adaptations to racial oppression and economic exploitation.

> Eventually, the habits cease to be mere responses. They acquire the status of cultural prescriptions . . . [that] harden into ingrained attitudes – routines of thought, feeling, and action – that over time become unexamined and unquestioned traditions.[5]

The search for solutions to the economic and social problems outside of ourselves and of our community is perhaps the most atrophying habit that Dominicans have learnt. We have constructed ourselves in an 'oppressor's ideology' as individuals dispossessed of a productive and creative mentality, of a will to struggle against the historiography fabricated by the intellectual elite. (This is not to say that there are no alternative voices in Dominican society. We would argue, however, that the above scenario is the preponderant one.)

But the African roots of the Dominican people are present, alive, and tenacious. From them comes the 'strange wailing of voices' that surrounds the poet (like the wind) and gnaws at her 'gut' during the journey through her inner self. It is the strange wailing that guides the little girl *not* to mold herself in racist ideology. The girl's challenge is to examine critically what the teacher represents. The strange wailing of those voices symbolises the possibility of *coming to be* in self knowledge and self-production.[6] The poetic writing of Chiqui Vicioso makes the African-rooted liberation struggle come alive in the collective voice of the masses. Stanza three enunciates this desire and this intent. Through the image of the 'seventh empire of the lizard', Vicioso challenges Dominicans with another vision. The lizard symbolises the poetic word, the word of liberation. Together with the seventh empire, symbol of a transformed world, these images call for Dominicans to develop a consciousness in which the resistance, struggle and survival of African peoples is a dynamic aspect of Dominican identity. Our African ancestors must be revered as present and active members in our everyday lives, rather than as a group of un-named persons, remote and silenced. The *question* that announces new possibilities in our history is the central one of who are we fundamentally, a question that is still asked in numbness and confusion.

The poem responds insightfully to that question. The notion of 'self' in the poem acquires a more profound humanity when it engages in an internal dialogue of justice and solidarity in the communal spaces to which the drums of Yemayá and Ochún summon us (stanza four). In this act of introspection, Vicioso alludes to the 'deterritorialisation' of a monologic 'national self' that the intellectual and political elites sell to the majority of Dominicans. In the African images that appear in stanza four, Vicioso articulates her vision of a simultaneous identity in the Bakhtinian sense of 'being with', meaning the development of an awareness of the 'other'.[7] In this case, the 'other' is Africa and her descendants in all parts of the world. In Dominican society the consciousness and knowledge of the 'other' translates into the necessity to vindicate historical fact, disfigured by the colonialist mentality, in which the customs, religious practices, and rebellion of people of African descent are legitimate. Within this necessity, the poetic voice seems to enunciate a new social and political practice that must be cultivated, one that re-configures the consciousness of our negritude.

Muamba Tujibikile explains that, since the discovery of America, there has been a concealment, a deformation of the legitimate black roots of our people. Thus, the conception of a national identity that transcends the limits of whiteness fabricated by the ruling classes goes hand in hand with the process of *self-disconcealment* that each Dominican should undertake.[8] This *autodesencubrimiento* is simultaneously an intimate and public process that is both sociological and psychological.

Chiqui Vicioso wisely captures the complexity of this process through which many of us have passed and understand all too well. Stanza five shows how the issue of identity is not simply a sociological problem; it is also an issue of the human soul. In changing the word *identity* to the word *love*, Vicioso takes us to spaces as much intimate as public, where we can create an alternative discourse to that of the dominant classes. The suggestive play on words 'the clear darkness of instinct' is lost in the English translation. The Spanish communicates the nature of this alternative discourse: the *darkness* in the sense of 'negritude' as an answer to *who are you?* The clear darkness of instinct evokes the intimate, the personal, the private, where one finds the truth we Dominicans forget, deny, and disdain in our daily lives. Vicioso also privileges instinct over the purely intellectual as a valid way toward self-knowledge, especially when this intellect is used to distort Dominican reality. The poet creates a counterpoint between palm trees, sea, architecture – images relatively static and devoid of human presence – and gatherings, trains, speeches, Amilcar – images that are alive with social, cultural and political activity. Again, Vicioso attempts a deterritorialisation in which debates and discourses about national identity are rescued from the domain of the ruling classes and re-conceputalised in the spaces of the majority.

These images suggesting political consciousness lead into the humanist activity of the revolutionary leader Amilcar Cabral. In the figure of the Guinean leader, Vicioso insists on the possibility of the Dominican majority being 'renamed', that is to say, that values that we use to construct our identity must be re-configured. In evoking Amilcar Cabral, the poetic voice recontextualises her personal experiences to place herself in the collective struggle at the national level. But more important, she attempts to understand the struggles of the Dominican masses from a transnational perspective that appreciated the peoples and communities of the African diaspora.

The presence of Amilcar in the poem speaks to us of cultural frontiers of (self)knowledge that transcend the atrophy and pendantry of traditional Dominican historiography. At these frontiers the little girl and her teacher respond, first through intuition, later with the certainty and faith of those who recognise in their heart the falsity of a supposed superior European origin ('It is this! said the heart / it is this! they repeated for the first time / in agreement the little girl and the teacher / clinging to the airplane / as one does a pencil'). This is one of the moments in which we best appreciate the acumen of Chiqui Vicioso.

The simile with which the poetic voice evokes the experience of the little girl and the teacher is quite interesting. The pencil, and by extension poetry, suggests the poet's desire to seek refuge from a sociocultural and political reality that stifles the masses in general and women in particular. Writing for Vicioso can be seen as an intimate recess into which she escapes from the lack of *autodesencubrimiento* by the Dominican majority. Yet, Vicioso articulates a public discourse in favour of an identity regarded by most as other. The beauty (and utility) of the work is this convergence of the public and the private. The interweaving of personal and public leaves no doubt that the ideological transformation implied in *autodesencubrimiento* must begin in the subjective spaces of each Dominican. As long as Dominicans embrace the myth of European culture as our essential inheritance, we will not understand that we already have the capacity to develop strategies for liberation.

Stanza seven supports this analysis. The number five – symbol of mutability, of self-transformation – in its deep and profound breathing becomes an asthmatic wheezing that ends up being muzzled. The *S* converted to silence symbolises the collective voice of the Dominican masses, concealed, subjugated, and excluded from participating in the processes that form national identity. Until now the experience of *autodesencubrimiento*, to which Vicioso calls our attention, appears enveloped in a space of *darkness*, meaning here the repressed, which is associated with *Is it this?, distance, strangeness*. This experience acquires form; it is established consciously as a part of Dominican historical and social experience the moment it is raised as a forceful answer to the practices and ideologies of the institutions of power. The active knowledge of our African roots, far from being an adornment or an exotic element, becomes a weapon to fight the silencing to which Dominicans are subjected.

The first lines of stanza seven articulate the strength and the spirit of the struggle that is found, but not necessarily consciously, in the masses; identity and love emerge tenaciously against the 'walls' of corruption that fetter the fullest development of the people. The aberration of a mentality that privileges Hispanic descent resounds in the repetition of the 'Is it this?' with its 'absurdity', with its triviality and its slavery to habit ('ant') with its desperate lack of vitality ('imploring cadaver'). The stanza ends rather abruptly with the declaration: 'the universe became the number nine / and there was a strange wailing of voices in the wind'. The universe that Vicioso captures in the number nine conveys the idea of a space of re-encounter with communities of the African diaspora, of a beginning emerging from a dynamic political awareness where the wailing in the wind ceases to be a strange element and becomes a feature of our 'quotidian-ness'. The voices brought by the wind make up a fundamental part of the answer to the question 'Who are you?' This is why the enunciation of the phrase 'a strange wailing in the wind' comes to us as a form of relief, of a liberation from prejudice, from false myths, from a deformed consciousness. As stated earlier, Vicioso abruptly propels us to a conception of a society that recognises itself in terms of a new solidarity, of *another* sensibility that links intellectual power to the historical tasks of the African diaspora.

The affirmation 'This we are! This you are!', no longer in the single voice of the little girl, but in the *ronda* of the multitude of school children and teachers, now educates us. The humanistic values of the last stanza become evident upon analysing them in light of the thinking of Cheikh Anta Diop:

> The essential thing, for people, is to rediscover the thread that connects them to their most remote ancestral past. The erasing, the destruction of the historical conscience also has been since time began part of the techniques of colonization, enslavement, and debasement of peoples.[9]

Diop concludes that, because of this destruction, teaching must be elevated to the level of national activity. It is the proposal of Vicioso in representing an authentic dialogue from a countergenerational perspective in which school children teach and educate their teachers. The innocence that Chiqui Vicioso conveys through the little girl and the other school children in this social re-vision is neither a cliché nor cheap sentimentality; it is what makes us understand that a society that defines itself in terms of discrimination against and oppression of black people is an immoral one. With the images of roundness in the last lines of the poem, Vicioso returns to the idea of identity as 'simultaneous with'. The circularity of the space occupied by (female) teachers and school children creates a site in which identity, in the form of the struggle for liberty and prosperity of the 'self', is inseparable from the struggle for liberty and prosperity of the 'other'.

Still, the image of the universe becoming the number nine, symbol of comprehension, unity and harmony, and the shift from the imperfect tense in 'un extraño ulular *traía* el viento' to the preterite tense 'un extraño ulular de voces *trajo* el viento' (emphasis added) do not answer the imploring 'cadaver'. The last stanza implies a faith mitigated by the current conditions of the Dominican substrate[10] that populate the last lines. If, indeed, the substrate are the heart and soul of the country, in these final lines they come through with petrified voices, alienated bodies and restricted vision. In their efforts to organise themselves politically, the men and women of the substrate fight for their humanity, but their struggle is individual, isolated, and sporadic. The discursive strategy of simply listing types of working-class people suggests this.

In a society such as the Dominican Republic, where the powerful secure their privileges by humiliating and alienating women, it is important to note that the re-visionist journey of the poet is represented through the intuition of women. In the strange wailing of the wind, Chiqui Vicioso endeavours to vindicate the participation of women in the liberation struggle. The strength of women's voices is corroborated in the fertility of Yemayá, goddess of the seas, and her daughter Ochún, goddess of rivers. This fertility is the visionary depth from which the voices of women and girls shape an identity that challenges those who insidiously preach the inferiority of Blacks and the superiority of Whites.

Notes

1. *Symbolic advantage,* in how it differs from material advantage, refers to the power or authority that is exercised in the daily sociocultural practices, those which do not directly fall under the rubric of the 'politico-economic'. For example, a person says to another 'Shut up, nigger!' (¡Cállate, negro de mierda!). What gives force to this (social *and* linguistic) act is not the race of the individuals. It is, rather, the power that the phrase acquires in a society that privileges the white aesthetic. See Pierre Bourdieu, *Language and Symbolic Power* (Cambridge: Harvard UP, 1991); Bonnie Urciuoli, *Exposing Prejudice: Puerto Rican Experiences of Language, Race, and Class* (Boulder: Westview Press,1996).

2. The dynamic that is revealed in this reflection is not only limited to the context of the Dominican Republic in which the thinking of Vicioso has been formed but to one that can be seen, in one form or another, in almost all Latin American or Caribbean countries. Peter Wade, *Blackness and Race Mixture: The Dynamics of Racial Identity in Colombia* (Baltimore: Johns Hopkins UP, 1993); Michel-Rolph Trouillot, *Nation, State, and Society in Haiti, 1804-1984* (Washington: Woodrow Wilson Center for International Scholars, 1985); Stephen Gregory and Roger Sanjek, *Race* (New Brunswick: Rutgers UP, 1994); France Twine, *Racism in a Racial Democracy* (New Brunswick: Rutgers UP, 1998); Bienvenida Mendoza, ed., *Racismo en los medios de comunicación* (Santo Domingo: Casa por la Identidad de las Mujeres Afro, 1996), and *Por una sociedad libre de prejuicio racial* (Santo Domingo: Casa por la Identidad de las Mujeres Afro, 1998); and Abdias do Nascimento, *O Quilombismo: Documentos de una militância pan-africanista* (Petrópolis, RJ, Brasil: Vozes, 1980) discuss a series of cultural practices that create certain 'realities' at the social and psychological level: *whitening,*

willful forgetting, and the role of *white privilege and racism in formation of national identity.* Their theoretical assertions effectively explain the apparent contradiction between *mestizo* identity, that is, non-white or mixed identity, as the norm and the omnipresence of racial discrimination.

3. The necessity of re-configuring the way we understand our identity resonates with José F. Pequeño's argument that identity should always be a term in the plural which encompasses similarities but also differences. 'I constitute a whole because I possess components whose diversity permits them to be articulated with coherence. The identity of the parts that constitute me would reside, then, in their capacity to integrate themselves and function due to certain similarities, but also due to indispensable differences . . . identity is . . . is a process of interminable evolution ....' (my translation). 'La identidad de los distintos', *Rumbo* June 1998: 59.

4. Sherezada Vicioso, *Un extraño ulular traía el viento* (Santo Domingo: Alfa y Omega, 1985).

5. Kesho Scott, *Habit of Surviving* (New Brunswick: Rutgers UP, 1991): 8.

6. Maulana Karenga contends that a people whose achievements are minor or whose knowledge of its history and the possibilities it suggests is deficient, develop a self-consciousness of similar characteristics. See 'Society, Culture, and the Problem of Self-consciousness: A Kawaida Analysis', *Philosophy Born of Struggle*, ed. Leonard Harris (Dubuque, IA: Kendall/Hunt,1983): 213.

7. Mikhail Bakhtin, *Mikhail Bakhtin,* Eds. Katerina Clark and Michael Holquist (Cambridge: Harvard UP, 1984): 77.

8. The term *autodesencubrimiento* comes from Pedro Muamba Tujibikile, *Quinientos años: hacia un autodesencubrimiento de la identidad caribeña* (Santo Domingo: CEDEE, 1991).

9. Cheikh Anta Diop, *Civilization or Barbarism,* trans. Yaa-Lengi Meema Ngemi (Brooklyn: Lawrence Hill 1981): 212.

10. We find a great usefulness in the term *substrate* not simply as it appears in works on linguistics but as a description of cultural groups of which a given society is composed. The substrate, those without power, influence the cultural practices of the society in general, although they do not determine dominant ideology. See John Holm, *Pidgin and Creoles: Volume I, Theory and Structure* (Cambridge: Cambridge UP 1988).

Soleida Ríos

Soleida Ríos

CUBA

(b. 1950)

*With the publication of her first collection of poetry in 1977, Soleida Ríos
was hailed by critics as one of Cuba's new, talented voices. Born on 'La
Prueba', a farm in the eastern countryside, she grew up and attended
school in Santiago de Cuba. After her parents' divorce, she stayed for a
while with her mother and four siblings but moved out in her early teens.
Caught up in the fervour of the Revolution, she enrolled in a four-year
teacher training programme when she was only thirteen and became an
itinerant teacher and educational consultant in the Sierra Maestra, an
experience that had a profound impact on her writing and her professional
career. Although she has worked as an educator for most of her life, serving
as director of Professional Technical Education from 1972 to 1980, and
as an institutional relations specialist in the Ministry of Culture, travelling
throughout the country and leading what she calls an 'almost itinerant
life' from 1982 to 1995, Ríos has devoted much of her professional career
to writing. She worked for two years as a literary advisor on the Isle of
Youth, served as president of the Literature Section of the Saíz Brothers
Brigade, and is presently a specialist in the Cuban Book Institute's Centre
for Literary Advancement, a position that she has held since 1995.*

Soleida Ríos has published four collections of poetry, including De la
sierra *(Of the Sierra) in 1977,* De pronto abril *(Suddenly April) in 1979,*
Entre mundo y juguete *(Between World and Toy) in 1987, and* El libro
roto *(The Broken Book) in 1995. A poet committed to the struggle for
equality, she once said, 'I'm interested in poetry's capacity to change life
and I think it has a critical role to play in the struggle for women's full
equality'. While working in the Sierra Maestra in the late sixties, she wanted
to express what she calls the 'living magic of the mountains', so she stopped
writing journal entries and turned to poetry. Her early poetry describes a*

336

bucolic landscape of butterflies and palm trees, but, on a deeper level, it also reveals a subtle political subtext through allusions to war and revolution. This narrative, meditative, and self-reflexive poetry includes what have been called her paradigmatic poems, poems such as 'Agua de otoño' (Autumn Rains) and 'Pájaro de la bruja' (Witch Bird), which deal, profoundly and philosophically, with the conundrums and enigmas of life – the solitude of love and the darkness of light. Her later poetry is more plaintive, more mournful, more dream-like because there are constant references to death (scorpion, moribund arrows, scabrous bosom) and loss (farewells, birds in flight, falling bodies). Fear is pervasive, as Antón Arrufat notes, but there is also a strong sense of despair, of disillusionment, of hopes betrayed in poems such as 'Último rezo para los ojos del traidor' (Last Prayer for the Traitor's Eyes) and 'Un soplo dispersa los límites del hogar' (A Breath Scatters the Boundaries of Home), with its title derived from a line by Rimbaud. Her other publications, all of which appeared in 1999, include Libro cero *(Zero Book), a narrative;* El texto sucio *(Dirty Text), a work of prose; and* El Libro de los sueños *(Dream Book), a testimonial that includes the dreams of some one hundred individuals. Her dedication to writing is reflected not only in her own work, but also in her support of other writers, for Ríos has conducted workshops throughout the country and, in 1989, she edited* Poesía infiel, *an anthology of verse by young Cuban poets.*

Although her poetry does not deal explicitly with race, Ríos manifests in her life – through her dress, hair, beliefs, and lifestyle – pride in her African heritage. She notes that her 'Alto resuena el cuerno llamándonos' (The Horn Calls Out to Us Loudly) is based on an anonymous African poem, while 'Cuerpo presente' (Final Rites) contains allusions to Afro-Cuban mythology. In a letter to the editor, she explained, 'Ochún [goddess of the river and of eros] is my mother protector, but also Yemayá [goddess of the seas and of maternal love]. I am daughter of "the two waters". Oya [goddess of storms and ruler of the dead] has taken a liking to me and I believe that I have taken one to her too'. Aché!

I Also Sing of Myself

I celebrate myself, I sing.

W.W.

I sing of myself because by force of love
I stand,
squeezing this curve of time
between my hands.

The morning stretches out over silence
and my steps
call back the high sounds.

I sing of myself and beyond, I sing
of what I will become
when night is rent by sun
and another music fills my footprints as I go

I sing of myself
for having come from the breath of a summer
among these palms that will watch over me
I take my place among the living
I make infinite my thirst
striking myself, I sing.

Translated by Margaret Randall

Autumn Rains

I hadn't thought of calling the poem Autumn Rains.
Instead I'd say
I love this man and I protect him
against the autumn rains against all
(myopia, fear
of the habit of loving
of the moon's mysteries
even of my duties and rights)
I love this man and do not belong to him
and yet I've been his
and what have I not possessed
in that dark corner of his room
– alone and together as the world –

Then I realised this wasn't possible.

I'd thought of writing on this sheet of paper
Revolution magic rebel and new
we on this side are true to your faults
(what setback or victory
we make our way inland with no other heart
but yours
no descendants but your deaths
on the shoulders of all).

For you I rage when
I realise this wasn't possible
on this sheet of paper.

I know that my mother weeps there in her courtyard
when I decide to leave
touching the dust of memory.
But the drop of water has dried

and the hungry scorpion is there
beside her with its black oils
deadly and scandalous as lightning.
I call out to her in the night
and want to return to that place of hers
like coming home from school.

Forgive me mother
but I've realised this wasn't possible.

Accidentally I'd also thought of escaping.
Giving my bland goodbye
to those who climb the perfect step
to one side the broken verses
all mending to one side.
And then I saw that the wind flashed open and closed
a little door
and I saw that I followed the wind's course
rushing at that door where today I knock
and no one opened.

Here a bird has come to die
and a bird has taken flight.
Here is the thorny cactus
and right here its orange flower.
And here am I,
lip of stone of plant life.
Here I've remained since then
with you, bird or dream,
– that lifts and sustains me and lets me fall –
here to blot out my autumn rains.

Translated by Margaret Randall

Untitled

I can now watch her in the mirror with some peace. She stands on the tips of her toes in order to reach the square of light coming in through the window. And far beyond, the moon may be there or something that I perhaps cannot see.

At the beginning it was just a silence or the noise produced by the fall itself. At the beginning, fear opened its two halves all at once. At times a fleeting music bubbled back from memory, forcing her to show her head a little bit. Outside, there was probably the confused repetition of gestures and intents in which I took no part except to ignore or contradict them and which she may have treated with reverence like the host in the hands of fervent communicants.

I did not prevent her going astray ….

Should she ask for bread or shelter? Shall she go out into the world and seek some recompense? Shall she throw stones around? Gather stones? Hold herself back? Embrace? Must she restore her composure? The Old Book and not I advised her:

May your vestments be white at all times, and may you never want for ointment on your head.

Whatever you may have to do, do it with your utmost strength; because in the grave, where you are headed, there is no work, nor job, nor science, nor wisdom.

She left an inscription on the big wall: 'What denies me or holds me back sounds and resounds and I write down that rhythm – the rebound. But my two opposing sides live together. One will want to be perceived favourably, the other wants to look without a mask'.

For my sake or for hers and for the sake of those following her, I left this bold writing on the big wall: 'One bird has come here to die and another bird has taken flight'.

Translated by Gabriel A. Abudu

The Horn Calls Out to Us Loudly*

Oh father
those still to come will hear you
even those who will come no more
still hear your voice
far or near
your word still moves us
what good you do us what badness
what restraint and what madness
fleeing in one direction
you prepare the needle
with a frown you are spinning for our patience
a long line of thread
oh father
the magic still overwhelms us
we fix our gaze on you
on the image and inside the house
see how the light bolt is tearing us up
see how the light casts a shadow
see how the bristling top of the hillock alerts us
and we go on one by one
like a lonely masterly lamb
our legs get tangled and we trip
our legs as if made of foam
are carrying on with wounds and they drag on the road
with you we carried out the miracle
our house in the middle of the forest
with you we fought off the vultures the worms
we grew our baby teeth
waiting for the shafts of the rays and teeth of the
    wild animal
your hand was the door
your star-lit face was the only lamp
we are not a lonely masterly lamb

give us your blessings with the four winds
give us the thirsting with three stones of song
and not this calm like that of a cyclone

Translated by Gabriel A. Abudu

* From an anonymous African poem

Final Rites[1]

taut the string
frays into sixty moribund arrows
into sixty somnambulist garments
into one single
into one
into one body that falls

I do not want to die
I do not want to die
I do not see now I do not see
there are mounds of dirt
the electric rods of the world
the current of fear

in this grave I do not perceive
I cannot see I cannot
with all my strength I push these mounds of dirt
that retreat and return
return return

behind

no one helps god
no one comes
papa I now know that you are there
give me your old enormous hand
lift me up oh god
virgin of cobre[2]
I pray for you the juanes[3]
I pray for that orphan boy you bear

the grave opens
the hole opens where I am
but the water is so limpid
it is the dedication water

for your farewell in clear goblets
remember it father
it is now time
give me your old hand
I do not want to die
throw me the lily the bulb of the lily
the root of the ground
I do not want to die

oh the mounds
the mounds return father
look at them how they return to enclose me
in their dark scabrous bosom
I do not want to die I do not yet grieve
the mounds grieve
the water grieves
the sky is marble it grieves
close the door father
rest in peace
in peace

Editor's translation

Notes

1. Soleida Ríos wrote to the editor: 'Mi madre era devota de la Caridad (Ochún, como tú sabes). Este poema me relaciona con un sueño que mi madre me contó siete días antes de su muerte. Lo verás en mi libro *El libro de los sueños*' (My mother was a devotee of the Virgen de Caridad [Ochún, as you know]. This poem is related to a dream that my mother told me seven days before her death. You will see it in my *Book of Dreams*).

2. The *Virgen de la Caridad del Cobre*, depicted as a brown-skinned woman, is the patron saint of Cuba and she represents the Afro-Cuban female deity Ochún. Her statue is located in the town of El Cobre, the site of the first open copper mine in the Americas and the site, in 1733, of one of Cuba's largest slave rebellions.

3. The *juanes*: In 1608, three men, including an Indian, Juan de Hoyos, and a ten-year-old slave, Juan Moreno, were in a boat collecting salt for the copper mines, when they found floating in the water a foot-tall wooden statue of Mary carrying the Christ child. The statue became the venerated *Virgen de la Caridad del Cobre*. According to Soleida Ríos, images of the Virgin depict her accompanied by three men, including a Black, named 'Juan'.

Life[1]

I'll begin in reverse.

I didn't marry, I didn't have children. If marrying means signing before witnesses, no. In the country, where I was born and lived the first four years of my life and to which I frequently returned, they said Miss So-and-So put it off. Isn't that funny? I lived with a young Argentinian – for better or worse – for almost three years, which proves our love because the situation could not have been more difficult (Isle of Pines: 1980-1982).

I came to Havana in 1982, when my personal experiment gave out: the experiment of diluting myself in an almost homogeneous crowd, in a rootless place, with scarcely a past – the Isle of Pines. In order not to be the object of observation and criticism, not to be obviously 'different', I then threw myself haphazardly into a collective adventure that consisted of 'teaching' completely illiterate people to read, introducing them to books, authors, certain films, and certain tasteful examples of Universal Art. Having also ended the period of my 'marriage' to the young Argentinian, who was sent to the Malvinas War in June 1982, I didn't have sufficient reason to stay there trying 'to plough the sea', because an adventure like that is either collective or it's not. Nor was it plausible to return to Santiago de Cuba, where for four years I had led an iconoclastic life (nomadic and, as viewed from the outside, quite scandalous). A young woman, separated from her family, a Black woman with an Afro, unmarried and ambitious to become a poet? A serious danger for the machismo of the region. I am talking about 1980, when I left. If I could, I would have chosen to live and write in Santiago de Cuba. There, I had mentors, friends, and, I thought, protection.

I finished primary school. Not a single course of secondary education. I was attracted to the Revolution and entered what is called the Training Plan for Primary Teachers of the Revolution, which took me to three places: first, the Sierra Maestra. A place called Minas del Frío (impressive: clouds

346

over the land, heroes' footsteps still fresh on the ground, sports, patriotic songs, marches, almost 6,000 people on top of a hill, rustic classrooms built with our hands at the edge of precipices) 1963-1964. Another site in Topes de Collantes, in the Escambray Mountains (also a naturally beautiful place, crowned with pine forests and an army of future teachers, adolescents, open to all trades and sports and some arts, organised around a stern disciplinary base, including a rule against fraternising in pairs!) 1964-1966. And a third site in the 'Antón Makarenko' Pedagogical Institute, in Tarará Beach, to the east of Havana (a place, I remember, as dry as the worst desert, hard, lacking in spontaneity and grace). But the proximity to the city made possible – besides the obligatory and perhaps very useful teaching activities in neighbourhood schools – an anxious, more-than-hoped-for escape into the evocative novelty of neo-realistic Italian films) 1966-1968.

The motive for entering the Training Plan – for I had thirteen years left to finish when I entered – was little more than curiosity incited by those strange names and the desire to venture forth, to climb hills. Although I believe that I also derived something of a personal satisfaction in 'taking a step forward'. In the language of the period, it might be called 'moving up' or 'marching' toward History.

I didn't have an academic preparation for writing. In Topes de Collantes, at night, in the great, empty halls of the building called 'The White Elephant', built as a tuberculosis hospital by tyrant Fulgencio Batista, I read, stretched out on the floor, the stories of Edgar Allan Poe. A volume that I took out of the trash, without covers and probably without some pages. Before, on my days off, I went to the library and opened thick volumes containing magical stories about fairies, goblins, princes and paupers. Luckily, as an adolescent, through the encouragement of a sister, I read romantic fiction, but not with the same intensity as she.

When I was a child, there was no television nor books nor literary encouragement from my family. One of my uncles was crazy about Buesa's poetry and he had a book that I must have leafed through on occasion.

On the other hand, I always remember a marvellous scene when we (children) and our uncles and aunts and perhaps my mother, played on a beautiful patio under the moon. Games with songs and dances inherited from the Spanish tradition. I also remember that the older children used to sit at night and tell stories.

My literary formation (?) was primarily autodidactic.

I was really introduced to literature by Poe, Kafka, César Vallejo (whose poems first revealed my need for poetry), then José Martí, and today, lest I omit their significance, there are Borges, Lezama, Piñera, Octavio Paz, Rimbaud,

Sor Juana, Amos Tutuola, Quevedo, M. Duras, M. Yourcenar, Salinger, Maccullers, and the anonymous ones on this or that side of the ocean.

In 1973, after four years in the mountains (as teacher and then regional consultant), I returned, without neglecting my obligations, to that practice and enjoyment of my solitude (which I had engaged in before without 'being discovered' and, I suspect, without luck), writing now what someone helped me define as poems and, through them, I found myself enrolled in a literary workshop (an organisation created for the development of new writers).

My contact with that wondrous nature of the Sierra and perhaps the absolute dominion of the epic in those years led me to write *De la Sierra* (From the Sierra), published in 1977. I really struggled over only one poem entitled 'Pájaro de La Bruja' (Witch Bird), which I finally succeeded in writing when I was about to submit the collection for publication.

Among the people whose encouragement I received, I want to name Díaz Oduardo, a poet, prematurely dead, who founded the publishing house 'Uvero' (I worked for two years at the very place in the Sierra with that name; it is associated, transcendentally, with one of the Rebel Army's important battles); the Cuban novelist, also deceased, José Soler Puig; Joel James, novelist, essayist, and historical researcher; and the poet Eliseo Diego, who died in 1993.

Family: Mother, deceased: Four siblings on my mother's side. Because I consider my father almost a fiction, I would not know how to relate to the siblings that fate gave me on that side. A *mambí*[2] grandfather, a true family emblem. My mother's father.

Editor's translation

Notes

1. Soleida Ríos wrote this *testimonio* in response to the editor's questions about her family, work, writing, and literary formation.
2. *mambí*: a proud and brave African-descended warrior who fought in Cuba's nineteenth-century wars of liberation from slavery and independence from Spain.

Soleida's Reappearance

Antón Arrufat

Reina María Rodríguez was the first person who told me about Soleida Ríos. Among the things that she said to me, I remember this: that several of Soleida's poems ('Agua de otoño' [Autumn Rains] and 'Pájaro de la bruja' [Witch Bird], to be precise) were paradigmatic for her generation and that, after these wondrous poems, Soleida Ríos' work slipped into silence and, consequently, into oblivion. Either she had stopped writing or was not interested in publishing her writing. Rodríguez also said that Ríos' last book, *Entre mundo y juguete* (Between World and Toy) (1987), had received little attention. Almost nine years had passed between this book and the previous one, *De pronto abril* (Suddenly April), 1979. These large publishing gaps made Soleida Ríos' poetry lose some of its contemporary significance, made it indistinct and almost nonexistent in present-day Cuban poetry.

After the publication of *Entre mundo y juguete* in 1987, our country suffered from a shortage of paper, ink, and so-called consumer goods, and the publishing industry underwent several calamities. Sigfredo Ariel told me that Soleida Ríos is very exacting about her poems. She retains very few of those she has written; she keeps only those that she considers less opaque, while the in-between ones disappear. She also expresses a certain disenchantment with poetry, a disenchantment that many contemporary poets experience. Disenchantment, doubt, mistrust . . . and the desire, which I have noticed in my conversations with Soleida, to write something else, to mix genres and to produce a kind of superpoetry. It is as if the writing of poetry, as it has been practised, is not now enough.

In composing her books, Soleida Ríos has a fault common to other Cuban poets: she passes texts from one book to the next. In many cases, the poems are repeated so often that she seems to change only the book's title. Two of her books, *De pronto abril* and *Entre mundo y juguete*, contain some of the same poems, including the paradigmatic

349

ones that Reina María Rodríguez mentioned. One of those, 'Agua de otoño', exemplifies the best poetry of its period. It interests me more than 'Pájaro de la bruja', and I judge it the more lasting text. Other poems from that same period have great merit: 'La casa de la tranquilidad' (Tranquillity House), 'Voy subiendo' (I Continue Climbing), 'Antigua' (Ancient), and 'Augurio' (Augury). That stage of her poetry is indebted to colloquialism. The major poets of colloquialism have evolved in two clearly discernible directions: renovation of classical forms or metaphoric intensification. Before the demise of colloquialism, Soleida Ríos chose a somewhat eclectic solution: her present poetry seems to participate in both tendencies.

As the cover reveals, *El libro roto* (Broken Book) took two years to complete, 1987-1989. Furthermore, it is the first book by Soleida that does not include previously published poems. I believe, however, that its publication is late. Perhaps too late. A reader will note the absence of poems written between 1989, when *El libro roto* was completed, and 1994, the date on the copyright page. The cover also raises a question about the title of the collection. Why broken you might ask. The word *roto* (broken) appears in several of her poems; like a key word, it encodes meaning and it offers clues in the search for that meaning: '. . . perdido en dos el mundo, roto de pronto / no se explica por qué' (. . . split in two the world, broken suddenly / without explanation) and 'y hasta diós está roto y anda en trapos' (and even god is broken and goes about in rags) appear in two poems prior to this book. In 'Agua de otoño', to which I return, we also find the same adjective: 'a un lado el verso roto / todo remiendo a un lado' (to one side the broken verse / all mending to one side). And written in parentheses below the title, as if to attract the reader's attention, are the words: 'poesía incompleta y desunida' (incomplete and disconnected poetry). These words suggest that poems are missing, perhaps poems composed by the same date that have evidently been excluded. We are, therefore, looking at an incomplete book. Because the book is *broken,* its poetry is considered 'disconnected'. It seems that Soleida Ríos is not in conformity with her own poetry collection. It is broken. It is disconnected. It is incomplete: 'a un lado el verso roto / todo remiendo a un lado'. The rupture is what gives meaning to Soleida's new book but also what makes it unsatisfactory. *El libro roto* presents us with a kind of self-awareness, which is unusual in a poetry ensemble. On being titled as something broken, it presents itself as a double book: the one it might have been and the one it actually is. Something similar occurs in several of her poems: the poem is offered to the reader as a text. One sees the poet (in this case, the author whom the poet has invented); the reader sees the poet writing the poem.

I will stop for a minute to consider the emblematic 'Agua de otoño'. It deals with a page from her youth, and in it can be found evidence of Soleida Ríos' poetics. As a poem or as writing, 'Agua de otoño' is self-meditative. Before it is written on the page, it sees itself and, after being written, it becomes a kind of *puesta en escena* (stage set) of what was seen beforehand. Considering its period – around the seventies – 'Agua de otoño' begins in an unusual way. It starts off:

I hadn't thought of calling the poem Autumn Rains.
Instead I'd say
I love this man and I protect him
against the autumn rains against all

It is a poem that considers itself a poem, something written. There is also in it what we find later in *El libro roto*: a break in causal connection and the appearance of a broken narrative, scattered into fragments …. I say 'narrative' because narrative elements remain in Soleida's poetry, as they did in her colloquial texts. 'Agua de otoño' is a brief story. This characteristic scarcely exists in *El libro roto*: the poem is no longer reflexive or narrative. Its scattered fragments coalesce as if magnetised by some kind of tragic *élan*. The poems in *El libro roto* owe little to intelligence as an organising force. If each stanza proceeds according to an order in which art is visible, the whole stanza is not integrated into an evident order. Each poem is *broken*, in the sense that I indicated a moment ago. Like many books of modern poetry, *El libro roto* demonstrates that terms such as 'lucidity', 'reason', or 'intelligence' are not present in an uncomplicated way. They can be there and stop being there; at times, they can disappear and yet continue resonating after their disappearance into the deep underground of poetic creation. In 'Agua de otoño', a part of the drama of writing is masked: the poet leaning over the page trying to find the missing poem – 'who was it / who were they / they crossed to the blank page / to the page drowned in its forgotten cry / it is the page and it was not I'. In the poem 'Manuscript Found in a Trunk', at the beginning of *El libro roto*, she writes about the poem's impossibility as writing: 'when I feel that this was not possible / on this sheet of paper'. It is impossible for the poem to save the lover from the 'habit of loving' or to save the Revolution from frustrated promises. It is also impossible to return to childhood: 'Forgive me mother / I have found out that this was not possible'.

But the process does not end here. Because it concerns a broken book, the poetry extends in different directions, some more successful than others. Its rupture is part of its dynamism. Or, rather, of its freedom.

And it is this freedom – born of an impulse, of *fatum* – to which Soleida surrenders without feeling herself constrained to follow the precepts of a poetic school; in this freedom she finds a solution to the demise of the poetics of colloquialism. The best texts of *El libro roto* open her writing to a possibility: the freedom that extends from the use of spurious words such as 'mud', 'cover', and 'angel', – forbidden in the poetics of colloquialism – to the use of almost oneiric structures of discourse. Now her vision touches the dark side of things: political frustrations and negative characters, such as the traitor in 'a black light', who nevertheless burns brightly, reducing to ashes the paradises, which are presently lost paradises and oneiric gardens of delight.

Fear runs through *El libro roto*. Not the 'myopia of fear', not the kind that was intended – through a poem like 'Autumn Rains' – to save the lover from love's dangers, but now the fear is a light, a sane splendour: the lucidity between lost happiness and present terror. From the first poem – 'fear aborted me / when it was like a father to me / father of my rib' – and almost to the end of the book, with all its gradations, with its nightmares and sudden coldnesses, fear inhabits these poems and constitutes their profound reason for existing as writings. Fear of faults, fear of dying, fear hidden in 'the broken throat', fear of the unknown and fear of the known, of the unknown culpability and of the acknowledged guilt. Fear like an enemy and fear like a friend. Fear that makes us scream and the kind that makes us sleep. Before the end of *El libro roto*, one of the final lines reads, 'they lapidated fear in the melted ice of my face'.

Those sections of this book in which fear is not a performative presence nor a form of lucidity are less successful. There are two types of transcriptions in those sections: biblical prophesies (examples of poorly executed intertextuality), where the biblical text is usually cited as is or with slight changes, and where the force of the prophetic and comminatory spirit has been inexplicably softened; and transcriptions of the dreams of Soleida Ríos or of others, whose names are given in small letters. This simple transcription of certain dreams has little value: the dreamer turned into a bird, long hallways, a rain of fish, and decapitated heads, are the trite commonplaces of any oneiric writing. There are some excellent poems in the book, and this seems enough to me. Let me mention 'Cuerpo presente' (Final Rites), 'Maleva y los niños en el Paraiso' (Maleva and the Children in Paradise), 'Ultimo rezo para los ojos del traidor' (Last Prayer for the Traitor's Eyes), 'Martes 13 en el mar de los sargazos' (Tuesday 13 in the Sargasso Sea), and 'Un soplo dispersa los límites del hogar' (A Breath Scatters the Boundaries of Home). Although they are not many, I believe that they are enough to justify the importance of *El libro roto*. The last two have to be included among the great Cuban poems of recent years.

Among the things that Reina María Rodríguez told me about Soleida Ríos, there is another that I have not forgotten: 'When she comes to my house, I hide the plants. I'm afraid that she'll dry them with her look'. Shortly after, I met Soleida, and it was the first thing that I remembered. I looked into her eyes. What could have possibly happened to dry up Reina's sweet-basil plants? The eyes in Soleida's dark face have a singular, fixed radiance. As soon as we met, she invited me to her house, which she calls The Asteroid, and she asked me to tell her one of my dreams. She jotted down some details and then interpreted them. Not like Freud, but like ancient magicians and sorcerers. In the course of our friendship, she often read my future in the Celtic runes that she carries in her wallet inside a small purse, or in Tarot cards or hexagrams from the *Libro de las mutaciones* (Book of Mutations). She has the voice and gestures of a fortune-teller. When she wants to, she creates around her an ambience of augury, dressed in clothes down to her ankles and with her hair in braids like an African goddess.

Now, finally, I bring to the attention of those who forgot her. I bring to the attention of those who know her, those who disparage her without having read her or read her carelessly. I bring to the attention of young poets who look down on her or look at her as one does a piece of junk in a dusty corner. I bring to the attention of readers of good will and bad: the silence about Soleida Ríos has been broken.

Editor's translation

Edelma Zapata Pérez

EDELMA ZAPATA PÉREZ

COLOMBIA

(b. 1954)

In a short, personal narrative, 'The Coming to Consciousness of an Afro-Indo-Mulatto Woman Writer in the Multi-Ethnic Society of Colombia', poet Edelma Zapata Pérez traces the outlines of her life: shifts in family relationships, questions about identity, exposure to different cultures, and development as a creative writer. Born in the small town of La Paz, she visited Cartagena and moved, at age five, to Bogotá after her parents' separation. She was raised in a multi-racial family by her mother, a zamba *of African and Native American origin, her father, a prominent Afro-Colombian novelist, anthropologist, and medical doctor, and her stepmother, a Spaniard. As children, she and her sister Harlem Segunda de la Paz often visited their extended family, which included Amerindian-descended relatives living on Colombia's Atlantic coast as well as Spanish grandparents, who exposed the girls to the Catalonian language and heritage. The Zapata home was a centre of creative and intellectual activity, where Afro-Colombian culture, particularly music, dance, religion, and literature, was celebrated. It was there that the young poet, who began writing at age twelve, was introduced to books and became an avid reader; it was there that she met and dialogued with some of Colombia's most distinguished writers; it was there that she developed a strong social conscience and became interested in anthropology. She participated in discussions about racial identity, learned about African history, and read the works of Afro-Colombian writers such as Jorge Artel, Candelario Obeso, and Arnoldo Palacios.*

Zapata Pérez's exposure to various cultures was also enhanced by extensive travel. As a young girl, she accompanied her father to Mexico, where she lived with a Catholic family and learned many of the country's customs; later, on a trip to the United States, she spent several months at a

Catholic boarding school in Texas and met girls from other countries. She visited the United States again, when her father was a visiting professor at Howard University in Washington, DC. On her return to Bogotá in the early 1960s, she began reading the works of African, Caribbean, and African American writers such as Malcolm X and Frantz Fanon, and, through literature, became interested in the Civil Rights and Black Power movements. Her reading inspired action: while a university student, she read Marxist philosophy and participated in protest demonstrations and confrontations with the police. An anthropologist by training, Zapata studied at the National University in Bogotá, and she and her husband, a former classmate, attended graduate school in Barcelona for two years. On her return to Colombia, she started working in communications, particularly in radio and journalism. She also began research on popular culture at the Colombian Foundation of Folkloric Research, directed by Manuel Zapata Olivella.

Zapata Pérez's first collection of poetry, Ritual con mi sombra *(Ritual With My Shadow), was published in 1999. It contains thirty-seven poems written over a ten-year period, and it includes several poems that were published previously in literary journals such as* Letras Nacionales. *Divided into five sections with titles such as 'Miedos ancestrales' (Ancestral Fears) and 'Plegaria ciega' (Blind Prayer), the collection moves thematically from personal feelings and intimate relationships to more political concerns: violence and bloodshed. Although the poet alludes frequently to a bucolic landscape of forests, butterflies, and mangoes, the predominant mood of her work is sombre. With a muted voice, she writes of solitude, loneliness, pain, and lost love. Her short poems – sometimes no more than three lines – reveal a preoccupation with death, for her poetry is haunted by the ghosts of the departed.*

Death

Alone death arrives
white or dark,
bereft of beauty.

She steps heavily
or at times she steps so lightly
that she never feels herself.

I imagine her skinny,
her body arid and deserted
transparent and dressed.

Deep and tearing wound,
long like the night.
it sinks within the soul
calm and silent.

Life's lonely companion
mysterious coin of luck
deep the calm when you arrive.

Translated by Laurence E. Prescott

The Final Drop

You will be the next drop of river
that nourishes this sea of violent bloods.
You will be at the portal of those who do not exist
when your eyes blind yet still warm
open to the mystery of death
and anonymous mouths praise your deeds
of noble knight.

Ritual marches will evoke infinite nostalgias
accompanying your solitary night ...
the sand will fall like a rain of stars
on the solitude of your home,
but you will be forgotten the same day
on which they dig your tomb.

A prayer opens the road to affliction
and we tremble with fear when death
can surprise us once more,
and its arrival
can still be inopportune and perfect.

We keep silent, and a slow sadness
overflows in us.

Translated by Laurence E. Prescott

Ancestral Fears

I come from ancestral fears
metallic symbols imprison me
in the vast solitude of daydreams,
I listen to the voice of the drums conversing
with the flight of the dead.

I convoke you:
Totems,
Gods,
the invisible and visible world!
Come all with your thundering lightning
to liberate my tribe!

Translated by Laurence E. Prescott

The Consciousness-Raising of an Afro-Indo-Mulatto Woman Writer in Colombia's Multiethnic Society[1]

Many years have passed since that long-ago moment when I uttered my first shout, accompanied by tears that were destined, from the beginning, to become a river. That's what my mother says over and over again: 'We did not know how to quiet you, crying night and day. There was no way to distract you and no lullaby to put you to sleep. It was as if you did not want to join the kingdom of this world'.

Perhaps I should mention that the little town in which I was born – La Paz, César – became, because of its geographic position, a much-travelled thoroughfare for native migrations, Spanish exploratory and colonising expeditions, and African captives.[2] Extensive cattle estates, farms, and craft industries developed in the area. A thriving market in European goods emerged during the colonial period, when there was a substantial mixing of races and cultures; trade was important to feed the colonists and to carry raw materials to the large cities on the Iberian Peninsula.

My placenta is buried in this land of musicians and poets; I have always known that the inhabitants are marked by the continuous movement of humans and beasts, and by routes that direct the traveller toward adventure. As its name (La Paz) suggests, it is a tranquil place, but that name seems a contradiction today, because those large grassy plains have become fields of violence and death. The sun, when it spreads across this land, disperses all the shade. The mixed-race women of African and indigenous ancestry, who move – bodies erect like banners – from their houses to the river carrying washtubs on their heads, seem to dance to the swaying of their hips.

Colombian culture, a mixture of beliefs and customs that nurtured my early childhood, left a deep impression on me. My maternal core – an overwhelmingly indigenous and mulatto blend – consisted of grandparents and uncles and aunts who were and are black-skinned, but their features, their hair, and their customs are essentially Amerindian. Profoundly religious with rigid moral values (from their Spanish forefathers), they acquired their own unique blend of magical-religious ideas, songs, and music that were influenced by African beliefs. These are some of the elements that comprise this cultural tri-ethnicity, and of course culture shapes one's true identity.

My maternal grandparents, Ana and Diogenes, who died while I was still very young, were careful to leave lands and properties to their sons, but they also left their daughters well cared for. My mother, Maria, a beautiful and febrile fifteen-year-old zamba,[3] bewitched my father beneath the flame of a burning torch in the passionate steps of the *cumbia* dance.[4] I know for certain that this occurred, because my wanderer of a father would not have let himself be ensnared by her charms.

My paternal grandparents – Antonio, who was of African descent, and Edelmira, the daughter of a Spanish immigrant with Indian blood – had seven children. Their third youngest child was my father Manuel, who had two daughters with my mother María. My sister, Harlem Segunda de la Paz, inherited such a long name for a number of reasons: 'Harlem' for the Black community of New York; 'Segunda' because there was another Harlem before her, who died when barely a year old; and 'de la Paz' needs no explanation. Harlem never liked our father's vivid imagination. Our distinct and separate personalities have always marked the difference between us, and were the cause of our childhood squabbles. While I was always restless by nature, she was focused and little given to sentimentality. A mulatto, I inherited my African forefathers' looks; while I am slender, delicate, and dark-skinned, she received the sallow complexion, high cheekbones, and straight hair of the Indians.

We lived with our parents for the first five years, but I have just a few memories of family life during this period: occasions when we rode on our father's knees; outings decked out in our Sunday best; recollections of the narrow streets of historic Cartagena, where we spent some time.

Change of Abode

The early break-up of our home caused sudden changes in our lives. Separated from our mother, we moved to Bogotá to become part of a new family that included my father and his second wife, Rosa, a Catalonian recently arrived from Spain. We were six and seven years old then. This change in geographic and cultural setting would have profound repercussions on our identity.

The Bogotá that we came to know in 1964 was a cold, rainy, and sombre city. The night that we arrived, we went straight to an apartment in the downtown area, very close to the Central Cemetery. I will never forget how surprised I was by an advertisement of a bar called 'The Last Tear', where men and women in dark, heavy *ruanas* and felt hats drank beer and shed their last tears for their deceased loved ones.

An important cultural event was to occur. Rosa was waiting for us at home. She had sewn for us white sheets adorned with a beautiful lace edging woven by our new Spanish grandmother. My mother María used to fix our hair, straightening it with grease made out of *corozo* oil, which was called 'black butter' in keeping with an African tradition.[5] The next day, the beautiful white pillowcases were black with grease, so Rosa washed our hair until the last drop of oil had disappeared. From that day on, my curly hair would be permanently arranged in braids.

My life in the capital marked the discovery of my blackness – a slow, painful, and anguished road toward my origins. There were few persons of my colour in this city then, so we – my sister and I – , accompanied by a white, blonde mother, became the objects of covert stares and comments by those who feigned a mordant show of pity: 'What pretty little Black girls!' Harlem paid no attention to the colour of her skin, but I reacted differently, perhaps because my African features included more than colour. Slowly, I became insecure and uncertain of my identity, and I also had a vague desire to have lighter skin. One factor that later resulted in a feeling of self-marginalisation was the longing to have straight hair. When my friends' hair would move in the wind that blew through the school bus window, I would be pierced right to the core. I longed for that movement: 'My hair was always so still!' I recognise now that such behaviour created inhibitions that confirmed doubts about my identity.

The Mirror of Electra

The image that I have of my father is of someone who loves his craft – literature. In the course of my life, I have seen him stick to a rigid discipline of work and research. I recall conversations carried on with friends such as Germán Espinosa, Héctor Rojas Herazo, Enrique Posada, Eduardo Pachón, and others when they visited our home.[6] Thus, I understood that one of man's most pleasant satisfactions is to make a passion of his work. Another thing to which my father has devoted part of his life is the study of Afro-Colombian culture. Identity was a topic that I heard since I was little. I cannot help but smile now, because identity seems to be a banner for cultural development and programmes created by the Ministry of Culture to be broadcast throughout the country. Suddenly 'culture' seems to be the fashionable topic, and the word 'identity', like so many others – 'democracy' and 'liberty' – has lost its original meaning. Nevertheless, it is important to emphasise here some elements of cultural difference and racial assimilation with respect to my parents, because their views on race influenced my childhood immensely.

My mother María never thought of identity as an integral part of her life, because she, like many others in this country, showed a lack of interest in her origins. One of my clearest memories is of my arrival for vacations at my mother's home in La Paz. The first person that my mother, who has straight, Indian hair, would call when we got home was the woman in charge of straightening kinky hair like mine. From my curly hair would emerge a completely transformed head, a head of straight hair, the ends of which fell like arrows on my shoulders. This comforted my mother, because she could never put up with the curly hair that I wore with a certain pride.

From Rosa, our new mother, we received influences from Catalan culture. We used to listen to stories about her life, her travels, the Spanish Civil War, and everyday family experiences. Hispanic influences nourished our upbringing.

A Look at the Old World

Two years later, our parents took us to Europe on a merchant ship, where we were the only passengers on board. It was a voyage of wonderful surprises: the sea, an expanse that enveloped me like a fish with no more horizons than the waves and the depth of the sky; my gaze lost in the infinite was no longer a fish but a flexible bird flying over the twilight. The sailors would surprise us when we stealthily peeked out from our bunks at compasses, caps, pictures, and wooden ships – all strange and mysterious toys that spoke to us of their travels. The penetrating odours of the ship and the sea lurked in the corners along with the creaking noises of the wood. When the ocean's swells coincided with meal times, the unfastened glasses, plates, and silverware began an indescribable dance; we screamed and laughed in the midst of the tension, while trying to grab the dishes.

We landed at Le Havre, France. From there we travelled by train to Paris and then to Barcelona. Family life with our grandparents – Emilio Bosch Roger, a painter, and Teresa Pérez, a small woman of delicate features – and their son Francisco, shaped the Spanish home. When my parents took a trip to Germany, we were left alone for the first time in a place that was totally unfamiliar to us. Rosa's father, who was blind for several years, and our grandmother, who was diligent and obliging, began introducing us to an unknown world. We felt like strangers in a place where everything was new and different: the meals; the trolley that disappeared like a worm into the Tibidabo Mountain; the seasons, especially winter with its bare trees and frightening snow, which my sister would throw at my head in fistfuls; the buildings with their large windows reflecting dark sunsets; the elevators; and a little jack-in-the-box, which everyone opened and closed in a different way. Inside the box anything could happen; Jack could remain suspended in air or he could peek from the cracks of inner rooms while waiting for a visitor.

In the afternoons we went religiously with Emilio and Teresa to the same café where they had lunch. The light that radiated from the table lamps and the warm reception of the employees, who treated us with friendliness and affection, surprised us. Finally, we took the place over.

First Readings and Adolescence

Reading always captivated me. As a child, I had many storybooks at my disposal. We used to go with Rosa to the bookstore. I was attracted to books with drawings that illustrated the fantastic world of the story. I was obliged more than once to stop reading at dinner time, because of my flights to the land of imagination. Around the time that I was twelve years old, I began trying to write, and my awkward narratives, which I could barely understand, were shaped by fantastic plots and unreal characters, such as fairies and princes.

Although I barely noticed it, adolescence began some years later, bringing with it different conflicts. It was an age of defiance and contradictions. During this period, I travelled with my father to Mexico, and this contact with a different culture made me appreciate its strong indigenous heritage. I lived with a Catholic family and learned their customs: their dances, mariachis, dress, foods, et cetera. I have a vague recollection of the parochial school that I attended, but do not remember the experience that undoubtedly influenced my spiritual development. At the end of my stay, I travelled to El Paso, Texas on the Mexican-North American border, where I spent the first month with a Chicana friend, who worked at a university high school. Through her and her friends, I became acquainted somewhat with the situation of the Mexican resident in the United States. During my six months in that city, I was enrolled in a boarding school run by nuns, where the girls were of different nationalities: North American, Japanese, Chilean, Spanish, Argentine, Peruvian, Venezuelan, and others.

The dialogues about our respective countries enriched my knowledge of the differences and similarities between people. This was the period when I used wigs and make-up. I don't know if that was indicative of the affectation that is characteristic of youth, or if it was an echo of Black American alienation. The visit gave me a taste of America, which I added to my cultural experiences.

I was having experiences and emotions that were foreign to my origin as a country girl who was born in a Valledupar province. I remember my astonishment at finding myself in brightly lit cities that contrasted with the darkness of my birthplace.

Back to My Roots

On my return to Bogotá I continued my secondary school studies. Around that time, an African American researcher named Laurence Prescott used to visit our home. A young friend of my father's who was interested in his literary work, Prescott used to plunge into the library to consult notes and writings. A tall man, he looked like a long-legged giraffe whose body extended above my eyes. His clear, hearty laughter, which flooded the house with joy, still resounds in my ears. His interest in Afro-Colombians reinforced my curiosity about my forebears. For the first time, I saw the image of a woman who proudly revealed her beauty rather than the faceless image of the Afro-Colombian woman who was disfigured by an ugly, servile stereotype.

My curiosity about race led me to read African American literature about the 1960s: the repercussions of Martin Luther King's non-violent movement, protests and demonstrations against discrimination and racial violence, militant and radical movements such as that of the Black Panthers, Communist political action as represented by Angela Davis, and Malcolm X's autobiography. I also have to mention Frantz Fanon's book, *The Wretched of the Earth*. Works would appear in my father's library, and I would read them without any particular orientation. I devoured those texts, and they strengthened my understanding of my ancestors and enhanced my father's sermons about the history of Africa, which was presented in school as a land of 'savages' without any reference to the great splendour of its ancient cultures.

From that moment, I knew the source of the discriminatory opinions that people held about Indians and Africans in Colombia; I understood that the history we learned was the coloniser's history, and that a new version had to be written.

Elegba, the god who opens roads, protects my steps, and for the second time I visited the United States with my father. I admired the city of

Washington with its beautiful monuments, museums, and neighbourhoods. My father gave a lecture at Howard University on his novel *Chambacú, corral de negros*. I realised that the students wanted to know about Afro-Colombians, about their potential and their opportunities in a society that oppresses and discriminates against them. In spite of this oppression, my people – whether they live in the country or the city – are equally authentic and creative in their daily struggle. In his spirituality, the contemporary and universal 'Afro' man bears witness to his ancient roots. When I gaze into my ancestors' mirror, I see harmony of movement and the sound of a slow, plaintive saxophone that echoes the lament of a far-flung prayer.

Times of Re-encounter

My admission to the National University's College of Anthropology in Bogotá opened up an unsuspected field of new possibilities, philosophies, attitudes, and commitments: human sciences, exposure to different cultures, my first experience in political militancy, student demonstrations, police confrontations, readings in Marxist philosophy, study sessions, and ideological beliefs.

Student living also offered me another dimension of life: marriage to a classmate, with whom I travelled a year later to Barcelona to continue our studies. At that time, Spain was experiencing a period of democratisation, after forty years of dictatorship and repression under Franco: restoration of the monarchy, legalisation of political parties, the election of Felipe Suárez as president, the awakening of a people who had been silenced for so many years.

The interaction with different nationalities allowed me to see myself in many mirrors: Catalonian, Basque, Galician, Andalusian, Aragones, and so forth. Dynamic vernacular languages were used freely after many years of censorship. One sensed this freedom spirit in the festive atmosphere of flags waving in the wind and the unbridled joy of young people. The boulevards were swarming with people and colours, and the air was fragrant with promise. The academic ambience of Barcelona nurtured my intellectual life with its pronounced Catalonian nationalist heritage. Most of the classes were taught in the Catalan language. The warm and generous instructors gave me criteria for analysis and an understanding of anthropological theory and praxis. Occasionally, I felt some racial discrimination, but, more often, I experienced friendship and other human values.

Eager to know European culture, I visited Paris, London, and the French and Spanish Mediterranean on furtive trips, and I finally landed in Morocco.

My arrival in that country coincided with the holy period of Ramadan. The streets of Tangiers were silent, while the mosques teemed with worshippers. The pilgrims were praying on their knees in the courtyards. The city of Fez, with its Arabic architecture, revealed to me a world different from that of the West, one which spoke to me with ancestral voices about the creativity of mankind.

Poetry, An Open Window

Loaded as I was with so many strange and personal experiences, my return to Colombia was a rebirth of forgotten roots. I began work at the Colombian Foundation of Folkloric Research, headed by my father, on projects related to the collection of popular culture, especially the oral tradition. I discovered the ancient philosophy of Colombia, one that brings together the indigenous, African, and European traditions – all the currents that commingle in my blood. I naturally gravitated toward the reading of poets and novelists who write about the ancestors, the drums, and the rattling of chains.

Afro-Colombian poetry led to my acquaintance with the most outstanding negritude writers in Colombia: Jorge Artel, who evoked adolescent boatmen, Indian flutes, and drums; Helcias Martán Góngora, navigator of lost coasts; Candelario Obeso of Mompós, the awakening of freedom; Arnoldo Palacios, excavator of bloodstained alluvia; Manuel Zapata Olivella, nearer in his fictional narration than in his physical geography; and Rogerio Valásquez, explorer of the Afro-Colombian under social injustice.[7]

My adolescent verses were a loud scream that did not resonate in the work of Afro-Colombian poets, who were more concerned with singing about a woman's physical and sensuous attributes than about her spirituality. It bothered me that this poetic expression was written solely by men in a society that oppresses and marginalises us. My poetic dabbling was notable primarily as an expression of my new awareness. The flowing of this river was slow and tortuous over the course of painful years. The violence expressed in Colombian literature of the past – a past that was apparently forgotten – rekindled the fire of political and social passions. Death appeared under another name but with the same hatred and rancour. It was not easy for an anthropologist to go about the countryside with a notebook and tape recorder on her shoulder interviewing widows and orphans about their trampled traditions.

In spite of this tragic loss of identity, *Letras Nacionales* emerged to herald literary nationalism.[8] Unpublished as well as established writers were invited to contribute to the journal, to examine their surroundings, and to affirm their patriotism in poems, novels, and short stories. I was not insensitive to the literature that passed through my hands before being printed on the small rotary press that besmeared with ink those of us who operated it. The beehive of my imagination began to swarm with blind verses in search of light. My poem 'Death' is from that period.

Today, I write poems about man: his solitude, dehumanisation, light, and darkness. My verse is a small, live coal that I keep burning in spite of the passage of time; my song is a cosmic chant/dance in my search for the magical word; my skin is moistened by all the seas; my blood is the depth of the wind that passed by and fertilised my womb; my name is the magic amulet of my forebears. All of that I express in 'Ancestral Fears', while 'The Final Drop' is about the violence that intoxicates a country. In conclusion, let us ponder what an ancient poet from deepest Africa wrote more than three thousand years ago:

> *To think that I am unable to say anything new which our*
> *ancestors have not said!* (Speech of Ankú, 1900)

Translated by Laurence E. Prescott

Notes

1.   This translation is based on the paper 'Toma de consciencia de una escritora afroindomulata: en la sociedad multiétnica colombiana', presented at the IX meeting of the Association of Colombianists (University of the Andes, Bogotá, Colombia, July 1995), and on a revised version published in *América Negra* [Bogotá] 11 (1996): 175-185.
2.   The small town of La Paz (which means Peace) is located in the Department of Cesar on Colombia's Atlantic coast.
3.   *Zamba/o* is a person of mixed African (Black) and Indian parentage or ancestry.
4.   The *cumbia,* a centuries-old popular dance that originated among Colombia's Atlantic coast peoples, manifests a blend of African, Amerindian, and European elements. Female dancers carry and hold aloft lighted candles, while male dancers, doffing hats, pursue them. Some scholars speculate that the *cumbia*, whose name may derive from *cumbé*, referring to a dance of African origin, is rooted in fertility rites. See Delia Zapata Olivella, 'La cumbia, síntesis musical de la nación colombiana. Reseña histórica y coreográfica,' *Revista Colombiana de Folclor* 3.7 (1962): 187-204.
5.   *Coroza* (from the indigenous word *corojo*) refers to a palm tree (possibly *Elaeis melanococca* or *Alfonso oleifera*) found in Colombia, whose fruit

yields a greasy substance from which an oil (cf. African palm oil) is extracted or made.

6. Germán Espinosa (1938), poet, novelist, and short story writer, Hectór Rojas Herazo (1921), poet and prize-winning novelist, and Eduardo Pachón Padilla (1920), a noted literary critic, historian, and compiler of several major collections of Colombian short stories, are all natives of the Atlantic coast. Enrique Posada (1936), is a journalist, novelist, and short story writer from the city of Medellín in the Department of Antioquía.

7. Jorge Artel (1909, Cartagena to 1994, Barranquilla), Colombia's leading poet of negritude, whose publications include *Tambores en la noche* (1940; 1955; 1986); Helcias Martán Góngora (1920, Guapi to 1984, Cali), known as the poet of Colombia's Pacific Coast and author of more than thirty books of poetry and prose; Candelario Obeso (1849, Mompós to 1884, Bogotá), whose *Cantos populares de mi tierra* (1877) earned him recognition as the nation's first Black poet who expressed the sentiments and condition of the Negroid masses; Arnoldo Palacios (1924, Certegui, Chocó), author of *Las estrellas son negras* (1949) and other works of fiction; Manuel Zapata Olivella (1920), internationally noted writer, whose many publications include the prize-winning novel *Changó el gran putas* (1938); Rogerio Velásquez (1918, Sipi, Chocó to 1965, Bogotá), anthropologist, educator, poet and author of *Las memorias del odio* (1953).

8. *Letras Nacionales* is the literary journal founded and published by Manuel Zapata Olivella in Bogotá. Its initial period lasted from 1965 to 1970; the second series ran from 1973 to approximately 1979.

Yvonne-América Truque

✐vonne- América Truque

COLOMBIA/CANADA

(1955–2001)

One of the most important contemporary Latino-Canadian writers, Truque was born in Santa Fe de Bogotá, Colombia, where she grew up in an activist, literary family that included her mother Nelly, a trade unionist, two sisters – Sonia, a short story writer, and Colombia, a poet and editor of the bilingual literary review Vericueto – *and her father Carlos Arturo Truque, the noted Afro-Colombian writer. In 1974, the nineteen-year-old began writing poetry and moved to Spain, where she studied sociology at the Universidad Complutense in Madrid for two years. On her return to Colombia in 1979, she became seriously interested in writing while working at the National Library; she gave poetry readings and published her work in three anthologies. A committed writer who was disturbed by conditions in her homeland, Truque dealt with issues of social justice – poverty, urban blight, and political corruption – in language that is passionate, unadorned, and uncomplicated.*

Truque published her first collection of poetry, Proyección de los silencios *(Projecting Silences) in Bogotá in 1983, a second edition in 1984, and a bilingual (Spanish/French) edition in Montreal in 1986. The twenty-four poems, including the sombre 'Debatiéndome en el mundo' (Debating Myself in the World) and the rebellious 'Mujer batalla' (Warrior Woman), which she wrote for the 1983 International Year of the Woman, describe the pain of lost love, economic exploitation, abuse of political power, and the struggle for self-actualisation. After moving to Montreal, Quebec in 1984, Truque became active in literary and cultural circles: she sponsored poetry readings, organised Montreal's largest Spanish-speaking poetry event, and with her husband Jean Gauthier, whom she later divorced, founded the Centre d'Etudes et de Diffusion des Amériques Hispanophones (Centre for the Study and Dissemination of the*

Hispanophone Americas), a Spanish-language publishing company. Besides Truque's books, the CEDAH has published over fifteen titles by Latino-Québécois writers.

Ironically, it was in Canada that the poet began exploring the African roots of her identity, particularly those of the predominantly Black Chocó region on Colombia's Pacific coast, where her father originated. She began performing her poetry to the rhythms of the jembé *drum and, in 1994, she participated in Toronto's Mixed Art Festival, accompanied by Afro-Colombian musician Diego Marulanda. These performances brought critical acclaim to the writer, whose poems, essays, and prose pieces have been frequently anthologised. The poem 'Sin fronteras' (Without Boundaries) was a finalist in the 1986 contest of* Humanitas *magazine and a year later, 'Eliminando el sin embargo' (Eliminating the However) won first prize in the same contest. In 1991, Truque published* Retratos de sombras y perfiles inconclusos: *the first part 'Shadow Portraits', contains ten eight-line elegies to the dead and the disappeared, while the poems in 'Unfinished Portraits' suggest, through images of light and flight, the possibility of freedom from oppression. As the titles of her books indicate, Truque is concerned with the silence and shadows into which those at the bottom of society – the beggars, prostitutes, criminals, derelicts, and abandoned children – retreat out of alienation, despair, and hopelessness. Her poetry is a powerful and passionate instrument in the defence of human dignity and social justice. On April 27, 2001, shortly before Yvonne América-Truque's death from lung cancer, Howard University's Department of Modern Languages and Literatures organised a seminar at which she was honoured as a major Afra-Hispanic writer.*

Warrior Woman

To Julia Abril

It was she. I saw her one day
she seemed the same and I . . .
and I, did not know her.

She came out of years
disrobing her footsteps.
Her belly world-swollen
she was a So! So! of freedom
        missing
entoning her angry rebelliousness

She came out of time and in her eyes
the sun, the moon, the sky
had settled
in an infinite longing to live her life.

Then, I saw her running the streets
with rage lodged in her bowels
breaking Silence-Fetters
Institution-Home
        Falsehood ! ! !

She said live to future-dream
She said: I will live to tomorrow-wander

It was she. Yes! I saw her one day
There I recognised myself and we said to be embattled
I recognised myself in her
and we said to be barricaded.
We left riding horseback over our desires
to become woman-future
to become woman-tomorrow.

International Day of the Woman: March 8, 1983
Editor's translation

. . . Being a Woman and Writing

*. . . Being a woman and writing is being the heroine
who has escaped from the flames. It is being the
conjurer who uncovers and transforms secret terrains
in a sacred word-ritual.*

*. . . Being a woman and writing is awakening from
the spell of a thousand-year-old dream, invoking
consequent words that come back and remind us of
the real meaning of life.*

*. . . Being a woman and writing is accepting
knowledge of the occult in each phase of life. It is
being the female messenger who reestablishes the
cognitive link that reason has broken.*

*. . . Being a woman and writing is ceasing to exist in
order to Live. It is living in order to understand. It is
learning in order to know. It is knowing in order to
reveal, it is revealing in order to transform.*

Editor's translation

On that Underbrush that has Entrapped Us

I walk
alone, my steps lost
in the interlacing streets
of the sleeping city.

I breathe
air of cars honking
nauseous gas
fetid rotting garbage.

Tango music comes
from an ancient bar on the corner.

Arcades
cradle curled up children, the homeless, drunks,
one man hidden like a hungry wolf
lying waiting for its prey
Someone's just been knifed!!!

Whores
and customers in the shadows
all blur into the night.

Stoplights, streets
streets, noise
noise, bars
bars, soldiers
Bullets!!
I walk
silently
on the humid asphalt
The clocks have stopped.

Tomorrow
I'll read the newspapers, and on the front page
the headline will be
'NEW QUEEN CHOSEN FOR COFFEE FESTIVAL'

Someone is Sleeping

Moon
   rolling
      cautiously
Embracing
        flicker
   of
      lights
Grey satin,
   the rain has stopped
My street is gleaming again

As I smoke a cigarette
far-off silences surround me
perhaps detecting
an unexpected event
Wind
   battering
      fragile
        windowpanes

Fine
   brush
      of wind
mute brush painting in silence
coagulating words with no meaning
Today I don't know how to say anything
it's midnight
and somewhere
a child is wandering in silence
walking aimlessly through his loneliness
while
   in great houses
the executioners sleep peacefully

Untitled
From 'Retratos de Sombras' (Portraits of Shadows)

There is no promised land, nor paradise
No homeland to cling to
After the long voyage
And a seedless return
Anger unites with nostalgia
For what might have been but in which so many failed
I walk past ruins, rubble, muddy corpses
My people are being murdered and I call out to them

VI

From 'Perfiles inconclusos' (Unfinished Profiles)

Ah! No, No, No, No!
This time…
I will not give you the pleasure
of drinking my blood
drop by drop
Nor of playing with my dreams
Or appropriating my words

No, No, No, No!
This time…
I am moulding wings of greater strength
and none of you
shall hold me back
from this final flight

VII
From 'Perfiles inconclusos' (Unfinished Profiles)

For you, I have just ended
my world in yours
and I skilfully separate
a past full of solitudes both voluntary and imposed

I
deliberately
destroy my world

For you, I will forever invent
whatever moon you desire and put it in your hands
the fulfilment of games
places all our own

For you, my love is different
though as tomorrows and years pass
and distance approaches
in your illusion of creating yourself
you may possibly even
hate me

for my daughter Isabelle

Yvonne-América Truque: A New Female Voice From Colombia

Marvin A. Lewis

In the introduction to the anthology *Woman Who Has Sprouted Wings: Poems by Contemporary Latin American Women Poets*, Mary Crow, the editor, states:

> The question of the specific contributions of contemporary women poets to the larger world of poetry is difficult and problematic. If we measure Latin American women poets by their appearance in national and international anthologies, they have clearly been judged wanting – if, indeed, they have been judged at all, since their work is frequently not even considered. To what degree is this their invisibility as women and to what degree their measurement against a false standard? Are there themes, kinds of imagery, language, particular to women poets generally or to Latin American women poets specifically? (23)

The issue of the representation of women writers from Latin America is certainly not new. There have been, and still are, efforts to make their works better known to the reading public. Although Yvonne-America Truque's poetry is not included in the anthology *Woman Who Has Sprouted Wings*, it is interesting to note that she shares many of the concerns expressed as being characteristics of contemporary Latin American women poets, especially in Truque's attitudes toward language, nature, urban life, and the poor and oppressed. In her poems, Truque does not appear to concentrate specifically upon developing a female sensibility at the expense of other human issues. Rather, as a woman writer, her commitment is inextricably bound to problematic issues in Colombia, in particular, and Latin America, in general. Consequently, her writing cannot be limited to the 'themes, kinds of imagery, [and] language, particular to women poets'.

Yvonne-América Truque, who emigrated from Bogotá, Colombia to Montreal, Canada is the daughter of Carlos Arturo Truque, one of the most renowned Afro-Colombian writers. Her major publication, *Proyección de los silencios* (Projecting Silences), has appeared in several chapbook editions and was published in Canada in a definitive bilingual Spanish / French edition. Truque was very active in the Colombian literary scene since she first began to give readings in 1982; her works appeared in periodicals, and she was affiliated with the literary group 'Arbol de Tinta' (Ink Tree). The present volume of poetry is an expanded version of *Projección de los silencios* and *Selección poética, 1977-1982* (Selected Poetry). This brief presentation is a discussion of some of the major themes and techniques prevalent in the poetry of Truque.

Proyección contains twenty-four poems of exceptional artistic quality, which express a profound degree of disillusion with the human condition. Alienation, the urban experience, solitude, and existence are primary thematic concerns of the author. Truque's message is conveyed most often through the techniques of surrealism and contrasts: between light and shadow, day and night, life and death. Several selections will suffice to demonstrate these tendencies. 'Poema 4' (Poem 4), in spite of its brevity, is concerned with human destiny and the precariousness of existence:

Eramos tan frágiles y livianos
como una gaviota en el aire,
o como la hoja que en otoño
el viento arrastra . . . y cae. (28)

(We were as fragile and light
as sea gulls in the air
or like the leaf which in autumn
the wind carries . . . and drops.)*

In this instance, human frailty and grace are juxtaposed through similes of non-permanence; the gazelle, which is pure form and agility, contrasts with the archetypal leaf, a metaphor that symbolises life's passing. Both images are analogous to the human condition.

Similar in tone is the poem, 'Y que bella ha sido' (And how beautiful has been), which is an expression of existential anguish, occasioned by an uncaring urban environment:

. . . y que bella ha sido esta noche
de sueños, divagaciones y añoranzas
esperando el aullido rudo de la mañana

que inclemente volverá a entregarme
al doloroso vacío, de esta ciudad
B A S U R E R O ! ! ! ! (11)

(. . . and how beautiful this night has been
of dreams, digressions and longings
awaiting the rude howl of morning
which unceremoniously will return to deliver me
to the painful emptiness, of this city
G A R B A G E   D U M P !)

The sense of estrangement, exacerbated by the urban experience expressed in this selection, is reflective of the concerns of many of the poems in *Proyección de los silencios*. By contrasting the beauty of the nocturnal poetic ambience with the impending ugliness of daily reality, the poet expresses disenchantment with the inevitable cycles of the universe. On a more concrete level, in this poem the dreams, digressions, and longings of the nocturnal contemplative mood are overshadowed by the surreal emptiness of an urban, human wasteland.

Indeed, the city is not presented as a positive force in *Proyección*. For instance, 'De ese maraña que nos ha atrapado' (About That Undergrowth That's Trapped Us) is a metaphorical walk on the wild side from the perspective of an outsider:

> Camino
> solitaria, paso perdido
>
> . . . .
>
> Prostitutas
> maleantes y señores
> todos confundidos en la noche.
> Semáforos, calles
> calles, ruidos
> ruidos, bares
> bares, militares
> !Balas!! (19-20)
>
> (I walk
> alone, my steps lost
>
> . . . .

                    Whores
        and customers in the shadows
        all blur into the night.
                    Stoplights, streets
                    streets, noise
                    noise, bars
                    bars, soldiers
                        Bullets!)

In the first stanza, 'alone' and 'steps lost' reflect the initial distance – physical
and psychological – between object and observer. There is a sense of
suffocation, of claustrophobia generated by both human and non-human
contaminants of the environment. This compounds the sense of degradation
felt in a dehumanised and violent milieu in which humans are cast aside
and criminals stalk their prey. Thus, the underbelly of the city is exposed,
meshing the haves and the have-nots in a nauseating amalgam of sights,
sounds, and smells. This experience is timeless, on the periphery, however,
because the players are anonymous and their suffering is not as meaningful
as the positive, superficial images presented by the official media as the
protagonist dares to look into the future.

    Not all of the selections from *Proyección* deal with bleak, exterior
situations. There are moments reserved for the emotions and meaningful
human interactions. Those poems interpreting love, memory, absence,
and time are exemplary. To illustrate, 'Poema 3' reads:

    Abrí indistintamente
    de mi memoria una página.
    Encontré tus ojos escrutándome
    y una perla que por mi mejilla rodaba. (27)

    (I opened vaguely
    a page from my memory.
    I found your eyes examining me
    and a pearl that rolled down my cheek.)

This process of remembrance and discovery involves peeling off layers of
unpleasant experiences in an effort to examine one of the most fundamental
human emotions. The point of departure is a past amorous encounter that
surfaces in the present. The sense of longing is most profound in the poem
'A un amigo ausente' (To an Absent Friend):

Qué tristeza!
     Esta tarde
mis pasos se perdieron
en los angostos corredores
de esta ciudad impía.
En hojas muertas
        ya pisadas. (37)

(How sad!
     This evening
my steps were lost
in the wide corridors
of this godless city
In already dead and
        treaded leaves.)

In this instance, the tension inherent in the urban environment helps to exacerbate the sense of aloneness and sadness experienced by the protagonist. The physical reality of a 'ciudad impía' (godless city) filled with 'hojas muertas / pisadas' (dead / treaded leaves) stands in stark contrast to the mental escape projected in 'imaginarias nubecillas de algodón' (imaginary little cotton clouds). This dialectical relationship between the real and the imagined still results in frustration because the reciprocal response that the persona is seeking appears to be blowing in the wind. These same sentiments are conveyed in the poems, 'Un recuerdo' (A Memory) and 'Tu rostro' (Your Face).

The only poem in *Proyección* that is devoted specifically to the situation of women is 'Mujer batalla' (Warrior Woman), which was written to celebrate the International Women's Day on March 8, 1983. An image is presented of a combative female who is out to right some societal wrongs. She is an archetypal person, who is not impeded by temporal or spatial limitations: 'Venía del tiempo y en sus ojos / se habían instalado el sol / La luna, el cielo / en un infinito desear vivir su vida' (She came out of time and in her eyes / were implanted the sun / The moon, the sky / in an infinite desire to live her life) (9). The challenge, for the narrator, is to convert this image into meaningful experience. She reacts:

Me reconocí en ella
y dijimos ser barricada.
Salimos cabalgando en nuestros deseos

para ser mujer futuro
para ser mujer mañana. (10)

(I recognized myself in her
and we were said to be a barricade.
We left riding our desires
to be future women
to be women of tomorrow.)

There is total identification with this symbolic female, who represents ideals toward which one should aspire in order to forge a more promising future for women. Significantly, this affirmation of the positive values of struggle takes place in a militant environment rather than in the domestic sphere or within the confines of motherhood.

From these examples, one can conclude that *Proyección de los silencios* is composed of a number of intense, human poems. For the most part, these selections are cerebral, meditative works of silence and introspection. Their overall meaning is best summed up in the book's central metaphor, the poem 'Debatiéndome en el mundo' (Debating Myself in the World), which assesses the plight of human beings as it relates to poetic creation:

Vuelvo aquí, a mi lámpara y papeles
para susurrar, decir, gritar!!
Que un fuego me abrasa todos los rincones.
Y sigo vagando y recorriendo mis moradas
como recorrer las calles en tardes de soles. (26)

(I return here, to my lamp and papers
in order to whisper, to talk, to shout!
That a fire burns all of my being
And I keep drifting and searching my resting place
like roaming the streets on sunny afternoons.)

The attempt to transform lived and observed experience into words is a difficult process. The poet's inability to articulate the sentiments of the less fortunate often results in disillusion and discontent. 'No habrá paz. Para mi alma / no hay sosiego' (There will be no peace. For my soul / there is no rest) (25) is the expressed attitude. This degree of anguish results in the characteristic restlessness that is prevalent throughout *Proyección de los silencios*, thereby expressing a desire for many positive changes.

* Editor's Note: All translations from Spanish into English are by Marvin A. Lewis, except for the poem 'De ese maraña que nos ha atrapado', which was translated by Hugh Hazelton.

Works Cited

Crow, Mary, ed. *Woman Who Has Sprouted Wings: Poems by Contemporary Latin American Women Poets*. Pittsburgh: Latin American Literary Review Press, 1984.
Truque, Yvonne-América. *Proyección de los silencios*. Montreal: CEDAR, 1986.

Cristina Cabral

CRISTINA CABRAL

URUGUAY

(b. 1959)

Called one of the most talented Afro-Uruguayan writers since Virginia Brindis de Salas and Pilar Barrios, Cristina Rodríguez Cabral is one of the first Black women in Uruguay to earn a university degree and to pursue graduate study in the United States. She is a highly educated professional, who obtained a nursing degree, completed a bachelor's in sociology at the Universidad de la República Oriental del Uruguay, received a master's in English from Indiana University of Pennsylvania, and is presently a doctoral candidate at the University of Missouri-Columbia. She has been actively involved in literary and cultural events in both Latin America and the United States, lecturing at universities in Sao Paolo and Rio de Janeiro, representing Uruguay at conferences such as the Second Profile of Black Literature and the First Centenary of the Abolition of Slavery in Brazil, and participating in Afro-Hispanic research conferences in Missouri and the Yari Yari Black Women's Conference in New York.

Cabral began writing at age twelve but did not become serious about her work until ten years later, when she began writing prose pieces that reflected her extensive reading of novels. At a writer's conference in Brazil, when participants insisted on calling her a poet, Jorge Amado explained, 'Don't fool yourself. You are a poet. You want to run from poetry. Why?' Although she has written a novel and essays such as 'Literature as a Form of Resistance', '100 Years of Abolition', and 'Afro-Uruguayan Literature', she has made her mark as a poet. In 1986, her novel Bahía, mágica Bahía *won first prize in Cuba's Casa de las Américas literary contest, and in 1989,* De par en par *(Wide Open), a collection of poetry and poetic prose was published by* Mundo Afro *(Black World) in Uruguay. Her poetry has also appeared in journals such as the* Afro-Hispanic Review *and* PALARA *(which also published her interview with Costa Rican novelist Quince Duncan), as well as in Alberto Britos'* Antología de poetas negros *(1990), the first anthology of Black Uruguayan poetry. Although she has written nine books of poetry, only one,* Desde mi trenchera *(From My Trench), has been published. Some of the others include* Pájaros sueltos *(Loose Birds),* Entre giros y mutaciones *(Between Turns and Changes),* La del espejo y yo *(The Woman in the Mirror and I), and the recent* Memoria y resistencia *(Memory and Resistance), which was written in the United States.*

Although Cristina Cabral's intellectual and literary formation occurred in Uruguayan schools and universities, her ideas, particularly those relating to race, gender, and identity, matured in Brazil and the United States, where she was exposed to Afrocentric culture and philosophy. Her early work, patterned after more mainstream writers, focused on love, intimate feelings, and feminine experiences, while her mature verse, particularly that written after 1995, reveals her increased militancy and views on social issues: racism and poverty, sexism in machista societies, psychic and cultural alienation, Uruguay's African roots, and her identity as a Black woman. Her experiences in Brazil, particularly her exposure to the African-centred culture of Bahía, introduced her to negritude; it was there and in the United States that she discovered her own identity. She wrote, 'I defined myself as a Black woman, a broader concept than that of an Afro-Uruguayan. In the United States, I feel more Afro-Latina, or rather a minority among other minorities'. As an Afro-Latina, Cristina Cabral has been exposed to a new language, an alien space, and overt racism – experiences that are powerfully reflected in her most recent poetry.

25 August 1988

Ah, this winter that so slowly takes its leave, with its days on which whirlwinds alternate with radiant sun, intermittent drizzle with great storms. August is a burgeoning of flowering trees, rose petals bursting forth; the greening once again of shiny leaves that had withdrawn into themselves, hiding from the cold, sleeping, enclosed in their coffers of live sap. And now they waken; they lazily shake themselves, yawn, heavy with dew in the gardens of Montevideo.

El Prado presents to my eyes its new carpet of pale green grass, cool green, newly green, tender green; on brown tree trunks, pink and white buds are opening; these trees, like opaque skeletons where suddenly spring appears, dressing them in colours and poetry.

The afternoon is cold, windy, with a sky that is spattered with clouds like tufts of cotton batting, swiftly crossing.

It is August 25, Declaration of Independence Day. A national holiday: the drums are out, Black folks are partying in the street, dancing, lighting bonfires, drinking wine, talking intensely and joyfully; there is also a protest demonstration downtown, where the people demand justice. How many years have we been celebrating this so-called independence, knowing full well that we Uruguayans have not been freed from anything. The drums continue to sound loudly; taut skin bloodied by hands as enslaved now as back around 1825. The different sounds of drums fuse, mixing with the *atabaques*, those tall, slender Brazilian drums used in *capoeira*. Together, they leave the slave quarters,[1] take command of the main square, take over the night, and once more seek the hidden door leading to the Quilombo.[2]

Nightime:

Night, bathing her moon in silver, discovers me walking towards the drums. You can hear them from afar. I stop; they fall silent again; the wind has carried away their voices. The furious roar of the sea dominates the southern walkway they call the Rambla Sur. The drums return now, directing my steps, guiding my steps to where they ought to go. The drums know me, the strong beating of their drumheads has kissed my feet for a long time now. It has bound them to hundreds of feet that keep dancing from afar; ever since they seized our land from us; beating the drums powerfully, strongly, has never summoned silence.

And now today, caressed by night, we are here surging forward once again, performing *candomblé* openly out in the streets, as in olden days.

The stars flicker boldly in the deep blue sky; the moon commands with majesty and spills mother-of-pearl light on drums fired with passion, on calloused hands aflame with passion, on bodies writhing in anguish, unleashing their age-old pain.

We must not forget that we are the children of kings and warriors; that is why they beat the drums loudly when we are born, when we marry, when we die, whenever there are national festivities celebrated with bombastic speeches made by White men[3] who utterly forbid any Black participation. As the children of kings and warriors, for centuries we have resisted whitening, that racist philosophy that yesterday prohibited us from going out into the street, and today attempts to keep us divided and dispersed.

There they are: the line of drums snakes its way through the crowd slowly, surrounded by dozens of children, men, and women who brave the winter weather; *fiesta* in the streets; *chico*, the small guitar, *repique*, the bells, and the piano mark the rhythm. My ears are inundated quickly with music that springs from the bloodied hands of Black men.

That is the rhythm of Cuareim, a rhythm both tender and violent; people are dancing, neighbours, musicians, poets, prostitutes, homosexuals; the painters, the professionals, the bums, the drunkards, the executives, the starving. Everyone is present at the huge street party celebrated throughout the country, the only autochthonous celebration that lives and vibrates in Montevideo, the only one that crosses the walls of Carnival and flows into the streets. Drums are not bound by a calendar; their art is not spent on an improvised board. The neighbourhoods of Sur and Palermo make up their scenography, and the old street where houses, vast mansions, and crumbling buildings, barely surviving, alternate with sumptuous colonial grandeur and modern construction. We are the choreographers: neighbours, drummers, dancers, the one with the calm look who tranquilly just comes along, accompanying the group with tape-recorder in hand; the one who prefers to march next to the line, his ears drinking in the sounds, the ones who are moved to dance only in front of their own house, those who carry the paper necessary to temper the drum-skins: tourists, gawkers – everyone makes up the *comparsa* group. Good musicians and composers come here to listen, to drink at the fountain, at the source, to go from the hand of Ansina, Cuareim, or Buceo, several blocks running slightly downhill, to let loose before the music of the *son*, to stop on some street corner, tuning the anguished sounding drums.

This celebration reminds me of Bahia as far as its spontaneity and joyousness goes; its streets are like those in the Pelourinho.[4] I think it is the only opportunity in Uruguay to shake off a little bit of our classic, old, grey, traditional suit, so formal and polite.

It is unbelievable to discover that most Uruguayans do not know about this magnificent spectacle that is so unique in our country. Other people ridicule it (the same as they do with any expression of Black culture) or they try to eliminate it: 'Going out in the street with drums doesn't look right'. Everything that is not 'Europeanising', that is not European, is denied entry into the narrow Uruguayan mentality.

The huge grin of the Lobo (the Wolf) opens like a magic fan on Cuareim; it spills starlight on the Island of Flowers and loses itself in the moonlight on its way to Ansina.

Sea wolf. Wild wolf of the high plains. Captive wolf that throws off the twisted chains under the spell of drums.

We must never forget that we are the children of kings and warriors.

Translated by Carol A. Beane

Notes

1. *senzala*: slave quarters near the Big House.
2. *Quilombo*: free territory inhabited and organised by Blacks, racially mixed people, Whites and Indians who fled the sugar plantations. The greatest of these was Quilombo dos Palmares / Quilombo of the Palm Trees in Alagoas (Brazil), 1595-1694.
3. The original Spanish contains a neologism *blanqui-discursos,* which involves a play on *blanco* – White man – and *yanqui*, referring to the often intrusive role that North Americans have played in Latin American history, economics, and politics.
4. *Largo de Pelourinho*: A street and neighbourhood in the Brazilian city of Salvador de Bahia, named after the whipping post used for the public punishment of slaves.

From My Trench

From my trench, I fight lies and false stories
from my trench, I sing to kill agony
I plant flowers
and hurl lightning from the stars
I lose battles and win wars.
From my trench, I soar day by day
like an eagle, a woman warrior
My soul trembles as I carry my banner
From here, I extend my hand
and touch waves
I believe in life
and the hereafter
From my trench, I light stars and lightning bolts
I battle life
and silence goodbyes
From my trench, I hear your voice,
and your song
echoing in the wind
frightening away fears
taking away pain.

Translated by Caroll Mills Young

Five Hundred Years After

To five hundred years of conquest, indigenous genocide, and African slavery

Dry summer / hot summer
sombre / shadows / empty streets
Montevideo / MONTE / VI / DEO
Radios wail:
'you have to tighten your belts
to fight inflation'
radios wailed:
'it's going to end / it's going to end'
and it's over;
only to start again
this thing called inflation.
Montevideo / capital seat
of carnival,
Five hundred years of what / 'they discovered us'
Five hundred years of what / 'they civilised us'
Five hundred years after
they tore us from our land,
Five hundred years stained
with indigenous blood / and black sweat.
And we are going to celebrate / like good
sons of . . . / immigrants / and slaves,
welcoming the caravels
naked / hungry / in war paint
with feathers on our heads
waiting for new images
like good
sons of . . . / the Motherland,
the one who birthed us / so badly.
They say they're going to polish
up the bronze
on those shackles
and chains / that they still keep for us Blacks.

Translated by Caroll Mills Young

Memory and Resistance

To those always,
Pioneers
Tireless
Daughters of the night,
Black Women
Who ennoble history
And for those men
Who also do so. AXÉ.

Black Man
If you only look for
A woman who warms
Your food and your bed,
Keep on blinding
Your handsome eyes
With the white blindfold.
The one of battle and dreams
It is who speaks to you.
That is my kingdom.

I am resistance and memory.
I built the master's road
Just like the one to freedom.
I died in the Big House
As well as in Senzala.
I left the plantation and barefoot
Became a runaway slave.
Alone I was community, home and government
Because you were rarely there,
Black man without memory,
Shoulder to shoulder
Back to back
You went on without being there.

Black Man,
Our always absent,
Generation after generation.
I gave birth to you
As well as to your father
And your brothers
I bent over
Strapping you to me during the harvest.
I bleed, I struggle, I resist
Yet you don't know my voice.

Missing from your memory
And found guilty
I live
Prisoner of time
And of stereotype
They were my breasts
That fed you
And the master's child too
I was blood mixed in the mud
With whip, humiliations
And then rape.
From there I unfolded
My wings to the wind
Mother,
Black woman,
Runaway slave
Iemanjá.
Oxum,
E Iansá a la vez.

Sometimes legend reminds me
But never history,
Although you might write it.
Black Man
What did they do to your memory
That makes my quiet walk unknown to you
Untamed
By the earth

Man who looks for me in
The picture of a Hollywood star
Or of your blonde office-mate
Forget it;
I am the warrior queen
Who freed you under the stars
The one who taught you as a child
To love the land
And shoot the gun.
I,
Lost memory
That passes through your windows
I,
Jet black skin and wrinkled hands
I,
Black woman
I,
Mestiza
Warm heart and bare feet.
I,
Torn clothes and wild hair,
I with my thick lips
I proclaimed you king.
I,
Companion of struggle and dreams
To whom your absence and life
Taught you
Demanded of you
Much more than warming
Your bread
And your pillow.

They taught you to sing
To our Gods,
To prepare tomorrow's children
So that their lives as freed men
And women
Would testify
Faithfully

To the full nobility
Of our battles.

I,
Mother,
Black Woman,
Runaway Slave,

Iemanjá
Oxum,
E Iansá a la vez.

Translated by Caroll Mills Young

Glossary

Casa Grande: Afro Brazilian slave master's house.
Senzala: Afro Brazilian slave quarters.
Ingenio: sugarcane plantation.
Cimarrona: runaway slave who fled to mountains to live as a free woman.
Iemanjá (Yemajá): the most popular female deity of the Yoruba religion; goddess
    of the sea who symbolises fertility and maternity.
Oxum (Osún): female deity of Yoruba religion, goddess of rivers who symbolises
    feminine beauty.
Iansa: woman warrior.

Crossing Borders / Crossing Boundaries: Cristina Cabral's *Memoria y resistencia*

Caroll Mills Young

Books by Uruguayan women writers such as Delmira Agustini (1886-1914), Maria Eugenia Vaz Ferreira (1875-1924), Juana de Ibarbourou (1895-1979), Teresa Porzekanski (1945), and Cristina Peri Rossi (1941) appear in bookstores throughout Uruguay. However, works by popular Black Uruguayan women writers such as Virginia Brindis de Salas and Cristina Cabral are out of print or are unavailable in spite of the fact that they are part of the corpus of Latin American literature. Their unavailability reveals much about the marketing, publishing, and textual production of Uruguay. Adverse social and economic conditions contribute to the silence and silencing of Black Uruguayan women writers, but these writers refuse to remain voiceless. Through their lectures, writing, and social activism their voices are heard.

Although Brindis de Salas died in 1958, she was significant as the first and only Black female writer in the Southern Cone (Uruguay, Argentina, Chile) until the late 1980s, when there was a resurgence of writing by Afro-Uruguayan women. These new writers represent a continuum of a Black female literary tradition that began in the early 1930s. Recently, many of the works by these contemporary writers have been published in the Black Uruguayan periodical *Mundo Afro (Black World)*, which introduced Cabral to the Uruguayan public in 1988. With the publication of her poetry in *Mundo Afro* and her poetry readings in Brazil, Cabral was hailed as the most talented Black writer since Pilar Barrios and Virginia Brindis de Salas. Cabral's work has since appeared in Uruguay's first anthology of Black poetry, *Antología de poetas negros* (1990), edited by Alberto Britos. In 1995, her work was introduced to scholars in the United States. My article 'New Voices of Afro-Uruguay', published in the *Afro-Hispanic Review*, traces her evolution as an Afro-Uruguayan writer. In the same year, Lorna Williams' 'Difference and Identity in the Poetry of Cristina Rodríguez Cabral' appeared in the fall issue of the *Afro-Hispanic Review*. Since 1995, Cabral's work has attracted greater attention. In 1997, she was invited to participate, along with Maya Angelou, Angela Davis, and Nancy Morejón, in the Yari Yari Black Women's Conference at Columbia University.

In this paper, I shall focus on Cabral as a leading Uruguayan writer who is a part of the Latin American literary tradition. I shall examine several issues that are central to a discussion of postcolonial discourse, particularly as these relate to Cabral's experiences as an Afro-Uruguayan woman living in the United States. I shall discuss the themes of race, gender, resistance, and cultural displacement as the writer confronts her new experiences. I shall also attempt to answer the question: Which is most important to the writer, her race, gender or identity as a Latin American? However, before I begin a discussion of Cabral's 1998 collection of poetry, *Memoria y resistencia* (Memory and Resistance), I shall provide an overview of the sociohistorical context that has shaped her life and writing.

According to Nathaniel C. Nash, the history of African-descended people in Uruguay began in 175l, when the first slave ships docked in Montevideo. At one point, he writes, Blacks outnumbered Whites in the Banda Oriental. Although Uruguay abolished slavery in 1842, Blacks continued to occupy subservient positions in the society. Today, there are approximately 180,000 Blacks in a country of some three million people, but most Afro-Uruguayans still reside in Montevideo. They remain primarily in jobs that they held during slavery as domestic servants, gardeners, and chauffeurs. Nash comments that there are no Black members of Congress, no Black union leaders, and less than 50 Black professionals. The number of college graduates is one-tenth of one per cent of the population or only 65 Blacks, and Cristina Rodríguez Cabral is one of those college graduates. In 1995, she earned a degree in sociology from the Universidad de la República Oriental del Uruguay in Montevideo. In 1996, she left Uruguay to study English at the American Language Institute in Indiana, Pennsylvania, and, after an intensive summer of study, she returned to Montevideo. One year later, she was admitted to Indiana University of Pennsylvania as a master's degree candidate. In 1998, she completed the master's degree in English and is presently a full-time doctoral student at the University of Missouri-Columbia in the Department of Romance Languages. Cabral is the first Black woman in her country to pursue advanced university degrees abroad.

Cabral's literary contributions now extend over a decade. Her works include the travel journal, *Bahía – Mágica Bahía* (1985); three essays: 'La literatura como forma de resistencia' (1988), '100 Años de Abolición?' (1988), 'La literatura Afro-Uruguaya' (1993), and nine books of poetry: *Pájaros sueltos* (Loose Birds),1987; *Entre giros y mutaciones* (Between Gyrations and Mutations), 1988; *Desde el sol* (From the Sun), 1989; *Entre sones y poesía* (Between Sounds and Poetry), 1989; *De par en par* (Wide Open), 1989, *Cuento y canto de par en par* (Story and Song Wide Open), 1990; *La del espejo y yo* (The One in the Mirror and I), 1990; *Desde mi trinchera* (From My Trench),1993; and *Memoria y resistencia* (Memory and Resistance), 1998. Most of Cabral's work remains unpublished; her only published collection of poetry is *Desde mi trinchera*.

In an interview with Lorna Williams, she discussed her role as a writer: 'I began a struggle to vindicate, to recover, Black culture that was then hidden; I began to express what I was feeling in the form of verse, already in progress, for example, as a form of racial protest' (57).[1] Her three essays, in particular, argue that Uruguayan culture has African roots, and her poetry protests the racist treatment of Black Uruguayans by European descendants. Themes of racism, oppression, poverty, and the destruction of the Afro-Uruguayan community abound in her work. She recognises that resistance and reconstruction must first take place in the Black community if it is to move forward in a positive direction. Overall, Cabral's work deals with the urgent issues and cultural problems that plague the Black Uruguayan community. Her work, she explains, is 'una herramienta de lucha' (a tool of struggle).

Most of Cabral's life has been spent writing in her own space, a *space* or *place* in consonance with Uruguayan culture. For the first time, Cabral is writing while living in the United States, in a new environment, a new place, and a society with a complex mixture of cultures, language, and history. *Memoria y Resistencia* represents that complexity. Geographically displaced, Cabral is now a Black Uruguayan woman confronted by the other – a country that most South Americans consider exploitative and hegemonic. This new, complex experience dictates the voice we hear. It contradicts the poetic voice of her earlier poetry, which expressed the experiences of being Black and female in Uruguay. Cabral now views with amazement the economic waste, racial dissension, and gender tensions of the dominant culture, as well as the similarities and differences between the Afro-American and Afro-Uruguayan cultures. She has to reconcile her false constructions of the United States and to find her place and space within the cultural, racial, and gender framework of the society in which she now lives. For that reason, *Memoria y resistencia* is the story, in poetry, of her struggle with *otherness*; it reveals her struggle to define herself and to survive in this new world.

Dedicated to her mother, whom she calls la primera querrera que conocí / y que me enseñó a andar (the first warrior woman that I knew /

who taught me how to walk), the collection is divided into two parts: 'Memoria' a series of eight snapshots of her life experiences, and 'Resistencia', nine poems that deal with conflicts and cultural battles. In this volume, her poetic form turns away from Eurocentric poetic models. Cabral opens the book with 'Memoria', a poem written in the United States, which expresses isolation, loneliness, and love. Although the protagonist does not identify the absent lover, it is clear that the two are separated geographically and that the speaker longs to be physically in his presence. The female persona recollects every part of his body with sensual imagery: 'el perfume de sus labios' (the perfume of his lips), 'mi boca lentamente se cubrió de néctar' (my mouth was slowly covered with nectar), and 'que luces destellan tus ojos' (what lights twinkle in your eyes). As she reconstructs a mental image of his body, the verses move as if the speaker slowly and thoughtfully traces his frame. Suddenly, the daydream ends. At that point, the verses end abruptly with the realisation that the lover and their relationship will never exist. The poet's attempts to resist the mental and physical images of her lover fail as she longs to be loved again.

> Que la memoria descorre su velo
> Y me imprime tu fragancia.
> El amor, más veloz que los tiempos
> Y que las aguas
> Abre tu boca madura
> Y canta . . .

> (How memory traces your face
> And prints your fragrance in me.
> Love, faster than time
> And the waters
> Your strong mouth opens
> And sings . . .)

'Memoria' is reminiscent of Cabral's earlier verse; it is very private, like an intimate conversation with the poet. It has overtones of the poetry of Juana Ibarbourou and Delmira Agustini, poets whose intimate and sensuous verses express anguish, love, passion, and hope. In a recent conversation, Cabral explained that the poetry of both Ibarbourou and Agustini greatly influenced her writing and that many of her former poems were written to 'record the mystic world that she held inside'. These poems, she says, served as a form of therapy to deal with her aloneness and loneliness.[2] 'Memoria' expresses the poet's vitality, joy, and desire, while she struggles to survive in the United States. In general, the poetry in this collection deals primarily with love, race, displacement, resistance, rebellion, loneliness, and cultural representation.

In 'En la clase de literatura americana' (In American Literature Class), Cabral searches for words to describe her new life outside of Uruguay. Here, we see the poet immersed in a world of English-speakers, where she struggles with the words of an alien tongue.

De momento
no intento traducirlas;
Solo paladear el sabor
de la poesía
liberada.

(At the moment
I don't try to translate them
Only to savour the taste
Of liberated
poetry.)

Struggling with a new language, a new academic environment, and the reality of living in the United States, Cabral wants to continue to express herself freely and poetically. There is now a conflict between the English-speaking environment and the Spanish-speaking one; she grapples with raw words while trying to shape them into poetry. She feels 'out of place', and this displacement blocks the creative process. Attempts to overcome cultural displacement produce a tension that she has never experienced. Cabral is now faced with her circumscribed identity as a Black Uruguayan professional woman and her new identity as a graduate student / single mother in a small rural town in western Pennsylvania. According to Bill Ashcroft, place and displacement are crucial features of post-colonial literature. This sense of displacement, he explains, creates tension in the creative process:

A sense of displacement, of the lack of fit between language and place may be experienced by both those who possess English as a mother tongue and those who speak it as a second language. In both cases, the sense of dislocation from an historical 'homeland' and that created by the dissonance between language and the experience of 'displacement' generates a creative tension within the language. Place is thus the concomitant of difference, the continual reminder of the separation, and yet of the hybrid interpenetration of the coloniser and colonised. (391)

In her new space, Cabral wrestles with multiple identities. Her physical movement from Uruguay to the United States forces her to deal with new racial and gender positions. Although she is a Black woman who is geographically removed from Uruguay, she has crossed boundaries in search of opportunities for growth and access to more resources – for both herself and her daughter. In this new space and place, she must re-negotiate who she is and what she wants to be, as she becomes part of an English-speaking world, a world whose imperialism and economic dominance she has resisted. Poetry is the vehicle with which she escapes the dissonant language and the hegemonic practices of the United States, while searching for a new definition of self.

Resistance and difference are recurring themes in the title poem, 'Memoria y resistencia', which celebrates blackness. Race and gender are at the forefront. Here, we see the poet's views on race and representation. The poem, divided into three parts, echoes the themes of Maya Angelou's 'Phenomenal Woman' and Nikki Giovonni's 'Ego Tripping'. Like Angelou and Giovonni, Cabral affirms, in bold language, the beauty, wisdom, and courage of Black women. The female protagonist speaks in the first person throughout the poem, reminding the reader of her historical accomplishments and the spirit of her ancestors. The poetic voice challenges the reader to embrace and love blackness, to reject the negative image of Black people that has been passed down for generations. Cabral begins with a salutation to Black men and women.

Mujeres Negras
que enoblecen la historia
Y para aquellos hombres
que también lo hacen. *Axé.*

(Black Women
who ennoble history
and for those black men
who also do so. Axé.)

Rebelling against the Spanish language of the European coloniser, Cabral ends the stanza with the Yoruba word 'Axé', which means life force, divine authority, and the power to make things happen (Lindsay 292).[3] *Axé* is commonly used in *candombé*, the Afro-Brazilian religion, to honour the *orixas* or deities, because it evokes positive energy and strength for African-descended people. Cabral's use of Yoruba language and customs is an identity marker that locates her poem in an African framework. For the poet, the Yoruba language and Afro-Brazilian culture epitomise the strength and courage of Black people.

Cabral's use of Yoruba as a literary and cultural device underscores the significance of her residence in Brazil's Salvador de Bahía, which is second only to Nigeria in the size of its Black population. In her *Bahía – Mágica Bahía*, she writes about Afro-Brazilian poetry and its relationship to African-derived religions such as *umbanda* and *candomblé* (spelled *candombé* in Uruguay).[4] Her experiences in Brazil encouraged the poet to acknowledge her African heritage and her identity as a Black Uruguayan woman. To that end, Cabral also began to address the systematic exclusion and marginalisation of Blacks in Uruguay. Because Bahía has the largest Black population in South America, she was impressed by the solidarity of the Afro-Brazilian community and its efforts to achieve racial and social equality. The use of Yoruba and Bantu words indicates the writer's desire to connect Uruguay to its religious heritage and its African origins. Both the aesthetics of her poetry and the representation of self undergo a radical change; her poetics, at first expressed through lyrical and pastoral images, becomes bolder and more dramatic, affirming her identity as a rebellious, Black, South American woman.

In the next part of 'Memoria y resistencia', Cabral focuses on the Black male and his treatment of Black women, whom he devalues, according to the poet.

Hombre Negro
Si tan solo buscas
Una mujer que caliente
Tu comida y tu cama,
Sigue blanqueando
Tus bellos ojos
Con la venda blanca.

(Black man
If you only look for
A woman who warms
Your food and your bed

You are blinding
Your handsome eyes
With the white blindfold.)

In contrast, the following verses serve as an historical summary of the female protagonist's slave past. This history lesson becomes an instrument of cultural, social, and political resistance. Remembering these historical events underscores the valour and courage of the speaker, while it also erases negative racial images, particularly of Black women.

Soy resistencia y memoria.
Construí el camino del amo
Así como el de la libertad.
Morí en la Casa Grande
Igual en la Senzala.
Dejé el ingenio y descalza
Me hice cimarrona.

(I am resistance and memory
I built the master's road
Just like the one to freedom.
I died in the Big House
As well as in Senzala.
I left the plantation and barefoot
Became a runaway slave.)

Cabral chronicles, as does Cuban poet Nancy Morejón in her seminal 'Mujer negra', the physical and psychological violence that Black women have experienced but resisted throughout history. The poet continues to place the Black man at the centre of this history, reminding the reader of his denial of the repression and oppression of Black women. The poet ends the stanza by juxtaposing Spanish and Yoruba words that praise the Black 'woman warrior'.

Madre,
    Negra,
        Cimarrona
Iemanjá,
    Oxum,
        E Iansá a la vez.

This construction reinforces the Black female's identity: 'madre' reflects her divine life force and her ability to procreate; 'negra' affirms, in a strong and uncompromising voice, her blackness; and 'cimarrona' signifies her resistance to slavery and male domination. Finally, the evocation of African female deities – 'Iemanjá' (goddess of fertility), 'Oxum', (goddess of beauty), and 'Iansá', (woman warrior) – highlights the spiritual sisterhood of all Black women.

Cabral continues her protest by challenging Black men's superficial concept of female beauty, as evidenced in their desire for White women.

> Hombre que buscas en mí
> El retrato de una estrella de Hollywood
> O de tu rubia compañera de oficina,
> Olvídalo;

> (Man who looks for me in
> The picture of a Hollywood star
> Or of your blonde office-mate,
> Forget it;)

The binary relationship of black/white and male/female shows that they coexist in a paradoxical relationship. To reinforce this idea, the poet juxtaposes the physical image of the Black woman – with her jet black skin, thick lips, and wild hair – to that of the White woman, who is depicted as a Hollywood star or a blonde office-mate. As Frantz Fanon notes, these 'superficial differences of the body (skin colour, body shape, hair texture) are read as indelible signs of the "natural" inferiority of the possessor. This is the inescapable "fact" of blackness, a "fact" which forces on "Negro" people a heightened level of bodily self-consciousness, since it is the body which is the inescapable, visible sign of their oppression and denigration' (qtd. by Ashcroft 321). However, these bodily differences are cultural signifiers that counteract the signs of inferiority. In her description of the Black woman, Cabral attempts to dismantle Eurocentric notions of the ideal female body as that of the blonde, blue-eyed, straight-haired, White woman. The poet encourages the reader to eliminate self-hatred by focusing on the historical role of Black women. The repetition of 'yo' underscores the movement from individual to collective – and shared – experiences that deconstruct notions of male supremacy and domination. The historical testimony of the speaker is a vehicle to instill race pride and to eradicate racial hatred and male domination. Cabral has a responsibility, she believes, as an artist to voice social and political issues that are often concealed behind closed doors. Living in the United States has allowed her to view Uruguay's Black and White communities from a distance and to see more clearly Uruguay's social and racial problems.

In analysing Cabral's latest collection of poetry, I have attempted to determine the primacy of race, gender or Latin American identity. Cabral, herself, best answers this question when she writes, 'Soy negra sudamericana decidida a caminar con la honorable sonrisa del guerrero' (I am a Black South American woman determined to walk with the honourable smile of a warrior).[5] The poet indicates that race, gender, and national identity are not separate but are interconnected. Cabral reveals a personal story through her poetic artistry, because her poems deal with the meaning of feminist consciousness, political resistance, and racial identity. She moves both women and Blacks from margin to centre. Hers is a story of self-discovery and a tribute to Black women who move beyond boundaries. It is the poet's message of a new beginning, one of hope and promise.

Notes

1. Unless otherwise indicated, all translations are mine.
2. When she completed the manuscript in 1998, the poet said that 'en los momentos más difíciles de mi vida siempre escribo poesía. Es mi terapía, mi forma de desconectarme de lo cotidiano' (In the most difficult moments of my life, I always write poetry. It is my therapy, my way of disconnecting from the routine events of my life) (Interview with Cabral, May 7, 1998).
3. The poet commented, 'Mi relación con Brasil, especialmente con Bahía, está directamente relacionada al descubrimiento de mi etnicidad y de mi religiosidad. En Brasil me di cuenta de que era negra, de que tenía un bagaje cultural que estaba por encima de mi "ser uruguayo"'. (My relationship with Brazil, especially with Bahía, is directly related to the discovery of ethnicity and religiosity. In Brazil, I realised that I was a Black woman, that I had a lot of cultural baggage, that I was more than my 'Uruguayan being'). She went on to say, 'In Bahía, I discovered the presence of the Orixas in my life; it was there where I became another person'. (Interview with Cabral August 16, 1999).
4. Cabral retains the Yoruba names, but the spellings are Portuguese and not Spanish.
5. This line is from an untitled poem written in March 1993.

Works Cited

Ashcroft, Bill et al, eds. *The Post-Colonial Studies Reader*. New York: Routledge, 1995.

Britos Serrat, Alberto. *Antología de los poetas negros uruguayos*. Montevideo: Ediciones Mundo Afro, 1990.

Cabral, Cristina. *Memoria y resistancia*. Unpublished manuscript, 1998.

Lindsay, Arturo, ed. *Santería Aesthetics in Contemporary Latin American Art*. Washington, DC: Smithsonian Institute Press, 1996.

Nash, Nathaniel C. 'Uruguay is On Notice: Blacks Want Recognition'. *The New York Times* May 7, 1993: A4.

Williams, Lorna V. 'Entrevista con Cristina Rodríguez Cabral en Montevideo en Julio de 1993'. *Afro-Hispanic Review* 14 (Fall 1995): 57-63.

Young, Caroll Mills. 'New Voices of Uruguay'. *Afro-Hispanic Review* 14 (Spring 1995): 58-64.

Shirley Campbell

$\mathcal{S}$HIRLEY $\mathcal{C}$AMPBELL

COSTA RICA

(b. 1965)

A third-generation Costa Rican of Jamaican descent, Shirley Campbell studied drama, literature, and creative writing at the Conservatorio de Castilla. She became active in social and cultural programmes: she taught at the Conservatory, organised writing workshops for children for Costa Rica's Ministry of Education, conducted summer programmes through the Association for the Development of Afro-Costa Rican Culture, and served as Founding Director of the Group for the Promotion and Diffusion of Afro-Costa Rican Culture (DADISI). In 1993, she graduated from the University of Costa Rica and later took postgraduate courses sponsored by the University of Syracuse in Zimbabwe. After living in Africa with her family from 1993 to 1995, she spent several years in El Salvador and Honduras before moving to Jamaica.

Campbell's education, work, travel, and contact with diverse ethnic groups find expression in her writing, which reveals her concern for children, interest in women's issues, and pride in Black culture and history. In her first collection of poetry, Naciendo *(Being Born), birth serves as a metaphor for the creative process. Written in the first person, many of the untitled, numbered poems are deeply introspective; they deal with questions of race, gender, and personal relationships from the point of view of a Black, Costa Rican woman. With sensual images and concise language, the poet treats themes of birth, death, migration, religion, and family. Indeed, two of her most important archetypes are grandparents, who represent the ancestors – the nurturers, village elders, and culture bearers who bind families together. Since the publication of* Naciendo, *Campbell has participated in conferences, radio and television interviews, and poetry readings at home and abroad. In 1992, she attended a conference of Caribbean women writers in Curaçao, where she was* acknowledged as a poet with an Afro-Caribbean worldview. Considered a post-negritude writer whose views on race have been shaped by her family and by Afro-Creole writers such as Nicolás Guillén and Quince Duncan, Campbell explains, 'I have learned the art of being Black throughout my life. The task of making myself understood as a Black and a woman has been, after all, most satisfactory'. She does indeed reveal the sensitivity of a Race Woman in her 1994 publication, Rotundamente negra *(Unequivocal Black Woman)*.

The poet is presently working on a collection of forty poems entitled Descifrando siglos e historia desde la piel *(Deciphering Centuries of History Through the Skin), and she is preparing another anthology about women who have shaped her life. A committed writer, Shirley Campbell explains: 'I see my work as a form of educating people about negritude, about loving themselves and fighting for the things in which they believe'.*

Closing the Circle that Began in Africa

I was born in Costa Rica thirty-five years ago in the capital city of San José, the fifth of seven brothers and sisters in an immigrant family. My parents are from the Costa Rican Caribbean Coast, although they moved to San José when they were very young, seeking better educational and employment opportunities. As for the preceding generation, both my grandmothers were born in Jamaica and, with their parents, came to Costa Rica as young children. They were one of the many waves of Caribbean immigrants who were brought in to build the railroad and, later, to provide the mind and muscle for the development of the banana plantation economy. Political constraints and mobilisation limitations kept my grandparents in Limón, isolated from the more developed central provinces of San José, Heredia and Alajuela. From their generation, we inherited Jamaican culture, including Jamaican English, which is still the mother tongue of most of Costa Rica's Black population.

Thanks to my parents' dedication, we all received an education and were brought up with pride in our African heritage. While working hard to raise and maintain six children, my father obtained a university degree through his own effort and my mother's support. He always liked the performing arts and was a member of several choruses, so he encouraged us to develop our artistic abilities. My eldest sister is a modern dancer and my youngest is a singer. Although the others did not pursue their talents, each was involved in an artistic activity at some point in time.

I completed my elementary and high school training at an arts institute, where I studied acting and literary creation. It was there that I started writing. I participated in acting and writing workshops throughout elementary and secondary school. At the university, I continued training and took some courses in literature. I graduated with a degree in anthropology from the Social Sciences Department of the University of Costa Rica (my country's most important institution of higher education). I was always interested in this field, because studying the culture and traditions of other people was always my passion. Later, I took graduate-level courses in African history and feminism in Harare, Zimbabwe.

I have always been a passionate advocate in the fight against discrimination and racism, so I have joined study groups and organisations working to that aim. Participating in such groups in Costa Rica, Zimbabwe and Honduras, I developed a global vision of the anti-racism movement and of the struggle of Black people, in general. It was through my involvement with the Black consciousness movement that I met my husband, a Costa Rican who shares my interest in the cause. His work with the United Nations allowed me to move to and live in Zimbabwe for two years. This was perhaps the most important experience of my life and, as such, it had a profound impact on my life and on my writing. Living in Africa had a great impact on my husband and me. Being part of the majority was a new and delightful experience. It was wonderful living in an environment where it was no longer necessary to justify ourselves or defend ourselves for being different. We also discovered that being the product of five hundred years of western history had made us hybrids; so it was sometimes difficult for us to understand Africans or for Africans to understand us. At times, we did not feel that we belonged.

After living in Africa, we moved to El Salvador for two and a half years and then to Honduras. Each experience was valuable. In El Salvador, the population is a mixture of indigenous, White, and Black people, but there are no Black groups as such. In Honduras we developed very close ties with the Garifuna population (a group of African-descended people, 800,000 strong, who live on the Caribbean Coast of Guatemala, Honduras, and Nicaragua). We tried to support many Garifuna causes, and their rich culture taught us a great deal. The Garifuna have preserved a lot of their African heritage, including language, which was derived from the Yoruba. They live, however, in dire conditions; they are among the poorest of the poor in one of the poorest countries in the hemisphere.

Six months ago, we arrived in Jamaica, where we now live. Harold and I agree that coming to Jamaica is like closing a circle. After more than one hundred years, we are back in the land of our forefathers. This cycle that began in Africa starts to make sense when destiny gives us the opportunity to recover part of our history and give it back to our children. Just as our grandparents went to Costa Rica, we came to Jamaica with the promise of a good job and a better future. Arriving here, we learned that, after several generations, there is still a strong bond and many similarities between the culture inherited from our forefathers and the Jamaican one.

Moving from one place to another has allowed me to become an independent consultant and to expand my professional skills. I have worked on short assignments for various agencies of the United Natons, private businesses, and women's organisations. I work in different areas, but primarily on gender, reproductive health, and population and development. I have organised and evaluated projects, and conducted research on cultural issues, et cetera. Currently I organise my life so that I can work, travel around the world, raise my children, write, and live with great intensity. We travel to Costa Rica frequently so that the children have a sense of belonging and can maintain a link with the extended family. I also return there to participate in poetry readings and other events to which I am invited.

While I am not sure which authors have actually influenced my work, I admire several writers. Nicolás Guillén is very important to me, and I like the poetry of Nicaraguan Rosario Murillo. Quince Duncan and Jorge Debravo are my favourite Costa Rican authors, and I enjoy reading works by female Costa Rican authors who are very good. I also like Mario Benedetti and Simone de Beauvoir. I particularly like erotic literature written by women. I also like Milan Kundera and Gabriel García Márquez. Nowadays, I am discovering a world of excellent Caribbean writers.

I have gathered my recent poems into a new book, which I want to get published. This group of forty poems examines the process of searching within to discover history through the eyes of a Black woman. I am also working on another collection of poems – more like narratives – about women. It is dedicated to all those women who have passed through my life, who have lived with me, through whom I have lived, and who have helped me define myself as a human being. I also have other projects. I want to write a narrative about what I have learned through these years of travelling, and how those experiences have affected my perception of myself and my concept of this world.

In my work, I see a way of educating people about Black consciousness and helping them to gain self-respect and to fight for the things they believe in. My poetry, which I write for my children, is something like thinking aloud. I hope that, through my writing, my children will develop self-appreciation and show others how nice it is to be Black in a world that tries to teach us otherwise. It has worked so far. Tiffany and Malcolm, eleven and eight years old respectively, are happy and self-confident. I am happy doing what I do, and I continue working to change the world. Let's see if I can do it. I keep working to see if, through my poetry, I can make more people happy about their own skin, whatever colour it may be.

Abuelo *

Abuelo,
usted no nos contó historias
ni nos acuñó en sus brazos
deletreándonos el atardecer
no nos durmió cantando
ni nos besó la frente
cuando hubo quien
nos recordara el color de la piel
usted fue distinto abuelo
es ahora cuando lo comprendo
se tardó más de medio siglo
para empezar a amarnos
para empezar a evocar
los duros y malheridos
senos de su historia
usted fue distinto abuelo
de verdad lo comprendo
cuando miro
este pueblo de los dos
sostenido a la música de un grito
mirando aun por las ventanas
y deletreando
el amanecer.

---

* Shirley Campbell requested that her original poems, in Spanish, be published
along with the translations. She wrote: 'This is of great importance to me
because the poems were conceived in this language and the feelings and
sensations can't be translated'.

Grandpa

Grandpa
you did not tell us stories
nor did you cuddle us in your arms
nor kiss us on the forehead
when there were those
who would be mindful of the colour of our skin
you were different grandpa
only now do I comprehend it
after more than half a century
to begin to love ourselves
to begin to evoke
the harsh and badly wounded
bosoms of his history
you were different grandpa
truly do I comprehend it
when I behold
this people of us both
nurtured to the music of a shout
still looking through the windows
and spelling out
the dawn.

Translated by Donald K. Gordon

VIII

Entonces crecí
me hice grande
y tenía responsabilidades distintas
debía hacer esfuerzos por llorar
con menos frecuencia
debía entender adecuadamente
como nacían los niños
debía poder explicar a otros
cosas como el sol o las estrellas
debía poder explicar concretamente
por qué no debían los niños
ver novelas en la televisión.
Fue que crecí
ya era una persona adulta
y debía dominar al menos someramente
la existencia.
Fue entonces cuando sentí el vacío
fue el mismo día
el de la existencia
me sentí sin nada
fue caminando por la calle
cuando encontré mujeres
caminé otro poco
y de nuevo
encontré mujeres
y sentí el vacío
y miré en los otros.
Y no me encontraba
y sentí el vacío
fue el día de la existencia
sí
lo recuerdo
que la historia sonrió y dijo

mujeres
me faltaba algo
tuve una hija y algo me faltaba
me sentía vacía
me miré la piel con marcas y estrellas
y un color distinto
me miré la piel
con un tono oscuro
con un tono inmenso
descubrí en mi sangre
de pronto una abuela
a una hembra
y una hilera larga
de madres cantando
y una tierra negra
sembrada por ellas
y entonces crecí
y me hice grande
como las estrellas.
Me hice larga
como los caminos
me entendí mujer
una mujer negra

Then I grew

VIII

I became big
and I had different responsibilities
I ought to strive to cry
with less frequency
I ought to understand absolutely
how children were born
I ought to be able to explain
things like the sun or the stars
I ought to be able to explain concretely
why children ought not
to view the soaps on television.
The reality was I grew
now I was an adult person
and I ought to master at least superficially
existence.
It was then that I felt the emptiness
it was the same day
that of existence
I felt a nothingness
it was walking through the street
when I met women
I walked a bit more
and again I met women
and I felt the emptiness
and I looked at others
and I could not find myself
and I felt the emptiness
'twas the day of existence
yes
I recall it
history smiled and said
women
something was alack in me

I had a daughter and something was lacking in me
I felt myself empty
I beheld my skin with its marks and pips
and a different colour
I beheld my skin
with a dark tone
with an immense tone
I discovered in my blood
with a suddenness a grandmother
a female
and an extended line
of mothers singing
and a black land
sown by them
and then I grew
and I became big
like the stars
I became long
like the roads
I understood myself to be a woman
a black woman

Translated by Donald K. Gordon

XIII

Me niego rotundamente
a negar mi voz
mi sangre y mi piel
y me niego rotundamente
a dejar de ser yo
a dejar de sentirme bien
cuando miro mi rostro en el espejo
con mi boca
rotundamente grande
y mi nariz
rotundamente hermosa
y mis dientes
rotundamente blancos
y mi piel
valientemente negra
y me niego categóricamente
a dejar de hablar
mi lengua mi acento y mi historia
y me niego absolutamente
a ser parte de los que se callan
de los que temen
de los que lloran
porque me acepto
rotundamente libre
rotundamente negra
rotundamente hermosa.

XIII

I unequivocally refuse
to refute my voice
my blood and my skin
and I unequivocally refuse
to desist from being me
to desist from feeling good
when I behold my face in the mirror
with my mouth
unequivocally large
and my nose
unequivocally beautiful
and my teeth
unequivocally white
and my skin
valiantly black
and I categorically refuse
to desist from speaking
my language in my accent and of my history
and I absolutely refuse
to be part of those who keep silent
of those who fear
of those who weep
because
I accept myself
unequivocally free
unequivocally black
unequivocally beautiful

Translated by Donald K. Gordon

'Patches of Dreams': The Birth of Shirley Campbell's Oeuvre

Dellita Martin-Ogunsola

Shirley Campbell made her literary debut in 1988 with *Naciendo* (Being Born), and that work, together with her 1995 collection *Rotundamente negra* (Unequivocally Black), gives voice to the Black female presence in Costa Rica. Donald Gordon comments that 'Campbell is at one and the same time a deeply introspective writer who gives outward expression to the realities of black life. She is a lyricist conscious of her past, reflective on the present, and meditative on the future' (23). As a contributor to an emerging Black poetry in Costa Rica, Campbell is part of the post-negritude current flowing throughout the Caribbean and Latin America, for her works diverge from negritude in significant ways. First, the uniqueness of *Naciendo* and *Rotundamente negra* is that they address exclusively the Black female historical experience in Costa Rica, while channelling race, gender, and aesthetics into a powerful expression of the personal. Second, the lyrics of both collections explore the emotional landscape of the village in both a private and public sense, creating a discourse that runs counter to the prevailing notions of race, gender, and aesthetics in the canon. Janet Hampton identifies this process in American literatures when she observes that African-ancestored writers like Rita Dove and Shirley Campbell 'create portraits of their communities as subjects, not objects, of discourse . . . [and] construct images of diasporan people who define themselves rather than be defined by others ...' (33). Third, like the lyricism of Nancy Morejón, Campbell's poetry is celebratory, contemplative, and subtle, rather than plaintive, strident, and explicit, as is so much of the work of the negritude movement. This essay examines the interweaving of race, gender, and aesthetics in *Naciendo*, another solid contribution to Black female discourse in Latin America.

Myriam Díaz-Diocaretz identifies a tradition of writing by women in Spanish-speaking America that traces the formation of the female voice as individual and collective subject, a development she refers to as the 'matriheritage of founding discourses' (91-92). In spite of this tradition, the voices of women of colour, particularly those of African descent, have been misappropriated, omitted, or silenced. *Naciendo* represents the creative coming of age of a young, gifted, Black poet in the wake of the Afro-creolist movement. Specifically, the work's connection to the diaspora corpus of literature in the Caribbean is evident in Campbell's choice of an epigraph that contains famous lines from the poetry of Claude Mckay, Nicolás Guillén, and Aimé Césaire, respectively.[1] On the one hand, Gordon views Campbell's evocation of the Black diaspora through referencing these writers as a way of expressing signature themes like '. . . death and blood, fraternity, rage' (23-24). On the other hand, Hampton delineates a semiotic and feminist perspective in Campbell's poetry, which she compares to that of Rita Dove: 'The themes of migration, dislocation and exile, of sisterhood and generational connectedness, and of defiance and empowerment, both political and physical, are evident in their poems' (33). These two points of view are not mutually exclusive, for both sets of themes are manifest in *Naciendo*. If anything, the two thematic streams merge at times, then separate, and are ultimately rejoined as Campbell paints an imaginary landscape that is refreshing and uplifting. Furthermore, the examination of race, gender, and aesthetics in *Naciendo* enables literary critics and readers to comprehend the postcolonial ideology through which women artists and intellectuals 'center' themselves and 'reconfigure present arrangements' to better explore their connections with their societies (Davies 1). Campbell confirms this posture in her *Presentación* (5).

Naciendo is an appropriate title for Campbell's first book of poems because it emphasises the idea of new birth (Gordon 26). Moreover, 'De frente' (Forward March) is the heading for part one, which contains a series of eight untitled poems. The poet's technique of not assigning specific titles to individual selections captures the imagery of the main title *Naciendo* (Being Born) while also suggesting the amorphous, anonymous state of gestation that human beings experience before birth. The opening lines of the first poem refer to the return from a journey, possibly from a voyage of self-discovery:

He vuelto
dispuesta a restregarme
de caricias con el tiempo
a descalzar la vida
empapada en besos
y calzada de miseria (9)

(I have come back
ready to scrub myself
with caresses in time
to unshod life
impregnated with kisses
and shod in misery.)

In the above passage, the image of rebirth is associated with the personal act of cleansing, as seen in verbs and verbal phrases like 'restregarme' (to scrub myself) and 'descalzar la vida' (to unshod life). 'Descalzar' personifies and concretises the noun 'vida'. Thus, the new self that is so eager to offer caresses ('caricias') and kisses ('besos') awaits its birth with great expectation, and this is reinforced through the image of the birth canal: 'He vuelto / por este pasillo estrecho / de la esperanza' (I have come back / through this narrow passage / of hope). The idea of a rite of passage is implicit in the trope. The theme of purification is presented toward the end of the poem: 'Hoy regreso / para limpiar las rodillas / al pasado' (Today I am returning / to cleanse my knees / of the past). This suggests that cleansing must precede rebirth (ll. 16-18): 'para entregarme limpia / como naciendo / frente a mis entrañas' (to devote myself wholly / like being born / from my own essence). Using knees as a key symbol, the poet evokes both the historical pose of the slave who kneels in humiliation before the master, and the metaphysical posture of one who wilfully bends down in an act of praise and thanksgiving. In essence, this new birth is designed to cleanse the muddy waters of a troublesome life, which is expressed by 'calzada de miseria' (shod with misery). The latter image evokes the poignant 'no crystal stair' metaphor of Langston Hughes's famous poem 'Mother to Son', where life has '. . . tacks in it, / And splinters, / And boards torn up, / And places with no carpet on the floor – / Bare' (187). Furthermore, the convergence of these two figures of speech is consequential because of the shared history and vision of African-descended writers in the Americas (Jackson 89-92).

The fifth poem of the 'De Frente' series (p. 13) continues the image of life as a new creature: 'No les traigo / la vida entre palabras / ni los dioses contra balas que nos arrebataron' (I do not bring you / life wrapped in words / nor gods against bullets / that they wrested from us). In addition, the birth process becomes a metaphor for artistic creativity, as the poetic voice expresses the agony and ecstasy of lyrical composition:

Les traigo hijos sin pañales blancos
les propongo estos pechos negros

sin blanca leche
pero con remiendos de sueños (13)

(I bring you babies without white diapers
I offer you these black breasts
bereft of white milk
but turgid with patches of dreams)

Here, Campbell compares the poet to a mother of naked babies ('hijos sin pañales blancos'), symbolising the birth of poems not bound by the trappings of the hegemonic culture. Instead, the poetic 'I' must rely on patches of dreams ('remiendos de sueños') to nourish its own creativity, or the resilient bits and pieces of individual and communal life that have survived and flourished in the soil of the African diaspora. Although the lack of white milk and tattered dreams hint at deprivation and paucity, they also imply that true fulfilment and wealth do not depend on possessions, especially forced ones. Thus, the antithesis that contrasts black breasts / patched dreams with white milk / white diapers is significant, for it suggests that one way of facing ('De frente') the conflictive relationship between African diaspora and European dominant cultures is to strip and cleanse oneself of the harmful elements, save the healthy portions, and start over. On the one hand, the fact that black breasts are 'bereft of white milk' is healthy, because it means the artist must search the recesses of her individual soul and ethnic memory (the journey) to produce a new sensibility (the return) that emanates from the specific context of Afro-Caribbean history. On the other hand, the act of writing ironically links the poet to the very context (Western culture/Costa Rican history) that is the source of her blues.

The lyrics of the 'De frente' series evoke the intimate and personal aspects of Campbell's world. Part two of *Naciendo* focuses on the village, or '. . . the neighborhoods and the population of those neighborhoods', within the city (Morrison 37), for throughout this untitled section is articulated implicitly or explicitly the renowned African adage: 'It takes a whole village to raise a child'. This part begins with an epigraph that is a poeticised version of Quince Duncan's short story 'Una carta' (A Letter):

. . . Más fuerte que el sonido
de los hierros carcomidos
por el uso y el tiempo,
se elevan los gritos;

monótona plegaria
de un pueblo que hierve. (17)

(. . . Stronger than the sound
of iron rusted
by use and time.
shouts rise up
monotonous plea
of a town that is seething.)

Campbell replicates the structure of the blues poem by arranging the prose
into a six-line stanza, thus capturing the antiphonal interplay of vocalic
phonemes (i-o, a-a, i-e) that convey a sense of endurance, urgency, and
pent-up energy. The monotonous plea metaphor depicts a community
that is seething in its own prostration even as it awaits the opportunity to
rise up and take control of its destiny. This epigraph provides a stage for
what Morrison calls 'the advising, benevolent, protective, wise Black ancestor
. . .' (39), or the place/space where the moral values and manners of the
village are evident. ² In *Naciendo* that ancestor is represented by a
grandparent.

'De noche' (Night-time) presents the figure of the grandmother, who
suggests roots and routes:

las abuelas viven sus vestidos claros
y llenos de luces
sus sexos negros
y llenos de historias. (22)

(grandmothers wear their pastel dresses
and their dark genitals
filled with radiance
and replete with stories.)

In keeping with the new birth metaphor sustained in *Naciendo*, this poem
portrays grandmothers as flesh-and-blood people who nurture the body
and the spirit with their loving presence. Moreover, the contrast between
pastel dresses, which are symbols of beauty and delicateness, and black
sexuality, which represents fecundity and lineage, illustrates the lasting
impressions grandmothers leave on their grandchildren. Essentially, these
surrogate mothers function as guardian angels who guide, inspire, and protect

their young charges, but who also pass on knowledge about real life through the fascinating stories they tell:

> De noche
> estas abuelas
> nos arropan el corazón
> con su viejo tiempo (22)

> (At night
> these grandmothers gently wrap
> up and tuck in our hearts
> with old times)

Unlike the subjects of formal schooling, these lessons in history are full of joy and sorrow, hope and despair, defeat and triumph, thus providing the children with an education that authentically reflects their circumstances, or Duncan's *afro-realismo* ('Taller', n.p.). Furthermore, it is the kind of training that will help them keep a strong sense of identity even when challenged by a world that tells them otherwise.

Part Three of *Naciendo* is '. . . las mujeres . . . y los hombres' (. . . Women . . . and Men), which contains ten titled as well as untitled poems. There are three that constitute what I call the 'Grandparent Trilogy', where Campbell paints some rather unconventional portraits of certain elders in the community. For example, in the touching poem 'A una abuela negra cualquiera' (To Anybody's Black Grandmother), the poet contextualises the life of a character who has experienced hard times, who, in fact, has hit rock bottom, but who has managed to salvage a measure of dignity:

> La vieja . . .
> ....
> Se ha detenido
> a recoger un trozo de llanto
> que cayó de su cartera (40)

> (The old woman . . .
> ....
> Stooped down
> to retrieve a piece of weeping
> that fell out of her purse)

The concrete representation of the persona's emotional life as a piece of weeping ('llanto') is so poignant that the reader feels compassion rather than scorn for her. Moreover, her specific role – whether she is nanny, domestic, street vendor, rejected lover, abandoned wife, or prostitute – is less significant than her capacity to endure, which is underscored by her upright stance: 'Camina erguida / aprisionando los besos / de todos los hombres necesarios' (She walks upright / imprisoning the kisses of / all the necessary men) (41). In contrast to the character Miss Spence in Duncan's 'Una carta', the grandmother of 'A una abuela' seems to have lost all hope. The woman's lack of real joy is symbolised by the 'imprisoned kisses' she remembers from loveless relationships and the major battles and minor victories she faces daily, represented by beating ('golpea') and caressing ('acaricia') her children, in the futile pursuit of happiness ('los sueños / sin verdad posible'). Nevertheless, 'a piece of weeping', 'an empty purse', 'imprisoned kisses', and 'blows and caresses' are all signs of the embattled life this elder endures heroically.

The nurturing role of the grandparent is underscored by its absence in 'Abuelo' (Grandfather), which Hampton views as an 'accusatory poem' (37). In this poem the grandfather is too embittered with life to cradle little ones on his lap, tell them stories, or sing lullabies: 'Abuelo / usted no nos contó historias / ni nos acunó en sus brazos' (Grandfather / you did not tell us stories / nor cradle us in your arms) (43). In the total context of this lyric, however, the tone in lines 1–8 is more plaintive than accusatory, for in lines 9–16 there is understanding, acceptance, and forgiveness: 'Usted fue distinto abuelo / es ahora cuando lo comprendo' (You were different, Grandfather / now I understand why) (42). 'De caricias en el tiempo' (With timely caresses), the adult persona attempts to heal the wounds of Black history, 'los duros y malheridos / senos de su historia'. This image recalls 'el padre acurrucado' (the hunchbacked father) of Morejón's 'La cena' (Suppertime) (12). By recording the saga of the ancestors, Campbell, like Morejón, assumes the role of the African griot in the diaspora – to remember, celebrate, and praise.

'A grany' (To Granny) is a poem about a visceral love for one of the village ancestors:

A fuerza de querer escucharla rezar
primero rezaron ellos
y luego cantaron (44)

(Because they wanted to hear her pray
they prayed first
and then sang)

Perhaps Granny is in mourning or on her death bed, but the family does not
want to let her go. Through faith they sing and pray her back to life again. The
pronouns 'she' (ella) and 'they' (ellos) show generational connectedness in
the poem (Hampton 33), for the grandmother's ability to sing and pray has
been transmitted to her family members, who, in turn, use this legacy to
revive her. The concretisation and personification of abstractions with select
verbs and ambiguous pronouns are techniques that highlight Campbell's
adeptness with concise language: 'ellos besaron a Dios / acariciaron el cielo
con la mirada / y palmearon la espalda de la felicidad' (they kissed God /
caressed heaven with one look / and patted joy on the back) (44). In short,
the characters in the 'Grandparent Trilogy' illustrate the varied responses to
suffering by women and men who are victims of migration, dislocation and
exile, as well as the exploration of family and community. These multifaceted
themes are characteristic of African diaspora literature.

'A grany' is a perfect transition between ' . . . las mujeres . . . y los
hombres' and the final part of *Naciendo*: 'Confesión' (Confession). This
part of the collection is a re-affirmation of faith, arrived at after an intense
period of questioning traditional beliefs. On the one hand, 'Invocación a
Dios' (Invocation to God) presents an interlocutor who challenges the
Supreme Being to reveal himself in human dimensions:

Por qué no venís Dios Mío
a interpretarnos la vida
vení a concluirnos las verdades
y a amarnos
con amor de hombre (47)

(Dear God, why don't you come
unravel life's mysteries for us
come settle certain truths for us
and love us
with human passion)

Although the issue is presented as a rhetorical question, it contains a note
of defiance. The failure to understand why evil and suffering exist weighs
heavily on the griot's shoulders, and she feels compelled to provide solutions

or restore hope to a defeated nation. This poem illustrates a personal relationship with God, as seen in the use of the familiar verb form 'venís', but it also shows the persona's attempt to communicate with the Supreme Being on a level that is accessible to the community. Both private and public anguish emerge in the phrases 'monótona plegaria' (monotonous plea) and 'sangrar nuestro sudor' (bleed our sweat). The latter also evokes the drops of blood-like sweat shed by Jesus on the Mount of Olives (Luke 22:44). In contrast, the poem 'Creer' (Believing) is more traditional in its affirmation of faith in an omnipotent, omnipresent, and omniscient being: 'Creo en Dios . . . / creo que existe / en el cielo / en la tierra / en el rostro del vecino / en mis senos sin madre / y en la vida / creo en Dios . . .' (I believe in God . . . / I believe He exists / whether in Heaven / or on earth / in my neighbour's face / and in my motherless bosom / and in life / I believe in God) (49). The use of ellipsis and economy of words underscore Campbell's attempt to articulate the joy and pain of spiritual rebirth and healing, which is its own reward.

In conclusion, *Naciendo* expands female discourse in Latin America, where the oeuvres of Black women writers have often been omitted from the canon. This situation indicates a general problem for the Afro-Hispanic author, who does not always have access to a publishing industry that would make his/her works available, or whose readership is almost always hindered by the lack of education, affordability, or interest (DeCosta-Willis 248). No matter what obstacles they face, Campbell and other Black women writers are developing a 'matriheritage of founding discourses'[3] in Latin America, but they also contribute to the upsurge in writing by females that is taking place in African-ancestored communities throughout the diaspora. In the words of Abena P.A. Busia:

> the growing body of works by black women writers of the African diaspora, collectively, has strategic impact, for within these works our writers re/collect the separated fictions of our lives, in order to reclaim our stories and to re-write our histories. In doing this, they legitimize lives and world views which have become for us the manifestations of the voice re-found. (289)

Race, gender, and aesthetics are pivotal in the poetry of Shirley Campbell in that the first two factors have impacted the cultural traditions on which she draws to create the aesthetics of a new Black female discourse in the private and public spheres. Through the motifs of birth, death, rebirth, return, passage, nurture, healing, and restoration, and through the use of figures of speech like imagery, metaphor, symbolism, understatement, ellipsis, detachment, allusion, and conciseness, Campbell spins a delicate and exquisite cocoon out of which a powerful and unique voice emerges, even as it gives testimony to the bilingual/bicultural heritage of post-negritude writing in Costa Rica. Furthermore, the mental, emotional, and spiritual liberation that comes from the validation of the Afro-Caribbean worldview ensures Campbell a prominent place in the canon of that tremendous global 'voice-refound' in literature.

Notes

1. Shirley Campbell, epígrafo, *Naciendo* (San José, Costa Rica: UNED, 1988) n.p. Even though the three poets wrote in English, Spanish, and French, respectively, Campbell translates them into Spanish: 'Si hemos de morir, que sea notablemente / para que nuestra cara sangre no se vierta en vano' (Claude McKay); 'Eh, compañeros, aquí estamos' (Nicolás Guillén); 'Quien no me comprenda no comprenderá el rugido de un tigre' (Aimé Césaire). All quotes from this edition will be cited parenthetically.

2. Toni Morrison, 'City Limits, Village Values', in *Literature & the Urban Experience: Essays on the City and Literature*, eds. Michael C. Jaye and Ann Chalmers Watts (New Brunswick, New Jersey: Rutgers University Press, 1981), 35-43. Morrison is careful to distinguish between the concept of village presented by White writers and Black authors. In much fiction and poetry by writers of the dominant culture, the city is an evil from which they seek escape, for it tends to restrain the freedom (rugged individualism) of the alienated, lonely hero. African American writers do not idealise either the city or the country, since both spaces hold their share of challenges, ugliness, terrors, and discomfort. Morrison observes about Black writers:

    > The general hostility to the city is not the result of the disappearance of grandeur or the absence of freedom. And the idealization of the country is not a pastoral delight in things being right with God. Writer after writer concedes explicitly or implicitly that the ancestor is the matrix of his yearning. The city is wholesome, loved when such an ancestor is on the scene, when neighborhood links are secure. The country is beautiful – healing because more often than not, such an ancestor is there (39).

3. Myriam Díaz-Diocaretz, ' "I Will Be a Scandal in Your Boat": Women Poets and the Tradition', In *Knives and Angels: Women Writers in Latin America*, ed., Susan Bassnett (London: Zed Books, 1990), 86-109. Quoted in Myriam Yvonne Jehenson, preface, *Latin American Women Writers: Class, Race, and Gender* (Albany: State University of New York Press, 1995), xi. Jehenson devotes a great deal of discussion to the tradition of writing among female

authors who identify as caucasian in Latin America, but tokenises indigenous authors like Domitila Barrios de Chungara and Rigoberta Menchú, as well as the Afro-Brazilian writer Carolina María de Jesus. Jehenson omits any reference to Afro-Hispanic women writers. Thus, I use Díaz-Diocaretz's 'matriheritage of founding discourses' to signify, i.e., to comment on the hypocritical posture of White women who complain about being excluded from the canon, but who commit the same sin where Black female authors are concerned.

Works cited

Busia, Abena P.A. 'This Gift of Metaphor: Symbolic Strategies and the Triumph of Survival in Simone Schwartz-Bart's *The Bridge of Beyond*'. In *Out of the Kumbla*. Eds., Carole Boyce Davis and Elaine Savoy Fido, 289-303. Trenton, New Jersey: Africa World Press, 1990.

Campbell, Shirley. *Naciendo*. San José, Costa Rica: UNED, 1998.

Davies, Carole Boyce, ed. 'Black Women's Writing: Crossing the Boundaries'. In *Matatu* 3.6 (1989): 1-4.

DeCosta-Willis, Miriam. 'Afra-Hispanic Writers and Feminist Discourse'. In *Women in Africa and the African Diaspora: A Reader*. Eds., Rosalyn Terborg-Penn and Andrea Benton Rushing, 247-62. Washington, DC: Howard University Press, 1996.

Díaz-Diocartez, Myriam. ' "I Will Be a Scandal in Your Boat": Women Poets and the Tradition'. In *Knives and Angels: Women Writers in Latin America*. Ed., Susan Bassnett, 86-109. London: Zed Books, 1990.

Duncan, Quince. Taller sobre el proceso creativo', Quince Duncan Symposium. Afro-Latin Research Conference. University of Pennsylvania, Indiana, Pennsylvania, March 21, 1998.

Gordon, Donald K. 'Expressions of the Costa Rican Black Experience: The Short Stories of Dolores Joseph and the Poetry of Shirley Campbell'. *Afro-Hispanic Review* 10 (September 1991): 21-6.

Hampton, Janet. 'Portraits of a Diasporan People: The Poetry of Shirley Campbell and Rita Dove'. *Afro-Hispanic Review* 14 (Spring 1995): 33-9.

Hughes, Langston. 'No Crystal Stair'. In *Selected Poems of Langston Hughes*. New York: Vintage Books, 1974.

Jehenson, Myriam Yvonne. *Latin-American Women Writers: Class, Race and Gender*. Albany: State University of New York Press, 1995.

Morejón, Nancy. 'La cena'. In *Richard trajo su flauta*. Havana: Cuadernos, 1967.

Morrison, Tony. 'City Limits, Village Values: Concepts of the Neighborhood in Black Fiction'. In *Literature and the Urban Experience: Essays on the City and Literature*. Eds., Michael C. Jaye and Ann Chalmers Watts, 35-43. New Brunswick, New Jersey: Rutgers University Press, 1981.

Shirley Campbell's *Rotundamente negra:* Content and Technique

Donald K. Gordon

Shirley Campbell Barr is a figure of increasing importance in Central American literature. Her first collection of poetry, *Naciendo* (Being Born), was published in 1988, and her second, *Rotundamente negra* (Unequivocally Black), in 1994. Three thematic strands – cultural, historical, feminist – combine to form an integrated whole that reflects her experiences as a Black Costa Rican woman, her prescription for change, and her hopes for the future. Hers is both an activist and a reflective voice, which portrays a keen consciousness of the situation of Blacks in general and of Black women in particular. Campbell's search for identity, centred on the Black-woman-as-mother, is part of a larger canvas that embraces cultural and historical aspects of Black people both inside and outside of Costa Rica. Her racial consciousness involves the elaboration of specific themes such as humanity, skin colour, racism, fear, love, sensuality, eroticism, religion, struggle, hope, solitude, time, and nature. In her representation of these themes, she utilises a variety of stylistic devices, including imagery, similes, personification, anaphora, polysyndeton, and repetition.

With respect to content and style, *Naciendo* and *Rotundamente negra* share characteristics, but there is no doubt that in its intensity and emotion, in its social and political message, *Rotundamente negra* is, as Campbell says 'blacker' than her first book. Campbell's racial consciousness stems from her life experiences, which have had an enormous influence on her and which have left an indelible mark on her poetry. Three aspects of her life are of crucial importance to her work, because they are part of the cultural framework in which her vision of herself as a Black woman is rooted. The history of Black people in Costa Rica, the culture of her people, the education of women and children, are of prime importance to Campbell. The first defining influence on Campbell has been her reconnection with the Port City of Limón, which Campbell's parents left for the capital San José. Campbell returned to Limón to work on United

Nations projects, her own focus being to educate indigenous women from Talamanca, Siguirres, and Matina, which she did between 1991 and 1993, striving to improve their level of education, and to make them aware of their rights. As part of a group dedicated to the study and diffusion of Black culture, she feels impelled to effect change because 'Costa Rican society, full of prejudices, has left us marginalized' (Monestel 25). Specifically, she is determined to break the stereotype of the Limonese as shiftless and devoted only to eating patties and playing dominoes. Her racial awareness is the most compelling factor, the essential basis of her poetry. She has said, 'I never lose sight of the fact that I am Black, this is basic for what I have to say in my poetry… from this starting point of who and what I am I launch out on more universal themes'(Monestel 24).

The second experiential and motivating force has been the Conservatorio de Castella. Campbell studied there and subsequently became an instructor in the Workshop for Literary Expression under the auspices of Costa Rica's Ministry of Education. She places great store by her work with adolescents and young children, and she often dedicates poems to the young children from her summer workshop at Castella. Poem I, for example, is dedicated to 'my little ones at the Castella workshop, 1990' *(RN 55)*, and poem VI is also dedicated 'to the little ones from the 1990 summer workshop because little by little we are retrieving our dreams and history' *(RN 119)*. The third imperative in Campbell's poetry, inextricably linked to her hopes for children and her nexus with Limón, is a need to relate to Africa, to feel an affinity with the motherland, the source of the black diaspora. She spent almost two years, 1994–1996, in Zimbabwe with her partner Harold Robinson, who worked for the United Nations, and their two children Tiffany and Nakei. While in Zimbabwe, Campbell did postgraduate work in African history and feminism in a programme run by New York's Syracuse University. Taking her children to Africa when they were young was of vital importance to Campbell, given her own experience. She has said, 'As any Black person in this country could tell you, growing up as a minority is a very traumatic experience. Ever since I was five years old I've wanted to go somewhere where I was in the majority, where no one would say to me, "Damn Black woman, why don't you go back to Africa"' (Pratt np). Campbell's Black consciousness has been heightened because she 'grew up in a white neighbourhood, went to a white school and eventually to a white university' (Pratt np). Going to Africa was the fulfilment of a dream for a woman who was conscious of her identity and aware of Africa as 'the land of an ancestry that has been denied us all our lives' (Pratt np).

Although the themes of race, colour, love, and struggle are evident in *Naciendo,* her second collection of poetry is more resolute in tone. *Rotundamente negra* has three sections. 'The Promised Land' includes ten poems, as well as a subsection, 'When Words Are Born', with two poems dedicated to children. This first section is inspired by Campbell's children and is prefaced by a short poem: 'To my children / because for them / is all that I do'. The second section, 'Now That I Can Shout It Out', contains eleven poems, primarily about love, and it begins: 'To you / companion in faith and in desire' (63). It seems inspired by Harold Robinson. She suggests that with the passage of time love is no longer clandestine (67), and no one has the right to deem the lovers culpable (85). The third section, 'Unequivocally Black', has 13 poems that deal with Black consciousness and her experiences as a Black woman. She is a Black woman – a mother and lover, as well as a participant in the fight for equality and justice – who writes: 'I declare myself an active member / of the struggle' (114–115). This section is dedicated 'to all of you, whom I am certain, share these principles'. Interspersed throughout the book are pencil sketches of women's faces that reflect two key elements in Campbell's work: women and colour, or specifically, women of colour.

The Black woman is central to Campbell's poetry and the nexus Black-woman-mother is an important theme in *Rotundamente negra,* because Campbell wants the reader to know that her poetry is by a Black woman who is a mother. She once said, 'I am exceptionally proud to be a Black woman. I want people to know just by reading my work, without hearing my name or seeing my picture, that my poems were written by a Black woman-mother. For me, there's nothing more important' (Pratt n.p.). A poem that describes her passage to adulthood concludes: 'I understand I was a woman / a Black woman' (129). In another poem, she expresses the complexity of her identity, for she wants readers 'to understand that I am Black / woman / lover / to understand that I am mother' (114). The theme of the Black-woman-as-mother is so important in her poetry that it has led one commentator to write that 'Campbell...describes herself first as a mother and then as a Black woman' (Pratt np). The distinction between these two aspects of her being is not necessary, because Campbell feels no contradiction between the two: motherhood and blackness are the forces that drive Campbell's poetry.

Rotundamente negra is intensely personal. She writes about giving birth in poem VI – 'my life began/ when I gave you life', and in poem IX she recounts how Tiffany and Malcom changed her life. Her poem on Tiffany (III) depicts a new and loving mother and the miracle of a wondrous newborn daughter, but with the caveat 'we are black / and while we endeavour to grasp that truth / we shall always have kisses to give / and unsullied hands / to be kissed'. The poem has received widespread publicity because it appeared in *La Nación* with a photograph of mother and daughter. In another autobiographical poem, Campbell reveals that she gave birth at ages 23 and 26, and she describes the joy and pain of becoming a mother: 'I do not lament having given birth to them with blood / and much / much pain' (113). Campbell delves deeply into family relationships in *Rotundamente negra*, particularly in the second section, which deals with love. The poet views sensuality and the expression of sexual intimacy as the highest manifestation of love. The persona wants her lover 'to sink me in your body / … to feel me as part of you' (75), 'with all this passion / ablaze in my organ' (92), 'my breasts afire / and my organ' (95).

Campbell's relationship with her partner made it easy for her to accompany him to Zimbabwe, a trip which fulfilled her dream of going to Africa, the cradle of her ancestry. Campbell is keenly aware of her history and of her role as an active participant in the struggle for equality. The resolve to struggle is militantly affirmed in *Rotundamente negra*: 'I declare myself an active member / of this struggle… an indefatigable worker / and the blackest in the world' (114–115). The demonstrative adjective 'this' suggests that the battle is not yet won, and the adjective in the superlative gives an aura of militant pride. Campbell's insistence on her blackness emanates from her awareness of prejudice based on skin colour. In *Rotundamente negra*, she returns frequently to the question of colour and the reality of raising children 'of this colour' (30). For a Black person, survival is an art: 'it requires daily skill / having skin of this colour' (42). 'To live day after day / in this skin' (101) suggests the prolongation and intractability of racial discrimination. Campbell addresses the problem in a poem written 'To Carlos, because he is beginning to understand', an apparent reference to Carlos Manuel Morera, who wrote the prologue to *Rotundamente negra*. Her poem is a gentle rebuke to her friend, who is just 'beginning to understand', and it suggests that he would have to be part of her history to understand. The racism that Carlos acknowledges in the disparagement of Black women is anathema to Campbell, who regards her skin (22), eyes, and lips (113) as beautiful.

Campbell attributes her self-esteem and sense of history to her grandparents, legendary figures whom she portrays as strong caregivers and nurturers. In *Rotundamente negra*, she depicts the strength and femininity of the women: 'our grandmothers / who never wept / who were women all their lives' (119–120). Her homage to her forebears is similar to that of Nicolás Guillén, who acknowledged his dual ancestry, Spanish and African, in such celebrated poems as 'Ballad of the Two Grandfathers' and 'My Name'. In Poem VI, Campbell gives Shamara the words to say her name, her true name. The Costa Rican poet, like Guillén, respects a person's worth regardless of colour. There is also a similarity in the two poets' concept of humanity, particularly in Guillén's 'Execution' and 'The Wall'. Campbell's poetry suggests that universal human values must take precedence over skin colour, which Guillén affirms in 'Eh, companions, here we are', the epigraph to *Naciendo*. Campbell's admiration for Guillén is evident in poem X of the section 'Rotundamente negra'. The long elegy to Guillén is significant because it synthesises elements of his poetry while lamenting his death. The poet addresses the Cuban in the second person, as a friend, recognising that he depicted 'the blows of our history' (135). She reflects on the question of colour and of common ideals: 'those of us who have / the colour of your skin / who share your aggrieved dream' (134). She captures the cadence of Guillén's verse: 'Nicolás Guillén has died / he who sang to you in Yoruba / sóngoro cosongo / and depicted you in black / the colour of hope' (135). Finally, she pleads: 'do not die / as yet this world / is still not ready / to live without you' (135-136).

For Guillén, black was the colour of hope, and the idea of hope is pervasive in Campbell's poetry. It appears with great frequency in *Naciendo* and is continued in *Rotundamente negra* in a figurative house 'called hope' (6). If Campbell emphasises hope, she also projects the essential loneliness of the human being. The concept of solitude is pervasive in her first collection and is reiterated in the second, where the poet writes of her 'emptiness' (128). Loneliness engenders fear, and the poet expresses a fear of dusk and of being alone at daybreak (81). The antidote to fear is love, and in poem X, love conquers fear. Campbell also writes about love of God. A manifestation of Campbell's belief in a higher power is her frequent depiction of nature: rain, sea, ocean, moon, and sun. In *Naciendo,* nature evokes sadness, but in *Rotundamente negra* the mood is more optimistic: 'to believe that dawn / is more imminent / than night / ... to make the sun / sing to us / a beautiful song / of welcome / to be able to believe in the following day' (104). References to 'dawn' and 'night' indicate the passage of time, which marks the progression of her personal suffering. The poet uses stylistic devices, such as repetitions, anaphora, oxymorons, personification, and similes to underscore the themes of time, love, and death.

Whether dealing with love or hope, the poet uses specific stylistic devices to enhance her sentiments. She employs polysyndeton to depict a dream, which recalls 'I Have a Dream' by Martin Luther King, whom she mentions by name. Campbell has a dream to share with children: 'and they rise at dawn / and they sing / and they dream / and when the children dream ...' (125). Polysyndeton is also employed in VIII, an autobiographic poem about growing up, which reflects the solitude of her search for self. She writes, 'and I felt the emptiness / and I looked at others / and I could not find myself / and I felt the emptiness' (128). Just as polysyndeton underscores the poet's lonely struggle for self-identity, it also highlights the problem of racism 'in Africa / and in Haiti / and in the Southern United States / and in the world' (141).

In elaborating on the themes of humanity, liberty, hope, solitude, time, nature, love, family, God, and, especially, Black women, Campbell employs a variety of stylistic devices: polysyndeton, symbolism, repetition, anaphora, paronomasia, imagery, simile, and metaphor. Content and form thus coalesce in the projection of her message. Janet J. Hampton understands the significance of Campbell's poetry when she writes that the poet joins 'the chorus of voices ... of sisters, scattered throughout the world, in revealing, recounting and celebrating their communities'. Ultimately, self-acceptance and pride are most important. In *Rotundamente negra,* the poet reiterates her message in the last poem, XIII, from which comes the book's title: 'I unequivocally refuse / to refute my voice / ... because / I accept myself / unequivocally free / unequivocally black / unequivocally beautiful' (143 – 144). 'Free', 'black', and 'beautiful' are crucially significant adjectives, which garner more force individually and collectively through the repetition of the adverb 'unequivocally'. Technique and content combine to make the poetry of Shirley Campbell increasingly important.

Works Cited

Campbell, Shirley. *Naciendo.* San José, Costa Rica: Departamento de Publicaciones de la UNED, 1988.
___. *Rotundamente Negra.* San José, Costa Rica: Arado, 1994.
Hampton, Janet J. 'Portraits of a Diasporan People: The Poetry of Shirley Campbell and Rita Dove'. *Afro-Hispanic Review* 14 (Spring 1995): 33-9.
Monestel, Manuel. '¡Yo También Canto, Patria!' *Aportes* (October 1987): 25
Pratt, Christine. 'Costa Rican Black Poet Shirley Campbell Bound for Africa'. In *The Tico Times* (July 29, 1994): 24

Mayra Santos-Febres

ℳAYRA 𝒮ANTOS-FEBRES

PUERTO RICO

(b. 1966)

One of Puerto Rico's most prolific and internationally renowned writers, Mayra Santos-Febres is a poet, essayist, novelist, editor, short story writer, and university professor, who has published five books and completed a doctorate – all before age thirty-five. She grew up surrounded by books and the tools of writing in a family of teachers that included her mother, father, aunts, and uncles, who nurtured her mind and spirit with words and images. She began writing at five and decided to become a writer at fifteen because, as she explained, 'Words are the medium through which I understand the worlds that I inhabit'. Her narratives, the products of extensive reading and research, reveal the dignity and beauty of the down-and-out – the prostitutes, domestics, obese men, homosexuals, Blacks, and poor people who cling to the margins of society. She commented in a recent interview, 'I don't know if it has to do with my personal experiences as a Black woman but I have always searched for beauty in what people usually discard as useless'. In that search, she creates magic through wondrous tales, haunting characters, and sensuous, poetic language evoking the sounds and rhythms and textures of her island homeland; at the same time, she deals subtly and profoundly with serious issues such as racism, sexism, homophobia, colonialism, and capitalism.

Santos-Febres' writing is characterised by humour, irony, stylistic innovations, nuanced characterisations, erotically charged language, and complete control of her craft. Bilingual in Spanish and English, she writes in Spanish, and her works have been translated into French, English, Italian, Portuguese, and Slovenian. She has published two collections of critically acclaimed poetry: El orden escapado *(Escaped Order), in 1988, which won first prize in* Tríptico *magazine's contest in honour of Evaristo Rivera Chevremon; and* Anamú y manigua, *published in 1991, which celebrates the contributions of Black women to Puerto Rican culture. Her first collection of short stories,* Pez de Vidrio *(Stained Glass Fish), translated as* Urban Oracles *(1994), won the Letras de Oro Prize, while the short story 'Oso blanco' (White Bear) from her 1998 collection* El cuerpo correcto *(Correct Body) won France's Juan Rulfo Prize. Noted for her original and subversive treatments of race, gender, and sexuality, Santos-Febres published her first novel in 2000.* Sirena Selena Vestida de Pena *(Siren Selena Dressed in Sorrow) deals, poignantly and humorously, with the ambiguities of sexuality as depicted by a sixteen-year-old tranvestite, gifted with a seductive, siren-like voice. The novel, which has received rave reviews and was on Puerto Rico's bestselling list, reveals, according to one critic, the deep desire of the human being to transcend reality and discover beauty. Particularly compelling are her portraits of women, which are inspired by memories of ordinary women, forgotten mothers and grandmothers, as well as political and literary heroines, such as Lolita Lebrón, Julia de Burgos, and Angela María Dávila.*

Currrently an associate professor at the University of Puerto Rico, she was awarded Mellon and Ford Foundation grants for graduate study at Cornell University, from which she received a doctorate in 1991. An artist, intellectual, and cultural worker, she has given readings and performances of her work throughout the world, organised and conducted writing workshops, attended seminars and conferences to promote literature, assisted with journals such as Piso 13 *and* Página Robada, *affiliated herself with poetry circles like En la Mirilla and La Iguana Dorada, and collaborated with a group investigating 'Racism and Identity'. In 1995, she received a grant to conduct a Youth Forum on Puerto Rican Literature and to edit the anthology* Mal(h)ab(l)ar: nueva literatura puertorriqueña. *With a second work of fiction underway – this time, a detective novel – Santos-Febres is living up to her words: 'I haven't started dropping my fat pieces yet'.*

The Institute of Culture Says

The Institute of Culture says
that Puerto Rican women are
Taino, Spanish and African
perhaps
but perhaps we are also those
who squat with our backs to the wind
without memory of anything but
the dress put on lay-away a week ago
or the touch of relaxer we should apply to our
hair, maybe some highlights
or to find the perfectly matching nail enamel . . .
The latest demographic census says
that Puerto Rican women are
nine for every man
perhaps
but perhaps we are also
a sweaty confusion in mid air
attempting to look between our legs
without shame, or scorn,
without fury, or sorrow
just as one watches a passerby
finish his coffee and smile,
a guerrilla warfare against loneliness
against pungent men
who always leave us for
taller, thinner, blonder girls
against a fear to love other women a bit too much
to get pregnant, to get fat.
The Commission on Women's Issues says
that Puerto Rican women are
more than 37 per cent of the country's labour force
perhaps
but also, perhaps we are those who support

three children and a husband
with miserable wages,
or we who sell cosmetics and tupperware
on our lunch breaks
to pay the phone and electricity
those who bear the bosses' stained hands
and laugh
laugh desperately
we who laugh to keep from sending all to hell
to keep from running
towards fury's eye
away from statistics
that can never quantify
that inner rainstorm that never ends
that leaves everything faceless without edges
that corrodes the nail by which we hang
our last hope, once we get home.

Translated by author

Marina's Fragrance

Doña Marina Paris was a woman of many charms. At forty-nine her skin still breathed those fragrances which when she was young had left the men of her town captivated and searching for ways to lick her flanks to see if they tasted as good as they smelled. And every day they smelled of something different. At times, a delicate aroma of witch's oregano would drift out of the folds of her thighs; other days, she perfumed the air with masculine mahogany or with small wild lemons. But most of the time she exuded pure satisfaction.

From the time she was very little, Doña Marina had worked in the Pinchimoja take-out restaurant, an establishment opened in the growing town of Carolina by her father Esteban Paris. Previously, Esteban had been a virtuoso clarinetist, a road builder and a molasses sampler for the Victoria Sugarcane Plantation. His common-law wife, Edovina Vera, was the granddaughter of one Pancracia Hernandez, a Spanish shopkeeper fallen on hard times, for whom time had set a trap in the form of a black man from Canovanas. He showed her what it meant to really enjoy a man's company, after she had lost faith in almost everything, including God.

Marina grew up in the Pinchimoja. Mama Edovina, who gave birth to another sister every year, entrusted Marina with the restaurant and made her responsible for watching Maria, the half-crazy woman who helped Mama move the giant pots of rice and beans, the pots of *tinapa* in sauce, of chicken soup, roasted sweet potato, and salt cod with raisins, the specialty of the house. Her special task was to make sure that Maria didn't cook with coconut oil. Someone had to protect the restaurant's reputation and keep people from thinking that the owners were a crowd of sneaky blacks from Loiza.

From eight to thirteen years of age, Marina exuded spicy, salty, and sweet odors from all the hinges of her flesh. And since she was always enveloped in her fragrances, she didn't even notice that they were bewitching every man who passed close to her. Her pompous smile, her kinky curls hidden in braids or kerchiefs, her high cheekbones, and the scent of the day drew happiness from even the most decrepit sugarcane-cutter, from the skinniest road-worker burnt by the sun, from her father, the frustrated clarinetist, who rose from his stupor of alcohol and daydreams to stand near his Marina just to smell her as she passed by.

Eventually, the effect Marina had on men began to preoccupy Edovina. She was especially worried by the way she was able to stir Esteban from his alcoholic's chair. The rest of the time he sat prostrate from five o'clock every morning, after he finished buying sacks of rice and plantains from the supplier who drove by in his cart on the way down to the Nueva Esperanza market. Marina was thirteen, a dangerous age. So one day Edovina opened a bottle of Cristobal Colon Rum from Mayaguez, set it next to her partner's chair, and went to look for Marina in the kitchen, where she was peeling sweet potatoes and plantains.

'Today you begin working for the Velazquezes. They will give you food, new clothes, and Doña Georgina's house is near the school.' Edovina took Marina out of the back of the Pichimoja over towards Jose de Diego Street. They crossed behind Alberti's pharmacy to the house of Doña Georgina, a rich and pious white woman, whose passion for cassava stewed rich with shrimp was known throughout the town.

It was at about this time that Marina began to smell like the ocean. She would visit her parents every weekend. Esteban, a bit more pickled each time, reached the point where he no longer recognized her, for he became confused thinking that she would smell like the daily specials. When Marina arrived perfumed with the red snapper or shrimp that they ate regularly in the elegant mansion, her father took another drag from the bottle which rested by his chair and lost himself in memories of his passion for the clarinet. The Pinchimoja no longer attracted the people that it used to. It had lapsed into the category of breakfast joint; you could eat *funche* there, or corn fritters with white cheese, coffee and stew. The office workers and road-builders had moved to a different take-out restaurant with a new attraction that could replace the dark body of the thirteen-year-old redolent with flavorful odors – a jukebox which at lunch time played Felipe Rodriguez, Perez Prado, and Benny Moore's Big Band.

It was in the Velazquez house that Marina became aware of her remarkable capacity to harbor fragrances in her flesh. She had to get up before five every morning so she could prepare the rice and beans and their accompaniments; this was the condition that the Velazquezes imposed in exchange for allowing her to attend the public school. One day, while she was thinking about the food that she had to prepare the next morning, she caught her body smelling like the menu. Her elbows smelled like fresh *recaillo;* her armpits smelled like garlic, onions and red pepper; her forearms like roasted sweet potato with butter; the space between her flowering breasts like pork loin fried in onions; and further down like grainy white rice, just the way her rice always came out.

From then on she imposed a regimen of drawing remembered scents from her body. The aromas of herbs came easily. Marjoram, pennyroyal and mint were her favourites. Once she felt satisfied with the results of these experiments, Marina began to experiment with emotional scents. One day she tried to imagine the fragrance of sadness. She thought long and hard of the day Mama Edovina sent her to live in the Velazquez household. She thought of Esteban, her father, sitting in his chair imagining what could have been his life as a clarinetist in the mambo bands or in Cesar Concepcion's combo. Immediately an odor of mangrove swamps and sweaty sheets, a smell somewhere between rancid and sweet, began to waft from her body. Then she worked on the smells of solitude and desire. Although she could draw those aromas from her own flesh, the exercise left her exhausted; it was too much work. Instead, she began to collect odors from her masters, from the neighbours near the Velazquez house, from the servants who lived in the little rooms off the courtyard of hens, and from the clothesline where Doña Georgina's son hung his underwear.

Marina didn't like Hipolita Velazquez, junior, at all. She had surprised him once in the bathroom pulling on his penis, which gave off an odor of oatmeal and sweet rust. This was the same smell (a bit more acid) which his underpants dispelled just before being washed. He was six years older than she, sickly and yellow, with emaciated legs and without even an ounce of a bottom. 'Esculapio' she called him quietly when she saw him passing, smiling as always with those high cheekbones of a presumptuous Negress. The gossips around town recounted that the boy spent almost every night in the Tumbabrazos neighborhood, looking for mulatta girls upon whom he could 'do the damage.' He was enchanted by dark flesh. At times, he looked at her with a certain eagerness. Once he even insinuated that they should make love, but Marina turned him down. He looked so ugly to her, so weak and foolish, that just imagining Hipolito laying a finger upon her made her whole body begin to smell like rotten fish and she felt sick.

After a year and a half of living with the Velazquezes, Marina began to take note of the men around town. At Carolina's annual town fair that year, she met Eladio Salaman, who with one long smell left her madly in love. He had a lazy gaze and his body was tight and fibrous as the sweet heart of a sugarcane. His reddish skin reminded her of the tops of mahogany tables in the Velazquez house. When Eladio Salaman drew close to Marina that night, he arrived with a tidal wave of new fragrances that left her enraptured for hours, while he led her by the arm all around the town square.

The ground of the rain forest, mint leaves sprinkled with dew, a brand-new washbasin, morning ocean spray… Marina began to practice the most difficult odors to see if she could invoke Eladio Salaman's. This effort drew her attention away from all her other duties, and at times she inadvertently served her masters dishes that had the wrong fragrances. One afternoon the shrimp cassava came out smelling like pork chops with vegetables. Another day, the rice with pigeon peas perfumed the air with the aroma of greens and salt cod. The crisis reached such extremes that a potato casserole came out of the oven smelling exactly like the Velazquez boy's underpants. They had to call a doctor, for everyone in the house who ate that day vomited until they coughed up nothing but bile. They believed they had suffered severe food poisoning.

Marina realized that the only way to control her fascination with that man was to see him again. Secretly she searched for him on all the town's corners, using her sense of smell, until two days later she found him sitting in front of the Serceda Theater drinking a soda. That afternoon, Marina invented an excuse, and did not return to the house in time to prepare lunch. Later she ran home in time to cook dinner, which was the most flavorful meal that was ever eaten in the Velazquez dining room throughout the whole history of the town, for it smelled of love and of Eladio Salaman's sweet body.

One afternoon, while strolling through the neighborhood, Hipolito saw the two of them, Marina and Eladio, hand in hand, smiling and entwined in each other's aromas. He remembered how the dark woman had rejected him and now he found her lost in the caresses of that black sugarcane cutter. He waited for the appropriate moment and went to speak with his esteemed mother. Who knows what Hipolito told her – but when Marina arrived back at the house, Doña Georgina was furious.

'Indecent, evil, stinking Black woman.'

And Mama Edovina was forced to convince the mistress not to throw her daughter out of her house. Doña Georgina agreed, but only on the condition that Marina take a cut in her wages and an increase in her supervision. Marina couldn't go to the market unaccompanied, she couldn't stroll on the town square unaccompanied, she could only communicate with Eladio through messages.

Those were terrible days. Marina couldn't sleep; she couldn't work. Her vast memory of smells disappeared in one fell swoop. The food she prepared came out insipid – all of it smelled like an empty chest of drawers. This caused Doña Georgina to redouble her insults. 'Conniving little thing, Jezebel, polecat.'

One afternoon Marina decided she wouldn't take any more. She decided to summon Eladio through her scent, one that she had made in a measured and defined way and shown to him one day of kisses in the untilled back lots of the sugar plantation. 'This is my fragrance,' Marina had told him. "Remember it well." And Eladio, fascinated, drank it in so completely that Marina's fragrance would be absorbed into his skin like a tattoo.

Marina studied the direction of the wind carefully. She opened the windows of the mansion and prepared to perfume the whole town with herself. Immediately the stray dogs began to howl and the citizens rushed hurriedly through the streets, for they thought they were producing that smell of frightened bromeliads and burning saliva. Two blocks down the street, Eladio, who was talking to some friends, recognized the aroma; he excused himself and ran to see Marina. But as they kissed, the Velazquez boy broke in on them and, insulting him all the way, threw Eladio out of the house.

As soon as the door was closed, Hipolito proposed to Marina that if she let him suck her little titties he would maintain their secret and not say anything to his mother. 'You can keep your job and escape Mama's insults, too,' he told her, approaching her.

Marina became so infuriated that she couldn't control her body. From all the pores wafted a scaly odor mixed with the stench of burned oil and acid used for cleaning engines. The odor was so intense that Hipolito had to lean on the living room's big colonial sofa with the medallions, overwhelmed by a wave of dizziness. He felt as if they had pulled the floor out from under him, and he fell squarely down on the freshly mopped tiles.

Marina sketched a victorious smile. With a firm tread she strode into Doña Georgina's bedroom. She filled the room with an aroma of desperate melancholy (she had drawn it from her father's body) that trampled the sheets and dressers. She was going to kill that old woman with pure frustration. Calmly she went to her room, bundled her things together, and gazed around the mansion. The pest, the Velazquez boy, lay on the floor in a state from which he would never fully recover. The master bedroom smelled of stale dreams that accelerated the palpitations of the heart. The whole house gave off disconnected, nonsensical aromas, so that nobody in town ever wanted to visit the Velazquez house again.

Marina smiled. Now she would go see Eladio. She would go resucitate the Pinchimoja. She would leave that house forever. But before exiting through the front door a few filthy words – which surprised even her – escaped from her mouth. Walking down the balcony stairs, she was heard to say with determination,

'Let them say *now* that blacks stink!'

'The Page on Which Life Writes Itself'
A Conversation with Mayra Santos Febres

Elba D. Birmingham-Pokorny

EB-P: I want to begin this interview with a very broad question: Why do you write?

MS-F: Why do I write? Mainly because I cannot stop doing it, nor can I imagine wanting to do anything else with more passion and purpose. There is nothing that makes more sense to me, nothing that nourishes me more. Words are the medium through which I understand the worlds that I inhabit, visit, or dream about. So, basically, I write because I have to. It is the way in which I live this life of mine.

EB-P: When did you begin writing and in what genre?

MS-F: I began writing poetry when I was very young; I must have been five or six years old at the time. I decided to become a writer when I was fifteen years old. Since then, I have been assisting at workshops, organising small poetry journals and other publications, and participating in literary life.

EB-P: Is writing an integral part of your existence?

MS-F: Yes. Better still, literature is a part of my existence. When I am not writing, I read. When I am not reading, I edit. When I am not editing, I teach literature, or write diaries, or make notes for a project. I must not get carried away, though, because there are other activities that I enjoy and live for: taking care of my mother, for instance, enjoying my relationships with family and friends, loving my husband, going to my step aerobics class. But, yes, writing is an essential part of my existence.

EB-P: Is writing painful for you? Do you find that you have to go to certain places in your imagination or in reality before you come to terms with what it is that you want to write or say?

MS-F: It is very difficult to ask a writer about his or her creative process. I cannot describe it, except through the use of vague metaphors, such as 'beyond reason' or 'mystical' and so on. I sincerely hate those phrases; they are filled with false glitter. So, I don't know if I have to go to a certain place in reality or in my imagination to come to terms with what I want to say. I can only tell you that the creative process is not painful to me. It is somewhat difficult, a bit exasperating, but never painful. Not yet. Besides, I am deeply convinced that pain is overrated in the literary world. For the Romantics it became a marker (sometimes a substitute) for intelligence, for depth. I think that pleasure and laughter can be as shallow or as deep as pain can be. That is why I prefer to refer to the creative process as challenging. To translate life into literature and sensations into memory is a difficult task. But I enjoy every minute of it.

EB-P: Is there anything that you have a fear of when you write?

MD-F: When I write, what I fear the most is to tell the truth, my deepest-felt truth, in a way so innocuous that it could easily be mistaken for a Sprite commercial.

EB-P: What is your writing process composed of? Do you make notes and compile them or do you sit down and write until the work is completed?

MS-F: Pulse, sensation, and resonance – those are the main ingredients in my writing process. First, a feeling has to be awakened. Then, I have to find the sensations that translate that feeling into meaning, a corporeal meaning. And from there, I go into language. Therefore, when I write, I take notes, draw maps of departures and destinations, and find routes into the page. But I always start with that initial thrust, that pulse that I write down like a maniac, fearful of losing the raw experience of that initial feeling.

EB-P: What particular experiences have influenced you as a writer?

MS-F: It is very difficult to pinpoint one experience as the beginning of my career as a writer. *Fue azaroso, como todo en la vida, llegar hasta la página* (It was risky, like everything in life, to get to the page). I grew up, However, surrounded by writing materials. Pens, paper, and blackboards were my first toys. You see, my mother, father, five aunts, and three uncles were teachers. There were books in my house, but they were not valued as 'Art'. They were working tools. Maybe that is why literature is not sacred to me; it is a way of life.

EB-P: Many well known writers have had their work translated into other languages. Have your works been translated and, if so, which ones and into which languages?

MS-F: They have been translated into English, Portuguese, Slovenian, and French. A newspaper in Slovenia and *Revue Noire* in Paris published a selection of poetry from *Anamú y Manigua*. *The Latin American Review of Arts and Literature* and the *Review of the National Library* in Brasil have also published some things. Last year, Lumen Books in Boston published an English translation of my short story collection, *Pez de vidrio,* which was given the title *Urban Oracles*. But I hope that all of my work will be available in translation in many languages, including Esperanto, Yoruba, Slavic, and Braille.

EB-P: Have you used any woman from your immediate family as a model for some of your texts and, if so, who and for what reason?

MS-F: I use all the women in my family and most of my women friends as models in my writing. I measure myself against them and the world.

EB-P: Which writers have had a major influence or impact upon you as a writer?

MS-F: All the writers I have read influence me in one way or another, even the ones that I dislike. But, if you ask me which are my favourite writers, I would say that LATELY my favourites are Toni Morrison, Manuel Ramos Otero, Allen Ginsburg, and Jean Genet. I like very few heterosexual male writers: just some short stories by Jorge Luis Borges, Julio Cortázar, Octavio Paz's *Piedra del sol,* and most of César Vallejo. I also like Ayi Kweyi Armah and Salman Rushdie, but that is about it.

EB-P: What do you have in common with contemporary Puerto Rican writers such as Rosario Ferré, Ana Lydia Vega, Carmen Lugo Filippi, and others, and what distinguishes your persona from theirs?

MS-F: I honestly don't know. We all write about Puerto Rico quite a bit. And we do share similar preoccupations about gender. But, aside from those sociological coincidences, I don't think that our work is similar at all. Then again, Ana Lydia Vega's concern with popular slang is very different from Rosarito's use of linguistic irony in her critique of the island's sugarcane aristocracy, or Carmen Lugo Filippi's elliptic narration of intimate worlds. There is one thing, though, that sets me apart from all the other writers: I am Black. My take on race as a literary theme goes beyond its use as a trope or a symbol of nationhood.

EB-P: What do you perceive as the major differences between the Puerto Rican women writers who live outside of Puerto Rico and those who continue to live on the island? Do you see any aesthetic differences in the works of writers from the Puerto Rican diaspora? What is the importance of the site of creation to the creative act?

MS-F: I think that the main difference between mainland and island-based Puerto Rican writers, in general, is the centrality of ethnic definitions. In Puerto Rico, you do not have to defend your Puerto Ricanness; it is a given. There are, however, other struggles such as the fight for political independence, the experience of racism and sexism, and the liberation of our imagination from colonialism. For US-based Puerto Rican writers, the point of reference is different. They have to deal with issues of language, culture, and identity. It is all a question of location. The site of creation is central to the creative act, definitely. But it is only central when that site is charged with an existential meaning. What I mean by this is that for a French or British writer to write from, let's say, Singapore, might not mean much in the manner of creation, but for a Latin American, African, or Indian writer, it can make all the difference in the world. Colonisation has charged our sites – our territories, countries, neo-colonies, ethnicities, et cetera – with a tense meaning. Aside from that, a place is also a point of intersection for many experiences: light, sound, climate, culture. In my case right now, I honestly prefer to write from Puerto Rico. Living on the island is fundamental to me.

EB-P: How has your work been received here in Puerto Rico? How have critics here reacted to your work as compared to those who live outside of Puerto Rico?

MS-F: From the beginning, the reception of my work inside and outside of Puerto Rico has been great. Many critics have commented on the plasticity and sensuality of my language, and on the importance of race and gender as major themes in my work.

EB-P: Would you discuss what you see as the status of women writers, particularly contemporary women writers, in Puerto Rican literature?

MS-F: Women are not marginal in Puerto Rico. We now define the canon of contemporary literature. That is a fact that nobody can deny. Rosario Ferré, Ana Lydia Vega, Magali García Ramos, Mayra Montero are major voices in our literature. Then again, the same goes for all of Latin American literature. The best known writers who emerged after the boom of the 1960s are all women: Luisa Valenzuela, Isabel Allende, Diamela Eltitt, Angeles Mastretta .... There has been a shift in the international evaluation of women writers. I am not arguing, though, that there is no sexism in the worlds we inhabit as women writers. We are expected to deal with certain themes and to write according to a certain formula: the 'women's literature' formula. In other words, we are supposed to write about domestic abuse, sexual harassment, the home, tradition, et cetera, as if that is all that we know and can relate to. The thing is that the world of a woman is vaster than her gender. Gender is but a standpoint from which one sees the world, an important perspective but one of many, nevertheless. The same goes for race, sexual preference, class, nationality.... I believe that the way to go is to stress difference as one erases it through writing. Because, yes, I am a Black Puerto Rican woman writer (and proud of it!), but I will always be more than those categories, which will never be able to define me completely. The day that happens, I am done for. Because I have the right to be more than a Black Puerto Rican woman writer. I have the right to be 'universal' and 'human', just as a White French male writer does. Why not?

EB-P: In your opinion, what does it mean to be a Black woman in the Spanish-speaking Caribbean, in a US colony such as Puerto Rico? On the basis of this experience, what do you see as the position of the Black writer in Puerto Rico and in Latin America?

MS-F: I don't know what it means to be a Black woman in the Spanish-speaking Caribbean. I know how it feels. It feels as if you exist in virtual reality, as a symbol of 'our shared African heritage', as if you passed out of an episode of *Roots* and started roaming around the island without any connection whatsoever to the transformations that you see unravelling in front of your eyes. You are the past.

In our island nations, the future is not black. Nor is the present. Each of the contemporary manifestations of race in the Dominican Republic, Puerto Rico, and Cuba is criminalised or brushed away as fashion, assimilation, or plain craziness. Rap, for instance, international hip-hop culture, Afro-Antillean religion. All of these manifestations of race become domesticated through the rhetoric of the nation. *Merengué* and *bachata* become Dominican, and since Dominicans are not Black, according to the nation's rhetoric, then the genre miraculously becomes White. The same goes for the rumba and salsa. But something weird happens when the genres are needed to attract tourism. In such cases, the nation folklorises the musical expressions, dresses Black musicians and dancers in funny costumes, and *Voilá!* The origins become theatricalised and blackness becomes a performance from the distant past.

I believe that something very similar happens in the rest of Latin America, especially in places such as Bolivia or Ecuador or Uruguay, where these countries selected another symbol to define their origins: the native Amerindian. So, the existence of a Black writer in Latin America, or in the Caribbean to a lesser extent, is pretty precarious. If he or she does not become a token, s/he becomes a symbol of national origin, of the past. I refuse to be one or the other. I still haven't figured out how I will manage not to fall into those categories, but I am trying hard not to become Tembandumba de la Quimbamba.

EB-P: You are one of the youngest women writers in Puerto Rican literature. How do you view yourself and those of your immediate generation of writers in relation to the tradition of Puerto Rican literature? By this I mean, do you see yourself as involved in the tradition as well as doing something new or making a contribution to Puerto Rican literature?

MS-F: I think that Ezra Pound was right when he said that each writer reinvents literary tradition by engaging in a conversation with his or her literary ancestors. My imaginary conversations with Julia de Burgos, Angela María Dávila, Luis Palés Matos, José I de Diego Padró, and others have provoked entire books. You can read *Anamú y manigua* as a response to Correijer's 'Alabanza a la Torre de Ciales', Julia's 'Farewell to Welfare Island', and Palés' *Tuntún de pasa y grifería*. You could also read *Pez de vidrio* as a response to Ana Lydia Vega's *Encancaranublado* and to Manuel Ramos Otero's 'El cuento de la mujer del mar.' And then again, you can trace other conversations in those books to many other traditions. I speak with Puerto Rican writers of the present and the past as much as I speak with Toni Morrison, Salman Rushdie, Jean Genet, Masaweta Devi, Jorge Luis Borges, Octavio Paz, Patrick Suskind, Luisa Valenzuela, Alejandra Pizarnik, Elena Poniatowska, and Angélica Gorodischer, to name but a few.

As to my contribution to the Puerto Rican literary tradition, I think it is too soon to say what it is. I haven't started dropping my fat pieces yet.

EB-P: You are a woman and one of the major new writers of Puerto Rico. How has writing through the affective filters of sexism and racism affected you professionally?

MS-F: They haven't affected me at all. Racism and sexism have not interfered with my profession as a writer or university professor. If I say otherwise, I would be lying. I am not arguing that there is no sexism or racism in Puerto Rican universities or in our literary community. There are very few Black professors, very few Black writers, very few Afrocentric courses. But there are hundreds of people – Black, White, mulatto, men, women, gay, and straight – who want things to change, and they are working for that change. It is starting to occur. I am the living proof of that.

EB-P: Toni Morrison once said, 'I write the books that I want to read'. Is this also true in your case? If so, are you trying to clarify your perceptions or others' perceptions of the multiple ways that the history, experiences, and identities of women, especially women of African ancestry, have been represented in Latin American literature?

MS-F: I agree with Toni Morrison. I, too, write the books that I want to read. But it is not because I want to clarify perceptions about blackness, gender, or nationality. There is some of that underneath what drives me. What drives me is the need to say my version of things, to add my version to the myriad of perceptions that are out there.

EB-P: Can you discuss the reception of *Anamú y manigua* in Puerto Rico?

MS-F: It was well received. The book sold out after six months, and for a book of poetry that is an accomplishment. Now it is taught regularly in courses on literary genres and contemporary literature in many Puerto Rican universities.

EB-P: In *Anamú y manigua* and *El orden escapado,* there is a profound preoccupation with the body. To what extent is this 'autobiography of the body' tied or linked to the ongoing project of exploration, construction, and affirmation of self – racial, gendered, and/or [concerning] national identities?

MS-F: The body is the site of perception, the filter, and the page on which life writes itself. The body reflects the way in which history touches a person. If writing defies oblivion, if it is a way of constructing memory, then the body is the quintessential instrument of literature. All one has to do is try to translate what one perceives through the senses into words. Without the body I cannot write, because I perceive the world through it. Needless to say, I don't believe in that old mind-body separation. I discarded that myth a long time ago.

EB-P: In *Anamú y manigua,* do you see gender – a basic principle of social classification – as a site and/or landscape for self-exploration and for an examination of the multiple forms of oppression that confront women? Do you also see gender as a part of the ongoing project to discover strategies of survival and resistance, to render visible the invisible, and to establish an identity for those on the periphery of patriarchal discourse?

MS-F: For me, gender is a definite point of departure for talking about politics. However, I cannot see it in a hierarchical way. I guess that is because the feminism that I practice comes from the Third World, and in the Third World the predominant way in which many women experience oppression is not gender. Sexual oppression is always linked to race, to class, to ethnicity, to sexual preference, to migratory status, to so many things. To pinpoint gender as such a central element would be an error. My understanding of womanhood is organically intertwined with my experiences of other oppressions, of colonialism, and also of the privileges that I have experienced as an intellectual, a writer, a college graduate, a financially independent woman, etc.

EB-P: Can you explain to what extent you see the probing into the African roots and culture, which takes place in *Anamú y manigua* as forming part of the awakening of national consciousness and the process of investigation into the sociocultural construct of identity?

MS-F: I wrote *Anamú y manigua* as a way to describe the participation of Black women in the construction of nationhood in Puerto Rico. I needed to feel that my mother, my grandmother, the women of my family, and I were a part of Puerto Rico; for we had worked so hard and suffered and conquered so much that Puerto Rico would be incomplete without us. This book does not address the issue of the awakening of national consciousness, but of the ways in which Black women have always been Puerto Rican, because their/our work is a thread in the construction of the nation. Maybe in critical analysis it is difficult to explain the ways in which race, gender, class, and nation intersect, but in the lives of my mother, my grandmother, and me, those identities go hand in hand and place us in a particular locus within the history of our country, of this planet. *Anamú y manigua* is an attempt to understand those places and to celebrate them.

EB-P: The image of the mirror seems to be ever-present in your work, particularly in *Pez de vidrio*. What is the function and significance of this image to you?

MS-F: I wasn't aware until now of the presence of the mirror image in my work. So, I can only guess what it means. Maybe it signifies the confrontation of the self in the construction of gender. But I would have to read my work again to tell you what the mirror really means, what my reading of it is. And to tell you the truth, I don't like to read the books I write, once they are published. I read them while I am writing them, and then I forget them. It is the only way to keep on writing other books that I would like to read.

EB-P: In *Pez de vidrio,* the character in the short story 'La escritora' (The Woman Writer) oscillates between reality and possibility – her need to survive and her overwhelming need to create, to write, to communicate … To what extent does this character capture the problematic and/or dilemma of the creative woman facing a patriarchal society that frustrates her need for self-realisation and artistic creativity?

MS-F: Your question answers itself. In our societies, a creative woman has to face many obstacles in order to let her voice be heard. All because she is a woman. There are many other creative people who face similar obstacles that result from other types of oppression. What I tried to do with 'La escritora' was to explore the layers of possibilities for self-realisation and the series of obstacles that a creative person faces when she is a woman. There are three *escritoras* in the tale: the one who is writing, the one the story is about, and a third worker who intervenes in the story. Supposedly, that writer is me. The dialogue and intersections between those three voices reveal the insecurities of the creative process and the way it fits into its social milieu. Because, let's face it, creative writing is not a very lucrative activity and women have many responsibilities to face. However, for some women, to stop creating is to die. What to do about the dilemma? I tried to offer one answer in 'La escritora'.

EB-P: Because the bar operates as a nexus of exchange on multiple levels, to what extent does the space of the bar in the short story 'Nightstand' disclose the protagonist's internalisation of a sexist economy of the female body?

MS-F: The link between the bar and internalised sexism is not direct. What I mean by this is that I don't think that the protagonist of 'Nightstand' goes to a bar because she has internalised her own objectification. The proof is that the protagonist of the title story, 'Pez de vidrio' (Stained Glass Fish), also goes to the bar and there she finds her liberation. There are many ways to go to a bar, just as there are women who go there for different reasons. I go to bars, but I don't go there looking for Mr Right (i.e. Mr Money). Then again, I don't go to universities, press conferences, art exhibits, or church for that reason either. 'Pez de vidrio' deals with the lives of contemporary urban Caribbean women, and the bar is another place where our stories unfold. In my stories, I want to take women out of the house.

I want literary women to inhabit the same spaces that we inhabit. And that is why I chose the bar as a setting for this story.

EB-F: There are different forms or classes of feminism that arise from various types of literary, social, racial, historical, cultural, and political pressures. What do you understand as feminism? To what extent is *Pez de vidrio* a feminist text? If so, can you explain how feminism has impacted your way of writing?

MS-F: I have already answered this question, and I don't feel comfortable labelling *Pez de vidrio* as a feminist text. It is in a way, but I imagine the book to be more than that. Let me explain myself. I am a feminist. I support Puerto Rican independence. I am anti-racist. I am against homophobia and lesbophobia. I hate the fact that there are sixteen Puerto Rican political prisoners in US federal prisons. I don't like injustice of any kind. I don't like capitalism a whole lot. I am against the US embargo of Cuba, and I don't agree with Castro's totalitarian regime. I don't like military interventions, and I abhor violence. My work reflects all of that. But a literary text will always be more than politics. It has to be. Because literature is about imagination and freedom of expression, it can serve political purposes, but it is fuelled by struggles of the soul. That is why I hope that *Pez de vidrio* exceeds all those categories in which critics try to place it. That is why it is and it is not a feminist text.

EB-P: I understand that you are currently working on your first novel. Are you free to discuss it at this moment?

MS-F: No. I don't care to talk about the novel that I am working on. I consider that bad luck.

EB-P: One last question. You have worked in various genres: poetry, short story, journalism, and now, the novel. What are you hoping to achieve with your work? What do you, as a person and as a woman, want most of all to achieve in your lifetime?

MS-F: I am a writer. To work in many genres is no big deal to me. Different genres pose different challenges that I am more than happy to accept. I learn from those challenges; they make me a better writer. When I go back to poetry after winning an award in short story writing, I go with a different perspective. I become a different poet. The same happens when I write novels or essays. Writing is a process and, although I am very concerned about the final product and its reception by the reading public, as a writer, what fascinates me is the process. What I hope to achieve with my work is excellence. To make beauty. To touch people's hearts.

To give back what César Vallejo, Toni Morrison and Octavio Paz and Pizarnik and Julia de Burgos and Manuel Ramos Otero and Palés Matos gave to me: magic.

You also ask me what do I, as a person and as a woman, want most of all to achieve in my lifetime. That is a tough question, the toughest you have asked so far. I guess that I want what everybody else wants: to be happy. To die knowing that I gave life my best shot. I cannot imagine a better way to achieve this than by writing.

Reclaiming the Female Body, Culture, and Identity in Mayra Santos-Febres's 'Broken Strand'

Elba D. Birmingham-Pokorny

> *Cultural identity . . . is a matter of 'becoming' as well as 'being'. Cultural identities come from somewhere, have histories. But, like everything, which is historical, they undergo constant transformation. Far from being eternally fixed in some essentialised past, they are subject to the continuous 'play' of history, culture, and power.*
>
>

Stuart Hall (223)

For more than three decades, feminist scholars have challenged the notion that women are important only in relation to men and can be defined only in terms of male discourse. They also have made women's need to search for an individual and collective identity, for a sense of agency, and for a history of their own, central concerns in their writings. Yet, these concerns have never been more compelling and meaningful than at this time, when women of colour and others on the periphery have begun to find a literary and scholarly voice with which to seek social and political equality, to understand the connection between domination and representation, to explore new forms of subjectivity, to discover strategies for survival and resistance, and to establish their own identities.

By making such issues as identity, voice, and the representation of the female body central preoccupations of her work, the Puerto Rican writer Mayra Santos-Febres appears to question the socio-cultural constructs of female identity and subjectivity. In *Pez de vidrio* (1995), a collection of short stories translated into English with the title *Urban Oracles*, Santos-Febres deconstructs the notion of a fixed, essentialist, female identity and, in the process, creates multiple visions of women searching for their own images. This search brings into focus women's struggle to define themselves as subjects, to invent and create their own identities, and ultimately to voice themselves into being. In so doing,

Mayra Santos-Febres responds to bell hooks' challenge to interrogate images of race and representation, as well as ways of looking and seeing. hooks states:

> As radical intervention we must develop revolutionary attitudes about race and representation. To do this we must be willing to think critically about images. We must be willing to take risks. We must be willing to challenge and unsettle, to disrupt and subvert …. That is the idea – to provoke and engage (7).

In keeping with these intents, Santos-Febres deconstructs the notion of woman as a relational sign and frees her from the constraint and containment imposed upon her image, body, identity, and sexuality by patriarchal and hegemonic official discourse. Each of the stories in *Urban Oracles* explores, in the author's words:

> the lives and miracles of city dwelling women. Desire, reality and cultural impediments interweave in the narrative discursive spaces of these short stories to reveal the urban setting from a feminine point of view. All the protagonists of these short stories – lonely and eager – search for themselves and for each other at the city's crossroads. Divorce, forced solitude, aesthetic perplexities, poverty, passion, and writing intersect to delineate the urban body of woman (*Pez* 73).

The discursive spaces of these stories relate the lives of a diverse group of women who struggle to break away from hegemonic modes of existence, to reinvent themselves, and to attain subjectivity by writing the texts of their lives. Accordingly, each of these women conducts her search for identity within the context of: (a) the national debate over Puerto Rico's political future; (b) the Puerto Rican people's struggle for a national and cultural identity; (c) the history of US colonial domination and exploitation of the island; and (d) the various modes of subjugation underscoring the patriarchal society's representation of woman's history, voice, body, and identity.

In her article 'Reclaiming the Body', Santos-Febres chronicles the ways in which patriarchal society's repressive binary system of oppositions and colonialism's discursive and institutional apparatuses of domination and exploitation have, on the one hand, kept women forever split between what they feel themselves to be and what they perceive society wants them to be, and, on the other hand, impacted woman's desire and her relationship with her body. According to Santos-Febres, the recognition and retrieval of the body from discursive erasure is central to the processes of writing new forms of subjectivity, elaborating a narrative of liberation and accepting one's corporeality and sexuality. More important, the reappropriation of the body is essential in making one aware of the multiple experiences and groups that constitute the heterogeneous ensemble of Caribbean culture and identity. Regarding these two points, Mayra Santos-Febres remarks:

> So now the body I live with is much more in tune with the history that has made me who I am. It is a history that surpasses the individual, that claims many other people with many different experiences of blackness and gender. I would love to hear those stories since they are the departing point from which words can be born to create a critical discourse about the matter, a discourse that can help us define the contours of that body still waiting to be fully explored – not as a conquered territory, but as home ('Reclaiming the Body' 20).

The short story 'Broken Strand' tells the story of a pre-adolescent Black girl named Yetsaida, who is obsessed with the way she looks and the way that others see her. The story chronicles both her dreams and her efforts to conform to an ideal of beauty that devalues her and obscures her identity. Yetsaida dreams of a new self:

> Under Miss Kety's hands, the neophyte has become pensive. She dreams of her new hair, dyed Auburn Copper red and floating in the breeze as she appears before the Sky Academy for Looks and Beauty in Miami, recounting in perfect English the trajectory of her success (I was a small girl with a dream, a dream of beauty that has come true. Thank you, Sky Academy!). Miss Kety looks at Yetsaida's broken nose, and with one eye closed looks at her own, and she raises the girl from her seat before the sunset (*Urban Oracles* 8).

But Yetsaida's dreams are mediated by the distorted lens of hegemonic discourse and by the mass media in a consumer society. More important, Yetsaida's efforts to give shape to her dreams of beauty, independence, and success are mediated through the images and aesthetic constructs of an invasive US culture. The politics of domination embedded in these images force the Other into a position of inferiority. From this position of domination, the invader uses language to relate to the Other, to establish or destroy its identity, to induce him/her to self-deprecation and/or racial self-hatred. The physical and textual violence inflicted on the Other by the modes of representation of this hegemonic discourse of otherness is evident in the racial self-hatred in the following quote: '– Oh, renaissance fairies, nymphets from the projects, who at four already know about alcoholic breath and dried-out condoms on the sidewalk, and want to straighten their hair so they won't be so black and so ugly and so low-class' (*Urban Oracles* 2).

Unfortunately, this point is lost on Yetsaida because she has been seduced by these images, by the products of a consumer society, and by the voice that tells her how she should be: 'now she can wait her turn at Kety's Beauty Parlor … to make herself over just like she always knew that she should be' (4). To achieve – if only symbolically – this ideal of beauty she is willing to camouflage her blackness by an 'hallucinatory' whiteness that not only negates her presence but also contributes to her dislocation from history and from the world itself. In other words, if one's identity is fashioned by the public symbols that represent one's culture or what one intellectualises and practices as one's culture, denials of cultural symbols can be interpreted as a rejection of one's presence in the world.

Accordingly, the subversive possibilities of Yetsaida's dreams and attempts to create a space for the representation of her own identity vanish because of her inability to break away from White representation. All that remains is a broken strand of hair, the map of the world on Miss Kety's forearm, broken noses, and the Centre for Psychiatric Treatment as a canvas upon which to sketch the destructive history of enslavement, colonisation, and subjugation of the colonised other. These dreams remain in stark contrast to the physical and emotional terrorism imposed on people, particularly African people and their descendants, who have been enslaved and marginalised in New World cultures. These people denounce the annihilating politics of domination that informs the ideology of representation in Euro-American hegemonic discourses, while acknowledging the potentiality of resistance and subjectivity embedded even in the elements of deliberate misrecognition.

Paradigmatically, these elements of deliberate misrecognition function in the narrative space of 'Broken Strand' as a platform from which to thematise the inconsistencies, irreconcilable divisions, absences, and samenesses embedded in patriarchal and hegemonic discourses on national identity, sexuality, and woman's body. Speaking about the 'sameness' that has silenced and erased the body of the other – particularly the Black woman's body – from the hegemonic construct of Puerto Rican national identity, Mayra Santos-Febres remarks:

> I don't know what it means to be a Black woman in the Spanish speaking Caribbean. I know how it feels like. It feels like you exist in virtual reality, as a symbol of 'our shared African Heritage' . . . (See 'The Page on Which Life Writes Itself' in this volume).

The elements of deliberate misrecognition are used in the narrative space of 'Broken Strand' as a vehicle from which to explore the possibility of new subjectivities through: (a) the deconstruction of the concepts of race, gender, and identity; (b) the interrogation of the disruptive social, historical, and ideological intents embedded in the notion of sameness; and (c) the retrieval of the abused body from and within Euro-American discursive erasure. It is within these contexts – deconstruction, interrogation, and retrieval – that the title of the story, the images of the broken strand, broken noses, the map of burns on Miss Kety's forearm, and the stray fist – acquire full significance as sites of knowledge, resistance, and freedom. Standing outside the boundaries of the true universal ideal of beauty and womanhood of the Euro-American dominant discourse, the wounded and rejected Black body, borrowing Mayra Santos-Febres' words, reflects the various ways in which history touches a person.

Yetsaida's and Miss Kety's broken noses underscore the brutal history of physical and psychological abuse that informs the lives and experiences of people of African ancestry in the New World and the uneven gender difference of this history of domination on the Black female body; and ultimately link Yetsaida's and Miss Kety's private experience as victims of domestic abuse to the collective experience of victimisation and abuse that punctuates the history of Black people. One aspect of this history includes the violence embedded in the dominant discourses – discourses of colonisation, subjugation, sexism, exploitation, discrimination, and disenfranchisement – and the acts of male violence committed against the Black female. These gendered acts of violence are thematised in 'Broken Strand' through graphic descriptions and re-enactments of male violence and abuse – verbal and psychological abuse, sexual exploitation, and physical violence — suffered and endured by Yetsaida, Miss Kety, and other women of the neighbourhood.

These harsh accounts of male violence against Black females reflect the effects of the internalisation of the Euro-American colonial discourse of domination and of the extent to which patriarchal society's dissymmetrical gender arrangements perpetuate the structures of authority that contain, confine, and silence women within the domestic domain. The devastating impact of the internalisation of a discourse – that sees the body of the other as expendable and as something that can be invaded and violated with no fear of retribution and retaliation – is summed up in the insensitive and aggressive behaviour of Yetsaida's father and in the violent abuses that mark the domestic lives of the female characters. The protagonist offers a vivid account of this violence in the following passage:

> She insists to the father, who arrives from the street stumbling, who
> yells at her, to whom she yells back, who chases her to hit her and

grabs her by the neck, who makes Mama cry and grabs her nose just in case he throws a fist – 'Whose nose?' All the screaming bewilders her so; the blood bewilders so. . . ah and the river that comes out of the nose, red, neon red like Miss Kety's comb (*Urban Oracles* 4).

It is in light of this history of violence against the Black female that the map of burns on Miss Kety's forearm acquires full meaning and symbolic significance. Indeed, the map of burns on Miss Kety's forearm not only functions in the narrative space of 'Broken Strand' as a vehicle to call attention to the historical experience of being Black and female in a specific society but, more important, it also denounces the capture and inscription of the Black body in the context of the brutal history of the slave trade and of a market economy grounded in the commodification and branding of the Black body.

The idea of the Black body as a 'possession' is further reelaborated in the 'Broken Strand' through the images of the broken strand, nappy curls, and Yetsaida's dreams. Both the images and the longing for straight hair indicate the internalisation of a white racist aesthetic that privileges blondeness and straight hair as tokens of beauty. On the other hand, these images also underscore the crushing violence against the body, image, and identity of the other, by a racist Euro-American discourse of domination that seeks to erase the public symbols and physical traits of the other's culture and race. More importantly, this Euro-American discourse of domination intends to remove the presence of the other from the world itself and, in the process, to compel the other to act as an accomplice to his/her own subjugation and disappearance.

Mayra Santos-Febres uses Yetsaida's longing for straight hair to disclose the shame and stigma associated with 'nappy hair' in a racist society, to indicate the extent to which Black women have been manipulated by Euro-American languages and images to conform to White beauty standards. In so doing, Santos-Febres focuses on the politics of dominance and deterritorialisation embedded in a racialised aesthetic that suggests that Black women, while appealingly 'different', must resemble White women to be considered really beautiful. The author explores, through images of broken strands and nappy hair, what it means to be Black, female, and nappy-headed in a racist society. In the process, she also calls attention to the need to develop an oppositional look that challenges and interrogates our ways of looking and our ways of being seen, and to understand how fear and repression work by turning parts of ourselves into our enemies.

In conclusion, with the reappropriation of the female body, the claim of subjectivity, and a subversion of the dominant phallocentric 'official' discourse through voices, figures, and bodies from the margins, Mayra Santos-Febres seeks to reconstruct and offer a more realistic representation of the female body. She seeks to question 'difference' and to explain what it means to be female, poor, and Black in contemporary Latin American society. In 'Broken Strand', she proposes a more realistic representation of the various strands of society, one that reveals experiences and cultures of the various groups that constitute the heterogeneous ensemble of the Caribbean.

In an act that is tantamount to the reconstruction of Latin American identities, Santos-Febres calls for the recognition and retrieval of the Black body from erasure in order to write and inscribe a multi-layered identity in the still undefined space of the Puerto Rican social landscape. In so doing, she creates out of the various strands representative of the body, experiences, history, culture, image, and identity of the African presence in the New World an inclusive and all-embracing range of identities. These identities exceed all categories and defy the prevailing belief in a fixed, essentialist female identity and a homogeneous national culture in Puerto Rico.

Works Cited

Birmingham-Pokorny, Elba. '"The Page on Which Life Writes Itself": A Conversation with Mayra Santos-Febres'. *Daughters of the Diaspora: Afra-Hispanic Writers*. Ed., Miriam De Costa-Willis, Kingston: Ian Randle Publishers, 2003.
Hall, Stuart. 'Cultural Identity and Cinematic Representation'. In *Ex-Iles: Essays on Caribbean Cinema*, edited by Mbye Cham, 220-236. Trenton, N.J.: Africa World Press, 1992.
hooks, bell. *Black Looks: Race and Representation*. Boston, MA: South End Press, 1992.
Santos-Febres, Mayra. *Pez de vidrio*. Miami: North South Center, 1995.
___. 'Reclaiming the Body'.*The San Juan Star*, October 22, 1995.
___. *Urban Oracles*. Trans., Nathan Budoff and Lydia Platon Lázaro. Cambridge, Massachusetts: Lumens Edition, 1997.

Selected Bibliography

Acosta-Belén, Edna. 'Beyond Island Boundaries: Ethnicity, Gender, and Cultural Revitalization in Nuyorican Literature'. *Callaloo* 15 (Fall 1992): 979-998.

Adams, Clementina R. *Common Threads: Afro-Hispanic Women's Literature.* Miami: Ediciones Universal, 1998.

Agosín, Marjorie, ed. *A Dream of Light and Shadow: Portraits of Latin American Women Writers.* Albuquerque: University of New Mexico Press, 1995.

_____. *Silencio e imaginación.* Santiago de Chile: Editorial Universitaria, 1985.

_____, ed. *These Are Not Sweet Girls.* Fredonia, N.Y.: White Pine Press, 1994.

Algarín, Miguel and Miguel Piñero. *Nuyorican Poetry: An Anthology of Puerto Rican Words and Feelings.* New York: William Morrow & Co., 1975.

Anglesey, Zoë, ed. *Ixok Amar-Go: Central American Women's Poetry for Peace.* Penobscott, Maine: Granite Press, 1987.

Anim-Addo, Joan. *Framing the Word: Gender and Genre in Caribbean Women's Writing.* London: Whiting and Birch, 1996.

Anzaldúa, Gloria. *Borderlands: The New Mextiza.* San Francisco: Aunt Lute Books, 1991.

_____. *Making Face, Making Soul/Haciendo Caras: Creative and Critical Perspectives by Feminists of Color.* San Francisco: Aunt Lute Foundation Books, 1990.

Anzaldúa, Gloria and Cherrié Moraga. *This Bridge Called My Back: Writings by Radical Women of Color.* Watertown, Mass.: Persephone Press, 1981.

Arnedo, Miguel. 'The Portrayal of the Afro-Cuban Female Dancer in Cuban *Negrista* Poetry'. *Afro-Hispanic Review* 16 (Fall 1997): 26-33.

Balutansky, Kathleen M. 'Naming Caribbean Women Writers: A Review Essay'. *Callaloo* 13 (1990): 539-50.

Bankay, Anne María. 'Contemporary Women Poets of the Dominican Republic: Perspectives on Race and Other Social Issues'. *Afro-Hispanic Review* 12 (Spring 1993): 34-41.

Barradas, Efraín. *Herejes y mitificadoes: muestra de poesía puertorriqueña en los Estados Unidos.* Río Piedras: Ediciones Huracán, 1980.

Bassnett, Susan, ed. *Knives and Angels: Women Writers in Latin America.* London: Zed Books, 1990.

_____. *Para entendernos: inventario poético puertorriqueño de hoy.* Hanover, N. H.: Ediciones del Norte, 1983.

Behar, Ruth, ed. *Bridges to Cuba / Puentes a Cuba.* Ann Arbor: The University of Michigan, Press, 1995.

Bejel, Emilio. *Escribir en Cuba: entrevistas con escritores cubanos, 1979-1989.* Río Piedras: Editorial de la Universidad de Puerto Rico, 1991.

Benítez-Rojo, Antonio. *The Repeating Island: The Caribbean and the Postmodern Perspective*. Trans. James E. Maraniss. Durham: Duke University Press, 1992.

Busby, Margaret, ed. *Daughters of Africa*. New York: Pantheon, 1992.

Carter, June. 'La Negra as Metaphor in Afro-Latin American Poetry'. *Caribbean Quarterly* 31 (1985): 73-82.

Castillo, Debra. *Talking Back: Toward a Latin American Feminist Literary Criticism*. Ithaca: Cornell University Press, 1992.

Castro-Klaren, Sara et al. *Women's Writing in Latin America*. Boulder, Colorado: Westview Press, 1991.

Cocco de Filippis, Daisy. 'Indias y trigueñas No Longer: Contemporary Dominican Women Writers Speak'. *Cimarrón* 1 (Spring 1988): 132–150.

_____, ed. *Combatidas, combativas y combatientes: Antología de cuentos escritos por mujeres dominicanas*. Santo Domingo: Editora Taller, 1992.

_____, ed. *Literatura dominicana al fin del siglo: Diálogo entre la tierra natal y la diáspora*. New York: Dominican Studies Institute, City College of New York, 1999.

_____, ed. *Sin otro profeta que su canto: Antología de poesía escrita por dominicanas*. Santo Domingo: Taller, 1988.

Crow, Mary, ed. *Woman Who has Sprouted Wings: Poems by Contemporary Latin American Women Poets*. Pittsburgh: Latin American Literary Review Press, 1987.

Cudjoe, Selwyn R., ed. *Caribbean Women Writers: Essays from the First International Conference*. Wellesley: Calaloux Publications, 1990.

Cunningham, Lucia Guerra, ed. *Splintering Darkness: Latin American Women Writers in Search of Themselves*. Pittsburgh: Latin American Literary Review Press, 1990.

Cypess, Sandra Messinger. 'Tradition and Innovation in the Writings of Puerto Rican Women'. In *Out of the Kumbla*, edited by Carole Boyce Davies and Elaine Savory Fido. Trenton: Africa World Press, 1990.

Davies, Carole Boyce. *Black Women, Writing and Identity: Migrations of the Subject*. New York: Routledge, 1994.

_____, ed. *Moving Beyond Boundaries: Black Women's Diasporas*. Washington Square, N. Y.: New York University Press, 1995.

Davies, Carole Boyce and Elaine Savory Fido, eds. *Out of the Kumbla: Caribbean Women and Literature*. Trenton: Africa World Press, 1990.

Davies, Carole Boyce and Molara Ogundipe-Leslie, eds. *Moving Beyond Boundaries: International Dimensions of Black Women's Writing*. Washington Square, New York: New York University Press, 1995.

Davies, Catherine. 'Madre Africa y memoria cultural: Nancy Morejón, Georgina Herrera, Excilia Saldaña'. *Revolución y Cultura* 2-3 (March-June 1999): 56-67.

_____. *A Place in the Sun? Women Writers in XXth-Century Cuba*. London: Zed Books, 1997.

Díaz Castro, Tania. *Todos me van a tener que oir / Everyone Will Have to Listen.* Princeton: Linden Lane Press, 1990.

Espada, Martín. *Poetry Like Bread: Poets of the Political Imagination from Curbstone Press.* Willimantic, Conn.: Curbstone Press, 1994.

Feal, Rosemary Geisdorfer. 'The Afro-Latin American Woman Writer: Drumming with a Difference'. *Afro-Hispanic Review* 14 (Fall 1995): 10-12.

_____. 'Poetas afrohispánicas y la "política de la identidad"'. In *Literatura, historia e identidad: Los discursos de la cultura de hoy,* edited by Lilia Granillo Vásquez. Mexico: Universidad Autónoma Metropoplitana Azcapotzalco, 1996.

Fenwick, M. J., ed. *Writers of the Caribbean and Central America.* New York: Garland, 1992.

Fernández, Roberta. *In Other Words: Literature by Latinas of the United States.* Houston: Arte Público, 1994.

Flores, Angel and Kate Flores. *The Defiant Muse: Hispanic Feminist Poems from the Middle Ages to the Present.* New York: The Feminist Press, 1988.

Gallazo, Rubén and Alberto Britos Serrat. *Antología de poetas negros uruguayos.* Montevideo: Ediciones Mundo Afro, 1990.

Guerra Cunningham, ed. *Splintering Darkness: Latin American Women Writers in Search of Themselves.* Pittsburgh: Latin American Literary Review Press, 1990.

Gutiérrez, Franklin. *Evas terrenales: Biobibliografías de 150 autoras dominicanas.* Santo Domingo: Comisión Permanente de la Feria del Libro, 2000.

Hopkinson, A., ed. *Lovers and Comrades: Women's Resistance Poetry from Central America.* London: Women's Press, 1989.

Horno-Delgado, Asunción, et al. *Breaking Boundaries: Latina Writings and Critical Readings.* Amherst: The University of Massachusetts Press, 1989.

Ippolito, Emilia. *Caribbean Women Writers: Identity and Gender.* Rochester: Camden House, 2000.

Jehenson, Myriam Yvonne. *Latin-American Women Writers: Class, Race, and Gender.* Albany: State University of New York Press, 1995.

Jones, Anny Brooksbank and Catherine Davies. *Latin American Women's Writing: Feminist Readings in Theory and Crisis.* New York: Oxford University Press, 1996.

Kaminsky, A. *Reading the Body Politic: Feminist Criticism and Latin American Women Writers.* Minneapolis: University of Minnesota Press, 1995.

Kutzinski, Vera M. *Sugar's Secrets: Race and the Erotics of Cuban Nationalism.* Charlottesville: University Press of Virginia, 1993.

Lewis, Marvin A. *Afro-Hispanic Poetry, 1940-1980: From Slavery to 'Negritud' in South American Verse.* Columbia: University of Missouri Press, 1983.

Liddell, Janice Lee and Yakini Belinda Kemp, eds. *Arms Akimbo: Africana Women in Contemporary Literature.* Gainesville: University Press of Florida, 1999.

López-Springfield, Consuelo, ed. *Daughters of Caliban: Twentieth Century Caribbean Women.* Bloomington: Indiana University Press, 1997.

Luis, William. *Dance Between Two Cultures: Latino Caribbean Literature Written in the United States*. Nashville: Vanderbilt University Press, 1997.

Martínez Echázabal, L. *Para una semiótica de la mulatez*. Madrid: Porrúa Turranzas, 1990.

Martínez, Julio A. *Dictionary of Twentieth-Century Cuban Literature*. New York: Greenwood Press, 1990.

Marting, Diane E., ed. *Spanish American Women Writers: A Bio-Bibliographical Source Book*. New York: Greenwood, 1990.

Marzán, Julio. *Inventing a Word: An Anthology of Twentieth-Century Puerto Rican Poetry*. New York: Columbia University Press, 1980.

Meyer, Doris. *Reinterpreting the Spanish American Essay: Women Writers of the 19th and 20th Centuries*. Austin: University of Texas Press, 1995.

Meyer, Doris and Margarite Fernández Olmos. *Contemporary Women Authors of Latin America*. Brooklyn: Brooklyn College Press, 1983.

Miller, Beth, ed *Women in Hispanic Literature: Icons and Fallen Idols*. Berkeley: University of California Press, 1983.

Minority Rights Group, ed. *No Longer Invisible: Afro-Latin Americans Today*. London: Minority Rights Publications, 1995.

Moore, Robin. *Nationalizing Blackness: Afrocubanism and Artistic Revolution in Havana, 1920-1940*. Pittsburgh: University of Pittsburgh Press, 1997.

Nasta, Susheila, ed. *Motherlands: Black Women's Writing from Africa, the Caribbean and South Asia*. New Brunswick, N. J.: Rutgers University Press,1992.

Ndongo-Bidyogo, Donato and Mbaré Ngom, eds. *Literatura de Guinea Ecuatorial (Antología)*. Madrid: Casa de Africa - SIAL Ediciones, 2000.

Newson, Adele S. and Linda Strong-Leek. *Winds of Change: The Transforming Voices of Caribbean Women Writers and Scholars*. New York: Peter Lang Publishing, 1998.

Pérez Firmat, Gustavo. 'Mulatto Madrigals'. In *The Cuban Condition: Translation and Identity in Modern Cuban Literature*, 80-94. Cambridge: Cambridge University Press, 1980.

Pérez Sarduy, Pedro and Jean Stubbs, eds. *AfroCuba: An Anthology of Cuban Writing on Race, Politics and Culture*. Melbourne: Ocean Press, 1993.

_____. *Afro-Cuban Voices: On Race and Identity in Contemporary Cuba*. Gainesville: University Press of Florida, 2000.

Phaf, Ineke, ed. *Presencia criolla en el Caribe y América Latina / Creole Presence in the Caribbean and Latin America*. Madrid: Iberoamericana, 1996.

Prescott, Laurence E. 'Negras, morenas, zambas y mulatas: Presencia de la mujer afroamericana en la poesía colombiana'. In *Colombia: literatura y cultura del Siglo XX*, edited by Isabel Rodríguez Vergara. Washington: Organization of American States, 1995.

Radhakrishnan, R. *Diasporic Mediations: Between Home and Location*. Minneapolis: University of Minnesota Press, 1996.

Ramos Rosado, Marie. *La mujer negra en la literatura puertorriqueña: Cuentística de los setenta*. San Juan: Editorial de la Universidad de Puerto Rico, 1999.

Rafuls, Pedro Monge. *Lo que no se ha dicho*. Jackson Heights, N. Y.: Ollantay Press, 1994.

Randall, Margaret. *Breaking the Silence: An Anthology of 20th-Century Poetry by Cuban Women*. Vancouver: Pulp Press, 1982.

_____. *Estos cantos habitados: These Living Songs*. Fort Collins, Colorado: Colorado State Review Press, 1978.

Rodríguez, María Christine. 'Women Writers of the Spanish-Speaking Caribbean: An Overview'. In *Caribbean Women Writers*, edited by Selwyn R. Cudjoe. Wellesey: Calaloux Publications, 1990.

Rodríguez de Laguna, Asela. *Images and Identities: The Puerto Rican in Two World Contexts*. New Brunswick: Transaction, 1987.

Rody, Caroline. *The Daughter's Return: African-American and Caribbean Women's Fictions of History*. New York: Oxford University Press, 2001.

Rose Green-Williams, Claudette. 'The Myth of Black Female Sexuality in Spanish Caribbean Poetry: A Deconstructive Critical View'. *Afro-Hispanic Review* 12 (Spring 1993): 16-23.

Smart, Ian. *Central American Writers of West Indian Origin, A New Hispanic Literature*. Washington, DC: Three Continents Press, 1984.

Smorkaloff, P. M. *Readers and Writers in Cuba: A Social History of Print Culture 1830s-1990s*. New York: Garland, 1997.

Stavans, Ilan. *The Hispanic Condition: Reflections on Culture and Identity in America*. New York: Harper Collins Publishers, 1995.

Steady, Filomina Chiona. *The Black Woman Cross-Culturally*. Rochester, Vermont: Schenkman Books, 1981.

Torres-Saillant, Silvio. *Caribbean Poetics: Toward an Aesthetic of West Indian Literature*. New York: Cambridge University Press, 1997.

_____, ed. *Hispanic Immigrant Writers and the Identity Question*. Jackson Heights, N. Y.: Ollantay Center for the Arts, 1989.

_____. 'The Tribulations of Blackness: Stages in Dominican Racial Identity'. *Callaloo* 23 (Summer 2000): 1086-111.

Turner, Faythe. *Puerto Rican Writers at Home in the USA: An Anthology*. Seattle: Open Hand Publishers, 1991.

Valis, Noel et al. *In the Feminine Mode: Essays on Hispanic Women Writers*. London: Bucknell University Press, 1990.

Virgillo, Carmelo and Naomi Lindstrom. *Woman as Myth and Metaphor in Latin American Literature*. Columbia: University of Missouri Press, 1988.

Williams, Claudette M. *Charcoal and Cinnamon: The Politics of Color in Spanish Caribbean Literature*. Gainesville: University Press of Florida, 2000.

Young, Ann Venture. 'The Black Woman in Afro-Caribbean Poetry'. In *Blacks in Hispanic Literature: Critical Essays,* edited by Miriam DeCosta. Port Washington, N.Y.: Kennikat Press, 1977.

_____. 'Black Women in Hispanic American Poetry: Glorificaion, Deification and Humanization'. *Afro-Hispanic Review* 1 (January 1982): 23-8.

Bibliography Of Afra-Hispanic Writers
Cristina Ayala

Ayala, Cristina. *Ofrendas mayabequinas: Recopilación de poesías publicadas en distintos periódicos de esta y otras provincias.* Prólogo de Valentín Cuesta Jiménez. Güines: Imprenta Tosco Heraldo, 1925.

Cervantes, Carlos Alberto. *Plácido y Cristina Ayala: disertación histórico-crítica, leída en la noche del 28 de junio de 1927 en el salón de actos de Unión Fraternal.* Havana: Imprenta Estrella, 1927.

Morejón, Nancy. 'Breve nota sobre Cristina Ayala'. *Revista del Vigia* 7 (1996).

Eulalia Bernard

Bernard, Eulalia. *Griot.* San José, Costa Rica: Adventist Foundation, 1998.

_____. *My Black King.* Eugene, Oregon: World Peace University, 1991.

_____. *Ritmohéroe.* San José, Costa Rica: Editorial Costa Rica, 1982.

McKinney, Kitzie. 'Costa Rica's Black Body: The Politics and Poetics of Difference in Eulalia Bernard's Poetry'. *Afro-Hispanic Review* 15 (Fall 1996): 11-20.

Sharman, Russell Leigh. 'Poetic Power: The Gendering of Literary Style in Puerto Limón'. *Afro-Hispanic Review* 19 (Fall 2000): 70-79.

Smart, Ian I. *Central American Writers of West Indian Origin: A New Hispanic Literature.* Washington, D. C.: Three Continents Press, 1984.

_____. 'Eulalia Bernard: A Caribbean Woman Writer and the Dynamics of Liberation'. *Letras Femeninas* 13 (Spring-Autumn 1987): 79-85.

Virginia Brindis de Salas

Barrios, Pilar. 'Fue homenajeada la autora de *Pregón de Marimorena* Virginia Brindis de Salas'. *Nuestra Raza* (June 1946): 9.

Brindis de Salas, Virginia. *Cien cárceles de amor.* Montevideo: Compañía Impresora, 1949.

_____. *Pregón de Marimorena: Poemas.* Montevideo: Sociedad Cultural Editora Indoamericana, 1946.

DeCosta-Willis, Miriam. 'Afra-Hispanic Writers and Feminist Discourse'. *NWSA Journal* 2 (Summer 1993): 204-17.

Johnson, Lemuel A. ' "Amo y espero": The Love Lyric, Virginia Brindis de Salas, and the African-American Experience of the New World'. *Afro-Hispanic Review* 3 (September 1984): 19-29.

Lewis, Marvin A. 'Virginia Brindis de Salas: The Call of Mary Morena'. In *Afro-Hispanic Poetry, 1940-1980: From Slavery to 'Negritud' in South American Verse*, 13-25. Columbia: University of Missouri Press, 1983.

Young, Caroll. 'The New Voices of Afro-Uruguay'. *Afro-Hispanic Review* 14 (Spring 1995): 58-64.

_____. 'Virginia Brindis de Salas vs. Julio Guadalupe: A Question of Authorship'. *Afro-Hispanic Review* 12 (Fall 1993): 26-30.

Julia de Burgos

Actas del Congreso International Julia de Burgos. San Juan: Ateneo Puertorriqueño, 1993.

Barradas, Efrain. 'Entre la esencia y la forma: El momento neoyorquino en la poesía de Julia de Burgos'. *Explicación de Textos Literarios* 15 (1986-1987): 138-52.

Burgos, Julia de. *Antología poética*. Río Piedras: Editorial Coquí, 1967.

_____. *Canción de la verdad sencilla*. Río Piedras: Ediciones Huracán, 1982.

_____. *El mar y tú: otros poemas*. Río Piedras: Ediciones Huracán, 1981.

_____. *Poema en veinte surcos*. Río Piedras: Ediciones Huracán, 1982.

_____. *Roses in the Mirror*. San Juan: Ediciones Mairena, 1992.

_____. *Song of the Simple Truth: Obra completa poética: The Complete Poems*. Williamantic, Conn: Curbstone Press, 1997.

_____. *Yo misma fui mi ruta*, edited by María M. Solá. Río Piedras: Ediciones Huracán, 1986.

Esteves, Carmen. 'Julia de Burgos: Woman, Poet, Legend'. In *A Dream of Light and Shadow: Portraits of Latin American Women Writers*, edited by Marjorie Agosín. Albuquerque: University of New Mexico Press, 1995.

Friis, Ronald J. 'Vision of the Muse in *Canción de la verdad sencilla* and *Veinte poemas de amor*'. *Chasqui: Revista de Literatura Latinoamericana* 23 (May 1994): 10-17.

González, José Emilio. 'Julia de Burgos: La mujer y la poesía'. *Sin Nombre* 7 (October-December 1976): 86-100.

Jiménez de Báez, Yvette. *Julia de Burgos: Vida y poesía*. Río Piedras: Editorial Coquí, 1966.

Julia de Burgos. Río Piedras: Ediciones Mairena, 1986.

Julia de Burgos. San Juan: Instituto de Cultura Puertorriqueña, 1990.

Julia de Burgos: Amor y soledad. Madrid: Ediciones Torremozas, 1994.

Julia de Burgos: Periodista en Nueva York. San Juan: Ateneo Puertorriqueño, 1992.

Kattau, Colleen. 'The Plural and the Nuclear in "A Julia de Burgos"'. *Symposium: A Quarterly Journal in Modern Literatures* 48 (Winter 1995): 285-93.

López, Ivette. 'Julia de Burgos o el silencio del poema sin palabras'. *Revista del Colegio Universitario de Humacao-UPR* 13 (2000): 36-41.

Morales, Belén Román. 'La poesía política de Julia de Burgos y Lolita Lebrón'. *Revista del Ateneo Puertorriqueño* 4 (Jan-Dec 1994): 281-91.

Rivera Villegas, Carmen. 'La modernidad puertorriqueña . . . y la poética de Julia de Burgos'. *Revista de la Universidad Metropolitana* 13 (1996): 166-77.

_____. 'Sobreviviendo en la metropoli: El multiculturalismo en la prosa de Julia de Burgos'. *Bilingual Review / La Revista Bilingüe* 23 (Sept-Dec 1998): 214-22.

Springfield, Consuelo López. ' "I Am the Life, the Strength, the Woman": Feminism in Julia de Burgos' Autobiographical Poetry'. *Callaloo* 17 (Summer 1994): 701-14.

Torres-Robles, Carmen. 'Social Irredentism in the Prose of Julia de Burgos'. *The Bilingual Review/La Revista Bilingüe* 17 (Jan.-Apr. 1992): 43-9.

Tracy, Mary Jane. 'Julia de Burgos: Woman, Poet, Legend'. In *A Dream of Light and Shadow,* edited by Marjorie Agosín. Albuquerque: University of New Mexico Press, 1995.

Umpierre, Luz María. 'Metapoetic Code in Julia de Burgos' *El mar y tú*: Towards a Revision'. In *Retrospect: Essays on Latin American Literature,* edited by Elizabeth S. Rogers and Timothy J. Rogers. York, S.C.: Sp. Lit. Pubs. Co., 1987.

Vicioso, Sherezada. 'Entrevista con Don Juan Bosch, sobre Julia de Burgos'. In *Algo que decir: Ensayos sobre literatura femenina (1981-1991).* Santo Domingo: Editora Búho, 1991.

_____. 'An Interview with Don Juan Bosch'. *Callaloo* 17 (Summer 1994): 694-700.

_____. 'Julia de Burgos: La nuestra'. *Algo que decir: Ensayos sobre literatura femenina (1981-1991).* Santo Domingo: Editora Búho, 1991.

_____. 'Julia de Burgos: Our Julia'. *Callaloo* 17 (Summer 1994): 674-83.

_____. 'El rival de Río Grande de Loíza (Entrevista con el Sr. Juan Isidro Jimenes Grullón)'. In *Algo que decir: Ensayos sobre literatura femenima (1981-1991).* Santo Domingo: Editora Búho, 1991.

_____. 'The Rival to the Río Grande of Loíza: An Interview with Juan Isidro Jimenes Grullón'. *Callaloo* 17 (Summer 1994): 684-93.

Zavala-Martínez, Iria. 'A Critical Inquiry into the Life and Work of Julia de Burgos'. In *The Psychosocial Development of Puerto Rican Women,* edited by Cynthia García Coll and María de Lourdes Mattei. New York: Praeger, 1989.

Cristina Cabral

Cabral, Cristina. 'A Conversation with Quince Duncan'. *PALARA* 2 (Fall 1998): 113-18.

_____. 'Devenir desigual'. *Mundo Afro* (August 1988) n, p.

_____. *Desde mi trenchera.* Montevideo: Ediciones Mundo Afro, 1993.

_____. 'Memoria y resistencia'. Trans. Antonio D. Tillis. *PALARA* 4 (Fall 2000): 104-07.

_____. 'Poemas: "Cimarrones", "Hoy más que nunca", "Quinientos años después"'. *Afro-Hispanic Review* 12 (Fall 1993): 41-2.

Galloza, Rubén and Alberto Britos Serrat. *Antología de poetas negros uruguayos.* Montevideo: Ediciones Mundo Afro, 1990.

Williams, Lorna V. 'Difference and Identity in the Poetry of Cristina Rodríguez Cabral'. *Afro-Hispanic Review* 14 (Fall 1995): 27-34.

_____. 'Entrevista con Cristina Rodríguez Cabral en Montevideo en Julio de 1993'. *Afro-Hispanic Review* 14 (Fall 1995): 57-63.

Young, Caroll Mills. 'New Voices of Uruguay'. *Afro-Hispanic Review* 14 (Spring 1995): 58-64.

Shirley Campbell

Campbell, Shirley. *Naciendo*. San José, Costa Rica: UNED, 1988.

_____. 'A Nicolás Guillén'. *Afro-Hispanic Review* 12 (Spring 1993): 48.

_____. *Rotundamente negra*. San José, Costa Rica: Arado, 1994.

Gordon, Donald K. 'Expressions of the Costa Rican Black Experience: The Short Stories of Dolores Joseph and Poetry of Shirley Campbell'. *Afro-Hispanic Review* 10 (September 1991): 21-6.

Hampton, Janet Jones. 'Portraits of a Diasporan People: The Poetry of Shirley Campbell and Rita Dove'. *Afro-Hispanic Review* 14 (Spring 1995): 33-9.

_____. 'The Voice of the Drum: The Poetry of Afro-Hispanic Women'. *Afro-Hispanic Review* 14 (Fall 1995): 13-20.

Sharman, Russell Leigh. 'Poetic Power: The Gendering of Literary Style in Puerto Limón'. *Afro Hispanic Review* 19 (Fall 2000): 70-9.

Aida Cartagena Portalatín

Alvarez, Julia. 'Doña Aída, with Your Permission'. *Callaloo* 23 (Summer): 821-23.

Back, Michelle. ' "En tiempo puro": The Search and Discovery of Territory in the Life and Work of Aida Cartagena Portalatín'. *Lucero: A Journal of Iberian and Latin American Studies* 6 (Spring 1995): 44-52.

Brown, Isabel Zakrzewski. 'Autora en busca de expresión en *Escalera para Electra*'. *Romance Review* 12 (1993): 130-38.

Cartagena Portalatín, Aida. *Culturas africanas: Rebeldes con causa*. Santo Domingo: Colección Montesinos, 1986.

_____. *Danza, música e instrumentos de los indios de la Española*. Santo Domingo: Editora Universidad Autónoma de Santo Domingo, 1974.

_____. *Del desconsuelo al compromiso. From Desolation to Compromise: A Bilingual Anthology of Poetry by Aida Cartagena Portalatín*, edited by Daisy Cocco de Filippis. Santo Domingo: Editora Taller, 1988.

_____. *Del sueño al mundo*. Santo Domingo: Ediciones La Poesía Sorprendida, 1945.

_____. *Dos técnicas cerámicas indoantillanas: Diagnóstico del Orígen de los Yacimientos de las Antillas Mayores*. Santo Domingo: Instituto Dominicano de Antropología, 1971.

_____. *En la casa del tiempo*. Santo Domingo: Colección Montesinos, 1984.

_____. *Escalera para Electra*. Santo Domingo: Editora Universidad Autónoma de Santo Domingo, 1970.

_____. *Estudio etnológico remanentes negros en el culto del Espíritu Santo de Villa Mella.* Santo Domingo: Editora Universidad Autónoma de Santo Domingo, 1975.

_____. *José Vela Zanetti.* Santo Domingo: Colección La Isla Necesaria, 1954.

_____. *La mujer dominicana y el quehacer literario.* Santo Domingo: Editora Universitaria, 1988.

_____. *La tarde en que murió Estefanía.* Santo Domingo: Editora Taller, 1983.

_____. *La tierra escrita.* Santo Domingo: Ediciones Brigadas Dominicanas, 1967.

_____. *La voz desatada.* Santo Domingo: Brigadas Dominicanas, 1962.

_____. *Llámale verde.* Santo Domingo: Ediciones La Poesía Sorprendida, 1945.

_____. 'Mambru Did Not Go to War'. *Callaloo* 23 (Summer 2000): 1076-79.

_____. *Mi mundo el mar.* Santo Domingo: Colección La Isla Necesaria, 1953.

_____. *Tablero.* Santo Domingo: Editora Taller, 1978.

_____. *Una mujer está sola.* Santo Domingo: Colección La Isla Necesaria, 1955.

_____. *Víspera del sueño, poemas para un atardecer.* Ciudad Trujillo: Ediciones La Poesía Sorprendida, 1944.

_____. *Yania tierra: A Documentary Poem,* edited and translated by M.J. Fenwick. Washington, D. C.: Azul Editions, 1995.

_____. *Yania tierra: Poema documento.* Santo Domingo: Colección Montesinos, 1981.

_____, ed. *Narradores dominicanos.* Caracas: Monte Avila Editores, 1978.

Cocco de Filippis, Daisy. 'Aída Cartagena Portalatín: A Literary Life. Moca, Dominican Republic, 1918-94'. In *Moving Beyond Boundaries: Black Women's Diasporas,* edited by Carole Boyce Davies. Port Washington, N. Y: New York University Press, 1995.

DeCosta-Willis, Miriam. 'Afra-Hispanic Writers and Feminist Discourse'. *NWSA Journal* 2 (Summer 1993): 204-17.

_____. 'Can(n)on Fodder: Afro-Hispanic Literature, Heretical Texts, and the Polemics of Canon-Formation. *Afro-Hispanic Review* 19 (Fall 2000): 30-9.

González, Carolina. 'A Poet on Her Own: Aída Cartagena Portalatín's Final Interview'. *Callaloo* 23 (Summer 2000): 1080-85.

Hampton, Janet Jones. 'The Voice of the Drum: The Poetry of Afro-Hispanic Women'. *Afro-Hispanic Review* 14 (Fall 1995): 13-20.

Heredia, Aida L. 'Lamento por *Yania Tierra* de Aida Cartagena Portalatín'. In *Encuentro, Re Encuentro, Déjà vu,* edited by Margarita Vargas and Henry J. Richards. Proceeding of the University of Buffalo (SUNY) Sesquicentennial Symposium on Hispanic Studies, April 11-12, 1997.

Sosa, José Rafael, ed. *La mujer en la literatura, homenaje a Aida Cartagena Portalatín.* Santo Domingo: Editora Universitaria, 1986.

Williams, Lorna V. 'The Inscription of Sexual Identity in Aida Cartagena's *Escalera para Electra'. Modern Language Notes* 112 (March 1997): 219-31.

Lourdes Casal

Burunat, Silvia. 'El arte literario de Lourdes Casal (1938-1981)'. *Confluencia: Revista Hispánica de Cultura y Literatura* 1 (Fall 1985): 107-11.

Casal, Lourdes. *El caso Padilla: Literatura y revolución en Cuba: Documentos*. Miami: Ediciones Universal, 1971.

_____. *Everyone has Their Moncada: 10 Poems*. New York: Center for Cuban Studies, 1982.

_____. 'The Founders: Alfonso', translated by Margaret Jull Costa. In *The Voice of the Turtle: An Anthology of Cuban Stories*, edited by Peter Bush. New York: Grove Press, 1997.

_____. 'Images of Cuban Society Among Pre- and Post-Revolutionary Novelists'. *DAI* 37 (1975): 715.

_____. *Itinerario ideológico: Antología*. Miami: Instituto de Estudios Cubanos, 1982.

_____. 'Lo que dice Caliban: Relectura'. *Areito* 9 (1984): 15-6.

_____. *Los fundadores: Alfonso y otros cuentos*. Miami: Universal, 1973.

_____. *La novela en Cuba, 1959-1967: Una introducción*. New York: Exilio, 1970.

_____. *Palabras juntan revolución: Poesía*. Havana: Casa de las Américas, 1981.

_____. 'Race Relations in Contemporary Cuba'. In *The Position of Blacks in Brazilian and Cuban Society*, edited by Anani Dzidizienyo and Lourdes Casal. London: Minority Rights Group, 1979.

_____. *Revolution and 'conciencia': Women in Cuba*. New York: Women's Interntional Resource Exchange Service, 1980.

_____. *Revolution and Race: Blacks in Contemporary Cuba*. Washington, D.C: Wilson Center, Latin American Program, 1979.

_____. *The Role of the Urban Working Class in the Cuban Revolution: Insurrectional Stage*. Washington, D.C.: Wilson Center, 1979.

Consejo de Dirección de *Areito*. 'El Instituto de Estudios Cubanos o los estrechos límites del pluralismo'. *Areito* 9 (1984): 120-22.

'Dos semanas en Cuba: Entrevista a Lourdes Casal'. *Areito* 9 (1983): 9-11.

Rafaela Chacón Nardi

Chacón Nardi, Rafaela. *La alfabetización en México, una experiencia educativa que pudiera utilizarse en Cuba*. Mexico: Ediciones Lyceum, 1951.

_____. *Coral del aire*. Havana: Letras Cubanas, 1982.

_____. *Del silencio y las voces*. Havana: Letras Cubanas, 1978.

_____. *Imágenes infantiles de Cuba revolucionaria: Testimonio gráfico, 1970-1975*. Havana: Gente Nueva, 1983.

_____. *Martí: Momentos importantes*. Havana: Editorial Gente Nueva, 1984.

_____. *Mínimo paraiso*. Matanzas, Cuba: Ediciones Matanzas, 1997.

_____. *Una mujer desde su isla canta*. Havana: Ediciones Hispasón; Ediciones Artex, 1994.

_____. *Viaje al sueño*. Havana: Cofre, 1948.

Hernández Menéndez, M. *La poética de Rafaela Chacón Nardi*. Havana: Letras Cubanas, 1996.

Luz Argentina Chiriboga

Beane, Carol. 'Chiriboga: A Conversation'. *Moving Beyond Boundaries: Black Women's Diasporas*, edited by Carole Boyce Davies. Washington Square, N.Y: New York University Press, 1995.

_____. 'Entrevista con Luz Argentina Chiriboga'. *Afro-Hispanic Review* 12 (Fall 1993): 17-23.

_____. 'Strategies of Identity in Afro-Ecuadoran Fiction: Chiriboga's *Bajo la piel de los tambores / Under the Skin of the Drums*'. In *Moving Beyond Boundaries: Black Women's Diasporas,* edited by Carole Boyce Davies. Washington Square, N.Y: New York University Press, 1995.

Chiriboga, Argentina. *Bajo la piel de los tambores*. Quito: Editorial Casa de la Cultura Ecuatoriana, 1991.

_____. *La Contraportada del deseo*. Quito: Talleres Gráficos, 1992.

_____. *Diáspora por los caminos de Esmeraldas*. Quito: Ardilla Editores, 1997.

_____. *Drums Under My Skin,* translated by Mary Harris. Washington, D.C: Afro-Hispanic Institute, 1996.

_____. *En la noche del viernes*. Quito: SINAB Colección País Secreto, 1997.

_____. 'Epístola a Orula'. *Afro-Hispanic Review* 10 (January 1991): 24.

_____. *Escritores esmeraldeños: raíces, biografía, producción y crítica*. Quito: Amigos de la Genealogía, 1995.

_____. 'Excerpt from the Novel *Jonatás y Manuela* by Luz Argentina Chiriboga'. Translated by Rosemary Geisdorfer Feal. *Afro-Hispanic Review* 17 (Fall 1998): 30-45.

_____. *Jonatás y Manuela*. Quito: Abrapalabra Editores, 1994.

_____. *Manual de ecología*. Quito: Abrapalabra Editores, 1992.

_____. *Palenque: Décimas*. Quito: Editorial Instituto Andino de Artes Populares, 1999.

_____. 'Vituperio'. *Afro-Hispanic Review* 10 (January 1990): 24.

DeCosta-Willis, Miriam. 'The Poetics and Politics of Desire: Eroticism in Luz Argentina Chiriboga's *Bajo la piel de los tambores'*. *Afro-Hispanic Review* 14 (Spring 1995): 18-25.

Feal, Rosemary Geisdorfer. 'Entrevista con Luz Argentina Chiriboga'. *Afro-Hispanic Review* 12 (Fall 1993): 12-6.

_____. 'The Legacy of Ba-Lunda: Black Female Subjectivity in Luz Argentina Chiriboga's *Jonatás y Manuela'*. *Afro-Hispanic Review* 17 (Fall 1998): 24-9.

_____. 'Poetas afrohispánicas y la "política de la identidad"'. *Literatura, historia e identidad: Los discursos de la cultura,* edited by Lilia Granillo Vázquez. Mexico City: Univ. Autónoma Metropolitana, 1996.

_____. 'Reflections on the Obsidian Mirror: The Poetics of Afro-Hispanic Identity and the Gendered Body'. *Afro-Hispanic Review* 14 (Spring 1995): 26-32.

Feracho, Lesley. 'Women's Diasporic Dialogues: Redefining Afro-Caribbean and Afro-Latin American Identity in Rojas' *El columpio de Rey Spencer* and Chiriboga's *Jonatás y Manuela'*. *PALARA* 5 (Fall 2001): 32-4.

Richards, Henry and Aida L. Heredia. 'Entrevista con Luz Argentina Chiriboga'. In *Narradoras ecuatorianas de hoy*, edited by Adelaida López de Martínez and Gloria de Cunha-Giabbai. San Juan: Editorial de la Universidad de Puerto Rico, 2000.

_____. 'Luz Argentina Chiriboga'. *Narradoras ecuatorianas de hoy*, edited by Adelaida López de Martínez and Gloria de Cunha Giabbai. San Juan: Editorial de la Universidad de Puerto Rico, 2000.

Seales Soley, LaVerne M. and Sharon P. Seales Soley. 'Entrevista con Luz Argentina Chiriboga: escritora afro-ecuatoriana'. *Afro-Hispanic Review* 17 (Fall 1998): 64-6.

Josefina de la Cruz

Cruz, Josefina de la. *Agua secreta*. Santo Domingo: Editora Cosmos, 1977.

_____. *Una casa en el espacio: novela*. Santo Domingo. n. p., 1980.

_____. *Debajo de la piel (y otros poemas anónimos)*. Santo Domingo: Editora Cosmos, 1978.

_____. *Gineceo: poemas*. Santo Domingo: n.p., 1988.

_____. *La sociedad dominicana de finales de siglo a través de la novela*. Santo Domingo: Editora Cosmos, 1978.

Angela María Dávila

Dávila, Angela María. *Animal fiero y tierno*. Río Piedras, Puerto Rico: Ediciones Huracán, 1981.

López, Ivette. '*Animal fiero y tierno*: Apuntes para una lectura'. *Revista/Review Interamericana* 10 (Fall 1980): 398-408.

Sandra María Esteves

Azize, Yamila. 'Poetas puertorriqueñas en Nueva York'. *Cupey: Revista de la Universidad Metropolitana* 4 (Jan.-June 1987): 17-24.

Barradas, Efraín. 'Conciencia femenina, conciencia social: La voz poética de Sandra María Esteves'. *Third Woman* 1 (1982): 31-4.

Esteves, Sandra María. 'Ambivalence or Activism from the Nuyorican Perspective in Poetry'. In *Images and Identities: The Puerto Rican in Two World Contexts*. New Brunswick: Transaction, 1987.

_____. *Bluestown Mockingbird Mambo*. Houston: Arte Público, 1990.

_____. 'For Noel Rico'. *Revista Chicano-Riqueña* 10 (Winter-Spring 1982): 1.

_____. 'The Feminist Viewpoint in the Poetry of Puerto Rican Women in the United States'. *Images and Identities: The Puerto Rican in Two World Contexts*, edited by Asela Rodríguez de Laguna. New Brunswick: Transaction Books, 1987.

_____. 'Open Letter to Eliana'. In *Breaking Boundaries: Latina Writing and Critical Readings*, edited by Asunción Horno-Delgado, et al. Amherst: University of Massachusetts Press, 1988.

_____. *Tropical Rains: A Bilingual Downpour*. Bronx, N.Y.: African Caribbean Poetry Theater, 1984.

_____. *Yerba Buena*. Greenfield Center, N.Y.: Greenfield Review Press, 1980.

Fernández Olmos, Margarita. 'Sex, Color, and Class in Contemporary Puerto Rican Women Authors'. *Heresies* 4 (1982): 46-7.

_____. 'From the Metropolis: Puerto Rican Women Poets and the Immigration Experience'. *Third Woman* 1 (1982): 40-51.

Luis, William. 'María C(h)ristina Speaks: Latina Identity and the Poetic Dialogue Between Sandra María Esteves and Luz María Umpierre'. *Hispanic Journal* 16 (Spring 1997): 137-49.

Ortega, Eliana. 'Poetic Discourse of the Puerto Rican Woman in the U. S.: New Voices of Anacaonian Liberation'. In *Breaking Boundaries*, edited by Asunción Horno-Delgado, et al. Amherst: University of Massachusetts Press, 1989.

Umpierre, Luz María. 'La ansiedad de la influencia en Sandra María Esteves y Marjorie Agosín'. *Revista Chicano-Riqueña* 11 (Fall-Winter 1983): 139-47. [Reprinted in *Nuevas aproximaciones críticas a la literatura puertorriqueña contemporánea*. Río Piedras. Ed. Cultural, 1983.]

_____. 'De la protesta a la creación: Una nueva visión de la mujer puertorriqueña en la poesía'. *Imagine: International Chicano Poetry Journal* 2 (Summer 1985): 134-42.

Georgina Herrera

Argüelles, Lydia de and Gabriela Díaz-Cortez. *Afro-Hispanic Review* 18 (Spring 1999): 53-7.

Davies, Catherine. 'Madre Africa y memoria cultural: Nancy Morejón, Georgina Herrera, Excilia Saldaña'. *Revolución y Cultura* 2-3 (March-June 1999): 56-67.

_____. 'Mother Africa and Cultural Memory: Nancy Morejón, Georgina Herrera, Excilia Saldaña'. In *A Place in the Sun? Women Writers in XXth Century Cuba*. London. Zed Books, 1994.

_____. 'Writing the African Subject: The Work of Two Cuban Women Poets'. *Women: A Cultural Review* 4 (Spring 1993): 32-48.

Herrera, Georgina. *Gentes y cosas*. Havana: Ediciones Unión, 1974.

_____. *GH*. Havana: Ediciones El Puente, 1962.

_____. *Grande es el tiempo*. Havana: Ediciones Unión, 1986.

_____. *Granos de sol y luna*. Havana, Ediciones Unión, 1978.

_____. *Gustadas sensaciones*. Havana: Ediciones Unión, 1997.

_____. 'Introducing Georgina Herrera'. Translated by Lydia de Argüelles and Gabriela Díaz-Cortez. *Afro-Hispanic Review* 16 (Spring 1999): 53-8.

_____. 'Poetry, Prostitution, and Gender Esteem'. *Afro-Cuban Voices*, edited by Pedro Pérez Sarduy and Jean Stubbs. Gainesville: University Press of Florida, 2000.

Raquel Ilonbé

Ilonbé, Raquel. 'Ceiba' and 'Los tres hermanos'. In *Literatura de Guinea Ecuatorial*, edited by Donato Ndongo-Bidyogo and M'baré N'gom. Madrid: Casa de Africa, 2000.

N'gom Faye, M'baré, ed. 'Raquel Ilonbé'. In *Diálogos con Guinea: Panorama de la literatura guineoecuatoriana de expresión castellana a través de sus protagonistas*. Madrid: Labrys 54 Ediciones, 1996.

Juanita Mitial

Mitil, Juanita. 'My Shadow is Blue'. *Afro-Hispanic Review* 3 (January 1984): 29.

_____. 'I Have a Memory'. In *Erotique Noire / Black Erotica*, edited by Miriam DeCosta-Willis, et al, 414-15. New York: Doubleday, 1992.

Nancy Morejón

Abudu, Gabriel A. 'Nancy Morejón's *Mutismos*: The Philosophical and Ethical Foundation of Her Poetic Discourse'. *Afro-Hispanic Review* 15 (Spring 1996): 12-21.

Barradas, Efraín. 'Nancy Morejón o un nuevo canto para una vieja culebra'. *Afro-Hispanic Review* 15 (Spring 1996): 22-8.

Behar, Ruth and Lucia Suarez. 'Two Conversations with Nancy Morejón'. In *Bridges to Cuba / Puentes a Cuba,* edited by Ruth Behar. Ann Arbor: The University of Michigan Press, 1995.

Cordones-Cook, Juanamaría. 'Voz y poesía de Nancy Morejón'. *Afro-Hispanic Review* 15 (Spring 1996): 60-71.

Davies, Catherine. 'Madre Africa y memoria cultural: Nancy Morejón, Georgina Herrera, Excilia Saldaña'. *Revolución y Cultura* 2-3 (March-June 1999): 56-67.

_____. 'Mother Africa and Cultural Memory: Nancy Morejón, Georgina Herrera, Excilia Saldaña'. In *A Place in the Sun? Women Writers in XXth-Century Cuba*. London: Zed Books, 1994.

DeCosta-Willis, Miriam. 'The Craft of the Essay: Nancy Morejón's *Fundación de la imagen'*. In *Diáspora*, edited by Elba Birmingham-Pokorny. Magnolia, Arkansas: Southern Arkansas University, 2000.

_____. 'Orishas Circling Her House: Race as (Con)Text in Morejón's Poetic Discourse'. In *Moving Beyond Boundaries: Black Women's Diasporas*, edited by Carole Boyce Davies. Port Washington Square, N. Y: New York University Press, 1995.

_____, ed. *Singular Like a Bird: The Art of Nancy Morejón*. Washington: Howard University Press, 1999.

Feal, Rosemary.Geisdorfer. 'Poesía afrohispánica y la "política de la identidad"'. In *Literatura, historia e identidad: Los discursos de la cultura hoy*, edited by Lilia Granillo Vázquez. Mexico City: Universidad Autónoma Metropolitana, Azcapotzalco, 1996.

_____. 'Reflections on the Obsidian Mirror: The Poetics of Afro-Hispanic Identity and the Gendered Body'. *Afro-Hispanic Review* 14 (Spring 1995): 26-32.

Feracho, Leslie. 'Arrivals and Farewells: The Dynamics of Cuban Homespace through African Mythology in Two Eleggua Poems by Nancy Morejón'. *Hispania* 83 (Mar 2000): 51-8.

Hampton, Janet Jones. 'The Voice of the Drum: The Poetry of Afro-Hispanic Women'. *Afro-Hispanic Review* 14 (Fall 1995): 13-20.

Hernández, Sandra. 'La poesía de Nancy Morejón: Memoria, identidad y creación'. In *Celebración de la creación literaria de escritoras hispanas en las Américas*, edited by Lady Rojas-Tempe and Catharina Vallejo. Ottawa: GIROL Books, 2000.

Howe, Linda S. 'The Fluid Iconography of the Cuban Spirit in Nancy Morejón's Poetry'. *Afro-Hispanic Review* 15 (Spring 1996): 29-34.

James, Conrad. 'Patterns of Resistance in Afro-Cuban Women's Writing: Nancy Morejón's "Amo a mi amo"'. In *Framing the Word: Gender and Genre in Caribbean Women's Writing*, edited by Joan Anim-Addo. London: Whiting and Birch, 1996.

Luis, William. 'The Politics of Aesthetics in the Poetry of Nancy Morejón'. *Afro-Hispanic Review* 15 (Spring 1996): 35-43.

Maloof, Judy. 'Nancy Morejón'. *Hispamérica: Revista de Literatura* 25 (April 1996): 0363-0471.

Morejón, Nancy. *Amor, ciudad atribuída, poemas*. Havana: Ediciones El Puente, 1964.

_____. *Baladas para un sueño*. Havana: Unión de Escritores y Artistas de Cuba, 1989.

_____. *Le Chaînon Poètique*. Translated by Sandra Monet-Descombey. Champigny-sur-Marne, France: Edition L.C.J., 1994.

_____. *Cuaderno de Granada*. Havana: Casa de las Américas, 1984.

_____. *Dos poemas de Nancy Morejón*. Drawings and Design by Rolando Estévez. Matanzas, Cuba: Ediciones Vigia, 1989.

_____. *Elogio de la danza*. Mexico City: La Universidad Nacional Autónoma de México, 1982.

_____. *Elogio y paisaje*. Havana: Ediciones Unión, 1996.

_____. *Fundación de la imagen*. Havana: Editorial Letras Cubanas, 1988.

_____. *Grenada Notebook / Cuaderno de Granada*. Translated by Lisa Davis. New York: Círculo de Cultura Cubana, 1984.

_____. 'Grounding the Race Dialogue: Diaspora and Nation'. In *Afro-Cuban Voices*, edited by Pedro Pérez Sarduy and Jean Stubbs. Gainesville: University Press of Florida, 2000.

_____. *Lengua de pájaro*. With Carmen Gonce. Havana: Instituto Cubano del Libro, 1971.

_____. *Mutismos*. Havana: Ediciones El Puente, 1962.

_____. *Nación y mestizaje en Nicolás Guillén*. Havana: Ediciones Unión, 1982.

_____. *Nancy Morejón*. New York: Center for Cuban Studies, 1983.

_____. *Octubre imprescindible*. Havana: Ediciones Unión, 1982.

_____. *Ours the Earth*. Translated by J. R. Pereira. Mona, Jamaica: Institute of Caribbean Studies, 1990.

_____. *Paisaje célebre*. Caracas: Fundarte, Alcaldia de Caracas, 1993.

_____. *Parajes de una época*. Havana: Editorial Letras Cubanas, 1979.

_____. *Piedra pulida*. Havana: Editorial Letras Cubanas, 1986.

_____. *Pierrot y la luna: Divertimento, 31 de diciembre de 1990. Afro-Hispanic Review* 15 (Spring 1996): 56-9.

_____. *Poemas*. Mexico City: Universidad Autónoma de México, 1980.

_____. *Poemas de amor y de muerte*. Toulouse: Caravelle, 1993.

_____. 'Las poéticas de Nancy Morejón'. *Afro-Hispanic Review* 15 (Spring 1996): 6-9.

_____. *Richard trajo su flauta y otros argumentos*. Havana: Unión de Escritores y Artistas de Cuba, 1967.

_____. *El río de Martín Pérez y otros poemas*. Drawings and Design by Rolando Estévez. Matanzas, Cuba: Ediciones Vigia, 1996.

_____. *Where the Island Sleeps Like a Wing*. Translated by Kathleen Weaver: San Francisco: The Black Scholar Press, 1985.

_____, ed. *Recopilación de textos sobre Nicolás Guillén*. Havana: Casa de las Améicas, 1974.

Mullen, Edward. 'Introducing Nancy Morejón to the Reader'. *Afro-Hispanic Review* 15 (Spring 1996): 4-5.

Rivera-Valdés, Sonia. 'Celebración para un siete de agosto'. *Afro-Hispanic Review* 15 (Spring 1996): 10-1.

Rosario-Sievert, Heather. 'Nancy Morejón's Eye/I: Social and Aesthetic Perception in the Work of Nancy Morejón'. *Afro-Hispanic Review* 15 (Spring 1996): 44-9.

Smart, Ian. 'Nancy Morejón as Guillén's Mujer Nueva'. *Afro-Hispanic Review* 15 (Spring 1996): 50-5.

West, Alan. 'The Stone and Its Images: The Poetry of Nancy Morejón'. *Studies in 20th Century Literature* 20 (Winter 1996): 193-219.

Trinidad Morgades Besari

Morgades Besari, Trinidad. "Antigona." *Africa 2000 14* (1991)

_____. 'Antigona'. In *Literatura de Guinea Ecuatorial*, edited by Ndongo-Bidyogo and M'baré N'gom. Madrid: Casa de Africa, 2000.

_____. 'Para ti, mujer'. *El Patio* 27 (January 1999).

_____. 'Poder legítimo y cambio social'. *El Patio* 18 (January 1993).

_____. 'La puesta en escena de *Antigona*'. *El Patio* 15 (July-August 1992).

_____. 'La vuelta a casa'. *El Patio* 21 (February 1992).

N'gom, M'baré. 'Teatro y escritura femenina en Guinea Ecuatorial: Entrevista a Trinidad Morgades Besari'. *Afro-Hispanic Review* 19 (Spring 2000): 104-05.

María Nsue Angüe

N'gom, M'baré, ed. 'María Nsué Angüe'. *Diálogos con Guinea: Panorama de la literatura guineoecuatoriana de expresión castellana a través de sus protagonistas*. Madrid: Labrys 54 Ediciones, 1996.

_____. 'Novelística y espacio femenino: entrevista a María Nsue Angüe'. *Afro-Hispanic Review* 19 (Spring 2000): 102-3.

_____. 'Relato de una vida y escritura femenina: *Ekomo*, de María Nsue Angüe'. *The Jounral of Afro-Latin American Studies and Literature* 3 (Spring 1995): 77-92.

Nsue Angüe, María. 'Adagu'. *Cultura Africana* 3 (1993): 20-2.

_____. 'Delirios'. *Africa 2000* 15 (1991): 27-29.

_____. *Ekomo*. Madrid: Universidad Nacional de Educación a Distancia, 1985.

_____. 'Ekomo; Adugu'. *Literatura de Guinea Ecuatorial*, edited by Donato Ndongo-Bidyogo and M'baré N'gom. Madrid: Casa de Africa, 2000.

_____. 'Nuevos Cuentos de María Nsue: "Cena de desamor", "Una historia terrible"'. *El Patio* 3 (January 1997): 33-8.

_____. *Relatos*. Malabo, Equatorial Guinea: Centro Cultural Hispano-Guineano, 2000.

Osubita, Juan Bautista. 'La muerte de Ekomo en *Ekomo*'. *Africa 2000* 15 (1992): 48-50.

Zielina, María. '*Ekomo*: Representación del universo mítico, la magia y la psicología de un pueblo "fang"'. *Afro-Hispanic Review* 19 (Spring 2000): 93-101.

Juana Pastor

Cervantes, C. A. 'Juana Pastor: La primera poetisa cubana'. In *Sobre la poesía negrista*, edited by Oscar Fernández de la Vega, 11-16. New York: n.p., 1985.

Pastor, Juana. 'Décimas (November 27, 1815)'. *Parnaso Cubano*, 1881.

Loida Maritza Pérez

Pérez, Loida Maritza. 'From *Geographies of Home*'. *Callaloo* 23 (Summer 2000): 910-17.

_____. *Geographies of Home*. New York: Viking Penguin, 1999.

María Caridad Riloha

Gusano, Exilio. *Literatura de Guinea Ecuatorial*, edited by Donato Ndongo-Bidyogo and M'baré N'gom. Madrid: Casa de Africa, 2000.

Soleida Ríos

Arrufat, Antón. 'Reaparición de Soleida'. *Unión* 24 (July-September 1996): 89-91.

Ríos, Soleida. *De la sierra*. Santiago de Cuba: Uvero, 1977.

_____. *De pronto abril*. Havana: Ediciones Unión, 1979.

_____. *Entre mundo y juguete*. Havana: Editorial Letras Cubanas, 1987.

_____. *Libro cero*. Havana: Editorial Letras Cubanas, 1998.

_____. *El libro roto: Poesía*. Havana: Ediciones Unión, 1994.

_____. *El libro roto. Poesía incompleta y desnuda 1987-1989*. Havana: Instituto del Libro, 1996.

_____. *El texto sucio*. Havana: Ediciones Unión, 1999.

_____. *El libro de los sueños*, edited by Soleida Ríos. Havana: Editorial Letras Cubanas, 1999.

_____, ed. *Poesía infiel: Selección de jóvenes poetisas cubanas*. Havana: Editora Abril, 1989.

Beatriz Rivera

Rivera, Beatriz. *African Passions and Other Stories*. Houston: Arte Público Press, 1995.

_____. *Midnight Sandwiches at the Mariposa Express*. Houston: Arte Público Press, 1997.

_____. *Playing With Light*. Houston: Arte Público Press, 2000.

_____. 'Santería'. *Afro-Hispanic Review* 16 (Spring 1997): 5-10.

Marta Rojas

Birmingham-Pokorny, Elba D. 'Re-writing Cuban History and Identity: The Legitimization of Love, Culture, and Otherness in Marta Rojas' *El columpio de Rey Spencer'*. *Revista Diáspora* 11 (2001): 20-7.

DeCosta-Willis, Miriam. 'Can(n)on Fodder: Afro-Hispanic Literature, Heretical Texts, and the Polemics of Canon-Formation'. *Afro-Hispanic Review* 19 (Fall 2000): 30-9.

Feracho, Lesley. 'Women's Diasporic Dialogues: Redefining Afro-Caribbean and Afro-Latin American Identity in Rojas' *El columpuo de Rey Spencer* and Chiriboga's *Jonatás y Manuela'*. *PALARA* 5 (Fall 2001): 32-41.

Rojas, Marta. *Antes del asalto al Moncada*. Havana: Unión de Escritores y Artistas de Cuba, 1979.

_____. *El aula verde*. Havana: Unión de Escritores y Artistas de Cuba, 1982.

_____. 'Canciones (voces) del ser americano, cuerpos olvidados, textos rescatados, voces subalternas e identidad del milenio'. *Revista Diáspora* 11 (2001): 7-19.

_____. *El columpio de Rey Spencer*. Havana: Editorial Letras Cubanas, 1993.

_____. *La cueva del muerto*. Havana: Unión de Escritores y Artistas de Cuba, 1983.

_____. *Dead Man's Cave*. Havana: José Martí Publishing House, 1988.

_____. *El que debe vivir*. Havana: Casa de las Américas, 1978.

_____. *Escenas de Viet Nam (entrevistas)*. Havana: Instituto Cubano del Libro, 1971.

_____. *La generación del centenario en el juicio del Moncada*. Havana: Editorial de Ciencias Sociales, 1979.

_____. 'Holy Lust: Whiteness and Race Mixing in the Historical Novel'. In *Afro-Cuban Voices*, edited by Padro Pérez Sarduy and Jean Stubbs. Gainesville: University Press of Florida, 2000.

_____. *El juicio del Moncada*. Havana: Editorial de Ciencias Sociales, 1988.

_____. *El médico de la familia en la Sierra Maestra*. Havana: Editorial Ciencia Médica, 1986.

_____. *Reportajes de la nueva vida*. Havana: Editorial Letras Cubanas, 1980.

_____. *Tania, guerrillera heroica*. Buenos Aires: R. Cedeno Editor, 1993.

_____. *Tania la guerrillera inolvidable*. Havana: Instituto del Libro, 1970.

_____. *Tania, the Unforgettable Guerrilla*. New York: Random House, 1971.

_____. 'El testimonio en la revolución cubana'. In *Testimonio y literatura*, edited by Rene Jara. Minneapolis Institute for the Study of Ideologies, 1986.

_____. *Viet Nam del Sur*. Havana: Instituto del Libro, 1967.

Excilia Saldaña

Abudu, Gabriel A. 'African Oral Arts in Excilia Saldaña's *Kele Kele*'. *Afro-Hispanic Review* 19 (Fall 2000): 21-9.

Davies, Catherine. 'Cross-Cultural Homebodies in Cuba: The Poetry of Excilia Saldaña'. In *Latin American Women's Writing: Feminist Readings in Theory and Crisis*, edited by A. Brooksbank Jones and C. Davies. New York: Oxford University Press, 1996.

_____. 'Hybrid Texts: Family, State and Empire in a Poem by Black Cuban Poet Excilia Saldaña'. In *Comparing Postcolonial Literatures: Dislocations*, edited by Ashok Bery and Patricia Murray. New York: St. Martin's Press, 2000.

_____. 'Madre Africa y memoria cultural: Nancy Morejón, Georgina Herrera, Excilia Saldaña'. *Revolución y Cultura* 2-3 (March-June 1999): 56-67.

_____. 'Mother Africa and Cultural Memory: Nancy Morejón, Georgina Herrera, Excilia Saldaña'. In *A Place in the Sun? Women Writers in XXth-Century Cuba*. London: Zed Books, 1997.

_____. 'Women Writers in Twentieth Century Cuba: An Eight-Point Survey'. In *Framing the Word: Gender and Genre in Caribbean Women's Writing*, edited by Joan Anim-Addo, 138-8. London: Whiting and Birch, 1996.

González, Flora M. 'El afán de nombrarse en la obra poética de Excilia Saldaña'. *Afro-Hispanic Review* 16 (Fall 1997): 34-42.

_____. 'De la tradición épico-lírica a la yoruba en *Kele Kele* de Excilia Saldaña'. In *Actas del Congreso Beresit II*, vol. II. Toledo, Spain: Cofradía Internacional de Investigadores, 1992.

_____. 'Excilia Saldaña, In Memoriam 1946-1999'. *Afro-Hispanic Review* 19 (Fall 2000): 3-7.

_____. 'Reviews of *Kele Kele* and *Mi Nombre'*. *Afro-Hispanic Review* 19 (Fall 2000): 12-3.

González, Flora and Rosamond Rosenmeier, eds. and trans. *In the Vortex of the Cyclone: Selected Poems by Excilia Saldaña*. Gainesville: University Press of Florida, 2002.

Gutiérrez, Mariela A. 'Excilia Saldaña: Cultivando una 'traslación' inviolada de su poesía negra'. In *Celebración de la creación literaria de escritoras hispanas en las Américas*, edited by Lady Rojas-Trempe and Catharina Vallejo. Ottawa: GIROL Books, 2000.

Saldaña, Excilia. 'Autobiografía'. *Breaking the Silence: An Anthology of 20th Century Poetry by Cuban Women*, translated by Margaret Randall, 200, 202. Vancouver: Pulp Press, 1982.

_____. *Bulgaria, el país de las rosas*. Havana: Editorial Gente Nueva, 1987.

_____. *Cantos para un Mayito y una paloma*. Havana: Editorial Unión, 1984.

_____. *Cine de horror y misterio*. Havana: Universidad de La Habana, 1975.

_____. *Compay Tito*. With D. Chericián. Havana: Editorial Gente Nueva, 1988.

_____. *De la isla del tesoro a la isla de la juventud*. Havana: Editorial Gente Nueva, 1978.

_____. 'Deus'. *Lovers and Comrades*, edited by Amanda Hopkinson, 121. London: The Women's Press, 1989.

_____. *Flor para amar*. Havana: Editorial Gente Nueva, 1980.

_____. *Kele Kele*. Havana: Editorial Letras Cubanas, 1987.

_____. 'Lo cotidiano trascendente: Reflexiones sobre mi obra poética'. *Afro-Hispanic Review* 19 (Fall 2000): 8-11.

_____. *Mi Nombre (Antielegía Familiar)*. Havana: Ediciones Unión, 1991.

_____. 'My Name (A Family Anti-Elegy)', edited by Ruth Behar and Juan León. *Michigan Quarterly Review* 33 (Summer 1994): 543-47.

_____. *El misterioso caso de los maravillosos cascos de Doña Cuca Bregante*. Havana: Editorial Capitán San Luis, 1992.

_____. *La Noche*. Havana: Editorial Gente Nueva, 1989.

_____. 'Poesía de Excilia Saldaña: "Tríptico de los contrasonetos anacrónicos" y "Vieja Trova sobre soporte CD ROM"'. *Afro-Hispanic Review* 19 (Fall 2000): 14-20.

_____. 'Ofumelli'. In *AfroCuba*, edited by Pedro Pérez Sarduy and Jean Stubbs, 163-8. Brooklyn: Ocean Press, 1993.

_____. *Poesía de amor y combate*. Havana: Editorial Gente Nueva, 1981.

_____. *El refranero de La Víbora*. Havana: Editorial Letras Cubanas, 1989.

_____. *Soñando y viajando*. Havana: Editorial Gente Nueva, 1980.

_____. *Un testigo de la historia*. Havana: Editorial Gente Nueva, 1978.

Beatriz Santos Arrascaeta

Santos, Beatriz, and Nene Lorriaga. *Africa en el Río de la Plata*. Buenos Aires: Editorial Amerindia, 1995.

_____. 'Afro-Uruguayan Poetry'. *Afro-Hispanic Review* 12 (Fall 1993): 37-47.

_____. 'Mujeres'. *Mundo Afro* 1 (August 1988): 32.

_____. *La herencia cultural africana en las Américas.* Montevideo: Ediciones Populares para América Latina, 1998.

_____. *Historia de vida: Negros en el Uruguay.* Montevideo: Ediciones Populares para América Latina. 1994.

_____. 'El tipo de discriminación que hay en Uruguay es sútil y solapado. Es en silencio'. *El Día* 8 (October 1989): 22.

Mayra Santos-Febres

Santos-Febres, Mayra. *Anamú y manigua.* Río Piedras, Puerto Rico: Editorial La Iguana Dorada, 1991.

_____. *El cuerpo correcto.* San Juan, Puerto Rico: R & R Editoras, 1998.

_____. 'Ensayos ardientes'. *Revista de la Universidad Metropolitana* 10 (1990):189-92.

_____. *El orden escapado.* San Juan, Puerto Rico: Editorial Tríptico, 1991.

_____. *Pez de vidrio.* North South Center: University of Miami, 1995.

_____. 'Reclaiming the Body'. *The San Juan Star.* October 22, 1995.

_____. *Sirena Selena vestida de pena.* Barcelona: Grijalbo Mondadori, 2000.

_____. *Sirena Selena,* translated by Stephen A. Lytle. New York: Picador, 2000.

_____. *Urban Oracles: Stories,* translated by Nathan Budoff and Lydia Platón Lázaro. Cambridge: Lumen Editions, 1997.

_____, ed. *Mal(h)ab(l)ar: Antología de nueva literatura puertorriqueña.* San Juan, Puerto Rico: Yagunzo Press International, 1997.

Colombia Truque Vélez

Truque Vélez, Colombia. '*Louvabagu (el otro lado lejano)* o un teatro latinoamericano de la identidad–entrevista realizada por Colombia Vélez a Rafael Murillo-Selva Rendón'. *Afro Hispanic Review* 18 (Spring 1999): 34-7.

_____. 'Navego'. *Afro-Hispanic Review* 1 (January 1982): 16.

_____. *Otro nombre para María y otros cuentos.* Bogota: Colcultura, 1993.

Yvonne-América Truque Vélez

Truque Vélez, Yvonne-América. 'A mi padre'. *Afro-Hispanic Review* 6 (September 1987): 7.

_____. 'A modo de introducción [Homenaje a Carlos Arturo Truque]'. *Afro-Hispanic Review* 6 (September 1987): 5.

_____. 'Poemas'. *Afro-Hispanic Review* 5 (Jan., May, and Sept.1986): 17, 20, 24, 27, 30, 42.

_____. 'Poemas: "Debatiéndome en el mundo", "Hojas de sol", "Sin fronteras"'. *Afro-Hispanic Review* 2 (May 1983): 22, 26, 31.

Proyección de los silencios / Projection des silences, translated by Colombia Truque and Jean Gauthier. Montreal: Centre d'Etudes de Diffusion des Amériques Hispanophones, 1986.

Salomé Ureña de Henríquez

Cocco de Fillippis, Daisy. 'Salomé Ureña de Henríquez'. In *Documents of Dissidence.* 16-21. New York: Cuny Dominican Studies Institute, 2000.

Gutiérrez, Franklin. 'Análisis de *Anacaona'.* In *Enriquillo: Radiografía de un héroe galvaniano,* 66-69. Santo Domingo: Editora Buho, 1999.

Ureña de Henríquez, Salomé. *Poesías.* Santo Domingo: Imprenta García Hermanos, 1880.

_____. *Poesías.* Madrid: Tipográfica 'Europa', 1920.

_____. *Poesías completas.* Ciudad Trujillo: Impresora Dominicana, 1950.

_____. *Poesías completas.* Santo Domingo: Editora Taller, 1988.

_____. *Poesías completas.* Santo Domingo: Editora Corripio, 1989.

Vicioso, Chiqui. 'A cien años: Salomé Ureña o la praxis entre poesía y feminismo'. In *The Women of Hispaniola,* edited by Daisy Cocco De Filippis, 61-73. New York: York College, 1993.

_____. *Salomé Ureña de Henríquez, a cien años de un magisterio.* Santo Domingo: Comisión Permanente de la Feria del Libro, 1997.

Sherezada (Chiqui) Vicioso

Vicioso, Sherezada. *Algo que decir: ensayos sobre literatura femenina, 1981-1991.* Santo Domingo: Editora Buho, 1991.

_____. 'Between the Milkman and the Fax Machine: Challenges to Women Writers in the Caribbean'. *Winds of Change,* edited by Adele S. Newson and Linda Strong-Lee. New York: Peter Lang, 1998.

_____. *Bolver a vivir: imágenes de Nicaragua.* Santo Domingo: Editora Buho, 1986.

_____. 'Dominicanyorkness: A Metropolitan Discovery of the Triangle'. *Callaloo* 23 (Summer 2000): 1013-16.

_____. *Un extraño ulular traía el viento.* Santo Domingo: Editora Alfa y Omega, 1985.

_____. 'Falling off the Wagon' and 'S-Word'. *Callaloo* 23 (Summer 2000): 1012-16.

_____. 'An Interview with Don Juan Bosch'. *Callaloo* 17 (Summer 1994): 694-700.

_____. *Julia de Burgos: la nuestra.* Santo Domingo: Editora Alfa & Omega, 1987.

_____. 'Julia de Burgos: Our Julia'. *Callaloo* 17 (Summer 1994): 674-83.

_____. 'An Oral History: Testimonio'. In *Breaking Boundaries: Latina Writing and Critical Readings,* edited by Asunción Horno-Delgado, et al. Amherst: Univ. of Massachusetts Press, 1989.

_____. 'The Rival to the Río Grande of Loíza'. *Callaloo* 17 (Summer 1994): 684-93.

_____. *Viaje desde el agua*. Santo Domingo: Fundación del Libro Casa de Teatro, 1981.

Irene Zapata Arias

Lagos, Ramiro. *Poesía liberada y deliberada de Colombia*. Bogota: Tercer Mundo, 1978.

Zapata Arias, Irene. 'Muchacho campesino'. *Poesía liberada y deliberada de Colombia*, edited by Ramiro Lagos. Bogota: Ediciones Tercer Mundo, 1976.

_____. 'Negro, no mueras por las calles' / 'Nigger Don't Die on the Streets'. In *Black Poetry of the Americas,* edited by Hortensia Ruiz del Vizo. Miami: Ediciones Universal, 1972.

Edelma Zapata Pérez

Fueger, Kathleen M. 'La sombra luminosa: La postura afirmativa de *Ritual con mi sombra* de Edelma Zapata Pérez'. *Afro-Hispanic Review* 20 (Spring 2001): 104-14.

Manzini, Giorgio M.'Il tema dell' identità negra nell' attuale poesia afro-colombiana'. *Humanitas* (February 1983): 40-51.

Zapata Pérez, Edelma. *Ritual con mi sombra*. Bogota: El Astillero Editorial, 1999.

_____. Toma de conciencia de una escritora afroindomulata en la sociedad multiétnica colombiana'. *América Negra* 11 (1996): 175-85.

Contributors

Gabriel A. Abudu earned his BA degree in Spanish and French from the University of Ghana, an MA from Queen's University, and a PhD from Temple University. Currently an assistant professor of Spanish at York College of Pennsylvania, he has a research interest in Afro-Caribbean literature, particularly that of Cuba, and he has published several articles on the Afro-Cuban poets Nancy Morejón and Excilia Saldaña.

Jack Agüero served as Director of the Museo del Barrio in East Harlem for eight years. An award-winning poet, essayist, and short story writer, he has published two collections of poetry, *Correspondence Between the Stonehaulers* and *Sonnets for the Puerto Rican,* as well as *Dominoes and Other Stories from the Puerto Rican.* He edited *Immigrant Experience: The Anguish of Becoming American,* and his translation of Burgos' poetry, *Song of the Simple Truth: The Complete Poems of Julia de Burgos,* appeared in 1991.

Antón Arrufat, author of the provocative *Los siete contra Tebas,* is a poet, novelist, playwright, and literary critic who lives and writes in Havana. The Instituto Cubano del Libro (Cuban Book Institute) recently awarded him the Alejo Carpentier Prize for Best Novel at Havana's International Book Fair. His most recent collections of poetry include *Lirios sobre un fondo de espada* (1996) and *Ejercicios para hacer de la esterilidad virtud* (1998).

Carol A. Beane received a doctorate in Romance Languages and Literature from the University of California at Berkeley. Currently, she is an associate professor of Spanish at Howard University with specialties in African diaspora studies and literature of the Caribbean and Latin America. Her publications, which have appeared in the *Afro-Hispanic Review, Revista Iberoamericana,* and other journals, focus on rereadings of canonical texts in Afro-Hispanic, Latin American, and Caribbean literature. She has also translated from Spanish into English the poetry and prose of Caribbean and Latin American writers of African descent.

Elba D. Birmingham-Pokorny, professor of Spanish at Southern Arkansas University, teaches courses in Latin American and Afro-Hispanic literature and culture. The founding editor of *Diáspora,* she has published *Denouncement and Reaffirmation of the Afro-Hispanic Identity in Carlos Guillermo Wilson's Works, An English Anthology of Afro-Hispanic Writers* *of the Twentieth Century, Critical Perspectives in Enrique Jaramillo-Levi's Work*, and *The Demythologization of Language, Gender and Culture and the Re-Mapping of Latin American Identity in Luis Rafael Sánchez's Works*. Founder of the Annual Conference on Afro-Hispanic Literature and Culture, she is currently completing a manuscript on the works of Mayra Santos-Febres.

Nathan Budoff has translated, in addition to Mayra Santos-Febres' *Urban Oracles* (1997), Antonio López Ortega's collection of short stories, *Moonlit* (1998), *Too Late for Man: Essays (New Voice from Latin America)* (1995) by William Ospina, and *The Joy of Being Awake* (1996), a novel by the Colombian writer Hector Abad.

Daisy Cocco de Filippis is a professor and former chair of the Department of Foreign Languages at York College (CUNY), where she specialises in Dominican literature, particularly that of women writers. She has published *Estudios semióticos de poesía dominicana* and *Para que no se olviden: The Lives of Women in Dominican History*, and she has edited or co-edited *Sin otro profeta que su canto: Antología de poesía escrita por dominicanas*, *Poemas del exilio y otras inquietudes: Antología de poetas dominicanos en New York*, *Del desconsuelo al compromiso: La poesía de Aída Cartagena Portalatín*, *Combatidas, combativas y combatientes: Antología de cuentos escritos por mujeres dominicanas*, and eight other collections.

Linda R. Collins is an instructor of Spanish in the Department of Foreign Languages at Georgia Southern University. Her research interests include Afra-Hispanic literature, contemporary Latin American literature, and women writers of the diaspora. In 1975, she received the master's degree in Spanish language and literature from the University of Wisconsin-Milwaukee, and she is completing a doctorate at the University of Kentucky, where she is writing her dissertation on the work of Aida Cartagena Portalatín.

Margaret Jull Costa was co-winner, in 1992, of the Texeira Gomes Portuguese Translation Prize for her translation of Fernand Pessoa's *The Book of Disquiet*. Among the Spanish, Portuguese, and Latin American writers whose novels and short stories she has translated are Bernardo Atxaga, Javier Marías, Juan José Saer, and Carmen Martín Gaite.

Miriam DeCosta-Willis, former professor of Africana Studies at the University of Maryland, Baltimore County, edited *Blacks in Hispanic Literature*, *The Memphis Diary of Ida B. Wells*, and *Singular Like a Bird: The Art of Nancy Morejón*. She co-edited *Homespun Images: An Anthology of Black Memphis Artists and Writers*; *Double Stitch: Black Women Write About*

Mothers and Daughters; and *Erotique Noire / Black Erotica* . Her essays have appeared in journals such as the *Afro-Hispanic Review, National Women's Studies Journal,* and *College Language Association Journal.*

Rosemary Geisdorfer Feal, formerly a professor of Spanish at the State University of New York at Buffalo, is now executive secretary of the Modern Language Association. She specialises in Caribbean and South American literature and literary theory, including Afro-Hispanic studies, feminist criticism, and queer theory. She is associate editor of the *Afro-Hispanic Review.* Her books include *Novel Lives: The Fictional Autobiographies of Guillermo Cabrera Infante and Mario Vargas Llosa* (1986) and *Painting on the Page: Interartistic Approaches to Modern Hispanic Texts* (1995). Feal's latest research focuses on women's erotic writing in Spanish.

David Frye has worked since 1880 as an anthropologist, historian and translator in Spain, Mexico and Cuba. The author of *Indians into Mexicans: History and Identity in a Mexican Town,* he is also an accomplished translator, whose work has appeared in *Bridges to Cuba/Puentes a Cuba* and *Memoria: Cuban Art of the Twentieth Century.* His article 'The Joy of Translation' was published in the *Journal of the International Institute,* and he recently translated Abilio Estévez's *Thine is the Kingdom: A Novel.*

Flora M. González is associate professor of Writing, Literature and Publishing at Emerson College. She has published articles on Afro-Cuban literature and culture in journals such as *Revista Iberoamericana, Afro-Hispanic Review* and *Cuban Studies.* Her most recent publication is *In the Vortex of the Cyclone,* a translation, with Rosamond Rosenmeier, of the poetry of Cuban writer Excilia Saldaña.

Donald K. Gordon, former professor of Spanish at the University of Manitoba in Canada, has published *Los cuentos de Juan Rulfo* and *Lo jamaicano y lo universal en la obra del costarricense Quince Duncan.* His scholarly essays have appeared in such journals as the *Afro-Hispanic Review, Hispania, The Canadian Modern Language Review, Canadian Journal of Latin American Studies,* and *Revista Canadiense de Estudios Hispánicos.* The former secretary-treasurer of the Canadian Association of Hispanists, he has served since 1981 as Jamaican Honorary Consul at Winnipeg.

Mary Arthurlene Harris, a native of Guyana, South America, received the PhD degree in Spanish from the University of Oklahomo and presently teaches Spanish at Bowie State University. The author of *La estructura como apoyo temático e ideológico en la poesía de Blas de Otero* (Pliegos, 1992) and the translator of *Bajo la piel de los tambores* (Drums Under My Skin) by Luz Argentina Chiriboga (Afro-Hispanic Institute, 1996), she has also translated articles for *Catalan Review* and *Cimarrón.*

Aida L. Heredia specialises in Latin American and Caribbean literature and culture. She has published a book, *De la recta a las cajas chinas: la poesía de José Kozer*, and written articles on national identity, memory, transculturation, and religion as counter-colonial practice. Her research interests extend to cultural representaton and the African Diaspora in Latin America. An assistant professor of Hispanic Studies at Connecticut College, she received the BA degree from Queens College and the MA and PhD degrees from SUNY, Buffalo.

Linda Howe received her MA and PhD degrees from the University of Wisconsin, Madison, where her dissertation was entitled 'The Representation of Afro-Cuban Culture and Identity in the Poetry of Nancy Morejón and Miguel Barnet: The Question of Gender and Race in Revolutionary Cuba'. Her essays have been published in the *Afro-Hispanic Review, Crítica de Textos Literarios*, and the *Journal of Afro-Latin American Studies and Literatures*.

Shirley Jackson, professor of Spanish in the Department of Languages and Communication Disorders at the University of the District of Columbia, has published two books, *Estudios selectos sobre obras literarias del mundo hispánico* and *La novela negrista en Hispanoamérica* as well as articles in such journals as the *Afro-Hispanic Review, Cuadernos Iberoamericanos*, and *América Negra*. Co-editor of the *Journal of African Roots*, she is founder and president of the Center for the Interdisciplinary Study of Languages and Cultures in Africa and the African Diaspora.

Marvin A. Lewis, co-editor of the *Afro-Hispanic Review* and of *Palara*, is professor of Spanish at the University of Missouri-Columbia as well as founder/director of the Institute for Languages and Literatures of the African Diaspora. He is the author of *Afro-Hispanic Poetry, 1940-1980: From Slavery to 'Negritud' in South American Verse* (1983); *Treading the Ebony Path: Ideology and Violence in Contemporary Afro-Colombian Prose Fiction* (1987); and *Ethnicity and Identity in Contemporary Afro-Venezuelan Literature: A Culturalist Approach* (1992).

Consuelo López-Springfield, a specialist in Caribbean, Latino Studies, and Women's Studies, is assistant dean at the College of Letters and Science at the University of Wisconsin-Madison. The editor of *Daughters of Caliban: Twentieth-Century Caribbean Women*, she guest-edited a 1994 issue of *Callaloo* on Puerto Rican women writers, as well as a 2000 issue on the literature and culture of Dominica.

Dellita Martin-Ogunsola is former professor of Spanish and chairperson of the Department of Foreign Languages and Literatures at the University of Alabama at Birmingham. A specialist in Afro-Hispanic and Caribbean literature, she has published articles in *Black American Literature Forum, MELUS, CLAJ*, and *Afro-Hispanic Review*. She recently published

Las mejores historias de Quince Duncan / The Best Short Stories of Quince Duncan and authored of the forthcoming *Female Calibans in the Fiction of Quince Duncan*. She is past president of the College Language Association, founded in 1937 by a group of Black scholars and educators.

M'baré N'gom is associate professor of Spanish and Latin American Studies, and French and Francophone Studies, and Chairperson of the Department of Foreign Languages at Morgan State University. His articles have appeared in *Hispania, Canadian Journal of Hispanic Studies, Diáspora, Francofonía, Australian Journal of French Studies, Caribe, Afro-Hispanic Review,* and *Quimera,* among others. He is the author of *Diálogos con Guinea: panorama de la literatura guineoecuatoriana de expresión castellana a través de sus protagonistas.*

Antonio Olliz Boyd, a Cuban-American who specialises in semiotic studies of the Afro-Latino image in Latin American literature, is professor emeritus of Hispanic and Portuguese languages and literatures and former director of the Portugese Program at Temple University. His publications include a monograph, 'Manuel Zapata Olivella', for the *Dictionary of Literary Biography* and two articles co-authored with Gabriel Abudu: 'Afro-Iberian Identity in the Early Literature of Spain: Precursor to the Afro-Hispanic Identity' and '*Piedra Pulida*: Nancy Morejón's Tribute to Nicolás Guillén', published in *Singular Like a Bird: The Art of Nancy Morejón.*

Lydia Platón Lázaro collaborated with Nathan Budoff in the translation of *Urban Oracles* by Mayra Santos-Febres.

Laurence E. Prescott teaches in the Department of Spanish, Italian, and Portuguese at Penn State University. The author of *Candelario Obeso y la iniciación de la poesía negra en Colombia* and *Without Hatreds or Fears: Jorge Artel and the Struggle for Black Literary Expression in Colombia,* he has also published several articles on Afro-Hispanic and Caribbean literatures.

Margaret Randall is a critically acclaimed poet, editor, translator, author, photographer, and publisher. In 1984 she returned to the United States after twenty-three years in Latin America, but the INS ordered her deported because of opinions expressed in some of her books. A number of well-known writers helped in her five-year fight to remain in the country of her birth. She won her case and now resides in New Mexico. Some of her many publications include *Cuban Women Now; Women in Cuba: Twenty Years Later; Sandino's Daughter; Breaking the Silences: An Anthology of 20th Century Poetry by Cuban Women; Christians in the Nicaraguan Revolution; Risking a Somersault in the Air: Conversations with Nicaraguan Writers; Gathering Rage: The Failure of 20th Century Revolutions to Develop* *a Feminist Agenda; Sandino's Daughter's Revisited;* and the forthcoming *When I Look in the Mirror and See you: Women, Torture and Resistance..*

Rosamond Rosenmeier is retired from the University of Massachusetts and presently teaches writing and poetry at Andover Newton Theological School. Her collection of poetry, *Lines Out*, was published by Alice Jane Books in 1989, and she is working on a second volume of poetry. She has collaborated with Flora M. González on a translation of the poetry of Excilia Saldaña of Cuba.

John A. Scott is a Fulbright scholar and doctoral candidate in linguistic anthropology from the University of Iowa.

Ian I. Smart, professor of Spanish at Howard University, has published *Central American Writers of West Indian Origin: A New Hispanic Literature; Nicolás Guillén, Popular Poet of the Caribbean; Amazing Connections: Kemet to Hispanophone Africana Literature;* a novel, *Samni Mannitae: A Tall Tale for Our Times;* and two translations, *Short Stories by Cubena* and *Pastrana's Last River.* A founding editor of the *Afro-Hispanic Review,* he recently co-edited *Ah Come Back Home: Perspectives on the Trinidad and Tobago Carnival.*

Claudette Williams is currently senior lecturer and head of the Department of Modern Languages and Literatures at the Mona Campus of the University of the West Indies in Jamaica. She is the author of *Charcoal and Cinnamon: The Politics of Color in Spanish Caribbean Literature* and of several articles on Spanish Caribbean and Spanish American literature.

Ann Venture Young is a former associate professor of foreign languages at Morgan State University, editor/translator of the anthology *The Image of Black Women in 20th Century South American Poetry,* co-founder of the Afro-Hispanic Institute, and past president of the College Language Association.

Caroll Mills Young is associate professor of Spanish at Indiana University of Pennsylvania. Her major teaching and research interests are Afro-Latin literature and culture, Black women writers, comparative literature, and multicultural education. She has been awarded several grants to study the Black experience in Argentina and Uruguay, and has published articles in journals such as the *Afro-Hispanic Review* and *College Language Association Journal.* Her recent publications include 'New Voices of Afro-Uruguay' and 'The Unmasking of Virginia Brindis de Salas: Minority Discourse of Afro-Uruguay' in Dolan Hubbard's *Recovered Writers / Recovered Tests.*

Permissions

The editor and publisher would like to thank the authors and translators who contributed their work for publication in this volume. In addition, they thank and acknowledge the following for permission to reproduce the material in this volume:

Virginia Brindis de Salas:

Reprinted by permission of The University of Tennessee Press. Carol Mills Young, 'The Unmasking of Virginia Brindis de Salas: Minority Discourse of Afro-Uruguay' from *Recovered Writers / Recovered Texts: Race, Class, and Gender in Black Women's Literature*, edited by Dolan Hubbard, Tennessee Studies in Literature, Volume 38. Copyright © 1997 by The University of Tennessee Press.

Carmen Colón Pellot:

'Oh Lord, I Want to be White', 'Roots of *Mulata* Envy' and 'The Land is a Mulatto Woman' from *Charcoal and Cinnamon: The Politics of Color*, ed. and trans. Claudette Williams. Reprinted courtesy of University Press of Florida, Copyright © 2000.

Julia de Burgos:

'Cry of the Kinky Haired Girl' from *Charcoal and Cinnamon: The Politics of Color,* ed. and trans. Claudette Williams. Reprinted courtesy of University Press of Florida. Copyright © 2000.

'Río Grande of Loiza', 'To Julia de Burgos' and 'Pentachrome' from *Song of the Simple Truth: The Complete Poems of Julia de Burgos*, ed. and trans. Jack Agüeros. Copyright © 1996. Published by Curbstone Press. Distributed by Consortium.

López-Springfield, Consuelo. "'I Am the Life, the Strength, the Woman": Feminism in Julia de Burgos' Autobiographical Poetry'. *Callaloo* 17 (1994), 701-714. Copyright © Charles H. Rowell. Reprinted by permission of Johns Hopkins University Press.

Eulalia Bernard:

Smart, Ian. 'Eulalia Bernard: A Caribbean Woman Writer and the Dynamics of Liberation'. *Letras Femeninas*. 13 (1987) 79-85. Copyright © 1987. Reprinted courtesy of *Letras Femeninas*.

Lourdes Casal:

'Ana Veldford' from *Bridges to Cuba / Puentes a Cuba*, ed. Ruth Behar, trans. David Frye. Copyright © 1995. Reprinted by permission of the *Michigan Quarterly Review*.

Argentina Chiriboga:

'Poems by Chiriboga', trans. Rosemary Geisdorfer Feal. *Afro-Hispanic Review* 12 (Fall 1993): 16. Copyright © 1993. Reprinted by permission of the *Afro-Hispanic Review*.
   Drums Under My Skin, trans. Mary Arthurlene Harris. Washington: Afro-Hispanic Institute, 1996.

Nancy Morejón:

'Ana Mendieta' from *Bridges to Cuba / Puentes a Cuba,* ed. Ruth Behar, trans. David Frye. Copyright © 1995. Reprinted by permission of the *Michigan Quarterly Review*.

Excilia Saldaña:

González, Flora M.'The Zeal for Self-Denomination in the Poetic Works of Excilia Saldaña', trans. Mary A. Harris. *Afro-Hispanic Review*16 (Fall 1997): 34-42. Copyright © 1997. Reprinted by permission of the *Afro-Hispanic Review*.

Beatriz Santos:

'Negro Griot' [Black Griot], 'Fuego' [Fire], trans. Miriam DeCosta-Willis. *Afro-Hispanic Review*. 12 (Fall 1993): 47. Copyright © 1993. Reprinted by permission of the *Afro-Hispanic Review*.

María Nsue Angüe:

N'gom, M'baré. 'Relato de una vida y escritura femenina: *Ekomo*, de María Nsue Angüe' [Narrative of a Woman's Life and Writing: María Nsue Angüe's *Ekomo*]. *The Journal of Afro-Latin American Studies and Literatures, JALAS&L.* 3 (Spring 1995): 77-92. Copyright © 1995. Reprinted by permission of the *JALAS&L*.

Mayra Santos-Febres:

'Marina's Fragrance' from *Urban Oracles,* trans. Nathan Budoff and Lydia Platon Lázaro. Copyright © 1997. Reprinted by permission of Lumen Editions.
   While every effort has been made to trace the copyright holders of the material included in this volume, the editor and publishers would be pleased to hear from any interested parties.

INDEX

CPSIA information can be obtained at www.ICGtesting.com
Printed in the USA
LVOW08s1308080315

429659LV00004B/287/P